W9-CZZ-218

THE BLAIR HANDBOOK

FOURTH EDITION

Toby Fulwiler
University of Vermont

Alan R. Hayakawa
The Patriot News
Harrisburg, Pennsylvania

Prentice Hall

Upper Saddle River, New Jersey 07458

Library of Congress Cataloging-in-Publication Data

Fulwiler, Toby (date)
   The Blair handbook / Toby Fulwiler, Alan R. Hayakawa.—4th ed.
      p. cm.
   Includes index.
   ISBN 0-13-098142-7—ISBN 0-13-099350-6 (pbk.)
      1. English language—Rhetoric—Handbooks, manuals, etc.   2. English
   language—Grammar—Handbooks, manuals, etc.   3. Report writing—Handbooks,
   manuals, etc.   I. Hayakawa, Alan R.   II. Title.

PE1408 .F78 2002
808'.042—dc21   2002021430

Editor in Chief: Leah Jewell
Editorial Assistant: John Ragozzine
Assistant Editor: Karen Schultz
*VP/Director of Production and
   Manufacturing:* Barbara Kittle
Production Editor: Joan E. Foley
Production Assistant: Elizabeth Best
Copyeditor: Kathryn Graehl
Permissions Researcher: Tracy Metivier
Manufacturing Manager: Nick Sklitsis
Assistant Manufacturing Manager: Mary
   Ann Gloriande

Director of Marketing: Beth Mejia
Senior Marketing Manager: Brandy
   Dawson
Marketing Assistant: Christine Moodie
Art Director: Anne Bonanno Nieglos
Interior and Cover Designer: Kenny Beck
Cover Art: John S Dykes Illustration
Art Production Manager: Guy Ruggiero
Electronic Artist: Mirella Signoretto

This book was set in 9/11 Bookman Light by The Clarinda Company
and was printed and bound by RR Donnelley & Sons Company.
Covers were printed by Phoenix Color Corporation.

For permission to use copyrighted material, grateful
acknowledgment is made to the copyright holders listed
on page 940, which is considered an extension of this copyright page.

 © 2003, 2000, 1997, 1994 by Pearson Education, Inc.
Upper Saddle River, New Jersey 07458

Printed in the United States of America
10 9 8 7 6 5 4 3 2 1

ISBN 0-13-099350-6 (paper)
ISBN 0-13-098142-7 (case)

Pearson Education LTD., London
Pearson Education Australia PTY, Limited, Sydney
Pearson Education Singapore, Pte. Ltd
Pearson Education North Asia Ltd, Hong Kong
Pearson Education Canada, Ltd., Toronto
Pearson Educación de Mexico, S.A. de C.V.
Pearson Education—Japan, Tokyo
Pearson Education Malaysia, Pte. Ltd
Pearson Education, Upper Saddle River, New Jersey

What you need to know, when you need to know it.

www.prenhall.com/fulwiler

Every new copy of *The Blair Handbook, Fourth Edition,* is packaged with an online solutions access card that allows you to register for instant access to the book's Companion Website™. Key features of this site include the following:

E-Book
- ◆ Search the Contents
- ◆ Search by key word
- ◆ Search by rule number

Assessment
- ◆ Chapter exercises
- ◆ Blue Pencil editing exercises
- ◆ Diagnostic tests

Research and Documentation Styles
- ◆ MLA
- ◆ APA
- ◆ *Chicago Manual*
- ◆ CSE
- ◆ Columbia Online

Teacher Resources
- ◆ Turnitin.com
- ◆ Instructor's Area
- ◆ Online Catalog and Rep Locator

CONTENTS

Preface   **xxii**

* The ESL symbol indicates sections that have ESL boxes.

PART FIVE

Revising   271

EDITING FOR EFFECTIVENESS   331

Boxes

CHECKLIST

💡 CRITICAL THINKING

ESL

PREFACE

This fourth edition of *The Blair Handbook*, like its predecessors, focuses on the needs of contemporary college writers. Our goal is the same: to offer clear explanations of language conventions, practices, and guidelines that govern good writing; to provide strategies for learning your own approach to the writing process; and samples of writing by both published authors and student writers that model both good practices and successful products. As the field of English studies continues to evolve—particularly with the growth of the computer as a writing and research tool—we have revised the text to make it as up-to-date as possible.

We remain committed to the process-oriented approach that has characterized all previous editions. We have simplified the treatment of the writing process and expanded the coverage of research. The result is a handbook that continues to offer the most practical and jargon-free guidance available on the crafting of expository prose.

PRINCIPLES UNDERLYING THE BLAIR HANDBOOK

Writing as a process

The organization of *The Blair Handbook* corresponds to the stages of the writing process, so all chapters are contextualized, as much as possible, within the process. We have presented traditional handbook material—information on style, grammar, punctuation, and mechanics—as part of the "editing process," where writers check their final-draft language for clarity and correctness.

- **Part One, Writing in College** (Chapters 1–3), introduces students to the five interrelated but discrete stages of the writing process—planning, drafting, researching, revising, and editing—explored in more detail in each of the next five parts.

- **Part Two, Planning** (Chapters 4–6), discusses planning as an informal yet focused activity where writers work out their voice in relation to their purpose and audience.

- **Part Three, Drafting** (Chapters 7–10), explains strategies for finding topics, formulating arguments, making claims, using evidence, and developing drafts for four specific writing purposes: reflecting, explaining, arguing, and interpreting.

- **Part Four, Researching** (Chapters 11–17), explores research methods and examines field, library, and online resources for writing lively research papers.

- **Part Five, Revising** (Chapters 18–21), focuses on a variety of strategies that make revision both the most demanding and creative part of the writing process.

- **Part Six, Editing** (Chapters 22–49), presents guidelines to make finished work as clear and correct as possible. An overview of "Editing" is introduced in Chapter 22, while subsequent chapters cover effectiveness (Chapters 23–31), grammar (Chapters 32–37), punctuation (Chapters 38–44), and mechanics (Chapters 45–49).

- **Part Seven, Presenting Your Work** (Chapters 50–53), covers topics ranging from the formatting of papers to publishing class books and Web pages to developing writing portfolios and making oral presentations.

- **Part Eight, Writing Across the Curriculum** (Chapters 54–61), discusses the distinguishing characteristics of writing in different academic disciplines and includes guidelines for documentation according to MLA, APA, and other disciplinary systems.

- **Part Nine, A Grammar Reference** (Chapters 62–64), is a concise resource for students who seek technical explanations of parts of speech and grammatical structure of sentences.

Treatment of students as writers

Because writing skills are essential to success in college and beyond, we encourage students to think of themselves as writers as well as being technically proficient in all phases of the writing process. We stress that writing is a dynamic activity in which writers make choices, experiment with language, evaluate the results, and rewrite as necessary. Thus, we include information to help students write for their readers as well as for themselves.

- **Plentiful samples of student writing.** *The Blair Handbook* includes an abundance of authentic student writing samples ranging from journal entries and rough drafts to nine finished essays presented in class books and writing portfolios.

- **Four types of essays.** In Part Three, we outline four types of commonly assigned essays: reflections Chapter 7), explanations (Chapter 8), arguments (Chapter 9), and interpretations (Chapter 10). Each of these essay types is illustrated by a complete student paper and extracts from other student papers. In Part Four we demonstrate how research can be conducted and applied to college essays serving any of these four purposes. In addition, we include a sampler of three innovative research essays.

- **Hand-edited examples.** Examples in the editing part of *The Blair Handbook* use handwritten corrections to show students how problems in clarity, grammar, punctuation, and mechanics can be resolved.

Innovative approach to research

Research is something people do in their everyday lives. People do research to plan trips, shop for products, and look for jobs, for instance. We explain how these same research skills can be practiced in academic settings. We believe our research coverage is the most imaginative and comprehensive in any college handbook on the market.

Research is a natural part of many writing assignments. It is conducted from early to late stages in the development of serious academic papers, so we feature it early in the handbook.

Library, Internet, and field research may be equally important. Beneficial research occurs not only in the textual sources that students consult via computers and books, but also in the field, as both interviews and site observations add imaginative and informative life to research papers.

Research sources need to be evaluated. The easy accessibility of millions of Internet resources intensifies the researcher's need to discriminate among sources of information; our new edition provides guidelines for thinking critically about *all* sources.

Writing and learning activities

The Blair Handbook features meaningful activities that help students work through their own versions of the writing process. Students explore their experiences as writers in "Explorations." Students practice editing techniques on sample student texts in "Practices." They apply the principles discussed to papers they are working on in "Applications." In addition, "Suggestions for Writing and Research," are made at the end of chapters in Parts One through Five, offering both individual and collaborative writing assignments.

Emphasis on the conventions of effective writing

Good writing must be clear, vital, and stimulating to read— what we call "effective." *The Blair Handbook* explains features of standard, written English as conventions that facilitate effective communication, not as arbitrary rules. And it spends less time instructing students in grammar jargon and more time showing students how to identify, analyze, and solve problems that cause reader confusion. Where grammatical terms or technical language is useful, the words are introduced in boldface and defined. Because the handbook is a reference work, definitions and explanations are restated each time they are mentioned in a new chapter. A glossary of terms at the end of the book provides further reinforcement.

Boxes

Three types of boxes highlight special features.

- **Checklist boxes.** A check mark in the upper left corner of a box indicates a summary of key information in the preceding section. These lists range from composing strategies, to figures of speech, to logical fallacies.

- **Critical thinking boxes.** Critical thinking boxes, indicated by a lightbulb icon, prompt students to reassess their writing for clear and logical interpretations and explanations.

- ESL boxes. Over forty ESL boxes, easily identified by their ESL icon, contain information on all aspects of planning, drafting, researching, and revising that prove troublesome for nonnative speakers of English. In addition to the ESL boxes, a strand of special writing suggestions in Parts One through Three asks students to draw on their experiences as nonnative speakers and writers of English in order to improve their writing.

Emphasis on contemporary pedagogy

The Blair Handbook emphasizes the best practices of current writing classes, including multiple-draft assignments, peer writing workshops, an abundance of ungraded informal writing, the publishing of final drafts, and portfolio assessment.

- **Journals.** Because writing-to-learn is recognized as an important part of learning to write, *The Blair Handbook* includes a whole chapter (Chapter 4) that provides students with ideas for journal writing.

- **Voice.** The writer's stance or voice is treated comprehensively in Chapter 6, as writers shape it according to purpose and audience; the drafting, revising, and editing sections all reinforce the development of a writer's personal voice.

- **Revising.** Serious writing classes are rewriting classes. Revising is presented as the key to creating successful critical and imaginative papers. *Blair* provides concrete suggestions—some conventional and some surprising—to help students learn, once and for all, that revising is serious business.

- **Writing across the curriculum.** The use of writing in disciplines other than English is treated comprehensively in Part Eight. Detailed information includes why particular formats and conventions have developed in five major disciplinary areas: languages and literature, humanities, social sciences, physical sciences, and business.

NEW TO THE FOURTH EDITION

This new fourth edition of *The Blair Handbook* pays special attention to keeping up-to-date with the ever-expanding computer literacy of our readers and the increased availability of ever more powerful hardware and software to them.

- **Publishing on the World Wide Web.** Part Six includes a new chapter, 52, on writing for the World Wide Web. It contains updated and expanded ideas to improve document design, transmission of papers by e-mail, publication on the World Wide Web, and the establishment of personal Web pages.

- **Creative nonfiction.** A new chapter at the end of the Revising section takes a serious look at the imaginative factual prose commonly called creative nonfiction. For interested instructors and students, the ideas here lead to lively and provocative writing by students of all ability levels.

- **A research sampler.** Our new collection of sample research essays in Chapter 17 provides samples of creative nonfiction and collaborative writing, with different essays emphasizing field, Internet, and library research.

- **The updated formats of both MLA and APA documentation,** including the latest (and most sensible) guidelines for documenting electronic sources. In addition, we have included a separate chapter on Columbia Online Style for instructors who prefer this latest documentation system.

- **A new Web site,** located at www.prenhall.com/fulwiler, accompanies this edition. The site provides a complete e-book, linked to hundreds of self-grading exercises and other Web material. The e-book is easily searchable by keyword, index, or section number/letter code for a rule or other information. Also included are diagnostic tests and "Blue Pencil" exercises, which provide grammar and punctuation practice in the context of complete paragraphs.

SUPPLEMENTS

Supplements for instructors

The *Instructor's Manual for The Blair Handbook, Fourth Edition,* by Megan Fulwiler, Kate Hoffman, and Kuhio Walters, a helpful resource with answers for activities, additional activities, teaching tips, strategies for word-processing activities, ESL advice, background information on writing, and interesting quotations.

www.turnitin.com an innovative service free to qualified adopters of *The Blair Handbook, Fourth Edition.* The program helps professors easily identify instances of Web-based student plagiarism. Each paper submitted to a professor's "drop box" is cross-referenced with millions of possible online sources. Within 24 hours, teachers receive a customized, color-coded "Originality Report," complete with live links to suspect Internet locations for each submitted paper.

BlackBoard, Course Compass, and WebCT adapted for *The Blair Handbook.* These course management programs provide extensive book-specific content, which enable professors to create online courses easily and quickly. Access codes to all online course management content is available at a discount price when packaged with this handbook. Contact your local Prentice Hall representative for ordering information.

Prentice Hall Resources for Teaching Writing, individual booklets presenting information on some of the most effective approaches and important concerns of composition instructors today, each written by an expert on the particular topic: *Distance Education,* by W. Dees Stallings; *Computers and Writing,* by Dawn Rodrigues; *Classroom Strategies,* by Wendy Bishop; *Portfolios,* by Pat Belanoff; *Journals,* by Christopher C. Burnham; *Collaborative Learning,* by Harvey Kail and John Trimbur; *English as a Second Language,* by Ruth Spack; *Writing Across the Curriculum,* by Art Young.

Supplements for students

Editing Activities for *The Blair Handbook, Fourth Edition,* includes both the editing activities in the handbook and additional activities, with ample space to edit on the page (Answer Key available).

Evaluating Online Resources: English 2003 helps students critically evaluate the material they research on the Internet. Free when packaged with this handbook.

A Writer's Guide to Research and Documentation, ISBN 0-13-032641-0

A Writer's Guide to Writing in the Disciplines and Oral Presentations, ISBN 0-13-018931-6

A Writer's Guide to Document and Web Design, ISBN 0-13-018929-4

A Writer's Guide to Writing About Literature, ISBN 0-13-018932-4

Special offers

The New American Webster Handy College Dictionary or the *Roget's College Thesaurus* can be packaged free with *The Blair Handbook, Fourth Edition*. Please contact your local Prentice Hall representative for more details and a special package ISBN for bookstore orders.

ACKNOWLEDGMENTS

To our colleagues nationwide who agreed to share their collective wisdom on the teaching of writing in the Blair resource pamphlets: Pat Belanoff, State University of New York at Stony Brook; Wendy Bishop, Florida State University; Chris Burnham, University of New Mexico at Las Cruces; Deborah H. Holdstein, Governors State University; Harvey Kail, University of Maine; Ruth Spack, Tufts University; Dees Stallings, University of Maryland; John Trimbur, Worchester Polytechnic Institute; and Art Young, Clemson University.

To Megan Fulwiler; Kuhio Walters, University of New Hampshire; and Kate Hoffman, University of Vermont, for writing the fourth edition of the *Instructor's Manual* to reflect the latest methods in teaching composition; Heidi Schultz of the University of North Carolina at Chapel Hill, who judiciously prepared new bibliographic references in "Useful Reading"; Jan Frodesen of the University of California, Santa Barbara, and Barbara Matthias, Iowa State University, who prepared and revised the **ESL** boxes, incorporating the newest understandings of how students learn English as a second language; Sean McDowell and Dave Carlson of Indiana University, who prepared many of the activities in the text.

To the many students at the University of Vermont who asked and answered questions about learning to write and especially to those who allowed us to reprint samples of their essays, freewrites, and journal entries.

To Leah Jewell, editor in chief, whose vision of contemporary writing instruction guided *The Blair Handbook, Fourth Edition*, to completion; to Karen Schultz, assistant editor, who facilitated everything; to John Ragozzine, editorial assistant; to Brandy Dawson, our fearless, relentless, and savvy marketing manager; to Christine Moodie, marketing assistant. We'd also like to thank Beth Mejia, director of marketing, and Yolanda de Rooy, president of humanities and social sciences, for their enduring support of this project.

To our expert Prentice Hall production team, who took our handbook from manuscript to bound book: Joan Foley, production editor; Anne Nieglos, art director; Kenny Beck, interior and cover designer; Guy Ruggiero, art production manager; Mirella Signoretto, electronic artist; and Mary Ann Gloriande, assistant manufacturing manager.

To the many thoughtful, critical, and experienced reviewers or users of our four editions, whose comments guided the major manuscript revisions: Kimberly Abels, University of North Carolina, Chapel Hill; Marsha E. Ackermann, Michigan State University; James Allen, College of DuPage; Melanie Almeder, University of Florida; Steve Anderson, University of Arkansas at Little Rock; Richard Bullock, Wright State University; William Carroll, Texas A & M University; Veronica Cruz, University of Florida; Jay R. Curlin, Ouachita Baptist University; Janet Cutshall, Sussex County Community College; Carol David, Iowa State University; Bernard J. Gallagher, Louisiana State University at Alexandra; Virginia Gibbons, Oakton Community College; Thomas Haley, University of Minnesota; James Hallemann, Oakland Community College; Maureen Hoag, Wichita State University; Francis A. Hubbard, Marquette University; John Johnston, Yavapai Colllege; Leila Kapai, University of the District of Columbia, Washington; Frances Kostarelos, Governors State University; Victoria Lague, Miami-Dade Community College, Kendall; David Lashmet, University of Florida; Michelle LeBeau, University of New Mexico, Valencia; Erin Lebofsky, Temple University; Kelley Logan, Southwestern Oklahoma State University; Thomas Marshall, Robert Morris College; Michael J. Martin, Illinois State University; Lynn Langer Meeks, Utah State University; Lamata Mitchell, Rock Valley College; Michael Moran, University of Georgia; Katy Norton, Indiana University; J. S. Renau, University of Florida; Sarah Rodgers, Owens Community College; Bryan Sandoval, Utah State University; Lucille M. Schultz, University of Cincinnati; Eileen Seifert, DePaul University; Linda Sneed, Indiana University; Josephine Koster Tarvers, Winthrop University; Richard Veit, University of North Carolina, Wilmington; Lisa Walmsley, University of Florida; Sam Watson, University of North Carolina, Charlotte; Sarah M. Williamson, University of Wisconsin-Stout; John Woznicki, Fairmont State College; and Kathy Wyss, San Jose State University.

To John Harvey of *The Oregonian*, who instilled respect for the language and for a writer's style; to John A. Kirkpatrick of *The Patriot-News* of Harrisburg, for his dedication to excellence in newspapering; to Ichiro Hayakawa and Frederick Romer Peters, who never met but shared a love of the English language that they passed on to their children; and to Barbara, for her boundless patience, support, and love.

And thanks finally and always to Laura for her continued patience and with this important, yet never-ending project.

Toby Fulwiler
Alan R. Hayakawa

THE
BLAIR
HANDBOOK

Peel off these self-stick tabs and place them on the edge of the related text pages for quick location of key concepts. Use the plain white write-on tabs to mark your frequently used areas of the text.

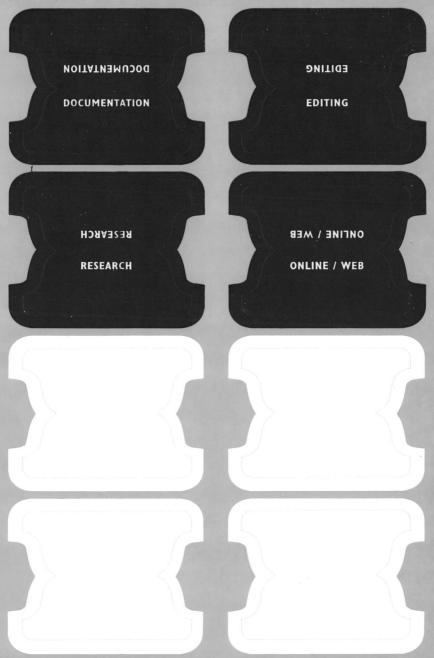

PART ONE

Writing in College

www.prenhall.com/fulwiler

Writing In College
www.prenhall.com/fulwiler

**On *The Blair Handbook, Fourth Edition,*
Web site you can find**

- Tips for drafting and planning
- Discussion of the writing process
- Exercises on revising your work

Questions and Answers About Writing

You can count on one thing—attending college will mean writing papers. Whether you are enrolled in a writing course or any other course, you'll be asked to write critical essays, research reports, position papers, book reviews, essay exams, and laboratory reports and sometimes to keep a journal. You may have tackled similar writing assignments in high school, so you've had some practice. Now that practice will be put to a test.

Recently we asked a class of first-year college students to talk about themselves as writers. Several began by describing where they wrote. Amy, for example, said she did most of her writing "listening to classical music and, if it is a nice day, under trees," while Jennifer felt "most comfortable writing on [her] bed and being alone." Others described their attitudes. John, for example, said he wrote best "under pressure." Becky, however, preferred writing when she "felt strongly or was angry about something," while Kevin "hated deadlines." In fact, there proved to be as many different perspectives on being a writer as there were students in the class. To continue our conversation, we asked more specific questions.

1 a What is difficult about writing?

Everything about writing can seem difficult, from getting started to organizing, revising, and editing. Our own experience tells us this is so—and every published writer we know says the same thing. How, we wondered, would first-year college writers characterize their difficulties? Here is what they told us:

Jennifer: "I don't like being told what to write about."

Amy: "I never could fulfill the page requirements. My essays were always several pages shorter than they were supposed to be."

Jill: "I always have trouble starting off a paper . . . and I hate it when I think I've written a great paper and I get a bad grade. It's so discouraging, and I don't understand what I wrote wrong."

Omar: "Teachers are always nitpicking about little things, but I think writing is for communication, not nitpicking. I mean, if you can read it and it makes sense, what else do you want?"

Ken: "Putting thoughts down on paper as they are in your mind is the hardest thing to do. It's like music—anyone can play a song in his head, but translating it to an instrument is the hard part."

We weren't surprised by these answers since we too remember wondering: What did teachers want? How long was enough? How do you get thoughts into words? Why all the nitpicking?

WRITING 1: EXPLORATION ─────────────────────

What do you find difficult about writing? Do you have a problem finding subjects to write about? Or do you have trouble getting motivated? Or does something about the act of writing itself cause problems for you? Explain in your own words by writing quickly for five minutes without stopping.

ESL: Are any of your writing difficulties related to writing in a second language? For example, do you need to translate some ideas from your native language to English? Do problems with grammar or vocabulary make it difficult for you to communicate?

1 **b**   What do you enjoy about writing?

Though any writer will tell you writing isn't easy, most writers will also describe it as interesting and exciting. So we asked our first-year students what it was about writing that gave them pleasure:

Jolene: "If I have a strong opinion on a topic, it makes it so much easier to write a paper."

Rebecca: "On occasion I'm inspired by a wonderful idea. Once I get going, I actually enjoy writing a lot."

Casey: "I enjoy most to write about my experiences, both good and bad. I like to write about things when I'm upset—it makes me feel better."

Darren: "I guess my favorite kind of writing is letters. I get to be myself and just talk in them."

Like our students, we prefer to write about topics that inspire or interest us, and we find personal writing such as letters especially easy, interesting, and enjoyable.

WRITING 2: EXPLORATION ────────────────────────────

What kind of writing do you most enjoy doing? What do you like about it: communicating? exploring a subject? playing with words? something else?

I **c** What surprises are in store?

After talking with first-year students, we asked some advanced students about their writing experiences: "What has surprised you the most about writing in college?"

Carmen: "Papers aren't as hellish as I was told they'd be. In fact, I've actually enjoyed writing a lot of them—especially after they were done."

Aaron: "My style has changed a lot. Rather than becoming more complex, it's become simpler."

Kerry: "The most surprising and frustrating thing has been the different reactions I've received from different professors."

Rob: "I'm always being told that my writing is superficial—that I come up with good ideas but don`t develop them."

John: "The tutor at our writing lab took out a pair of scissors and said I would have to work on organization. Then she cut up my paper and taped it back together a different way. This really made a difference, and I've been using this method ever since."

Chrissie: "Sharing papers with other students is very awkward for me. But it's extremely beneficial when I trust and like my group, when we all relax enough to talk honestly about one another's papers."

As you can see, most advanced students found ways to cope with and enjoy college writing. Several of them reported satisfying experiences when they shared their writings with each other. We are sorry that some students, even in their last year, could not figure out what their instructors wanted; we think there are ways to do that.

WRITING 3: EXPLORATION ━━━━━━━━━━━━━━━━━━━━━━

Think about your experience with writing in the last school you attended. What surprised you—pleasantly or not—about the experience? What did you learn or not learn?

I **d** Why is writing important?

We also asked these advanced students why, in their last year, they had enrolled in an elective writing class: "What made the subject so important to you?"

Kim: "I have an easier time expressing myself through writing. When I'm speaking, my words get jumbled—writing gives me more time, and my voice doesn't quiver and I don't blush."

Rick: "Writing allows me to hold up a mirror to my life and see what clear or distorted images stare back at me."

Glenn: "The more I write, the better I become. In terms of finding a job after I graduate, strong writing skills will give me an edge over those who are just mediocre writers."

Amy: "I'm still searching for meaning. When I write I feel I can do anything, go anywhere, search and explore."

Angel: "I feel I have something to say."

We agree with virtually all of these reasons. At times writing is therapeutic, at other times it helps us clarify our ideas, and at still other times it helps us get and keep jobs.

WRITING 4: EXPLORATION ━━━━━━━━━━━━━━━━━━━━━━

Look over the various answers given by the college seniors and select one. Do you agree or disagree with the student? Explain.

I **e** What can you learn from the experience of others?

Since our advanced students had a lot to say about writing, we asked them to be consultants: "What is your advice to first-year college writers?" Here are their suggestions:

Aaron: "Get something down!! The hardest part of writing is starting. Forget the introduction, skip the outline, don't worry about a thesis—just blast your ideas down, see what you've got, then go back and work on them."

Christa: "Plan ahead. It sounds dry, but planning makes writing easier than doing laundry."

Victor: "Follow the requirements of the assignment to a T. Hand in a draft for the instructor to mark up; then rewrite it."

Allyson: "Don't think every piece you write has to be a master-piece. And sometimes the worst assignment turns into the best writing. Don't worry about what the instructor wants—write what you believe."

Carmen: "Imagine and create; never be content with just retelling a story."

Rick: "When other people trash your writing, thank them and listen to their criticism. It stings, but it helps you become a better writer."

Jason: "Say what you are going to say as clearly and as straight-forwardly as possible. Don't try to pad it with big words and fancy phrasing."

Angel: "Read for pleasure from time to time. The more you read, the better you write—it just happens."

Kim: "When choosing topics, choose something that has a place in your heart."

These are good suggestions to any writers: start fast, think ahead, plan to revise and edit, listen to critical advice, consider your audience, be clear, read a lot. We hope, however, that instructors respond to your writing in critically helpful ways and don't "trash" it. Whether or not you take some of the advice will depend on what you want from your writing: good grades? self-knowledge? personal satisfaction? clear communication? a response by your audience? When we shared these suggestions with first-year students, they nodded their heads, took some notes, and laughed—often with relief.

WRITING 5: EXPLORATION ────────────────────────────

What else would you like to ask advanced college students about writing? Find one and ask; report back.

1 f What else do you want to know about writing?

Realizing that our first-year college writers had already received twelve years' worth of "good advice" about learning to write, we asked them one more question: "What do you want to learn about writing that you don't already know?" In parentheses, we have provided references to chapters of this handbook that answer these questions.

Emma: "Should I write to please the instructor or to please myself?" (See Chapter 6, "Assuming a Rhetorical Stance.")

Jose: "I'm always being told to state my thesis clearly. What exactly is a thesis, and why is it so important?" (See 6a; also Chapters 8, "Explaining Things"; 9, "Arguing Positions"; and 10, "Interpreting Texts.")

Jolene: "How do I develop a faster way of writing?" (See Chapter 5, "Inventing and Discovering.")

Amy: "Is there a trick to making a paper longer without adding useless information?" (See especially Chapter 19, "Focused Revising.")

Sam: "How do I learn to express my ideas so they make sense to common intelligent readers and not just to myself?" (See suggestions in Part Six, "Editing.")

Scott: "How can I make my writing flow better and make smooth transitions from one idea to the next?" (See Chapters 23, "Shaping Strong Paragraphs," and 25, "Strengthening Sentence Structure.")

Terry: "I want to learn to like to write. Then I won't put off assignments until the last minute." (See Chapter 3, "The Writing Process," and Part Two.)

Jennifer: "I have problems making sentences sound good. How can I learn to do that?" (See Chapters 23–31.)

John P.: "I would like to develop some sort of personal style so when I write, people know it's me." (See 6c.)

John K.: "I want to become more confident about what I write down on paper. I don't want to have to worry about whether my documentation is correct or my words spelled right." (See Chapters 16, "Using Sources," and 45, "Spelling.")

Woody: "Now that I'm in college, I would like to be challenged when I read and write, to think and ask good questions and find good answers." (See Chapter 2, "Reading Critically to Think Critically.")

Pat: "I don't want to learn nose-to-the-grindstone, straight-from-the-textbook rules. I want to learn to get my mind into motion and pencil in gear." (See Chapters 3, "The Writing Process," and 5, "Inventing and Discovering.")

Heidi: "I would love to increase my vocabulary. If I had a wider range of vocabulary, I would be able to express my thoughts more clearly." (See Chapter 30, "Choosing the Right Word.")

Jess: "I'm always afraid that people will laugh at my writing. Can I ever learn to get over that and get more confident about my writing?" (See Chapter 3, "The Writing Process.")

We can't, of course, guarantee that if you read and use *The Blair Handbook* your writing will get easier, faster, longer, clearer, or more correct. Or, for that matter, that your style will become more personal and varied, or that you will become a more confident and comfortable writer—no handbook can do that for you. Becoming a better writer depends on your own interest and hard work. It will also depend on your college experience, the classes you take, and the teachers with whom you study. However, whether in class or on your own, if you read *The Blair Handbook* carefully and practice its suggestions, you should find possible answers to all these questions and many more.

We admit that there was at least one concern for which we really had no good response. Jessica wrote, "My biggest fear is that I'll end up one semester with four or five courses that all involve writing and I'll die." Or maybe we do have a response: If you become comfortable and competent as a writer, you'll be able to handle all the writing assignments thrown your way. Even if you can't, Jessica, you won't die. It's just college.

SUGGESTIONS FOR WRITING AND RESEARCH

INDIVIDUAL

I. Interview a classmate about his or her writing experiences, habits, beliefs, and practices. Include questions such as those asked in this chapter as well as others you think may be important. Write a brief essay profiling your classmate as a writer. Share your profile with a classmate.

2. Over a two-week period, keep a record of every use you make of written language. Record your entries daily in a journal or class notebook. At the end of two weeks, enumerate all the specific uses as well as how often you did each. What activities dominate your

list? Write an essay based on this personal research in which you argue for or against the centrality of writing in everyday life.

COLLABORATIVE

As a class or in small groups, design a questionnaire to elicit information about people's writing habits and attitudes. Distribute the questionnaire to both students and faculty in introductory and advanced writing classes. Compile the results. Compare and contrast the ideas of students at different levels and disciplines and write a report to share with the class. Consider writing a feature article for your student newspaper or faculty newsletter reporting what you found.

Reading Critically to Think Critically

2

College-level assignments ask you to expand your reading, thinking, and writing skills. That means being able to analyze the distinctions, interpretations, biases, and conclusions of others and
make sense of their writing. **Critical reading** for research assignments involves evaluating the relative importance or credibility of
each of your sources and placing them in a context of related opinions or findings.

This process is sometimes called **critical thinking**. More
than just thinking, however, it includes gathering information,
synthesizing it, and reaching new conclusions or findings of your
own. College instructors expect you to make distinctions, develop
interpretations, and render conclusions in your own writing that
stand up to the critical reading of others, including your instructors. Becoming a critical thinker requires you to exercise reason
and judgment in both reading and writing. Although most of
The Blair Handbook is about writing, this chapter is about critical reading and its relationship to, and influence on, critical
thinking.

2 a Reading to understand

Before you can read any text critically, you need to understand
what you're reading. To do so, you need some context for the new
ideas you encounter, some knowledge of the text's terms and ideas,
and some awareness of the rules that govern the kind of writing
you are reading.

Imagine, for example, reading Mark Twain's *The Adventures of
Huckleberry Finn* with no knowledge of American geography, the
Mississippi River, or the institution of slavery. Imagine reading
about the national debt without understanding basic mathematics,
principles of taxation, or the meaning of deficit spending. The more
you know about any subject, the more you are capable of learning.

The more you learn, the more you know—and the more careful and critical will be your reading, writing, and thinking about that subject.

Many college instructors will ask you to read about subjects that are new to you, so you won't be spending much time reading about what you already know. As you read one unfamiliar text after another, how can you manage to read successfully? How can you create a context, learn the background, and find the rules to help you read unfamiliar texts in unfamiliar subject areas? Let's look at how this might be done.

As an experiment, read the following short opening paragraph from an eight-paragraph *New York Times* story titled "Nagasaki, August 9, 1945." When you have finished, pause for a few moments and think about what you learned, how you learned it, and what you think the rest of the story will be about.

> In August 1945, I was a freshman at Nagasaki Medical College. The ninth of August was a clear, hot, beautiful, summer day. I left my lodging house, which was one and one half miles from the hypocenter, at eight in the morning, as usual, to catch a tram car. When I got to the tram stop, I found that it had been derailed in an accident. I decided to return home. I was lucky. I never made it to school that day.
>
> MICHAITO ICHIMARU

How did you do? Below, we've slowed down our own reading process to show what it was like:

1. We read the first sentence carefully, noticing the year 1945 and the name of the medical college, "Nagasaki." Through our prior historical knowledge, we *identified* Nagasaki, Japan, as one of the two cities on which the United States dropped atomic bombs at the end of World War II—though we did not remember the precise date.

2. We noticed the city and the date (August 9) and wondered if that was when the bomb was dropped. We *asked* (silently), "Is this a story about the bomb?"

3. Still looking at the first sentence, a reference to the writer's younger self ("I was a freshman"), we guessed that the author was present at the dropping of this bomb. We *predicted* that this would be a survivor's account of the bombing of Nagasaki.

4. The word *hypocenter* in the third sentence made us pause again. We *questioned* what the word meant. The language seemed oddly out of place next to the "beautiful, summer day" described in the second sentence. It sounded technical enough to refer to the place where the bomb went off. Evidence was mounting that the narrator

may have lived one and a half miles from the exact place where the atomic bomb detonated.

5. In the next to last sentence of the paragraph, the author says that he was "lucky" to miss school. Why, unless something unfortunate happened at school, would he consider missing it "lucky"? We *predicted* that had the author gone to school "as usual," he would have been closer to the hypocenter, which we now surmised was at Nagasaki Medical College.

6. We then *tested* our several predictions by reading the rest of the essay—something that you, of course, can't do here. They proved correct: Michaito Ichimaru's story is a firsthand account of witnessing and surviving the dropping of the bomb, which in fact killed all who attended the medical college, a quarter of a mile from the hypocenter.

7. Finally, out of curiosity, we *consulted* an encyclopedia for "Nagasaki" and *confirmed* that 75,000 people were killed by this second dropping of an atomic bomb on August 9, 1945.

It is possible that your reasoning went something like ours, which we have reconstructed here as best we could. Of course, these thoughts didn't occur in a seven-step sequence at all, but rather in split-second flashes, simultaneously. Even as we read a sentence for the first time, we found ourselves reading backward as much as forward to check our understanding.

You'll notice that in our example, some parts of the pattern of identifying/questioning/predicting/testing/confirming occur more than once, perhaps simultaneously, and not in any predictable order. No two readers would—or could—read this passage in exactly the same way. However, our reading process may be similar enough to yours to show that reading is a messy trial-and-error process for everyone and that it depends as much on prior knowledge as on new information.

Whenever you read a new text or watch an unfamiliar event, you give it meaning by following a procedure similar to the one we did in the above example, trying to identify what you see, question what you don't understand, make and test predictions about meaning, and consult authorities for confirmation or information. Once you know how to read successfully for basic comprehension, you are ready to read critically.

WRITING I: APPLICATION ─────────────────────────────

Select a book you have been assigned to read for one of your courses and find a chapter that has not yet been covered in class. Read the first page of the chapter and then stop. Write out any predictions you have about where the rest of

READING STRATEGIES ACROSS LANGUAGES

If you learned to read in your native language before learning English, you can use some of the same strategies to read English. For example, some features of stories, explanations, or arguments may be the same in English as in your native language. Whenever you feel that you do not have a good understanding of the purpose or important features of something you are reading in English, take a moment to reflect on how you would have approached a similar text in your native language, and see whether you can use some of those same strategies.

You can also take advantage of information you gained through reading in your native language when you read in English. All readers relate new information in a text to what they already know; this helps them understand the text better and allows them to make predictions about what it will contain. As you read, try to be aware of any relevant information you know about the subject, whether you gained this information in English or in your native language.

 READING TO UNDERSTAND

1. Identify. Read first for what you recognize, know, and understand. Identify what you are reading about. Read carefully—slowly at first—and let meaning take hold where it can.

2. Question. Pause, and look hard at words and phrases you don't know or understand. See whether they make sense when you reread them. Compare them to what you do know, or place them in a context you understand.

3. Predict. Make predictions about what you will learn next: How will the essay, story, or report advance? What will happen? What theme or thesis will emerge? What might be the point of it all?

4. Test. Follow up on your predictions by reading further to see if they are correct or nearly correct. If they are, read on with more confidence; if they are not, read further, make more predictions, and test them. Trial and error are good teachers.

5. Confirm. Check your reading of the text with others who have also read it and see if your interpretations are similar or different. If you have questions, ask them. Share answers.

the chapter is going. (Ask yourself, for example: What is its main theme or argument? How will it conclude?) Finish reading the chapter and check its conclusion against your predictions. If your predictions were close, you are reading well for understanding.

2 **b** Reading critically

People read in different ways at different times. When they read a novel for pleasure or a newspaper to learn about current events, they read to find out "what happens." Doing this is reading for understanding. However, when they read a novel to write a paper on it or a newspaper to find evidence for an argument, they must read beyond the basic facts. They must analyze what they've read and assess the validity of the author's assumptions, ideas, and conclusions. Doing this is reading critically.

The rest of this chapter describes three strategies that lead readers from simply understanding texts to evaluating and interpreting them: previewing, responding, and reviewing. Although we will discuss this process of critical reading as three separate activities, it will become clear that they seldom occur in a simple one-two-three order.

One of our students, Richard, kept a detailed journal when he read a book titled *Iron John*. Richard shared with us both his thoughts and journal entries, some of which are reproduced here as an example of critical reading.

WRITING 2: EXPLORATION

Describe how you read a text when you need to understand it especially well, say, before an examination on it or when you plan to use its ideas in a paper.

Previewing

To preview a text, either look it over briefly before reading it or read it rapidly through once to get a general sense of what it says.

First questions

You should begin asking questions of a text from the moment you pick it up. Your first questions should be aimed at finding general, quickly gleaned information, such as that provided by the title, subtitle, and table of contents.

- What does the title suggest?

- What does the table of contents promise?

- What can I learn from the chapter titles or subheads?

- Who is the author? (Have I heard of him or her?)

- How current is the information?

You may not ask these questions methodically, in this order, and you don't have to write down your answers, but you should ask them before you read the whole text. If your answers to these questions suggest that a text is worthy of further study, continue with the previewing process.

Here are the notes Richard took in response to his first questions:

The title itself, *Iron John*, is intriguing, suggests something strong and unbreakable. I already know and admire the author, Robert Bly, for his insightful poetry but have never read his prose.

The table of contents looks like fun:

1. The Pillow and the Key

2. When One Hair Turns Gold

3. The Road of Ashes, Descent, and Grief

4. The Hunter for the King in Time with No Father

5. The Meeting with the God-Woman in the Garden

Second questions

Once you've determined that a book or article warrants further critical attention, it's helpful to read selected parts of it rapidly to see what they promise. Skimming leads to more questions. Capture your answers on note cards or in a journal.

- Read the prefatory material: What can I learn from the book jacket, foreward, preface?

- Read the introduction, abstract, or first page: What theme or thesis is promised?

- Read a sample chapter or subsection: Is the material about what I expected?

- Scan the index or notes: What sources have informed this text? What names do I recognize?

- Note words or ideas that you do not understand: Do I have the background to understand this text?

- Consider: Will I have to consult other sources to obtain a critical understanding of this one?

In skimming a text, you make predictions about coverage, scope, and treatment and about whether the information seems pertinent or useful for your purpose.

Here are the notes Richard took in response to his second group of questions:

> According to the blurb on the jacket: "*Iron John* is Robert Bly's long-awaited book on male initiation and the role of the mentor, the result of ten years' work with men to discover truths about masculinity that get beyond the stereotypes of our popular culture."

> There is no introduction or index, but the chapter notes in the back of the book (260–67) contain the names of people Bly used as sources. I recognize novelist D. H. Lawrence, anthropologist Mircea Eliade, poet William Blake, historian Joseph Campbell, and a whole bunch of psychologists—but many others I've never heard of.

These preview notes confirmed that *Iron John* is a book about men and male myths in modern American culture by a well-known poet writing a scholarly prose book in an informal style. Richard learned that Bly will not only examine current male mythology but also make some recommendations about which myths are destructive and which constructive.

Previewing is only a first step in a process that now slows down and becomes more time-consuming and critical. As readers begin to preview a text seriously, they often make notes in the text's margin or in a journal or notebook to mark places for later review. In other words, before the preview stage of critical reading has ended, the responding stage has probably begun.

WRITING 3: APPLICATION ─────────────────────────

Select any unfamiliar book about which you are curious and preview it, using the two kinds of questions outlined here. Stop after ten minutes and write what you know about the text.

2 Responding

Once you understand what a text promises, you need to examine it more slowly. You need to begin the work of evaluating its ideas, assumptions, arguments, evidence, logic, and coherence.

You need to start developing your own interpretation of what the text is all about. The best way to do this is to **respond,** or "talk back," to the text in writing.

Respond to passages that cause you to pause for a moment to reflect, to question, to read again, or to say "Aha!" If the text is informational, try to capture the statements that summarize ideas or are repeated. If the text poses an argument (and many of the texts you'll be reading in college will do so), you need to examine the claims the text makes about the topic and to consider each piece of supporting evidence. (See Chapter 9 for more on arguments.) If the text is literary (a novel, play, poem, or essay), pay extra attention to language features such as images, metaphors, and dialogue. In any text, notice boldfaced or italicized words—they have been marked for special attention.

Ask about the effect of the text on you: How am I reacting? What am I thinking and feeling? What do I like? What do I distrust? Do I know why? But don't worry too much about answering all your questions at this point. (That's where reviewing comes in.)

Responding can take many forms, from margin notes to extensive journal entries (See Chapter 4 for more about journal writing), but it should involve writing. The more you write about something, the more you will understand it. If you own the article or book, write any questions or comments in the margins. If you don't—or even as an additional strategy if you do—try writing in a journal. A reading journal gives you a place to record responses to what you read. (Write each response on a fresh page, with the date, the title, and the author noted. In these entries, write any and all reactions you have to the text, including summaries, notes on key passages, speculations, questions, answers, ideas for further research, and connections to other books or events in your life. Note especially the ideas with which you agree or disagree. Explore ideas that are personally appealing. Record memorable quotations (with page numbers) and indicate why they strike you as memorable.

To read any text critically, begin with pen or pencil in hand. Mark places to be examined further, but be aware that mere underlining, checking, or highlighting does not yet involve you in a conversation with the text. To converse with the text, you need to engage actively in one or more of three activities: probing, freewriting, or annotating and cross-referencing.

In discussing these three activities, we will use the following brief passage from *Iron John*, a text that Richard responded to in a variety of ways:

The dark side of men is clear. Their mad exploitation of earth's resources, devaluation and humiliation of women, and obsession with tribal warfare are undeniable. Genetic inheritance contributes to their obsessions, but also culture and environment. We have defective mythologies that ignore masculine depth of feeling, assign men a place in the sky instead of earth, teach obedience to the wrong powers, work to keep men boys, and entangle both men and women in systems of industrial domination that exclude both matriarchy and patriarchy. . . .

I speak of the Wild Man in this book, and the distinction between the savage man and the Wild Man is crucial throughout. The savage soul does great damage to soul, earth, and humankind; we can say that though the savage man is wounded he prefers not to examine it. The Wild Man, who has examined his wound, resembles a Zen priest, a shaman, or a woodsman more than a savage.

Although Richard's responses to *Iron John* illustrate all three activities, most students would use only one or two of these techniques to examine critically a single text.

Probing

In **probing,** ask deeper questions than you asked before. Here, for example, are the questions Richard raised about the passage from *Iron John*:

Bly refers to the dark side of men; does he ever talk about the dark side of women? How would women's darkness differ from men's? What evidence for either does he provide?

Bly suggests that part of men's dark behavior is genetic, part cultural; where does he get this information? Does he think it's a 50/50 split?

What "defective mythologies" is Bly talking about? Does he mean things like religion and politics, or is he referring to nursery rhymes and folktales?

I like the distinction Bly makes between "Wild" and "savage" men. Did he coin the terms, or are they used pervasively in mythology in the same way? I wonder how sharp the line really is between the two.

Those seem like reasonable questions to ask about the passage; however, any other reader could easily think of many more. These questions are "critical" in the sense that they not only request further information from the book but also challenge the author's terms, statements, and sources to see whether they will stand up under scrutiny.

The questions are also written in Richard's own language. Using your own words helps in at least three ways:

1. It forces you to articulate precisely.

2. It makes the question your question.

3. It helps you remember the question for future use.

Freewriting

Write fast about an idea and see where your thoughts go. This **freewriting** often helps you clarify your own thoughts about the ideas in the text. When you freewrite, write to yourself in your own natural style, not worrying about sentence structure, spelling, or punctuation. Nobody else need ever read this; its purpose is to help you tie together ideas from your reading with the thoughts and experiences in your own mind. (For more details on freewriting, see 5b.)

In thinking about the passage from *Iron John*, Richard made the following entry in his journal:

> 9/30 Bly praises the "Wild Man" in us, clearly separating "wildness" from barbarism and savagery—hurting others. Also suggests that modern men are wounded in some way—literally?—but only those who examine their wounds gain higher knowledge. In an interview I once heard him talk about warriors—men who seek action (mountain climbing? skiing? Habitat for Humanity?) to feel whole and fulfilled. So men (why not women too?) test themselves—not necessarily against other men—against nature or even themselves. Harvey says sailing is his warrior activity. Is backpacking mine?

Richard's freewriting shows the writer reacting to one idea in the text (*wildness*), moving to another (*being wounded*), digressing by remembering a TV interview, raising a question (*why not women too?*), and concluding by raising a question about himself (*Is backpacking mine?*). Freewriting generates questions at random, catches them, and leaves the answering for later.

Annotating and cross-referencing

Annotating, or talking back to a text by writing in the margins, is an excellent way to make that text your own. Annotating is easier if you have your own copy of the text; otherwise you can make your annotations on Post-it notes or in a notebook with page numbers marked. As a critical reader, what would you write in these annotations?

- Points of agreement or disagreement
- Supporting examples

The Fifties male had a clear vision of what a man was, and what male responsibilities were, but the isolation and one-sidedness of his vision were dangerous.

Examples in film? Books?

During the 1960s, another sort of man appeared. The waste and violence of the Vietnam war made men question whether they knew what an adult male really was. If manhood meant Vietnam, did they want any part of it? Meanwhile, [the feminist movement encouraged men to actually look at women,] forcing them to become conscious of concerns and sufferings that the Fifties male labored to avoid. As men began to examine women's history, and women's sensibility, some men began to notice what was called their *feminine* side and pay attention to it. This process continues to this day, and I would say that most contemporary men are involved in it in some way.

How did they see it?

There's something wonderful about this development—I mean the practice of men welcoming their own "feminine" consciousness and nurturing it—this is important—and yet I have the sense that there is something wrong. The male in the past twenty years has become more thoughtful, more gentle. But by this process he has not become more free. He's a nice boy who pleases not only his mother but also the young woman he is living with.

Examples? Easy Rider? Platoon?

Why is pleasing people wrong? contradiction?

female-associated word—loaded

In the seventies I began to see all over the country a phenomenon that we might call the "soft male." Sometimes even today when I look out at an audience, perhaps half the young males are what I'd call soft. They're lovely, valuable people—I like them—they're not interested in harming the earth or starting wars.

How would Bly define free?

Should they be?

An annotated text page

- Implications and consequences
- Personal associations and remembrances
- Connections to other texts, ideas, and courses
- Recurring images and symbols

To move beyond annotating (commenting on single passages) to **cross-referencing** (finding relationships among passages), use a coding system to show that one annotation or passage is related to another. Some students write comments on different features of the text in different colors, such as reserving green for nature images, blue for key terms, red for interesting episodes, and so on. Other students write their notes first and then go back and number them, perhaps 1 for plot, 2 for key terms, and so on.

WRITING 4: APPLICATION _____

Keep a reading journal for an assigned reading from one of your courses. Write something in the journal after every reading session, including probing questions and freewriting. Annotate the text and create a cross-referencing system as you go along to see what patterns you can discover. Write about the results of these response methods in your journal: Did they help? Which ones worked best?

3 Reviewing

To review, you need both to reread and to *re-see* a text, reconsidering its meaning and the ideas you have about it. You need to be sure that you grasp the important points within the text, but you also need to move beyond that level to a critical understanding of the text as a whole. In responding, you started a conversation with the text so you could put yourself into the book's framework and context; in reviewing, you should consider how the book can fit into your own framework and context. As you review, keep responding, talking back to the text, but this time do so with more purpose and focus.

Reviewing will take different forms depending on how you intend to use the text—whether or not you are using it to write a paper, for example. In general, there are two ways to review a text you have read critically: you can interpret what it means, or you can evaluate its soundness or significance.

When you review to interpret or evaluate a text, you slow your reading down and ask critical questions. You move beyond an appreciation of what the text says and build your own theory of what the text means and how good or useful it is. (For more information on writing to interpret, see Chapter 10; for more on evaluating texts, see Chapter 15.)

If you plan to write a critical paper about a text, it's a good idea to confirm your interpretation by consulting what others have said about that text. The interpretations of other critics will help put your own view in perspective as well as raise questions that may not have occurred to you. Try to read more than one perspective on a text. However, it is better to consult such sources after you have established some views of your own so that you do not simply adopt the view of the first expert you read.

When you review a text, you examine its meaning and weigh its merits: What does it say? Is it credible? Why or why not? What's debatable? Texts with different purposes need to be examined accordingly. For example, an argument text tries to do one thing, an informational text something else, and a literary text something else again.

Argument texts. Argument texts make certain claims in advance and then support those claims with evidence. When you first respond to such a text, you simply identify and comment on the text's argument. When you review it, you examine and evaluate each part of the argument to see whether it is sound. If the text argues that *Huckleberry Finn* is a racist book, look closely at the evidence, the claims, and the whole argument.

Review the **evidence.**

• Is it is a **fact**—something that can be verified and that most readers will accept without further argument?

• Is it an **inference**—a conclusion drawn from an accumulation of facts?

• Is it an **opinion**—an idea that reflects an author's personal beliefs and may be based on faith, emotion, or myth?

While all three types of evidence have their place, the strongest arguments are based on accurate facts and reasonable inferences. Look out for opinions that are masquerading as facts and for inferences that are based on insufficient facts.

Review the **claims.** A claim is a statement that something is true or should be done.

• Is the claim stated clearly? (On what page?)

• Is every claim supported by sufficient evidence?

• Are you aware of counterclaims or contradictory evidence?

If a claim is important or daring, one fact is not enough. Look for any claims that are unsupported or that are supported by insufficient evidence.

Review the logic of the argument. For an argument to be logical, it must be based on reason, not emotion.

• Does the argument advance step by step to a reasonable conclusion?

• Are there any unexplained gaps or mistakes in reasoning?

(See Chapter 9 for more on argument writing.)

Informational texts. Reviewing informational texts requires making sure the facts are true, the inferences are based on facts, and the opinions are based on knowledge. Informational texts don't make arguments, but they often draw conclusions from the facts they present. For example, a geology text explaining the theory of continental glaciation should explain the evidence that supports the theory. Ask these kinds of questions of informational texts:

• Do the facts justify the conclusions?

• Is any information that you expect to be there missing?

• Is the author's tone fair and reasonable?

• What is the basis for the author's expertise?

(See Chapter 8 for more on informational writing.)

Literary texts. Essays, short stories, poems, and plays may contain arguments and information, but their primary goal is more elusive—to make you feel, imagine, empathize, or understand. One good way to interpret or evaluate literature is to write journal entries in response to questions about different elements of the text:

• What is the *plot*?

• Are the *characters* believable?

READING CRITICALLY

1. Preview a text first by questioning the title, table of contents, author's reputation, and date: do they seem relevant to you? If you are still interested in the source, ask similar questions of the preface or foreword, the introduction, sample pages, and index: does this text provide useful information?

2. Respond to a text by writing back to some of its assertions: ask further questions, freewrite possible answers, and write margin notes next to interesting or puzzling passages.

3. Review an argument text by examining the logic of the argument, the claims it makes, and the evidence that is presented to support these claims.

　　Review an informational text by checking whether the facts justify the conclusion.

　　Review a literary text by explaining in your own words its plot, character, setting, point of view, and theme.

- Is the *setting* convincing?

- From what *point of view* is the text written?

- What *images* or *themes* are repeated?

Interpreting and evaluating literature is often very personal, relying on individual associations and responses, but the strongest critical evaluations are based on textual evidence. (For information on analyzing and interpreting literary texts, see Chapter 10.)

SUGGESTIONS FOR WRITING AND RESEARCH

INDIVIDUAL

Select a short text. First read it briefly for *understanding*, to be sure it makes sense to you. Second, read it *critically* according to the methods described in this chapter. Finally, write a short (two-page) *review* of the text in which you explain its meaning and recommend or don't recommend it to other readers.

COLLABORATIVE

As a class or small group, agree on a short text to read and write about, following the suggestions in the individual exercise above. Share your written reviews in small groups, paying particular attention to the claims and evidence each writer uses. Rewrite your review, using the response you received from your group. (For more information about responding to other writers' texts, see Chapter 20.)

3 The Writing Process

While there is no one best way to write, some ways do seem to work for more people in more situations than do others. Learning what these ways are may save you some time, grief, or energy—perhaps all three. This chapter describes the messy business we call the **writing process.** It takes a close look at how writers write from the time they select something to write about through their efforts at drafting, revising, and editing, until they send this writing out into the world. If you're interested in improving your writing, examine closely your own writing process: describe how you do it, identify what works and what doesn't, then study the ideas and strategies that work for others—some of these are bound to help you.

It's time to examine your own writing habits: What do you do, for example, when you are assigned to write a paper due in one week? Do you sit down that day and start writing the introduction? Or do you sit down but do something else instead? If you don't work on the assignment right away, do you begin two days before deadline, or is your favorite time the night before the paper is due? Do you write a few pages a day, every day, and let your paper emerge gradually? Or do you prefer to draft it one day, revise the next, and proofread it just before handing it in?

What writing conditions do you seek? Do you prefer your own room? Do you like to listen to certain kinds of music? Do you deliberately go somewhere quiet, such as the library? Or do you prefer a coffee shop, a cafe, or a booth at McDonald's?

With what do you write? Your own computer or the school's? A pencil on tablets of lined paper? Or do you first write with a favorite pen and then copy the result onto a computer?

Editing symbols

ABB	abbreviation **49**		REF	pronoun reference **36a–e**
ADJ	adjective **35a, 39f, 61d**		REP	repetitious **21d, 26e**
ADV	adverb **35a, 61d**		S-V AGR	subject-verb agreement **34**
AWK	awkward		SLANG	slang **30g**
BIAS	biased language **31**		SP	spelling **46**
CAP, ≡	capital letter **46**		SP OUT	spell out
CASE	pronoun case **36**		SUB	subordination **25b–c, 33e**
CLICHE	cliché **30i**		T	verb tense **34d–e**
COH	coherence **23c**		TONE	tone **29**
CONCL	conclusion **24**		??	unclear
COORD	coordination **25a, 25c**		VERB	verb **34**
CS	comma splice **33**		W	wordy
DM	dangling modifier **35g**		'	apostrophe **42**
EMPH	emphasis		[ ]	brackets **44d**
FRAG	sentence fragment **32**		:	colon **33c**
FS	fused sentence **33**		,	comma **39**
HYPH	hyphen **47**		$\frac{1}{M}$	dash **44b**
ITAL	italics **48**		. . .	ellipsis points **44c**
JARG	jargon **30g**		!	exclamation point **38c**
LC	lowercase letter		( ) parens	parentheses **44a**
MIXED	mixed construction **37b**		⊙	period **38a**
MM	misplaced modifier **35f**		?	question mark **38b**
MOOD	verb mood **34f–g**		" "	quotation marks **43**
MS	manuscript		;	semicolon **33b**
NUM	number **49**		/	slash **44e**
OPEN	opening **24**		⌒	close up space
¶	paragraph **23**		#	add space
//	parallelism **25e-f**		^	insert
P	punctuation **38–44**		ℐ	delete
P-A AGR	pronoun-antecedent agreement **36f–j**		~	transpose
			X	obvious error
PASS	passive voice **27c**			

Which of the habits or methods described here is the right one? Which technique yields the best results? These are trick questions, since different ones work best for different individuals. There is no single best way to write. People manage to write well under wildly different conditions.

The rest of this chapter identifies five discrete but overlapping and often nonsequential phases of the process of writing—planning, drafting, researching, revising, and editing—and explains how this handbook reflects this process.

ESL USING YOUR NATIVE LANGUAGE WHEN COMPOSING IN ENGLISH

You may want to compose in both your native language and English when working on a writing assignment. For example, you might brainstorm, make notes, or create outlines in your native language, or you could use native-language words or phrases when you're not sure of the English equivalents. Using your native language this way may help you avoid writer's block and develop fluency in English. However, because you want as much practice writing in English as possible, don't compose a whole essay first in your native language and then try to translate it into English. Periodically you should evaluate the effectiveness of your composing strategies. For instance, if you find that using a native language–English dictionary often results in unidiomatic constructions, you may want to become more familiar with a good English dictionary.

WRITING I: EXPLORATION

Answer the questions posed on the opening pages of this chapter. Where, when, and how do you usually write? What are the usual results? With what do you need some extra help?

ESL: If you sometimes write in your native language, compare the process you use when writing in it with the process you use when writing in English. Are any parts different? Why do you think this is so?

3 b Planning

Planning consists of creating, discovering, locating, developing, organizing, and trying out ideas. Writers are doing deliberate planning when they make notes, turn casual lists into organized outlines, write journal entries, compose rough drafts, and consult with others. They also are doing less deliberate planning while they walk, jog, eat, read, browse in libraries, converse with friends, or wake up in the middle of the night thinking. Planning involves both expanding and limiting options, locating the best strategy for the occasion at hand, and focusing energy productively.

Planning comes first. It also comes second and third. No matter how careful your first plans, the act of writing usually necessitates that you keep planning all the way through the writing process, that you continue to think about why you are writing, what you are writing, and for whom. When writers are not sure how their ideas will be received by someone else, they often write to themselves first, testing their ideas on a friendly audience to find a good voice for communicating with others in later drafts.

During the planning process for *The Blair Handbook*, for instance, we were trying out ideas and exploring broadly and also narrowing our thinking to focus both on our purpose as writers and the purposes that handbooks serve. We had to consider our audience: who uses handbooks? We had to find our voice not only as classroom teachers but as writers: would we be friendly and casual or authoritative and serious? We spent some time inventing and discovering ideas—figuring out what kind of information you, our readers, require in a handbook, how much of this information we already knew, and where to find what we didn't know.

Part Two of this handbook focuses on the concerns that most writers face at the initial stages of a writing project: using a journal to help you create and discover ideas (Chapter 4), using invention and discovery techniques (Chapter 5), and focusing on your purpose, audience, and voice to guide your writing style (Chapter 6).

WRITING 2: APPLICATION _____

Describe the strategies you commonly use when you plan papers. How much does your planning vary from time to time or assignment to assignment? Now use your favorite planning strategy for twenty minutes to plan one currently assigned paper.

3 **C** **Drafting**

At some point all writers need to move beyond thinking, talking, and planning and actually start writing. Many writers like to schedule a block of time—an hour or more—to draft their ideas, give them shape, see what they look like. One of the real secrets to good writing is learning simply to sit down and write.

Drafting is the intentional production of language to convey information or ideas to an audience. First drafts are concerned with ideas, with getting the direction and concept of the piece of writing clear. Subsequent drafting, which includes revising and editing, is concerned with making the initial ideas ever sharper, more precise and clearer.

While most writers hope their first draft will be their final draft, it seldom is. Still, try to make your early drafts as complete as possible at the time—that is, give each draft your best shot: compose in complete sentences, break into paragraphs where necessary, and aim at a satisfying form. At the same time, allow time for second and third drafts and maybe more.

Sometimes it's hard to separate drafting from planning, researching, revising, and editing. Many times in writing *The Blair Handbook*, we sat down to explore a possible idea in a notebook and found ourselves drafting part of a chapter instead. Other times, when we were trying to advance an idea in a clear and linear way, we kept returning instead to revise a section just completed. While it's useful to separate these phases of writing, don't worry too much if they refuse to stay separate. In most serious writing, every phase of the process can be considered *recursive*—that is, moving back and forth almost simultaneously and maybe even haphazardly, from planning to revising to editing to drafting, back to planning, and so on.

The four chapters in Part Three describe strategies for drafting different college writing assignments: reflecting on experience (Chapter 7), explaining things (Chapter 8), arguing positions (Chapter 9), and interpreting texts (Chapter 10). Each chapter contains samples of student writing, in both draft and finished stages. While there are more than five kinds of college papers, the approaches to drafting in Part Three apply to any number of other writing assignments.

WRITING 3: APPLICATION _____

Describe the process you most commonly use to draft a paper. Is your way of starting consistent from paper to paper? Now write the first draft for the paper you planned in Writing 2: sit down, and for half an hour compose as much of the

paper as you can, noting in brackets as you go along where you need to return with more information or ideas.

Writers need something to write about. Unless they are writing completely from memory, they need to locate ideas and information. Even personal essays and experiential papers can benefit from additional factual information that substantiates and intensifies what the writer remembers.

As a college student, you do a form of **research** every time you write an analysis or an interpretation of a text: reading and rereading the text is the research. You do research when you compare one text to another. You do research to track down the dates of historical events. You do research when you conduct laboratory experiments, visit museums, interview people, or surf the Web.

Whenever you write about unfamiliar subjects, you have two choices: to research and find things out, or to bluff with unsupported generalizations. Which kind of paper would you prefer to read? Which kind of writing will you profit by doing?

The seven chapters in Part Four describe how to write papers that require research. We encourage you to consider research as a natural part of almost every writing assignment: the truth is, writers should know what they are writing about rather than limiting themselves to writing what they already know about. However, one common college assignment—the research essay—will require you to do more extensive research, use a more formal style and format, and write a longer paper than most other assignments; Chapter 11 provides guidance on writing research essays. Research for college papers is conducted in the library (Chapter 12), on the Internet (Chapter 13), or in the field (Chapter 14). After locating possible sources, you need to evaluate their usefulness (Chapter 15), select strategies for including these sources in your paper (Chapter 16), and document them appropriately. Part Four concludes by presenting a variety of student-written research papers on different subjects and in different styles and formats (Chapter 17).

Because the documentation system appropriate for a paper depends largely on the discipline in which it is written, we include specific instructions and models for documenting research papers in Part Eight, "Writing Across the Curriculum" (Chapters 54–61). This section presents each documentation system within the context of the aims and styles of its discipline: the Modern Language Association (MLA) for languages and literature the Chicago system

for the humanities, the American Psychological Association (APA) system for the social sciences, and so on.

WRITING 4: APPLICATION

Describe the kind of research assignments you have done in the past. Now locate additional research information to add to the paper you began drafting in Writing 3, using any research process with which you are familiar.

3 e Revising

Somewhere in the midst of their writing, most writers revise the drafts they have planned, drafted, and researched. **Revising** involves rewriting to make the purpose clearer, the argument stronger, the details sharper, the evidence more convincing, the organization more logical, the opening more inviting, the conclusion more satisfying.

We consider revising to be separate from editing, yet the two tasks may not always be separable. Essentially, revising occurs at the level of ideas, whereas editing occurs at the level of language. Revising means re-seeing the drafted paper and thinking again about its direction, focus, arguments, and evidence. In writing this fourth edition of *The Blair Handbook,* we revised ceaselessly to get each chapter even sharper than it was in the first and second editions.

While it is tempting to edit individual words and sentences as you revise, revising before you edit saves time and energy. Revising to refocus or redirect often requires that you delete paragraphs, pages, and whole sections of your draft, actions that can be painful if you have already carefully edited them.

Each of the four chapters in Part Five covers a different aspect of revising. Chapter 18 ("The Revising Process") discusses the overall goals of revising. Chapter 19 ("Focused Revising") explores systematic revision options. Chapter 20 ("Responding to Writing") examines how writing groups aid revising. Chapter 21 ("Creative Nonfiction") provides imaginative strategies for revising college essays.

WRITING 5: APPLICATION

Does your usual process for revising a paper include any of the ideas discussed in this section? Describe how your process is similar or different. Now revise the paper to which you added research information in Writing 4, using any revision techniques with which you are comfortable.

3 f Editing

Whether writers have written three or thirteen drafts, they want the last one to be perfect—or as near perfect as time and skill allow. When **editing,** writers pay careful attention to the language they have used, striving for the most clarity and punch possible. Many writers edit partly to please themselves, so their writing sounds right to their own ears. At the same time, they edit hoping to please, satisfy, or persuade their intended readers.

You edit to communicate as clearly as possible. After you've spent time drafting and revising your ideas, it would be a shame for readers to dismiss those ideas because they were poorly expressed. Check the clarity of your ideas, the logic and flow of paragraphs, the precision and power of your words, and the correctness and accuracy of everything from facts and references to spelling and punctuation.

In finishing *The Blair Handbook*, we went over every word and phrase to make sure each one expressed our ideas precisely. Then our editors did the same. Then they sent the manuscript to other experts on writing, and they too went over the whole manuscript. Then we revised and edited again.

Because there are so many different things to look for when you edit your writing, Part Six of *The Blair Handbook*, the editing

---

REVIEWING THE WRITING PROCESS

1. Plan to write by practicing invention strategies to help you find and clarify ideas. (See especially Chapters 4 and 6.)

2. Start a first draft of your paper early to see where your ideas are taking you. Plan to write later drafts to clarify, substantiate, or change those ideas. (See specific guidelines for drafting different papers in Chapters 7–10.)

3. Add current research to your papers by locating authoritative, accurate, and detailed information in the library, on the Internet, or through interviews and observations. (See specific suggestions in Chapters 11–17.)

4. Revise each paper (all good writers revise their writing!) by returning to its central idea and questioning its accuracy, evidence, and conclusions. (See Chapters 18–21.)

5. Edit your paper for clarity, grammar, punctuation, and mechanics. (See Part Six for specific editing help.)

section, occupies more than half
several subparts for easy referen
ers strategies for attracting a
"Editing Grammar" explains
dard English. "Editing Pun
periods, commas, semico
covers additional conv
form. The principles t
cate effectively with
Handbook is desi
learn and use th

Writing wit is organized into
r Effectiveness" cov-
our readers' attention.
tical conventions of stan-
escribes the conventions of
so on, and "Editing Mechanics"
presenting language in written
rs (and speakers) apply to communi-
udiences are called **rhetoric.** *The Blair*
o be a convenient reference to help you
inciples in your writing.

3 g Writing with computers

Computers are great writing tools. Unlike typewriters, pens, and pencils, computers allow writers to change their writing infinitely and easily before the words are ever printed on paper. Writers are not committed to final copy until they print it out, and even then they can work on it again and again without retyping the whole thing over.

All word processing programs work in pretty much the same way: You type the words on the computer screen—plan, draft, revise, edit. When finished, you store the file, with a brief descriptive name, on your hard drive or a disk. When you want to work on the document again, you call the file back to the screen and start all over.

Improving your writing process

Computers make it easier for you to move back and forth freely as you compose. If you are like most writers, you probably jump around—planning, drafting, and researching whenever you need to. Computers facilitate this process by keeping everything fluid and endlessly changeable.

Creating distance

Computers create instant distance from your thoughts, setting them in good-looking electronic type, where they seem less personal and easier to revise and edit. Most word processors give you access to type styles (fonts), graphic images, and page layouts that can produce professional-looking and visually exciting papers with good readability and aesthetic appeal.

WRI **writing process**

1. Plan with **...PUTERS**
maintaining a separ... keeping your journal on a disk and by
discover ideas related... paper you write. As you invent and
abling you to copy useful... record them in the paper's file, en-
2. Draft with a computer ...and easily to your paper itself.
screen and saving each draft to b... ...ing directly on the monitor
3. Research with a computer b... ...d edited later.
catalogue and searching the Internet with... your library's online
(See Chapters 12–13.) ...iate search engines.
4. Revise with a computer by adding, deleting, ...ng, and pasting
to focus and advance ideas.
5. Edit with a computer by reviewing each sentence a... playing
with word constructions on screen so that each sentence car...s its
own weight and says exactly what you mean.
6. Format finished copy on a computer by selecting the appropriate type font and size; by using boldface, italics, and underlining judiciously; and by including graphics where appropriate.

Conducting research

Computers allow access to research resources via the Internet. You may also be able to access your local library through a computer connection. Instead of traveling physically to locate information, books, periodicals, and special collections, you can search for, find, and receive printouts from sources within the collections of many libraries, museums, electronic bulletin boards, and the World Wide Web.

Consulting reference sources

Computer programs allow you to check dictionaries, encyclopedias, thesauruses, grammar books, and style manuals, automatically coordinated with whatever text you are working on. In the future such tools will only become more numerous and better.

3 h Writing in English as a second language

All students in a writing class can grow as writers, those with extensive writing experience as well as those who have

never written much. However, the ones faced with the greatest challenge may be students whose first language is not English. In addition to learning new strategies for composing and new forms for expressing what they know, nonnative speakers must attend to the conventions of language that native speakers take for granted.

Besides possible grammar and vocabulary difficulties, students who grew up speaking another language may have to adjust to the expectations and traditions of the American classroom. For example, American academic prose is often less formal than that in many other countries. Students who have learned to write in more formal systems may find instructors suggesting that they make their writing more lively or personal. Also, while U.S. schools increasingly treat writing as a multiple-draft process, instructors in many other countries may expect a piece of writing to be finished correctly the first time through.

If English is not your native language, you need to read, write, speak, and listen attentively to as much English as you can. Use your writing class as a place to try out new ideas about writing, revising, and editing, and don't be afraid to ask your instructor and classmates for help.

Throughout *The Blair Handbook* blue boxes provide information about the English language of particular interest to nonnative speakers. The gold letters "ESL" in the contents identify each section that includes one of these specially marked boxes. This symbol in blue also appears before the special ESL writing suggestions found in many chapters in Parts One, Two, and Three. Finally, an ESL index is provided at the back of the book to help you locate topics that you may find helpful.

If English *is* your native language, you may still benefit from skimming the ESL boxes. They may give you a broader appreciation of foreign languages as well as English.

SUGGESTIONS FOR WRITING AND RESEARCH

INDIVIDUAL

Study your own writing process as you work on one whole paper from beginning to end, taking notes in your journal to document your habits and practices. Write an analytic sketch describing the way you write and speculating about the origins of your current habits.

COLLABORATIVE

With your classmates, form interview pairs and identify local professional writers or professors who publish. Make an appointment with one of these practicing writers, interview him or her about the writing process he or she practices, and report back to the class. Write a collaborative report about writers in your community; make it available to other writing classes or interested faculty.

PART TWO

Planning

www.prenhall.com/fulwiler

Planning

www.prenhall.com/fulwiler

On *The Blair Handbook, Fourth Edition,* Web site you can find

- Exercises on keeping a journal
- Drafting and planning tips
- Audience and voice discussion

4 Keeping a Journal

Journals allow people to talk to themselves without feeling silly. They help college students figure out and reflect on what is happening in their personal and academic lives. Sometimes students focus their journal writing narrowly, on the subject matter of a single discipline; other times they speculate broadly, on the whole range of academic experience; and still other times they write personally, exploring their private thoughts and feelings. College instructors often recommend or require that students keep journals to monitor what and how the students are learning. Just as often, however, students require journals of themselves, realizing that journals are more useful for the writer than for the reader.

4　a　Understanding journals

Journals are daily records of people's lives (*jour* is French for "day"). Of course, journals don't need to be written in every day, and sometimes they go by other names: daybooks, logs, learning logs, commonplace books, or simply writer's notebooks. No matter what you call them, their function is similar—to capture ideas and events that are on your mind. In this sense, a journal can be whatever you want it to be, recording whatever snippets of life you find interesting and potentially useful. What makes a journal a journal?

Sequence

Journals capture thoughts sequentially, from one day or time period to the next. Dating each entry allows you to compare ideas to both later and earlier ones and provides an ongoing record of your constancy, change, or growth. You thus end up documenting your learning over the course of a semester or a project.

Audience

Journals are written for the writer, not some distant reader. A journal is a place to explore what's important to *you*, not to communicate information or ideas to someone else. While you may choose to share entries with people you trust, your main audience remains yourself. An assigned journal, however, may initiate an informal conversation between you and your instructor. In this role, it has much in common with notes, letters, and other informal means of communication.

Language

The language of journals is whatever writers want it to be. Since your audience is yourself, you should use whatever language you feel most comfortable with. (The exception would be a journal assigned by somebody else who wants also to read it.) Your focus should be on ideas rather than on style, grammar, spelling, or punctuation. In journal writing, focus on what you want to say rather than on the language of your thought.

Ownership

You are free to get things wrong in journals and not be penalized. It's your notebook. Journals are practice and discovery books: you can put new concepts into your own words, try out new lines of reasoning, and not worry about completing every thought. If something doesn't work the first time, try it again in subsequent entries—or abandon it entirely.

Academic journals differ from diaries, daybooks, and private journals in important ways. Whereas diaries record any and all events of the writer's day, academic journals focus more consistently on ideas under study in college. Academic journals might be described as a cross between private diaries, written solely for the writer, and class notebooks, which record an instructor's words. Like diaries, journals are written in the first person about ideas important to the writer; like class notebooks, they focus on a subject under study in a college course.

Diary ———————→ Academic journal ◄——————— Class notebook

Your journal includes your thoughts, reactions, reflections, and questions about your classes and ideas, written in your own language. Think of your academic journal as a personal record of your educational experience.

Describe your experiences with journals. Have you ever kept one for school before? In which class? With what result? Have you ever kept one on your own? With what result? Do you still keep one? What is it like? If you are unfamiliar with journals, what do you think of the idea of journal writing?

ESL: Have you ever kept a journal in your native language? What was it like?

4 **b** Keeping college journals

Both personal and academic journals are useful to college writers because they provide places to record and play with thought and experience. In our classes, we recommend that students keep both, one about their private lives, one about academic matters; sometimes they do this with separate notebooks, other times by dividing a loose-leaf notebook into two sections.

1 Journals in the writing class

Journals are often assigned to help student writers discover, explore, advance, and critique their writing projects and to help instructors monitor and informally assess students' development as writers.

Use your journal to find topics to write about, to try out introductions and arguments, to record relevant research and observations, to assess how the paper is turning out, and to make plans for what to do next. In the following journal entry, John tells himself what to do in the next draft of a paper describing his coaching of an eighth-grade girls' soccer team:

> 9/16   I'm going to try to use more dialogue in my paper. That is what I really think I was missing. The second draft is very dull. As I read it, it has no life. I should have used more detail.
>
> I'll try more dialogue, lots more, in draft 3. I'll have it take place at one of my practices, giving a vivid description of what kids were like.
>
> I have SO MUCH MATERIAL. But I have a hard time deciding what seems most interesting.

John uses his journal to critically evaluate his most recent paper draft and to catch ideas for revising next time.

Use your journal to record what you've learned about writing through class discussions, reading of other student papers, and

reviewing your own writing. Near the end of the semester, John reflected in his journal about what he had learned so far:

> 11/29   I've learned to be very critical of my own work, to look at it again and again, looking for big and little problems. I've also learned from my writing group that other people's comments can be extremely helpful—so now I make sure I show my early drafts to Kelly or Karen before I write the final draft. I guess I've always known this, but now I actually do it.

WRITING 2: APPLICATION

Keep a journal for the duration of a writing project, recording in it all of your starts, stops, insights, and ideas related to the project. At the end, consider whether the journal presents a fair portrait of your own writing process.

2 Journals across the curriculum

Journals are useful in any course, to clarify course purposes, pose and solve problems, keep track of readings, raise questions to ask in class, practice for exams, and find topics for paper assignments.

In science or mathematics, when you switch from numbers to words, you often see the problem differently. In addition, putting someone else's problem or question into your own language makes it yours and so leads you one step further toward a solution.

One of the best uses for journals is making connections between college knowledge and personal knowledge. For example, when you record personal reflections in an academic journal, you may identify with and perhaps make sense of the otherwise distant and confusing past. When you write out trial hypotheses based on personal observations, you may eventually discover good ideas for research topics, designs, or experiments.

3 Personal journals

While *The Blair Handbook* emphasizes academic writing, we believe that personal journal writing has many powerful benefits for college writers. In personal journals, feel free to explore your feelings about college, prospective majors, roommates, grades, parties, dates, friends. When you keep a journal in a writing class, mark off a section for personal entries. Whether you share these with your instructor should be up to you.

Keep a personal journal for two weeks, writing faithfully for at least ten minutes each day. Write about whatever is on your mind. Follow the "Guidelines for Keeping a Journal" at the end of this chapter. After two weeks, reread your entries and assess the worth of such writing to you.

4 Double-entry journals

Double-entry journals can help you separate initial observations from later, more reflective observations. To make such a journal, divide each page in a notebook with a vertical line down the middle. On the left side of the page, record initial observations of data; on the right side, reflect on the meaning of what you first recorded, either at the same time or later. In other words, double-entry journals let you observe and reflect upon your prior observations and reflections.

Although such notebooks originated in the sciences, allowing lab scientists to collect data at one time and to speculate about them later, these notebooks also serve well in other courses. In an English class, for example, you can make initial observations about the plot of a story on the left while raising questions and concerns on the right, as we see in Susan's entry about Alice Walker's novel *The Color Purple* shown on page 44. In the left column, she recorded the plot; in the right column; she noted her personal reaction to what she was reading.

4 c Ideas for college journals

Journals are useful even when you're not in an academic environment, since good ideas, questions, and answers don't always wait for convenient times. We suggest that you write often, in your most comfortable voice, and not worry about someone's evaluating you. The following selection of journal entries illustrates some of the ways journals can be used.

Planning

Journals can help you plan any project by providing a place to talk it over with yourself. Whether it's a research paper, a personal essay, or a take-home examination, you can make journal notes about how to approach it, where to start, or who else to consult

Summary	What I think
pp. 3–12. Celie's mother is dying so her father starts having sex with her. She got pregnant by him twice and he sold both of her babies. Celie's mother died and he got married again to a very young girl. Mr. is a man whose wife died and he has a lot of children. He wants to marry Celie's sister Nettie. Their father won't let him. He says Nettie has too much going for her so he let him have Celie.	Why did Celie's father sell her kids? How could Mr. take Celie if he wanted Nettie so much? I think Celie's father is low-down and selfish. A very cruel man.
pp. 13–23. Celie got married to Mr. and his kids don't like her and he beats her. While Celie was in town she met the lady who has her kids. She was a preacher's wife. Nettie ran away and came to stay with Celie. Mr. still likes her and puts her out because she shows no interest in him. Celie tells her to go the preacher's wife's house and stay with them because she was the only woman she saw with money.	I think it's wrong to marry someone to take care of your children and to keep your home clean. I think Celie was at least glad to know one of her children was in good hands. I am glad Nettie was able to get away from her dad and Mr., hopefully the preacher & wife will take her in.
pp. 24–32. Shug Avery, Mr.'s old girlfriend and also an entertainer, came to town. Mr. got all dressed up so he could go see her, he stayed gone all weekend. Celie was very excited about her.	How could he go and stay out with another woman all weekend? Why didn't he marry Shug? Why was Celie so fascinated with Shug?

A sample of a double-entry journal on the novel *The Color Purple*

before actually beginning a draft. Here is an entry from Peter's journal kept for his first-year writing class:

> 10/12 Well, I switched my research topic to something I'm actually interested in, a handicapped children's rehabilitation program right here on campus. My younger brother was born deaf and our whole family has pitched in to help him—but I've never really studied what a college program could do to help. The basis of my research will be interviews with people who run the program—I have my first appointment tomorrow with Professor Stanford.

Sometimes planning means venting frustration about what's going wrong; other times it means exploring a new direction or topic. Journal writing is ultimately unpredictable: it doesn't come out neat and orderly, and sometimes it doesn't solve your problem, but it does provide a place where you can keep trying to solve it.

2 Learning to write

Part of the content of a writing course is the business of learning to write. You can use a journal to document how your writing is going and what you need to do next to improve it. In the following example, Bruce reflects on his experience of writing a report:

> 10/3 I'm making this report a lot harder than it should be. I think my problem is I try to edit as I write. I think what I need to do is just write whatever I want. After I'm through, then edit and organize. It's hard for me though.

Bruce chastises himself for making his writing harder than it need be and reminds himself about the process he learned in class. Journals are good places to monitor your own version of the writing process and to document what helps you the most.

3 Writing to learn

The act of regular writing clarifies ideas and causes new ones to develop. In that sense, journal writing is an invention and discovery technique. (See Chapter 5.) Julie, who kept a journal about all the authors she studied in her American literature course, noticed a disturbing pattern and wrote in her journal to make some sense of it:

> 2/4 So far, the first two authors we have to read have led tragic, unhappy lives. I wonder if this is just a coincidence or if it has something to do with the personality of successful writers. Actually, of all people, writers need a lot of time

alone, by themselves, thinking and writing, away from other people, including, probably, close family members. The more I think about it, writers would be very difficult people to live with, that's it—writers spend so much time alone and become hard to live with.

Julie used the act of regular journal writing to process and figure out ideas, make interpretations, and test hypotheses. To *write to learn* is to trust that as you write, ideas will come—some right, some wrong; some good, some bad.

ESL **JOURNALS FOR SECOND LANGUAGE WRITING**

Journals are useful when you are writing in a language other than your native language. Since you don't have to be concerned with correctness, your can work on developing fluency, experimenting with language, and trying out new vocabulary or sentence structures.

In an academic journal, your instructor will probably expect you to do more than summarize assigned reading. Consider using a double-entry journal.

To help you develop your English vocabulary, keep an ongoing list of new words as described in 30c. Include both vocabulary you learn in your classes and words or idioms that you hear outside class.

 Gaining social and political awareness

Writing in a journal is a good way to examine the social and political climate in which you grew up and which perhaps you took for granted. In the following example, Jennifer uses her journal to reflect on sexist language:

3/8 Sexist language is everywhere. So much so that people don't even realize what they are saying is sexist. My teacher last year told all the "mothers-to-be" to be sure to read to their children. What about the fathers? Sexist language is dangerous because it so easily undermines women's morale and self-image. I try my hardest not to use sexist language, but even I find myself falling into old stereotypes.

Note that Jennifer recorded both her awareness of sexist language in society and her own difficulty in avoiding it.

5 Evaluating classes

Journals are good places in which to assess your classes, including both what you're learning and what you're not learning. In the following entry, Brian seemed surprised that writing can be fun:

> 10/28   English is now more fun. When I write, the words come out more easily and it's not like homework. All my drafts help me put together my thoughts and retrieve memories that were hidden somewhere in the dungeons of my mind. Usually I wouldn't like English, like in high school, but I pretty much enjoy it here. I like how you get to hear people's reactions to your papers and discuss them with each other.

Your journal is one place where you can raise critical questions about a class or, by sharing it, let your instructor know what is happening in class from your point of view.

6 Letting off steam

Journals are good places to vent frustration when things aren't going well, personally or academically. College instructors don't assign journals to improve students' mental health, but they know that journals can help. Kenyon writes about the value of keeping his journal for one semester:

> 12/1   This journal has saved my sanity. It got me started at writing. . . . I can't keep all my problems locked up inside me, but I hate telling others, burdening them with my problems—like what I'm going to do with the rest of my life.

In many ways, writing in a journal is like talking to a sympathetic audience; the difference, as Kenyon noted, is that the jounal is always there, no matter what's on your mind.

7 Reporting progress

Sometimes it's hard to see how much you've learned until you reread your journal at the end of a term and notice where you began and where you ended. Your writing may have been casual and fast, your thinking tentative, your assessments or conclusions uncertain, but the journal gives you a record of who you were, what you thought, and how you've changed. Rereading a term's worth of entries may be a pleasant surprise, as Jeff found out:

> 11/21   The journal to me has been like a one-man debate, where I could write thoughts down and then later read them. This seemed to help clarify many of my

ideas. To be honest there is probably fifty percent of the journal that is nothing but B.S. and ramblings to fulfill assignments, but that still leaves fifty percent that I think is of importance. The journal is also a time capsule. I want to put it away and not look at it for ten or twenty years and let it recall for me this period of my life.

GUIDELINES FOR KEEPING A JOURNAL

- Choose a notebook you are comfortable with. A small loose-leaf binder allows you to add, delete, and rearrange entries or share selected samples with an instructor.

- Consider using a computer. One advantage of computer journals is that they make it easy for you to copy interesting or useful entries directly into the paper you are working on.

- Date each entry. Also include the day of the week and the time if you like having more complete records. A journal allows you to watch your thoughts change over time.

- Write long entries. Plan to write for at least ten minutes, preferably longer, to allow your thoughts to develop as fully as possible. The more you write, the more you find to say.

- Include both "academic" and "personal" entries. Put a divider in your loose-leaf notebook to separate them.

WRITING 4: APPLICATION

Look over the examples in this section and see if you can think up additional uses for journals. Can you provide any concrete examples from your own journal?

SUGGESTIONS FOR WRITNG AND RESEARCH

INDIVIDUAL

I. Select a well-known writer in your intended major who kept a journal (for example, Mary Shelley, Ralph Waldo Emerson, or Virginia Woolf in literature; Leonardo da Vinci, Georgia O'Keeffe, or Edward Weston in the arts; B. F. Skinner or Margaret Mead in the social sciences; Charles Darwin or Marie Curie in the natural sciences). Study the writer's journals to identify important

characteristics and the purpose they probably served. Write a report on what you find, and share it with your class.

2. Review your journal entries for the past two weeks, select one entry that seems especially interesting, and write a reflective essay of several pages on it. How are the entry and the essay different? Which is better? Is that a fair question?

COLLABORATIVE

Bring duplicated copies of one journal entry written during the term. Exchange entries and discuss interesting features of the entries.

Inventing and Discovering

Good writing depends on good ideas. When ideas don't come easily or naturally, writers need techniques for finding or creating them. Writers need to invent new ideas or discover old ones at all phases of the writing process, from finding and developing a topic to narrowing an argument and searching for good evidence. And knowing how to invent and discover ideas when none seems apparent is also the best antidote for writer's block, helping you get going even when you think you have nothing to say.

The main premise behind the techniques discussed in this chapter is "The more you write, the more you think." Language begets language, and more language begets more ideas. Virtually all writers have had the experience of starting to write in one direction and ending up in another; as they wrote, their writing moved their thinking in new directions—a powerful, messy, but ultimately positive experience and a good demonstration that the act of writing itself generates and modifies ideas. This occurs because writing lets people see their own ideas, on paper or on a computer monitor, and doing that, in turn, allows them to change those ideas. This chapter suggests ways to harness the creative power of language and make it work for you.

WRITING I: EXPLORATION

Describe the procedures you usually use to start writing a paper. Where do you get the ideas—from speaking? listening? reading? writing? Do you do anything special to help them come? What do you do when ideas don't come?

5 a Personal brainstorming

Brainstorming is rapid list making. You ask yourself a question and then list as many answers as you can think of. The point is to get out lots of possible ideas for later examination and review.

Do not try to evaluate your ideas. Just record them as they occur to you, even those you think you will eventually reject. Sometimes you can generate ideas best by setting goals for yourself: what are five possible topics for a paper on campus issues?

I. overcrowding in campus dormitories

2. prohibiting cars for first-year students

3. date rape

4. multiculturalism and the curriculum

5. attitudes toward alcohol on campus

Sometimes you can brainstorm best by leaving the question open-ended: in thinking about the fourth topic, what do you already know about multiculturalism and the curriculum that interests you?

•   racial diversity high among campus students

•   racial diversity low among faculty

•   old curriculum dominated by white male agenda

•   new curriculum dominated by young feminist agenda

•   how to avoid simplistic stereotypes such as those I've just written

In making such lists, jotting down one item often triggers the next, as is seen above. Each item becomes a possible direction for your paper. By challenging yourself to generate a long list, you force yourself to find and record even vague ideas in concrete language, where you can examine them and decide whether or not they're worth further development. You can also record the ideas you generate in your personal brainstorming sessions by drawing clustering diagrams. (See 5f.)

5 b Freewriting

Freewriting is fast writing. You write rapidly, depending on one word to trigger the next, one idea to lead to another, without worrying about conventions or correctness. Freewriting helps you find a focus by writing nonstop and not censoring the words and

ideas before you have a chance to look at them. Try the following suggestions for freewriting:

- Write as fast as you can about an idea for a fixed period of time, say five or ten minutes.

- Do not allow your pen to stop moving until the time is up.

- Don't worry about what your writing looks like or how it's organized; the only audience for this writing is yourself.

If you digress in your freewriting, fine. If you misspell a word or write something silly, fine. If you catch a fleeting thought that's especially interesting, good. If you think of something you've never thought of before, wonderful. And if nothing interesting comes out—well, maybe next time. The following five-minute freewrite shows John's attempt to find a topic for a local research project:

> I can't think of anything special just now, nothing really comes to mind, well maybe something about the downtown mall would be good because I wouldn't mind spending time down there. Something about the mall . . . maybe the street vendors, the hot dog guy or the pretzel guy or that woman selling T and sweatshirts, they're always there, even in lousy weather—do they like it that much? Actually, all winter. Do they need the money that bad? Why do people become street vendors—like maybe they graduated from college and couldn't get jobs? Or were these the guys who never wanted anything to do with college?

John's freewrite is typical: he starts with no ideas, but his writing soon leads to some. This kind of writing needs to be free, unstructured, and digressive to allow the writer to find thoughts wherever they occur. For John, this exercise turned out to be a useful one, since he ultimately wrote a paper about "the hot dog guy," a street vendor.

ESL   **FREEWRITING TO DEVELOP FLUENCY**

Writing in a second language can be frustrating when you are trying to pay attention to your ideas, sentence structures, word choices, spelling, grammar, and so on. Many ESL writers have discovered that freewriting helps tremendously with this problem. If you haven't tried freewriting before, you might find it hard at first not to stop and carefully check each sentence, but with continued practice this activity should help you to postpone editing and improve your fluency in English. If you have access to a computer, try invisible writing.

A computer can help you freewrite more freely by making your words invisible. This guarantees that you won't try to revise and edit at this early stage. Simply turn off your monitor or turn down the brightness until it is dark, and type away, focusing only on your current thoughts. After ten minutes, turn the brightness up and see what you have written.

5 c Looping

Looping is a sequenced set of freewrites. Each freewrite focuses on one idea from the previous freewrite and expands it. To loop, follow this procedure:

1. Freewrite for ten minutes to discover a topic or to advance the one you are working on.

2. Review your freewrite and select one sentence closest to what you want to continue developing. Copy this sentence, and take off from it, freewriting for another ten minutes. (John might have selected "Why do people become street vendors?" for further freewriting.)

3. Repeat step 2 for each successive freewrite to keep inventing and discovering.

5 d Asking reporters' questions

Writers who train themselves to ask questions are training themselves to find information. Reporters ask six basic questions about every news story they write: who? what? where? when? why? and how? Following this set of questions leads reporters to new information and more complete stories:

- *Who* or what is involved? (a person, character, or thesis)

- *What* happened? (an event, action, or assertion)

- *Where* did this happen? (a place, text, or context)

- *When* did it happen? (a date or relationship)

- *Why* did it happen? (reason, cause, or explanation)

- *How* did it happen? (a method, procedure, or action)

While these questions seem especially appropriate for reporting an event, the questions can be modified to investigate any topic:

Who or *what* is my central focus?

What happens as the paper progresses?

Where do I make my main point? On what page?

Are my *reasons* (my answers to the *why* question) ample and documented?

How well does my strategy work?

Outlines are, essentially, organized lists. In fact, outlines grow out of lists, as writers determine which ideas go first, which later, which are main, which subordinate. Formal outlines use a system of Roman numerals, capital letters, Arabic numerals, and lowercase letters to create a hierarchy of ideas. Some writers prefer informal outlines, using indentations to indicate relationships between ideas.

When Carol set out to write a research essay on the effect of acid rain on the environment in New England, she first brainstormed a random list of areas that such an essay might cover:

- What is acid rain?
- What are its effects on the environment?
- What causes it?
- How can it be stopped?

After preliminary research, Carol produced this outline:

I. Definition of acid rain

II. The causes of acid rain

    A. Coal-burning power plants

    B. Automobile pollution

III. The effects of acid rain

    A. Deforestation in New England

        1. The White Mountain study

        2. Maple trees dying in Vermont

    B. Dead lakes

Note how Carol rearranged the second and third items in her original list to talk about causes before effects. The very act of making the outline encouraged her to invent a structure for her ideas. Moving entries around is especially easy if you are using a computer, because you can see many combinations before committing yourself to any one of them. The rules of formal outlining also cause you to search for ideas: if you have a Roman numeral I, you need a II; if you have an A, you need a B. Carol thought first of coal-burning power plants as a cause, then brainstormed to come up with an idea to pair with it.

Writing outlines is *generative*: In addition to recording your original thoughts, outlines actually generate new thoughts. Outlines are most useful if you modify them as you write in accordance with new thoughts or information.

After an outline has been revised and is in its final form, it can be shared with the reader in the form of headings. In long papers— or textbooks such as this one—headings help readers follow the structure of the writer's presentation.

5 **f** Clustering

Clustering is a method of organizing ideas visually to reveal their relationships. Clustering is useful both for inventing and discovering a topic and for exploring a topic once you have done all your preliminary research. To use clustering, observe the following procedure:

1. Write a word or phrase that seems to be the focus of what you want to write about. (Carol wrote down "acid rain.")

2. Write ideas related to your focus in a circle around the central phrase and connect them to the focus phrase. If one of the ideas suggests others related to it, write those in a circle around *it* (Carol did this with her idea "solutions").

3. If one idea (such as "solutions") begins to accumulate related ideas, start a second cluster with the new term in the center of your paper.

5 **g** Talking with peers

One of the most powerful invention techniques is simply talking with a partner or small group with the deliberate intention of helping each other find ideas. The directions are simple: sit across from each other for five or ten minutes and begin talking about

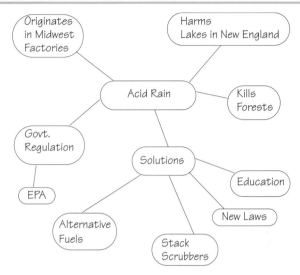

A clustering diagram

possible topics or approaches or ways of finding sources. It doesn't matter who starts or finishes, since the principle at work here is that oral language, like written language, begets ideas. At some point it will be helpful to write down what you are talking about so that you have a record to return to.

 SUGGESTIONS FOR INVENTION AND DISCOVERY

- **Brainstorm** a list of five possible topics to write about.
- **Freewrite** for ten minutes about the most interesting topic on your list
- **Loop** back in your freewriting, selecting the most interesting or useful point, and freewrite again with that point as the focus.
- Ask the **reporters' questions** about the topic: who? what? when? where? why? and how?
- Make an **outline** of a possible structure for your paper.
- **Cluster** ideas about your topic and then on a related idea that occurs during the initial clustering.
- **Talk** with a partner or small group for ten minutes, helping each other find or advance one idea each.

SUGGESTIONS FOR WRITING AND RESEARCH

INDIVIDUAL

Explain your own most useful invention technique for finding ideas. Explain your technique and support it with samples from your own earlier papers. Give clear directions to teach other writers how to use it.

COLLABORATIVE

Find a common writing topic by having each person in the group or class select one of the invention and discovery techniques described in this chapter and practice using it for ten minutes. Make a collective list of the topic ideas generated this way. Then ask each individual to select one topic and write for another five minutes. Again make a list of topics and the important ideas generated about them. Discuss the ideas together and try to arrive at a consensus on a common writing topic for the whole class to pursue. The most interesting part of this assignment will be comparing the variety of approaches chosen by different students on the same topic. This exercise is an excellent way to generate a *class book* (see 51d).

Assuming a Rhetorical Stance

The focus, structure, and style of every paper you write is determined by why you are writing **(purpose),** to whom **(audience),** and under what circumstances **(situation).** Taken together, purpose, audience, and situation largely determine the voice in which you write. (See 6d.) While this chapter asks you to consider each of these elements analytically and in isolation, in truth, writers usually think about these elements intuitively and simultaneously. In any case, we believe the following discussion may be useful when you are assigned to write an academic paper.

6 a Writing for a purpose

People write to discover what's on their minds, figure things out, vent frustrations, keep records, remember things, communicate information, shape ideas, express feelings, recount experiences, raise questions, imagine the future, create new forms, and simply for pleasure. They also write when they're required to in school, to demonstrate knowledge and solve problems. But no matter what the task, writers write better when they do so purposefully—when they know what they want to accomplish.

This section examines three broad and overlapping reasons for writing—discovering, communicating, and creating—and discusses strategies to accomplish each one effectively.

Writing to discover

Writing helps people discover ideas, relationships, connections, and patterns in their lives and in the world. In college, students write to discover paper topics, develop those topics, expand and explain ideas, and connect seemingly unrelated material in coherent patterns. In this sense, writing is one of the most powerful learning tools available.

Writing is especially powerful because it makes language—and therefore thought—stand still, allowing it to be examined slowly and deliberately, allowing the ideas to be elaborated, critiqued, re-arranged, and corrected. Playwright Christopher Fry once said, "My trouble is that I'm the sort of writer who only finds out what he is getting at by the time he's got to the end of it." In other words, his purpose and plan become clear only after he's written a whole draft; he knows that the act of writing will help him find his way. But rather than considering this inventive power of writing "trouble"—to use Fry's word—you can consider it a solution to many other problems. Once you know that writing can generate ideas, advance concepts, and forge connections, then you can use it deliberately and strategically to help you write college papers.

Discovery can happen in all writing. Anytime you write, you may find new or lost ideas, implications, and directions. However, sometimes it pays to write with the specific intention of discovering. Discovery writing is often used before actual drafting to explore the subject and purpose of a paper or to solve writing problems once drafting and revising have begun. (See Chapter 5.)

WRITING I: EXPLORATION _____

Describe a time when you used writing for discovery purposes. Did you set out to use writing this way, or did it happen accidentally? Have you used it deliberately since then? With what results?

2 Writing to communicate

The most common reason for writing in college is to say something to an audience. College students write essays, exams, and reports to instructors, as well as letters, applications, and résumés to potential employers. To communicate to instructors and employers alike, writing needs to be *purposeful* so both writer and reader know where it's going; it needs to be *clear* in order to be understood; and it needs to be *correct* in order to be believable.

Thesis-based writing

Many academic assignments require a **thesis,** a statement of the writer's purpose, which the paper is expected to assert, explain, support, or defend. A thesis, broadly speaking, summarizes the main idea of a paper and makes that idea explicit to readers.

A *thesis statement* is a generalization in one or more sentences, early or late in the paper, that summarizes the paper's point. For example, the thesis of this chapter, that *the focus, structure, and style of papers are determined by purpose and audience,* is stated in the first paragraph and supported throughout the rest of the chapter.

Some papers, like this chapter, present the *thesis first,* in the first paragraph or somewhere on the first page. A thesis-first paper summarizes for the readers in advance what the paper will be about. Other papers present the thesis later in what might be called a *delayed-thesis* arrangement. Delayed-thesis papers show readers different sides or aspects of an idea before presenting the writer's conclusion about that idea.

Whether first or delayed, a thesis answers the critical reader question: So what? Why does this paper exist? What's it about? A thesis first sums up what will be demonstrated if the readers continue reading; a delayed thesis explains the point they should have gotten if their reading is nearly finished. Common thesis-based assignments in college include the following:

- **Reflecting on experience.** The purpose of sharing an experience with somebody else is to explain something about yourself and, in the process, teach them something they don't already know. (For more on recounting experience, see Chapter 7.)

- **Explaining ideas.** The purpose of explaining something is to make it clear to somebody who knows less about the subject than you do. You explain best by following a logical order, using simple language, and providing illustration and examples of what you mean. (For more on explaining, see Chapter 8.)

- **Arguing positions.** The purpose of arguing is to persuade readers to agree with your position. College assignments frequently ask you to explore opposing sides of an issue or several different interpretations of a text and then to take a stand advocating one point of view. (For more on argument, see Chapter 9.)

- **Interpreting texts.** The purpose of interpreting a text is to explain what the text means, to tell why you believe it means this, and to support your reading with reasons based on evidence from the text. (For more on interpreting texts, see Chapter 10.)

Some papers, such as those that recount personal experience and those that are reflective in nature, may not state theses directly. Instead, they often have an *implied thesis;* by the paper's end, the reader understands the point of the paper without the writer's stating it explicitly.

WRITING 2: EXPLORATION

When is the last time you wrote to communicate something? Describe your purpose and audience. How successful were these acts of communication? How do you know?

3 Writing to create

When you write to create, you pay special attention to the way your language looks and sounds—its form, shape, rhythm, images, and texture. Though the term *creative writing* is usually associated with poetry, fiction, and drama, it's important to see all writing, from personal narratives to research essays, as creative (see Chapter 21).

When you write to create, you pay less immediate attention to your audience and subject and more to the act of expression itself. Your goal is not so much to change the world or to transmit information about it but to transform an experience or idea into something that will make your readers pause, see the world from a different angle, and perhaps reflect upon what it means. You want your writing itself, not just the information it contains, to affect your readers emotionally or esthetically as well as intellectually.

In most college papers, your primary purpose will be to communicate, not to create. However, nearly every writing assignment has room for a creative dimension. When writing for emotional or esthetic effect in an otherwise communicative paper, be especially careful that your creativity serves a purpose and that the communicative part is strong on its own. You want your creative use of language to enhance, not camouflage, your ideas.

Intensifying experience

When Amanda recounted her experience picking potatoes on board a mechanical potato harvester on her father's farm, she made her readers feel the experience as she did by crafting her language to duplicate the sense of hard, monotonous work:

> Potatoes, mud, potatoes, mud, potatoes, that was all I saw in front of me. They moved from my right side to my left, at hip level. A conveyor belt never stopping. On and on and on.
>
> The potatoes passed fast, a constant stream. My hands worked deftly, pulling out clods of dirt, rotten potatoes, old shaws, and anything else I found that wasn't a potato. It was October, the ground was nearly frozen, the mud was hard and solid. Cold. Dirt had gotten into my yellow and yet brown rubber gloves, had wedged under my nails, increasing my discomfort.

This is a creative approach to essay writing because the writer uses a graphic, descriptive style to put readers at the scene of her experience rather than summarizing it or explaining explicitly what it meant to her.

Experimenting with form

Keith created a special language effect in an otherwise traditional and straightforward academic assignment by writing a poetic prologue for a research essay about homeless people in New York City. The full essay contains factual information derived from social workers, agency documents, and library research.

> The cold cement
>   no pillow
> The steel grate
>   no mattress
> But the hot air
>   of the midnight subway
> Lets me sleep.

Using the poetic form creates a brief emotional involvement with the research subject, allowing readers to fill in missing information with their imaginations. Note, however, that the details of the poem (cold cement, steel grate, subway) spring not from the writer's imagination but from his research notes and observations. For more information on experimenting with form, style, or language, see Chapter 21, "Creative Nonfiction."

WRITING 3: EXPLORATION ─────────────────────────

Describe a time when your primary purpose in writing was to create rather than to discover or communicate. Were you pleased with the result? Why or why not?

---

6 b Addressing audiences

The better you know your **audience,** the better you're likely to write. Whether your writing is judged "good" or not depends largely on how well it's received by the readers for whom it's intended. Just as you change the way you speak depending on whom you're

addressing—your boss, mother, professor, or between friend and younger brother—so you change the way you write depending on to whom you're writing. You don't want to overexplain and perhaps bore the audience, or underexplain and leave it wanting.

Speakers have an advantage over writers in that they see the effect of their words on their listeners and can adjust accordingly. A puzzled look tells the speaker to slow down, a smile and nod says keep going full speed ahead, and so on. However, writers can only imagine the reactions of the people to whom they're trying to communicate.

We believe all college papers need to be written to at least two audiences, maybe more: first, to yourself, so you understand it; second, to your instructor who has asked you to write it in the first place. In addition, you may also be writing to other students or for publication to more public audiences. This section examines how expectations differ from one audience to the next.

Understanding college audiences

It might help to think of the different audiences you will address in college as existing along a continuum, with those closest and best known to you (yourself, friends) at one end and those farthest from and least known to you (the general public) at the other end:

Self——Family——Friends——Instructor——Public

While the items on your continuum will always differ in particulars from somebody else's, the principle—that you know some audiences better than others—will always be the same and will influence how you write. The audience of most concern to most college students is the instructor who will evaluate their learning on the basis of their writing.

WRITING 4: EXPLORATION _____

Think back over the past several weeks and list all the different audiences to whom you have written. To whom did you write most often? Which audiences were easy for you to address? Which were difficult? Why?

ESL: Do you think English-speaking audiences have expectations that differ from the expectations of audiences who speak your native language?

Shaping writing for different audiences

To shape your writing for a particular audience, you first need to understand the qualities of your writing that can change according to audience. The context you need to provide; the structure, tone, and style you use; and your purpose for writing can all be affected by your audience. (Structure, tone, and style are important elements of voice. See 6d.)

Context

Different audiences need different **contexts**—different amounts or kinds of background information—in order to understand your ideas. Find out whether your audience already knows about the topic or whether it's completely new to them. Consider whether any terms or ideas need explaining. For example, other students in your writing group might know exactly who you mean if you refer to a favorite singer, but your instructor might not. Also consider what sort of explanation would work best with your audience.

Structure

Every piece of writing is put together in a certain way: some ideas are discussed early, others late; transitions between ideas are marked in a certain way; similar ideas are either grouped together or treated separately. How you **structure** a paper depends in large part on what you think will work best with your particular audience. For example, if you were writing an argument for someone who disagrees with your position, you might begin with the evidence with which you both agree and then later introduce more controversial evidence.

Tone

The **tone** of a piece of writing conveys the writer's attitude toward the subject matter and audience. How do you want to sound to your readers? You may, of course, have a different attitude toward each audience you address. In addition, you may want different audiences to hear in different ways. For example, when writing to yourself, you won't mind sounding confused. When writing for instructors, though, you will want to sound confident and authoritative.

Style

Style is largely determined by the formality and complexity of your language. You need to determine what style your readers

expect and what style will be most effective in a given paper. Fellow students might be offended if you write in anything other than a friendly style, but some instructors might interpret the same style as disrespectful.

Purpose

The explicit purpose of your writing depends more on you and your assignment than on your audience. (See 6a.) However, certain purposes are more likely to apply to particular audiences than others. Also, there are unstated purposes embedded in any piece of writing, and these will vary depending on whom you're addressing. For example, is it important that your readers like you? or that they respect you? or that they give you good grades? Always ask yourself what you want a piece of writing to do for—or to—your audience and what you want your audience to do in response to your writing.

Let's follow the way writing generally needs to change as you move along the scale away from the audience you know best, yourself.

Writing to yourself. Every paper you write is addressed in part to yourself, and some writing, such as journals, is addressed primarily to yourself. However, most reports, essays, papers, and exams are also addressed to other people—instructors, peers, parents, or employers. Journal writing is your opportunity to write to yourself and yourself alone. When you write to yourself alone, you don't need to worry about context, structure, tone, or style; only purpose matters if you are the sole reader. However, if you make a journal entry that you might want to refer to later, it's a good idea to provide sufficient background and explanation to help you remember the event or the idea described if you do return to it. When you are the reader of your own writing, choose words, sentences, rhythms, images, and punctuation that come easiest and most naturally to you. (For more information, see Chapter 4.)

Writing to peers. Your peers are your equals, your friends and classmates, people of similar age, background, or situation. Some of your assignments will ask you to consider the other students in the class to be your audience: for example, when you read papers to each other in writing groups or exchange papers to edit each other's work.

The primary difference between writing to yourself and writing to peers is the amount of context and structure you need to provide to make sure your readers understand you. If your paper is about a personal experience, you need to provide the explanations and

details that will allow readers who did not have your experience to understand fully the events and ideas you describe.

If your paper is about a subject that requires research, be sure to provide background information to make the topic comprehensible and interesting in a structure (e.g., chronological, logical, cause-effect) that makes sense. Be direct, honest, and friendly; peers will see right through any pretentious or stuffy language.

You usually write to peers to share a response to their writing, to recount an experience, to explain an idea, or to argue a position. In a writing class, the most important implicit purpose is probably to establish a good working rapport with your classmates by being honest, straightforward, and supportive.

Writing to instructors. Instructors are among the most difficult audiences for whom to write. First, they usually make the assignments, so they know what they want, and it's your job to figure out what that is. Second, they often know more about your subject than you do. Third, different instructors may have quite different criteria for what constitutes good writing. And fourth, each instructor may simultaneously play several different roles: a helpful resource, a critic, an editor, a coach, and finally, a judge.

It is often difficult to know how much context to provide in a paper written for an instructor, unless the assignment specifically tells you. For example, in writing about a Shakespearean play to an English professor, should you provide a summary of the play when you know that he or she already knows it? Or should you skip the summary information and write only about ideas original with you? The safest approach is to provide full background, explain all ideas, support all assertions, and cite authorities in the field. Write as if your instructor needed all this information and it were your job to educate him or her.

When writing papers to instructors, be sure to use a structure that suits the type of paper you are writing. For example, personal experience papers are often chronological, reports may be more thematic, and so on. (The chapters in Part Three describe conventional structures for each type of paper discussed there.)

One of your instructor's roles is to help you learn to write effective papers. But another role is to evaluate whether you have done so and, from a broader perspective, whether you are becoming a literate member of the college community. Therefore your implicit purpose when you write to instructors is to demonstrate your understanding of conventions, knowledge, reasoning ability, and originality.

Writing to public audiences. Writing to a public audience is difficult for all writers because the audience is usually both diverse

Structure. The structure of a text is how it's put together: where it starts, where it goes next, where the thesis occurs, what evidence fits where, how it concludes. Structure is the pattern or logic that holds together thoughtful writing, revealing something of the thought process that created it. For example, a linear, logical structure may characterize the writer as a linear, logical thinker, while a circular, digressive structure may suggest more intuitive, less orderly habits of mind. Skillful writers, of course, can present themselves one way or the other depending on whom they're addressing and why.

The easiest way to gain control of an essay's structure is to make an outline that reveals visually and briefly the organization and direction you intend. Some writers outline before they start writing and stick to the outline all the way through the writing. Others outline only after writing a draft or two to help control their final draft. And still others start with a rough outline which they continue to modify as the writing modifies thought and direction. (For more on outlining, see 5e.) Also consider the structure of your paragraphs and sentences. (See Chapters 23 and 25.)

Values and beliefs. Your values include your political, social, religious, and philosophical beliefs. Your background, opinions, and beliefs will be part of everything you write, but you must learn when to express them directly and when not to. For example, including your values would enhance a personal essay or other auto-biographical writing, but it may detract attention from the subject of research essay.

To gain control of the values in your writing, consider whether the purpose of the assignment calls for an implicit or explicit state-ment of your values. Examine your drafts for words that reveal your personal biases, beliefs, and values; keep them or take them out as appropriate for the assignment.

Authority. Your authority comes from confidence in your knowledge and is projected through the way you handle the ma-terial about which you are writing. An authoritative voice is often clear, direct, factual, and specific, leaving the impression that the writer is confident about what he or she is saying. You can exert and project real authority only over material you know well, whether it's the facts of your personal life or carefully re-searched information. The more you know about your subject, the more clearly you will explain it, and the more confident you will sound.

To gain control over the authority in your writing, do your homework, conduct thorough research, and read your sources of information carefully and critically. (See Chapter 2.)

QUESTIONS FOR EXAMINING YOUR VOICE

- **Tone.** Read drafts aloud and listen to the attitude you hear. Is it what you intend? If not, how could you change it?
- **Style.** What image of yourself do you create through your language? Is it formal or informal? complex or simple?
- **Structure.** What does your structure say about your manner of thinking? Is it careful and tight? loose and flexible? logical? intuitive? Which do you want it to be?
- **Values.** Do your beliefs show through when you speak on paper? Do you want them to?
- **Authority.** Where does your writing voice sound especially knowledgeable and confident? Where does it sound tentative and unsure? What can you do to be more consistently authoritative?

WRITING 7: APPLICATION

Describe your own writing voice in terms of each of the elements outlined in this section (tone, style, structure, values, authority). Then compare your description with a recent paper you have written. In what ways does the paper substantiate your description? In what ways does it differ from your description? How do you account for any differences?

ESL: Is your writing voice in English different from your writing voice in your native language? If you are aware of any differences, try to describe them in terms of the elements discussed in this chapter. Are there qualities of your voice in one language that you would like to transfer to your voice in the other language?

SUGGESTIONS FOR WRITING AND RESEARCH

INDIVIDUAL

1. Select a topic that interests you and write about it in each of the three modes described in this chapter. First, begin with discovery writing to yourself, perhaps in a journal. Second, write a letter to communicate with somebody about this interest. Third, write creatively about it in a short poem, story, or play. Finally, describe your experience writing in these different modes.

2. Select a paper written recently for an instructor audience and rewrite it for a publication, choosing either a student newspaper or

a local magazine. Before you start, make notes about what elements need to be changed: context, structure, tone, style, or purpose. When you finish recasting the paper to this larger, more public audience, complete collaborative assignment 3. Make final revisions, taking into account your partner's observations, and send your paper to the publication.

3. Collect and examine as many samples of your past writing as you have saved. Also look closely at the writing you have done during this term. Write a paper in which you describe and explain this history and evolution of your voice and the features that most characterize your current writing voice.

COLLABORATIVE

I. Select a topic that your whole writing group is interested in writing about. Divide your labors so that some of you do discovery writing, some do communicative writing, and some write creatively. With scissors and tape, combine your efforts into a single coherent, creative piece of college writing, making sure that some of every member's writing is included in the finished product. Perform a reading of this collage for the other groups; listen to theirs in return.

2. In a group of five students, select a topic of common interest. Write about the topic (either as homework or for fifteen minutes in class) to one of the following audiences: yourself, a friend who is not attending your school, your instructor, an appropriate magazine or newspaper. Share your writing with one another, and together list the choices you needed to make for each audience.

3. Exchange recently written papers with a partner. Examine your partner's paper for the elements of voice. In a letter, each of you describe what you find. How does your partner's perception of your voice match or differ from your own? Now do individual assignment 2, including your partner's assessment as part of your analysis.

PART THREE

Drafting

www.prenhall.com/fulwiler

Drafting

www.prenhall.com/fulwiler

On *The Blair Handbook, Fourth Edition,* Web site you can find

- Tips for writing an argument paper
- Exercises on thesis statements
- Hints for writing various types of essays

Reflecting on Experience

Good stories can be told about virtually anything. Not only can good stories be about any subject, they can be quite simple and can take place in your own backyard—and *you* can tell them. Potential stories happen all the time—daily, in fact. What makes them actually become stories is recounting them, orally or in writing. Good stories are entertaining, informative, lively, and believable; they will mean something to you who write them and to your audience, who will read them.

All stories, whether they're true (nonfiction) or imagined (fiction), are accounts of something that happened—an event or series of events, after which something or somebody is changed. Whether the story is about "The Three Little Pigs" or *Huckleberry Finn* (both fiction), or about Darwin's *Voyage of the Beagle* or your own trip last winter to Mexico (nonfiction), it includes the following elements: a character (who?) to whom something happens (what?) by some method (how?), in some place (where?), at some time (when?), for some reason (why?). In other words, any time you render a full account of a personal experience, you answer questions about who, what, how, where, when, and why. Whether your story is engaging or not depends on the subject, your interest in telling it, and the skill with which you weave together these story elements.

WRITING 1: EXPLORATION ─────────────────────────────

Think about the best stories you have read or listened to. What makes them memorable? What makes them believable?

ESL: You might want to reflect on stories you have read or heard in your native language; do they translate well into English? Why or why not?

In personal experience writing, your main character is yourself, so try to give your readers a sense of who you are through your voice, actions, level of awareness, and description. The characters in a good story are believable and interesting; they come alive.

Voice

Your language reveals who you are—playful, serious, rigid, loose, stuffy, honest, warm, or whatever. In the following excerpt, in which Beth relates her experience playing oboe during a two-hour Saturday morning orchestra rehearsal, we learn she's serious, fun loving, impish, and just a little lazy:

> I love that section. It sounds so cool when Sarah and I play
> together like that. Now I can put my reed back in the water and
> sit back and listen. I probably should be counting the rests.
> Counting would mean I'd have to pay attention and that's no
> fun. I'd rather look around and watch everyone else sweat.

Actions

Readers learn something about the kind of person you are from your actions. For example, when Karen recalls her thoughts playing in a basketball tournament, we learn something of her insecurity, fears, and skills all at once:

> This time, don't be so stupid, Karen—if you don't take it
> up court, you'll never get the ball. Oh, God, here I go. Okay,
> they're in a twenty-one—just bring it up—Sarah's alone—
> fake up, bounce pass—yes, she hits it! I got the assist!

Insight

One of the best ways to reveal who you are is to show yourself becoming aware of something, gaining a new way of seeing the world, a new insight. While such awareness can occur for apparently unexplainable reasons, it most often happens when you encounter new ideas or have experiences that change you in some way. In writing a paper about why she goes to the library to write a paper, Judith clarifies first for herself—then for her readers—the relationship between feeling safe and being creative.

Two weeks ago, a female student was assaulted not far from where I live—that's why I've taken to locking my door so carefully. I am beginning to understand the importance of feeling safe in order to be creative and productive. Here, in the library, I feel secure, protected from real violence and isolated from everyday distractions. There are just enough people for security's sake but not so many that I feel crowded. And besides, I'm surrounded by all these books, all these great minds who dwell in the hallowed space! I am comfortable, safe, and beginning to get an idea.

4 Telling details

Describe yourself and other participants in your story in such a way that the details and facts help tell your story. A telling detail or fact is one that advances your characterization of someone without your having to render an obvious opinion. For example, you could characterize your little sister by pointing out the field hockey stick in the corner of her room, the photograph of the seventh-grade field hockey team on the wall, and the teddy bear next to her pillow. You could characterize her coach by pointing to the logo on her sweatshirt: "Winning isn't everything. It's the only thing."

WRITING 2: APPLICATION _____

Start to characterize yourself. Write four paragraphs, and in each one, emphasize one of these individualizing elements: voice, actions, awareness, and any telling details of your life. Select any or all that seem worthy of further exploration and write a few more paragraphs.

7 b Finding a subject (what?)

People write about their personal experiences to get to know and understand themselves better, to inform and entertain others, and to leave permanent records of their lives. Sometimes people recount their experiences casually, in forms never intended for wide circulation, such as journals, diaries, and letters. Sometimes they write in forms meant to be shared with others, such as memoirs, autobiographies, or personal essays. In college, the most common narrative forms are personal experience essays.

Subjects for good stories know no limits. You already have a lifetime of experiences from which to choose, and each experience is a potential story to help explain who you are, what you believe, and how you act today. Here are some of the topics selected by a single first-year writing class:

- playing oboe in Saturday orchestra rehearsals

- counseling disturbed children at summer camp

- picking strawberries on a farm

- visiting the library

- clerking at a drugstore

- playing in a championship basketball game

- solo camping in Outward Bound

- touring Graceland in Memphis

- painting houses during the summer

When you write a paper based on personal experience, ask yourself: Which experience do I *want* to write about? Will *anybody else* want to read about it? Here are some suggestions. (See Chapter 6 for specific strategies.)

Winning and losing

Winning something—a race, a contest, an award—can be a good subject, since it features you in a unique position and allows you to explore or celebrate a special talent. At the same time, the exciting, exceptional, or highly dramatic subjects such as scoring the winning goal in a championship game or placing first in a creative writing contest may be difficult to write about because they've been used so often that readers have very high expectations.

The truth is that in most parts of life there are more losers than winners. While one team wins a championship, dozens do not. So there's a large, empathetic audience out there who will understand and identify with a narrative about losing. Although more common than winning, losing is less often explored in writing because it is more painful to recall. Therefore there are fresher, deeper, more original stories to tell about losing.

Milestones

Perhaps the most interesting but also the most difficult experience to write about is one that you already recognize as a turning

point in your life, whether it's winning a sports championship, being a camp counselor, or reading in the library. People who explore such topics in writing often come to a better understanding of them. Also, their very significance challenges writers to make them equally significant for an audience that did not experience them. When you write about milestones, pay special attention to the physical details that will both advance your story and make it come alive for readers.

Be cautious, however, in choosing topics about intimate personal relationships, such as a romantic attachment, the death of someone you care about, or a divorce within your family, especially if the experience is recent. Writing about these and other close or painful experiences in your journal or diary can be immensely cathartic, but sharing them with instructors and classmates in a paper may be inappropriate. Because these emotional milestones evoke such intense reactions, it is difficult to write about them in a way that goes beyond the expression of strong feelings. Before you begin a paper on one of these sensitive topics, ask yourself—and your instructor—these questions: Can I present a fair and accurate account? Will my paper bring useful insights to my audience? Will it betray the confidence or invade the privacy of the other people mentioned?

3 Daily life

Commonplace experiences make fertile subjects for personal narratives. You might describe practicing for, rather than winning, the big game, or cleaning up after, rather than attending, the prom. If you are accurate, honest, and observant in exploring a subject from which readers expect little, you are apt to surprise them pleasantly and draw them into your story. Work experiences are especially fruitful subjects, since you may know inside details and routines of restaurants and retail shops that the rest of us can only guess: How long is it before McDonald's tosses its unsold hamburgers? How do florists know which flowers to order when?

WRITING 3: APPLICATION _____

Make a list of a dozen experiences about which you could tell stories. Think of special insight you gained as well as commonplace events that were instructive or caused change. Share your list with classmates and find out which they would most like to hear about.

ESL: You might want to reflect on your experiences learning English or adjusting to a new culture.

7 C Establishing perspective (how?)

The term *perspective* refers to the vantage point or position from which one is telling a story. Perspective addresses this question: How close—in time, distance, or spirit—are you to the experience? Do you write as if it happened long ago or yesterday? Do you summarize what happened or put readers at the scene? Do you explain the experience or leave it mysterious? In other words, you can control, or at least influence, how readers respond to a story by controlling the perspective from which you tell it.

Authorial perspective is established largely by **point of view.** Using the **first person** (*I*) puts the narrator right in the story as a participant. This point of view is usually the one used in personal experience writing, as Beth, Karen, and Judith do in earlier examples.

The **third person** (*he* or *she*) establishes a distinction between the person narrating the events and the person experiencing them and thus tends to depersonalize the story. This perspective is more common in fiction, but it has some uses in personal essays as well. In the following example, for instance, Karen opens her personal experience essay from the imagined perspective of the play-by-play announcer who broadcasts the championship game; the point of view is first person, but from the perspective of a third person:

> 2:15 Well folks, it looks as if Belmont has given up, the coach is preparing to send in his subs. It has been a rough game for Belmont. They stayed in it during the first quarter, but Walpole has run away with it since then. Down by twenty with only six minutes left, Belmont's first sub is now approaching the table.

Verb **tense** establishes the time when the story happened or is happening. The tense used to relate most of the events in a story is called the **governing tense.** Personal experience stories are usually set in either the present or the past.

Once upon a time: past tense

The most natural way to recount a personal experience is to write in the past tense; whatever you're narrating *did* happen sometime in the past. Lorraine uses the past tense to describe an automobile ride with her Native American grandfather to attend a tribal conference:

> I sat silently across from Grandfather and watched him
>
> slowly tear the thin white paper from the tip of the

cigarette. He gathered the tobacco in one hand and drove
the van with the other. I memorized his every move as he
went through the motions of the prayer, which ended
when he finally blew the tobacco out of the window and
into the wind.

Even though the governing tense for your personal narrative
may be the past tense, you may still want to use other tenses for
special purposes.

2 Being there: present tense

The present tense provides the illusion that the experience is
happening at the moment; it leaves no time for your reflection. This
strategy invites readers to become involved with your story as it is
happening and invites them to interpret it for themselves.

If you want to portray yourself thinking rather than talking—in
what is called **interior monologue**—you may choose to use fragment sentences and made-up words since the flow of the mind
doesn't obey conventional rules of language. For example, when
Beth describes her thoughts during orchestra rehearsal, she writes
an interior monologue; we hear her talking to herself while trying to
blow her oboe (note how she provides clues so that we understand
what is going on around her):

> No you don't really mean that, do you? You do. Rats.
> Here we go ... Pfff ... Pff ... Why isn't this playing?
> Maybe if I blow harder ... HONK!! Great. I've just made
> a total fool of myself in front of everyone. Wonderful.

3 Mixing tenses

Writers often need more than one tense to tell a complete story.
A writer telling most of a story in the present tense may switch to
the past tense to provide additional important information, as
Judith does in the opening paragraph of an essay on page 90 about
personal safety:

> It is already afternoon. I fiddle with the key to lock the
> apartment door after me. I am not accustomed to locking
> doors. Except for the six months I spent in Boston, I have
> never lived in a place where I did not trust my neighbors.

When I was little, we couldn't lock our farmhouse door;
the wood had swollen and the bolt no longer lined up
properly with the hole, and nobody ever bothered to fix it.
I still remember the time our baby-sitter, Rosie, hammered
the bolt closed and we had to take the door off the hinges
to get it open.

WRITING 4: APPLICATION _____

Write one page of a possible story using the first person, past tense, and a second page using the first person, present tense. From which perspective do you prefer to tell the story? Why?

7 d   Describing the setting (where?)

Experiences happen in some place at some time, and good stories describe these settings. To describe a believable physical setting, you need to re-create on paper the sights, sounds, smells, and physical sensations that allow readers to experience it for themselves. In addition to telling details that support your plot or character development, try to include **evocative details,** colorful details of setting and character that will let your readers know you were really there.

In the following example, Heather portrays details of the farm where she spent the summer picking strawberries:

The sun is just barely rising over the treetops and there
is still dew covering the ground. In the strawberry patch,
the deep green leaves are filled with water droplets and
the strawberries are big and red and ready to be picked.
The patch is located in a field off the road near a small
forest of Christmas trees. The white house, the red barn,
and a checkerboard of fields can be seen in the distance. It
is 5:30 a.m. and the day has begun.

The evocative details are those which appeal to your senses, such as sight, touch, and smell: *"dew covering the ground," "deep green leaves," "strawberries . . . big and red," "white house," "red barn,"* and *"checkerboard of fields."*

The telling details of a setting reveal something essential about your story without your explaining them (see also 7a4). For example, in telling a story about your sister, you might describe the physical objects in her room, which in turn describe important elements of her character: *"hockey stick," "soccer ball," "gym bag," "sweatpants," "baseball jersey," "life-size posters of Michael Jordan and Tiger Woods."* In other words, skillful description helps you "tell" the story without interpreting its meaning for the reader.

WRITING 5: APPLICATION _____

Describe in detail one of the settings in which your experience took place. Appeal to at least three senses, and try to include details that "tell" some of your story without needing further explanation or overt value judgments on your part.

7 **e** **Narrating a sequence of events (when?)**

In every story, events are ordered in some way. While you cannot alter the events that happened in your experience, as a writer you need to decide which events to portray and in what order to present them.

Selecting events

You have dozens of places to start and end any story, and at each point along the way, many possible details and events are worth relating. Your final selection should support the theme of your story. To decide which events to portray, figure out how much detail you intend to devote to each one. In writing about her basketball career, Karen could have told about her four years playing in high school, her senior year alone, one game, or even less. Because she wanted to focus on a climactic point in great detail, she selected "even less"—she writes her entire six-page paper about the final six minutes in her final game.

In selecting events, consider using one of two strategies that writers commonly use to maintain reader interest: showing cause and effect and building suspense. When writers recount an experience to show **cause and effect,** they relate one event as bringing about another or several others (having an accident causing one to undergo physical therapy, meeting a person resulting in making a friend, taking a trip leading to the learning of a new language and new customs).

In using **suspense,** writers raise questions or pose problems but delay answering or solving them. If the writer can make the question interesting enough, the problem pressing enough, readers will keep reading to learn the answers or solutions—in other words, to find out what happens. Karen's paper asks indirectly, "What is it like to play a championship game from the perspective of a substitute player?"

2　Ordering events

The most common way to order events is to use **chronological order,** presenting events in the sequence in which they happened. Chronological order can be straightforward, following a day from morning to night as Heather does in her narrative about picking strawberries. Chronology orders Karen's six minutes at the end of one basketball game, and it orders Judith's evening trek to the library to study in safety. Sometimes, however, the sequence of events might be broken up, so that readers are introduced to an event in the present, with the rest of the story being a narrated flashback—an especially common strategy in films such as *Saving Private Ryan* and many others. In an experiential essay, for example, Judith might have begun her essay already sitting in the library and reflecting back on how she got there and why. In telling a story, the order of events is always a writer's choice.

WRITING 6: APPLICATION ───────────────────────────

Outline the sequence of events of your story in the order that makes the most sense. Is the arrangement chronological? If not, what is it? How do you decide which event to begin with? Which one to end with?

7　f　Developing a theme (why?)

We can talk about the "why" of a story on two levels: First, *why* did the events occur in the story? What motivated or caused them? Well-told stories will answer this question, directly or indirectly. But we can also ask the writer. Of all the many stories you could write, *why* did you write this one? Or, more bluntly, every reader asks, at least tacitly: So what? What's the meaning or significance of this story? What did I learn by reading it? Well-told stories will also answer this question; readers will see and understand both why you wrote it and why they read it.

However, first drafts of personal experience narratives often do not reveal clear answers to these questions, even to the writers themselves. The purpose of a first draft is to get the events down on paper for a writer to look at; the reason for writing may not yet be apparent, even to the writer. In subsequent drafts, the meaning of these events—the **theme**—should become clearer to the writer because a major reason for writing about personal subjects is to put them in some kind of perspective, to reflect on them and find out how they contribute to the writer's current self. If some meaning doesn't emerge in the course of exploring the topic, the writer is well advised to switch topics.

In experiential stories, the theme isn't usually explicitly stated in the first paragraph as is the thesis statement in expository or argumentative writing. Instead, writers reflecting on personal experience may create a meaning that is not directly stated anywhere and that becomes clear only at the end of the narrative. Although any and all themes are possible, we will describe three broad categories that make especially good stories: slices of life, insights, and turning points.

Slices of life

Some stories simply let readers see what life is like for someone else. Such stories exist primarily to record the writer's memories and to convey information in an interesting way. Their primary theme is "This is what my life is like."

Beth's story of the Saturday orchestra rehearsal is a slice of life, as she chooses to focus on a common "practice" rather than a more dramatic "performance." After using interior monologue for nine paragraphs, in the last paragraph she speaks to the readers directly, explaining what the meaning of music is in her everyday life:

> As hard as it is to get up every Saturday morning, and as hard as it is to put up with some people here, I always feel good as I leave rehearsal. A guest conductor once said: "Music sounds how feelings feel." It's really true. Music evokes emotions that can't be described on paper. Every human feeling can be expressed through music— sadness, love, hatred. Music is an international language. Once you learn it you can't forget it.

2 Insights

In contrast to the many but routine experiences that reveal slices of life is the single important experience that leads to a writer's new insight, change, or growth. Such an experience is deeply significant to the writer, and he or she makes sure that readers see the full value of the experience, usually by explicitly commenting on its meaning. In the following passage, near the end of her essay (see pp. 90–92), Judith locates a place in the library where she will study for her philosophy exam, reflecting that she needs not only comfort but safety in order to concentrate fully:

> I find my place, an empty chair near a window, and slouch down into it, propping my legs on the low table in front. If my mother could see me, she'd reprimand me for not sitting up straight. I breathe deeply, close my eyes for a moment, and become centered, forgetting both last night's pizza and tomorrow's philosophy exam. I need a few minutes to acclimate to this space, relax, and feel safe before starting my work.

3 Turning points

Turning points are those moments in one's life when something happens that causes the writer to change or grow in some large, or small way—more than routine, less than spectacular—perhaps somewhere in between slices of life and profound insights. In fact, many of the best personal experience stories have for themes a modest change or the beginning of growth. Although such themes may be implied throughout the story, they often become clear only in a single climactic moment or episode. Mary's camp counselor story shows her progress from insecurity to confidence in gaining the trust of a ten-year-old. The following excerpt takes place after she has rescued Josh from ridicule by other campers:

> He ran in and threw himself on my bed, crying. I held him, rubbing his head for over an hour. "I love you, Mary. You're the best big sister in the whole world and you're so pretty! I love you and don't ever want you to leave."

WRITING FROM PERSONAL EXPERIENCE

After writing a first draft, address the following questions and revise accordingly:

- **Who** are you? What distinguishes you from others? How much of you is revealed in this story?
- **What** actually happens in this story? Is it clear to somebody who wasn't there with you?
- **How** do you choose to tell the story: first or third person? present or past tense?
- **Where** does this story take place? Will readers be able to see or feel it?
- **When** does this story take place? Is there a logical order for revealing these events?
- **Why** are you telling this story? What makes it significant? What do you want your readers to take from reading it?

WRITING 7: APPLICATION _____

Freewrite for ten minutes about the meaning of your story as you have written it so far, addressing some of these questions: What have you discovered about yourself? Were there any surprises? Does your story interest you? Why or why not? What do you want readers to feel or know at the end?

7 **g** Shaping the whole paper (student essay)

The finished draft of Judith's personal reflective essay, "Writing in Safety," opens and closes with a walk to and from the library. It has a loosely narrative pattern and is written in the present tense to convey a sense of the events unfolding as we read them. Her essay tells a very simple story, since it's mainly about walking and sitting down. The journey emerges as a mental, almost spiritual, quest for safety—safety in which to think and create without fear. At the same time, the physical dimensions of her journey and the attention to descriptive detail make her journey believable.

Writing in Safety

Judith Woods

It is already afternoon. I fiddle with the key to lock the apartment door after me. I am not accustomed to locking doors. Except for the six months I spent in Boston, I have never lived in a place where I did not trust my neighbors. When I was little, we couldn't lock our farmhouse door; the wood had swollen and the bolt no longer lined up properly with the hole, and nobody ever bothered to fix it. I still remember the time our baby-sitter, Rosie, hammered the bolt closed and we had to take the door off the hinges to get it open.

I heft the book bag onto my shoulder and walk up College Street toward the library. As I pass and am passed by other students, I scrutinize everything around me, hoping to be struck with a creative idea for a topic for my English paper. Instead, my mind fills with a jumble of disconnected images, like a bowl of alphabet soup: the letters are there, but they don't form any words. Campus sidewalks are not the best places for creativity to strike.

Approaching the library, I see skateboarders and bikers weaving through students who talk in clusters on the library steps. A friendly dog is tied to a bench, watching for its owner to return. Subjects to write about? Nothing strikes me as especially interesting, and besides, my heart is still pounding from the walk up the hill. I wipe my damp forehead and go inside.

Inside the smoke-colored doors, the loud and busy atmosphere vanishes, replaced by the soft, soothing hum of air-conditioning and the hushed sound

of whispering voices. The repetitive sound of the copy machine has a calming

effect as I look for a comfortable place in which to begin my work.

I want just the right chair, with a soft cushion, and a low sturdy table for

a leg rest. The chairs are strategically positioned with comfortable personal

space around each one, so you can stretch your arms fully without touching a

neighbor. I notice that if there are three chairs in a row, the middle one is

always empty. If seated at a table, people sit staggered so they are not

directly across from one another. People seem to respect each other's need

for personal space.

Like a dog who circles her bed three times before lying down, I circle the

reading room looking for the right place to sit. I need to feel safe and

comfortable so I can concentrate on mental activity. Some students, however,

are too comfortable. One boy has moved two chairs together and covered

himself with his coat, and he is asleep in a fetal position. A girl sits at a table,

head down, dozing like we used to do in first grade.

I find my place, an empty chair near a window, and slouch down into it,

propping my legs on the low table in front. If my mother could see me, she'd

reprimand me for not sitting up straight. I breathe deeply, close my eyes for a

moment, and become centered, forgetting both last night's pizza and

tomorrow's philosophy exam. I need a few minutes to acclimate to this space,

relax, and feel safe before starting my work.

Two weeks ago, a female student was assaulted not far from where I

live—that's why I've taken to locking my door so carefully. I am beginning to

understand the importance of feeling safe in order to be creative and

productive. Here, in the library, I feel secure, protected from real violence and isolated from everyday distractions. There are just enough people for security's sake but not so many that I feel crowded. And besides, I'm surrounded by all these books, all these great minds who dwell in this hallowed space! I am comfortable, safe, and beginning to get an idea.

Hours later—my paper started, my exam studied for, my eyes tired—I retrace the path to my apartment. It is dark now, and I listen closely when I hear footsteps behind, stepping to the sidewalk's edge to let a man walk briskly past. At my door, I again fumble for the now familiar key, insert it in the lock, open the door, turn on the hall light, and step inside. Here, too, I am safe, ready to eat, read a bit, and finish my reflective essay.

SUGGESTIONS FOR WRITING AND RESEARCH

INDIVIDUAL

Write a personal experience essay based on Writings 2–6 in this chapter. Find a subject that will let you show some change or learning on your part. Plan to write this narrative in several drafts, each one exploring a different aspect of your experience.

COLLABORATIVE

As a class, write the story of your writing class so far in the semester. Each class member contributes one chapter (one page) to this tale. Each member chooses any moment (funny, momentous, boring, routine) and describes it so that it stands on its own as a complete episode. Choose two class members to collect all the short narrative chapters and weave them into a larger narrative with a beginning, middle, and end.

8 Explaining Things

To explain something is to make it clear to somebody else who wants to understand it. Explaining is fundamental to most acts of communication and to nearly every type of writing, from personal to argumentative and research writing. Explanatory writing is also a genre unto itself: a newspaper feature on baseball card collecting, a magazine article on why dinosaurs are extinct, a textbook on the French Revolution, a recipe for chili, or a laboratory report.

8 a Writing to explain

Explanatory writing (also called *expository* or *informational* writing) answers questions such as these:

- What is it?

- What does it mean?

- How does it work?

- How is it related to other things?

- How is it put together?

- Why did it happen?

- What will its consequences be?

To write a successful explanation, you need to find out first what your readers *want* to know, then what they *already know* and what they *don't know*. If you are able to determine—or at least make educated guesses about—these audience conditions, your writing task becomes clear. When you begin to write, keep in mind three general principles that typify much explanatory writing: (1) it focuses on the idea or object being explained rather than on the writer's beliefs and feelings: (2) it often—not always—states its

objective early in what might be called an informational thesis; and (3) it presents information systematically and logically.

In writing classes, explanation usually takes the form of research essays and reports that emphasize informing rather than arguing, interpreting, or reflecting. The assignment may be to "describe how something works" or to "explain the causes and effects" of a particular phenomenon. This chapter explains how to develop a topic, articulate your purpose, and use strategies appropriate for your audience.

WRITING I: EXPLORATION

How good are you at explaining things to people? What things do you most commonly find yourself explaining? What is the last thing you explained in writing? How did your audience receive your explanation?

ESL: How is explaining things in your native language different from or similar to explaining things in English?

8 b Focusing on a topic

Topics with a limited, or specific, scope are easier to explain carefully and in detail than topics that are vague, amorphous, or very broad. For example, general subjects such as mountains, automobiles, or music sound systems are so broad that it's hard to know where to begin. However, a specific aspect of sound systems, such as compact discs (CDs) is easier. Within the subject of CDs, of course, there are several topics as well (design, manufacturing process, cost, marketing, sound quality, comparison to tape and vinyl recordings, etc.). If your central question focuses on how CDs are manufactured, you might well address some of these other issues (cost, marketing, comparison) as well, but only in so far as they illuminate and advance your focus on manufacturing. Effective explanations are detailed and developed, include examples, and are focused around a central question ("How are CDs made?" or "How do CDs differ from LPs?"). Of course, there may be other questions to be answered along the way ("How do CDs work?" "Why do CDs cost so much?"), but these are secondary.

Once you have a focused topic on a central question, you need to assemble information. If you're not an expert yourself, you'll need to consult authorities on the topic. Even if you are already an expert, finding supporting information from other experts will help make your explanation clear and authoritative. Keep your audience in mind as you begin your research. You don't want to waste time researching and writing about things your audience already knows or issues that are beyond the scope of your focused topic.

WRITING 2: APPLICATION ─────────────────────

What would you like to explain? for what purpose? to whom? If you're not sure, do some freewriting or journal writing to help you discover a question.

8 c Developing a thesis

The **thesis** statement in an explanatory paper is simply the writer's declaration of what the paper is about. Stating a thesis early in an explanatory work lets readers know what to expect and guides their understanding of the information to be presented. In explanatory writing, the thesis states the answer to the implied question your paper sets out to address: What is it? How does this work? Why is this so?

QUESTION   Why do compact discs cost so much?

THESIS   CDs cost more than cassette tapes because the laser technology required to manufacture them is so expensive.

The advantage of stating a thesis in a single sentence is that it sums up the purpose of your paper in a single idea that lets readers predict what's ahead. Another way to state a single-sentence thesis is to convey an image, analogy, or metaphor that provides an ongoing reference point throughout the paper and gives unity and coherence to your explanation—a good image keeps both you and your readers focused.

QUESTION   How are the offices of the city government connected?

THESIS   City government offices are like an octopus, with eight fairly independent bureaus as arms and a central brain in the major's office.

The thesis you start with may evolve as you work on your paper—and that's okay. For example, suppose the more you learn about city government, the less like an octopus and the more like a centipede it seems. So, your first thesis is really a **working thesis,** and it needs to be tentative, flexible, and subject to change; its primary function is to keep your paper focused to guide further research.

WRITING 3: APPLICATION ━━━━━━━━━━━━━━━━━━━

Write out a working thesis for the topic you are explaining. If you are addressing a *when* or *how* question, find a controlling image or analogy that will hold all of the elements together.

8 d   Using strategies to explain

Good strategies that can be used to explain things include defining, describing, classifying and dividing, analyzing causes and effects, and comparing and contrasting. Which strategy you select depends on the question you are answering as well as the audience to whom you are explaining. You could offer two very different explanations to the same question depending on who asked it. For example, if asked "Where is Westport Drive?" you would respond differently to a neighbor familiar with local reference points ("One block north of Burger King") than to a stranger who would not know where Burger King was either. With this caution in mind on considering who is the receiver of the explanation, here is a brief overview of possible strategies:

QUESTION	STRATEGY
What is it?	Define

Example: A CD is a small plastic disc containing recorded music.

What does it mean?	Define

Example: Today, when you talk about a "recording," you mean a cassette tape or a CD, not a grooved vinyl disc.

What are its characteristics?	Describe

Example: A vinyl disc is round with tiny grooves covering its surface in which a needle travels to play sound.

QUESTION	STRATEGY
How does it work?	Describe process

Example: On a CD, a laser beam reads the tiny dots on the spinning disk and sends back sound.

How is it related to other things?	Compare and contrast

Example: A CD transmits clearer sound than a cassette tape.

How is it put together?	Classify and divide

Example: A basic stereo system includes an input (to generate sound), a processor (to amplify and transmit sound), and an output (to make sound audible).

To what group does it belong?	Classify and divide

Example: CD players, along with record players and tape cassette decks, are sources of music in a stereo system.

Why did it happen?	Analyze cause and effect

Example: The CD skips because either its surface is dirty or the player is broken.

What will its consequences be?	Analyze cause and effect

Example: If you scratch a vinyl record with a knife, it will skip.

If your paper is on a tightly focused topic and answers a narrow, simple question, you may need to use only one strategy. More often, however, you will have one primary strategy that shapes the paper as a whole and several secondary strategies that can vary from paragraph to paragraph or even sentence to sentence. For example, to explain why the government has raised income taxes, your primary strategy would be to analyze cause and effect, but you might also need to define terms such as *income tax,* to classify the various types of taxes, and to compare and contrast raising income taxes to other budgetary options. In fact, almost every explanatory strategy makes use of other strategies: How, for example, do you describe a process without first dividing it into steps? How can you compare and contrast without describing the things compared and contrasted?

ESL **VOCABULARY FOR EXPLAINING THINGS**

- Description

consists of	has
displays	characterized by

Example: The gardenia *has* a sweet fragrance.

- Division

consists of	separated into
divided into	composed of

Example: The curriculum is *divided into* the humanities, the social

sciences, and the natural sciences.

- Classification

categorized according to	categorized as
classified according to	classified as
grouped according to	

Example: History can be *classified as* a humanities discipline.

- Comparison

also	resembles
both . . . and . . .	similar to
like	the same as

Example: *Like* English, Spanish uses articles before nouns.

- Contrast

but	on the other hand
however	unlike
in contrast	yet

Example: *Unlike* English, Spanish does not always state the subject

of a sentence.

- Cause and effect

as a result	so
consequently	therefore
for this reason	thus

Example: Some marathon runners do not pace themselves well, and

as a result they may be unable to finish a race.

Defining

To define something is to identify it, to set it apart so that it can be distinguished from similar things. Writers need to define any terms central for reader understanding in order to make points clearly, forcefully, and with authority.

Formal **definitions** are what you find in a dictionary. They usually combine a general term with specific characteristics:

> A computer is a programmable electronic device [*general term*] that can store, retrieve, and process data [*specific characteristics*].

Usually, defining something is a brief preliminary step accomplished before you move on to a more important part of the explanation. When you need to define something complex or difficult or when your primary explanatory strategy is definition, you will need an extended definition consisting of a paragraph or more. This was the case with Mark's paper explaining computers, in which he defined each part of a typical computer system. After defining the central processor unit (CPU), he defined computer memory:

> Computer storage space is measured in units called "Kilobytes" (K). Each K equals 1,024 "bytes" or approximately 1,000 single typewriter characters. So 1 K equals about 180 English words, or a little less than half of a single-spaced typed page, or maybe three minutes of fast typing.
>
> Personal computers generally have their memories measured in "megabytes" (MB). That means 1 MB equals 1,048,567 bytes (or 1,000 K), which translates into approximately 400 pages of single-spaced type. One gigabyte (GB) equals 1,000 MB or 400,000 pages of single-spaced type.

Describing

To describe a person, place, or thing means to create a verbal image so that readers can see what you see; hear what you hear; or taste, smell, and feel what you taste, smell, and feel. In other words, effective descriptions appeal to the senses. Furthermore, good descriptions contain enough sensory detail for readers to

understand the subject, but not so much as to distract or bore them. Your job, then, is to include just the right amount of detail so that you put readers in your shoes.

To describe how processes work is more complicated than describing what something looks like: in addition to showing objects at rest, you need to show them in sequence and motion. You need to divide the process into discrete steps and present the steps in a logical order that will be easy for readers to follow. This is easier to do with simple processes, such as making a peanut butter and jelly sandwich, than for complex processes, such as manufacturing an automobile.

To help orient your readers, you may also want to number the steps, using transition words such as *first, second,* and *third.* In the following example, taken from an early draft of his paper, Keith describes the process of manufacturing compact discs:

> CDs start out as a refrigerator-sized box full of little plastic beads that you could sift your hands through. They are fed into a giant tapered corkscrew—a blown-up version of an old-fashioned meat grinder. As the beads pass down the corkscrew, they are slowly melted by the heated walls.
>
> At the bottom of their descent is a "master recording plate" onto which the molten plastic is pressed. The plastic now resembles a vinyl record, except that the disc is transparent. The master now imprints "pits," rather than grooves, around the disc, the surface resembling a ball of Play-Doh after being thrown against a stucco wall—magnified five thousand times.

3 Comparing and contrasting

To compare two things is to find similarities between them: to contrast is to find differences. **Comparing and contrasting** at the same time helps people understand something two ways: first, by showing how it is related to similar things, and second, by showing how it differs. College assignments frequently ask you to compare and contrast two authors, books, ideas, and so on.

People usually compare and contrast things when they want to make a choice or judgment about them: books, food, bicycles,

presidential candidates, political philosophies. For this reason, the two things compared and contrasted should be similar: you'll learn more to help you vote for president by comparing two presidential candidates than one presidential candidate and a senate candidate; you'll learn more about which orange to buy by comparing it with other oranges (*navel, mandarin*) than with apples, plums, or pears. Likewise, it's easiest to see similarities and differences when you compare and contrast the same elements of each thing. If you describe one political candidate's stand on gun control, describe the other's as well; this way, voters will have a basis for choosing one over the other.

Comparison-and-contrast analysis can be organized in one of three ways: (1) a *point-to-point analysis* examines one feature at a time for both similarities and differences; (2) a *whole-to-whole analysis* first presents one object as a whole and then the other as a whole: (3) a *similarity-and-difference analysis* first presents the similarities, then the differences between the two things, or vice versa.

Use a point-to-point or similarity-and-difference analysis for long explanations of complex things, such as manufacturing an automobile, in which you need to cover everything from materials and labor to assembly and inspection processes. But use a whole-to-whole analysis for simple objects that readers can more easily comprehend. In the following whole-to-whole example, a student explains the difference between Democrats and Republicans:

> Like most Americans, both Democrats and Republicans believe in the twin values of equality and freedom. However, Democrats place a greater emphasis on equality, believing equal opportunity for all people to be more important than the freedom of any single individual. Consequently, they stand for government intervention to guarantee equal treatment in matters of environmental protection, minimum wages, racial policies, and educational opportunities.
>
> In contrast, Republicans place greater emphasis on freedom, believing the specific rights of the individual to be more important than the vague collective rights of the masses. Consequently, they stand for less government

> control in matters of property ownership, wages and the
> right to work based strictly on merit and hard work, and
> local control of schools.

Note how the writer devotes equal space to each political party, uses neutral language to lend academic authority to his explanation, and emphasizes the differences by using parallel examples as well as parallel sentence structure. The careful use of several comparison-and-contrast strategies makes it difficult for readers to miss his point.

An *analogy* is an extended comparison which shows the extent to which one thing is similar in structure and/or process to another. Analogies are effective ways of explaining something new to readers, because you can compare something they are unfamiliar with to something they already know about. For example, most of us have learned to understand how a heart functions by comparing it to a water pump. Be sure to use objects and images in analogies that will be familiar to your readers. (See the box on pp. 122–124 in Chapter 9 for a discussion of *false analogies*, arguments that inaccurately portray things that are different as being similar.)

4 Classifying and dividing

People generally understand short more easily than long, simple more easily than complex. One way to help readers understand a complicated topic is to **classify and divide** it into simpler pieces and to put the pieces in context.

To *classify* something, you put it in a category or class with other things that are like it:

> Like whales and dolphins, sea lions are aquatic mammals.

To *divide* something, you break it into smaller parts or subcategories:

> An insect's body is composed of a head, a thorax, and an abdomen.

Many complex systems need both classification and division to be clear. To explain a stereo system, for example, you might divide the whole into parts: headphones, record player, graphic equalizer,

tape deck, CD player, preamplifier, amplifier, radio, and speakers. To better understand how these parts function, you might classify them into categories:

Inputs	Radio
	Record player
	Tape deck
	CD player
Processors	Preamplifiers
	Amplifiers
	Graphic equalizers
Outputs	Speakers
	Headphones

Most readers have a difficult time remembering more than six or seven items at a time, so explaining is easier when you organize a long list into fewer logical groups, as in the preceding example. Also be sure that the categories you use are meaningful to your readers, not simply convenient for you as a writer.

5 Analyzing causes and effects

Few things happen all by themselves. Usually, one thing happens because something else happened; then it, in turn, makes something else happen. You sleep because you're tired, and once you've slept, you wake up because you're rested, and so on. In other words, you already know about cause and effect because it's a regular part of your daily life. A **cause** is something that makes something else happen; an **effect** is the thing that happens.

Cause-and-effect analyses are most often assigned for college papers to answer *why* questions: Why are the fish dying in the river? The most direct answer is a *because* statement:

Fish are dying *because* oxygen levels in the lake are too low.

The answer, in other words, is a thesis, which the rest of the paper must defend and support:

There are three reasons for low oxygen level . . .

Cause-and-effect analyses also try to describe possible future effects:

If nitrogen fertilizers were banned from farmland that drains into the lake, oxygen levels would rise, and fish populations would be restored.

Unless there is sound, widely accepted evidence to support the thesis, however, this sort of analysis may lead to more argumentative writing. In this example, for instance, farmers or fertilizer manufacturers might complicate the matter by pointing to other sources of lake pollution—outboard motors, paper mill effluents, urban sewage runoff—making comprehensive solutions harder to reach. Keep in mind that most complex situations have multiple causes. If you try to reduce a complex situation to an overly simple cause, you are making the logical mistake known as *oversimplification*. (See the box on pp. 122–124 in Chapter 9 for further discussion of errors in logic to avoid in cause-and-effect explanations.)

WRITING 4: APPLICATION ─────────────────────────

Decide which of the five strategies described in this section best suits the primary purpose of the explanatory paper you are drafting. Which additional or secondary strategies will you also use?

8   e   Organizing with logic

If you explain to your readers where you're taking them, they will follow more willingly; if you lead carefully, step by step, using a good road map, they will know where they are and will trust you.

Your method of organization should be simple, straightforward, and logical, and it should be appropriate for your subject and audience. For example, to explain how a stereo system works, you have a number of logical options: (1) you could start by putting a CD in a player and end with the music coming out of the speakers; (2) you could describe the system technically, starting with the power source to explain how sound is made in the speakers; (3) you could describe it historically, starting with components that were developed earliest and work toward the most recent inventions. All these options follow a clear logic that, once explained, will make sense to readers.

WRITING 5: APPLICATION ─────────────────────────

Outline three possible means of organizing the explanatory paper you are writing. List the advantages and disadvantages of each. Select the one that best suits your purpose and the needs of your audience.

8 f Maintaining a neutral perspective

First, you need to understand that absolute neutrality or objectivity is impossible when you write about anything. All writers bring with them assumptions and biases that cause them to view the world—including this explanatory project—in a particular way. Nevertheless, your explanations will usually be clearer and more accessible to others when you present them as fairly as possible, with as little bias as possible—even though doing this, too, will depend on who your readers are and whether they agree or disagree with your biases. In general, it's more effective to emphasize the thing explained (the object) rather than your personal beliefs and feelings. This perspective allows you to get information to readers as quickly and efficiently as possible without you, the writer, getting in the way.

To adopt a neutral perspective, write from the third-person point of view, using the pronouns *he, she,* and *it*. Keep yourself in the background unless you have a good reason not to, such as explaining your personal experience with the subject. In some instances, adopting the second-person *you* adds a friendly, familiar tone that keeps readers interested.

Be fair; present all the relevant information about the topic, both things you like about it and things you dislike. Avoid emotional or biased language. Remember that your goal is not to win an argument, but to convey information.

8 g Shaping the whole paper (student essay)

In the following essay, Keith Jordan asks the question "How is the music that our generation listens to and takes for granted actually made?" He says, in effect, read my essay ("Let me fill you in") and I'll explain how CD players operate and how the discs are manufactured. His organization is simple as he starts with the playing of the disc and backtracks to how they are made. Keith's voice throughout is that of a knowledgeable tour guide. Although his personality is evident ("How much can you screw up a yes or no?"), his biases do not affect the report. Although the primary explanatory strategy in Keith's essay is cause and effect, he uses most of the other strategies discussed in this chapter as well: definition, process description, and comparison and contrast. His essay is most remarkable for its effective use of analogy. At various points, he asks his readers to think of radar, the game of telephone,

jimmies on an ice cream cone, corkscrews, meat grinders, player pianos, and Play-Doh.

The Sound Is Better than the Music: The Making of Compact Discs

Keith Jordan

Our generation is the music generation. We buy and listen to more music more often than any generation before us, but few of us actually understand how this music is made. The purpose of your whole sound system, from recording to speaker, is to reproduce music that sounds as much like the original source as possible. The compact disc (CD) technology that we take for granted reproduces music better than previous recording systems because it's both simpler and more complicated than they were. Let me fill you in.

A CD player operates by sending out a laser beam of light that bounces off an object, like radar, and returns with a message, which becomes the music. On one CD there are hundreds of thousands of tiny pits that resemble those of a player piano scroll, telling the piano which keys to hit. The CD player reads either a simple "yes" or a "no"—a pit or no pit—from the disc. The laser in your CD player detects the distance to the disc to determine whether there's a pit, which will be farther away, or not.

What's the difference, you ask, in receiving music from tiny pits versus the grooves on vinyl records or magnetic deposits on tapes? The result is less interference between the message sent and the message received. Do you remember playing the "telephone game" in fifth grade? You know, the one where someone on one side of class whispers something in your ear and it gets passed along until it gets to the last person, who says what he or she

was told? This is much the way in which your sound system works: a recording—either a disc or a tape—is like the first person, and your speakers are like the last. In the case of the vinyl records or magnetic tapes, I whisper some line in your ear and you pass it on, but by the time it reaches the last person, it's been touched and twisted and has a few more words attached. However, in the case of the CD, I whisper either a "yes" or "no," and by the time it reaches the last person it should be exactly the same—this is where the term "digital" comes from, meaning either there is a signal ("yes") or there isn't one ("no"). How much can you screw up a yes or a no?

The CD manufacturing process, however, is not so simple. To guarantee that almost nothing will interfere with (scratch or break) the digital message encoded on the plastic, the disc is metallized, a process that deposits a thin film of metals, usually aluminum, on the surface; you see it as a rainbow under a light. Since light won't bounce back from transparent plastic, the coating acts as a mirror to bounce back the laser beam. The disc is mirrored by a precise spray-painting process called "sputtering." You couldn't just dip the thing because then the pits would fill in or melt. The clear disc is inserted into a chamber and placed opposite a piece of pure aluminum called "a target," which is bombarded with electricity, causing the aluminum atoms to jump off and embed themselves into the surface of the disc, like jimmies on an ice cream cone. Then the disc is "spin-coated" yet again with a fine film of resin, which becomes the outer coating on the CD.

Once the resin is cured by a brief exposure to ultraviolet light, your CD is pretty much idiot-proof. As long as you don't interrupt the light path in the

film, your CD will perform perfectly, even with small scratches, so long as

they don't diffract the laser beam—and even then you may be able to rub

them smooth with a finger. No object, other than a ray of light, comes in

contact with the recorded surface of a compact disc.

The CD is finished when it is stamped with the appropriate logo and

allowed to dry. In other words, the way CDs are played and made eliminates

the interference that cause distortion in earlier music systems. These steps,

which have taken me several hours to explain on paper, take a mere seven

seconds on the assembly line from materials that cost no more than a pack of

gum. The technology behind CD systems guarantees a faithful sound

recording and a disc that will last virtually forever—longer, perhaps, than

some of the music we listen to.

WRITING TO EXPLAIN

When you have finished a first draft of your explanatory paper, address the following questions:

- Did you state in one sentence the goal or **thesis** of this paper? Is this stated on your first page or toward the end? Is the thesis statement where it should be? If not, where should it be moved?
- What **strategies** (see 8d) did you use to explain your topic? Would other strategies, in addition to in place of the ones you used, help to make the explanation clearer?
- Is there a clear logic in the **order** of your explanation? What is it? Can you think of an alternative order?
- Is your explanation **objective?** Do you have a **bias** or opinion about this topic? Does your bias show? Do you want it to?
- If you knew little or nothing about this topic, at what points would you have difficulty understanding the paper?

SUGGESTIONS FOR WRITING AND RESEARCH

INDIVIDUAL

1. Write a paper explaining any thing, process, or concept. Use as a starting point an idea you discovered in Writing 2. When you have finished one draft of this essay, look back and see whether there are places where your explanation could be improved through use of one of the explanatory strategies explained in this chapter.

2. Select a writer of your choice, fiction or nonfiction, who explains things especially well. Read or reread a passage of explanatory writing in his or her work and write an essay in which you analyze and explain the effectiveness of the explanation you find there.

COLLABORATIVE

Form writing groups based on mutual interests; agree as a group to explain the same thing, process, or concept. Write your explanations separately and then share drafts, comparing and contrasting your different ways of explaining. For a final draft, either (1) rewrite your individual drafts, borrowing good ideas from others in your group, or (2) compose a collaborative single paper with contributions from each group member.

9 Arguing Positions

Argument is deeply rooted in the American political and social system, in which free and open debate is the essence of the democratic process. Argument is also at the heart of the academic process, in which scholars investigate scientific, social, and cultural issues, hoping through the give-and-take of debate to find reasonable answers to complex questions. Argument in the academic world, however, is less likely to be about winning or losing—as it is in political and legal systems—than about changing minds or altering perceptions about knowledge and ideas.

Argument as rational disagreement, rather than as quarrels and contests, most often occurs in areas of genuine uncertainty about what is right, best, or most reasonable. In disciplines such as English, history, and philosophy, written argument commonly takes the form of interpretation, in which the meaning of an idea or text is disputed. In disciplines such as political science, engineering, and business, arguments commonly appear as position papers in which a problem is examined and a solution proposed.

The purpose of writing argument papers is to persuade other people to agree with a particular point of view. Arguments focus on issues about which there is some debate; if there's no debate, there's no argument. College assignments commonly ask you to argue one side of an issue and defend your argument against attacks from skeptics.

9 a Understanding the elements of argument

In a basic position paper assignment, you are asked to choose an issue, argue a position, and support it with evidence. Sometimes your investigation of the issue will lead you beyond polar positions toward compromise—a common result of real argument and debate in both the academic and political worlds. In other words, such a paper may reveal that the result of supporting one position

(thesis) against another **(antithesis)** is to arrive at yet a third position **(synthesis),** which is possible now because both sides have been fully explored and a reasonable compromise presents itself.

This chapter explains the elements that constitute a basic position paper: an arguable issue, a claim and counterclaim, a thesis, and evidence.

1 Issues

An issue is a controversy, something that can be argued about. For instance, mountain bikes and cultural diversity are things or concepts, not in themselves issues. However, they become the foundation for issues when questions are raised about them and controversy ensues.

ISSUE   Do American colleges adequately represent the cultural diversity of the United States?

ISSUE   Should mountain bikes be allowed on wilderness hiking trails?

These questions are issues because reasonable people could answer them in different ways; they can be argued about because more than one answer is plausible, possible, or realistic.

Virtually all issues can be formulated, at least initially, as yes/no questions about which you will take one position or the other: pro (if the answer is yes) or con (if the answer is no).

ISSUE   Should mountain bikes be allowed on trails in Riverside Park?

PRO   Yes, they should be allowed to share pedestrian trails.

CON   No, they should not be allowed to share trails with pedestrians.

2 Claims and counterclaims

A **claim** is a statement or assertion that something is true or should be done. In arguing one side of an issue, you make one or more claims in the hope of convincing an audience to believe you. For example, you could make a claim that calls into question the educational experience at Northville College:

CLAIM   Northville College fails to provide good education because the faculty is not culturally diverse.

Counterclaims are statements that oppose or refute claims. You need to examine an opponent's counterclaim carefully in order to refute it or, if you agree with the counterclaim, to argue that your claim is more important to making a decision. For example, the following counterclaim might be offered against your claim about the quality of Northville College education:

COUNTERCLAIM   The Northville faculty are good scholars and teachers; therefore, their cultural backgrounds are irrelevant.

You might agree that "Northville faculty *are* good scholars and teachers" but still argue that the education is not as good as it would be with more diversity. In other words, the best arguments provide not only good reasons for accepting a position but also good reasons for doubting the opposition. They are made by writers who know both sides of an issue and are prepared for the arguments of the opposition.

3 Thesis

In an argument, the major claim your paper makes is your **thesis:**

THESIS   Northville College should enact a policy to make the faculty more culturally diverse by the year 2010.

In taking a position, you may make other claims as well, but they should all work to support this major claim or thesis:

CLAIM   The faculty is not culturally diverse now.

CLAIM   A culturally diverse faculty is necessary to provide a good education for today's students.

CLAIM   The goal of increased cultural diversity by the year 2010 is achievable and practical.

In arguing a position, you may state your thesis up front, with the remainder of the paper supporting it (*thesis first*), or you may state it later in the paper after weighing the pros and cons with your reader (*delayed thesis*). As a writer, you can decide which approach is the stronger rhetorical strategy after you fully examine each claim and the supporting evidence. Each strategy, thesis first or delayed, has its advantages and disadvantages (see 9f).

4 Evidence

Evidence makes a claim believable. **Evidence** consists of facts, examples, or testimony that supports a claim. For example, to support a claim that Northville College's faculty lacks cultural diversity, you might introduce the following evidence:

EVIDENCE   According to the names in the college catalog, 69 of 79 faculty members are male.

EVIDENCE   According to a recent faculty survey, 75 of 79 faculty members are Caucasian or white.

EVIDENCE   According to Carmen Lopez, an unsuccessful candidate for a position in the English department, 100 percent of the faculty hired in the last ten years have been white males.

Most arguments become more effective when they include documentable source material; however, shorter and more modest argument papers can be written without research and can profitably follow a process similar to that described here.

WRITING 1: EXPLORATION ———————————————————

An issue debated by college faculty is whether or not a first-year writing course should be required of all college students. Make three claims and three counterclaims about this issue. Then select the claim you most believe in and write an argument thesis that could form the basis for a whole essay.

ESL: Consider similarities and differences in how arguments are developed in English and in your native language. Do arguments in your native language use claims and counterclaims?

9 b Finding an issue

You'll write better and have a more interesting time if you select an issue that interests you and about which you still have real questions. A good issue around which to write a position paper will meet the following criteria:

• It is a real issue about which there is controversy and uncertainty.

• It has at least two distinct and arguable positions.

• Resources are available to support both sides.

• It is manageable within the time and scope of the assignment.

In selecting an issue to research and write about, consider both national and local issues. You are likely to see national issues explained and argued in the media:

Are SAT scores a fair measure of academic potential?

Should handgun ownership be outlawed in the United States?

Does acid rain kill forests?

The advantages of national issues include their extensive coverage by television and radio, national newspapers such as the *New York Times* and *Washington Post,* and national newsmagazines. The broad coverage of national news is likely to provide evidence and supporting claims from many sources. In addition, you can count on your audience's having some familiarity with the subject. The disadvantage is that it may be difficult to find local experts or a site where some dimension of the issue can be witnessed.

Local issues derive from the community in which you live. You will find these issues argued about in local newspapers and on local news broadcasts:

Should a new mall be built on the beltway?

Should mountain bikes be allowed in Riverside Park?

Should Northville College require a one-semester course introducing students to diverse American cultures?

The advantage of local issues is that you can often visit a place where the controversy occurs, interview people who are affected by it, and find generous coverage in local news media. The disadvantage is that the subject won't be covered in the national news. Evidence and claims in support of your thesis may be more limited.

Perhaps the best issue is a national issue (hikers versus mountain bikers) with a strong local dimension (this controversy in a local park). Such an issue will enable you to find both national press coverage and local experts (see 9g).

WRITING 2: APPLICATION ─────────────────────────────

Make a list of three national and three local issues about which you are concerned. Next, select the three issues that seem most important to you and write each as a question with a yes or no answer. Finally, note whether each issue meets the criteria for a good position paper topic.

9 C Analyzing an issue

The most demanding work in writing a position paper takes place *after* you have selected an issue but *before* you actually write the paper. To analyze an issue, you need to conduct enough research to explain it and identify the arguments of each side.

In this data-collecting stage, treat each side fairly, framing the opposition as positively as you frame the position. Research as if you are in an honest debate with yourself. Doing so may even cause you to switch sides—one of the best indications of open-minded research. Furthermore, empathy for the opposition leads to making qualified assertions and heads off overly simplistic right versus wrong arguments. Undecided readers who see merit in the opposing side respect writers who acknowledge an issue's complexity.

1 Context

Provide full context for the issue you are writing about, as if readers know virtually nothing about it. Providing **context** means answering these questions: What is this issue about? Where did the controversy begin? How long has it been debated? Who are the people involved? What is at stake? Use a neutral tone, as Issa does in the essay on pages 130–136 in discussing the mountain bike trail controversy:

> With all these new riders, there is a need for places to ride, and this is where the wilderness trail controversy begins. The mountain bike is designed to be ridden on dirt trails, logging roads, and fire trails in backwoods country. However, other trail users who have been around much longer than mountain bikers prefer to enjoy the woods at a slow, leisurely pace. They find the rapid and sometimes noisy two-wheel intruders unacceptable. . . .

2 Claims for (pro)

List the claims supporting the pro side of the issue. Make each claim a distinctly strong and separate point, and make the best possible case for this position, identifying by name the most important

people or organizations that hold this view. Issa makes the following claims for opening up wilderness trails to mountain bikes:

1. All people should have the right to explore the wilderness so long as they do not damage it.

2. Knobby mountain bike tires do no more damage to hiking trails than Vibram-soled hiking boots.

3. Most mountain bike riders are respectful of the wilderness and courteous to other trail users.

3 Claims against (con)

List the claims supporting the con side of the issue—the counterclaims. It is not important to have an equal number of reasons for and against, but you do want an approximate balance.

1. Mountain bike riders ride fast, are sometimes reckless, and pose a threat to slower moving hikers.

2. Mountain bike tires damage trails and cause erosion.

4 Annotated references

Make an alphabetical list on note cards or computer files of the references you consulted during research, briefly identifying each according to the kind of information it contains. The same article may present claims from both sides as well as provide context. Following are two of Issa's annotated references:

Buchanan, Rob. "Birth of the Gearhead Nation." Rolling Stone 9 July 1992:

80-85. Marin Co. CA movement advocates more trails open to mountain

bike use. Includes history. (pro)

Schwartz, David M. "Over Hill, Over Dale on a Bicycle Built for . . . Goo."

Smithsonian June 1992: 74-84. Discusses the hiker vs. biker issue,

promotes peaceful coexistence; includes history. (pro/con)

Annotating your list of references allows you to check and rearrange your claims at any time during the writing process. In addition, if you write and organize your references now, your

reference page will be ready to go when you've finished writing your paper.

Select one of the issues you are interested in, establish the necessary context, and make pro and con lists similar to those described in this section, including supporters of each position. Make the best possible case for each position.

9 d Taking a position

Once you have examined the two positions fairly, weigh which side is the stronger. Select the position that you find more convincing and then write out the reasons that support this position, most compelling reasons last. This will be the position you will most likely defend; you need to state it as a thesis.

Start with a thesis

Formulate your initial position as working thesis early in your paper-writing process. Even though it is merely something to start with, not necessarily to stick with, it serves to focus your initial efforts in one direction and it helps you articulate claims and assemble evidence to support it.

WORKING THESIS   Hikers and mountain bikers should cooperate and support each other in using, preserving, and maintaining wilderness trails.

Writers often revise their initial positions as they reshape their paper or find new evidence. Your working thesis should meet the following criteria:

- It can be managed within your confines of time and space.

- It asserts something specific.

- It proposes a plan of action.

Take a position on the issue you have identified. Formulate a working thesis that you would like to support. Test your thesis against the criteria listed for good theses.

Your argument is the case you will make for your position, the means by which you will try to persuade your readers that your position is correct. Good arguments need solid and credible evidence and clear and logical reasoning.

Assembling evidence

A claim is meaningless without evidence to support it. Facts, examples, inferences, informed opinion, and personal experience all provide believable evidence.

Facts and examples

Facts are verifiable and agreed upon by everyone involved regardless of personal beliefs or values. Facts are often statistical and recorded in some place where anybody can look them up:

> Water boils at 212 degrees Fahrenheit.

> Northville College employed 79 full-time faculty and enrolled 1143 full-time students in 1999.

> Five hundred Japanese-made "Stumpjumper" mountain bikes were sold in the United States in 1981.

Examples can be used to illustrate a claim or clarify an issue. If you claim that many wilderness trails have been closed to mountain biking, you can mention examples you know about:

> The New Jersey trails at South Mountain, Eagle Rock, and Mills Park have all been closed to mountain bikes.

Facts and examples can, of course, be misleading and even wrong. For hundreds of years malaria was believed to be caused by "bad air" rather than, as we know today, by a parasite transmitted through mosquito bites; however, for the people who believed the bad-air theory, it was fact.

Inferences

The accumulation of a certain number of facts and examples should lead to an interpretation of what those facts mean—an *inference* or a **generalization.** For example, if you attend five different classes at Northville College and in each class you find no minority students, you may infer that there are no minority

students on campus. However, while your inference is reasonable, it is not a fact, since your experience does not allow for your meeting all the students at the college.

Facts are not necessarily better or more important than inferences; they serve different purposes. Facts provide information, and inferences give that information meaning.

Sometimes inference is all that's available. For example, statistics describing what "Americans" believe or do are only inferences about these groups based on information collected from a relatively small number of individuals. To be credible, however, inferences must be reasonable and based on factual evidence.

Expert opinion

Expert opinion makes powerful evidence. A forest ranger's testimony about trail damage caused by mountain bikes or lug-soled hiking boots reflects the training and experience of an expert. A casual hiker making the same observation is less believable. To use expert opinion in writing arguments, be sure to cite the credentials or training that makes this person's testimony "expert."

Personal testimony

A useful kind of evidence is testimony based on personal experience. When someone has experienced something firsthand, his or her knowledge cannot easily be discounted. If you have been present at the mistreatment of a minority student whether as the object or an observer of the incident, your eyewitness testimony will carry weight, even though you are not a certified expert of any kind. To use personal testimony effectively, provide details that confirm for readers that you were there and know what you are talking about.

2 Reasoning effectively

To build an effective argument, consider the audience you must persuade. If you were writing about the mountain bike controversy and taking a pro-biker position, for example, you would ask yourself these questions:

- Who will read this paper?

  Members of an environmentally conscious hiking club? members of a mountain bike club? your instructor?

- Where do I think my readers stand on the issue?

Hikers are often opposed to mountain bikes, and mountain bikers are not, but you would need more information to predict your instructor's position.

- How are their personal interests involved?

  Hikers want the trails quiet and peaceful; bikers want to ride in the wilderness, and your instructor may or may not care.

- What evidence would they consider convincing?

  A hiker would need to see convincing examples of trails not being damaged by mountain bike use; bikers would accept anecdotal testimony of good intentions, and you're still not sure about your instructor.

The more you know about the audience you're trying to sway, the easier it will be to present your case. If your audience is your instructor, you'll need to make inferences about his or her beliefs based on syllabus language, class discussion, assigned readings, or personal habits. For example, if your instructor rides a mountain bike to work, you may begin to infer one thing; if he or she assigns Sierra Club readings in the course, you infer something else; and if the instructor rides a mountain bike *and* reads Sierra Club publications, well, you've got more homework ahead. Remember that inferences based on a single piece of evidence are often wrong; find out more before you make simple assumptions about your audience. And sometimes audience analysis doesn't work very well when an instructor, in an effort to help you learn to develop a persuasive position paper, assumes a deliberately skeptical role, no matter which side of an issue you support. It's best to assume you will have a critical reader and to use the best logic and evidence available. Following are some ways to marshal careful and substantial evidence.

First, establish your credibility. Demonstrate to your audience that you are fair and can be trusted. Do this by writing in neutral, not obviously biased, language—avoid name-calling. Also do this by citing current sources by respected experts—and don't quote them out of context. Do this also by identifying elements that serve as common ground between you and the audience—be up front and admit when the opposite side makes a good point.

CREDIBLE — Northville College offers excellent instruction in many areas; however, its offerings in multicultural education would be enhanced by a more diverse faculty.

LESS CREDIBLE — Education at Northville College sucks.

Second, use logic. Demonstrate that you understand the principles of reasoning that operate in the academic world: Make each claim clearly and carefully. Make sure you have substantial, credible evidence to support each claim. Make inferences from your evidence with care; don't exaggerate or argue positions that are not supported by the evidence. Use **logic** to infer reasonable relationships between pieces of evidence.

LOGICAL

Because 75 of 79 faculty members are white and 69 of 79 are male, hiring more blacks, Hispanics, Native Americans, and women, when they are available, would increase the cultural diversity of the faculty.

ILLOGICAL

Because most of the Northville faculty are white men, they must be racists and should be sent to another country.

Third, avoid false arguments. For more than two thousand years, since the time of the ancient Greeks and Romans, the principles of false logic have been recognized by careful debaters and audiences alike. Study these logical **fallacies** (see the box "False Arguments"). Avoid using them in making your arguments, and also recognize when others try to use them on you. Although false arguments do not necessarily lead to false conclusions, they weaken the writer's credibility with readers who recognize the faulty logic. The illogical argument above contains three fallacies. It "begs the question" (it has not been established that the whole faculty is racist); it "does not follow" that racists should be sent to another country; and it "oversimplifies" by proposing a simplistic solution to a complex problem.

Fourth, appeal to your audience's emotions. It's fair to use means of persuasion other than logic to win arguments. Write with vivid details, concrete language, and compelling examples to show your audience a situation that needs addressing. It is often helpful, as well, to adopt a personal tone and write in friendly language to reach readers' hearts as well as minds

EMOTIONAL
APPEAL

When Bridgett Jones, the only black student in Philosophy 1, sits down, the desks on either side of her remain empty. When her classmates choose partners for debate, Bridgett is always the last one chosen.

WRITING 5: APPLICATION ————————————————————————

Develop an informal profile of the audience for your position paper by answering the questions posed in this section. Make a list of the kinds of evidence most likely to persuade this audience.

FALSE ARGUMENTS (FALLACIES)

The following false arguments are often made when a writer does not have enough evidence to support his or her claims. Learn to recognize faulty logic and avoid it.

- **Ad hominem (to the person) and false authority.** Bases claims on who supports them rather than on the content or logic of the premise. Ad hominem arguments attempt to refute a statement by attacking a supporter, and false authority arguments suggest that the opinion of a particular person, often a celebrity, is authoritative, even though that person is not known as an expert in the subject being debated.

AD HOMINEM
> Professor Jones is worried about keeping his job, so you can't believe his argument that Northville's hiring policies aren't biased.

Perhaps Professor Jones has other reasons—logical or illogical—for believing the policies are not biased. He may have been part of a failed effort to attract more female and minority faculty members, or perhaps he is a bigot.

FALSE
AUTHORITY
> My roommate has lived in this town for fifteen years, and she says the college has favored white men in its hiring for as long as she can remember.

The writer's roommate is not in a position to know why the majority of faculty members are white men. There may be reasons other than a biased hiring policy.

- **Bandwagon.** Encourages people to accept a position simply because others already have.

More than three-fourths of American colleges have required courses on cultural diversity; so should Northville College.

Is there convincing evidence that these courses are beneficial? Maybe offering separate courses is not the best way to introduce more cultural diversity into Northville College's curriculum.

- **Begging the question.** Treats a questionable statement as if it had already been accepted.

Northville College must change its discriminatory hiring policies if the administration wants to attract a more culturally diverse faculty.

(Continued)

Are the policies discriminatory, or could the disproportionate number of white male faculty members be due to other causes such as a lack of applications from women and minority candidates?

- **False analogy.** Uses analogy incorrectly to claim that two things which are alike or similar in one way are also alike or similar in other ways.

  Just as polar bears don't hang around with black panthers, so white students shouldn't be part of a community that includes black students.

  The only characteristics that are shown to be similar between the animals and students are the fur color of polar bears and skin color of white students and the fur color of panthers and the skin color of black students. The writer has not shown that fur color is the reason the two species of animals don't "hang around" to-gether, much less that humans resemble either species in other ways.

- **False cause (post hoc, ergo propter hoc).** The translation of the Latin is "after this, therefore because of this." Assumes that if one event happened after another, the earlier event must have caused the later one.

  When Fay Wong transferred from culturally diverse Southfield College to predominantly white Northville College, her grade point average dropped dramatically. Being a token minority student must have distracted her from her studies.

  There could be other explanations for the drop in her grades, such as a heavier course load or family problems, to name just two possibilities.

- **False dilemma (either/or argument).** Presents a situation as allowing only two options when there are actually more.

  Northville College will have to fire some of its white male faculty members and replace them with minority and female instructors or give up on the idea of making the faculty more culturally diverse.

  The college could also hire minority and female instructors in the course of re-placing retirees, and it could add new positions to the faculty.

- **Non sequitur (does not follow).** Presents a conclusion that does not logically follow from its premises.

  Bill Cosby is a great comedian, so he would be an excellent college teacher.

(Continued)

Cosby's talents as a comedian don't either prove or disprove that he would perform well as a college teacher.

- **Oversimplification.** Reduces a complex system of causes and effects to an inaccurate generalization.

  The teaching of traditional American values will be eroded if the Northville faculty becomes more culturally diverse.

  Some American values, such as equality and tolerance for differences, may be strengthened by the hiring of a more diverse faculty.

- **Slippery slope.** Assumes that if an action or event is allowed to occur, it will lead to more extreme actions or events.

  If Northville College offers a course in cultural diversity, pretty soon it will have to offer a whole range of courses in ethnic studies.

  Have all the colleges that offer a course in cultural diversity subsequently been compelled to add courses in ethnic studies to their curriculum?

9   f   Organizing a position paper

To organize your paper, you need to know your position on the issue: what is the main point of your argument? In other words, move from a *working thesis* to a *final thesis:* confirm the working thesis that's been guiding your research so far, or modify it, or scrap it altogether and assert a different one. You should be able to articulate this thesis in a single sentence as the answer to the yes/no question you've been investigating. (See 9d.)

THESIS   Wilderness trails should be open to both mountain bikers and hikers.

THESIS   Wilderness trails should be closed to mountain bikes.

Your next decision is where in this paper you should reveal your thesis to the reader—in your opening or strategically delayed until later?

Thesis-first organization

Leading with a thesis, the most common form of academic argument, tells readers from the beginning where you stand on the

LIMITING GENERALIZATIONS

When you make general claims, you should carefully limit your statements so that the generalizations are accurate and believable. Claims that are too broad may cause your readers to doubt the strength of your argument. Use these techniques to limit your general claims:

- Use adverbs such as *often, usually, seldom*, or *frequently* if something is not always true.

> *often*
> Due to the recent budget cuts, students cannot enroll in the courses
> ^
> they need for graduation.

- Add *many, most*, or *a majority of* to limit the subject's range.

> *many*
> Because of the recent budget cuts, students cannot enroll in the
> ^
> courses they need for graduation.

- Use *may, might*, or *could* if you are not certain of a claim about the future.

> *may*
> Raising tuition ~~will~~ deprive some students of a college education.
> ^

- Add an expression of probability (*it is possible/probable/likely that . . .*) before the general claim to show that you cannot be absolutely sure of the result.

> *It is very likely that raising*
> ~~Raising~~ tuition will prevent some students from getting a college edu-
> ^
> cation.

issue. One good way to organize a thesis-first argument is to make the remainder of the essay defend your claim against counterclaims, support your thesis with evidence, and close with a restatement of your position. In this organization, your thesis occupies both the first and last position in the essay, making it easy for your readers to remember.

I. **Introduce and explain the issue.** Make sure there are at least two debatable sides. Pose the question that you see arising from this issue; if you can frame it as a yes/no, for/against construction, both you and your reader will have the advantage throughout your answer of knowing where you stand.

> Minority students, supported by many majority students at Northville College, have staged a week-long sit-in to urge the hiring of more minority faculty across the curriculum. Is this a reasonable position? Should Northville hire more minority faculty members?

2. **Assert your thesis.** Your thesis states the answer to the question you have posed and establishes the position from which you will argue. Think of your thesis as the major claim the paper will make.

> Northville College should enact a policy to make the faculty more culturally diverse as soon as reasonably possible.

Writers commonly state their thesis early in the paper, at the conclusion of the paragraph that introduces the issue.

3. **Summarize the counterclaims.** Before elaborating on your own claims, explain the opposition's counterclaims. Doing that gives your own argument something to focus on—and refute— throughout the rest of the paper. Squeezing the counterclaims between the thesis (2) and the evidence (5) reserves the strongest places—the opening and closing—for your position.

> COUNTERCLAIM 1 Northville College is located in a white middle-class community, so its faculty should be white and middle-class also.

> COUNTERCLAIM 2 The Northville faculty are good scholars and teachers; therefore, their race is irrelevant.

4. **Refute the counterclaims.** Look for weak spots in the opposition's argument, and point them out. Use your opponent's language to show you have read closely but still find problems with the claim. To refute counterclaim 1, you could make a statement like this:

> If the community in which the college is located is "white middle-class," all the more reason to offer that diversity in the college.

Your refutation is often stronger when you acknowledge the truth of some of the opposition's claims (demonstrating your fairness) but point out the limitations as well. To refute counterclaim 2, you could say this:

It's true that Northville College offers excellent instruction in many areas; however, its instruction in multicultural education would be enhanced by a more diverse faculty.

5. **Support your claims with evidence.** Spell out your own claims clearly and precisely, enumerating them or being sure to give each its own full-paragraph explanation, and citing supporting evidence. This section will constitute the longest and most carefully documented part of your essay. The following evidence supports the thesis that Northville needs more cultural diversity:

> According to the names in the college catalog, 69 of 79 faculty members are male.

> According to a recent faculty survey, 75 of 79 faculty members are white.

> According to Carmen Lopez, an unsuccessful job candidate for a position in the English department, all faculty hired in the last ten years have been white males.

6. **Restate your position as a conclusion.** Near the end of your paper, synthesize your accumulated evidence into a broad general position, and restate your original thesis in slightly different language.

> While Northville College offers a strong liberal arts education, the addition of more culturally diverse faculty members would make it even stronger.

2 Delayed-thesis organization

Using the delayed-thesis type of organization, you introduce the issue and discuss the arguments for and against, but you do not obviously take a side until late in the essay. In this way, you draw readers into your struggle to weigh the evidence, and you arouse their curiosity about your position. Near the end of the paper, you explain that after carefully considering both pros and cons, you have now arrived at the most reasonable position. Concluding with your own position gives it more emphasis. The following delayed-thesis argument is derived from the sample student essay at the end of this chapter.

1. **Introduce the issue and pose a question.** Both thesis-first and delayed-thesis papers begin by establishing context and posing

a question. Following is the question for the mountain bike position paper:

> Should mountain bikes be allowed on wilderness trails?

2. **Summarize the claims for one position.** Before stating which side you support, explain how the opposition views the issue:

> To traditional trail users, the new breed of bicycle [is] alien and dangerous, esthetically offensive, and physically menacing.

3. **Refute these claims.** Still not stating your own position, point out your difficulties with believing this side:

> Whether a bicycle—or a car or horse for that matter—is "alien and . . . esthetically offensive" depends on your personal taste, judgment, and familiarity. And whether it is "dangerous" depends on how you use it.

In addition, you can actually strengthen your position by admitting that in some cases the counterclaims might be true:

> While it's true that some mountain bikers—like some hikers— are too loud, mountain biking at its best respects the

---

 ARGUING A POSITION

After composing the first draft of your argument paper, address the following questions:

- Can you formulate the issue as a question answered yes or no? Have you done this early in your paper? Should you?
- What claim are you making about this issue? Where in your paper do you make this claim?
- What evidence supports your claim? Is it based on fact, inference, or opinion?
- What counterclaims will the opposition make about this issue? Where in your paper do you address these counterclaims?
- What evidence supports the counterclaims? How and where do you refute this evidence?
- Is you paper organized as a thesis-paper or a delayed-thesis paper? Is this the most effective strategy for your paper? Why?

environment and promotes peace and conservation, not noise and destruction.

4.   **Summarize the counterclaims.** You are supporting these claims and so they should occupy the most emphatic position in your essay, last:

> Most mountain bikers respect the wilderness and should be allowed to use wilderness trails.

5.   **Support your counterclaims.** Now give your best evidence; this should be the longest and most carefully documented part of the paper:

> Studies show that bicycle tires cause no more erosion or trail damage than the boots of hikers and far less than horses' hooves.

6.   **State your thesis as your conclusion.** Your rhetorical strategy is this: after giving each side a fair hearing, you have arrived at the most reasonable conclusion:

> It's clear that mountain bikers don't want to destroy trails any more than hikers do. The surest way to preserve America's wilderness areas is to establish strong cooperative bonds among the hikers and bikers, as well as those who fish, hunt, camp, canoe, and bird-watch, and encourage all to maintain the trails and respect the environment.

WRITING 6: APPLICATION ━━━━━━━━━━━━━━━━━━━━━━━━

Make two outlines for organizing your position paper, one with the thesis first, the other with a delayed thesis. Share your outlines with your classmates and discuss which seems more appropriate for the issue you have chosen.

9 **g** **Shaping the whole paper (student essay)**

In the following paper, Issa explores whether or not mountain bikers should be allowed to share wilderness trails with hikers. In the first part of the paper he establishes the context and background of the conflict; then he introduces the question his paper will address: "Is any resolution in sight?" Note his substantial use of sources, including the Internet and interviews, cited in the MLA documentation style. (See Chapter 55 for a discussion of documentation in MLA style.) Issa selects a delayed-thesis strategy, which

allows him to air both sides of the argument fully before revealing his solution, a compromise position: so long as mountain bikers follow environmentally sound guidelines, they should be allowed to use the trails.

On the Trail: Can the Hikers Share with the Bikers?

By Issa Sawabini

The narrow, hard-packed dirt trail winding up the mountain under the spreading oaks and maples doesn't look like the source of a major environmental conflict, but it is. On the one side are hikers, environmentalists, and horseback riders who have traditionally used these wilderness trails. On the other side, looking back, are the mountain bike riders want to use them too. But the hikers don't want the bikers, so trouble is brewing.

The debate over mountain bike use has gained momentum recently because of the increased popularity of this form of bicycling. Technology has made it easier for everyone to ride these go-anywhere bikes. These high-tech wonders incorporate exotic components including quick gear-shifting derailleurs, good brakes, and a more comfortable upright seating position— and they can cost up to $2,000 each (Kelly 104). Mountain bikes have turned what were once grueling hill climbs into casual trips, and more people are taking notice.

Mountain bikes have taken over the bicycle industry, and with more bikes come more people wanting to ride in the mountains. The first mass-produced mountain bikes date to 1981, when 500 Japanese "Stumpjumpers" were sold; by 1983 annual sales reached 200,000; today the figure is 8.5

million. In fact, mountain biking is second only to in-line skating as the fastest-growing sport in the nation: "For a sport to go from zero to warp speed so quickly is unprecedented," says Brian Stickel, director of competition for the National Off Road Bicycle Association (Schwartz 75).

With all these new riders, there is a need for places to ride, and this is where the wilderness trail controversy begins. The mountain bike is designed to be ridden on dirt trails, logging roads, and fire trails in backwoods country. However, other trail users who have been around much longer than mountain bikers prefer to enjoy the woods at a slow, leisurely pace. They find the rapid and sometimes noisy two-wheel intruders unacceptable: "To traditional trail users, the new breed of bicycle [is] alien and dangerous, esthetically offensive and physically menacing" (Schwartz 74).

"The problem arises when people want to use an area of public land for their own personal purpose," says Carl Newton, forestry professor at the University of Vermont. "Eventually, after everyone has taken their small bit of the area, the results can be devastating. People believe that because they pay taxes for the land, they can use it as they please. This makes sense to the individual, but not to the whole community." Newton is both a hiker and a mountain biker.

When mountain bikes first came on the scene, hikers and environmentalists convinced state and local officials to ban the bikes from wilderness trails (Buchanan 81; Kelly 104). The result was the closing of many trails to mountain bike use: "Many state park systems have banned

bicycles from narrow trails. National Parks prohibit them, in most cases, from leaving the pavement" (Schwartz 81). These trail closings have separated the outdoor community into the hikers and the bikers. Each group is well organized, and each group believes it is right. Is any resolution in sight?

The hikers and other passive trail users have a number of organizations, from conservation groups to public park planning committees, who argue against allowing mountain bikes onto narrow trails traditionally traveled only by foot and horse in the past. They believe that the wide, deeply treaded tires of the mountain bikes cause erosion and that the high speeds of the bikers startle and upset both hikers and horses (Hanley; Schwartz 76).

The arrival of mountain bikes during the 1980s was resisted by established hiker groups, such as the Sierra Club, which won debate after debate in favor of closing wilderness trails to mountain bike activities. The younger and less well organized biking groups proposed compromise, offering to help repair and maintain trails in return for riding rights, but their offers were ignored. "Peace was not given a chance. Foes of the bicycle onslaught, older and better connected, won most of the battles, and signs picturing a bicycle crossed with a red slash began to appear on trailheads all over the country" (Schwartz 74).

In Millburn, New Jersey, trails at South Mountain, Eagle Rock, and Mills Park have all been closed. Anyone caught riding a bike on the trails can be arrested and fined up to $100. Local riders offered an amendment calling for trails to be open Thursday through Sunday, with the riders helping maintain the trails on the other days. The amendment was rejected. According to hiker

Donald Meserlain, the bikes "ruin the tranquillity of the woodlands and drive out hikers, bird watchers, and strollers. It's like weeds taking over the grass. Pretty soon we'll have all weeds" (Hanley).

Many areas in western New York, such as Hunter's Creek, have also been closed to mountain bike use. Anti-biking signs posted on trails frequently used by bicyclists caused a loud public debate as bike riding was again blamed for trail erosion.

Until more public lands are opened to trail riding, mountain bikers must pay fees to ride on private land, a situation beneficial to ski resorts in the off season: "Ski areas are happy to open trails to cyclists for a little summer and fall income" (Sneyd). For example, in Vermont, bike trails can be found at the Catamount Family Center in Williston, Vermont, as well as at Mount Snow, Killington, Stratton, and Bolton Valley. At major resorts, such as Mount Snow and Killington, ski lifts have actually been modified to the top of the mountains, and each offers a full-service bike shop at its base.

However, the real solution to the conflict between hikers and bikers is education, not separation. In response to the bad publicity and many trail closings, mountain bikers have banded together at local and national levels to educate both their own member bike riders and the nonriding public about the potential alliance between these two groups (Buchanan 81).

The largest group, the International Mountain Bike Association (IMBA), sponsors supervised rides and trail conservation classes and stresses that mountain bikers are friends, not enemies of the natural environment. "The IMBA wants to change the attitude of both the young gonzo rider bombing

downhill on knobby tires and the mature outdoorsman bristling at the

thought of tire tracks where boot soles alone did tread" (Schwartz 76).

IMBA published guidelines it hopes all mountain bikers will learn

to follow:

1. Ride on open trails only.
2. Leave no trace.
3. Control your bicycle.
4. Always yield trail.
5. Never spook animals.
6. Plan ahead. (JTYL)

The New England Mountain Bike Association (NEMBA), one of the

largest East Coast organizations, publishes a home page on the Internet

outlining goals: "NEMBA is a not-for-profit organization dedicated to

promoting land access, maintaining trails that are open to mountain

bicyclists, and educating riders to use those trails sensitively and

responsibly. We are also devoted to having fun" (Koellner).

At the local level, the Western New York Mountain Bike Association

(WNYMBA) educates members on proper trail maintenance and urges its

members to cooperate with local environmentalists whenever possible. For

instance, when angry cyclists continued to use the closed trail at Hunter's

Creek, New York, WNYMBA used the Internet to warn cyclists against

continued trail use: "As WNYMBA wishes to cooperate with Erie County

Parks Department to the greatest extent possible on the use of trails in open

parks, WNYMBA cannot recommend ignoring posted signs. The first IMBA

rule of trail is 'ride on open trails only'" (JTYL).

Educated mountain biking, like hiking and horseback riding, respects the environment and promotes peace and conservation, not noise and destruction. Making this case has begun to pay off, and the battle over who walks and who rides the trails should now shift in favor of peaceful coexistence. "Buoyed by studies showing that bicycle tires cause no more erosion or trail damage than the boots of hikers, and far less than horses' hooves, mountain bike advocates are starting to find receptive ears among environmental organizations" (Schwartz 78).

Even in the Millburn, New Jersey, area, bikers have begun to win some battles, as new trails have recently been funded specifically for mountain bike use: "After all," according to an unnamed legislator, "the bikers or their parents are taxpayers" (Hanley).

The Wilderness Club now officially supports limited use of mountain bikes, while the Sierra Club also supports careful use of trails by riders so long as no damage to the land results and riders ride responsibly on the path. "In pursuit of happy trails, bicycling organizations around the country are bending backward over their chain stays to dispel the hell-on-wheels view of them" (Schwartz 83).

Education and compromise are the sensible solutions to the hiker/biker standoff. Increased public awareness as well as increasingly responsible riding will open still more wilderness trails to bikers in the future. It's clear that mountain bikers don't want to destroy trails any more than hikers do. The surest way to preserve America's wilderness areas is to establish strong cooperative bonds among the hikers and bikers, as well as those who fish,

hunt, camp, canoe, and bird-watch, and to encourage all to maintain the trails and respect the environment.

Works Cited

Buchanan, Rob. "Birth of the Gearhead Nation." Rolling Stone 9 July 1992: 80-85.

Hanley, Robert. "Essex County Mountain Bike Troubles." New York Times 30 May 1995: B4.

JTYL (ed.) Western New York Mountain Bike Association Home Page. Western New York Mountain Bike Association. 4 Oct. 1995 <http://128.205.l66.43/public/wnymba/wnymba.html>.

Kelly, Charles. "Evolution of an Issue." Bicycling May 1990: 104-105.

Koellner, Ken (ed.). New England Mountain Bike Association Home Page. 19 Aug. 1995. New England Mountain Bike Association. 30 Sep. 1995 <http://www.ultranet.com/~kvk/nemba.html>.

Newton, Carlton. Personal interview. 13 Nov. 1995.

Schwartz, David M. "Over Hill, Over Dale on a Bicycle Built for . . . Goo." Smithsonian June 1992: 74-84.

Sneyd, Ross. "Mount Snow Teaching Mountain Biking." Burlington Free Press 4 Oct. 1992. E1.

SUGGESTIONS FOR WRITING AND RESEARCH

INDIVIDUAL

1. Write a position paper on the issue you have been working with in Writings 2–6. Follow the guidelines suggested in this chapter, using as much research as you deem appropriate.

2. Write a position paper on an issue of interest to your class. Consider topics such as (1) student voice in writing topics, (2) the seating plan, (3) the value of writing groups versus instructor conferences, or (4) the number of writing assignments.

COLLABORATIVE

1. In teams of two or three, select an issue: divide up the work so that each group member contributes some work to (1) the context, (2) the pro argument, and (3) the con argument (to guarantee that you do not take sides prematurely). Share your analysis of the issue with another group and receive feedback. Finally, write your position papers individually.

2. Follow the procedure for the first collaborative assignment, but write your final position paper collaboratively.

10 Interpreting Texts

To interpret a text is to explain what it means. To interpret a text also implies that the text can be read in more than one way: your **interpretation** is your reading; others may read it differently. The word *text* implies words, writing, books; however, virtually all works created by human beings can be considered as texts open to interpretation: films, music and dance performances, exhibits, paintings, photographs, sculptures, advertisements, artifacts, buildings, and even whole cultures. Perhaps the most popular forms of interpretive writing are published reviews of movies, music, books, and the like.

In college, the most common form of *interpretive essay* assignment is to write analytical essays about reading assignments in humanities and social science courses. Since words can mean more than one thing, texts composed of written words have multiple meanings: they can mean different things depending on who is reading them, and there is no one right answer.

To find out what a poem, essay, play, or story means, you need to hear it, look at its language, examine how it is put together, compare it with similar things, notice how it affects you, and keep asking why.

10 a Writing interpretive essays

The best texts to select for an interpretive assignment are those that are most problematic—texts whose meaning seems to you somewhat slippery and elusive—since these give you, the interpreter, the most room to argue one meaning against another. Your job is to make the best possible case that your interpretation is reasonable and deserves attention.

A typical assignment may be to interpret a poem, story, essay, or historical document—a complex task that draws upon all of your reasoning and writing skills: you may have to *describe* people and

situations, *retell* events, *define* key terms, and *analyze* passages and *explain* how they work, perhaps by *comparing* or *contrasting* the text with others. Finally you will *argue* for one meaning rather than another—in other words, develop a *thesis,* and defend this *thesis* with sound *reasoning* and convincing *evidence.*

This chapter explores numerous ways of developing textual interpretations, using for illustrative purposes Gwendolyn Brooks' poem "We Real Cool." Brooks' poem is especially useful because it is short and quickly read, yet full of potential meanings. Our questions about this text, as well as the strategies for finding answers, are virtually the same ones we would use with any text—fiction, nonfiction, or poetry.

Read, now, this poem by Gwendolyn Brooks about pool players at the Golden Shovel pool hall, and follow along as we examine different ways of determining what it means.

We Real Cool

THE POOL PLAYERS.
SEVEN AT THE GOLDEN SHOVEL.

We real cool. We
Left school. We

Lurk late. We
Strike straight. We

Sing sin. We
Thin gin. We

Jazz June. We
Die soon.

WRITING 1: EXPLORATION ⎯⎯⎯⎯⎯⎯⎯⎯⎯⎯⎯⎯⎯⎯⎯⎯

After reading "We Real Cool," freewrite for ten minutes to capture your initial reaction. Ask yourself these questions: What did it remind me of? Did I like it? Do I think I understand it? What emotions did I feel?

10 b Exploring a text

A good topic for an interpretive essay addresses a question that has several possible answers. If you think the text is overly simple, you will have no real need to interpret it. In addition, choose a topic

that interests or intrigues you; if it doesn't, chances are it won't interest or intrigue your readers either.

No matter what text you are interpreting, however, you need to figure out what it means to you before you can explain it well to someone else. Plan to read it more than once, first to understand what it's like, where it goes, what happens literally. As you read, mark passages that interest or puzzle you. Read the text a second time, more slowly, making marginal notes or journal entries about the interesting, questionable, or problematic passages. As you do this, look for answers and solutions to your previous concerns, rereading as many times as necessary to further your understanding.

In selecting a text to interpret, ask yourself these questions:

- Can this text be read in more than one way?

- What are some of the different ways of reading it?

- With which reading do I most agree?

- Where are the passages in the text that support this reading?

- Whom does my interpretation need to convince? (Who is my audience?)

WRITING 2: APPLICATION ─────────────────────────

Select a text that you are interested in interpreting, and write out the answers to the questions above. Do not at this time worry about developing any of these answers thoroughly.

10 c Joining an interpretive community

How you read and interpret a text depends upon who you are. Who you are depends on the influences that have shaped you—the communities to which you belong. All of us belong to many communities: families, social and economic groups (students or teachers, middle or working class), organizations (Brownies, Boy Scouts, Democrats, Masons), geographic locales (rural or urban, North or South), and institutions (school, church, fraternity). Your membership in one or more communities determines how you see and respond to the world.

The communities that influence you most strongly are called **interpretive communities;** they influence the meaning you make

of the world. People who belong to the same community as you do are likely to have similar assumptions and therefore likely to interpret things as you would. If you live in an urban black community, jazz and rap music may be a natural and constant presence in your life; if you live in a rural white community, country and western music may be the norm; at the same time, as a member of either group you might also belong to a larger community that surrounds itself with classical music. All this means is that people who belong to different communities are likely to have different—not better or worse—perspectives from yours.

Before writing an interpretive essay, it is helpful to ask, "Who am I when I am writing this piece?" You ask this to examine the biases you bring to your work, for each of us sees the world—and consequently texts—from our own particular vantage point. Be aware of your age, gender, race, ethnic identity, economic class, geographic location, educational level, political or religious persuasion. Ask to what extent any of these identities emerges in your writing.

College is, of course, a large interpretive community. Various smaller communities exist within it called disciplines—English, history, business, art, and so on. Within any discipline there are established ways of interpreting texts. Often when you write an interpretive essay, you will do so from the perspective of a traditional academic interpretive community. Take care to follow the conventions of that community, whether you are asked to write a **personal interpretation,** in which you deliberately identify yourself and your biases, or an **analytical interpretation,** in which you remove your personal perspective as much as possible from your writing.

▇ Personal interpretation

In writing from a personal or subjective perspective, the interpreter and his or her beliefs and experiences are part of the story and need to be both expressed and examined. In examining "We Real Cool," for instance, you may bring your background into your writing to help your reader understand why you view the poem as you do. You may compare or contrast your situation to that of the author or characters in the text. Or you might draw upon particular experiences that cause you to see the poem in a particular way. For example, Mitzi's response (which is reprinted at the end of this chapter) begins with memories inspired by the poem:

> "We Real Cool" is a sad poem. It reminds me of the gang
>
> in high school who used to skip classes and come back

smelling of cigarette smoke and cheap liquor—not that I

knew it was cheap back then.

It is increasingly common for good interpretive essays to include both analytical and personal discussions, allowing you to demonstrate your skill at closely reading texts while acknowledging your awareness of the subjective nature of virtually all interpretive acts. To move in a more analytic direction, Mitzi would need to quote and discuss more lines directly from the poem, as she does later in her essay:

These "cool" dropouts paid for their rebellion in drug

overdoses, jail terms, police shootouts, and short lives.

They "Die soon," so we never know where else their

adventurous spirits might have taken them.

2 Analytical interpretation

In analyzing a text, writers often focus on the content and deliberately leave themselves, the interpreters, in the background, minimizing personal presence and bias. If you are asked to write this way—to avoid first-person pronouns or value judgments—do your best to focus on the text and avoid language that appears biased. In reality, of course, authors reveal their presence by the choices they make: what they include, what they exclude, what they emphasize, and so on. But when you are aware of your inescapable subjectivity, aware that your own situation affects the inferences and judgments you make about others, this awareness will help you keep your focus on the subject and off yourself.

In writing about "We Real Cool," for example, your first reaction may be more personal than analytical, focusing on your own emotions by calling it a *sad poem,* as Mitzi does, or by expressing value judgments about the poem's characters:

I think these guys are stupid, cutting their lives short

drinking, stealing, and fighting.

However, a more analytical response would be to drop the first person (*I think*) and the judgment (*these guys are stupid*) and to focus more closely on the text itself, perhaps quoting parts of it to show you are paying close attention:

The speakers in the poem, "The Pool Players", cut their

lives short by hanging out at "The Golden Shovel,"

fighting, drinking, stealing, and perhaps worse.

10 d Developing an interpretation

There is no formula for arriving at or presenting an interpretation in essay form, but readers, especially English instructors, will expect you to address and explain various elements of the text that usually contribute substantially to what it means.

Convincing interpretive essays often, but not always, include the following information, commonly in this order:

1. an overview of the text, identifying author, title, and genre and *briefly* summarizing the whole text

2. a description of form and structure

3. a description of the author's point of view

4. a summary of the social, historical, or cultural context in which the work was written

5. an assertion or thesis about what you believe the text means—your main business as an interpreter

Note that a **thesis,** whether explanatory (see 8c), argumentative (see 9a), or interpretive, is essentially a statement or passage that identifies the central point of the paper. To be persuasive and believable, any thesis needs to be supported with substantial and credible evidence. While some interpretive essays may include all of the elements listed above, others will emphasize some of the elements while downplaying others. For example, an interpretive essay that focuses on authorial point of view may not say much about form, structure, or historical context.

Identify and summarize the text

Interpretive essays, like all essays, should begin by answering basic questions. Interpretative essays usually address these questions: What genre is this text—poem, play, story, or essay? What is its title? Who is the author? When was it published? In addition, all such essays should provide a brief summary of the text's story, idea, or information. Summarize briefly, logically, and objectively to provide a background for what else you plan to say about the text, as in this example:

> "We Real Cool," a poem by Gwendolyn Brooks, condenses
>
> the life story of pool-playing high school dropouts to
>
> eight short lines and foreshadows an early death on the
>
> city streets.

2 Explain the form and organization

To examine the organizational structure of a text, ask: How is it put together? Why start here and end there? What connects it from start to finish? For example, by repeating words, ideas, and images, writers call attention to them and indicate that they are important to the meaning of the text. No matter what the text, some principle or plan holds it together and gives it structure. Texts that tell stories are often organized as a sequence of events in chronological order. Other texts may alternate between explanations and examples or between first-person and third-person narrative. You will have to decide which aspects of the text's form and organization are most important for your interpretation. The following example pays close attention to Brooks' overall poetic structure:

> The poem consists of a series of eight three-word
> sentences, each beginning with the word "We." The
> opening lines "We real cool. We / left school" explain the
> characters' situation. The closing lines "We / Jazz June.
> We / Die soon" suggest their lives will be over soon.

3 Describe the author's perspective

Authorial perspective is the point of view from which the text is presented. In an article, essay, textbook, or other work of nonfiction, you can expect the author to write about truth as he or she sees it—just as we are doing in this textbook, trying to explain writing according to our own beliefs about writing. However, in a work of poetry, fiction, or drama the author's point of view may be quite different from that of the character(s) who narrate or act in the story. If you can describe or explain the author's perspective in your interpretive esssay, you provide readers with clues about the author's purpose. For example, Kelly's essay (reprinted at the end of this chapter) opens by making a distinction between Brooks the poet and her characters, "Seven at the Golden Shovel":

> Gwendolyn Brooks writes "We Real Cool" (1963) from
> the point of view of the members of a street gang who
> have dropped out of school to live their lives hanging
> around pool halls—in this case "The Golden Shovel."
> These guys are semiliterate and speak in slangy street
> lingo that reveals their need for mutual support in their
> mutually rebellious attitude toward life.

What he doesn't say, but clearly implies, is that Brooks herself is a mature and highly skilled user of formal English, and that in the poem she adopts the persona or mask of semiliterate teenagers in order to tell their story more effectively.

4 Place the work in context

What circumstances (historical, social, political, biographical) produced this text? How does this text compare or contrast with another by the same author or a similar work by a different author? No text exists in isolation. Each was created by a particular author in a particular place at a particular time. Describing this context provides readers with important background information and indicates which conditions you think were most influential. "We Real Cool" could be contextualized this way:

> "We Real Cool" was published in 1963, a time when the
>
> civil rights movement was strong and about the time that
>
> African Americans coined the phrase "Black is beautiful."
>
> The poem may have been written to remind people that
>
> just because they were black did not mean they
>
> necessarily led beautiful lives.

5 Explain the theme of the text

In fiction, poetry, and reflective essays, the main point usually takes the form of an implicit **theme,** which in academic writing you might call a *thesis,* either stated or unstated. A main reason for writing an interpretive essay is to point out the text's theme. Examine what you think is the theme in the text. Ask yourself: So what? What is this really about? What do I think the author meant by writing this? What problems, puzzles, or ideas seem interesting? Good topics arise from material in which the meaning is not obviously stated.

When you write an interpretation from an objective or analytical perspective, you make the best case possible that, according to the evidence in the text itself, this is what the text means. In analytical writing, you generally state your thesis (about the text's theme) early in the essay, as Kelly does here about "We Real Cool" at the end of his first paragraph:

> The speakers in the poem, "We," celebrate what adults
>
> would call adolescent hedonism—but they make a

conscious choice for a short, intense life over a long, safe, and dull existence.

When you write from a subjective or personal perspective, you make it clear that your interpretation is based on your own emotional reactions and memories as much as on the content of the text, and that other readers will necessarily read it differently. The controlling idea or theme of Mitzi's subjective interpretation of "We Real Cool" is revealed in her opening paragraph, in which she compares the narrators of the poem to the gang members of her own high school.

6 Support your interpretation

Analytical interpretations are usually built around evidence from the text itself: summarize larger ideas in your own language to conserve space; paraphrase more specific ideas also in your own words; and quote directly to feature especially colorful or precise language. If you include outside information for support, comparison, or contrast reasons, document carefully where it came from. Most of the preceding examples referred to specific lines in the poem, as does this passage from Kelly's essay:

> Instead of attending school, planning for their future, or finding work, these seven "Lurk late," "Strike straight," "Sing sin," "Thin gin," and "Jazz June." Watch out for this bunch. If you see them coming, cross the street.

Subjective interpretations also include textual evidence, but often passages from the text are cited as prompts to introduce the writer's own memories, associations, or personal ideas, as in Mitzi's essay. The more specific and concrete your examples, the better.

> I think everybody who ever went to a public high school knows these guys—at least most of them were boys— who eventually "Left school" altogether and failed to graduate. They dressed a little differently from the rest of us—baggier pants, heavier boots, dirtier shirts, and too long hair never washed—and if there were girls—too much makeup or none at all.

Look at the text you plan to interpret, and make brief notes about each of the elements described in this section.

10 e Interpreting different genres

All the examples so far have come from a single short poem. If you are interpreting a work of fiction or nonfiction, or something else altogether such as an art exhibit, a concert, or a film, the basic elements of interpretation still apply—with a few differences.

1 Poetry

Of all language genres and forms, poetry exhibits the most intensive and deliberate use of language. With certain exceptions, poetic texts are far shorter than even short stories or one-act plays. Consequently, when interpreting poems, pay special attention to specific words, phrases, and lines; quote exactly to support your points; and familiarize yourself with the basic poetic terms you learned in high school: line, stanza, rhyme, rhythm, meter, metaphor, and image.

2 Fiction

To write about a novel or short story, explain how the main elements function: the *narrator* (who tells the story), *plot* (what happens in the story), one or more *characters* (who are acting or being acted upon), *setting* (where things are happening), and *theme* (the meaning of the story). Be sure to keep in mind that the author who writes the story is different from the characters in the story and that what happens in the story is different from the meaning of the story.

3 Drama

Plays are a special kind of fiction that are meant to be acted out on a stage; consequently, all the elements of fiction apply, except that since the characters are acting out the story, a narrator is seldom present. In drama, the setting is limited to what is contained on the stage, what the characters are thinking is usually not available to the audience, and the actors who play the parts are crucial to the play's success. Remember, too, that plays are structured

WRITING INTERPRETIVE ESSAYS

When you have completed the first draft of your interpretive essay, address the following questions:

- Do you identify the author, the title, and the date this text was published, early in your text? If not, should you?
- Have you provided a brief summary of what happens (plot) on the literal level in the text?
- Where do you explain the meaning or importance of this text?
- Is your approach to this interpretive essay objective or subjective? Why do you choose the one approach over the other?
- Have you provided evidence from the text itself for all assertions? If not, should you?
- Have you correctly documented any assertions not your own or any passages of text that you quote or paraphrase? (See 16g.)

according to acts (usually from one to five), which are in turn divided into scenes.

4 Movies

Fictional films are discussed in terms similar to those for fiction and drama (plot, character, setting, theme). However, additional elements also come into play: camera angles, special effects, and unlimited settings. Because of the complexity of orchestrating all of these elements, the film director rather than the screenwriter is often considered the "author" of a film.

5 Nonfiction

The elements of a nonfiction story are similar to those of fiction, except that everything in the text is supposed to have really happened. For this reason, the author and the narrator of the story are one and the same.

Informational nonfiction—essays, reports, and textbook chapters—is also meant to be believed; however, here you might say that "ideas" and "arguments" are the main characters to be discussed and evaluated.

6 Other media

In interpreting other kinds of texts—paintings, photographs, sculptures, quilts, buildings, concerts, and so on—always explain to your reader the basic identifying features, be they verbal, visual, musical, or something else: What is it? What is its name or title? Who created it? What are its main features? Where is it? When did it take place? As with your interpretation of literary works, your interpretation of works in other media can identify a theme and can respond to the theme in subjective, personal ways and more objective, analytical ways.

10 f Shaping the whole paper (student essay)

This chapter concludes with two sample interpretive papers from which some of the foregoing illustrations have been taken. The first one might be called an objective or *critical essay,* while the other might be called a subjective or *personal essay.*

Analytic response to "We Real Cool"

Kelly writes a brief analytical interpretation of "We Real Cool," called "High Stakes, Short Life," keeping himself in the background, writing in the third-person point of view. He presents his thesis early and supports it afterward with frequent quotations from the text, amplifying and explaining it most fully in his last paragraph.

High Stakes, Short Life

Kelly Sachs

Gwendolyn Brooks writes "We Real Cool" (1963) from the point of view

of the members of a street gang who have dropped out of school to live their

lives hanging around pool halls—in this case "The Golden Shovel." These

guys are semiliterate and speak in slangy street lingo that reveals their need

for mutual support in their mutually rebellious attitude toward life. The

speakers in the poem, "We," celebrate what adults would call adolescent

hedonism—but they make a conscious choice for a short, intense life over a long, safe, and dull existence.

For the "Seven at the Golden Shovel," companionship is everything. For many teenagers, fitting in or conforming to a group identity is more important than developing an individual identity. But for these kids, none of whom excelled at school or had happy home lives, their group is their life. They even speak as a group, from the plural point of view, "We," repeated at the end of each line; these seven are bonded and will stick together through boredom, excitement, and death.

From society's point of view, they are nothing but misfits—refusing to work, leading violent lives, breaking laws, and confronting polite society whenever they cross paths. Instead of attending school, planning for their future, or finding work, these seven "Lurk late," "Strike straight," "Sing sin," "Thin gin," and "Jazz June." Watch out for this bunch. If you see them coming, cross the street.

However, the most important element of their lives is being "cool." They live and love to be cool. Part of being cool is playing pool, singing, drinking, fighting, and messing around with women whenever they can. Being cool is the code of action that unites them, that they celebrate, for which they are willing to die.

The poet reveals their fate in the poem's last line. Brooks shows that the price of coolness and companionship is higher than most people are willing to pay. In this culture, the fate of rebels who violate social norms is an early death ("We / Die soon"), but to these seven, it is better to live life to the

fullest than hold back and plan for a future that may never come. They

choose, accept, and celebrate their lives and "Die soon."

Personal response to "We Real Cool"

In the following essay, "Staying Put," Mitzi writes about her personal reaction to Brooks' poem, describing how it reminds her of her own high school experience. Mitzi's theme, the sad lives of ghetto gangs, opens and closes the essay and provides the necessary coherence to hold it together. While she quotes the text several times, her primary supportive examples come from her own memories.

Staying Put

Mitzi Fowler

Gwendolyn Brooks' "We Real Cool" is a sad poem. It reminds me of the

gang in high school who used to skip classes and come back smelling of

cigarette smoke and cheap liquor—not that I knew it was cheap back then. I

think everybody who ever went to a public high school knows these guys—at

least most of them were boys—who eventually "Left school" altogether and

failed to graduate. They dressed a little differently from the rest of us—

baggier pants, heavier boots, dirtier shirts, and too long hair never washed—

and if there were girls—too much makeup or none at all.

They had their fun, however, because they stayed in their group. They

came late to assemblies, slouched in their seats, made wisecracks, and often

ended up like the characters in The Breakfast Club, in detention after school

or on Saturday morning.

And no matter how straitlaced and clean-cut the rest of us were, we

always felt just a twinge of envy at these careless, jaunty rebels who refused to

follow rules, who didn't care if they got detentions, who didn't do homework,

and whose parents didn't care if they stayed out all night. I didn't admit it very often—at least not to my friends—but some part of me wanted to have their pool hall or whatever adventures, these adult freedoms they claimed for themselves. However, I was always afraid—chicken, they would have said—of the consequences, so I practiced piano, did my algebra, and stayed put.

Then I think of the poem's last line and know why I obeyed my parents (well, most of the time), listened to my teachers (at least some of them), and stayed put (if you don't count senior cut day). These "cool" dropouts paid for their rebellion in drug overdoses, jail terms, police shootouts, and short lives. They "Die soon," so we never know where else their adventurous spirits might have taken them. In the end, this poem just makes me sad.

SUGGESTIONS FOR WRITING AND RESEARCH

INDIVIDUAL

1. Write an interpretive essay about a short text of your choice. Write the first draft from an analytic stance, withholding all personal judgments. Then write the second draft from a personal stance, including all relevant private judgments. Write your final draft by carefully blending elements of your first and second drafts.
2. Locate at least two reviews of a text (book, recording, exhibit) with which you are familiar, and analyze each to determine the reviewer's critical perspective. Write your own review of the text, and agree or disagree with the approach of the reviewers you analyzed. If you have a campus newspaper, consider offering your review to the editor for publication.

COLLABORATIVE

As a class or small group, attend a local concert, play, or exhibition. Have each student take good notes and, when he or she returns home, write a review of this event that includes both an interpretation and a recommendation that readers attend it (or not). Share these variations on the same theme with others in your class or group and explore the different judgments that arise as a result of different perspectives.

PART FOUR

Researching

www.prenhall.com/fulwiler

Researching

www.prenhall.com/fulwiler

On *The Blair Handbook, Fourth Edition,* Web site you can find

- How to evaluate online resources
- Discipline-specific Web site links
- Ways to plan and organize your research

Writing Research Essays

Before agonizing too long over your next research project, stop to consider what, exactly, research entails. Keep in mind that in your nonacademic life you conduct practical research of one kind or another every time you search the want ads for a used car, browse through a library in search of a book, or read a movie review. You may not make note cards or report the results in writing, but whenever you ask questions and then systematically look for answers, you are conducting research.

In college, the research you conduct is academic rather than practical. In other words, it's designed to result in a convincing paper rather than a purchase or an action. Academic research is part of the writing process for most of your papers.

You rarely begin writing an explanation, argument, or interpretation already knowing all the facts and having all the information you'll need: to fill in the gaps in your knowledge, you conduct research. In fact, one type of assignment, the **research essay,** is specially designed to introduce you to the process of conducting research and writing a paper based on your findings. Research essays are generally longer, require more extensive research, use a more formal style and format, and take more time than other papers.

Meaningful research results from real questions that you care to answer. It's exciting work. And if you're not now excited about something, once you start engaging in research activities you may surprise yourself: take a tour of your library and find out what's there; get on the Internet and start exploring the resources of the World Wide Web; above all, start thinking, writing, and talking to people about ideas, and exciting things will happen.

An example of practical research

In preparing to write this chapter, we asked ourselves about the last time we did research of a substantial nature. Toby recalled the amount of practical research he did recently when he bought a motorcycle. His current motorcycle was a small BMW that he used for riding to school and taking short trips. It was time, he thought, to buy a new motorcycle big enough for comfortable long-range touring. Finding the right machine meant shopping carefully, which meant asking good questions: What kind of motorcycle was best for touring? How large should it be? What make was most reliable? How much would it cost? Who were the best dealers?

Here's how Toby researched his questions about buying a new motorcycle:

• Toby approached the owner of Frank's Motorcycle Shop and asked about the virtues of certain BMW touring machines on display. He felt overwhelmed by the array of styles and models available. He looked at and sat on these machines, but he did not take any for a test ride.

• Toby visited other local dealers, who sold Honda, Yamaha, and Suzuki motorcycles, and listened to sales pitches explaining the features of their best touring machines. He found some too racy and others too large.

• He looked up back issues of *Rider* magazine in the local library and made photocopies of the most relevant articles, underlined key findings, and made notes in the margins of his photocopies.

• He searched the World Wide Web for information on touring motorcycles and found reprints critically reviewing the latest touring motorcycles, which he downloaded and studied, learning current motorcycle terminology (ABS, telelever), models (sport tourers, roadsters), and performance data (roll-on speed, braking distance).

• He wrote in his journal and talked to people who knew a lot about motorcycles—some old friends and the BMW mechanic at the shop where his old bike was serviced.

• Six weeks after beginning his investigation, he returned to Frank's and test-drove the two BMW models that most interested him: the R1150RT offered better wind protection while the K1200RS offered more performance. After weighing the relative merits of each machine, Toby bought a bright red BMW K1200RS.

What research outside school settings have you conducted recently? Think about major changes, moves, or purchases that required you to ask serious questions.

2 Activities in the research process

While the search for motorcycle knowledge is practical rather than academic, it serves nevertheless to introduce most of the activities common to all research projects, whether to gather information or to support an argument, in school or out.

- **The researcher has a genuine interest in the topic.** It's difficult to fake curiosity, but it's possible to develop it. Toby's interest in motorcycles was long-standing, but the more he investigated, the more he learned and the more he still wanted to know. Some academic assignments will allow you to pursue issues that are personally important to you; others will require that you dive into the research first and generate interest as you go.

- **The researcher asks questions.** Toby's first questions were general rather than specific. However, as he gained more knowledge, the questions became more sharply focused. No matter what your research assignment, you need to begin by articulating questions, finding out where the answers lead, and then asking still more questions.

- **The researcher seeks answers from people.** Toby talked to both friends and strangers who knew about motorcycles. The people to whom he listened most closely were specialists with expert knowledge. All research projects profit when you ask knowledgeable people to help you answer questions or point you in directions where answers may be found.

- **The researcher visits places where information may be found.** Toby went to dealerships not only to ask questions of experts but also to observe and experience firsthand. No matter how much other people told him, his knowledge increased when he made his own observations.

- **The researcher examines texts.** Toby looked up information on the Internet, visited the library, and read magazines to become more informed about his subject. While printed texts are helpful in practical research, they are crucial in academic research.

- **The researcher evaluates sources.** As the research progressed, Toby double-checked information to see if it could be confirmed by more than one source. In practical research, the researcher must evaluate sources to ensure that the final decision is satisfactory.

Similarly, in academic research, you must evaluate sources to ensure that your final paper is convincing.

• **The researcher writes.** Toby made field notes and margin notes and also wrote in his journal. In practical research, writing helps the researcher find, remember, and explore information. In academic research, writing is even more important, since the results must eventually be reported in writing.

• **The researcher tests and experiments.** In Toby's practical research, testing was simple and fairly subjective—riding different motorcycles to compare the qualities of each. Testing and experimentation are also regular parts of many research projects.

• **The researcher combines and synthesizes information to arrive at new conclusions.** Toby's accumulated and sorted-out information led to a decision to purchase one motorcycle rather than another. In academic research, your synthesis of information leads not to a purchase but to a well-supported thesis that will convince a skeptical audience that your research findings are correct.

What this researcher did not do, of course, is the step most directly concerned with the subject matter of this handbook: write down the results of his investigation in a formal report. The greatest difference between practical and academic research is that the former leads to practical knowledge on which to act, the latter to theoretical knowledge written for others to read. So, for academic research, there is one more activity to consider:

• **The researcher presents the research findings in an interesting, focused, and well-documented paper.** The remainder of this chapter explains how to select, investigate, and write about academic research topics.

11 b Managing the research process

A research paper is the end result of the process of finding, evaluating, and synthesizing information that is new to you from a wide variety of sources. Therefore, research essays occupy a span of weeks or months and are often the most important projects you work on during a semester. It pays to study the assignment carefully, begin working on it immediately, and allow sufficient time for the many different activities involved.

1 Considering the assignment

First, reflect on the course for which the paper is assigned. What is the aim of this field of study? What themes has the instructor

STRATEGIES FOR MANAGING THE RESEARCH PROCESS

- **Ask questions.** Begin by asking questions about a subject, both of yourself and of others. Preliminary questions lead to more specific inquiries.

- **Read extensively.** Texts of all kinds—books, journal and magazine articles, and studies—are the raw material from which you will build your research paper.

- **Question knowledgeable people.** Start with people you know. If they can't help, ask who can. Then broaden that circle to include people with specialized knowledge.

- **Seek out firsthand information and experience.** No matter how many answers other people offer you, seek out information yourself.

- **Evaluate your sources and double-check the information you find.** Sources vary in their accuracy and objectivity. Try to confirm the information you gather by checking more than one reliable source.

- **Write at every stage.** The notes you take on your reading, the field notes you write, and the research log you keep all help you gain control of your subject. Everything you have written also helps you when you start drafting.

emphasized? How would a research assignment contribute to the goals of this course? In other words, before even considering a topic, assess the instructor's probable reasons for making the assignment and try to predict what is expected from your finished paper.

Also study the assignment directions carefully. Identify both the subject words and the direction words. *Subject words* specify the area of the investigation. *Direction words* (verbs such as *write* or *explain*) specify your purpose for writing—whether you should explain or report or argue or do something else.

2 Finding a topic

To find a topic, think about how your interests dovetail with the content of the course. What topics of the course do you enjoy most? What discussions, lectures, or labs have you found most engaging? What has happened recently in the news that both interests you and relates to the course material? Do some freewriting to find the topic that seems most promising to you (see Chapter 5) or surf the Internet for ideas!

COLLABORATIVE RESEARCH PROJECTS

Of all writing assignments, those involving research profit most from collaboration. In the corporate, business, and scientific worlds, nearly all work is collaborative, including posing, processing, and solving problems; reaching decisions; evaluating production; and writing reports. For most complex problems, two heads are better than one, and three are better than two. If your assignment lends itself to collaboration, and if your instructor approves, find out with which classmates you could work. The following suggestions will aid collaboration:

- **Choosing a topic.** Either form a group you want to work with and then choose a topic you all want to research, or choose a topic that interests you and see whether you can interest others in joining you.

- **Determining group size.** Small groups (two to three people) work better than large groups, because they make it easier to find time to meet outside of class and to synthesize the information found.

- **Organizing the group.** Divide tasks early in your project, specifying who will do what when. Divide the tasks equitably so that everyone contributes an equal amount. Divide the tasks so that members make maximum use of their different skills, abilities, and interests.

- **Doing research.** Agree to take careful notes from texts or interviews and to duplicate the notes so that each group member has full sources of information. Someone should cover periodicals. Someone else should check the Internet, and someone else should find local experts to interview, in person, via telephone, or through e-mail.

- **Drafting.** A group writing a single paper can write together by (1) blending voices, passing the drafts back and forth, each writer overwriting the others each time; (2) sequencing voices, each writer writing a different section (as in chapters in a book); or (3) weaving voices, so that the final product has different writers' voices emerging at different times throughout the paper.

- **Agreeing on a thesis.** In the early stages of collaborative writing, each group member should write his or her own version of what the research suggests. These early drafts should be shared, with each writer reconsidering the thesis in light of points made by the other writers. If there is disagreement, continue to share the research, but write separate papers that reflect the different conclusions arrived at.

(Continued)

- **Revising and editing.** At the end, responsibilities can be divided equitably according to abilities, with different members volunteering to type, prepare references, edit, proofread, and reproduce the final paper. This is also a good time to even out the workload, if some have done more so far than others. However, for more complete group ownership of the project, conduct a round-robin reading, whereby each member looks at the final draft.

- **Evaluating responsibility and achievement.** We recommend some degree of self-assessment on all collaborative projects. The best way to achieve this is for each group member to assess both himself or herself and the group as a whole. These assessments should first be processed by the group; if disagreements arise, involve the instructor. When all group members meet their responsibilities and deadlines, all should receive the same grade. As a last resort, the instructor or another group could referee.

At the same time, limit or narrow your topic to one you can answer with real and specific information—information that catches attention in ways that loose generalities about vast subjects cannot. Besides, if you limit your topic, your chances of managing and answering it improve dramatically.

SUBJECT   The *environment* [too broad to be called a topic].

TOPIC   *Corporate practices that harm the environment* [narrower and better but still too broad].

TOPIC   *Do American companies exploit people's concern for the environment by misleading advertisements for "green" policies and products* [narrower, more neutral, and more focused].

3 Developing a research question

Since research essays are among the lengthiest and most complex of all college assignments, make the project interesting and purposeful by developing a research question that will be exciting for you to answer. What makes a good research question?

- **It's a question that you really want to know the answer to.**

- **It requires more than a yes or no answer.**

YES OR NO   Do companies misrepresent the environmental advantages of their products?

BETTER   How do companies represent or misrepresent the environmental advantages of their products?

- **It's sufficiently complex that you do not already know the answer.** Some of the ways companies misrepresent products as green are changing the names of chemical ingredients, hiding research that proves there are hazards, and creating advertising that suggests environmental purity.

- **It's a question that you have a reasonable chance of answering.** A quick survey of World Wide Web and library sources on false advertising reveals a wealth of books and periodicals on the subject. How have American companies capitalized in their advertising on American consumers' environmental consciousness?

4 Becoming an authority

Whenever you undertake research, you join an ongoing conversation among a select community of people who are knowledgeable about the subject. As you collect information, you too become something of an expert. You gain an authoritative voice, becoming a stronger, more powerful writer. Plan to become enough of an expert on your topic that you can teach your classmates and instructor something they didn't know before. The best way to exercise your new-found authority is to write in your own words all the major information and ideas connected with your research project, both periodically in your journal entries and later when you draft.

5 Keeping an open mind

Don't be surprised if, once you begin researching, your questions and answers multiply and change. Be prepared to travel in circles at times or find dead ends where you expected thoroughfares—but also thoroughfares where you expected dead ends. For example, suppose you start out researching local recycling efforts, but you stumble upon the problem of finding buyers for recycled material. One source raises the question of manufacturing with recycled materials, while another source turns the whole question back to consumer education. All of these concerns are related, but if you attempt to study them all with equal intensity, your paper will be either very long or very superficial. Follow your strongest interests, and try to answer the question you most care about.

ESL **BECOMING AN AUTHORITY**

If you have been educated outside the United States, you may feel it is inappropriate to act as an authority, especially on an unfamiliar topic. In U.S. colleges, however, students are expected to develop a sense of authority regarding their topics. This enables them to present interesting ideas of their own rather than repeating what others have said.

Becoming an authority means working hard to become an expert and thus master your writing project. The following guidelines should help:

- Learn enough about your topic to become the class expert.
- Read your sources critically, analyzing what they say and why they might be saying it. (See Chapter 2.)
- Think carefully about which sources to use and how to use them in your paper. (See 16a–16b.)
- Make sure your paper includes ideas of your own, not just summaries of what other people have said.

11 **c** **Formulating a working thesis**

When an answer to your research question starts to take shape, form a **working thesis,** that is, a preliminary answer from which you can investigate further. If additional research leads you in a different direction, be ready to redirect your investigation and revise your working thesis.

Whether or not you already have a working thesis will determine what type of research you undertake. **Informational research** is conducted when you don't know the answer to the question or don't have a firm opinion about the topic. You enter this kind of investigation with an open mind, focusing on the question, not on a predetermined answer. Eventually, you will need to develop a working thesis. Such research might be characterized as thesis-finding.

Argument research is conducted to prove a point. You enter the project with a working thesis—the tentative answer to your question, the side of the debate you want to support: should companies be held to stricter standards of truth in commercial advertising? You might argue yes and then conduct research to buttress your position. A research question helps focus your energies, but

argument research is really thesis-driven since you're hunting for support to prove your point.

The process of researching may lead to a revised or entirely different thesis, so remember that any thesis is subject to revision, redirection, and clarification. Nonetheless, whatever thesis you start with will point you in one direction rather than another. (For more on informational and argument papers, see Chapters 8–9.)

WRITING 2: APPLICATION

Select a topic that interests you and that is compatible with the research assignment. List ten questions that you have—or that you think others might have—about this topic. Select the question that most interests you and freewrite about it for ten or more minutes. Why does it interest you? Where would you start looking for answers?

11 d Keeping a research log

A **research log** can help you keep track of the scope, purpose, and possibilities of any research project. Such a log is essentially a journal in which you write to yourself about the process of doing research by asking questions and monitoring the results. Questions you might ask include the following:

What subject do I want to research?

What information have I found so far?

What do I still need to find?

Where am I most likely to find it?

What evidence best supports my working thesis?

What evidence challenges my working thesis?

How is my thesis changing from where it started?

Writing out answers to these questions in your log clarifies your tasks as you go along. It forces you to articulate ideas and examine supporting evidence critically. Doing this, in turn, helps you focus your research activities. Novice researchers often waste time tracking down sources that are not really useful. Answering questions in your research log as you visit the library, look for and read sources, review note cards, and write various drafts can make research more efficient.

When you keep notes in a research log, record them as if they were on separate note cards. Here, for example, are some entries from a first-year student's research log:

> 11/12   Checked the subject headings and found no books on ozone depletion. Ref. librarian suggested magazines because it takes so long for books to come out on new subjects. In the <u>General Science Index</u> I found about twenty articles— I've got them all on a printout. Need to come back tomorrow to actually start reading them.

> 11/17   Conference today with Lawrence about the ozone hole thesis—said I don't really have much of a thesis, rather a lot of information aiming in the same direction. Suggested I look at what I've found already and then back up to see what question it answers—that will probably point to my thesis.

When a project requires you to investigate only a few sources of information, you may keep all your bibliographic and research notes in your research log, in a separate part of your class note-book, or on a single computer file.

WRITING 3: APPLICATION _____

Keep a research log for the duration of your research project. Write in it daily and record everything you think of or find in relation to the project. When your project is finished, write an account of the role the log played.

11 **e** **Using the writing process**

Research writing, like all important writing, benefits from the multistage process of planning, drafting, revising, and editing. In research writing, however, managing information and incorporating sources present special problems.

Planning the research process

After developing some sense of the range and amount of information available, write out a schedule of when you will do what. For example, plan a certain amount of time for trips to the library. If any of the books you need are checked out, allow time for the library to call those in. Arrange needed interviews well in advance, with time to reschedule in case a meeting has to be postponed. And allow enough time not only for writing but also for revising and editing. If you keep an online journal for recording and organizing your materials, download any useful information into computer files created for planning or drafting as well as researching.

On one page of your research log, design a research plan that includes both library and field investigations. In this plan, list sources you have already found as well as those you hope to find.

2 Researching a range of sources

To conduct any kind of research, you need to identify appropriate sources of information, consult and evaluate these sources, and take good notes recording the information you collect. You also need to understand how each source works as evidence.

Primary sources contain original material and raw information. **Secondary sources** report on, describe, interpret, or analyze someone else's work. For example, if you were exploring the development of a novelist's style, the novels themselves would be primary sources and other people's reviews and critical interpretations of the novels would be secondary sources. What constitutes a primary source will differ according to the field and your research question. For example, the novel *Moby-Dick* is a primary source if you are studying it as literature and making claims about what it means. It is a secondary source if you are investigating nineteenth-century whaling and referring to chapters in it that contain descriptions of harpooning.

Most research essays use both primary and secondary sources. Primary sources ground the essay in firsthand knowledge and verifiable facts; secondary sources supply the context for your discussion and provide support for your own interpretation or argument.

Most research essays are based on library and Internet sources. However, some of the most interesting research essays are also based on **field research.** This research includes firsthand interviews with people who have expert knowledge of your subject. You can also conduct field research simply by going places, observing carefully, and reporting what you find.

3 Drafting a thesis statement

When you write your first draft, be sure to allow time for further research. (See Chapter 16 more information on using sources.)

You, not your audience, are the expert on your research topic, so plan to explain, define, and clarify new or unusual terms and concepts. To find out what your classmates and instructor already know, ask them to read and respond to your paper at several points during its development—for example, when you have a

detailed outline or thesis and when you have completed your first draft.

In research writing, as in most writing, you need to tell your reader what you're up to. An **argument thesis** statement takes a position on an issue. (See Chapter 9.)

> In order to reduce the annual number of violent deaths in the United States, Congress should pass a law to limit the number of handguns that can be purchased in a single retail transaction.

An **informational thesis** statement presents information but does not advance one position over another. (See Chapter 8.)

> Many American companies attempt to capitalize on Americans' concern for the environment by a variety of advertising strategies.

Most research essays are long and complex enough that the thesis should be stated explicitly rather than left implicit. However, the thesis that ends up in your final paper may be different from the one you developed to help you write the paper.

Many research essays give the thesis at the beginning, somewhere in the first or second paragraph, where it acts as a promise to the reader of what will follow. Some research papers present a delayed thesis at the end, where it acts as a conclusion or summary (see 9f). If you take the delayed-thesis approach, you still need to be sure that the topic and scope of your paper are clear to readers from the very beginning.

4 Writing an I-search essay

An **I-search essay** focuses on *the process of the search* instead of the result of the search, as do traditional thesis-driven research papers. An I-search essay tells *the story of a quest* to answer a question. It reveals a genuinely curious writer trying to answer a question—probably a *why* question—using all available resources (memory, texts, people, and places). In other words, I-search means you, the author, searching; you include yourself as part of the story, beginning with your curiosity—where it came from and why you are curious and what difference an answer might make. You begin such a paper by articulating your first question—the first version of your question—even if later your question becomes something else. Then, you describe exactly how you went about answering your question. Such papers commonly include language such as *I wondered . . ., I logged on to . . ., I was puzzled . . ., then I*

read . . ., next I talked to . . ., now I was really frustrated . . ., finally I visited . . ., and so on, including false leads and dead ends. Such a paper might answer questions like these:

- Where did I look first to answer my question? What did I find out? What did I not find out?

- When I checked the World Wide Web, how many sources did I find? How many useful sources did I find? What made a source useful? What did I not find?

- What places did I physically visit? What did each look like? What did I find out there? What was missing?

- What person or people did I talk to? Who granted me an interview? When, where? What did each person look like? What did the setting look like? What did I learn there? What other leads did I find?

- What further questions have occurred as I've tried to answer the first question?

- What dead ends have so far turned up?

- When did I turn to the library? What did I look for—books, periodicals, other sources? How many of what kind did I find? How many did I read? What did I learn?

- Where and when did one source contradict another? How did I decide which to believe?

- How did I conclude my search? How satisfied am I now? Did I find one answer to my question? More than one answer? No answer?

- What related questions would I pursue, had I more time? Another life?

Your finished paper should read like a mystery or detective story, beginning with a puzzle that you, the investigator, need to solve. You are the detective telling the story, deliberately leaving your reader in some suspense until the end, where you give your answer (or fail to answer or surprise yourself with the answer—all legitimate and real endings). It takes a delayed-thesis approach (see 9f2). First-year student Amanda began her I-search paper this way:

> College is an expensive time. Aside from tuition, which
>
> my parents are graciously paying, my monthly expenses
>
> are pretty steep—phone bills, books, laundry, movies,
>
> pizza, and so on. For this reason, earlier in the semester I

✔ **TESTING YOUR THESIS STATEMENT**

A good thesis statement not only help readers understand your paper; it also helps you organize your thoughts and energies when writing. To draft a working thesis statement, ask yourself the following questions:

- **Is it interesting?** An informational thesis should answer a question that is worth asking: *What techniques do advertisers use to persuade the public?* An argument thesis should take a position on a debatable issue and should include a proposal for change: *Mountain bikes should be allowed on wilderness trails.*

- **Is it precise and specific?** Try to sharpen both your understanding of the thesis and the language you use to express it. Instead of arguing in favor of more access to the wilderness in general, argue for mountain bikes on specific wilderness trails.

- **Is it manageable?** You may have collected more information than you can actually write about. If necessary, take this opportunity to narrow both the thesis and the paper you expect to write.

- **Does it adequately reflect my research and the expected shape of my paper?** Your thesis should state the major point of your paper.

---

took a job as a telemarketer calling alumni and asking for money. But I did not enjoy harassing people in their homes, so after three weeks, I quit. Now I am back to relying on my savings and considering another job, this time as an RA, a resident assistant in the university dormitories. Before I fill out an application, however, I want to know just what the new job will entail.

I started my research by looking on the University of Vermont's Web home page, where I found. . . .

(To read Amanda's complete paper, see 17b.)

5 Revising

When drafting, you must follow your strongest research interests and try to answer the question you most care about. However,

sometimes what began as informational research may become argument as the process of drafting the paper tips your original neutrality one way or another. Or a research investigation that starts out to prove a thesis may, as you draft, become a more neutral, informative paper of various perspectives, especially when multiple causes or complications surface in what had seemed a straightforward case.

Be ready to spend a great deal of time revising your draft, adding new research information, and incorporating sources smoothly into your prose. Such work takes a great deal of thought, and you'll want to revise your paper several times. Consult Part Five for helpful strategies on revising your draft.

6 Editing

Editing a research paper requires extra time. Not only should you check your own writing, but you should also pay special attention to where and how you use sources (see Chapter 16) and use the correct documentation style (see Part Eight). The editing stage is also a good time to assess your use of quotations, paraphrase, and summary to make sure you have not misquoted or used a source without crediting it.

SUGGESTIONS FOR WRITING AND RESEARCH

INDIVIDUAL

1. Select a research topic that interests you and write an exploratory draft about it. First, write out everything you already know about the topic. Second, write out everything you want to know about the topic. Third, identify experts you can contact. Finally, make a list of questions you need answered. Plan to put this paper through a process that includes not only planning, drafting, revising, and editing but also locating, evaluating, and using sources.

2. Keeping in mind the research topic you developed in assignment 1 above, visit the library and conduct a search of available resources. What do you find? Where do you find it? Show your questions to a reference librarian and ask what additional electronic databases he or she would suggest. Finally, don't forget the Internet, an ever-expanding source of information on virtually any topic you can think of. (Before you go much further, read Chapter 13.)

3. After completing assignments 1 and 2 above, find a person who knows something about your topic and ask him or her for leads

about doing further research: Whom else would this person recommend you speak with? What books or articles would he or she recommend? What's the first thing this expert would do to find out information? Finally, look for a "virtual" person, someone available through an e-mail listserv or on the Internet with whom you might chat to expand your knowledge.

COLLABORATIVE

1. Join with a classmate or classmates to write a collaborative research essay. Develop plans for dividing tasks among members of the group. (Refer to the box on pp. 160–61.)

2. After completing a collaborative research essay, write a short report in which you explain the collaborative strategies your group used and evaluate their usefulness.

12 Conducting Library Research

Libraries are the heart—or perhaps the head—of the academic community. They provide the primary knowledge base that allows professors to teach and to conduct research in their fields. They also provide students with the sources of information that allow them to investigate any area of study.

What is it like today, researching in a modern college library? When our first-year students finished a major research project, we asked them to describe their library research experience, and here are some of their comments:

> Frances: "I could find all the library sources from just one computer search instead of looking one place for books, another for periodicals, and still another for films and CDs. It was awesome!"

> David: "The quality of my research was much better when I went to the library ... the sources were more informative and more trustworthy."

> Lydia: "The Internet was good for learning about the variety of tattoos, but I got the most specific information from visiting the tattoo parlor on Church Street and interviewing Jim, who does the needle work."

> Elena: "Researching in the library puts you in a scholarly mood— you look harder and goof off less."

> Tammy: "The library lady helped me when I was stuck. When you research at the library, you never feel alone."

Some topics might favour Internet research while other topics might favor local field research. But the most comprehensive collection of *reliable* information for most college research assignments remains the library. Unlike information from the Internet and personal interview sources, library sources are screened by experts and critics before being cataloged, listed, and shelved. Just because it's cataloged, of course, doesn't certify that every source

found in the library is accurate, true, or the last word, but expert screening increases the odds that the information is trustworthy. In addition, the reference librarian is on your team and can usually guide you to the right places.

The modern library is complex and multifaceted; you should visit your college library early and get to know it well. At first, a college library may appear intimidating, but the more you use it, the more friendly it will become.

12 **a** Planning library research

To learn about the library, you need to go there, walk slowly through it, read the signs that identify special rooms and departments, poke your nose into nooks and crannies, and browse through a few books or magazines. If there is an introductory video explaining the library, pause to see it. If there is a self-paced or guided tour, take it. Read informational handouts and pamphlets. Be sure to locate the following:

The **book catalog,** a computerized database that tells you which books your library owns and where they are located

The **stacks,** where books and periodicals are stored

The **circulation desk,** where you check out and reserve books and get information on procedures and resources

The **periodical room,** which houses current issues of magazines, journals, and newspapers

The **reference room,** which contains general reference works, such as dictionaries and encyclopedias, along with guides and indexes to more specific sources information

To take full advantage for library resources, keep the following suggestions in mind:

Visit the library early and often. As soon as you receive a research assignment, visit the library to find out what resources are available for your project, and plan to return often. Even if your initial research indicates a wealth of material on your topic, you may not be able to find everything the first time you look. A book you need may be checked out, or your library may not subscribe to a periodical containing important information, and you may need to order it on interlibrary loan, a process that takes some time.

✔ PLANNING LIBRARY RESEARCH

- **Go to the library early.** Find and use resources on your subject as soon as you can because they might not be readily available.
- **Prepare to take notes.** Take careful notes the first time around so you won't have to retrieve the sources again to pick up bibliographic information.
- **Keep a research log.** Write in your research log as you work to help you keep track of what you've already done and what you still have to do.
- **Consult general sources before specific ones.** On your first visit, check general sources—dictionaries, encyclopedias, atlases, and yearbooks—for a quick overview of your topic and for guidance in locating additional sources.
- **Talk to library personnel.** Describe your assignment to your reference librarian and ask for help finding sources. Librarians often know about sources you don't—it's their job.

Prepare to take notes. If you take careful notes from the sources you find, you will save yourself time and write a better paper. Even in this computerized world it helps to bring index cards to the library—3″ × 5″ cards for bibliographical information and 4″ × 6″ cards for notes—from your first visit on. (See 12e for more on note taking.) Also keep a research log. Writing in it as you work on your research project will help you find ideas to research, plan your course of action, pose and solve problems related to your topic, and keep track of where you have been so far. (See 11d for more on research logs.)

Check general sources before specific ones. During your first or second visit to the library, check general sources—dictionaries, encyclopedias, atlases, and yearbooks—for information about your topic. An hour spent with these general sources will give you a quick overview of the scope and range of your topic and will lead you to more specific information.

Ask for help. Talk to librarians. At first you might show them your assignment and describe your topic and your research plans; later you might ask them for help in finding a particular source or ask whether they know of any sources that you have not checked yet. Keep in mind, however, that reference librarians are busy people; don't ask questions that you haven't tried to answer for yourself.

SUGGESTIONS FOR TALKING WITH LIBRARIANS

- Before you ask for help, try to answer your questions yourself.
- Bring with you a copy of the research assignment.
- Be ready to explain the assignment in your own words: purpose, format, length, number of sources, and due date.
- Identify any special requirements about sources: Should information come from government documents? rare books? films?
- Describe the particular topic you are researching and the tentative question you have framed to address the topic.
- Describe any work you have done so far: Web sites, books, or periodicals looked at, log entries written, people interviewed, and so on.

12 b Finding sources of information

Most of the information you need to find will be contained in reference books, in other books, in periodicals (journals, magazines, and newspapers), or in electronic sources called *databases.* (See 12b3.) Reference books are fairly easy to locate: there are relatively few of them, and they are usually placed in one room or section of the library. However, even a moderate-sized college library owns hundreds of thousands of books and periodicals. To simplify the researcher's task of finding the relevant ones, bibliographies and indexes have been developed, most of which are available in both paper and electronic sources. These resources either indicate which books or periodical articles have been published on a given topic or attempt to present comprehensive lists of sources in an easy-to-use format. Once you know which book or periodical might be useful, you still need to find it. The library's catalogs tell you whether the library owns the source. To use these resources efficiently, look for sources of information by following this five-step process:

1. Consult *general reference works* to gain background information and basic facts. (See 12b1.)

2. Consult *bibliographies* and *indexes* to learn which books, periodicals, and articles are relevant. (See 12b2.)

3. Consult *computerized databases* (electronic catalogs of information) relevant to your topic. (See 12b3.)

4. Consult *your library's catalogs* to see whether the library owns the books and periodicals you want. (See 12b4.)

5. Consult *other sources* as needed. (See 12b5.)

Searching through indexes, databases, and catalogs is much easier if you have identified the keywords for your research topic. A **keyword** is an important word describing your topic—either a word for the topic itself, a word for the general subject, or a word describing constituent parts of the topic.

Keywords are sometimes nothing more than authors' names or titles of books. For example, keywords for a research paper investigating the pottery of Native Americans in the western United States could include *Indian, art,* and *California.* The keywords you select can mean the difference between success and failure. For example, a search including the word *Sioux* might turn up nothing, but a search including the word *Dakota* (the preferred term for this group) might result in a number of sources. To find good keywords for your topic, consult the *Library of Congress Subject Headings,* the established list of subject headings assigned to books in most academic libraries. This multivolume set of books is usually found in the reference area.

Reference works

General reference works provide background information and basic facts about a topic. The summaries, overviews, and definitions in these sources can help you decide whether to pursue a topic further and where to turn next for information. The information in these sources is necessarily general and will not be sufficient by itself as the basis for most research projects; you will need to consult specialized sources as well. General reference works do not make strong sources to cite in research papers.

Specialized reference works contain detailed and technical information in a particular field or discipline. They often contain articles by well-known authorities and sometimes have bibliographies and cross-references that can lead to other sources. Two useful guides to finding specialized reference books are *Guide to Reference Books,* edited by Robert Balay et al. (12th ed., 1996), and *Walford's Guide to Reference Material* (8th ed., 1999).

While many reference works are published as books, increasingly they are available electronically. The following lists suggest

common and useful references, although there are many more in each category.

Almanacs and yearbooks. Almanacs and yearbooks provide up-to-date information on politics, agriculture, economics, and population along with statistical facts of all kinds.

Facts on File: News Digest (1940–present). A digest and index to current events reported in newspapers worldwide. (Also CD-ROM, 1980–present.)

Statesman's Year-Book (1864–present). Annual statistics about government, agriculture, population, religion, and so on for countries throughout the world.

World Almanac and Book of Facts (1868–present). Review of important events of the past year as well as data on a wide variety of topics, including sports, government, science, business, and education.

Atlases. Atlases such as the *Hammond Atlas of the World,* the *National Geographic Atlas of the World,* and the *Times Atlas of the World* can help you identify places anywhere in the world and provide information on population, climate, and industry.

Biographical dictionaries. Biographical dictionaries contain information on people who have made some mark on history in many different fields; biographical indexes tell you how to locate additional sources.

Contemporary Authors (1962–present). Contains short biographies of authors who have published during the year.

Current Biography (1940–present). Contains articles and photographs of people in the news.

Who's Who in America (1899–present). The standard biographical reference for living Americans.

Dictionaries. Dictionaries contain definitions and histories of words along with information on their correct usage. (See 30b.)

Encyclopedias. Encyclopedias provide elementary information, explanations, and definitions of virtually every topic, concept, country, institution, historical person or movement, and cultural artifact imaginable. One-volume works such as the *Random House Encyclopedia* and *The Columbia Encyclopedia* give brief overviews. Larger works such as *Collier's Encyclopedia* (24 volumes) and the *New Encyclopaedia Britannica* (32 volumes, also online) contain more detailed information.

Specialized reference works. Although these works provide information that is more detailed and technical than that found in general reference works, you should still use them primarily for exploratory research and background information. Each discipline has many reference works; here is a small sampling:

LANGUAGES AND LITERATURE

Cassell's Encyclopedia of World Literature

Handbook to Literature

McGraw-Hill Encyclopedia of World Drama

Oxford Companion to American Literature

Oxford Companion to English Literature

HUMANITIES

Cambridge Ancient History

Encyclopedia of American History

Encyclopedia of Philosophy

Encyclopedia of Religion

Encyclopedia of World History

New Grove Dictionary of Music and Musicians

Dictionary of Art

SOCIAL SCIENCES

Encyclopedia of Education

Dictionary of Anthropology

Encyclopedia of Crime and Justice

Encyclopedia of Psychology

Encyclopedia of Social Work

International Encyclopedia of the Social Sciences

Political Handbook and Atlas of the World

SCIENCES

Encyclopedia of the Biological Sciences

Encyclopedia of Chemistry

Encyclopedia of Computer Science and Technology

Encyclopedia of Physics

Grzimek's Animal Life Encyclopedia

McGraw-Hill Encyclopedia of Science and Technology

BUSINESS

Encyclopedia of Banking and Finance

Encyclopedia of Economics

McGraw-Hill Dictionary of Modern Economics

WRITING 1: APPLICATION ─────────────────────────

Look up information on your research topic, using at least three of the reference sources described in this section.

2 Bibliographies and indexes

Bibliographies and indexes are tools: they help you locate books and periodicals that contain the information you need. Periodicals consist of magazines, journals, and newspapers, which are published at set periods throughout the year. They focus on particular areas of interest, and their information is more current than that found in books. Because so many periodical issues are published each year and because every issue can contain dozens of articles on various topics, using a periodical index or database is essential to finding the article you need.

Many bibliographies and indexes are available in electronic form, either through an online service or on a CD-ROM disk.

Bibliographies

Bibliographies list books alphabetically by title, by author, or by subject. Many books include a bibliography of the works consulted by the author in researching the book; always consult the bibliography of a book you have found helpful. Other bibliographies are published separately as reference tools. Some of the most useful are listed here:

Bibliographic Index: A Cumulative Bibliography of Bibliographies (New York: Wilson, 1938–present). This index lists the page numbers of bibliographies in books over a wide variety of subjects. Such bibliographies provide you with lists of related sources already compiled by another author on a subject similar to your own.

Books in Print (New York: Bowker, 1948–present). The latest edition of this yearly index lists by author, subject, and title all books currently in print. It is also available electronically.

MLA Bibliography of Books and Articles in the Modern Languages and Literature (1921–present). This is also available electronically (1963–present).

Indexes

Indexes are guides to the material published within works, sometimes within books but more often within periodicals. Each index covers a particular group of periodicals. Make sure that the index you select contains the journals, magazines, and newspapers that you want to use as sources.

Indexes list works alphabetically by author or by subject. To conduct an effective subject search, use the keywords you have identified for your topic. Check under every subject heading that might be relevant. Many periodicals use the subject headings in the *Library of Congress Subject Headings,* but others use their own lists.

Most indexes are available both in printed and computerized forms. Many are also available on *microfiche* or *microfilm*—media that simulate the printed page but must be read on special machines. Indexes in book form are usually the most comprehensive; those presented on microfilm, microfiche, and computer usually cover only the past ten or twenty years.

Computerized indexes allow you to focus your search strategy most effectively. By combining keywords in certain ways, you can have the computer generate a list of works that closely match your topic. (See 13a.)

General periodical indexes. These indexes list articles published in a variety of periodicals of interest to the general public. Some are listed here:

InfoTrac. This index, available only electronically, contains seven separate indexes. The *Academic Index* covers over 1000 commonly used scholarly and general interest publications. The *General Periodical Index* covers over 1000 general-interest publications. The *National Newspaper Index* covers large-circulation newspapers. Many entries include summaries.

Readers' Guide to Periodical Literature (1900–present). This semi-monthly index lists articles in over 200 magazines of general interest, such as *Newsweek, Popular Science,* and *Rolling Stone.* Electronic versions are also available (1983–present).

Specialized periodical indexes. These indexes list articles in periodicals in specific disciplines or fields of interest. They are usually

much more helpful than general indexes for college-level research. Here are some of the most common:

America: History and Life

Applied Science and Technology Index

Art Index

Biological and Agricultural Index

Business Periodicals Index

Dissertation Abstracts International

Education Index

Essay and General Literature Index

General Science Index

Humanities Index

Music Index

Psychological Abstracts

Social Sciences Index

3 Computerized resources

Electronic **databases** are large structured collections of electronically stored information on related topics that may provide summaries in addition to bibliographic information on the sources they list; occasionally they contain copies of the sources themselves. You are familiar with noncomputerized databases of many kinds: the phone book, your file drawer, your college catalog. Be it a university catalog, a listing of magazine articles, or a compilation of government reports, a computer database is a familiar idea in electronic form. Whether they contain graphics files or magazine articles, computer databases are often organized like file cabinets, with a hierarchy of folders divided by subject. Electronic databases can be either online or on CD-ROM. Many library catalogs today are computerized as well, in the form of online databases. (For more on how to use these sources, see 12c.)

Dialog database

A major online system commonly found in college libraries is *Dialog,* which offers more than 400 databases. Some of the most commonly used databases within *Dialog* are Arts and Humanities

Search (1980–present), ERIC (Educational Resources Information Center, 1966–present), PsycINFO (1967–present), Scisearch (1974–present), and Social Scisearch (1972–present).

To use this database, you usually need the assistance of a reference librarian. The library is charged a fee for each search, calculated according to the time spent and the number of entries retrieved. Some libraries have the person requesting the search pay the fee; others limit the time allotted for each search. Be sure to ask what your library's policy is.

Some databases, including some of the specialized databases within *Dialog,* are also available on CD-ROM. You can usually search these databases without the aid of a librarian.

Internet links

Don't forget, as well, that Internet-to-library and library-to-library links (e.g., OhioLink) make exploring the vast resources of libraries such as Harvard's or the University of Michigan's almost as quick and easy as finding a book in your campus library's electronic catalog.

WRITING 2: APPLICATION ━━━━━━━━━━━━━━━━━━━━━━━━━━━

Use one of the bibliographies, indexes, or databases described in this section to find information on a relevant book or periodical. Locate the work, and take notes on the usefulness of the source and the process you used to obtain it.

4 The library catalog

The library online catalog lists every book a library owns; many libraries also catalog their periodicals. Most online catalogs can be accessed from locations outside the library.

All catalogs provide the same basic information. They list books by author, title, and subject; describe their physical format and content; and tell where in the library to find them.

Plan to use the library catalog in two different ways. If you already know the title of a work, the catalog can confirm that your library owns the work and tell you where to find it. At other times you will use the catalog as you would an index or a database, searching for works that are relevant to your topic; this process is called *browsing.* Online catalogs are particularly good for browsing and have several special features to facilitate it.

Even if you discover that your library doesn't own the source you want, don't despair. Many libraries can obtain a work owned by another library through an interlibrary loan. It may take

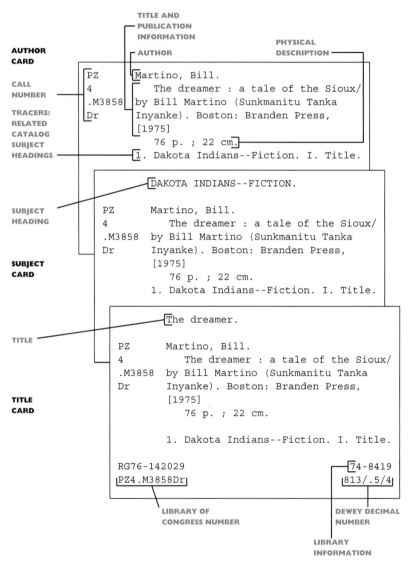

AUTHOR CARD

CALL NUMBER

TRACERS: RELATED CATALOG SUBJECT HEADINGS

TITLE AND PUBLICATION INFORMATION

AUTHOR

PHYSICAL DESCRIPTION

```
PZ        Martino, Bill.
4             The dreamer : a tale of the Sioux/
.M3858    by Bill Martino (Sunkmanitu Tanka
Dr        Inyanke). Boston: Branden Press,
          [1975]
              76 p. ; 22 cm.
          1. Dakota Indians--Fiction. I. Title.
```

SUBJECT HEADING

SUBJECT CARD

```
          DAKOTA INDIANS--FICTION.

PZ        Martino, Bill.
4             The dreamer : a tale of the Sioux/
.M3858    by Bill Martino (Sunkmanitu Tanka
Dr        Inyanke). Boston: Branden Press,
          [1975]
              76 p. ; 22 cm.
          1. Dakota Indians--Fiction. I. Title.
```

TITLE

TITLE CARD

```
          The dreamer.

PZ        Martino, Bill.
4             The dreamer : a tale of the Sioux/
.M3858    by Bill Martino (Sunkmanitu Tanka
Dr        Inyanke). Boston: Branden Press,
          [1975]
              76 p. ; 22 cm.

          1. Dakota Indians--Fiction. I. Title.

RG76-142029                          74-8419
PZ4.M3858Dr                          813/.5/4
```

LIBRARY OF CONGRESS NUMBER

DEWEY DECIMAL NUMBER

LIBRARY INFORMATION

Cards from a card catalog

anywhere from a few days to a few weeks to obtain your request, so start early.

Consulting online catalogs

Online catalog systems vary slightly from library to library, though all systems follow the same general principles. Locating works through author and title is much like the corresponding procedure with a card catalog, with one important exception: most online catalogs allow you to search with partial information. For example, if you know that the title of a novel begins with the words *Love Medicine* but you can't remember the rest of it, you can ask the catalog computer to search for the title *Love Medicine*. It will present you with a list of all works that begin with those words.

```
Search Request: T=LOVE MEDICINE
Search Results: 4 Entries Found                        Title Index
-----------------------------------------------------------------T257
1  LOVE MEDICINE: A NOVEL.  ERDRICH LOUISE <1984>        (BH)

   LOVE MEDICINE AND MIRACLES
2    SIEGEL BERNIE S <1986>  (BH)
3    SIEGEL BERNIE S <1988>  (DA)

   LOVE MEDICINE AND MIRACLES LESSONS LEARNED ABOUT SELFHEALING
   FROM A SURGEON'S EXPERIENCE WITH EXCEPTIONAL PATIENTS
4    SIEGEL BERNIE S <1986>  (BH)

-----------------------------------------------------------------
COMMANDS:    Type line # to see individual record
             O  Other options
             H  Help

NEXT COMMAND:
```

Results of a title search in an online catalog

Most online catalogs also allow you to perform keyword searches, much like the searches conducted on computerized databases. The advantage of this kind of search is that the computer can search different parts of the record at once. To perform a keyword search, use the words you've identified as describing your topic, linked by *and* or *or* as appropriate. (See 13c.) For example, if you're trying to research fictional accounts of Dakota Indians, you can search for *"Dakota Indians" AND "fiction."* (See 13a1.) The computer will present you with a list of works that fit that description. As with all computer searches, making your keyword search request as specific as possible will result in the most useful list.

```
Search Request: T=LOVE MEDICINE
BOOK - Record 1 of 5 Entries Found                       Long View
---------------------Screen-1-of-1----------------------------T259
Author:        Erdrich, Louise.
Title:         Love medicine : a novel
Edition:       1st ed.
Published:     New York : Holt, Rinehart, and Winston, c1984.
Description:   viii, 275 p. ; 22cm.
Subjects(LC):  Indians of North America--North Dakota--Fiction.
------------------------------------------------------------------
   LOCATION;           CALL NUMBER              STATUS
1  Halley Stacks       PS3555.R42 L6 1984       Not checked out

COMMANDS:       P  Previous screen
                O  Other options
                H  Help

NEXT COMMAND:
```

Full information on a book in an online catalog

Using call numbers

Once you have determined through the catalog that your library owns a book you want to consult, use the book's call number to locate it in the stacks. Most academic libraries use the Library of Congress system, whose call numbers begin with letters. Some libraries still use the older Dewey Decimal system, whose call numbers consist entirely of numbers. In either case, the first letters or numbers in a call number indicate the general subject area. Because libraries shelve all books for a general subject area together, this portion of the call number tells you where in the library to find the book you want.

Be sure to copy a book's call number exactly as it appears in the catalog. Most libraries have open stacks, allowing you to retrieve the book yourself; one wrong number or letter could lead you to the wrong part of the library. If your library has closed stacks, you will need to give the call number to a librarian, who will retrieve the book for you; the wrong call number will get you the wrong book.

WRITING 3: APPLICATION ─────────────────────────────

Use the library's catalog to see what holdings the library has on your topic. Retrieve one of these books from the stacks, and check to see whether it contains a bibliography that could lead you to other books. Record these findings in your research log.

5 Other sources of information

Many libraries own materials other than books and periodicals. Often these do not circulate. If you think one of the sources listed here might contain information relevant to your research, ask a librarian about your library's holdings.

Government documents. The U.S. government publishes numerous reports, pamphlets, catalogs, and newsletters on most issues of national concern. Reference books that can lead you to these sources include the *Monthly Catalogue of United States Government Publications* and the *United States Government Publications Index,* both available electronically. Many government documents are now available on the World Wide Web.

Nonprint media. Records, CDs, audiocassettes, videotapes, slides, photographs, and other media may also be located through the library catalog.

Pamphlets. Pamphlets and brochures published by government agencies and private organizations are generally stored in a library's vertical file. The *Vertical File Index: A Subject and Title Index to Selected Pamphlet Material* (1932/35–present) lists many of the available titles. Many are also available via the World Wide Web.

Special collections. Rare books, manuscripts, and items of local interest are commonly found in a special room or section of the library.

WRITING 4: APPLICATION ————————————————————————

Identify one relevant source of information in your library's holdings other than a book or periodical. Locate it and take notes on the usefulness of the source and the process you used to obtain it.

12 C Using electronic sources

Once libraries began to put their card catalogs on computers, it wasn't long before those libraries and other institutions began to make their resources available for remote searching via networks. You can find and retrieve documents by using an online catalog, searching a CD-ROM database, logging on to an access port at a university library or bulletin board system, exploring an online service such as CompuServe or America Online, or "surfing" the global network of computer interconnections known as the **Internet (Net).**

Some of the databases you can access through your computer are merely guides to where to find information. For example, a **bibliographic database,** like the online catalog of a library, lists articles or books by title, subject, and author, but it does not contain the full source text. An **abstract database** contains brief summaries of the article citations it lists, which can help you tell which articles might be most valuable to you. However, when researching, you cannot rely on summaries for information; too much is lost in the process of summarizing.

A **full-text database** often contains the complete text of the articles it lists. But beware: some texts are abbreviated when they are stored on the computer, and others omit accompanying information such as sidebars or graphics. Also, depending on how you are accessing the data, you may have to pay to retrieve the full text of an article.

A detailed discussion of the technical aspects of online research is beyond the scope of this book. However, an understanding of the basic online search tools and techniques will help you get started. (See Chapter 13.)

Whichever search tool you use, there is nothing magic about information transferred over a computer. You will need the same critical skills you use to evaluate printed materials, although the

```
SilverPlatter 3.11 Journal Articles (1/74 - 12/86)  F10=Commands
                                                     F1=Help
-------------------------------------------------------------------
                                                             1 of 3
TI: Teacher expressiveness: More important for male teachers than
female teachers?
AU: Basow.-Susan-A.; Distenfeld, -M.-Suzan
IN: Lafayette Coll
JN: Journal-of-Educational-Psychology; 1985 Feb Vol 77(1) 45-52
AB: 55 male and 62 female undergraduates viewed a videotape of a
male or female actor giving a short lecture using expressive or
nonexpressive communication and rated each teacher on a 22-item
questionnaire that yielded 5 factors (Rapport, Student Orientation,
Stimulates Interest, Organization, and Knowledge of Material).
Findings show that the expressive teacher received the highest student
evaluations on the basis of a global evaluation score and on the 5
factor scores. . . .
-------------------------------------------------------------------
MENU: Mark Record Select Search Term Options Find Print Download

Press ENTER to Mark records for PRINT or DOWNLOAD.
Use PgDn and PgUp to scroll.
```

Partial entry in a CD-ROM database (Sample record reprinted with permission of the American Psychological Association, publisher of PsycINFO® Database Copyright 1887–present by the American Psychological Association. All rights reserved. For more information contact <psycinfo@apa.org>.)

clues may be harder to understand when you find documents online. Is the author identified? Is that person a professional in the field or an interested amateur? What are his or her biases likely to be? Does the document you have located represent an individual's opinion or peer-reviewed research? (For more detailed discussion about evaluating electronic information, see 15b.)

12 d Reading library sources critically

So that you don't waste time and energy taking careful notes on sources that contain unimportant or unreliable information, make sure to read each source critically by previewing, responding, and reviewing. (See 2b.)

First, *preview* the source to get a general sense of it, to determine whether the source is related closely enough to your topic to be useful, and to decide whether to read further. If you determine that the source will be useful, read it more carefully and take notes on it. Critical reading at this stage consists of *responding* (entering into a conversation with a text while you read) and *reviewing* (coming to a critical understanding of the text as a whole).

Reviewing to evaluate is particularly important when you are writing a research essay, since you are trying to determine the worth or validity of the text and the information it contains. If you determine that a source is irrelevant, unreliable, or out of date, you'll need to find another. Because you want to know this as soon as possible, make the effort to evaluate each source continually: when reading, when taking notes, and when considering how to incorporate the source into your final paper.

You can get expert help in evaluating books by consulting book reviews. To avoid a hit-and-miss search, consult one of the several indexes that identify where and when a book was reviewed.

Book Review Index. This bimonthly index lists reviews of major books published in several hundred periodicals.

Current Book Review Citations. This annual index lists reviews published in more than 1000 periodicals.

For further discussion of approaches to evaluating library sources, see 15a.

WRITING 5: APPLICATION

For at least one source you are considering for your research paper, consult one of the book review indexes listed in this section. Look up some of these reviews and take careful notes.

12 e Taking notes

Taking good notes will make the whole research process easier, enabling you to locate and remember sources and helping you use them effectively in your writing. For short research projects requiring only a few sources, it is easy to take careful notes in a research log or class notebook and refer to them as needed when writing your paper. Or you can photocopy or print out whole articles or chapters and take them home for further study. However, for any research project requiring more than a few sources, you should develop a card-based system for recording your sources and the information you find.

1 Developing a working bibliography

When you locate a useful source, write all the information necessary to find that source again on a 3″ × 5″ index card, using a separate card for each work. If you create bibliographic cards as you go along, then at the end you can easily arrange them in alphabetical order and prepare your reference list. (For complete information on how to record bibliographic information using the appropriate documentation style, see MLA, APA, or other documentation conventions in Chapters 54–60.)

It is also easy to create bibliographic cards right on your computer, including all relevant information. (See the box on p. 191.) Some word processing programs make card shapes on the screen to simulate the restricted space of 3″ × 5″ or 4″ × 6″ file cards. The obvious advantage of electronic card entries is that they can be sorted and alphabetized to provide a typed draft of your reference page at the end of your paper.

Annotate your bibliography cards right from the start, noting the source, its point of view, information, or possible use later on. Otherwise, it's easy to forget what each source has to offer.

2 Creating note cards

Make note cards to record the relevant information found in your sources. When writing a research essay, you will be working

USING CRITICAL THINKING TO SELECT LIBRARY SOURCES

The more you research, the more expert you become at determining whether a source is useful. Note information from facts first: author, title, publisher, date, table of contents, section headings, chapter titles, and subheadings. Make inferences from surveying the text: tone of the foreword, preface, and introduction; direction of relevant sections, gleaned from reading first pages of chapters or abstracts or summaries of articles; bias inferred from references, indexes, and bibliography. When in doubt, confer with your instructor or a librarian. Here are some questions to ask yourself:

- **Subject.** Is the subject directly related to my research question? Does it provide information that supports my view? Does it provide helpful context or background information? Does it contain quotations or facts that I will want to quote in my paper?

- **Author.** What do I really know about the author's reputation? Does the book or periodical provide any biographical information? Is this author cited by other sources? Am I aware of any biases that might limit the author's credibility?

- **Date.** When was this source published? Is it sufficiently up to date to suit my purpose? If the purpose of using a source that is not current is to study ideas from the past, how does the source compare to other sources of its time? Does it represent common, widely accepted views or does it introduce a new perspective or discovery?

- **Publisher.** Who published this source? Is it a major publisher, a university press, or a scholarly organization that would subject material to a rigorous review procedure?

- **Counterauthority.** Does the source address or present counterarguments on issues I intend to discuss or take? Each point of view is essential for examining an issue completely.

from these note cards, so be sure they contain all the information you need from every source you intend to use. Also try to focus them on your research question, so that their relevance is clear when you read them later.

To have as much room as possible on each and every note card, use 4″ × 6″ index cards. For bibliography cards, use 3″ × 5″. These different sizes will also help keep the two sets separate. (Or put notes on the smaller cards to practice condensing ideas; put bibliographic references on the larger cards, using the extra space

for annotations.) A typical note card should contain only one piece of information or one idea. This system will allow you to arrange and rearrange the information in different ways as you write. At the top of each note card, identify the source through brief biblio-graphic identification (author and title), and note the page numbers on which the information appears. Many writers also include the category of information—a particular theme, subject, or argument for which the note provides support. Personal notes, including ideas for possible use of the information or cross-references to other information, should be clearly distinguished from material that comes from the source; they might be put at the bottom in parentheses.

3 **Using quotation, paraphrase, and summary**

When recording information on your card, you must take steps to avoid **plagiarism.** (See 16g.) Do this by making distinctions

---

**INFORMATION TO BE RECORDED
ON BIBLIOGRAPHIC CARDS**

FOR BOOKS

1. Call number or other location information
2. Full name(s) of author(s)
3. Full title and subtitle
4. Edition or volume number
5. Editor or translator
6. Place of publication
7. Publisher and date of publication
8. Inclusive page numbers for relevant sections in longer works

FOR PERIODICALS

1. Full name(s) of author(s)
2. Full title and subtitle of article
3. Periodical title
4. Perdiodical volume and number
5. Periodical date
6. Inclusive page numbers of article
7. Library call number or other location information

```
                                                              PE
                                                            1405
                                                             .U6
                                                             M55
                                                            1991

        Miller, Susan, Textual Carnivals.
        Carbondale: Southern Illinois UP, 1991.
```

Bibliographic card for a book using MLA documentation style

among quoting directly, paraphrasing, and summarizing. A **direct quotation** is an exact duplication of the author's words in the original source. Put quotation marks around direct quotations on your note cards so that you will know later that these words are the author's, not yours. (See 16d1.) A **paraphrase** is a restatement of the author's words in your own words. Paraphrase to simplify or clarify the original author's point. A paraphrase must restate the original facts or ideas fully and correctly. (See 16d2). A **summary** is a brief condensation or distillation of the main point of the original source. Like a paraphrase, a summary should be in your own words, and all facts and ideas should be accurately represented. (See 16d3.)

Deciding when to quote, when to paraphrase, and when to summarize in your notes will require judgment on your part. The major advantage of quoting is that it allows you to decide later, while writing the paper, whether to include a quotation or to paraphrase or summarize. However, copying down many long quotations can be time-consuming. Also, simply copying down a quotation may prevent you from thinking about the ideas expressed in a way that will benefit your understanding of the topic. In general, copy direct quotations only when the author's words are particularly lively or persuasive. Photocopying machines and computer printers make it easy to collect direct quotations, but be sure to highlight the pertinent material or make notes to yourself on the copy so you can remember later what you wanted to quote and why. For ease of organizing notes, many researchers cut out the pertinent quotation and paste it to a note card.

A good paraphrase can help you better understand a difficult passage by simplifying complex sentence structure and vocabulary into language with which you are more comfortable. Be careful not

> Lewis, <u>Green Delusions</u>, p. 230
> Reasons for overpopulation in poor countries
>
> Some experts believe that birth rates are linked to the "economic value" of children to their parents. Poor countries have higher birth rates because parents there rely on children to work for the family and to take care of them in old age. The more children, particularly sons, the better off the family is financially. In wealthier countries parents have fewer children because they cost more in terms of education and they contribute less.
>
> (Based on Caldwell and Cain—check these further?)

Note card containing a paraphrase

to distort the author's ideas. Use paraphrases when you need to record details but not exact words.

Because a summary boils a source down to its essentials, it is particularly useful when specific details in the source are unimportant or irrelevant to your research question. You may often find that you can summarize several paragraphs or even an entire article or chapter in just a few sentences without losing any useful information. It is a good idea to note when a particular card contains a summary so you'll remember later that it leaves out detailed supporting information.

 QUOTATION, PARAPHRASE, AND SUMMARY

As you take notes, use this box to help you choose which note-taking technique is best for your purposes.

- **Direct quotation** duplicates the exact words from a source. Keep direct quotations brief, and put prominent quotation marks around them on your note cards.
- **Paraphrase** restates the author's ideas in your own words simply, clearly, and accurately. This device captures content without exposing you to the risk of unacknowledged quotations, and thus your text may run as long as the original.
- **Summary** condenses the main point(s) of an original passage. Summarize in your own words, and use quotation marks around any of the author's language you include.

WRITING 6: EXPLORATION ───────────────────

Describe the most important, useful, or surprising thing you have learned about the library since exploring it as part of your research project. Share your discovery with classmates, and listen to theirs. Are you comfortable in the library? Why or why not? How does technology help or hinder the research process? Explain in an online journal entry and share this with the class.

SUGGESTIONS FOR LIBRARY RESEARCH PROJECTS

INDIVIDUAL AND COLLABORATIVE

Your school experience of a dozen or more years already tells you that library research can find information about a virtually unlimited number of topics. For the sake of exercise, see what type of library information you can locate to supplement the research you conducted at the end of Chapter 11 either individually or as a collaborative project.

13   Conducting Internet Research

The Internet provides a wide variety of information unavailable either in the library or in the field. Within the past decade, businesses and individuals have gained widespread access to the Internet, especially to that portion known as the World Wide Web (WWW). Although academic and scientific use of the Internet continues, commercial applications drive most Web development—which makes it a messy, crowded, but ever-so-useful place to conduct research, academic or otherwise. Many Web sites are secondary sources, written by people describing, analyzing, or interpreting the work of others. Less easy to find are primary sources, the original words and accounts of people describing their own experiences or findings.

Much of the difficulty and delight of the Internet stems from the fact that no one is in charge. No single agency or company is responsible for organizing or policing the Internet. No one knows exactly what is on it, nor is there a central card catalog or index showing what's available, from whom, or where it's located. The unscreened nature of the Internet makes it essential that you supplement Internet information with other sources. If you are unfamiliar with Web searching for noncommercial information, the following suggestions will help.

13 a   Select a search engine

A search engine ___ps you find Internet information. The two in most common use c___ntly are Google and Yahoo. However, be aware that no single ___h routine accesses the entire Internet. Because each search p___ each has its own methods and covers a different database, each ___h site will return different results from the same search ter___

1.   **Search options.** There are now so many specialized search sites that if you're not finding the information you need, it's often worthwhile to search for search engines.

Search evaluation sites will tell you the latest news about useful search engines and their everchanging status, functions, and power.

> **SearchIQ** <http://www.zdnet.com/searchiq/> from the online publisher ZDNet offers tips, ranks search sites, and provides extensive lists of specialty search tools by topic.

> **Search Engine Watch** <http://www.searchenginewatch.com/> uses search tools for users and describes how search sites select materials.

> **Lookoff** <http://www.lookoff.com/tactics/reviews.php3> gives detailed tables comparing the features and design of more than two dozen major search sites.

Metasearch engines retrieve results from many search sites simultaneously.

> **Dogpile** <http://www.dogpile.com>

> **Google** <http://www.google.com>

> **Ixquick** <http://www.ixquick.com>

> **Metor** <http://www.metor.com>

> **Queryserver** <http://www.queryserver.com>

> **Vivisimo** <http://www.vivisimo.com>

Directories index information by topic, much the way a library subject catalog or the telephone Yellow Pages is organized.

> **About** <http://www.about.com>

> **Looksmart** <http://www.looksmart.com>

> **Lycos** <http://www.lycos.com>

> **Open Directory** <http://dmoz.org/>

> **Yahoo!** <http://www.yahoo.com>

Search engines index sites according to words that appear in them.

AllTheWeb.com <http://www.alltheweb.com>

Alta Vista <http://www.altavista.com>

Hotbot <http://www.hotbot.com>

The following **search tools** are useful for searching specialized Internet databases:

FTP Search <http://computers.lycos.com/downloads/dindex.asp> searches File Transfer Protocol sites.

Liszt <http://www.liszt.com> searches e-mail list archives.

2. **Library and academic resources.** Many general-use search tools are weighted toward commercial and entertainment sites. (Some even charge listed sites a fee to be included in search results.) The following academically oriented tools often provide better results for writers.

Amazon.com <http://www.amazon.com>, an online bookstore, lists books in and out of print. Once you identify a useful title, you can often find it in your library.

Bartleby.com <http://www.bartleby.com> offers searchable, complete text of works of literature, poetry, and criticism.

Biographical Dictionary <http://www.s9.com/biography/> is searchable by name, year of birth and death, profession, works, and other terms.

Direct Search compiled by Gary Price of George Washington University <http://gwis2.circ.gwu.edu/~gprice/direct.htm> is an academically oriented set of links to sites overlooked by many commercial search engines, including archives, online library catalogs, and bibliographies.

Infoplease <http://www.infoplease.com> offers a collection of online almanacs.

Librarians' Index to the Internet <http://lii.org/> sponsored by the Library of California offers directories of searchable resources on academic topics.

RefDesk <http://www.refdesk.com/> provides links in the natural and social sciences, languages, geography, arts, and literature, plus dozens of dictionaries and encyclopedias.

Social Science Research Network <http://www.ssrn.com/> contains abstracts of current papers in accounting, economics, and legal scholarship.

U.S. Census Bureau <http://www.census.gov> is a primary source for government demographic and economic data.

WorldFactbook<http://www.odci.gov/cia/publications/factbook/index.html>, published by the U.S. Central Intelligence Agency, gives comprehensive background information on every country, from maps and rainfall totals to governmental organization and the telephone number of the country's embassy in Washington, D.C.

WRITING I ───

Search for a topic of special interest using three different search engines and/or directories from the list above. Compare the results and note both similarities and differences in the information each searching tool provides. Explain why, in future searches, one engine or directory *would* or *would not* provide you with adequate information.

13 b Check e-mail and newgroups

Once you have an e-mail address, you can correspond electronically with any of millions of people around the world who can, in turn, write to you. Of course, you need your correspondents' e-mail addresses. Try using a Web search site such as *Search.com* <http://www.search.com> that lists multiple e-mail search routines. Enter a name and check the search results against other information you already have. For example, if you were looking for Toby Fulwiler's address and found one with the domain *uvm.edu,* you could be fairly sure you had found the author of this book, who works at the University of Vermont (UVM), an educational institution.

E-mail can make a good interview tool. If you have questions for the author of an article you're citing in your research, you may be able to e-mail your questions and get quick answers. If you write to someone in search of information, be sure to identify yourself and describe your research project. In addition to your specific questions, don't forget to ask general questions such as "Can you think of other important sources (or questions or issues) I should be aware of?"

Another kind of continuing discussion group on the Internet is the *newsgroup* or *Usenet group.* A newsgroup consists of a collection of postings on a single topic. As with mailing lists, there are thousands of newsgroups. Most Internet service providers include newsgroup access as part of basic service. Dogpile <http://www.dogpile.com> and Google Groups <http://groups.google.com> both can search newsgroup archives.

Conduct an e-mail interview with an expert in your research field. Introduce yourself, explain your purpose, and ask three good questions. See Chapter 14 for tips on asking interview questions, then modify those for an online interview.

13 c A sample Web search

Depending on what kind of information you're looking for, searching the World Wide Web can be rewarding or frustrating. Many sites you'll find are **secondary sources,** written by people describing, analyzing, or interpreting the work of others. Less easy to find are **primary sources,** the original words and accounts of people describing their own experiences or findings. (See 11e2.)

One area where the Internet can excel, however, is in providing information on current events or contemporary issues. Here's what Jamie found in researching controversies about the safety of sport utility vehicles, a topic that had caught his interest in several news reports.

Jamie first tried searching the phrase *sport utility vehicle* and then *SUV,* but those searches returned used-car ads, new-car reviews, and all sorts of other commercial information he wasn't interested in.

To limit the search, he tried adding the word *rollover,* referring to a type of accident. That search produced few results. Since *rollover* was too limiting, he tried a more general term, *safety.* The search for *"sport utility vehicle" and safety* produced better results, including the following:

- The *National Highway Traffic Safety Administration* home page, including links to safety ratings of sport utility vehicles (rollover resistance rating) and technical papers on safety issues.

- A report by the National Highway Traffic Safety Administration called "Overview of Vehicle Compatibility/LTV Issues."

- A Web site produced by a pro-sport-utility group calling itself the Coalition for Vehicle Choice.

After studying materials these sites offered, Jamie concluded he had good primary data from the federal agency's studies and findings and useful secondary data in the opinions and reactions of people and organizations. There also were several e-mail addresses for people who might be able to answer questions. He decided to conclude his research by talking to owners of sport utility vehicles

DOCUMENTING A WEB SEARCH

Often it can be very difficult to retrace your steps to a valuable Internet resource. Use a notebook to keep track of which search engines and which search terms you use so that you can reproduce a search easily.

When you find a useful Web page, print a paper copy for your records. If your browser doesn't automatically do so, *write the URL of the page on your printout along with the date and time you acccessed the page.* This information will be helpful in documenting your sources and will be evidence of what you found on this site on the particular day you accessed it. (See Chapters 17 and 54–60 for styles of documenting electronic sources in various academic disciplines.)

and other recent car buyers to determine which, if any, of the safety issues influenced their decisions.

Troubleshooting

Following are frequently asked questions about Internet research.

- **What if I can't find a Web site?**

If you type in a URL but cannot locate the site, or you get an error message saying "Object not found," check your typing very carefully and try again. If you still get an error message, try a simplified version of the URL to take you to the site's home page, and then click on a link for more information. Even if the specific file you were seeking has been moved, chances are you can find related or updated information you can use.

Also try searching several different sites. No search engine or directory catalogs the entire Web, and no two engines search exactly the same way. So any comprehensive search effort requires several different search tools. Depending on your topic, you may find one search engine much more useful than the others. In any case, check the online help file that each search engine offers to find out the exact conventions of that engine.

- **How do I cite a Web source?**

It can be difficult to retrace your steps to a valuable Internet resource. Use a notebook to keep track of which search engines and which search terms you use so that you can reproduce a

National Highway Traffic Safety Administration
United States Department of Transportation

People Saving People
www.nhtsa.dot.gov

Search

GO!

| Hot At NHTSA | Crash Tests | Site Map |

| Recalls | Buying A Safer Car | Service Bulletins Database | Impaired Driving |

Popular Information

Air Bags
Auto Safety Hotline
Calendar
Child Passenger Safety
Child Seat Inspections
Complaint Form
Crash Statistics
Crash Tests
Disability Information
Docket Management System
E-Payment
Feedback
Firestone
FOIA
Grants
Hot@NHTSA
International Activities
NCSA
Press Releases
Publications Catalog
Real Videos
Recalls
Safety Materials
School Buses
Star Ratings
Table of Contents
What's New
Youth

Vehicle & Equipment Information
Problems & Issues
Testing Results
Regulations & Standards
Research & Development

Traffic Safety / Occupant Issues
Injury Prevention
Communications & Outreach
Driver Performance
Crash Information

Welcome To NHTSA
Announcements
What's NHTSA Doing?
DOT Auto Safety Hotline
Regional Offices

NEWS

NHTSA Publishes Proposed Model Year 2004 CAFE Standard - Press Release

NHTSA Announces Safety Recall Of Britax Child Safety Restraints - Press Release

NHTSA Publishes List of October 2001 Recalls - Press Release

U.S. Transportation Secretary Mineta Announces Launch Of Major Nationwide Campaign to Promote Tire Safety - Press Release

NHTSA proposes new standard for tire labeling to enhance consumer knowledge of tire safety and tire recall information. - Posted 12/20/2001

Buckle Up America
Child Passenger Safety Week

Feb 10-16, 2002

Winter Safety Tips

Rollover Resistance Rating

For more information dial NHTSA's toll-free hotline at
1-888-DASH-2-DOT
(1-888-327-4236)
8:00AM to 10:00PM ET Monday-Friday

Home page of the National Highway Traffic Safety Administration

search easily. When you find a useful Web page, print a copy for your records. If your browser doesn't automatically do so, write the URL of the page on your printout along with the date and time you accessed the page. These will help to document your paper and "freeze" the contents of a site that changes between visits.

USEFUL WEB RESOURCES

To explore the World Wide Web, log on to the Internet, type the URL you want into the command line of your browser, hit the "Enter" key, and see what you find. (When accessing a URL, always type the address exactly as it appears, and pay close attention to lower- and uppercase letters.)

Frequently asked questions (FAQs) about Web browsers	http://www.boutell.com/openfaq/browsers
Web history and resources from the nonprofit World Wide Web Consortium	http://www.w3.org
Web tours and training	http://www.learnthenet.com/english/index.html
Peterson's Education Center: Information on colleges	http://www.petersons.com
A list of libraries online, including *Internet Public Library,* Library of Congress, Public Libraries on the Internet, Presidential Libraries, Depository Libraries	http://www.microserve.net/~library/libraries.html
Medscape: a wealth of medical information written primarily for health professionals	http://www.medscape.com
The Gallup Poll	http://www.gallup.com
The New York Times (registration required)	http://www.nytimes.com
ABC News	http://www.abcnews.com
MSNBC (NBC News)	http://www.msnbc.com
ESPN (cable sports information)	http://espn.sportszone.com
The Blair Handbook by Toby Fulwiler and Alan R. Hayakawa	http://www.prenhall.com/fulwiler

14   Conducting Field Research

Research is an active and unpredictable process requiring serious investigators to find answers wherever those happen to be. Depending on your research question, you may need to seek answers by visiting museums, attending concerts, interviewing politicians, observing classrooms, or following leads down some other trail. Investigations that take place outside the library are commonly called **field research.**

After our first-year students completed a writing project in which field research played a central part, we asked them what they thought of this kind of research. Here is what they told us:

> Amanda: "Interviewing people adds authenticity and interest to any research paper."

> Lydia: "Without question, it was interviews that gave me the most current and interesting information for my tattoo paper. I could ask my own questions and not have to dig through useless information to get the answer."

> Angel: "When I quoted Congressman Sanders' personal views on gun control, his voice made my voice stronger and more believable."

> Jose: "Field research was very frustrating to me. No one would ever return my phone calls or answer my questions directly."

> Kate: "I enjoy field research because I'm more personally involved in it. It's harder than library or Web research—calling and making appointments and going places—but it is more entertaining."

Field research adds liveliness, immediacy, and credibility to a research paper, especially when used in conjunction with library and Internet research. In fact, it's always a good idea to learn as much as you can about the subject of your research via a library or Web search before conducting an interview; the people you talk to will see that you're informed and will give you more detailed

information. At the same time, good field research often takes more time and preparation than browsing the Web or an online catalog, so it can also be frustrating.

Field researchers collect information that is not yet recorded or assessed, and so they have the chance to uncover new facts and develop original interpretations. To conduct such research, you first need to determine which people, places, things, or events can give you the information you need. Then you must go out in the field and either **observe** by watching carefully or **interview** by asking questions of a particular person. You should take careful notes to record your observations or interviews and critically evaluate the information you've collected.

14 a Planning field research

Unlike a library, which bundles millions of bits of every kind of information in a single location, "fields" are everywhere. A college campus is an ideal place in which to conduct field research since there are many potential sites for investigation: academic departments, administrative offices, labs, libraries, dining and sports facilities, and dormitories. In the neighborhood beyond the campus, sites for field research include theaters, malls, parks, playgrounds, business offices, homes, and so on. Furthermore, accessing the Internet opens up the possibility of field research in cyberspace, from e-mail on your own campus to contact with a site halfway around the world. Field information is not cataloged, organized, indexed, or shelved for your convenience. Obtaining it requires diligence, energy, and careful planning.

- **Consider your research question as it now stands.** What sort of information will be most effective in your final paper?

- **Select your contacts and sites.** Find the person, place, thing, or event most helpful to you. Decide whether you will collect observations, conduct interviews, or do both.

- **Schedule field research in advance.** Interviews, trips, and events don't always work according to plan. Allow time for glitches, such as having to reschedule an interview or return for more information.

- **Do homework before you go.** Visit the library before conducting extensive field research. No matter from whom, where, or what you intend to collect information, there's background information at the library that can help you make more insightful observations or

formulate better interview questions. (For more information on using libraries, see Chapter 12.)

- **Take extensive notes in your research log.** Record visits, questions, phone calls, and conversations. Write in your log from the very beginning about topics, questions, methods, and answers. Record even dead-end searches, to remind yourself that you tried them.

WRITING 1: APPLICATION ⎯⎯⎯⎯⎯⎯⎯⎯⎯⎯⎯⎯⎯⎯⎯⎯

In your research log, write about the feasibility of using field research information to help answer your research question. What kind of field research would strengthen your paper? Where would you go to collect it?

14 b Interviewing

A good interview provides the researcher with timely, original, and useful information that often cannot be obtained by other means. Getting such information is part instinct, part skill, and part luck. If you find talking to strangers easy, then you have a head start on being a good interviewer; in many respects, a good interview is simply a good conversation. If you do not, you can still learn how to ask good interview questions that will elicit the answers you need. Your chances of obtaining good interview material increase when you've thought about what questions you want to pose ahead of time. The following guidelines should help you conduct good interviews:

Select the right person. People differ in both the amount and kind of knowledge they have. Not everyone who knows something about your research topic will be able to give you the information you need. In other words, before you make an appointment with a local expert because the individual is accessible, consider whether this is the best person to talk to. Ask yourself (1) exactly what information you need, (2) why you need it, (3) who is likely to have it, and (4) how you might approach this source to gain it.

Most research projects benefit from various perspectives, so you may want to interview several people. For example, to research Lake Erie pollution, you could interview someone who lives on the shore, a chemist who knows about pesticide decomposition, and a vice president of a paper company dumping waste into the lake. Just be sure the people you select are likely to provide you with information you really need.

Do your homework. Before you talk to an expert about your topic, make sure you know something about it yourself. Be able to define or describe your interest in it, know the general issues, and learn what your interview subject has already said about it. In this way, you will ask sharper questions, get to the point faster, and be more interesting for your subject to talk with. Plan appropriate questions.

Create a working script. A good interview doesn't follow a script, but it usually starts with one. Before you begin an interview, write out the questions you plan to ask and arrange them so that they build on each other—general questions first, specific ones later. If you or your subject digresses too much, your questions can serve as reminders about the information you need.

Ask both open and closed questions. Different kinds of questions elicit different kinds of information. Open questions place few limits on the answers given: Why did you decide to major in business? What are your plans for the future? Closed questions specify the information you want and usually elicit brief responses: When did you receive your degree? From what college? Open questions usually provide general information, while closed questions allow you to zero in on details.

Ask follow-up questions. Listen closely to the answers you receive, and when the information is incomplete or confusing, ask follow-up questions requesting clarification. Such questions can't be scripted; you just have to use your wits to direct your subject toward the information you consider most important.

Use silence. If you don't get an immediate response to a question, wait a bit before asking another one. In some cases, your question may not have been clear and you will need to rephrase it. But in many cases your interview subject is simply collecting his or her thoughts, not ignoring you. After a slight pause, you may hear thoughtful answers worth waiting for.

Read body language. Be aware of what your subject is doing while answering the questions. Does he or she look you in the eye? fidget and squirm? look distracted or bored? smile? From these visual cues you may be able to infer when your subject is speaking most frankly, doesn't want to give more information, or is tired of answering questions.

Take good content notes. Many interviewers take notes on a pad that is spiral-bound on top, which allows for quick page flipping. Don't try to write down everything, just major ideas and telling statements in the subject's own words that you might want to use as quotations in your paper. Omitting small words, focusing on the most distinctive and precise language, and using common

abbreviations (like *b/c* for *because* and *w/* for *with*) can make note taking more efficient.

Take good descriptive notes. Note your subject's physical appearance, facial expressions, and clothing, as well as the interview setting itself. These details will be useful later when you reconstruct the interview, helping you represent it more vividly in your paper.

Tape-record with permission only. If you plan to use a tape recorder, ask for permission in advance. The advantage of tape recording is that you have a complete record of the conversation. Sometimes on hearing the person a second time, you notice important things that you missed earlier. The disadvantages are that sometimes tape recorders make subjects nervous and that transcribing a tape is time-consuming work. It's a good idea to have pen in hand to catch highlights or jot down additional questions.

Confirm important assertions. When your subject says something especially important or controversial, read back your notes aloud to check for accuracy and to allow your subject to elaborate. Some interviewers do this during the interview, others at the end.

Review your notes. Notes taken during an interview are brief reminders of what your subject said, not complete quotations. You need to write out the complete information they represent as soon after the interview as you can, certainly within twenty-four hours. Supplement the notes with other remembered details while they're still fresh, recording them on note cards or directly into a computer file that you can refer to as you write your paper.

Interview electronically. It is possible, and useful, to contact individuals via telephone, electronic mail, or the Internet. Phone interviews are quick and obvious ways of finding out information on short notice. If your interviewee has an e-mail address, asking questions via this medium is even less intrusive than telephoning as your subject can answer when doing so is convenient—quickly, specifically, and in writing. Usenet newsgroups and listservs can also provide effective sites for initiating research conversations, and many World Wide Web sites are interactive, allowing questions and answers to flow back and forth. (For more on electronic sources, see Chapter 13.)

WRITING 2: EXPLORATION _____

Describe any experience you have had as either interviewer or interviewee. Drawing on your own experience, what additional advice would you give to researchers setting out to interview a subject?

ESL **CONDUCTING INTERVIEWS IN ENGLISH**

Interviewing someone, especially in a foreign language, can be challenging. Before you conduct an interview, consider whether you will feel comfortable taking notes and listening at the same time. If your interview subject doesn't object, you may want to use a tape recorder.

To take notes efficiently in an interview, develop a list of abbreviations beforehand to facilitate note taking. Don't hesitate to ask your interview subject to repeat or clarify information, but be polite. It is usually more polite to make a request than to use a command or statement.

POLITE REQUESTS Could you please repeat that statistic?
Would you please explain that to me?

WRITING 3: APPLICATION ──────────────────

Whom could you interview to find information useful and relevant to your project? Make a list of such people. Write out first drafts of possible questions to ask them.

14 C Conducting surveys

A type of field research commonly used in the social sciences is the **survey,** a structured interview in which respondents, representative of a larger group, are all asked the same questions. Their answers are then tabulated and interpreted. Researchers usually conduct surveys to discover attitudes, beliefs, or habits of the general public or segments of the population. They may try to predict how soccer moms will vote in an election, determine the popularity of a new movie with teenage audiences, compare the eating habits of students who live off campus to those of students who eat in college dining halls, or investigate an infinite number of other issues.

Respondents to surveys can be treated like experts for research purposes, because they are being asked for their own opinions or information about their own behavior. However, you must ask your questions skillfully to get useful answers. Wording that suggests a right or wrong answer does more to reveal the researcher's biases and preconceived ideas than to collect candid responses.

Furthermore, the questions should be easy to understand and answer, and they should be reviewed to make sure they are relevant to the research topic or hypothesis. The format for questioning and the way the research is conducted also have an influence on the responses. For example, to get complete and honest answers about a sensitive or highly personal issue, the researcher would probably use anonymous written surveys to ensure confidentiality. Other survey techniques involve oral interviews, in person or by phone, in which the researcher records each subject's responses on a written form.

Surveys are usually brief to gain the cooperation of a sufficiently large number of respondents. And to enable the researcher to compare answers, the questions are usually closed, although open-ended questions may be used to gain additional information or insights.

Surveys are treated briefly here because, in truth, the designing of good survey questions, distributing of surveys, and assessment of the results is a highly complex and sophisticated business. If you are interested in systematically surveying a given population, say, of a residence hall or a class, you would be wise to consult a social scientist or an education instructor for guidelines and help. A further complication arises if your surveys request sensitive information (such as personal experience with drugs, alcohol, or sex) from identifiable subjects; most colleges and universities have "human subject" boards or committees which need to approve any research that could compromise the privacy of students, staff, or faculty. Ask your instructor for guidelines before launching on any sensitive surveys.

However, the simple, informal polling of people to request opinions takes place quite often in daily college life, such as every time a class takes a vote or a professor asks the class for opinions or interpretations about texts. In one case, a student who was writing a self-profile wanted to find out how she was perceived by others. First, Anna made a list of ten people who knew her in different ways—her mother, father, older sister, roommate, best friend, favorite teacher, and so on. Next, she invited each to make a list of five words that best characterized her. Finally, she asked each to call her answering machine on a day when she knew she would not be home and name these five words. In this way, she was able to collect original outside opinion (field research) in a nonthreatening manner that she then wove into her profile paper, combining others' opinions with her own self-assessments. The external points of view added an interesting (and sometimes surprising) view of herself as well as other voices to her paper.

Invent a simple survey (no more than five questions) to generate external information about any paper topic you are working on. To implement the survey, plan to use a one-page paper handout, a brief e-mail message, or the telephone to collect responses.

14 d Observing

Another kind of field research calls for closely observing people, places, things, or events and then describing them accurately to show readers what you saw and experienced. While the term *observation* literally denotes visual perception, it also applies to information collected on site through other senses. The following suggestions may help you conduct field observations:

Select a good site to visit. Like interviewing, observing requires that you know where to go and what to look for. You need to have your research question in mind and then to identify those places where observation will yield useful information. For example, a research project on pollution in Lake Erie would be enhanced by on-the-scene observation of what the water smells, feels, and looks like. Sometimes the site you visit is the primary object of your research, as when the purpose of your paper is to profile the people and activities you find there. At other times the site is chosen to provide supplemental evidence.

Do your homework. To observe well, you need to know what you are looking for and what you are looking at. If you are observing a political speech, know the issues and the players; if you visit an industrial complex, know what is manufactured there. Researching background information at the library or elsewhere will allow you to use your site time more efficiently.

Plan your visit. Learn not only where the place is located on a map but also how to gain access; call ahead to ask directions. Find out where you should go when you first arrive. If relevant, ask which places are open to you, which are off limits, and which you could visit with permission. Find out about visiting hours; if you want to visit at odd hours, you may need special permission. Depending on the place, after-hours visits can provide detailed information not available to the general public.

Take good notes. At any site there's a lot going on that casual observers take for granted. As a researcher you should take nothing for granted. Keep in mind that without notes, as soon as you leave a site you forget more than half of what was there. Review and

rewrite your observation notes as soon after your site visit as possible.

Since you can't write everything down, be selective. Keep your research question in mind and try to focus on the impressions that are most important in answering it. Some of your observations and notes will provide the background information needed to represent the scene vividly in your paper. Some will provide the details needed to make your paper believable. Make your notes as precise as possible, indicating the color, shape, size, texture, and arrangement of everything you can.

THINKING CRITICALLY ABOUT FIELD SOURCES

When using field sources, it is important to analyze each source's underlying assumptions and reasoning, determine the reliability and credibility of the source, and develop an interpretation of your source's information that helps you answer your research question. To assess the value of field resources, ask yourself the following questions:

- **What is the most important point this source makes?** How does it address my research question? How might this point fit into my paper and how should I articulate it?

- **What evidence did the source provide that supports this point?** Is it strong or weak? Can I use it and build on it? Should I question or refute it?

- **Does the information support my working thesis?** If so, how? How can I express the support in writing?

- **Does the information challenge my working thesis?** If so, how? Can I refute the information or contradiction? Or should I revise my thesis to take the new information into account?

- **Does the information support or contradict information collected from other sources?** How so? How can I resolve any contradictions? Do I need to seek other sources for confirmation?

- **Is the source reliable?** Does any of the information from this source seem illogical or not credible? Has any of the information been contradicted by a more authoritative source?

- **Is the source biased?** Does the interview subject have a reason to be biased in any way? Would the selection of a different site have produced different information?

Use a notebook that has a stiff cover so you can write standing, sitting, or squatting; a table may not be available. Double-entry notebooks are useful for site visits because they allow you to record facts in one column and interpretations of those facts in the other. (See Chapter 4.)

If visual images would be useful, you can sketch, photograph, or videotape. If you speak your notes into a tape recorder, you will also pick up the characteristic sounds of the site.

WRITING 5: EXPLORATION ─────────────────────────

Describe a time when you used close observation in your writing. Was it deliberate or by accident? What was your readers' response?

WRITING 6: APPLICATION ─────────────────────────

List at least three physical sites to visit that would add relevant information to your study; list at least two virtual (electronic) sites as well. Then follow the suggestions in this chapter and visit at least one of each kind.

SUGGESTIONS FOR WRITING AND RESEARCH

INDIVIDUAL

1. Plan a research project that focuses on a local place (park, playground, street, building, business, or institution) and make a research plan that includes going there, describing what you find, and interviewing somebody. Make a similar plan for at least one electronic source. Conduct the research.

2. Plan a research project that begins with an issue of some concern to you. Identify a local manifestation of this issue that would profit from field research. Also consult the library or World Wide Web to place your issue in a larger context. Conduct the research, using field techniques appropriate to your topic.

COLLABORATIVE

Create a team of two to four classmates who would like to join you in researching the project you planned for individual assignment 1 or 2 above. Plan the necessary activities to make this project work. Divide the labor so that each of you brings some information to the group by next week's class meeting. Make a copy of your research information for each group member, including typed transcripts of interviews, copies of e-mail interviews, and photocopies of visual information. You may each write an individual paper based on your collective research, or you may team up and write a collaborative paper.

Evaluating Research Sources

15

In order for writers to use research sources to support claims made in research projects, they need to ask two critical questions of each source: (1) Is the source itself credible? (2) Is it useful in the paper I am writing? These are two very different questions, as the following discussion should make clear. This chapter provides guidelines for evaluating the credibility and usefulness of sources found in the library, on the Internet, and in the field.

15 a Evaluating library sources

Many of the books, periodicals, documents, special collections, and electronic sources have been recommended for library acquisition by scholars, researchers, and librarians with special expertise in each of the many subject areas the library catalogs. Some writers may be inclined to rely on Internet research in place of research in the library because the Net now provides additional and more easily accessed sources on every imaginable topic. However, Internet sources are not subject to the same screening and cataloging process as library sources; they require special critical appraisal (which we discuss in 15b).

All information sources, whether found in the library, on the Internet, or in the field, need to be questioned by your critical intelligence for credibility, need, and usefulness. The mere fact that some authorities judged a text to be credible at one time does not mean it is the only or best or latest viewpoint on the subject or that it is especially useful to the paper you are writing. Though the library remains the main repository of knowledge on a college campus, you cannot use library sources without subjecting each source to careful scrutiny. Two of the main reasons for questioning a source found in the library have to do with *time* (when was it judged true?) and *perspective* (who said it was true and for what reason?).

▮ Locating time

Most library documents, especially those created since the advent of copyright laws at the end of the nineteenth century, include their date of publication on or inside the cover of the document itself, and in most cases this will be a fact that you can rely on. In some cases, such as articles first published in one place and now reprinted in an anthology, you may have to dig harder for the original date, but it's usually there (check especially the permissions page). The first thing you should do when you locate a potentially useful source for your paper is notice and record its date of publication.

However, one of the main reasons library sources lose reliability, and hence credibility, is the simple passage of time. Sources become outdated and, therefore, unreliable. For example, geographical, political, or statistical information largely true for 1950 will be, of necessity, changed by the year 2002—in many cases, radically so. Compare any atlas or encyclopedia entry about Africa, Cuba, Russia, Israel, or the Baltic states from fifty years ago with the latest edition of the same work, and you'll find changes so striking as to make the older source, in today's terms, completely outdated. Yet when published, this source was accurate. Pay attention to the date a source was created, and reflect on what may have happened since then. Locate reviews of the work at the time it was published by consulting *The Book Review Digest* in the library: what was the critical reception? (See 12d.)

At the same time, dated information may still be highly useful—which is why old texts remain in the library. Once you know the source date, you can make an independent judgment about whether or not it will help your paper. For example, if you are studying change over time, you may need to know statistical information that was true decades ago to show what has changed since. But if you are studying current culture, the dated information may serve no purpose at all. Used one way, an old source will get you in trouble; used as a historical reference, it may make your case. In other words, when evaluating whether a dated source serves your purpose, you need to know what that purpose is.

▮ Identifying perspective

The second critical question to ask of any source is what point of view or perspective it represents. In other words, *who created the source* and *for what purpose?* Why has someone or some organization written, constructed, compiled, or otherwise recorded this

information? This second critical question is almost always more difficult to answer by reviewing the source itself. Most library texts include the dates they were published, but many do not identify the point of view of the creator—and when they do, this information, being a creation of the author, cannot always be believed.

The best way to evaluate the usefulness of a text to your purposes is to analyze a writer's assumptions, evidence, biases, and reasoning—which together constitute his or her perspective. Such analysis also helps you figure out to whom the writer was writing and why. In essence, you need to ask, *What is this writer's purpose?* Is it scholarly analysis, political advocacy, entertainment, or something else? Can you classify the writer by point of view or differentiate him or her from others with similar points of view? What does the writer assume about the subject or about the audience? Which statements are facts, which are inferences drawn from facts, and which are strictly matters of opinion? Are there relevant points the writer *doesn't* mention? How persuasive is the evidence? How compelling is the logic? Can you infer anything about the author's beliefs or biases? Do the answers to these questions make you more or less willing to accept the author's conclusions?

WRITING I: APPLICATION ──────────────────────────────────────

Find any text source in your current research that advocates a position or makes an argument. Deduce the author's purpose; identify any assumptions about the material or the reader; trace the logic of the argument. What makes the argument persuasive? What elements weaken it?

3 Cross-referencing

Although at first it may seem daunting or even futile to try to answer all these questions about every source, have patience and give the research process the time it needs. Keep in mind that *the more you learn, the more you learn.* Your ability to think critically about a given subject doesn't necessarily come quickly or easily. Often, at the beginning of a research project, when you're still trying to gain context and overview and you've looked at only one source, it's difficult to recognize an author's purpose. However, as you read further and begin to compare one source to another, you'll begin to notice differences, especially if you read extensively and carefully and take notes on cards or in a journal about all you find. The more differences you note, the more critically aware you become and the more you know why, how, and where a source might help you.

THINKING CRITICALLY ABOUT LIBRARY SOURCES

When you have selected your library sources (see the box in 12d) and are prepared to read them more thoroughly and take notes, apply your critical thinking skills to the following issues:

- **Publication date.** What is the significance of the publication date for your purposes? Consult the *Book Review Index* to locate reviews of the book sources at the time of publication to help you evaluate their credibility. For articles in general-interest magazines and scholarly or professional journals, you can often find useful commentary in letters to the editor of subsequent issues.

- **Perspective.** In each source, what are the author's point of view and purpose? Are the claims made in the text reasonable? Is the evidence based on fact, inference, or opinion? Is the language careful or careless, neutral or biased, calm or strident? Does the author take other perspectives into account?

- **Cross-references.** Does the information in one source support or contradict that in other sources? Do a subject search of the author in the library catalog, in a general periodical index, or on the World Wide Web to find out how the author is viewed by other experts and how your source fits in with the author's other works.

Consult the opinion of other experts about the published source by looking at reviews of the work when it was published or at later critical studies of the author. To find these, do a subject search for the author in the library's catalog, in a general periodical index, or on the World Wide Web.

4 **Critical reading**

To learn more about critically analyzing textual sources, especially those found in the library, review 2b on reading critically, and plan to ask both first and second questions of the text. (See pp. 14–15.) In short, the answers to first questions are generally factual, the result of probing the text (identifying the title, table of contents, chapter headings, index, and so on). The answers to second questions are more inferential, the result of analyzing the assertions, evidence, and language of the text (identifying the perspective of author and sources).

List three library sources you have consulted for a current research paper. Evaluate each according to timeliness and perspective. Which ones do you agree with? What is it about each source that makes you willing to rely on it or agree with it?

15 b Evaluating electronic sources

Anyone with a computer and a modem can publish opinion, advocacy, research claims, even bomb-making instructions on the Internet. That openness raises a caution for anyone relying on Internet sources for information. Material published on the Internet does not have to meet the standards of fairness, accuracy, or statistical validity demanded by, say, a peer-reviewed academic journal, a college library, or a daily newspaper. Much Internet material does meet such standards, but a great deal does not. How can you distinguish what is credible from what is questionable? And what do the differences mean for your research writing?

Evaluating a Web site

One indication of the type of information on a site comes from the electronic address (URL). The extension at the end identifies the type of organization that published the site. Six of these extensions, also called *top-level domain names,* have been in use since 1988.

commercial business	.com
educational	.edu
government	.gov
military	.mil
news and other networks	.net
nonprofit organization	.org

Seven new domain extensions are coming into use.

aviation	.aero
commercial business	.biz
cooperative businesses	.coop
informational sites	.info
licensed professionals	.pro
museums and museum staff	.museum
personal names	.name

The extension suggests the nature of the site. Sites with .gov and .mil can be expected to present official information from the sponsoring agencies. Nonprofit organizations usually have distinctive points of view that their sites are likely to reflect. (To see how an organization's viewpoint can saturate a site, visit the Sierra Club site <http://www.sierraclub.org> and the National Rifle Association site <http://www.nra.org>.) Commercial sites—*.com, .biz*—may be promotional, sales-oriented, or informational. Informational sites—*.inf*—are just coming into use at this time, but they will be open to all Internet users posting information of any type, including marketing, advocacy, entertainment, and promotion. An individual's site—signified by *.name* or a tilde ~ in the URL—usually represents one person's point of view, and in that case you have to determine how credible that individual is. Sites associated with educational institutions—*.edu*—may represent an entire university, a working group, a department, or an individual.

An address extension is not a complete indicator of a site's reliability or of its value to your research. Suppose you're writing about a topic in history and find a .edu site on the same topic made by a history class at another school. The site itself is a secondary source, so you may not want to rely on it directly. But it may contain useful references to primary or more authoritative sources that will be valuable to you. It also may give you a sense for what other students have to say about your subject. As another example, you may not feel comfortable relying on a commercial site as a secondary source for what it may say about history or particle physics, but such a site is a primary source for what the sponsoring company says about itself.

The domain name—the portion just before .com or .edu—may or may not indicate who owns the site. Sometimes the difference between one institution's official site and another, unrelated one is only a single letter or a hyphen. (See Identifying Ownership of Internet Resources, page 224.)

You should question every Internet source at least as exhaustively as you would any print source—evaluating its timeliness, its claims of authority, and its point of view. One good question is whether the electronic source has a print counterpart—a peer-reviewed journal, a respected periodical, or a book that might be chosen for a college library. Then you can assign roughly the same value to the Internet source as to its print cousin.

Most Internet sources are not so easy to evaluate. Ultimately you must be the judge of what materials you will rely on. We suggest asking **reporter's questions** of each source (*who, what, when, where, why,* and *how*). The answers to these questions will give you a basis for evaluating each source.

WHO IS THE AUTHOR OF THE SITE?

- Does the site say who created it?

- Is the author authoritative, by virtue of credentials, experience, or displayed knowledge?

- Does the author cite his or her credentials? (On a scientific site, for example, does the author have a degree in a relevant field? What level of degree?)

- Does the author speak in an official capacity for an organization, institution, or government agency?

- If no individual is named, is there a sponsoring organization? What do you know or what can you find out about the organization? Search the Web or your library for information.

- Does the site provide a link to the organization's or author's home page?

- Is there a way to contact the author or organization, by mail, telephone, or e-mail?

- If you cannot identify the author or sponsor of the site, how does that affect your estimate of its credibility? How will it affect your readers? (See box on Identifying Anonymous Internet Sources.)

WHAT IDEAS OR INFORMATION IS PRESENTED?

- Do you understand the ideas and the terms?

- Can you summarize the central ideas or claims in your own words?

- Would you judge the information to be substantial or superficial?

- Are reported facts supported by verifiable citations? If not, are you confident of their accuracy?

- Does the site contain facts, inference, analysis, opinion, speculation? Is the author careful to distinguish among these types of information? (See 9e.)

- Is the information balanced or one-sided? Are other points of view respectfully addressed, dismissed, or ignored? If other viewpoints are ignored or treated derisively, be wary.

- Does the site contain advertising? Is it clearly identified and separated from other material?

- What information is missing?

WHERE DOES THE INFORMATION COME FROM?

- Note the domain name and the extension—*.com, .edu, .gov, .org, .info.* Do you recognize the sponsoring organization? (See page 217.)

- Does the author identify the source of the information or describe how it was generated?

- Has the information appeared previously in print? Was there a reputable source?

- Can you tell whether the information has been peer-reviewed?

WHEN WAS THE SITE CREATED?

- How recently was the site updated, or when was the information posted?

- How does a missing date affect the information's credibility?

- Is the site complete or under construction? (If not complete, include that information in your citation.)

- Does the site appear to change frequently? In any case, make a printout including the date and URL so that if the site is revised, you have a record of what it said.

WHY IS THE INFORMATION PRESENTED?

- Does the purpose seem to be to inform, persuade, entertain, sell?

- Is the graphic presentation effective and unobtrusive? Does sound or animation contribute or detract?

- Are there links to other sites? Are the links current? Are the linked sites authoritative?

2 Asking critical questions of Web sources

Jordan was researching the early political career of Theodore Roosevelt. Here are some of the questions he raised and his evaluation of two Web sites he found.

The Theodore Roosevelt Association site:

- **Who?** the page <http://www.theodoreroosevelt.org/> says the Theodore Roosevelt Association was chartered by Congress in 1920 and that it provides "authoritative information on the life and ideals of Theodore Roosevelt." The *.org* domain name indicates a nonprofit organization. The mission statement—to inform the public of Roosevelt's "the great and historic contributions" suggest that the site will present an overwhelmingly positive view of the man. Will that view be balanced?

- **What?** The site has a wealth of relevant facts, such as a timeline of Roosevelt's life and images of pages from his diary. The dates are likely to be reliable, and the diary pages constitute a primary source. There is little reference to criticism of his work or policies,

Theodore Roosevelt Association home page

although biographies critical of Roosevelt are summarized in a bibliography.

- **Where?** The authors of the page are not named, but the site names the director and trustees and provides a mailing address, phone numbers, and e-mail addresses.

- **Why?** The mission statement says the organization exits "to instill in all who may be interested an appreciation for and understanding of the values, policies, cares, concerns, interests, and ideals that Theodore Roosevelt held." Again, the organization's point of view is clear.

- **How?** The site uses Roosevelt's own words, photographs, diary, and descriptions of his major actions as "achievements" to present a positive view of him. Jordan concluded he could rely on the site for many facts, some primary data, and a favorable view of Roosevelt. But he would have to look elsewhere for other perspectives on the man.

The Almanac of Theodore Roosevelt site:

- **Who?** The site <http://www.theodore-roosevelt.com/> doesn't identify its author, but it offers an e-mail link to its "webmaster." The site offers information about major segments Roosevelt's life, his achievements, and his family history. Links to other information are full of government sites, historical foundations, and reputable online publishers. The lack of an identified author is unsettling, but the wealth of facts displayed increases the site's credibility. A *whois* search found the registered owner of the name *theodore-roosevelt.com* and provided a mailing address. (See box on Identifying Anonymous Internet Sources on page 224.)

- **What?** The site is rich with historical photographs, political cartoons, film and sound clips, even a diagram of Roosevelt's famous charge up San Juan Hill. Not all sources are credited. There are numerous links to related materials, all of which seem to be reputable and authoritative. The site reproduces some primary documents, but Jordan felt more comfortable citing similar documents as reproduced on more carefully documented sites.

- **Where?** There is no mailing address apparent on the main site, only the e-mail link and a copyright line.

- **When?** Copyright is claimed for 1999 through 2002, and the site was updated less than three weeks before Jordan visited. That was encouraging.

- **Why?** There is no statement of purpose, but an enthusiasm for Theodore Roosevelt and his story shines through the pages.

T.R.

THEODORE ROOSEVELT
26th President of the United States of America

Theodore Roosevelt

BIOGRAPHY
Quick Facts
Biographical Summary
Genealogy—NEW

**Support
the
U.S.S. Theodore Roosevelt**
Click here for more information

TIMELINE—NEW
The Roosevelt Era: 1901-1909
Crossword Puzzle

Quote of the Week

Congressional
Medal of Honor

The Homes of
Theodore Roosevelt
Sagamore Hill
Birthplace in New York City
Maltese Cross - Ekhorn Ranches
Pine Knot
Bulloch Hall

The Star Spangled Banner Manuscript
U.S. Declaration of Independence
The U.S. Constitution

TR IN CARTOONS
Harper's Weekly
Puck
Opper's "Willie & His Papa" Series
Judge
Berryman's "Teddy Bear" Series
Other Cartoons

T.R.
in
Film and Sound

The Presidential Years
Accomplishments
Cabinet

Almanac of Theodore Roosevelt home page

- **How?** Although the site organization and execution are highly professional and the site is informative, Jordan concluded that the incomplete information about authorship, purpose, and sources weaken the site's usefulness as a resource for college-level research. He read the site carefully but resolved to check key facts against other sources.

WRITING 3: APPLICATION ────────────────────────────

List two Internet sources you have considered using for a current research paper. For each, answer the questions *who, what, when, where, why,* and *how.* Which site is more trustworthy? Which one do you agree with more? What about each source makes you more or less willing to rely on it?

IDENTIFYING THE OWNERSHIP OF INTERNET RESOURCES

Every Internet domain name, such as *google.com,* must be registered, and you can look up the name and address of each registered owner. Domain name registries also usually contain postal or e-mail addresses. The search tool for finding this information is called *WHOIS.* Click on the WHOIS link at Network Solutions, <http://www.netsol.com>. Enter only the second-level and top-level domain name (*google.com,* not *www.google.com*), and WHOIS returns the owner's name, address, and contact information. However, a site that makes you search for such information, rather than providing it, should not inspire confidence.

15 C Evaluating field sources

Everything said about critically questioning library sources would hold true for critically questioning field sources if people and places were as carefully documented, reviewed, and cataloged as library sources. Evaluation of your source is just as important when you are interviewing someone or visiting a Web site as it is when you are referring to printed texts. But you need to realize that verifiability—and therefore reliability and credibility—is more problematic for field sources than it is for multiple copies of cataloged texts that stay put in time and space. In other words, it is often more difficult for readers to track down field sources than text sources.

Interviews

An interview is usually a one-time event. The subject may no longer be available for cross-checking; a business or other place that provides you with information one day may change or become off limits the next day and so may become inaccessible. Be careful to find out whether an individual speaks for an organization or for him- or herself alone. Get permission in advance from the interviewee if you plan to tape-record. Then after the interview subject agrees to be recorded, start the recorder, and ask again for permission to record so you have confirming evidence of that agreement. Basically, what you will be doing is "freezing" the interview, but take copious notes anyway. With your recording to back you up, you do not need to be literal. Then transcribe the whole session. Having the transcript of an interview not only will allow you to quote exactly what was said but also will let you pick and choose from a variety of accurate statements. You can use only those that best support your case. Once an interview is taped, you can apply to it all the critical and analytical questions you would to a written source, asking for other opinions to verify certain statements or, if your interviewee is a public figure, looking up his or her record in a newspaper index or biographical review. If you cannot tape-record, take notes as carefully as possible; review main points with your subject before the interview ends, and then, at your leisure, apply as many as possible of the same analytical procedures to your notes as you would to a cataloged text.

For example, in writing a paper about local lake pollution, you might interview a biology professor who teaches a college course on lake pollution. In her office, she tells you that the most severe pollution is caused not by paper mills but by farm fertilizer—which surprises you. After transcribing your tape (or reviewing your notes), you cross-check her assertion by talking to other experts in the state department of natural resources and by reviewing text sources found in the library or on the World Wide Web. Note how you've been critical in two ways: first, you sought out an expert whose credentials gave her advance credibility; second you sought to verify her statements by confirming them with other reliable sources.

Site Visits

Any research essay written about a topic with local dimensions gains credibility when it shows evidence the writer has investigated it firsthand. For example, a recent first-year research paper

focused on the practical introduction of electric automobiles into America's car culture. Adam visited the local organization promoting these cars, interviewed the manager, and test-drove one of the electric vehicles. While his paper also included conventional sources from periodicals, it gained extra credibility from his personal account, his interview quotations, statements from brochures, and photographs of the vehicle he took for a test ride.

When you visit a place to locate evidence to support the claims you make in a paper, make photographic or video records of what it looks like and what you find. Take copious notes about time, sensory details, location, size, shape, color, number, and so forth. Pictures and careful verbal descriptions essentially freeze your visit and will help you in writing the paper in several ways. First, in writing your paper, you may include the photographs as well as specific details that would be difficult to invent had you not been present—both of which add credibility for original research. Second, even if you do not include photos or directly quote your notes, they will still jog your memory about what, exactly, you found and thus help you write more accurately. Finally, these recordings—assuming they are relatively objective in perspective and language—will help you maintain a neutral rather than a biased perspective.

On the one hand, evaluating the usefulness of an interview or site visit is simple: ask yourself whether the details gathered on your visit to the site support the assertions made by your paper. (See the box in 14d for tips on evaluating field research.) In his essay, for instance, Adam was able to testify positively to the electric car's quietness and ample acceleration as well as negatively, noting his fear the battery would run down before he returned to a charging station.

On the other hand, evaluating any field source becomes more complicated when you realize that you are both the creator and evaluator of the material at the same time. In site visits, the material is out there, and in and of itself, it has no meaning or value until you, the recorder, assign it. This material has not been filtered through the lens of another writer. *You* are the interpreter of what you witness, and when you introduce field evidence, it's your own bias that will show up in the way you use language; you will lead your reader one way or another depending on whether you describe the lake water as *cloudy, murky,* or *filthy* or label the electric car as *slow, hesitant,* or *a dog.* In other words, you assign a value to (evaluate) your field evidence by the way you present it in your paper.

THINKING CRITICALLY ABOUT YOUR ROLE IN FIELD RESEARCH

You participate directly in both the creation and the evaluation of interview and site-visit material you introduce into your research essays.

- You shape interview material through the questions you ask, the manner in which you conduct the interview, and the language of your notes.
- You shape on-site material through where you look, what you notice, and the language of your notes.
- You assign value to the field sources through the way you collect and record them; consequently, the primary bias you need to control and account for is your own.

WRITING 4: APPLICATION ━━━━━━━━━━━━━━━━━━

List two field sources for a current research paper. Examine each for evidence of your role in creating it and for evidence of your bias. Which source did you find more trustworthy? Which one helped your paper more? Why? Looking back, what would you have done differently during your interview or site visit? How do you plan to make up for any limitations of your field research?

16 Using Sources

Locating potential sources for a research project is one thing; deciding which ones to include, where to use them, and how to incorporate them is something else. Some writers begin making use of their sources in early exploratory drafts, perhaps by trying out a pithy quotation to see how it brings a paragraph into focus. Others prefer to sift and arrange all of their note cards in neat stacks before making any decisions about what to include in their essays. No matter how you begin writing with sources, there comes a time when you will need to incorporate them finally, smoothly, effectively, and correctly into your paper.

16 a Controlling your sources

Once you've conducted some research and are ready to begin planning and/or drafting your essay, you need to decide which sources you will use and how you will use them. You can't make this decision on the basis of how much time you spent finding and analyzing each source; you have to decide according to how useful the source is in answering your research question. In other words, you need to control your sources rather than letting them control you.

Real research about real questions is vital and dynamic, which means it's always changing. Just as you can't expect your first working thesis to be your final thesis, you can't expect to know in advance which sources are going to prove most fruitful. And don't think that you can't collect more information once you've begun drafting. At each step in the process you see your research question and answer more clearly, so the research you conduct as you write may be the most useful of all. Similarly, and perhaps especially when engaging in field research, writers of research essays often gain an increased sense of audience as their research progresses, which pays off in increasingly reader-oriented writing.

16 b Organizing your sources

One of the best strategies for maintaining personal control of your research essay is to make an outline first and then organize your notes accordingly. (If you compose an outline on a computer, it will be easier to make changes later on. The same goes for your notes if you've written them on a computer.) If you do it the other way around—organizing your notes in a logical sequence and then writing an outline based on that sequence—you'll be tempted to find a place for every note and to gloss over areas where you haven't done enough research.

1 Outline your research conclusions

If you **outline** your research conclusions first, you let the logical flow of ideas create a blueprint for your paper. (Of course, your outline may change as your ideas continue to develop.) If you can't outline before you write, then be sure to begin writing—if only by drafting a "topic sentence" outline to start major sections—before you arrange your note cards.

2 Organize your supporting evidence

Once you have outlined or begun drafting and have a good sense of the shape of your paper, **organize** your notes. Arrange the note cards so that they correspond to your outline, and put bibliographic cards in alphabetical order by the author's last name. Integrate field research notes as best you can, depending on their format. Finally, go back to your outline and annotate it to indicate which source goes where. By doing this, you can see whether there are any ideas that need more research.

16 c Synthesizing information from sources

As you prepare to draft, you need to assess all the information you have found and decide which sources are useful. Read your notes critically to evaluate each source, and **synthesize** the material into a new, coherent whole.

Synthesizing material involves looking for connections among different pieces of information and formulating ideas about what these connections mean. The connections may be similar statements made by several sources or contradictions between two sources. Try to reach some conclusions on your own that extend

beyond the information in front of you; then use those conclusions to form the goals for your paper.

Next, decide how you will use your source information; base your decisions on your goals for the paper and not on the format of your research notes. Papers written in an effort "to get everything in" are source-driven and all too often read like patch jobs of quotations loosely strung together. Your goal should be to remain the director of the research production, your ideas on center stage and your sources the supporting cast. By synthesizing your information into a unique presentation, you remain at center stage.

Also, keep in mind that referring more than two or three times to a single source—unless it is itself the focus of your paper—undercuts your credibility and suggests overreliance on a single point of view. On the other hand, using synthesis to show how ideas from different sources relate to each other as well as how they relate to your own stance greatly improves the coherence of your essay. If you find yourself referring largely to one source—and therefore one point of view—make sure that you have sufficient references to add other points of view to your paper.

WRITING 1: EXPLORATION

Describe your experience writing a recent research paper. What kind of clues can you recall that would indicate whether you or your sources controlled that paper?

WRITING 2: APPLICATION

Use your research log to draft a tentative thesis and working outline for your research paper. Then arrange your note cards according to that outline. If you can, work out a second option for essay arrangement. This procedure is simplified if your notes are computerized. If you do rearrange your notes via computer, however, be sure to save a copy of each arrangement in case you decide to return to it.

16 d Integrating information from sources

Once you know which sources you want to use, you still have to decide how the ideas from these sources will appear in your paper. The notes you made during your research may be in many forms. For some sources, you will have copied down direct quotations; for others, you will have paraphrased or summarized important information. For some field sources, you may have made

extensive notes on background information, such as your interview subject's appearance. Simply because you've quoted or paraphrased a particular source in your notes, however, doesn't mean you have to use a quotation or paraphrase from this source in your paper. Make decisions about how to use sources based on your goals, not on the format of your research notes.

At this point, it might be helpful for you to consider our suggestion that taking notes in your own words can pay major dividends in your research-based writing. Of major importance, of course, is the fact that drafting directly from quotations leads to a source-controlled essay—and frequently to a shortage of connecting information between ideas. As was explained in 12e3, taking notes in your own words also helps your comprehension of the ideas and arguments you've read. It encourages you mentally to digest material rather than simply copying, and it makes your rereading of the notes more meaningful. For these and other reasons, practices such as photocopying large chunks of material or downloading them via computer are no substitute for the note-*writing* portion of your research work.

Moreover, whether you quote, paraphrase, or summarize, you must acknowledge your source through documentation. Different disciplines have different conventions for documentation. The examples in this chapter use the documentation style of the Modern Language Association (MLA), the style preferred in the languages and literature field. (For documentation styles of specific disciplines, see Chapters 54–60.)

Quoting effectively

Direct quotation provides strong evidence and can add both life and authenticity to your paper.

To quote, you must use an author's or speaker's exact words. Slight changes in wording are permitted in certain cases, but these changes must be clearly marked. Although you can't change what a source says, you do have control over how much of it you use. Too much quotation can imply that you have little to say for yourself. Use only as long a quotation as you need to make your point. Remember that quotations should be used to support your points, not to say them for you.

Shortening quotations

Long quotations slow readers down and often have the unintended effect of inviting them to skip over the quoted material. Unless the source quoted is itself the topic of the paper (as in a literary

WHEN TO QUOTE

Direct quotation should be reserved for cases in which you cannot express the ideas better yourself. Use quotations when the original words are especially precise, clear, powerful, or vivid.

- **Precise.** Use quotations when the words are important in themselves or when the author makes fine but important distinctions.

Government, even in its best state, is but a necessary evil; in it worst state, an intolerable one.

THOMAS PAINE

- **Clear.** Use quotation when the author's ideas are complex and difficult to paraphrase.

Paragraphs tell readers how writers want to be read.

WILLIAM BLAKE

- **Powerful.** Use quotation when the words are especially authoritative and memorable.

You shall know the truth, and the truth shall make you free.

ABRAHAM LINCOLN

- **Vivid.** Use quotation when the language is lively and colorful, when it reveals something of the author's or speaker's character.

Writing, I'm more involved in it, but not as attached.

KAREN, A STUDENT

interpretation), limit brief quotations to no more than two per page and long quotations to no more than one every three pages.

Be sure that when you shorten a quotation, you have not changed its meaning. If you omit words within quotations for the sake of brevity, you must indicate that you have done so by using **ellipsis** points. Any changes or additions must be indicated with brackets. (See 44c–44d for more on ellipses and brackets.)

ORIGINAL   If they were candid, most magicians would say they are trying to entertain us by hiding the truth. They challenge us to discover what they have hidden. And we respond by trying to figure out the underlying causes of the magical effects and illusions we see. Like scientists, we search for the truth, for what might be hidden from our senses.

MICHAEL STRAUSS, *THE MAGICAL CLASSROOM* (2)

INACCURATE   In *The Magical Classroom,* Michael Strauss says that "most magicians . . . search for the truth" (2).

By omitting certain words, the writer has changed the meaning of the original source.

ACCURATE
QUOTATION   In *The Magical Classroom,* Michael Strauss says that "most magicians" attempt to entertain their audiences "by hiding the truth" (2).

Integrating quotations into your paper

Direct quotations will be most effective when you integrate them smoothly into the flow of your paper. You can do this by providing an explanatory "tag" or by giving one or more sentences of explanation. Readers should be able to follow your meaning easily and to see the relevance of the quotation immediately.

Using embedded or block format. Brief quotations should be embedded in the main body of your paper and enclosed in quotation marks. According to MLA style guidelines, a brief quotation consists of four or fewer typed lines.

> In *The Magical Classroom* Michael Strauss says, "If they were candid, most magicians would say they are trying to entertain us by hiding the truth" (2).

Longer quotations should be set off in block format. Begin a new line, indent ten spaces (for MLA), and do not use quotation marks.

> In *The Magical Classroom* Michael Strauss says:
>
> > If they were candid, most magicians would say they are trying to entertain us by hiding the truth. They challenge us to discover what they have hidden. And we respond by trying to figure out the underlying causes of the magical effects and illusions we see. Like scientists, we search for the truth, for what might be hidden from our senses. (2)

(See Chapter 43 for more on punctuating quotations.)

Introducing quotations. Introduce all quoted material so that readers know who is speaking, what the quotation refers to, and where it is from. If the author or speaker is well-known, it is especially useful to mention his or her name in an introductory signal phrase.

> Henry David Thoreau asserts in *Walden,* "The mass of men lead lives of quiet desperation" (5).

VERBS USED IN SIGNAL PHRASES

The verb you choose for a signal phrase should accurately reflect the intention of the source. Notice that some of these verbs require an object.

acknowledge	concede	illustrate	report
admit	conclude	imply [this idea]	reveal
agree	declare	insist	say
argue	deny	maintain	show
assert	emphasize	note	state
believe	endorse [this idea]	observe	suggest
claim	find	point out	think
comment	grant	refute [this idea]	write

There are certain *signal phrases* or *attributory phrases* to tell the reader that the words or ideas that follow come from another source. Choose a signal phrase that reflects the source's intentions, and to avoid monotony, vary the placement of the signal phrases you use.

If your paper focuses on written works, you can introduce a quotation with the title rather than the author's name, as long as the reference is clear.

> *Walden* sets forth one individual's antidote against the "lives of quiet desperation" led by the working class in mid-nineteenth-century America (Thoreau 5).

If neither the author nor the title of a written source is well known (or the speaker is a field source), introduce the quotation with a brief explanation to give your readers some context.

> Mary Catherine Bateson, daughter of anthropologist Margaret Mead, has become, in her own right, a student of modern civilization. In *Composing a Life* she writes, "The twentieth century has been called the century of the refugee because of the vast numbers of people uprooted by war and politics from their homes" (8).

Explaining and clarifying quotations. Sometimes you will need to explain a quotation in order to clarify why it's relevant and what it means in the context of your discussion.

> In *A Sand County Almanac,* Aldo Leopold invites modern urban readers to confront what they lose by living in the city: "There are

two spiritual dangers in not owning a farm. One is the danger of supposing that breakfast comes from the grocery, and the other that heat comes from the furnace" (6). Leopold sees city-dwellers as self-centered children, blissfully but dangerously unaware of how their basic needs are met.

You may also need to clarify what a word or reference means. Do this by using square brackets. (See 44d.)

Adjusting grammar when using quotations. A passage containing a quotation must follow all the rules of grammatical sentence structure: tenses should be consistent, verbs and subjects should agree, and so on. If the form of the quotation doesn't quite fit the grammar of your own sentences, you can either quote less of the original source, change your sentences, or make a slight alteration in the quotation. Use this last option sparingly, and always indicate any changes with brackets.

UNCLEAR
> In *A Sand County Almanac,* Aldo Leopold follows various animals, including a skunk and a rabbit, through fresh snow. He wonders, "What got him out of bed?" (5).

It is not clear whether him refers to the skunk or the rabbit.

CLEAR
> In *A Sand County Almanac,* Aldo Leopold follows various animals, including a skunk and a rabbit, through fresh snow. He wonders, "What got [the skunk] out of bed?" (5).

GRAMMATICALLY INCOMPATIBLE
> In *A Sand County Almanac,* Aldo Leopold said that living in the city is a "spiritual danger" if people "supposing that breakfast comes from the grocery."

To be grammatically correct, the writer needs to change supposing from a gerund (-ing word) to the verb form suppose. One way is to make the change inside the quotation marks with brackets.

GRAMMATICALLY COMPATIBLE
> In *A Sand County Almanac,* Aldo Leopold said that living in the city is a "spiritual danger" if people "[suppose] that breakfast comes from the grocery."

Another option is to start the quotation one word later.

GRAMMATICALLY COMPATIBLE
> In *A Sand County Almanac,* Aldo Leopold said that living in the city is a "spiritual danger" if people assume "that breakfast comes from the grocery".

Still another option is to recast the sentence completely.

GRAMMATICALLY
COMPATIBLE
According to Aldo Leopold, city dwellers who assume "that breakfast comes from the grocery" are out of tune with the world of nature (*A Sand County Almanac* 6).

WRITING 3: APPLICATION

Read through your research materials, highlighting any quotations you might want to incorporate into your paper. Use your research log to explore why you think these words should be quoted directly. Also note where in your essay a quotation would add clarity, color, or life; then see if you can find one to serve that purpose.

2 Paraphrasing effectively

Although it is generally wiser to write as many research notes as possible in your own words, you may have written down or photocopied many quotations instead of taking the time to put an author's or speaker's ideas into your own words.

To **paraphrase,** you restate a source's ideas in your own words. The point of paraphrasing is to make the ideas clearer (both to your readers and to yourself) and to express the ideas in the way that best suits your purpose. In paraphrasing, attempt to preserve the intent of the original statement and to fit the paraphrased statement smoothly into the immediate context of your essay.

The best way to make an accurate paraphrase is to stay close to the order and structure of the original passage, to reproduce its emphasis and details. However, don't use the same sentence

---

WHEN TO PARAPHRASE

Paraphrases generally re-create the original source's order, structure, and emphasis and include most of its details.

- **Clarity.** Use paraphrase to make complex ideas clear to your readers.
- **Details.** Use paraphrase to tailor the presentation of details that an author or speaker has described at great length to the goals of your paper.
- **Emphasis.** Use paraphrase when including an author's or speaker's point suits the emphasis you want to make in your paper.

STRATEGIES FOR PARAPHRASING

Writers who are inexperienced at paraphrasing in English sometimes just substitute synonyms for some of the author's words, keeping the sentence structure and many of the words the same. This kind of paraphrasing is unacceptable in academic writing; it can be considered a form of plagiarism. (See 16g.) Here are some suggestions that may help you write effective paraphrases:

- Before you begin writing a paraphrase of a sentence or passage, make sure that you understand the author's meaning. Look up in a dictionary any words you don't know, and ask a native speaker of English about any idioms or slang with which you are unfamiliar.

- Look away from the original source and put the ideas into your own words.

- If you are paraphrasing a passage, don't paraphrase the information one sentence at a time. Instead, try to express the meaning of the entire passage.

- Consider the context of the sentence or passage you are paraphrasing. Are there any references that are clear only from the surrounding sentences? Make sure you have given your readers enough information to understand your paraphrase.

- Use a thesaurus to find synonyms if you need to, but use only words you are familiar with. Not every synonym for a word listed in a thesaurus will be appropriate in your sentences.

patterns or vocabulary or you risk inadvertently plagiarizing the source. (See 16g2.)

If the original source has used a well-established or technical term for a concept, you do not need to find a synonym for it. If you believe that the original source's exact words are the best possible expressions of some points, you may use brief direct quotations within your paraphrase, as long as you indicate these with quotation marks.

Keep in mind why you are including this source; doing so will help you to decide how to phrase the ideas. Be careful, though, not to introduce your own comments or reflections in the middle of a paraphrase unless you make it very clear that these are your thoughts, not the original author's or speaker's.

ORIGINAL   The affluent, educated, liberated women of the First
             World, who can enjoy freedom unavailable to any woman

ever before, do not feel as free as they want to. And they
can no longer restrict to the subconscious their sense
that this lack of freedom has something to do with—with
apparently frivolous issues, things that really should not
matter. Many are ashamed to admit that such trivial
concerns—to do with physical appearance, bodies,
faces, hair, clothes—matter so much.

NAOMI WOLF, THE BEAUTY MYTH (9)

INACCURATE
PARAPHRASE

In *The Beauty Myth,* Naomi Wolf argues that First World
women, who still have less freedom than they would like
to have, restrict to their subconscious those matters
having to do with physical appearance—things that are
not really important to them (9).

ACCURATE
PARAPHRASE

In *The Beauty Myth,* Wolf asserts that First World
women, despite their affluence, education, and liberation, still do not feel very free. Moreover, many of these
women are aware that this lack of freedom is influenced
by superficial things having primarily to do with their
physical appearance—things that should not matter
so much (9).

WRITING 4: APPLICATION ─────────────────────────

Read through your note cards for any passages you quoted directly from an
original source. Find notes that now seem wordy, unclear, or longer than necessary. Paraphrase notes that you expect to use in your paper. Exchange your
paraphrases and the originals with a classmate, and assess each other's work.

3 Summarizing effectively

To **summarize,** you distill a source's words down to the main
ideas and state these in your own words. A summary includes only
the essentials of the original source, not the supporting details, and
is consequently shorter than the original.

Keep in mind that summaries are generalizations and that too
many generalizations can make your writing vague and tedious.
You should occasionally supplement summaries with brief direct
quotations or evocative details collected through observation to
keep readers in touch with the original source.

Summaries vary in length, and the length of the original source
is not necessarily related to the length of the summary you write.
Depending on the focus of your paper, you may need to summarize
an entire novel in a sentence or two, or you may need to summarize
a brief journal article in two or three paragraphs. Remember that

WHEN TO SUMMARIZE

As you draft, summarize often so that your paper doesn't turn into a string of undigested quotations.

- **Main points.** Use summary when your readers need to know the main point the original source makes but not the supporting details.
- **Overviews.** Sometimes you may want to devise a few sentences that will effectively support your discussion without going on and on. Use summary to provide an overview or an interesting aside without digressing too far from your paper's focus.
- **Condensation.** You may have taken extensive notes on a particular article or observation only to discover in the course of drafting that you do not need all that detail. Use summary to condense lengthy or rambling notes into a few effective sentences.

the more material you attempt to summarize in a short space, the more you will necessarily generalize and abstract it. Reduce a text as far as you can while still providing all the information your readers need to know. Be careful, though, not to distort the original's meaning.

ORIGINAL   For a long time I never liked to look a chimpanzee straight in the eye—I assumed that, as is the case with most primates, this would be interpreted as a threat or at least as a breach of good manners. Not so. As long as one looks with gentleness, without arrogance, a chimpanzee will understand and may even return the look.

JANE GOODALL, *THROUGH A WINDOW* (12)

INACCURATE SUMMARY   Goodall learned from her experiences with chimpanzees that they react positively to direct looks from humans (12).

ACCURATE SUMMARY   Goodall reports that when humans look directly but gently into chimpanzees' eyes, the chimps are not threatened and may even return the look (12).

WRITING 5: EXPLORATION ━━━━━━━━━━━━━━━━━━━

Review any sources on which you have taken particularly extensive notes. Would it be possible to condense these notes into a briefer summary of the entire work? Would it serve your purpose to do so? Why or why not?

16 e Using Internet sources

In 15b, we discussed at great length the pitfalls of relying on biased and anonymous Internet sources, stressing the importance of establishing the credibility of any Web source you intend to import into your academic writing. Because the Internet contains virtually every imaginable kind of information from every imaginable source, you need to introduce genuinely useful Web information in your papers with extra care.

One of the main features of academic writing is the assumption that it is based on critically examined sources of information. If sources are questionable to begin with, a paper relying uncritically on them will be questionable. Consequently, when you quote, paraphrase, or summarize *authoritative* sources from the World Wide Web—and there are many such sources on the Web—you need to be sure to emphasize the nature of that authority when you introduce the source. Although library and field sources also need to be introduced carefully, readers don't regard them with quite the skepticism and distrust they've learned while surfing the Net.

The best way to feature the credibility of your Web source is with an identifying signal phrase that emphasizes the quality of your source. For example, students investigating the recent trouble caused by the invasion of zebra mussels into Lake Champlain found more than a thousand sources of information listed on the Web, but the majority of them proved to be commercial sites that promised to solve a beach owner's problems with clogged water pipes or an infested beach.

The student researchers deemed the most credible information to come from nonprofit sources such as the U.S. Fish and Wildlife Service, so they made sure to feature the source name in a signal phrase:

> According to Madeleine Lyttle of the U.S. Fish and Wildlife
> Service, "The most imminent biotic threat from zebra
> mussel infestation is the decimation of native freshwater
> mussel populations."

Using the MLA documentation style, the researchers listed the full citation of this Web source alphabetically on the Works Cited page, complete with title, address, and date accessed:

Lyttle, Madeleine. "U.S. Fish and Wildlife Service, Lake Champlain Fish and
Wildlife Resources Complex." 14 Aug. 1998. Lake Champlain Ecosystem
Team. 17 Dec. 1998 <http:// 127.0.0.1:7654>.

More so than with government sources, readers may question the accuracy of information attributed to for-profit companies found on the Web, such as Lake Guard or Zebra-Tech, because of their obvious interest in selling a product or a service. However, such sources can still be useful to writers of research papers, especially if more disinterested sources are cited as well. For example, in using these sources in a paper, the writers increased their own credibility by pointing out their awareness of the commercial nature of the source:

> According to companies that specialize in fighting zebra
> mussels, such as Lake Guard and Zebra-Tech, multiple
> measures need to be taken to ensure the long-term
> eradication of zebra mussels from a given location.

No further in-text citation is necessary because interested readers may consult the Works Cited page to find the source of the Lake Guard or Zebra-Tech information—each of which will have an identifying URL.

16 f Using sources in an I-search essay

If you are writing an I-search paper, it is common to include the process of your search—where you found your information—along with its results. It is equally common to write such an essay in magazine style rather than academic style—that is, embedding the most necessary source information within the text as *The New Yorker* or *Newsweek* would and skipping the Works Cited or References page traditionally required in academic paper. Amanda's I-search essay (see 17b) introduces her book sources this way:

> A subject search turned up two books by M. Lee Upcraft
> that looked especially useful, Residence Hall Assistants in
> College and Learning to Be a Resident Assistant.
> According to Upcraft, before you sign on to become an RA,
> you need to ask yourself, "Can [I] turn in someone who is
> my friend?" (Learning 7).

16 g Understanding and avoiding plagiarism

Acknowledging your sources through one of the accepted systematic styles of **documentation** is a service to your sources, your readers, and future scholars. Knowledge in the academic community is cumulative, with one writer's work building on another's. After reading your paper, readers may want to know more about a source you cited, perhaps in order to use it in papers of their own. Correct documentation helps them find the source quickly and easily.

Failure to document your sources is a type of **plagiarism.** Plagiarism is taking someone's ideas or information and passing them off as your own. The practice of citing sources for "borrowed" ideas or words is both customary and expected in academic writing.

Most plagiarism is not intentional: many writers are simply unaware of the conventional guidelines for indicating that they have borrowed words or ideas from someone else. Nevertheless, it is the writer's responsibility to learn these guidelines and follow them.

Using a documentation style

Each discipline, or area of academic study, has developed its own conventions for documentation, a standardized set of guidelines that continue to evolve as the discipline evolves. The languages and literature disciplines use the style recommended by the Modern Language Association (MLA). (See Chapter 55.) Other humanities use a system of endnotes or footnotes. (See Chapter 56.) Social sciences use the style recommended by the American Psychological Association (APA). (See Chapter 57.) Natural sciences use the style recommended by the Council of Biology Editors (CBE) or a related style. (See Chapter 58.) You should use the documentation of the discipline for which you are writing; if you are in doubt, ask your instructor.

Basically, you must attribute any idea or wording you use in your writing to the source through which you encountered that idea or those words *if the material is not original to yourself.* You do not need to document *common knowledge,* that is, information that an educated person can be expected to know—knowledge commonly taught in school or carried in the popular media—or knowledge that can be found in multiple sources (encyclopedias, dictionaries). Examples include the dates of historical events, the names and locations of states and cities, the general laws of science, and so on. However, when you read the work of authors who have specific opinions and interpretations of a piece of common knowledge and you use their opinions or interpretations in your paper, you must give them credit through proper documentation.

It is also important to note that even "nonpublished" ideas or words should be attributed to their sources whenever such documentation is feasible. For example, if you use opinions from a

sidewalk poll, from conversation, or from Internet commentaries or a World Wide Web page in your writing, you must cite that original source.

2 Avoiding plagiarism

If you are not sure what you can take from a source and what you need to cite, ask a tutor or your instructor for help before you turn in your final paper. Also find out whether your school has a booklet on avoiding plagiarism.

Most campuses with online writing labs (OWLs) now have information about plagiarism available through the World Wide Web. Similarly, your campus OWL, if one exists, is also likely to provide an e-mail-based hot line for rapid, direct answers to important questions about plagiarism.

The most common incidence of inadvertent plagiarism is a writer's paraphrasing or summarizing of a source but staying too close to the wording or sentence structure of the original, sometimes lifting whole phrases without enclosing them in quotation marks. Keep in mind that when you paraphrase or summarize a source, you need to identify the author of those ideas just as if you had quoted directly.

To avoid plagiarism when you paraphrase, use your own words to replace language that is not important to quote exactly; in other

AVOIDING PLAGIARISM

- Place all quoted passages in quotation marks and provide source information, even if you are quoting only one phrase.
- Identify the source from which you have paraphrased or summarized ideas, just as you do when you quote directly.
- Give credit for any creative ideas you borrow from an original source. For example, if you use an author's anecdote to illustrate a point, acknowledge it.
- Replace unimportant language with your own, and use different sentence structures when you paraphrase or summarize.
- Acknowledge the source if you borrow any organizational structure or headings from an author. Don't use the same subtopics, for example.
- Put any words or phrases you borrow in quotation marks, especially an author's unique way of saying something.

words, you are attributing the ideas, but not the exact language, to the source. At the same time, make certain you cite *all* direct quotations, acknowledging that you are borrowing both the ideas *and the words*. Also, attribution does not prevent plagiarism if too much wording is borrowed directly.

ORIGINAL | The World Wide Web makes world-wide publishing possible to anyone who is able to arrange disk space on a server and has some basic knowledge of how pages are created.

CAROL LEA CLARK, *A STUDENT'S GUIDE TO THE INTERNET*

PLAGIARIZED PARAPHRASE | World-wide publishing is possible for anyone who has access to server disk space and who has knowledge of how Web pages are made. (Clark 77).

The above example uses too much language from the original source.

ACCEPTABLE PARAPHRASE | With the basics of Web page construction and storage space on a network server, Clark tells us, anyone can publish, at least potentially, for audiences around the world (77).

This example translates source language into the writer's own language.

WRITING 6: EXPLORATION ─────────────

Read the following quotation from Mike Rose's *Lives on the Boundary;* then explain why each of the three sentences that follow is an example of plagiarism.

> The discourse of academics is marked by terms and expressions that represent an elaborate set of shared concepts and orientations: alienation, authoritarian personality, the social construction of self, determinism, hegemony, equilibrium, intentionality, recursion, reinforcement, and so on. This language weaves through so many lectures and textbooks, it is integral to so many learned discussions, that it is easy to forget what a foreign language it can be. (192)

1. The discourse of academics is marked by expressions that represent shared concepts.
2. Academic discourse is characterized by a particular set of coded words and ideas that are found throughout the college community.
3. Sometimes the talk of professors is as difficult for outsiders to understand as a foreign language is to a native speaker.

17   A Sampler of Research Essays

Good nonfiction teaches you something you do not already know or shows you something you already know, but from a different angle. Such writing explores a world beyond the writer's private self (though it may include the writer's personal self) and delves into all matters of public interest, from the political and philosophical to the literary and historical. It goes beyond the general, the superficial, and the cliché-ridden toward something detailed, thoughtful, and original.

To write serious nonfiction that is both interesting and believable—which is, after all, what academic writing is supposed to be—you need to be willing to dig into a subject to know its center and make it come alive for your readers. When you write in this way, it doesn't matter whether or not readers are already interested in the topic or not, since its richness will create the interest, and its depth will do the teaching.

In most cases, writing that teaches readers something they did not already know includes ideas and information obtained through several kinds of research: making detailed observations, listening to expert testimony, taking notes from textual sources, or downloading judiciously from the Internet. Often, research writing uses all these sources. In other words, to write good nonfiction, you need to be genuinely curious, look hard for information, and craft persuasive prose.

When we make research-essay assignments in both first-year and advanced writing courses, students are free to select topics that interest them, with one condition: that it have some local dimension to allow for the possibility of field research. To explain

what we mean, consider the following subjects students have chosen to write about over the past few years:

1. **zebra mussels**
2. attics
3. handguns
4. cultural diversity
5. acid rain
6. front porches
7. graffiti
8. gargoyles
9. bowling
10. electric automobiles
11. **mannequins**
12. hawk watching
13. glass blowing
14. body piercing
15. weight lifting
16. dowsing
17. attention deficit disorder (ADD)
18. the Smurfs
19. platform shoes
20. **blue jeans**
21. Greyhound Rescue
22. city homeless shelter
23. student housing
24. Ronald McDonald House
25. typewriters
26. self-help books
27. **can collectors**
28. doors
29. yoga
30. astrology
31. witches
32. false I.D. cards
33. **resident assistants**
34. junior high dances

This list names only the general subjects that writers began to explore as they started their research, not the specific topics that emerged in their final paper drafts. Look at the way that imaginative and careful research shaped some of these topics.

The **zebra mussel** paper began when two first-year students in the School of Natural Resources teamed up to write a paper about pollution. At first, they weren't sure what kind of pollution to investigate. They started with water pollution and narrowed it to the major local water supply, Lake Champlain, which in turn led them to the invasion of zebra mussels that colonize and obstruct water intake pipes. Readers enjoyed the paper because of its up-to-date examination based on Internet resources, recent periodicals, and personal investigation of the lakeshore itself.

The **mannequin** paper emerged when one student explored her fear of mannequins, which originated from childhood memories of a headless mannequin in her parents' attic. To write the paper, she interviewed her mother, looked into the literature of phobia, and journeyed downtown to confront her fear firsthand by arranging with the owner of a women's clothing store to help dress a mannequin for a window display.

The general subject **blue jeans** became a focused topic when a first-year student investigated the history of Levi's, their differing popularity from decade to decade, and the social statement made

by people who wear tight versus baggy jeans and Levi's versus Lee, Wrangler, or Gap jeans. To do research, she went to the library, searched the Internet, and visited local clothing stores.

The **can collector** paper began as an editorial on the evils of capitalism, moved toward sympathetic generalizations about the plight of the homeless, but in its second draft, zeroed in on the life of can collectors when the writer, a junior in an advanced writing class, met a man collecting discarded soda and beer cans to earn the nickel deposit on each one. His paper gained its compelling authority when he followed the homeless man on his collection "route."

The **resident assistant** paper began when a first-year student wondered whether she should apply to be an RA in her sophomore year. To find out, she talked to the administration that supervised the RAs in the dormitories, the RAs themselves, and the students the RAs supervised. She also looked into the literature on RAs that she found both in the library and on the Internet. After conducting her research and writing her paper, she decided what she wanted to do—which you can find out by reading Amanda's whole paper reprinted in this chapter.

Three Research Essays

This chapter features three *research essays* written by college students exploring topics of personal interest, written to academic audiences. We call these research *essays* rather than research *papers* to emphasize their exploratory nature, informal style, and personal voice. All three papers pose questions early on that the subsequent research attempts to answer as the writers take readers through their research process, using the delayed-thesis approach most common in contemporary nonfiction (see 9f2). At the same time, each is documented according to formal academic conventions: two are individually written and use MLA format; one is team written and uses APA format.

For examples of more formal research papers, see the objective voice coupled with delayed-thesis organization in the research paper that concludes Chapter 9, "Arguing Positions," as well as the objective voice, thesis-first papers that illustrate both MLA (Chapter 55) and APA (Chapter 57) documentation formats.

17 b Personal research essay

The following research essay was the result of an assignment asking students to explore any topic of strong personal interest

about which they had substantial and real questions that could be answered by some combination of field, Internet, and library research. Students were asked to cast the paper in the form of an **I-search essay,** requiring the final draft to report as much on the process of the search as the answer or answers discovered. (See 11e4.) Amanda Kenyon Waite investigated what it would be like to work as a resident assistant (RA) in her college dormitory.

For a topic of personal interest that includes visiting places and interviewing people, writing often takes a first-person point of view in the writer's personal voice. Such a paper commonly omits a title page and includes on the first page, in the top left-hand corner, the author's name, instructor's name, course title, and date. The title is centered, followed by a double space, and the complete text, including quotations, is double spaced as well. Page numbers are included at the top right of each page. At the same time, Amanda followed the academic conventions of citing her sources according to *current MLA documentation style,* complete with brief in-text references to a Works Cited page at the end of her essay. She also followed current MLA conventions in citing sources drawn from field, library, and Internet sources.

To see a formal MLA style research paper, complete with annotations illustrating the use of MLA conventions, see the end of Chapter 55.

Resident Assistant: Responsible Job or Power Trip?

Amanda Kenyon Waite

College is an expensive time. Aside from tuition, which my parents are graciously paying, my monthly expenses are pretty steep--phone bills, books, laundry, movies, pizza, and so on. For this reason, earlier in the semester I took a job as a telemarketer calling alumni and asking for money. But I did not enjoy harassing people in their homes, so after three weeks, I quit. Now I am back to relying on my savings and considering another job, this time as an RA, a resident assistant in the university dormitories. Before I fill out an application, however, I want to know just what the new job will entail.

I started my research by looking on the University of Vermont's Web home page, where I found the following definition of an RA:

Primarily undergraduate students who live on each hall floor,

wing, or column and are trained to work with floor or column

residents to develop a community. They are also trained as

listeners, problem solvers, programmers, community builders,

referral agents, and peer advisors. ("Resident Life")

From my limited experience with resident assistants, this definition

seemed to make sense. I felt capable of learning the skills necessary to

become an RA. However, this definition included no mention of "policing

students," which I already predict will be my major hang-up with the job, so I

needed to find out more.

I made an appointment to talk to Sarah Daniels, a first-year RA who lives

nearby. When I asked why she became an RA, she explained:

Most of us do it for the money, but for me there was more to it. I

was sick of all the hate crimes in the residence halls. People

writing graffiti all over the place. I felt that by not doing anything

it might as well have been me who was writing it. I saw becoming

an RA as a way to educate people so that kind of stuff would stop.

After hearing Sarah's reasons, I felt a little guilty for thinking about this

job just for the money. However, since the pay for being an RA is free room

and board, it actually will be my parents, not I, who save money. (Of course,

if I do this, I'm sure I can talk them into paying my phone bills!) Still, I am all

for stopping students from messing up the walls, so this chance makes the

work meaningful. Sarah went on to describe the RA training as intense: "[It]

never really stops. All RAs have to take a ten-week course, too, and discuss a

theme each week. Last week we talked about sexuality. This week I think it's alcohol."

I knew that students can get written up for anything from lighting candles and incense to possessing a toaster or stumbling around drunk, but when I asked Sarah about busting students, she said, "I really haven't had too much experience with that."

Later, when I talked with friends in the dining hall, I found several who believed that RAs are just students on power trips, using their position to cause problems for people they don't like. I understood this bias, since RAs are in a position of authority over people the same age or even older, but I'm sure I would not use my position unfairly. I really do not enjoy getting other people into trouble, so if I were an RA, I don't think that students would feel this way about me.

I also learned that some students live much closer to RAs than they would like to. In the Living and Learning Center, for example, rooms are set up in suite style, with six rooms surrounding a common dining room, so residents sometimes live in the same complex as their RAs. One student in this situation who wished to remain anonymous said, "It feels like we need to sneak around, like she's our mom almost." Another, who also wants her name withheld, said, "They're so hypocritical. They bust you for being underage and drinking, but you can find the same 18-, 19-, 20-year-old RAs drinking off campus at their friends' houses." Karen Corey, however, went on record to say, "It's good to live with [an RA] because she keeps us informed about events and policies."

Still, I felt a little discouraged talking to these students--discouraged mostly because I tended to agree with them. I do not want to be the person who has to spoil everyone else's fun. I do not want to be a hypocrite who busts a student for something that I might do myself.

A few days later, I attended a meeting of the Future Educators program at which I had the chance to talk with Ben King, who had been an RA for two years. I asked him how much time he spent each week on RA duties. He answered in detail:

> It takes a fair amount of time from your schedule. Aside from the required class, I would say the job takes five to ten extra hours a week, attending meetings, preparing bulletin boards, counseling, being on duty--which means making rounds in your whole building four times a month. An average round takes half an hour to an hour and a half, depending on how rowdy the night is.

Ben's answer relieved some of my anxiety, since I know I could find the extra time to take on this job. I also have experience organizing activities and sending out information, so I know I can do that too. But hesitations about busting students were still on my mind, and Ben's comments didn't help:

> Enforcing policy--a nice way of saying busting--is a very small part of the job, but unfortunately, it's the thing RAs are most known for. I don't like busting students--it's definitely my least favorite part of the job. It is really confrontational, and I find that nerve-racking.

My search seemed to be leading me back and forth. Whenever I thought about my own leadership ability compared to that needed by an RA, I felt

encouraged. For instance, one site on the World Wide Web, "The Study of Leadership Behaviors of Resident Assistants," defined a leader as "someone who challenges the process, inspires shared vision, enables others to act, models the way, and encourages the heart" (DeBenedictis et al., pars. 6-7). I feel that I have all these positive skills--to challenge, inspire, enable, model, and encourage.

But when I looked beneath the positive aspects of the job, the enforcement elements made me anxious. Another Web site posted a letter from RA Kate Lupton to the Daily Stanford college newspaper that raised concerns similar to mine about the role of the RAs on college campuses:

> The greatest tragedy of all would be a change in the RA role from community builder to police [officer]. At Stanford, RAs have the opportunity to develop student trust; if the situation continues on its present track, forcing us to assume an enforcer role, we will no longer have that chance.

I finally visited the university library to see what else I could find on the enforcement duties of RAs. A subject search turned up two books by M. Lee Upcraft that looked especially useful, Residence Hall Assistants in College and Learning to Be a Resident Assistant. According to Upcraft, before you sign on to become an RA, you need to ask yourself, "Can [I] turn in someone who is my friend?" (Learning 7). After reading the question, I immediately felt uncomfortable. According to Upcraft, if you couldn't turn in your friends, you shouldn't be an RA. This is exactly what I was afraid of; I know I do not want to put myself in this situation.

Recently, a friend of mine was written up for drinking in a suite with seven other UVM students. The Incident Report described the event this way: "As we entered the suite we all noticed beer cans and bottles and people drinking. We asked them to collect all of the beer, and Chad watched them pour it down the sink" (Hart). No matter how hard I thought about it, I couldn't imagine myself doing this.

After this month-long search, I'm still undecided. Almost everything about being an RA sounds like something I could do. I have leadership, organizational, and communication skills. But I'm not sure I possess the ability to walk into students' rooms and force them to pour their good time down the drain. So, I have to answer one more question myself before I decide whether to apply: Is the risk of having to turn in my friends worth saving my parents $5000 next year?

Works Cited

Corey, Karen. Personal interview. 12 Oct. 1998.

Daniels, Sarah. Personal interview. 10 Oct. 1998.

DeBenedictis, Michelle, et al. The Study of Leadership Behaviors of Resident
     Assistants. West Chester U. Spring 1997. 13 pars. 15 Oct. 1998
     <http:// albie.wcupa.edu/ttreadwell/971gp4.html>.

Hart, Darrell. "Incident Report: U. of Vermont Resident Life Services." 1 Oct.
     1998.

King, Benjamin. Personal interview. 14 Oct. 1998.

Lupton, Kate. "Letter: Resident assistants fear role will include policing
     students' drinking." 5 Nov. 1996. Stanford U. 15 Oct. 1998
     <http//:www.dailystanford.org/Daily96-97/11-5/OP>.

Resident Life. Aug. 1998. U. of Vermont. 10 Oct. 1998

    <http://www.reslife.uvm.edu/resstaff/overview.htm>.

Upcraft, M. Lee. Learning to Be a Resident Assistant. San Francisco: Jossey,

    1982.

---. Residence Hall Assistants in College. San Francisco; Jossey, 1982.

17 **C** **Internet research essay**

    The following research essay by Katie Moll was written using research available exclusively on the World Wide Web and via electronic mail. She also investigated library sources but found nothing specific pertaining to her topic. While Internet research is often considered by students to be the easiest and most comfortable form of collecting information, in this case, Katie's topic itself originated on the Internet from controversial Web site postings that claimed the children's television show *The Smurfs* was Communist propaganda aimed at subverting the beliefs of American children. In other words, the Web posed the problem, and Katie used the Web to try to solve it.

    The essay opens with an explanation of how Katie discovered these controversial opinions on the Web. It follows her step-by-step investigation to find out whether these opinions might be true. The essay concludes with an especially interesting personal postscript that poses interesting questions for all who rely on Web-based research.

The Smurfs as Political Propaganda

Katie Moll

    Saturday morning cartoons were a large part of my childhood. They

brought enjoyment and laughter, and they sometimes taught moral lessons. I

grew up surrounded by shows like Fraggle Rock, Rainbow Brite, The Jetsons,

and Reading Rainbow. My personal favorite, however, was The Smurfs, a

cartoon focused on a village of small blue elf-like creatures that lived in

mushrooms and were always content with their lives. Much to my despair,

they were taken off the air after the 1980s. It wasn't until about a year ago that the Smurfs were brought to my attention again.

Recently, my sister and her boyfriend were going to a party where the theme was "cartoon characters." They wanted to attend the party dressed as Smurfette and Handy Smurf, but after checking every store in Philadelphia, they could find no costumes. When they checked the Internet for Smurf costumes, they found more hits than they expected: Web sites popped up with titles such as Sociopolitical Themes in the Smurfs and Papa Smurf Is a Communist. When I checked the Internet myself, I was both amazed and disgusted that someone would make such claims about my favorite cartoon, and I wondered, could this be true? Was the Smurf television show really political propaganda?

To check this story further, I searched the Web with the keyword "Smurfs," which took me to The Smurfs Official Site at <www.smurf.com/homepage.html>. It had nothing about the communist theory, but then again, why would it? This was the home page promoting the cartoon, so I doubted it would slander the program. However, I did obtain useful background information on the origin of The Smurfs. The creator of the Smurf characters was Peyo, the pen name of Pierre Culliford, who lived and worked in Brussels, Belgium. The Smurfs first appeared as a comic strip in 1958. It was not until 1981 that the The Smurfs became an animated television series designed by the team of William Hanna and Joseph Barbera, who also created Tom and Jerry, Ruff and Reddy, Huckleberry Hound, The Flintstones, The Jetsons, Jonny Quest, and Scooby-Doo. Nothing on the Smurf home page suggested that either Peyo or Hanna-Barbera had

subversive intentions, so I began to think the theory was a complete hoax.

But I wanted to find out more.

I also found numerous sites devoted to selling Smurfs: <u>Timeless</u>

<u>Trinkets.com</u> sells Smurf figures; "The Smurfs-Smurfy Pages" offers

<u>QuickTime</u> videos of the cartoon; <u>Smurf's Nightmare</u> offers reviews of the

Smurf video game; "Smurfs Wanted" was a page inquiring whether anyone

had figurines for sale. It was here, amid the jumble of commercial topics, that

I found what I was looking for.

A Web site called <u>The Smurfs as a Paradigm for Communist Society</u>

suggests, "The Smurfs were actually a well-devised piece of communist

propaganda to erode American society from within" (Gozer, para 2). Five

points of comparison between the Smurf cartoon show and a Russian

communist society make the author's case:

(1) Papa Smurf, the wise leader of the Smurf community, looks like Karl

Marx and (2) wears red pants; (3) all Smurfs work according to their

ability and receive according to their needs; (4) the villain, Gargamel,

acts like a greedy capitalist; and (5) his cat, Azreal, represents "third-world

despotisms that are clinging onto the coattails of first-world capitalism."

The author writes a short paragraph on each point and states that "these

five points provide very strong evidence pointing to the conclusion that

the TV show 'The Smurfs' is indeed a paradigm for communist society"

(para 8).

"Strong evidence"? It is hard to take this 500-word Web site very

seriously. It is short; the supporting detail in each paragraph is sketchy; some

of the arguments (Papa Smurf as Karl Marx!) are far-fetched; and the author

is not accountable, providing no name and no credentials, though an e-mail address <n9620080@cc.wwu.edu> is included.

However, a second Web site, Sociopolitical Themes in the Smurfs by J. Marc Schmidt, outlines in much more detail the basis for a Marxist interpretation of The Smurfs:

> Unlike many other cartoons, or indeed other television programmes, The Smurfs is about an entire society and its interactions with itself and with outsiders, rather than the adventures of a few characters. Hence, I believe it is, in short, a political fable, in much the same way that The Lion, the Witch and the Wardrobe was a fable about Christianity. Rather than Christianity, however, The Smurfs is about Marxism. (para 2)

Note that Schmidt does not label The Smurfs "communist propaganda" as does the Gozer Web site. Instead, he describes cartoon series in the same terms as other respected "political fables," such as C. S. Lewis's much admired The Lion, the Witch, and the Wardrobe--a comparison suggesting the program is something to be studied or learned from rather than be brainwashed by, as the term propaganda implies. In Schmidt's words, "I am not accusing The Smurfs of being some kind of subversive kiddie propaganda" (para 3).

Schmidt believes Peyo to be a socialist rather than a card-carrying communist, calling the Smurf village "a Marxist utopia" rather than a police state like the old Soviet Union (para 5). The evidence Schmidt assembles is thoughtful and far more convincing than Gozer's hasty claims. For example, he points out that Smurf village is "a perfect model of a socialist commune or

collective" (para 5), that "the Smurfs are all completely equal" (para 6), that "everyone is equally a worker and an owner" (para 7), and that "they wear the same kind and colour of clothes" (para 9).

In addition, Schmidt finds some of the same similarities between The Smurfs and a communist society as the Gozer Web site. Schmidt, too, suggests that the ruthless, greedy villain Gargamel "represents capitalism" and that he wants "metaphorically to devour socialism" or, perhaps, "to turn everything into a commodity" (para 12).

I found the Schmidt Web site to be quite convincing. For one thing, all that he says about the Smurfs and Smurf village matches what I remember about the show; once he points out those similarities, I can see his point. For another thing, the Schmidt article on the Web site is carefully written, with clear explanations and concrete examples. In addition, Schmidt includes his whole name along with an e-mail address <j_marc_s@hotmail.com>--an indication that he is willing to be responsible for his ideas. Because of the way Schmidt spells certain words (programme and colour), a first reading of his site suggests that his English is British rather than American, in which case he may have more objective distance from the cartoon show than an American author would.

However, when I looked at a third Web site that addressed this propaganda issue, Papa Smurf Is a Communist, I became momentarily confused again. At first glance, Papa Smurf seemed to have been written from an angry capitalist perspective, upset that communist connections are hidden in the children's cartoon. Even the feel of this Web page was

different, with a menacing black background and dark red letters as opposed to the more neutral tones on the other Web sites. This site's anonymous author pushed the conspiracy theory hard, as if trying to force the reader to believe the conspiracy theory.

At first, I was annoyed by the aggressive tone of the Papa Smurf Web site. But when I read it a second time, I found myself laughing. This Web site is not serious. Instead, it is making fun of the communist propaganda theory. Here, for example, is an excerpt from the site's opening paragraph:

> Yes, that is correct, Papa Smurf and all of his little Smurf minions are not the happy little characters Hanna-Barbera would have us believe! The cartoon was really created by the Russian government in order to indoctrinate the youngest members of Western society with communist beliefs and ideals, thus destroying their resistance to the imminent Russian invasion that was to occur when this generation (my generation) grew up.

"Imminent Russian invasion"? Wait a minute. While it is true that during the Cold War many Americans feared a nuclear war with Russia, no one feared an actual invasion.

A closer reading of this site reveals other laughable assertions. Here, for example, is the author's ridiculous pun about the villain's cat: "Another disturbing character was Gargamel's cat, Azrael, who represented the 'fat cat' American politician" (para 8). I began to think this site was a parody. Another obvious parody is the link called S.M.U.R.F., which reveals that the word Smurf is an acronym for "Small Men Under Red Father." In another

passage that is hard to take seriously, this anonymous author argues that Papa Smurf resembles Stalin, not Karl Marx:

> I feel that Stalin is most likely the man that Papa Smurf was modeled after. Marx believed more in the system of socialism, not communism. What is the difference, you may ask? Well, under both systems everything is supposedly shared equally among all members of the society; however, under the socialist system there are free elections for the leadership of the society, whereas under the communist system there are no elections. I sure as hell don't remember Papa Smurf being elected leader, nor was there ever an election to decide whether he should remain leader. Stalin's appearance also highly resembles that of Papa Smurf. His beard may not be as perfect as that of Marx, but look at that round face! (para 7)

The author does not reveal his or her identity but does provide an e-mail address <commiesmurfs@hotmail. com> to which readers can respond, along with twenty reader responses printed at the end of the site. Here is a sampling:

- "Your page was one of the funniest things I have read in a long time! Great job on it--I especially like the shot [an image on the Web page] of Papa Smurf with the hammer and sickle in his hat!"
- "The site made me open my eyes and realize that communism only exists not in society but in most of our pop culture as well. Being concerned, I am now proposing 'CASCO' (Canadians Against Smurf Communism) to rid the evils of the Smurfs on Sunday mornings; they are shown on a regular basis in Canada. Spread the news."

- "It is quite funny your point about Gargamel boiling the Smurfs and getting gold. Here in Central America he boiled enough Smurfs in the last 20 years, and believe me, he got a lot of cash out of it. In this case, Azrael turned out to be your beloved Marine Corps. Anyway, it is quite a good page."

To make sense of three different Web sites, each pointing to similarities between The Smurfs and Marxism, I looked more carefully at the sequence in which the sites were created. Who, in other words, started this comparison? Fortunately, each site was dated. The brief Gozer site was created in September 1997. The anonymous and obvious parody, Papa Smurf, was created in March of the same year--six months earlier than Gozer. The only serious site, Schimidt's, was not created until 1998 (the exact month is not available).

What does this chronology reveal? That the most obvious parody of the cartoon show, the anonymous Papa Smurf, was, in fact, published first. Its publication seemed to start a small chain reaction, with the Gozer site second and Schmidt's last.

Curious to see whether there were any connections among the three Web sites, I sent e-mail queries to each site. I never heard from the anonymous creator of the earliest site, Papa Smurf, but I received responses from the other two authors. J. Marc Schmidt responded promptly, identifying himself as a high school teacher living in Sydney, Australia (hence the British spellings), and explaining that he created his site after attending a museum exhibit on cartoon animation in which he found hard-to-believe interpretations of many animated shows. Schmidt writes, "I started thinking

more and more about socialism, and eventually the idea just clicked. Anyway, for good or bad, that incomprehensible blurb was the seed, which led me to write an essay called 'Sociopolitical Themes in the Smurfs.' I turned it into a Web site and put it on the Internet."

The author of the Gozer site also responded, providing his real name, Eric Lott, but asking me not to give out his personal e-mail address. Lott writes: "In honest truth, it was/is not intended as a parody. Personally, I am an anarcho-socialist. I began thinking this up . . . and developed it into a monologue. Most people I gave [it] to found it quite amusing."

After reading the comic, the amusing, and the serious interpretations of the socialist Smurfs, I realized I had to take another look at the cartoon myself. I obtained a copy of one Smurf episode by borrowing it from a friend's younger sister (who else would collect such videotapes?) and tried to watch it with an open mind, as if I were young again.

This untitled episode opens with Handy Smurf working on roofs, Baker Smurf making food, and Vanity Smurf idolizing himself in the mirror. Handy Smurf and Smurfette have a disagreement and Smurfette runs away into the woods. Papa Smurf rounds up the village to find her. Meanwhile, in the woods, Azreal (the cat) finds Smurfette sitting on a rock, crying, and Gargamel orders him to catch her. However, the Smurfs locate Smurfette just before the cat does, and a chase scene follows. The Smurfs escape by running underneath a low branch that knocks the cat unconscious. Back in the village, Handy and Smurfette make peace and live happily (I presume) until the next week.

After having read all the political ideas about The Smurfs, however, I found it difficult to watch an episode with an open mind. As soon as it was over, I began seeing possible socialist connections myself. For example, when Papa Smurf rounds up the village, is he a communist dictator taking charge? When Gargamel orders his cat to catch Smurfette, is he a capitalist dictator delegating his dirty jobs to the workers? Is the chase scene a reminder of the constant war between the free world and communism? Does the color red symbolize communism?

It was then I also realized that I could take virtually any children's story and make it mean something else. Do Santa Claus and Little Red Riding Hood wear red because they are communists? Do Santa's elves make toys because they are slaves? Is the Big Bad Wolf a greedy capitalist? While I can see the basis for these interpretations, I do not think children can--nor do I really think the show was deliberately meant to be subversive. The parallels are there only if you want them to be.

Postscript

Browsing the Internet after writing this paper, I found an interpretation of the popular children's television show Teletubbies, suggesting that one of the Teletubbies characters is a homosexual role model. According to "Parents Alert: Tinky Winky Comes Out of the Closet," an article published in the February 1999 edition of the National Liberty Journal--a newsletter edited and published by the Rev. Jerry Falwell--"Tinky Winky has the voice of a boy yet carries a purse . . . is purple--the gay-pride color; and his antenna is shaped like a triangle--the gay-pride symbol" (qtd. in Reed). At this point, however, I stopped reading. Who really cares whether or not Tinky Winky is

gay--or a Marxist, or a member of some other minority group? Not me.

Looking back at my research paper, I now think the real topic was neither the

Smurfs nor the Marxists. The real topic that emerges between the lines is

what I found out about the Internet itself. First, for anybody with access to a

computer, the Internet is the greatest medium ever devised for the unlimited

practice of free speech. Second, the Internet is also the greatest repository of

fact and fiction ever devised--but there's nobody to tell you for sure which is

which, sometimes not even the author! This idea clearly needs further

investigation and elaboration, but to tell the truth, I don't have the time. I'll

leave that topic, along with the Teletubbies, for my next paper.

Works Cited

Gozer. The Smurfs as a Paradigm for Communist Society. 27 Sep. 1997. 7 Oct.

    2001 <http://www.ac.wwu.edu/~n9620080/smurf.html>.

Lott, Eric. Personal e-mail. 4 Dec. 2001.

Papa Smurf Is a Communist. 16 Mar. 1997. 8 Oct. 2001 <http://geocities.com/

    CapitolHill/Lobby/1709>.

Reed, David. "Falwell's Newspaper Attempts to Label Teletubbies Character as

    Gay." 10 Feb. 1999. 9 Nov. 2001 <http://www.sfgate.com/cgibin/article.

    cgi?file=/ news/archive/1999/02/10/national0333EST0476.DTL>.

Schmidt, J. Marc. Sociopolitical Themes in the Smurfs. 7 Oct. 1998. 8 Oct.

    2001 <http://www.geocities.com/Hollywood/Cinema/3117/sociosmurf2.

    htm>.---. Personal e-mail. 3 Dec. 2001.

The Smurfs Official Site. 2000. 7 Oct. 2001 <http://www.smurf.com/

    homepage.html>.

Teletubbies. PBS kids. 2000. 8 Nov. 2001 <http://pbskids.org/teletubbies.

    html>.

The following essay was written by a team of first-year writers, Vanessa Cox, Jennifer Kirchoff, and Nathan McBryan, who teamed up to research the subject of glassblowing. While they used both library books and Internet sources, their primary and most exciting research occurred when they visited a glassblowing studio in downtown Burlington, Vermont. There is no controversy or issue in this paper; rather, it is an informational report written in an informal and collaborative voice. Establishing a consistent voice was one of the main problems in writing the paper; the authors solved it by writing from a "we" point of view and quoting each other in the third person to individualize perspectives. The version of the essay printed here has been condensed by half to emphasize the field-research portion of their investigation.

For a formal APA-style research paper, complete with annotations illustrating the use of APA conventions, see the end of Chapter 57.

The Modern Art of Glassblowing

Vanessa Cox, Jennifer Kirchoff, and Nathan McBryan

Of the many different types of art that express functional beauty, glassblowing is the one our research team is most curious about. Each of the three of us has an individual reason for learning more about glassblowing. Jen says, "When I was a little girl my mom kept all these beautiful glass vases, and I never understood why she kept them so clean and lined them up on the shelves so neatly. I picked one of them up one day and I accidentally dropped it. Instant tears came from my mother's eyes, and ever since, I wanted to learn why they meant so much to her." Vanessa had "seen only finished pieces of glass and wondered how you get the design, shape, and colors you want." Nate says, "Glassblowing is one of those things in life that I have too long taken for granted."

Before we look at the art of glassblowing, let us consider the magic of glass itself, one of the most fragile substances, yet one that can be made bullet-proof and heat-resistant. "The basic ingredients of glass have . . . remained the same for thousands of years. They are silica sand, lime, and soda. These ingredients are mixed . . . and heated to 2,800 degrees Fahrenheit. . . . The red-hot liquid is then ready to be drawn, pressed, or blown into shape" (Glass blowing secrets, 2001, para 2). How glass gets blown into shapes is the subject of this research essay.

What, exactly is glassblowing? A formal definition tells us it is "the art of working with molten glass from a furnace, using a long metal rod, either hollow (blowpipe) or solid (puntil iron) to gather the glass at the tip. Using various tools, the molten glass is shaped and manipulated to create a vast array of glass products, including tumblers, vases, perfume bottles, Christmas ornaments, and paperweights" (Glass Blowing, 1999). This information helps, but we want to witness the art of glassblowing firsthand and see how artisans actually use these "various tools" to create "tumblers, vases," and such. To learn about glassblowing firsthand, we made an appointment to tour downtown Burlington's only glassblowing studio, Church and Maple Glass Studio on October 7, 2001. As soon as we entered the studio, we noticed an increase in temperature--it was hot! Walking across the floor, we could feel the crunching of small pieces of broken glass beneath our feet. All around us we heard the hum of powerful fans blowing in outside air from the cool morning. We also heard two men shouting strange phrases back and forth: "Flip the rim and swing it." "Get me the

punty." "Put it in the annealer." We had entered the world of glassblowers--

hot, noisy, and perhaps even a little dangerous.

The men placed a finished piece of blown glass in an oven, closed the

oven door, and turned to greet us. The workers are Benny Giguere, 27 years

old, and Scott Tucker, 29, both of whom work full time at the Simon Pearce

Company in Quechee, Vermont (Mance, 2001). Benny has worked for the

company for five years, Scott for ten, jobs they each began after graduating

from high school. Today, however, they were not working for Simon Pearce

but for themselves, for personal enjoyment and to sell their personal work in

the downtown studio.

Scott told us, "Today, Benny is the master, and I am the apprentice." He

explained: "The master is the one who works with the piece and does the

blowing and swinging, and the apprentice makes the colors and gets tools

and other equipment ready for the master. You came on an interesting day,"

he continued. "I haven't worked as an apprentice in over ten years. I can't

believe it has been that long," he said, chuckling. "But I am more of a maker

of functional things and work from plans, while Benny is more of an artist

who plans as he goes. I will talk you through everything that Benny does as

he makes this flower vase."

The artisan, Benny, selected a 4-foot metal blowpipe, a long iron tube

with a heavy twine mouthpiece to insulate his lips. He dipped the blowpipe

into the molten glass inside the furnace. Benny explained that "different

types of tools are used for different types of glass, each one with a different

purpose for the work you are trying to do." (Moore, 1935) tells us that tools

such as Benny's blowpipe have been around for hundreds, perhaps thousands of years; the art of glassblowing has been traced to the ancient Syrians, around 25 B.C. (p. 14). In fact, "the first metal blowpipe came into widespread use in the first or second century before Christ, and glass production soared, particularly in the Roman world, where glass became available to the rich and the poor" (Thrall, n.d, para 1). The current tools are manufactured mostly in Seattle and Sweden.

The furnace that holds the hot glass is kept at "2050 degrees, but can range from 2000 to 2400 degrees to melt the glass," according to Scott. Every time Benny opens the furnace door, we feel the rush of heat on our faces.

After gathering a glob of molten glass the size of a tennis ball on the end of his blowpipe, Benny sat down on his bench and gently rolled the blowpipe back and forth on the pipe rest to center the melted glass on the pipe. Scott: "The key to glassblowing is keeping your piece centered and equal. To do this you must roll the blowpipe every second along the pipe rest." While Scott talked to us, Benny kept his eyes on his piece of glass; we could see the bright reflection of the glowing ball on his tinted glasses.

Benny now placed pieces of colored glass called "bit colors" on the small piece of glass on the blowpipe and put the pipe into the "glory hole"--a foot-wide opening in a 5-foot-long cylindrical furnace kept at 2500 degrees (McKearin, 1945). The glory hole kept the piece warm and manageable while Benny worked with it.

Scott explained, "The piece needs to be put into the glory hole every few minutes or else it will explode because the glass will cool too quickly if it is kept at room temperature." Once the color bit and glass were melted

together in a ball, Benny blew the piece into the shape of a tapered round flower vase.

Each glass piece is blown according to the number of glass layers it contains; the more layers, the harder it must be blown. To elongate the piece and make it even, the blowpipe must be swung in a circle. A tube with a nozzle filled with air is used to cool off an area of the piece that is complete. After finding the correct shape, the piece is colored. Scott: "To make the color of glass you want, the piece of glass must be rolled in either a fine powder color or a coarser grit color." For this piece, Scott added blue powder to the glass in the furnace, heating them together.

After decorating the vase with circles and swirls, Scott took another piece of hot glass, called a transfer bubble, from the furnace and stuck it on the bottom of the now-finished piece. Then Benny took a chisel-like tool and tapped along the blowpipe rim, separating the blowpipe from the glass object. He then affixed a new pipe--a pontil iron or punty--to the transfer bubble at the vase's bottom to hold it during the finishing process. "All that is left to do is to stick the finished piece in the glory hole to make sure everything is stuck together and will not break," Scott said. Benny took the piece out with wood-tipped metal tongs, and Scott held it with his thickly gloved hands while Benny tapped along the bottom to break off the punty. We noticed Benny and Scott, once finished with a particular tool, putting it in a bucket of water to stay cool for the next time they need it.

Scott's gloves were steaming as he placed the vase in the annealer--a finishing oven that starts out at 755 degrees but cools down progressively over an eight-hour period so that the new glass doesn't explode from a

drastic change in temperature. (Explosion is a common and dangerous problem for glassblowers.) In other words, by tomorrow the vase will be finished, cool, and ready to sell. Benny says with pride, "it will probably price out at fifty or sixty dollars because of the detail and time that went into it."

When we began this research, we knew only that blown-glass objects, from vases to glasses and Christmas tree ornaments, were usually sold in craft stores, gift shops, and art galleries, and that people bought them both for practical use and as art objects. Now we know more about the materials from which such objects are made, as well as the tools, time, and skills used to make them. We left Church and Maple Glass Studio with a new appreciation for the ancient yet modern art of glassblowing.

References

Glass Blowing. (1999). Colorado free university. Retrieved November 4, 2001,

   http://www.freeu.com/classes/1517.html

Glass blowing secrets. (2001, September 28). Retrieved November 4, 2001,

   from http://www.allsands.com/Hobbies/glassblowing_afi_gn.htm

Mance, D. (2001). See Vermont. Retrieved November 4, 2001, from

   http://seevermont.nybor.com/Made_in_ Vermont/Story/16201.html

McKearin, N. (1945). American glass. New York: Crown Publishers.

Moore, N. (1935). Old glass. New York: Tudor Publishing Co.

Thrall, A. (n.d.). A brief history of glass blowing. Glass act. Retrieved

   November 6, 2001, from www.neder.com/glassact/altframeset.html

PART FIVE

Revising

www.prenhall.com/fulwiler

Revising

www.prenhall.com/fulwiler

On *The Blair Handbook, Fourth Edition,* Web site you can find

- Revising strategies
- Exercises on focused revising
- Exercises on responding to writing

The Revising Process

A first draft is a writer's first attempt to give shape to an idea, argument, or experience. Occasionally, this initial draft is just right and the writing is done. More often, however, the first draft shows a broad outline or general direction that needs further thinking, further revision. An unfocused first draft, in other words, is not a mistake but rather a start toward a next, more focused draft.

No matter how much prior thought writers give to complex composing tasks, once they begin writing, the draft begins to shift, change, and develop in unexpected ways. Each act of writing produces new questions and insights that must be dealt with and incorporated into the emerging piece of writing; it is during this process that active and aggressive revision strategies can help. Inexperienced writers often view revising as an alien activity that neither makes sense nor comes easily. However, most experienced writers view revising as the essence of writing, the primary way of developing thoughts to be shared with others.

18 a Understanding revising

The terms *revising, editing,* and *proofreading* are sometimes used to mean the same thing, but there is good reason to understand each as a separate process, each in its own way contributing to good finished writing. **Revising** is re-seeing, rereading, rethinking, and reconstructing your thoughts on paper until they match those in your mind. It's conceptual work, generally taking place beyond the sentence, at the level of paragraph and higher.

In contrast, **editing** is changing language more than ideas. You edit to make precise what you want to say, testing each word or phrase to see that is accurate, appropriate, necessary. Editing is stylistic and mechanical work, generally taking place at the level of the paragraph, sentence, or word. The many dimensions of editing, including proofreading, are treated in Part Six.

Proofreading is checking a manuscript for accuracy and correctness. It is the last phase of the editing process, completed after conceptual and stylistic concerns have been addressed. When you proofread, you review spelling, punctuation, capitalization, and usage to make sure no careless mistakes have occurred that might confuse or distract readers.

There are two good reasons to revise before you edit. First, in revising you may cut out whole sections of a draft because they no longer suit your final purpose. If you have already edited those now-deleted sections, all that careful work goes for naught. Second, once you have invested time in carefully editing sentences, you become reluctant to cut them, even though these sections may no longer suit your purpose. Of course, writers are always circling back through the stages, editing when it makes more sense to revise, inventing when they mean to edit. Nonetheless, you will save time if you revise before editing and edit before proofreading.

ESL **REVISING VERSUS EDITING**

As this chapter explains, revising the content and organization of your ideas is different from editing for word choice and grammatical correctness. When a person writes in a second language, it is often difficult to postpone concerns about word choice and grammar. Consequently, ESL writers sometimes try to edit prematurely. Although you may want to do some editing in early drafts, remember that taking time to revise content is very important and that you should work on revision before you do any extensive editing.

WRITING I: EXPLORATION

Describe any experience you've had with revising papers: Was it for a school assignment or some writing on your own? Why did you revise? How many drafts did you do? Were you pleased? Was your audience?

18 b **Planning to revise**

You cannot revise if you haven't first written, so write early and leave time to revise later. Good college papers are seldom

written in one draft the night before they are due. When you plan in advance to revise, the following tools and techniques will serve you well:

- **Keep a revision notebook.** When you begin any substantial writing project, keep a notebook, journal, or computer file in which to capture all ideas related to your paper, including invention, drafting, research, and revision ideas. Over the span of several days or weeks, your revision may profit from your returning to earlier information, ideas, or insights. (See Chapter 4 for more about keeping a journal.)

- **Impose due dates.** Write the due date for a final draft on your calendar; then add earlier, self-imposed due dates for first, second, or third drafts. Your self-imposed intermediate due dates will guarantee you the time you need to revise well.

- **Write and rewrite with a computer.** Computers make revising easier and more effective. Any kind of word processing program allows you to change your text infinitely before ever calling it finished. The computer allows you to change words and sentences as well as move blocks of text from one part of your paper to another with ease—all essential acts of revising.

- **Read hard copy.** When revising with a computer, print out hard copies of your drafts and see how they read on paper. Hard copy lets you scan several pages at a time and quickly flip pages in search of certain patterns or information.

- **Save draft copies.** Make backup files of old drafts; if you become unhappy with your revisions, you can always return to the earlier copy.

WRITING 2: APPLICATION

Describe your approach to writing a paper from the time it's assigned to the time you hand it in. Do you do any of the prerevision work described above? Which of these general strategies makes sense in view of your current writing habits?

18 C Asking revision questions

To begin revising, return to the basic questions of purpose, audience, and voice: why am I writing? to whom? in what voice?

▮ Questions of purpose

It is often easier to see your purpose—or lack thereof—most clearly after you have written a draft or two. Ask the following questions:

• Why am I writing this paper? (Review the assignment.)

• Do all parts of the paper advance this purpose? (Outline by paragraph and make sure they do.)

• What is my rhetorical strategy: to narrate, explain, interpret, argue, reflect, or something else? (Review Chapter 6 to fine-tune strategy.)

• Have I stated the paper's theme or thesis clearly? (If not, do so, or have a good reason for not doing so.)

▮ Questions of audience

Make sure your paper is aimed accurately at your readers by asking the following questions:

• What does my audience know about this subject? (Avoid repeating elementary information.)

• What does my audience need to know to understand the point of my paper? (Provide full context and background for information your audience is not likely to know.)

CREATING TITLES

Titles catch the attention of readers and provide a clue to the paper's content. If a title doesn't suggest itself in the writing of your paper, try one of these strategies:

• Use one strong short phrase from your paper.
• Present a question that your paper answers.
• State the answer to the question or issue your paper will explore.
• Use a clear or catchy image from your paper.
• Use a famous quotation.
• Write a one-word title (or a two-word title, a three-word title, and so on).
• Begin your title with the word *On*.
• Begin your title with a gerund (*-ing* word).

- What questions or objections do I anticipate my audience raising? (Try to answer them before they are asked.)

3 Question of voice

Make sure your paper satisfies you. Revise so you say what you intend in the voice you intend by reading out loud and asking the following question:

Which passages sound like me speaking and which don't? (Enjoy those that do; fix those that don't.)

18 d Using revision strategies

For many writers, revising seems to be an instinctive or even unconscious process—they just do it. However, even experienced writers might profit by pausing to think deliberately about what plans and methods they use when they revise.

This section lists more than a dozen **revision strategies** that may be useful to you. While they won't all work for you all the time, some will be useful at one time or another. Notice that these suggestions start with larger concerns and progress toward smaller ones.

Some revision strategies are so important that we've treated them in a separate chapter (Chapter 19). *Limiting* is focusing on a narrow portion of a paper or concept and eliminating extraneous material; *adding* is incorporating new details and discussion to make writing more vivid and powerful. *Switching* and *transforming* are more innovative strategies for revision: by changing the tense, point of view, form, or format of a piece of writing, writers can gain insights into their writing and present their ideas in a new light.

1 Establish distance

Let your draft sit for a while, overnight if possible; then reread it to see whether it still makes sense. A later reading provides useful distance from your first words, allowing you to see whether there are places that need clarification, explanation, or development that you did not see when drafting. You can gain distance also by reading your draft aloud—hearing instead of seeing it—and by sharing it with others and listening to their reactions. No matter how you gain it, with distance you revise better.

2 Reconsider everything

Reread the whole text from the beginning: every time you change something of substance, reread again to see the effect of these changes on other parts of the text. If a classmate or instructor has made comments on some parts of the paper and not on others, do not assume that only the places where there are comments need revision.

3 Believe and doubt

Reread your draft twice, first as if you wanted to believe everything you wrote (imagine a supportive friend), putting check marks in the margins next to passages that create the most belief—the assertions, the discussion, the details, the evidence. Next, reread your draft as if you were suspicious and skeptical of all assertions (imagine your most critical teacher), putting question marks next to questionable passages. Be pleased with the check marks, and answer the question marks.

4 Test your theme or thesis

Most college papers are written to demonstrate a theme or thesis (to outlaw handguns; to legalize marijuana). However, revision generates other ideas, raises new questions, and sometimes reshapes your thesis (license handguns; legalize hemp as a cash crop). Make sure to modify other parts of your paper as necessary to keep up with your changing thesis.

5 Evaluate your evidence

To make any theme or thesis convincing, you need to support it with evidence. Do your facts, examples, and illustrations address the following questions?

- Does the evidence support my thesis or advance my theme? (In states that license handgun ownership, crime rates have decreased.)

- What objections can be raised about this evidence? (The decrease in crime rates has other causes.)

- What additional evidence will answer these objections? (In states that do not license handguns, crime has not decreased.)

(For more on evaluating evidence, see Chapters 2 and 9.)

6 Make a paragraph outline

The most common unit of thought in a paper is the paragraph, a group of sentences set off from other groups of sentences because they focus on the same main idea. Make a paragraph outline to create a map of your whole paper and see whether the organization is effective: number each paragraph and write a phrase describing its topic or focus. Does the subject of each paragraph lead logically to the next? If not, reorganize.

7 Rewrite introductions and conclusions

Once started, papers grow and evolve in unpredictable ways: An opening that seemed appropriate in an earlier draft may no longer fit. The closing that once nicely ended the paper may now fail to do so. Examine both introduction and conclusion to be sure they actually introduce and conclude. Sometimes it is more helpful to write fresh ones than to tinker with old ones. (For more on openings and conclusions, see Chapter 24.)

8 Listen for your voice

In informal and semiformal papers, your language should sound like a real human being speaking. Read your paper aloud and see whether the human being speaking sounds like you. If it doesn't, revise so that it does. In more formal papers, the language should sound less like you in conversation and more like you giving a presentation—fewer opinions, more objectivity, no contractions.

9 Let go

View change as good, not bad. Many writers become overly attached to the first words they generate, proud to have found them, now reluctant to abandon them. Learn to let your words, sentence, and even paragraphs go. Trust that new and more appropriate ones will come.

10 Start over

Sometimes revising means starting over completely. Review your first draft, then turn it face down and start fresh. Starting over generates your best writing, as you automatically delete dead-end ideas, making room for new and better ones to emerge. (Many writers have discovered this fact accidentally, by losing a file on a

computer and thus being forced to reconstruct, almost always writing a better draft in the process.)

 REMINDERS FOR REVISION

- Reread the **assignment** and state it in your own words. Does your paper address it?
- Restate your larger **purpose.** Has your paper fulfilled it?
- Consider your **audience.** Have you told your readers what they want and need to know?
- Read the text out loud and listen to your **voice.** Does the paper sound like something you would say?
- Restate the paper's **thesis** or **theme** in a single sentence. Is it stated in the paper? Does the paper support it?
- List the specific **evidence** that supports this thesis or theme. Is it sufficient? Is it arranged effectively?
- **Outline** the paper paragraph by paragraph. Is the development of ideas clear and logical?
- Return to your **introduction.** Does it accurately introduce the revised paper?
- Return to your **conclusion.** Does it reflect your most recent thoughts on the subject?
- Return to your **title** and write five alternative titles. Which is the best one?

WRITING 3: EXPLORATION ━━━━━━━━━━━━━━━

Look over the suggestions for revision in this section. Which of them have you used in the past? Which seem most useful to you now? Which seem most farfetched?

SUGGESTIONS FOR WRITING AND RESEARCH

INDIVIDUAL

Select any paper that you previously wrote in one draft but that you believe would profit from revision. Revise the paper by following some of the revision strategies and suggestions in this chapter.

In pairs or small groups, research the revision habits of a favorite or famous writer. If you cannot find such information, interview a professor, teacher, or person in your community who is known to write and publish. Find out about the revision strategies he or she most often uses. Summarize your findings according to the strategies described in this chapter and any others that your chosen writer uses. With your classmates, reorganize the research of individual members or teams by strategy. Each member or small group will assume responsibility for preparing a report on one strategy, discussing the information collected from all the chosen authors about that strategy. These reports can be assembled in a class book.

19 Focused Revising

Have you ever found yourself running out of ideas, energy, or creativity on what seemed to be a perfectly good topic for a paper? Have you ever been told to rewrite, revise, review, redo, or rethink a paper but not known exactly what those suggestions meant? Have you ever written a paper you thought was carefully focused and well researched but also was dull and lifeless?

Odds are you're not alone. When anyone writes a first draft—especially on an assigned topic to which he or she has given little prior thought—it's easy to summarize rather than analyze, to produce generalities and ignore specifics, to settle for clichés rather than invent fresh images, to cover too much territory in too little time. In fact, most first drafts contain more than their share of summary, generalization, superficiality, and cliché, since most first-draft writers are feeling their way and still discovering their topic. In other words, you seldom have a problem if your first draft is off the track, wanders a bit, and needs refocusing. However, you *do* have a problem if, for your second draft, you don't know how to reset your focus.

The best way to shape a wandering piece of writing is to return to it, reread it, slow it down, take it apart, and build it back up again, this time attending more carefully to purpose, audience, and voice. Celebrate first-draft writing for what it is—a warm-up, a scouting trip—but plan next to get on with your journey in a more deliberate and organized fashion. Sometimes you already know—or your readers tell you—exactly where to go. Other times, you're not sure and need some strategies to get you moving again. This chapter offers four specific strategies for restarting, reconceiving, and refocusing a stuck paper.

19 a Limiting

Broad topics lead to superficial writing. It's difficult to recount a four-week camping trip, to explain the meaning of *Hamlet,* or to

solve the problems of poverty, crime, or violence in a few double-spaced pages. You'll almost always do better to cover less ground in more pages. Instead, can you *limit* your focus to one pivotal day on the trip? Can you explain and interpret one crucial scene? Can you research and portray one real social problem in your own backyard?

1 Limit time, place, and action

When a first draft attempts to describe and explain actions that took place over many days, weeks, or months, try limiting the second draft to actions that took place on one day, on one afternoon, or in one hour. Limiting the amount of time you write about automatically limits the action (what happened) and place (where it happened) as well. For example, in the first draft of a paper investigating the homeless in downtown Burlington, Dan began with a broad sweep:

> In this land of opportunity, freedom takes on different meaning for different people. Some people are born to wealth; others obtain it by the sweat of their brows, while average Americans always manage to get by. But others, not so fortunate or talented, never have enough food or shelter to make even the ends of their daily lives meet.

While there is nothing inherently wrong with this start, neither is there anything new, interesting, or exciting. The generalizations about wealth and poverty tell us only what we already know; there are no new facts, information, or images to catch our attention and hold it for the pages still to come.

Before writing his second draft, Dan visited the downtown area, met some homeless people, and observed firsthand the habits of a single homeless man named Brian; then he limited his focus and described what he witnessed on one morning:

> Dressed in soiled blue jeans and a ragged red flannel shirt, Brian digs curiously through an evergreen bush beside a house on Loomis Street. His yellow mesh baseball cap bears no emblem or logo to mark him a member of any team. He wears it low, concealing any expression his eyes might disclose. After a short struggle,

> he emerges from the bush, a Budweiser can in hand, a
> grin across his face. Pouring out the remaining liquid, he
> tosses the can into his shopping cart among other
> aluminum, glass, and plastic containers. He pauses, slides
> a Marlboro out of the crumpled pack in his breast pocket,
> lights it, and resumes his expedition.

While only one small act happens in this revised first paragraph—the retrieving of a single beer can—that act anticipates Dan's forthcoming story of how unemployed, homeless people earn money. By starting with a single authentic scene, Dan writes more about less; in the process, he teaches his readers specific things about people he originally labeled "not so fortunate or talented." By describing instead of evaluating or interpreting this scene, he invites readers to make their own inferences about what it means. In other words, writing one specific, accurate, nonjudgmental scene asks readers to interpret and therefore engage more deeply in the text.

2 Limit scope

One technique for limiting the scope of any type of paper is to identify the topic of any one page, paragraph, or sentence in which something important or interesting is introduced. Begin your next draft with that specific topic, focusing close now and limiting the whole draft to only that topic. For example, in a paper arguing against the clear-cutting of forests, focus on one page describing the cutting of Western red cedar; limit the next whole draft to that single subject. In a paper examining the exploitation of women in television advertising, focus on one paragraph describing a single beer ad; limit the next whole draft to that single subject. In a paper examining your high school soccer career, focus on one sentence describing the locker room after the harrowing loss of the championship game. By limiting your scope in this fashion, you deepen your exploration.

WRITING 1: APPLICATION

Devote a portion of your journal or class notebook exclusively to exploring the revision possibilities of one paper. For your first entry, reread the paper you intend to revise, and limit either the time or scope that you intend to cover in the second draft.

 Adding

A sure way to increase reader interest in a paper, and your own interest as well, is to *add* new and specific material to that overly general first draft. Whether you are arguing about the effects of mountain bikes on the wilderness, explaining the situation of the homeless people downtown, or interpreting the poems of Gwendolyn Brooks, it is your job to become the expert on this subject in your writing class. It's your job to read the necessary articles, visit the appropriate places, interview the relevant people who will make you the authority to write the paper. On first drafts, neither your instructor nor classmates expect you to be this authority; on subsequent drafts, their expectations increase.

Add expert voices

Locate new information to add to your later drafts by reading widely and listening carefully. Get to the library and locate sources that supplement and substantiate your own voice. Quote the experts, identifying who they are and why they should be listened to. Also get out into the field and talk to people who are the local experts on your subject. Quote these experts and include their voices in your next draft.

Although textual quotations are helpful and expected in academic papers, they are seldom so lively as interview quotations from local people. In many instances where little may have been published on local issues, the only way to get up-to-date local information is to talk to people. Quoting people directly not only adds new and credible information to your paper; it invariably adds a sense of life as well. For example, as Dan continued his story of Burlington's homeless people, he interviewed a number of people, such as police officer Hardy, who had firsthand knowledge of the homeless can collectors:

> "They provide a real service to the community," he explains. "You'd see a lot more cans and bottles littering the streets if they weren't out here working hard each day. I've never had a problem with any of them. They are a real value."

While Dan himself could have made the same observation, it has greater authority and life coming from a cop on the beat.

In another instance, a team of first-year students collaborated to write a profile of the local Ronald McDonald House, a nonprofit organization providing free room and board for the families of hospital patients. In their first draft, they researched the local newspaper for introductory information on the origins of this institution. It was useful information, but without much life:

> The McDonald's corporation actually provided less than 5 percent of the total cost of starting the Ronald McDonald House. The other 95 percent of the money came from local businesses and special-interest groups.

For their second draft, the group interviewed the director of the Ronald McDonald House and used her as an additional and more current source of information. In fact, they devoted the entire second draft to material collected through interviews with the director and staff at the house. In the following sample, the director substantiates the information from the initial newspaper story but adds more specific, local, and lively details:

> "Our biggest problem is that people think we're supported by the McDonald's corporation. We have to get people to understand that anything we get from McDonald's is just from the particular franchise's generosity—and may be no more than is donated by other local merchants. Martin's, Hood, and Ben and Jerry's provide much of the food. McDonald's is not obligated to give us anything. The only reason we use their name is because of its child appeal."

Their final profile of the Ronald McDonald House included information ranging from newspaper and newsletter stories to site descriptions and interviews with staff, volunteers, and family.

2 Add details

If you quickly review this chapter's samples of revision by *limiting* and *adding,* you will notice the increase in specific detail. Focusing close, interviewing people, and researching texts all produce specific information that adds both energy and evidence to whatever paper you are writing. In the can collecting paper, the visual details make Brian come alive—"*the soiled blue jeans,*" "*red flannel*

shirt," "*yellow mesh cap*," "*Budweiser can*," "*Marlboro cigarette pack*." In the Ronald McDonald revisions, newspaper statistics add authority ("*5 percent McDonald's corporation contribution*") while the interview information adds specificity ("*Martin's*," "*Hood*," "*Ben and Jerry's*").

WRITING 2: APPLICATION ────────────────────────────

Identify texts, places, or people that contain information relevant to your paper topic and go collect it. If you are writing a paper strictly from memory, close your eyes and visit this place in your imagination: Describe the details and re-create the dialogue you find there.

19 **c** **Switching**

Another strategy for focusing a second or third draft is to deliberately alter your customary way of viewing and thinking about this topic. One sure way to change how you see a problem, experience, or idea is to *switch* the perspective from which you view it (the point of view) or the language in which you portray it (the verb tense).

1 Switch point of view

Switching point of view from which a story, essay, or report is written means changing the perspective from which it is told. For example, in recounting personal experience, the most natural point of view is the first person (*I, we*) as we relate what happened to us. Here Karen writes in the first person in reporting her experience participating in the Massachusetts women's basketball tournament:

> We lost badly to Walpole in what turned out to be our
>
> final game. I sat on the bench most of the time.

However, Karen opened the final draft of her personal experience basketball narrative with a switch in point of view, writing as if she were the play-by-play announcer broadcasting the game at the moment, in this case moving to third person *and* adopting a new persona as well:

> Well folks, it looks as if Belmont has given up; the
>
> coach is preparing to send in his subs. It has been a rough
>
> game for Belmont. They stayed in it during the first

quarter, but Walpole has run away with it since then.

Down by twenty with only six minutes left, Belmont's first

sub is now approaching the table.

In her final draft, Karen opened from the announcer's point of view for one page, then switched for the remainder of the paper to her own first-person perspective, separating the two by white space.

In research writing, as opposed to personal narrative, the customary point of view for reporting research results is third person (*he, she, it*) to emphasize the information and de-emphasize the writer. For example, the profile of the Ronald McDonald House begins, as you might expect, with no reference to the writers of the report:

The Ronald McDonald House provides a home away

from home for out-of-town families of hospital patients

who need to visit patients for extended periods of time

but cannot afford to stay in hotels or motels.

However, in one of their drafts, the writers switched to first person and explained their personal difficulties in reporting on this situation:

In this documentary, we had a few problems with

getting certain interviews and information. Since the

house is a refuge for parents in distress, we limited the

kinds of questions we asked. We didn't want to pry.

2 Switch tense

Switching verb tense means switching the time frame in which a story or experience occurs. While the present tense is a natural tense for explaining information (see the first Ronald McDonald example above), the most natural tense for recounting personal experience is the past tense, as we retell occurrences that happened sometime before the present moment—the same tense Karen adopted in draft one of her basketball essay. However, her final draft is written entirely in the present tense, beginning with the announcer and continuing through to the end of her own narrative:

It's over now, and I've stopped crying, and I'm very

happy. In the end I have to thank—not my coach, not my

team—but Walpole for beating us so badly that I got
to play.

The advantage of switching to the present tense is that it lets you reexperience an event, and doing that in turn allows you to reexamine, reconsider, and reinterpret it—all essential activities for successful revision. At the same time, readers participate in the drama of the moment, waiting along with you to find out what will happen next. The disadvantage is that the present tense is associated with fiction—it's difficult to be writing while you're playing basketball. It's also difficult to reflect on your experiences if you're pretending they are occurring as you are writing.

3 Switch sides

Another way to gain a new revision perspective is to switch sides in arguing a position: write one draft supporting the "pro" side, then write a second draft supporting the "con" side. For example, Issa, a dedicated mountain bike enthusiast, planned to write in favor of opening up more wilderness trails for use by mountain bikers. However, before writing his final draft, he researched the arguments against his position and wrote a draft of his paper from that point of view (compare it to the final version on page 130):

> The hikers and other passive trail users argue against
> allowing mountain bikes onto narrow trails traditionally
> traveled only by foot and horse. They point out that the
> wide, deeply treaded tires of the mountain bikes cause
> erosion and that the high speeds of the bikers startle and
> upset both hikers and horses. According to hiker Donald
> Meserlain, the bikes "ruin the tranquillity of the
> woodlands and drive out hikers, bird watchers, and
> strollers" (Hanley).

The real advantage of switching sides for a draft is that you come to understand your opponent's point of view better and so argue more effectively against it in your final draft. For his final draft, Issa argues his original position in favor of mountain bikes, but he does so with more understanding, empathy, and effectiveness

because he spent a draft with the opposition. His final draft makes it clear where he stands on the issue:

> Educated mountain biking, like hiking and horseback riding, respects the environment and promotes peace and conservation, not noise and destruction. Making this case has begun to pay off, and the battle over who walks and who rides the trails should now shift in favor of peaceful coexistence. "Buoyed by studies showing that bicycle tires cause no more erosion or trail damage than the boots of hikers, and far less than horses' hooves, mountain bike advocates are starting to find receptive ears among environmental organizations" (Schwartz 78).

The tone of the final draft of Issa's mountain bike essay is less strident and combative than it is conciliatory and compromising; it seems a very reasoned and sensible approach to a difficult problem and was, perhaps, brought about by his spending time seriously considering the objections of the opposition.

WRITING 3: APPLICATION ————————————————————

Write in your journal about a past experience, using the present tense and/or third-person point of view. Then reread the passage and describe its effect on you as both writer and reader.

19 d Transforming

To *transform* a text is to change its form by casting it into a new form or genre. In early drafts, writers often attend closely to the content of their stories, arguments, or reports but pay little attention to the form in which these are presented, accepting the genre as a given. However, recasting ideas and information into different genres presents them in a different light. The possibilities for presenting information in different genres are endless, since anything can become anything else. Consequently, keep in mind that some transformations are useful primarily to help you achieve a fresh perspective during the revision process, while others are appropriate for presenting the information to readers.

In the world outside of college, it is common for research information to be reported in different genres to different audiences. For example, in a corporate setting, the same research information may be conveyed as a report to a manager, a letter to the president, a pamphlet for the stockholders, and a news release for public media—and show up later in a feature article in a trade publication or newspaper. As in the working world, so in college: information researched and collected for any paper can be presented in a variety of forms and formats.

▮ Transform personal experience from essay to journal

The journal form encourages informal and conversational language, creates a sense of chronological suspense, is an ideal form for personal reflection, substitutes dates for more complex transitions, and proves especially useful for conveying experience over a long period of time. For example, Jeff used the journal format to tell the story of his month-long camping trip with the organization Outward Bound. Following is an excerpt, edited for brevity, in which he describes his reactions to camping alone for one week:

> Day 4   I find myself thinking a lot about food. When I haven't eaten in the morning, I tend to lose my body heat faster than when I eat. . . . At this point, in solo, good firewood is surprisingly tough to come by. . . .
>
> Day 5   Before I write about my fifth day of solo, I just want to say that it was damn cold last night. I have a −20 degree bag, and I froze. It was the coldest night so far, about −25. . . .
>
> Day 7   I haven't seen a single person for an entire week. I have never done this before, and I really don't want to do it again—not having anyone to talk to. Instead of talking, I write to myself. . . . If I didn't have this journal, I think I would have gone crazy.

▮ Transform to letters

An issue might be illuminated in a lively and interesting way by being cast as a series or exchange of letters. Each letter allows a different character or point of view to be expressed. For example, Issa's argument on mountain bike use in wilderness areas could be presented as a series of letters to the editor of a local paper arguing different sides of the controversy: from a hiker, a horseback rider, a mountain bike rider, a forest ranger, a landowner, and so on.

3 Transform to a documentary

Radio, film, and television documentaries are common vehicles for hearing news and information. Virtually any research paper could be made livelier by being cast as a documentary film or investigative feature story. Full research and documentation would be required, as for formal academic papers; however, writers would use the style of the popular press rather than the MLA or APA. In fact, the final form of the profile of the Ronald McDonald House was written as a script for *Sixty Minutes* and opened with a Mike Wallace–type reporter speaking into a microphone.

> Smith: Hello, this is John Smith reporting for *Sixty Minutes*. Our topic this week is the Ronald McDonald House. Here I am, in front of the house in Burlington, Vermont, but before I go inside, let me fill you in on the history of this and many other houses like it.

The final paper included sections with the fictional Smith interviewing actual staff members as well as some sections presented neutrally from the camera's point of view:

> Toward the back of the house, three cars and one camper are parked in an oval-shaped gravel driveway. Up three steps onto a small porch are four black plastic chairs and a small coffee table containing a black ashtray filled with cigarette butts.

4 Transform to a book with chapters

Teams of student writers can collaborate on writing a short book with "chapters" exploring an issue of common interest. Such a form could include a table of contents, preface, foreword, afterword, introduction, and so on. For example, Dan's report on the life of a can collector could become one chapter in a collaborative "book" investigating how the homeless live:

1. Housing for the Homeless
2. Dinner at the Salvation Army
3. Shopping at Goodwill

4. Brian: Case Study of a Can Collector

5. Winter Prospects

5 Transform to a magazine article

If you are investigating consumer products, such as mountain bikes, CDs, stereos, and the like, consider writing the final draft as a report for *Consumer Reports*. If you are investigating an issue such as homelessness, write it as an article for *Time* or *Newsweek*. Likewise, a story on dormitory security could be aimed at the campus newspaper. Before writing the final draft, be sure to study the form and conventions of the periodical for which you are writing.

6 Transform to a talk show debate

An especially good genre for interpretative or argument papers would be a debate, conversation, or panel discussion. For example, students recently wrote a paper as a debate on the advantages versus disadvantages of clear-cutting timber: on one side were the environmentalists and tourist industry, on the other side the paper companies and landowners; each side had valid points in its favor. The debate format was realistic, as it echoed very closely a similar debate in Congress.

7 Transform to any medium of expression

The possibilities are endless: song, play, poem, editorial, science fiction story, laboratory report, bulletin, brochure, commercial, public address, political speech, telephone conversation, e-mail exchange, World Wide Web page, poster, "Talk of the Town" for *The New Yorker,* sound bite, environmental impact statement, conference paper, video game, philosophical debate.

WRITING 4: APPLICATION ———————————————

Propose a transformation for a paper you are writing or have recently written. List the advantages and disadvantages of this transformation. Recast your paper (or a part of it) in the new genre and describe the effect.

Experimenting with revising versus academic convention

Standard academic **conventions** are accepted ways of doing certain things, such as using an objective voice in research reports and placing the thesis first in position papers. These conventions have evolved over time, for a reason. When carefully followed, they transmit ideas and information in a clear, predictable, and direct manner, avoiding confusion, complexity, and subjectivity. Although in many cases these conventions work well, successful writers sometimes invent unorthodox strategies and experiment with new forms to express their ideas. In order to decide whether a conventional or an unorthodox form is preferable in any part of your paper, try both to see which more appropriately presents your ideas in their best light. Sometimes an act as simple as changing time, tense, point of view, or genre can totally change the effect of a piece of writing.

The strategies described in this chapter are useful revising tools because they force writers to resee the events in their papers in different language and from different perpectives. Writing in new forms is also intriguing, exciting, and fun—an experience that writers often need after working long and hard to put together a first draft.

When and under what circumstances should you limit, add, switch, or transform? While there are no rules, you might try using these strategies whenever you feel stuck or in need of new energy or insight. But be sure to weigh gains and losses whenever you use new focusing techniques.

 FOCUSED REVISING

When you have finished the first draft of a paper, address one or more of the following questions:

1. How could this topic be **limited** so that it covers less in more detail?

2. What research information could I **add** to this paper to make it more convincing?

3. What would be the effect on this paper if I **switched** from past to present tense or from objective to subjective point of view?

4. In what **form** would the final draft of this paper be most effective?

Disregarding academic conventions in early drafts should seldom be a problem; however, disregarding them in final drafts is riskier, so check with your instructor. Be sure that in gaining reader attention in this way, you do not lose credibility or cause confusion.

SUGGESTIONS FOR WRITING AND RESEARCH

INDIVIDUAL

1. Write the first draft of a personal experience paper as a broad overview of the whole experience. Write the second draft by limiting the story to one day or less of this experience. Write the third draft using one of the other techniques described in this chapter: adding, switching, or transforming. Write the final draft any way that pleases you.

2. Write the first draft of a research-based paper as on overview of the whole issue you intend to deal with. In the second draft, limit the scope to something you now cover in one page, paragraph, or sentence. In the third draft, adopt one of the focused revision strategies described in this chapter: adding, switching or transforming. For your final draft, revise in any way that makes your presentation more effective.

COLLABORATIVE

For a class research project, interview college instructors in different departments concerning their thoughts about transforming academic papers into other genres. Write up the results in any form that seems useful.

20 Responding to Writing

All writers can use a little help from their friends. Few great books or good stories were written by one author in one draft without some kind of help along the way. This is not to say that individual authors do not compose their own work, for of course they do. But even the most skillful writers benefit from suggestions by editors, reviewers, teachers, and friends. In like manner, your writing will improve if you share it with classmates, consider their reactions, and revise accordingly. This chapter explores ways to give and get writing help.

20 a Asking for help

Writers can profit from help at virtually every stage of the writing process—brainstorming ideas, seeking research leads, proofreading—but it's while they're revising that most writers seek the help of potential audiences to find out what in their writing is strong, what weak, because then they still have a chance to do something about it. Following are some suggestions for getting help as you seek to finish your writing.

Identify the kind of help you want

When you share a draft with a reader, specify what you want. If you want help with ideas, tell your reader not to worry about grammar, mechanics, or style. If you are firm about your ideas but want help with style or proofreading, specify that need. If you do want a general reaction, say so—but be prepared to hear about everything and anything.

2 Ask specific questions

If you wonder whether you've provided enough examples, ask about that. If you want to know whether your argument is airtight, ask about that. If you are concerned about your tone, ask about that. Also mark specific places in your paper about which you have questions, whether a word, a sentence, or even a paragraph.

3 Ask global questions

Ask whether the larger purpose is clear. Ask whether the reader can identify your theme, thesis, or main point. Ask whether the paper seems right for its intended audience. Ask for general reactions about readability, evidence, and completeness. Ask what objections or problems your reader would anticipate from other readers.

4 Listen, don't defend

Pay close attention to what you hear. You have asked for help, so now listen to what's offered. While listening to oral comments, stay quiet and take notes, interrupting only when you don't understand something. When reading written responses, read them twice before accepting or rejecting them.

5 Maintain ownership

Don't act on responses with which you disagree. If you don't understand or believe what someone tells you to do, don't do it. This is your paper, and you will live with the results.

WRITING 1: EXPLORATION _____

Describe the best written or oral response to a piece of your writing that you remember. What were the circumstances? Who was the respondent? Explain whether the response was deserved or not.

20 b Giving constructive responses

When you find yourself in a position to help other writers, keep the following basic ideas in mind:

- **Respond to the writer's requests.** If you are asked whether the thesis is clearly stated, for example, address that question before

commenting on logic of the writer's reasoning, the accuracy or authority of the evidence, or other issues.

- **Follow the Golden Rule.** Give the kind of response that you would like to receive yourself. Remember how you feel being praised, criticized, or questioned. If you remember what helps, what hurts, and what makes you defensive, you'll give better help to others.

- **Attend to the text, not the person.** Focus on the text and not the writer's person. Writers, like all people, have egos easily bruised by careless or cruel comments.

- **Praise what deserves praise.** Most writers accept critical help when they also receive complimentary help, and in most papers

EVALUATIONS VERSUS SUGGESTIONS

When you are responding to an early draft of a classmate's writing, keep in mind that your purpose is to suggest ways to improve a work in progress rather than to evaluate a finished essay. Apply your critical thinking skills to identify strengths and weaknesses, but in communicating your reactions to the writer, express your opinions in a supportive rather than adversarial way.

The difference between an evaluation or judgment and a suggestion often depends on phrasing and sometimes on individual words. An **evaluation** or **judgment** places a value or a rating on the writing and is less helpful than a **suggestion** in providing details for revising. Try to concentrate on suggesting ways to improve any weakness you encounter.

EVALUATIVE	You should give more examples.
COMMENTS	Your introduction is too short.
SUGGESTIONS	You might consider giving other examples. I think your introduction could be better if you gave your reader some more background information.

Sometimes it is difficult to separate your own opinions or beliefs about the topic or content of the writer's work from your response to the presentation. This problem occurs especially when you care deeply about the topic and strongly disagree with the writer's thesis. In such situations, it is best to be open about your feelings so that the writer will be aware of their possible influence on your suggestions.

there is something that is praiseworthy. But writers can sense hollow praise, so avoid praising what doesn't deserve it.

- **Ask questions rather than give advice.** It's your turn, now, to respect ownership. Asking questions gives writers room to solve their own problems. Of course, when asked, give answers or suggest alternatives if you have them.

- **Focus on major problems first.** Address conceptual problems first, mechanical ones later on. Early drafts that are marked for every possible misspelling, typo, and grammatical slip can overwhelm writers, making them reluctant to revise at all. At the same

---

 THE LANGUAGE OF MAKING SUGGESTIONS

Here are some tips on writing suggestions for your classmates:

- Use words or phrases that indicate a statement is your opinion only.

I think   in my opinion   from my perspective
I feel   in my viewpoint

- Use *could* and *might* (suggestion) rather than *should* or *ought* (direction).

You *could* clarify the cause-effect relationship in the last paragraph.

> *Not: You should clarify. . . .*

- Avoid negative phrases unless you need them to state your opinion clearly.

I didn't understand how the second example was related to the first one.

> *Not: Your second example wasn't related to the first.*

- Use verbs like *seems* or *appears* to qualify your opinions.

The conclusion *seems* to shift to another topic.

The ideas at the end of your essay *appear* to be repeating ones that you stated earlier. Is that what you intended?

- Use questions if you are not sure that you interpreted the writer's ideas correctly.

You seem to be disagreeing with the author in one place but agreeing with her in another. *Did I misunderstand your point?*

time, most writers want such proofreading help on near-final drafts, so it pays to check what the writer wants when.

20 c Responding in writing

Responding to writing in writing, as most instructors do, is both common and convenient. "Talking back" to a piece of writing by commenting directly on the manuscript takes less time and is therefore more efficient than discussing every idea orally. You can annotate a classmate's manuscript as you would a published work. (See 2b2.) It is easy to make written comments specific, identifying particular words, sentences, paragraphs, or examples that need attention. Also, written comments leave a record for writers to refer to later, when they actually get around to the rewriting.

The disadvantage to writing comments directly on papers is the possibility that misunderstandings will arise because you are not present to clarify. Try to ask questions rather than give answers and, again, follow the Golden Rule. The following suggestions may help:

Comment in pencil. Ink is permanent. Red ink looks bloody. Pencil, on the other hand, is soft, gentle and erasable. Many writers have already developed negative associations from teacher's red ink comments that correct what's wrong rather than praise what's right. Don't do that to your classmates.

Use clear symbols. Consider using professional editing symbols to comment on a classmate's paper. (They are printed on the last page of this book.) Or use obvious symbols that anyone can figure out—underlining or circling phrases that puzzle you or writing question marks in the margin. Put brackets where a missing word or phrase belongs.

WRITING 2: EXPLORATION

Describe your most recent experience in receiving written comments from someone. Were the comments helpful? Did the respondent follow the suggestions given in this section? How did the comments influence your revisions?

20 d Responding through one-to-one conferences

One-to-one conferences provide the best and most immediate help writers can get. After reading a paper alone and quietly, sitting

together, you can read passages aloud and make both general and specific comments about the writing. An oral conference helps as a follow-up to written comments, as conversations between writer and reader promote community, friendship, and understanding.

Conferences also make it easy to address both global and specific writing concerns at the same time. Finally, writer and reader can clarify misunderstandings as soon as they arise, However, it is harder to make tough, critical comments face to face, so readers are often less candid than when they make written comments. Also, conferring together in any depth about a piece of writing takes time.

The suggestions for making effective written responses also apply to oral conferences; however, there are additional things to keep in mind:

Converse in a comfortable setting. A place that's warm and casual can make a great difference in creating a friendly, satisfying discussion. When digressions occur, as they will if you're relaxed together, use them to learn new things about the subject and about each other; many such digressions circle back and help the writer. Even in the friendliest setting, however, if you don't discuss the writing itself, the writer will not be helped.

Ask follow-up questions. Ask clarifying questions to help writers advance their revision. When you have already written out responses, use the oral conference time to ask deeper or follow-up questions so together you can search for appropriate solutions.

WRITING 3: APPLICATION _____

Confer with a writer about his or her paper. Follow the suggestions given in this section. Describe in a journal entry how they worked.

20 e Responding in writing groups

Many serious writers belong to writing groups in which members both give and receive help with their writing. When a particular writer's work is featured, that writer receives a response from each member of the group; in other sessions, this person gives responses.

Writing groups allow a single writer to hear multiple perspectives on a draft, which provide either more consensus or more options for revision. They also allow an interpretation to develop through the interplay of different perspectives, often creating a

ESL **PARTICIPATING IN WRITING GROUPS**

As a nonnative speaker of English, you may feel at a disadvantage in writing groups. Keep in mind, however, that participants usually give responses based on the content of a paper, not its grammar or word choice. Like your classmates, you can give valuable responses by pointing out what you think is successful in a paper and by providing suggestions for further developing a topic. As someone with a different cultural background, you may even be able to offer an interesting perspective on a topic that the writer hasn't considered.

cumulative response that existed in no single reader's mind before the session. Finally, writing groups can give writers more confidence by providing them with a varied and supportive audience.

At the same time, groups that meet outside of a classroom setting can be difficult to coordinate, since they involve people with varied schedules. Furthermore, the multiple audiences provided by groups may be intimidating and threatening to a writer. Since writing groups involve more people, require more coordination, take more time, and are less likely to be familiar than conferences with one other person, the following suggestions may help.

1 Form a group along common interests

Writing groups are useful in classes because the people are usually working on similar projects. You can take advantage of having everyone together at one time and place to give each other help. Writing groups can also be created outside of class by interested people who get together regularly to share their writing.

2 Focus on the writing

The goal of writing groups is to improve one another's writing and to encourage one another to write more. Pass out copies of the work in advance for silent reading prior to class, or read drafts aloud during the group meetings, with other group members following along on copies. After members have read or heard the paper, share your reactions, each in turn.

3 Keep groups small

In-class writing groups can have as few as three or as many as five members; time constraints make groups larger than five cumbersome. Smaller groups need less time, larger groups need more. Groups that meet outside of the classroom have fewer size and time limits.

4 Allocate time fairly

Sometimes a meeting is organized so that each member reads a paper or a portion of a paper. At other times a meeting may focus on the work of one member, and members thus take turns receiving responses at different meetings. If papers are to be read, it generally takes two minutes to read a typed, double-spaced page out loud. Discussion and comment time should match or exceed the oral reading time on each paper. Groups that meet on their own should experiment to determine how much they can read and

---

TEN QUESTIONS TO ASK WRITERS ABOUT THEIR WRITING

Although the specific questions you ask depend on the writer's particular paper, some of the following may be helpful:

1. Where did this idea come from? (The origin of the idea may provide useful clues as an aid to further revision.)

2. What idea holds the whole piece together? (Where's the center? Can you point to a page or paragraph?)

3. When you were writing, who were your imagined readers? (Is there any place you think your readers might still be confused?)

4. Where else could you find information to support or expand this topic? (All papers profit from research knowledge.)

5. Whom could you interview to provide more information or another perspective on this topic? (Interview quotations add life to most papers.)

6. Can you provide some background or context for this idea?

7. Can you provide any examples or illustrations to show what you mean?

8. Can you think of two alternative ways to begin this paper?

9. Can you think of two alternative ways to end this paper?

10. Can you think of two alternative titles?

discuss at each session, perhaps varying the schedule from meeting to meeting.

SUGGESTIONS FOR WRITING AND RESEARCH

INDIVIDUAL

Investigate what has been written about peer writing groups. Check, in particular, for work by Kenneth Bruffee, Peter Elbow, Anne Ruggles Gere, Thom Hawkins, and Tori Haring-Smith. Write a report to inform your classmates about your discoveries.

COLLABORATIVE

Form interview pairs and interview local published writers about the way in which response by friends, family, editors, or critics affects their writing. Share results orally or in a collaboratively written report.

21 Creative Nonfiction

The term *creative nonfiction* describes much of the good writing that appears in magazines such as *The New Yorker, Harper's,* and *GQ,* as well as many works on the nonfiction best-seller lists. Writers of creative nonfiction commonly borrow stylistic and formal techniques from the fast-paced visual narratives of film and television as well as from the innovative language of poetry, fiction, and drama. These influences encourage a multifaceted, multidimensional prose style. Many current nonfiction prose writers find the traditions of continuity, order, consistency, and unity associated with conventional prose insufficient to convey the chaotic truths of the postmodern world. This chapter examines some creative writing strategies and suggests appropriate venues within the academic curriculum where such prose strategies could be useful. (Many of the ideas presented here were first articulated by Winston Weathers in his groundbreaking book *An Alternate Style: Options in Composition* [Hayden, 1980]).

21 a Lists

Lists can break up and augment prose texts in useful, credible, and surprising ways. Lists of names, words, and numbers add variety, speed, depth, and humor to texts. And lists are everywhere we look, as Joan Didion illustrates in making the case that Las Vegas weddings are big business in this excerpt from "Marrying Absurd":

> There are nineteen such wedding chapels in Las Vegas, intensely competitive, each offering better, faster, and, by implication, more sincere services than the next: Our Photos Best Anywhere, Your Wedding on a Phonograph Record, Candlelight with Your Ceremony, Honeymoon Accommodations, Free Transportation from Your Motel to Courthouse to Chapel and Return to Motel, Religious or Civil Ceremonies, Dressing Rooms, Flowers, Rings, Announcements, Witnesses Available, and Ample Parking.

Didion's list of competitive wedding services convinces us she has observed carefully, she's not making this stuff up; without her saying it, we see some level of absurdity in the way this town promotes marriage.

Lists need not be clever so much as purposeful. That is, you include a list of names, items, quotations, and so on to show readers you know your stuff: you've done your homework, read widely or observed carefully, taken good notes, and made sense of what you've found. Lists deepen a text by providing illustrations or examples.

When first-year student Craig examined sexist stereotypes in children's toys, he made the following list of dolls on a single shelf at a local discount store:

> To my left is a shelf of Barbie: Animal Lovin' Barbie, Wet 'n Wild Barbie, Barbie Feelin' Pretty Fashions, Barbie Special Expressions, Super Star Barbie Movietime Prop Shop, Step 'n Style Boutique, My First Barbie (Prettiest Princess Ever), Action Accents Barbie Sewing Machine, Barbie Cool Times Fashion, Barbie and the All-Stars, Style Magic Barbie, a Barbie Ferrari, and tucked away in a corner, slightly damaged and dusty, Super Star Ken.

This list simply documents by name the products on the toy shelf, actually adding a dimension of authenticity and believability to the writer's case that, yes, the Barbie image has a considerable influence on children.

However, lists that are quick to read may not be quick to write; an effective list that appears to be written by free association may, in fact, have been laboriously constructed as the writer ransacked his memory or her thesaurus for words, then arranged and rearranged them to create the right sound or sense effect.

21 b Snapshots

Writing prose snapshots is analogous to constructing and arranging a photo album composed of many separate visual images. Photo albums, when carefully assembled from informative snapshots, tell stories with clear beginnings, middles, and endings, but with lots of white spaces between one picture and the next, with few transitions explaining how the photographer got from one scene to the next. In other words, while photo albums tell stories, they do so piecemeal, making the viewer fill in or imagine what happened between shots. Prose snapshots function the same way as visual snapshots; each is connected to the other by white space and leaps of reader logic and faith.

Sometimes individual snapshots are numbered to suggest deliberate connectedness; other times each is titled, to suggest an ability to stand alone like chapters within books; sometimes they appear on a page as block paragraphs, the reading alone revealing the lack of transitions and the necessity for active reader interpretation. As such, snapshots are satisfying for fast readers, each containing a small story unto itself, the whole a larger story, in part of the reader's making.

Margaret Atwood wrote snapshots to emphasize the dangers of men's bodies in the following passage from her essay "Alien Territory" (1983):

> The history of war is a history of killed bodies. That's what war is: bodies killing other bodies, bodies being killed.

> Some of the killed bodies are those of women and children, as a side effect you might say. Fallout, shrapnel, napalm, rape and skewering, anti-personnel devices. But most of the killed bodies are men. So are most of those doing the killing.

> Why do men want to kill the bodies of other men? Women don't want to kill the bodies of other women. By and large. As far as we know.

> Here are some traditional reasons: Loot. Territory. Lust for power. Hormones. Adrenaline high. Rage. God. Flag. Honor. Righteous anger. Revenge. Oppression. Slavery. Starvation. Defense of one's life. Love; or, a desire to protect the men and women. From what? From the bodies of other men.

> What men are most afraid of is not lions, not snakes, not the dark, not women. What men are most afraid of is the body of another man.

> Men's bodies are the most dangerous things on earth.

Note how the white space between one snapshot and another gives readers breathing space, time out, time to digest one thought before supping at the next. The white space between snapshots actually exercises readers' imagination as they participate in constructing some logic that makes the text make sense—the readers themselves supply the connectives, construct the best meaning, which, nevertheless, will be very close to what skillful authors intend.

Snapshots allow busy writers to compose in chunks, in five- and ten-minute blocks between appointments, schedules, classes, or coffee breaks. And, as we've seen, five or ten or twenty chunks— reconsidered, rearranged, revised—can tell a whole story. (For a

student example of composing in snapshots, see an excerpt from Paige's essay later in this chapter.)

While it's fun to write fast, random, and loose snapshots, the real secret to a successful snapshot essay is putting them together in the right order—some right order—some pattern that, by the end, conveys your theme as surely as if you had written straight narration or exposition. Writing snapshots on a computer is especially fun since you can order and reorder indefinitely until you arrive at a satisfying arrangement. Composing snapshot essays on easy-to-shuffle 3″ × 5″ cards also works. In either case, assemble and arrange as you would pictures in a photo album, playfully and seriously: begin at the beginning, alternate themes, begin in media res (in the middle), alternate time, begin with flashbacks, alternate voices, consider frames, alternate fonts, reinforce rhythms, experiment with openings and closings, type, and titles.

21 c Playful sentences

No matter what your form or style, sentences are your main units of composition, explaining the world in terms of subjects, actions, and objects, suggesting that the world operates causally: some force (a subject) does something (acts) that causes something else to happen (an object). English prose is built around complete and predictable sentences such as those in which this paragraph (and most of this book) is written. Sometimes, however, writers use sentences in less predictable, more playful ways.

Fragment sentences suggest fragmented stories. Stories different from the stories told by conventional subject-verb-object sentences. Fragment sentences, of course, can be used judiciously in conventional writing—even academic writing, so long as the purpose is crystal clear and your fragment is not mistaken for fragmentary grammatical knowledge. However, creative nonfiction writers use fragments to create the special effects they want. A flash of movement. A bit of a story. A frozen scene. Fragments force quick reading, ask for impressionistic understanding, suggest parts rather than wholes. Like snapshots, fragments invite strong reader participation to stitch together, to move toward clear meaning.

Fragment sentences suggest, too, that things are moving fast. Very fast. Hold on. Remember the snapshot passage from Margaret Atwood's "Alien Territory"? Note that she used fragments to emphasize the sharp dangers of men's bodies:

> Some of the killed bodies are those of women and children, as a side effect you might say. Fallout, shrapnel, napalm, rape and

skewering, anti-personnel devices. But most of the killed bodies are men. So are most of those doing the killing.

Why do men want to kill the bodies of other men? Women don't want to kill the bodies of other women. By and large. As far as we know.

Atwood's fragments make the reader notice sharply the brutal and jarring truths she is writing about; in this example, The lack of conventional connections between words mirrors the disconnectedness Atwood sees in her subject: men, violence, and war.

Write fragments so your reader knows they are not mistakes. Not ignorance. Not sloppiness or printer error or carelessness. Purposeful fragments can be powerful. Deliberate. Intentional. Careful. Functional. And brief.

A **labyrinthine sentence** is quite the opposite of the fragment sentence because it seems never to end; it won't quit, and goes on and on and on, using all sorts of punctuational and grammatical tricks to create compound sentences (two or more independent clauses joined by a comma and a conjunction such as *and* or *but*) and complex sentences (one independent clause with one or more dependent clauses) and is written to suggest, perhaps, that things are running together and are hard to separate—also to suggest the "stream of consciousness" of the human mind, in which thoughts and impressions and feelings and images are run together without the easy separation into full sentences or paragraphs complete with topic sentences—the power (and sometimes confusion) of which is illustrated in the passage below, by James Agee, as he imaginatively enters the thoughts of the people he is profiling in *Let Us Now Praise Famous Men* (1941), the poor Alabama tenant farmers:

But I am young; and I am young and strong and in good health; and I am young and pretty to look at; and I am too young to worry; and so am I for my mother is kind to me; and we run in the bright air like animals, and our bare feet like plants in the wholesome earth: the natural world is around us like a lake and a wide smile and we are growing: one by one we are becoming stronger, and one by one in the terrible emptiness and the leisure we shall burn and tremble and shake with lust, and one by one we shall loosen ourselves from this place, and shall be married, and it will be different from what we see, for we will be happy and love each other, and keep the house clean, and a good garden, and buy a cultivator, and use a high grade of fertilizer, and we will know how to do things right; it will be very different:) (?:)

Agee's long connected sentence creates the run-together, wishful, worried, desperate internal dream of his subjects in a way a conventional paragraph could not. Notice, too, that punctuation and grammar are conventional and correct—up to the end, where punctuation marks are used in unexpected ways to suggest something of the confusion and uncertainty these people live with daily. You may also write run-on or fused sentences in which punctuation does not function in expected ways, as Amy does in an essay about her evolution from grade school to college:

> My life is categorized by colors
>
>> sixth grade blue
>>
>> tenth grade red
>>
>> this year black
>>
>> the year before pink
>>
>> new favorites keep popping up
>>
>> next year will it be white?

Note that Amy uses indentation, as a poet might, instead of colons, commas, and periods, to signal readers how to read her text. Be careful that your playful sentences suggest "play" rather than "mistake." Use both fragment and labyrinthine sentences to create special effects, but be wary of grammatically incorrect sentences, such as run-ons and comma splices, since they make even liberal teachers suspicious.

21 d Repetition/refrain

Writers repeat words, phrases, or sentences for emphasis. They repeat words to remind us to think hard about the word or phrase repeated. They repeat words to ask us to attend and not take for granted. They repeat words to suggest continuity of idea and theme. They repeat words to hold paragraphs and essays together. And, sometimes, they repeat words to create rhythms that are simply pleasing to the ear.

The following paragraph opens Ian Frazier's book-length study *The Great Plains*:

> Away to the Great Plains of America, to that immense Western shortgrass prairie now mostly plowed under! Away to the still empty land beyond newsstands and malls and velvet restaurant

ropes! Away to the headwaters of the Missouri, now quelled by many impoundment dams, and to the headwaters of the Platte, and to the almost invisible headwaters of the slurped up Arkansas! Away to the land where TV used to set its most popular dramas, but not anymore! Away to the land beyond the hundredth meridian of longitude, where sometimes it rains and sometimes it doesn't, where agriculture stops and does a double take! Away to the skies of the sparrow hawks sitting on telephone wires, thinking of mice and flaring their tail feathers suddenly, like a card trick! Away to the airshaft of the continent, where weather fronts from two hemispheres meet and the wind blows almost all the time! Away to the fields of wheat and milo and Sudan grass and flax and alfalfa and nothing! Away to parts of Montana and North Dakota and South Dakota and Wyoming and Nebraska and Kansas and Colorado and New Mexico and Oklahoma and Texas! Away to the high plains rolling in waves to the rising final chord of the Rocky Mountains!

Frazier's singing chant invites us, in one sweeping passage, to think about the Great Plains as geography, biology, history, and culture. Along the way he uses fragments and lists and exclamation marks to invite readers to consider this arid and often overlooked part of America.

Repetition and refrain, along with lists, snapshots, fragments and labyrinthine sentences, are stylistic devices that add an emotional dimension to the otherwise factual material of nonfiction prose—without announcing, labeling, or dictating what those emotions need be. The word play of creative nonfiction allows nonfiction prose to convey themes more often conveyed through more obviously poetic forms.

21 e Double voice

Good nonfiction writing usually expresses something of the writer's voice. Writers can also project more than one voice from piece to piece of writing—sometimes within the same piece.

In any given essay, writers may try to say two things at the same time. Sometimes they question their own assertions; sometimes they say one thing out loud and think another silently to themselves; sometimes they say one thing that means two things; sometimes they express contradictions, paradoxes, or conundrums; and sometimes they establish that most of us have more than one voice with which to speak.

Double voices in a text may be indicated by parentheses—the equivalent of an actor speaking an "aside" on the stage (see what I

mean?) or in films, the internal monologue of a character revealed as voice-over or through printed subtitles while another action is happening on screen. Or it may be shown by changes in the size or **type of font,** a switch to *italics,* **boldface,** or CAPITAL LETTERS signaling a switch in the writer's voice. Or the double voice may occur without distinguishing markers at all. Or it may be indicated by simple paragraph breaks, as in the following selection from D. H. Lawrence in his critical essay on Herman Melville's *Moby-Dick* from *Studies in Classic American Literature,* where he uses fragments, repetition and double voice:

> Doom.
> Doom! Doom! Doom! Something seems to whisper it in the very dark trees of America.
> Doom of what?
> Doom of our white day. We are doomed, doomed. And the doom is in America. The doom of our white day.
> Ah, well, if my day is doomed, and I am doomed with my day, it is something greater than I which dooms me, so I accept my doom as a sign of the greatness which is more than I am.
> Melville knew. He knew his race was doomed. His white soul, doomed. His great white epoch, doomed. Himself doomed. The idealist, doomed. The spirit, doomed.

Here, Lawrence critiques Melville by carrying on a mock dialogue with himself, alternating his caricature of Melville's voice with his own whimsical acceptance of Melville's gloomy prophesy. Lawrence's essay seems written to provoke readers into reassessing their interpretations of literary classics, and so he provokes not only through the questions he raises but through his style as well—note his poetic use of repetition and sentence fragments that contribute to his double-voice effect.

Double voice may also be offset spatially, in double columns or alternating paragraphs. In trying to capture the experience of running a 26.2-mile marathon, student Paige alternated voices in separate snapshot-style paragraphs (one double stanza for each mile). In the following example from her third set of snapshots, her first voice is in the race (present tense, italics) while her second voice is remembering the training (past tense, non-italic, or roman, font):

> *Mile 3: Make sure you are going the right pace. Slow down*
> a little, you're going too fast. Let people pass you. Don't
> worry; they will burn out and you'll glide by later. Don't
> make a mistake.

My typical training week went like this:

Monday: a two-mile warm up at a slow pace; then three miles at a faster pace; finally, two miles slowing down, cooling off. After: a leg strength workout.

Tuesday: a medium long run, ten miles at a medium pace.

Wednesday: the dreaded speed workouts at the track, with mile runs alternating with quarter mile sprints. Afterwards, nausea and arm and leg strength workouts.

21 f Electronic style

Graphics capabilities included in word processing programs now allow writers to create varied page layouts with different fonts and styles. They make experimental writing easier, more possible, and more likely than at any other time in the history of print technology.

Clip art inserted from word processing programs enlivens many college papers and is something most instructors enjoy so long as it enhances or amplifies the content it accompanies and the content is solid, not fishy.

It is common for instructors to receive college papers that resemble professionally published articles in sophisticated journals.

A word of caution

Wise writers will master both conventional and unconventional styles and formats, using each as occasion and audience demand.

Proficiency in one is a poor excuse for sloppiness or neglect of the other. Creative nonfiction techniques, used carefully and judiciously on selected writing tasks, are fun to write and enjoyable to read, and at the same time they are able to convey the emotional and aesthetic dimension of ideas so difficult to express in conventional prose. Yet such stylistic devices are easy to overuse and exaggerate, resulting in predictable, routine, or overly cute expressions that lose the very edge they are trying to achieve and that made them effective in the first place. Check with your instructor before handing in an unconventional paper in response to a conventional assignment.

SUGGESTIONS FOR WRITING AND RESEARCH

INDIVIDUAL

I. Select one or more of the following techniques to compose your next essay: lists, snapshots, playful sentences, repetition, or double voice.

2. Recast an essay previously written in one or more of the experimental techniques above. Compare and contrast the effects created by each version.

COLLABORATIVE

As a class, compose a snapshot profile of your class, using one snapshot from each writer to piece together one thematically consistent but stylistically varied profile.

Editing

www.prenhall.com/fulwiler

Editing
www.prenhall.com/fulwiler

On *The Blair Handbook, Fourth Edition,* Web site you can find

- Improving your style
- Using commas, semicolons, and colons
- Eliminating sentence fragments

22 The Editing Process

Good writing communicates effectively with the writer's intended audience. As you plan, draft, and revise, you focus primarily on your **purpose**—on what you are trying to say. As you begin to edit, your focus shifts subtly to anticipating how your **audience**—your readers—will understand you.

To anticipate how readers will understand you, imagine yourself reading your work for the first time. Think about your intended readers: What do they already know about your subject? Which new ideas will you need to explain? If you are presenting an argument, will readers be sympathetic or skeptical?

Such anticipation—call it seeing with the eyes of the reader—can help you identify places where you haven't made your ideas clear, where readers may misunderstand, or where they are likely to raise the toughest questions. *Identifying potential problems* is the first step in **editing.**

The second step is *generating alternatives:* how could you clarify, explain, or anticipate questions? Think of two or three strategies that might help.

The third step is *choosing* which alternative best suits your purpose and your audience.

To edit well, you need a working knowledge of the conventions or standards of written English and the skill to apply those conventions according to your purpose, audience, and situation. Beyond following convention comes *polishing*—refining your writing to make paragraphs, sentences, and individual words communicate with clarity, style, and grace.

For your writing to be **effective,** your ideas need to come across with power and persuasiveness—and few wasted words. Strive for *clarity,* to make your purpose readily apparent to your audience. Seek a *style* appropriate for the subject, the audience, and your relation to that audience. Finally, edit for *grace*—a sense that the text is not only clear but enjoyable, moving, even memorable.

READING WITH THE EYES OF THE READER

Putting yourself in the place of your reader is a primary editing skill. Here's how to develop it:

- **Budget time for editing.** Don't assume you can rush through your paper in half an hour and make major improvements. Assume that editing will take at least as much time as drafting or revising did. Step back from your work by taking a break before you begin editing.

- **Exchange drafts with a trusted partner or with a writing group.** Jot down notes about what passages work well in your partner's writing and what elements slow your understanding. Notice how clearly such things stand out in someone else's writing. Share suggestions for improvement.

- **Work from large-scale issues to small.** Look at overall impressions, then the structure and development of ideas. Then move to paragraphs and last to sentences. The organization of this book generally follows that pattern.

- **Edit with a word processor.** Computerized text is infinitely changeable, so try different ways of expressing your ideas, then choose the best alternative. Also try changing formats and print out the paper; it's a good way to get a fresh look at your work.

- **Read with "fresh eyes" each time you sit down to edit.**

Most writers edit by attacking many issues at once, but to simplify discussion, we focus on one issue at a time. We have divided editing issues into four broad areas: effectiveness, grammar, punctuation, and mechanics.

22 a Editing techniques

This section outlines some major editing techniques to sharpen your writing. Each technique is cross-referenced to a subsequent chapter or section for more information.

Editing for unity

Edit paragraphs so that each advances and amplifies only one idea. One simple way to do this is to read each paragraph and make

sure each sentence illustrates the main idea in some logical way. For example, Issa discovered when writing his essay "On the Trail" (see Chapter 9) that the following paragraph would be better unified if he edited out the third sentence, which diverges into a different topic:

> When mountain bikes first came on the scene, hikers and environmentalists convinced state and local officials to ban the bikes from wilderness trails (Buchanan 81; Kelly 104). . . . These trail closings have separated the outdoor community into the hikers and the bikers. Each group is well organized, and each group believes it is right. Is any resolution in sight?

To test this editing technique, the writer read the paragraph through with and without the sentence in question and decided which was more effective. (See Chapter 23.)

2 Editing to grab readers' attention

The most attention-catching part of your paper—the opening paragraph—needs to be interesting enough to make readers want to continue reading. There is no one way to structure a good opening. Sometimes a colorful quotation or a surprising statistic works well. At other times a clear, direct thesis or a provocative question is needed. In the narrative example below, an internal monologue reveals the author's vulnerability in the middle of a championship tennis match:

> Bounce. Bounce. Bounce. The sound is driving me insane, but I just can't get the nerve to toss up the ball and serve. Am I scared? Yes. Of what, this girl or this match? This girl—this girl scares me. She's a natural talent. How many times is that crosscourt forehand shot going to rip past me? Well, if I'm going to lose, let's get on with it.

(See Chapter 24.)

3 Editing for rhythm

Reinforce the rhythm of your sentences. Readers notice sentences that please the ear. For example, parallel constructions create balanced, symmetrical rhythms that reinforce a comparison or contrast. A parallel construction repeats an identical grammatical pattern within the same sentence, paragraph, or passage. Note the several kinds of parallel constructions used in these sentences from "On the Trail":

Educated mountain biking, like ~~other environmental pursuits~~, *hiking and horseback riding,* respects the environment and promotes peace and conservation, not noise and destruction. Making this case has begun to pay off, and the battle over who walks and who rides the trails should now shift in favor of peaceful coexistence.

Other environmental pursuits was accurate, but altering the phrase to make it parallel to the first idea made the passage more rhythmic. (See Chapter 25.)

4 Editing for emphasis

The way you structure a sentence can emphasize one point over another. For example, in an essay, a paragraph, or a sentence, the most emphatic place is usually last. To end-weight a sentence, place less-essential information early; then end with the idea you want your reader to remember. Otherwise, it might get lost. For example, if we rewrote the second sentence of this paragraph with the most important information first, it would read this way: "*The most emphatic place is usually last in a whole essay, a paragraph, or a sentence, for example.*" Our point has nearly vanished. (See Chapter 25.)

5 Editing for variety

Varying sentence structures often makes paragraphs clearer and more enjoyable to readers. In the following example taken from her essay in 7g, Judith uses a variety of sentence lengths. She also varies sentence types.

It is already afternoon. I fiddle with the key to lock the apartment door after me. I am not accustomed to locking doors. Except for the six months I spent in Boston, I have never lived in a place where I did not trust my neighbors. When I was little, we couldn't lock our farmhouse door;

the wood had swollen and the bolt no longer lined up
properly with the hole, and nobody ever bothered to fix it.

(See Chapter 26.)

6 Editing for specific details

Nouns label or identify persons (*woman, ballet dancer*), places
(*room, dance studio*), and things (*clothes, leotards*). **Specific** nouns
(*ballet dancer, dance studio, leotards*) provide more detail than **general** nouns (*woman, room, clothes*). Adjectives that modify nouns
increase specificity by adding shape, size, color, texture, and so on.
In the following paragraph, Betsy describes members of a ballet rehearsal, using a variety of specific nouns and adjectives to let us
see her subjects:

> Dancers are scattered around the room, stretching,
> chatting, adjusting shoes and tights. Company members,
> the professionals who are joining us for this performance,
> wear tattered gray legwarmers, sweatpants that have lost
> their elastic, and old faded T-shirts over mismatched
> tights and baggy leotards. Their hair is knotted into buns
> or, in the case of male dancers, held tight with
> sweatbands. You can tell the students by the runless pink
> tights, dress-code leotards, and immaculate hair.

Specific nouns and adjectives create vivid and lively images—
"*tattered gray legwarmers*," "*baggy leotards*," and "*runless pink
tights*"—that would be lost with a more general description:
"*Dancers are scattered around the room, adults and students, each
group dressed differently.*" (See Chapter 27.)

7 Editing for dynamic verbs

Dynamic verbs show the subject of a sentence doing something: *walk, stride, run, jump, fly, sing, sail, swim, stop, look, listen,
hear, think, believe, doubt, sit, stumble,* or *fumble.* In contrast, **stative verbs** show the subject of a sentence in a state of being, existing rather than acting: *be, appear, become, seem,* or *exist.* Change

stative to dynamic verbs to make writing more vital and hold readers' attention.

swirls turbulently
The water is turbulent between the rocks.

The concluding paragraph of Judith's essay "Writing in Safety" (see 7g) uses dynamic verbs effectively (italics added):

> Hours later—my paper *started,* my exam *studied* for, my eyes *tired*—I *retrace* the path to my apartment. It is dark now, and I *listen* closely when I *hear* footsteps behind, *stepping* to the sidewalk's edge to let a man *walk* briskly past. At my door, I again *fumble* for the now familiar key, *insert* it in the lock, *open* the door, *turn* on the hall light, and *step* inside. Here, too, I am safe, ready to *eat, read* a bit, and *finish* my reflective essay.

Judith favors dynamic verbs. Her two stative verbs—*is* and *am*—provide a quiet contrast to the otherwise active paragraph. (See Chapter 27.)

8 Editing for conciseness

Delete words that do not add meaning, rhythm, or emphasis. Look at these sentences, each of which says essentially the same thing:

> In almost every situation that I can think of, with few exceptions, it will make good sense for you to look for as many places as possible to cut out needless, redundant, and repetitive words from the papers and reports, paragraphs and sentences you write for college assignments. [48 words]

> In most situations it makes sense to cut unneeded words from your college papers. [14 words]

> Whenever possible, omit unneeded words from your writing. [8 words]

> Omit unneeded words. [3 words]

In the first wordy sentence, the writer struggles for clarity. In the next two, the same idea is condensed by more than half and nearly by half again, then to a three-word command. (See Chapter 28.)

9 Editing for tone

Your **tone** reveals your attitude toward your subject and audience: whether you are distant or closely involved, neutral or partisan, dispassionate or emotional. To edit for tone, think of your purpose and imagine your audience: For whom are you writing? What effect do you want to create? For example, look again at the four sentences listed in 22a8 and notice how the tone increases in confidence and authority as you move from the tentative first version ("*In almost every situation that I can think of*"), through the gentle suggestion of the second ("*In most situations*"), to the stronger direction of the third ("*Whenever possible*"), to the command of the fourth ("*Omit*"). Choose a tone appropriate for your situation. (See Chapter 29.)

10 Editing to control bias

Using ethnic, racial, national, gender, or sex-preference stereotypes in your writing will make you appear **biased.** For example using the word *man* or *men* to stand for *human beings* or *people* is considered sexist because such terms ignore half of the population. Gender bias can appear to arise in your choice of pronouns and in terms for occupations (*policeman* rather than *police officer*). Texts written since the 1970s, when this issue began to receive widespread attention, usually avoid this gender bias. (See Chapter 31.)

11 Editing for grammar

Your audience for academic writing—instructors and fellow students—places a high value on **grammatical correctness** and the conventional use of language. Errors in sentence structure, verb agreement, or modifier placement will undermine your credibility and distract readers from your ideas. Sharpening your working knowledge of grammar will help you write better and keep you from writing nonsensical sentences such as this one:

> In a study of
> ~~Studying~~ the effects of cigarette smoking, monkeys smoked the
> equivalent of dozens of cigarettes a day.

The monkeys were not conducting the study. This first part of the sentence is a dangling modifier.

(See "Editing Grammar," Chapters 32–37.)

ESL | **THE LANGUAGE OF GENDER BIAS**

Languages vary in their conventions for indicating gender, so recognizing gender bias in English can be a challenge for speakers of other languages. For example the expression *man and wife* is considered biased because the term *wife* identifies the woman by her relationship to the man, but the word *man* does not refer to the relationship. Using parallel words, either *man and woman* or *husband and wife*, eliminates the gender bias.

When you are revising a paper, ask a native English speaker in your writing group or another trusted advisor to help you identify possible examples of gender-biased language in your writing.

12 Editing for punctuation

Correct **punctuation** also marks you as a skilled writer. Using commas, periods, quotation marks, colons, apostrophes, and other punctuation carefully will give you a familiarity with the rules so you will spot errors like this one:

> The Justice Department has expanded its investigation of
>
> Medicare fraud⁄and has launched several grand jury inquiries.

> *No comma is needed between parts of a compound predicate; the basic elements of the predicate in this sentence are* expanded . . . and . . . launched.

(See "Editing Punctuation," Chapters 38–44.)

13 Editing for mechanics

The term **mechanics** refers to issues that arise in presenting your finished writing, on paper or in electronic form. You must choose an appropriate and readable format. Other issues range from checking that every word is spelled correctly to capitalizing, abbreviating, and italicizing according to standard practice. The last editing act is **proofreading**—reading to make sure your manuscript is correct in every way. Good proofreading requires reading line by line, word by word, and letter by letter. (See "Editing Mechanics," Chapters 45–49.)

22 **b** Understanding the meaning of "error"

Getting facts wrong—identifying the North Star as Sirius rather than Polaris, for example—can destroy a reader's confidence in you. Readers also judge your reliability by your command of written language: mastery of the language implies mastery of the subject.

More important, writing problems can make it hard for a reader to understand you. The reader's only way of interpreting the words on a page is a knowledge of how those words have been used in the past. Every departure from **convention**—the way words are customarily used—presents a challenge to the reader. If that challenge proves too formidable, all but the most dedicated reader will turn away from reading in favor of, say, taking a nap.

Some conventions are so widely accepted that they are regarded as **rules,** and departures from them are considered **errors.** These rules do not result from any one person or committee deciding what ought to be right and issuing edicts accordingly. On the contrary, the rules are based on many writers' and grammarians' descriptions of how English has been written and spoken in the past. Other conventions are more flexible. However, if you stretch the boundaries of what readers expect, you risk being misunderstood or losing their attention.

EDITING I: EXPLORATION ————————————————

Look at the comments and corrections on a paper handed back to you by your instructor. Which comments concern rules, and which concern conventions? How could the changes suggested improve communication? For what other reasons might your instructor have made the comment? If you cannot understand the proposed change, discuss it with your instructor.

22 **c** Working with others

▊ **Editing someone else's work**

When you edit someone else's writing, make constructive suggestions that the writer can act on, not judgments that will leave the writer feeling attacked. The most effective editing relationship relies not on one person's authority but on cooperative efforts between writer and editor.

Read critically, trying to understand what the writer is attempting to do. Be alert to places where you as a reader have difficulty. Comment on the ways in which he or she has succeeded. Perhaps the writing employs good analysis, expresses a clear insight, or uses a compelling voice. Identifying such strengths helps the writer build on them. Then discuss the things you think the writer needs to clarify or correct. (See Chapter 20.)

2 Accepting editorial advice

Everyone has had the painful experience of having a paper returned with curt corrections in red ink. But being edited by others is a fact of life. In college, other students as well as teachers may comment on your writing. If you write for publication or at a job, staff editors or supervisors will edit your work. As a writer, you should accept comments with an open mind. Focus on how other people's reactions and verbal or written responses show what is working and not working in your writing. Adopt the suggestions you agree with and discuss the ones you don't. No matter how tactlessly or brusquely an editor communicates with you, remember that the comments are about a particular draft—not about all the writing you've ever done and certainly not about you yourself. Respond objectively and not defensively. Adopting a professional attitude will facilitate your interactions with those editing your work.

EDITING 2: EXPLORATION

Think of the teacher who has helped you most with your writing. How did he or she express comments and suggestions about your work? How did you respond? Can you also recall comments or corrections that hurt your feelings? What was the impact on your writing? Were you able to distinguish between the meaning of the comments and their effect on you? How?

22 d Editing with a computer

A word processing program greatly simplifies editing by making it easy to generate alternative versions by adding, deleting, moving and changing words. Most word processing programs have a "search and replace" or "find" function that allows you to locate every use of a word or phrase and change it with a few keystrokes.

Even more powerful is the computer's ability to copy or move chunks of text. You can "highlight" a block of text and then move,

copy, or delete the block. You can easily rearrange phrases, sentences, and even whole paragraphs.

A computer will store your work in a document or file each draft under a name you choose. When you begin editing a draft, save the new version under a different name, thus preserving both the original and the edited text. This practice also allows you to compare your most recent editing decisions with previous ones and then choose the best one.

Not least important, the ability to print any document easily eliminates the need to retype successive drafts, leaving you free to edit—and reprint—your work as many times as necessary.

EDITING 3: APPLICATION

Explore the use of computers as writing tools. If you have your own computer, ask about the word processing habits of your classmates. Do any of their

---

EDITING STRATEGIES USING COMPUTERS

Here are some strategies on how to use the computer to help you edit.

- **Change the look of your paper.** Radical changes in appearance give you the distance you need to edit effectively. Change the type font and print a draft. Doing this will help you recognize weaknesses as you review.

- **Alternate between hard copy and the screen.** This strategy also allows you to see with "fresh eyes." Edit first on a printed draft, marking any changes in pencil. Go back to the screen and transfer the changes, moving to other issues as you spot them.

- **Save each revision separately.** Later you can review the revisions for insights into your writing process.

- **Keep a file of personal trouble spots.** Keep a running list of overused words or frequent grammatical errors in a separate computer file. When editing, consult the list. Use computer search tools to find and remedy these trouble areas.

- **Use software tools, with care.** Many software packages contain a spell checker, dictionary, and thesaurus and sometimes a grammar checker and style checker. Take advantage of these features, but use them with care. Even the best spell checker cannot show you that you've written *two* for *to*, and no grammar checker can recognize every error.

methods have advantages over yours? What are their favorite editing strategies and techniques? If you don't have a computer, find out whether your college or community has computers that students can use and how to get access to them.

22 e Editing when English is your second language

Editing in English can be challenging for people who grew up speaking another language because they have had less time to develop an ear for what "sounds right"—something native speakers often rely on. Certain aspects of English are often confusing to nonnative speakers and writers, such as the sequence of verb tense used to illustrate the time at which events occurred:

By the time the sun *sets* tomorrow, I *will have been walking* for fifteen days.

The first part of the sentence uses the present tense to describe an action in the future; the second part describes an action that began in the past and will continue into the future but will be finished by the time indicated in the first part (sunset tomorrow).

In seemingly arbitrary ways, adjectives and articles (*the, a, an*)—or their absence—convey significant information about the nouns they precede:

ONE BOOK	*A book* is missing from the library.
AN INDEFINITE NUMBER	*Books* are missing.
ALL OF THE IDENTIFIED BOOKS	*The books* are missing.
NOT ALL OF THE BOOKS	*Some books* are missing.
ONE OF SEVERAL	*A biology book* is missing.
THE ONLY ONE OF ITS KIND	*The biology book* is missing.

To edit your writing for issues of this kind, try to improve your English-language skills in general. The best way to gain command of the language is by reading widely, listening and observing how language is used, and examining your own English to see how it resembles or differs from standard usage. Of course, this advice applies to all of us, native and nonnative speakers alike.

EDITING OTHER STUDENTS' WRITING

As a nonnative speaker of English, you may question your ability to edit your classmates' writing. Keep in mind, however, that you probably know a lot about what makes a piece of writing readable and effective. You are a part of the audience a classmate wants to reach. If something is unfamiliar or unclear to you, that information may be valuable to the writer. You can offer helpful feedback about clarity of purpose, variety of sentence structure, words or phrases that seem unnecessary, and many other elements of an essay that are discussed in this chapter.

In addition, read over your papers and attend to your instructors' comments carefully so that you will learn to recognize nonstandard usage or grammatical errors. Once you identify patterns in your writing, reread your papers, looking specifically for each trouble spot. The more you review grammar points and edit for grammar and usage, the easier it will become to make good choices.

Throughout *The Blair Handbook,* special boxes will help you understand certain aspects of the English language. Read the ESL boxes for tips about the grammatical structures and established patterns of standard written English.

22 f Using part six of *The Blair Handbook*

Many college instructors use a handbook like this one to show students how to make their writing stronger. Teachers reading dozens of student papers weekly will usually focus their written comments on large-scale issues, such as organization, logic, and the development of ideas. Rather than correct grammatical errors in detail, many instructors simply mark passages and refer students to the appropriate sections of the handbook for help.

What I liked most was/**the opportunity to explore different kinds**

of writing.   No comma between verb and complement.
          See commas, 39j.

This instructor suggests that the student refer to 39j to review the use of commas, in particular the rule that a single comma should

not separate a verb from a complement. Your instructor may also simply use a proofreading mark or correction symbol:

Every doctor has their own way of working.   *agr*

   Proofreading marks and correction symbols are widely used and largely standardized. The symbol *agr* here stands for agreement between a pronoun (*their*) and its antecedent (*doctor*). To see what a symbol means, look it up in the chart on the inside back cover of this book; the chart will refer you to a relevant section of the book. Standard proofreading marks are listed in 50c.

EDITING 4: APPLICATION ———————————————————

Select two or three comments that were marked on the last draft of a paper handed back to you by your instructor. Use the index or table of contents of *The Blair Handbook* to find out where the handbook addresses these issues, and then read those sections. Were the issues matters of effectiveness, of grammar, of punctuation, or of mechanics? What have you learned that you didn't know before? Use the editing advice in *The Blair Handbook* to edit the relevant sentences and correct any problems.

EDITING SECTION
Editing for Effectiveness

23 Shaping Strong Paragraphs

Paragraphs are the organizing units of writing, showing which ideas go together and how they relate to each other. Good paragraphing gives readers clues to how to read your paper. When a new paragraph begins, readers expect a new step in the development of your ideas.

Especially in academic writing, readers expect each sentence within a paragraph to develop a single main idea—that the paragraph will be **unified.** They expect the paragraph to present its ideas in a clearly perceptible order—that it will be well **organized.** And they expect each succeeding sentence to relate to what came before, advancing and supporting the central point—that the paragraph will be **coherent.**

23 a Ensuring that paragraphs are unified

In most college writing, each paragraph directly states a central idea, or **topic,** which is usually made explicit in a **topic sentence.** Sometimes a paragraph's topic can be communicated more subtly: readers may be able to infer a topic from a series of related sentences that do not include an explicit topic sentence.

In either case, a paragraph should contain only one main idea. Elements that do not support or clarify this idea should be eliminated. You can simply delete stray words or sentences; you can move them to another paragraph, or you can create a new paragraph where they will be more effective.

In a passage about minimizing the effect of divorce on children, Amy identified the first sentence as the topic sentence: *For various reasons, some unhappy couples remain married.* When she read each of the other sentences carefully to see whether they described reasons for staying married, she realized that the fourth sentence was out of place. She decided to move this sentence to the next paragraph, which dealt with a new topic.

For various reasons, some unhappy couples remain married. Some are forbidden to divorce by religion, others by social custom. Still others stay together "for the sake of the children," In recent years, psychologists and sociologists have studied families to determine whether more harm is done to children by divorce or by parents who stay together despite conflict. ~~But by~~

believing

~~staying together, such parents feel~~ they are sparing their children the pain of divorce.

In his study of family conflict, Robert S. Weiss found that children in such families were often happiest "when Daddy is at work" . . .

EDITING I: PRACTICE ────────────────────────

A. The following paragraph, part of an information manual for new employees at a college radio station, discusses gifts and promotions. With this audience in mind, edit the paragraph to improve unity.

> College radio stations do not receive lavish gifts, but they are not neglected in the grand sweep of promotions that back college-targeted records. This station has received everything from posters to gold records to bottles of liquor. Whether the promotions actually get the records played is hard to document at college radio stations, and ours is no exception. The most common gifts are passes to performances and free copies of records.

B. This paragraph is from an editorial that explains to local citizens the workings of the city planning board. With this audience in mind, edit the paragraph to improve unity.

> The idea of planning seems simple enough. Communities are asked to designate areas for specific purposes, such as commercial, residential, or industrial use. The state's new requirement that every city and township formulate a plan may create a shortage of planners. People take city planning very seriously. Sometimes such an innocuous topic as zoning leads to turmoil—for instance, when one group wants to open a restaurant in what others consider a residential zone. Trying to pinpoint exactly what a planner does is a little more complicated.

EDITING 2: APPLICATION

Select a paragraph from a paper you are working on. As you reread the paragraph, ask yourself these questions: (1) What is my topic sentence? and (2) How does this paragraph fit into my paper? If any sentences do not contribute to the main idea of the paragraph, try omitting or moving them. Eliminate any other elements that detract from the main point. If you find that some of your ideas need elaboration, write additional sentences with the above questions in mind.

How does your edited paragraph compare with the original? Does it advance your purpose more effectively?

23 b Organizing paragraphs

Ideas that are presented in no apparent order can confuse your readers, so clear organization within a paragraph is important. When editing, you must decide whether you have organized each paragraph in the way that most effectively accomplishes your purpose. You may decide to move your topic sentence or to reorganize the whole paragraph.

1 Placement of the topic sentence

Often the topic sentence or main idea is most effective at the beginning of a paragraph. If you find a topic sentence buried in the middle of a paragraph, consider moving it to the beginning.

> In 1987, a man lost his job for taking a few puffs of a cigarette during his lunch break because smoking on or off the job violated his department's policy. He took his employers to court to get his job back, but the judge ruled that smoking was not comparable to the privacy rights protected by the Constitution. Court decisions have limited smokers' rights to pursue their habit. Other cases have established nonsmokers' right to protection from secondhand smoke.

A topic sentence can also be placed at the end of a paragraph, which is another way of emphasizing it.

In 1987, a man lost his job for taking a few puffs of a cigarette during his lunch break because smoking on or off the job violated his department's policy. He took his employers to court to get his job back, but the judge ruled that smoking was not comparable to the privacy rights protected by the Constitution. Court decisions have limited smokers' rights to pursue their habit. Other cases have established nonsmokers' right to protection from secondhand smoke.

2 Common patterns of organization

The sentences and ideas within a paragraph should be arranged to convey the point of the paragraph effectively.

General to specific

One common pattern for organizing paragraphs is *general to specific*. Begin the paragraph by stating the principal idea; edit subsequent sentences to support, explain, or expand on that idea.

GENERAL STATEMENT

Many athletes have improved their performance by using steroids. One such athlete is track star Ben Johnson, who won the Olympic gold medal in 1988 in the hundred-meter dash. After a couple of days, Johnson's medal was taken away because he had tested positive for the use of steroids. His steroid use had increased his leg strength and therefore made him a faster runner. Another example is Benji Ramirez, a former student at Central State University. He played on the JV team for two years and wanted to be good enough for the varsity squad. He decided to do this by increasing his physical strength, and the method he chose was using steroids. By his senior year, he was a starter on the varsity team.

SPECIFIC EXAMPLE

Specific to general

A specific-to-general pattern of organization begins with a series of details or examples and ends with a general statement, the

topic sentence. In this personal narrative, Anita saved the topic sentence for last to give it impact:

SPECIFIC
EXAMPLE

I began by oversleeping—somehow I had forgotten to set my alarm clock. Then I had to drink my morning coffee black and eat my cereal dry becuse my roommate hadn't replaced the quart of milk she finished yesterday. After missing my bus and arriving late for my first class, I discovered that the paper I thought was due next week was actually due today. And because my lab partner was still mad at me about the mess I made of things last week, we accomplished almost nothing in two hours. All in all, it was a terrible day.

GENERAL
STATEMENT

Chronological order

Related events can be organized in **chronological order,** the order in which they happened. The topic sentence, a general statement summarizing the events and perhaps interpreting them, can appear at the beginning or, as in the paragraph above, at the end.

Sometimes paragraphs relating a series of events are better arranged in *reverse chronological order,* which looks back from the most recent to the most distant past, as in the example below. Here the topic sentence can appear at the end or at the beginning:

GENERAL
STATEMENT

At first a little hesitant to talk about painful memories, Leo started by describing his background. He ended the war as a refugee, he said, having escaped with only what he could carry. He then told me that on September 1, 1939, the Germans attacked Poland. They left his town alone for three days. On the third, they collected all the males from fifteen to sixty years of age and put them in a yard. The men were given trash and told to bury it with their hands. A friend of Leo's resisted and they shot him. He was buried along with the refuse.

EVENT 1

EVENT 2

EVENT 3

EVENT 4

In this vignette from a personal profile, Mark shows his interview subject opening up as he reaches farther into the past. Mark has structured the narrative to build up to its chilling conclusion.

Climactic order

An appeal to logic might be arranged in **climactic order,** beginning with a general statement, presenting specific details in order of increasing importance, and ending with a dramatic statement, a climax. Here Patrick is using scientific predictions to arouse and alarm a general, nonscientific audience:

GENERAL STATEMENT

Consider the potential effect of just a small increase in the earth's atmospheric temperature. A rise of only a few degrees could melt the polar ice caps. Rainfall patterns would change. Some deserts might bloom, but lands now fertile might turn to desert, and many hot climates could become uninhabitable. If the sea level rose only a few feet, dozens of coastal cities would be destroyed, and life as we know it would be changed utterly.

SPECIFICS IN INCREASING IMPORTANCE

CLIMAX

Spatial order

A physical description can be organized in **spatial order,** moving from one detail to another as the eye would move. As in the chronological paragraph, a topic sentence summarizing and interpreting the details can appear at the beginning or end. Janelle intended this description to give the reader the feeling of sitting in one place, observing carefully:

SPECIFICS ARRANGED SPATIALLY

Above the mantelpiece hung an ancient wheel lock musket that gave every indication of being in working order. A small collection of pewter, most of it dating from the colonial period, was arrayed across the mantel. To the left of the hearth stood a collection of wrought-iron fireplace tools and a bellows of wood and leather with brass fittings. At the right, a brass hopper held several cut limbs of what might have been an apple tree. On an iron hook above the coals hung a copper kettle, blackened with age and smoke. The fireplace looked as though it had changed little since the Revolution.

GENERAL STATEMENT

EDITING 3: PRACTICE

The following paragraph is from a news release that was sent to local newspapers in the townships near White Glen Park. Strengthen the paragraph by improving its organization.

One Saturday each month, Mike Perkins, a local golf pro, gives a free golf clinic at White Glen Park. Enthusiasts gather round while Mike discusses the finer points of the game. He addresses one aspect of the golf swing each session. He demonstrates the relevant concept, using someone from the crowd as a model. The public course donates six bushel baskets of golf balls and the use of its driving range for the event. Usually about sixty to eighty people show up. Saturday afternoons with Mike are always fun and informative. Last month he discussed proper hip movement in the iron swing. Then, after the lesson, Mike's monthly students hit practice shots until they use up the balls. The event is quite popular.

EDITING 4: APPLICATION ─────────────────────────

Make a copy of three paragraphs from a paper you are working on, and experiment to find the best possible organization for them. First, disassemble the paragraphs so that each sentence stands alone, either by cutting with scissors or by starting each sentence on a new line on the computer screen. Next, find the topic sentences and set them aside. Decide which sentences belong in which paragraph. Then play with the order of the sentences until you find one that seems particularly effective; you may want to try some of the patterns of organization discussed in 23b. Decide whether the topic sentence belongs at the beginning or the end of each paragraph. Finally, rewrite the paragraphs using the new organization, making any necessary changes in wording. How does this edited version compare with the original?

23 c Making paragraphs coherent

In a *coherent* paragraph, each sentence connects with the next in a way that readers can easily recognize. Shortening long paragraphs, using transitional expressions, and sparingly repeating key words can all help achieve coherence.

Shortening long paragraphs

Long paragraphs can lack coherence simply because readers may lose track of what you are saying. Breaking a long paragraph into several smaller ones can give the reader a chance to rest, and it often results in greater coherence within each of the new paragraphs.

During a divorce, parents have the ability to shield a child from most of the potential harm. Most couples who stay together believe that the two-parent structure is important to the child's well-being and that changing this pattern upsets a child. ¶ A child's security is based on his or her relationship with each parent individually, according to studies by Judith Wallerstein, who found that stable, caring relationships between a child and each parent are the most significant ingredient in raising a child. If these relationships are maintained, the effect of divorce on a

child's emotions is much reduced. Indeed, maintaining even one stable relationship would appear to be better than a weak connection with both parents. ¶ In the early stages of a breakup, both parents are often distracted by other issues. The child may suffer as a result. A child's performance in school and interactions with others may deteriorate, so everything should be done to aid the child in transition.

Breaking up the long paragraph helped us understand important points. Amy went on to add transitions between paragraphs as outlined in 23c2.

An essay consisting of many short paragraphs, however, can seem choppy and disjointed. If several small paragraphs develop what is essentially one idea, they might be better joined into larger paragraphs.

2 Using transitional expressions

Whenever your flow of ideas shifts, let the reader know which way you are headed. Otherwise readers may be confronted with a seemingly unrelated string of facts. Words that signal a change are called **transitional expressions.**

As you edit, examine each change of subject, time, point of view, or setting to see whether you have adequately marked the transition. Changes you make while restructuring paragraphs may make new transitions necessary. Look again at the edited example from the paper about divorce, in which one long paragraph was broken into three. To clarify how the three new paragraphs related to one another, Amy added two transitional sentences:

During a divorce, parents have the ability to shield a child from most of the potential harm. Most couples who stay together believe that the two-parent structure is important to the child's well-being and that changing this pattern upsets a child.

This, however, appears not to be the case.
A child's security is based on his or her relationship with
^
each parent individually, according to studies by Judith Wallerstein, who found that stable, caring relationships between a child

and each parent are the most significant ingredient in raising a child. If these relationships are maintained, the effect of divorce on a child's emotions is much reduced. Indeed, maintaining even one stable relationship would appear to be better than a weak connection with both parents.

The issue during divorce, then, is how well a child can maintain at In the early stages of a breakup, both parents are often distracted by other issues. The child may suffer as a result. A child's performance in school and interactions with others may deteriorate, so everything should be done to aid the child in transition.

least one secure relationship.

The first transitional sentence emphasizes a logical contrast. The second marks a shift of subject.

TRANSITIONAL EXPRESSIONS

Transitional expressions connect distinct ideas, indicating how one idea expands, exemplifies, summarizes, or relates to another:

- **Expanding:** also, and, besides, finally, further, in addition, moreover, then
- **Exemplifying:** as an illustration, for example, for instance, in fact, specifically, thus
- **Qualifying:** but, certainly, however, to be sure, only
- **Summarizing:** and so, finally, in conclusion, in short, in sum, this experiment shows, thus we see
- **Relating logically:** as a result, because, by implication, for this reason, from this we can see, if, since, so therefore
- **Comparing:** also, as well, likewise, similarly
- **Contrasting:** but, even though, nevertheless, still, yet, despite
- **Relating in time:** after, before, between, earlier, later, longer than, meanwhile, since
- **Relating in space:** above, adjacent to, behind, below, beyond, in front of, next to, north of, over, through, within

3 Using deliberate repetition

Selective repetition of key words or concepts creates a path for readers. The words that you want readers to remember become stepping-stones connecting one sentence to the next. In the following example, *controversy* and *dispute* as well as *opposes, opponents,* and *proponents* are key words that help readers follow the argument:

> The *controversy* over Northgate Mall has continued for five years. The *dispute* has divided the city into two camps. A small group *opposes* the mall, but its members are vocal and energetic. The *opponents* maintain that it would rob trade from existing businesses downtown and contribute to traffic congestion. *Proponents* say that the growth it would bring would be easily manageable.

STRATEGIES FOR EDITING PARAGRAPHS

Most writers paragraph intuitively when they draft. When you edit, make conscious decisions about paragraphs:

- **Look at length.** Does each paragraph begin and end in the appropriate place? Should it be shorter? Should it include part of the following paragraph? Are there too many long paragraphs or too many short paragraphs in a row?
- **Check for unity.** Does each paragraph express and develop a single idea? Eliminate or move distracting elements.
- **Consider organization.** Is the pattern of each paragraph appropriate for your purpose?
- **Assess coherence.** Check the flow from each sentence to the next to ensure that the paragraph is clear and logical.

EDITING 5: PRACTICE ────────────────────────

The following paragraph is from an oral report for a debate class. Strengthen the paragraph by editing to improve coherence. Consider the use of transitional expressions, the order of sentences, and the use of repetition. More than one edited version is possible. Be ready to explain your editing choices.

Accidents involving bicyclists usually increase when the college students—and their bicycles—return to classes. Many drivers in the city resent the high number of cyclists. They claim that the streets are too busy and too narrow for bike travel. Cyclists often will ignore traffic signals and stop signs and cut in and out of traffic without warning. If opposing traffic is slow in starting after a light changes, cyclists frequently will turn in front of it to move ahead. Usually few cyclists attempt to keep up with traffic, which creates a long line of cars unable to pass. These tendencies can be dangerous. At the corner of Tenth Street and Indiana the other day, a cyclist was struck by a car turning right when he tried to pass on the inside. He suffered no injuries, but some victims have to be hospitalized.

EDITING 6: PRACTICE

The following passage is from a newspaper account summarizing the history of a zoning proposal for a new mall and its impact on a mayoral election. Revise (1) to improve its unity, organization, and coherence and (2) to make it more interesting. You may have fun with your revision, so long as you do not alter the facts. You may begin new paragraphs as you see fit.

The zoning board rejected the proposal. The plan was the subject of three evenings of raucous debate. Then the city council took it up on appeal. The disagreement continued there for months. Some members said their first responsibility was to promote economic development in any form. The debate on the council reflected the divisions in the community. Growth should be regulated so that it does not harm existing businesses or the city as a whole, others believed. The project was approved two weeks after the new mayor took office. Amanda Robbins campaigned for mayor by rallying downtown businesspeople, historic preservationists, and neighborhood activists against the mall. Council member Steven McMillan ran on a pro-development, pro-mall platform. Both candidates said they wanted voters to end the deadlock on the proposal. The election was won by McMillian.

EDITING 7: APPLICATION

From a recent paper, select a passage of three or four paragraphs that does not quite read smoothly to you. Use your word processor or a photocopier to make several copies to experiment with. Try breaking paragraphs into smaller paragraphs or even individual sentences and rearranging them for better coherence, unity, and organization.

Try at least two new versions before deciding which is best.

24 Improving Openings and Conclusions

You never get a second chance to make a first impression. The **opening** of an essay must engage, stimulate, and challenge readers, enticing them to read further. Your opening should give readers a reliable guide to what will follow: it should introduce your topic and your thesis or main idea and give readers some idea of what you intend to say.

An essay's **conclusion** merits equal attention because your parting words will linger in the reader's mind. A conclusion that merely repeats generalities, that focuses only on a minor point, or that wanders off the subject will undermine your efforts. The conclusion provides your last opportunity to tie together everything you have covered and state it in clear, simple terms.

There are no all-purpose formulas for openings or conclusions; each must be carefully written to suit your purpose and audience. On rare occasions, the first words of an essay may spring to mind as you begin to write, or the last words may flow effortlessly from the preceding paragraphs, and you may never need to change them. More often, however, you will find it distracting, while drafting, to worry about an opening or conclusion. Put your efforts first toward drafting the main portion of the paper, and worry later about the opening and conclusion. After drafting and revising, go back to your openings and conclusions. The editing stage is the best time to sharpen your focus, check directness, and polish wording.

24 a Making openings engaging

In a short essay, you start like a sprinter and run flat-out for the full fifty meters. An opening no longer than one paragraph is standard in much college writing. In a longer paper, you can set off at a more leisurely pace, engaging readers' attention, then guiding it and focusing it by the time you state the main thrust of your argument.

In either case, readers should quickly be able to recognize both your **subject,** the general area you are writing about, and your **topic,** that particular aspect of the subject on which you are focusing. They should also understand your *main idea,* the central point you will make about that topic in your paper. In argument and research writing, this main point is presented in a **thesis,** an explicit statement usually placed in the opening paragraph. In personal experience and reflective writing, the thesis can take an unstated form as an implicit **theme** that is referred to throughout.

> Nikorn Phasuk, a Bangkok policeman who is also known as Plastic Man, steps onto a stage of asphalt under the glare of a blazing sun. He crouches, then retreats with mincing footwork as he coaxes vehicles toward him with fluid arm gestures, part of an artful ballet he uses to keep traffic rolling, no small feat in the city that may have the most congested streets in the world.
>
> As the last motorist accelerates by, the officer stabs a white gloved hand toward the heart of the city in a gesture that ends in a pirouette. Below dark sunglasses his teeth flash in a full grin, one that commuters irked by delays cannot help but emulate.
>
> "It relieves the tension, makes everybody less serious, and it's fun," Nikorn said. "And traffic seems to move faster."
>
> As he walked me back to my car, he held hands with a Bangkok journalist who had stopped by. Such intimacy, while common among Asian men, might be hard to imagine in New York City. But this was Thailand, where most actions seem choreographed for gentleness, and smiles are the expressions of choice.
>
> NOEL GROVE, "THE MANY FACES OF THAILAND"

Taking a few paragraphs to introduce a lengthy essay, Grove gives his readers a verbal film clip of downtown Bangkok that signals to his audience that they will be visiting an unfamiliar but delightful culture.

Your opening should be appropriate to your topic and main idea. Here are some techniques for matching your openings to specific purposes.

General-to-specific pattern

Many opening paragraphs for college papers start with a general statement of the main idea in a topic sentence. Subsequent sentences contain specific examples that support or expand on that statement, and the paragraph ends with a thesis statement.

> Language is the road map of a culture. It tells you where its people come from and where they are going. A study of the English

language reveals a dramatic history and astonishing versatility. It is the language of survivors, of conquerors, of laughter.

> RITA MAE BROWN, "TO THE VICTOR BELONGS THE LANGUAGE"

2 Striking assertion

This opening features a statement so improbable or far-reaching that the reader will want to see proof.

> John Milton was a failure. In writing "Paradise Lost," his stated aim was to "justify the ways of God to men." Inevitably, he fell short of accomplishing that and only wrote a monumental poem. Beethoven, whose music was conceived to transcend Fate, was a failure, as was Socrates, whose ambition was to make people happy by making them reasonable and just. The inescapable conclusion seems to be that the surest, noblest way to fail is to set one's own standards titanically high.

> LAWRENCE SHANIES,
> "THE SWEET SMELL OF SUCCESS ISN'T ALL THAT SWEET"

3 Anecdote

Try telling an **anecdote,** or brief story, about people or incidents to introduce your topic and illustrate your thesis.

> Once I met a woman who grew up in the small North Carolina town to which Chang and Eng, the original Siamese twins, retired after their circus careers. When I asked her how the town reacted to the twins marrying local girls and setting up adjacent households, she laughed and said: "Honey, that was nothing compared to what happened before the twins got there." Get the good gossip on any little mountain town, scratch the surface and you'll find a snake pit!

> FRANCINE PROSE, "GOSSIP"

Near the end of this paragraph, you see Prose's thesis coming and are ready to agree with it.

4 Interesting detail, statistic, or quotation

An interesting detail, statistic, or quotation can grab readers' attention and place them in an unfamiliar situation, making them eager for the context and explanation you are about to provide.

> People are often surprised, even alarmed, to learn that many of their cells crawl around inside them. Yet cell crawling is essential to our survival. Without it, our wounds would not heal; blood would not clot to seal off cuts; the immune system could not fight

infections. Unfortunately, crawling contributes to some disease processes, too, such as destructive inflammation and the formation of atherosclerotic plaques in blood vessels. Cancer cells crawl to spread themselves throughout the body: were cancer just a matter of uncontrolled cell growth, all tumors would be amenable to surgical removal.

THOMAS P. STOSSEL, "THE MACHINERY OF CELL CRAWLING"

Was your reaction the same as ours, "Yuck"? Then Stossel had you right where he wanted you!

5 Provocative question

After a few sentences of background information to establish the topic, a writer can ask a provocative question, which the essay attempts to answer.

> Look around you in most locations in the United States and Australia, and most of the people you'll see will be of European ancestry. At the same sites 500 years ago everyone without exception would have been an American Indian or an aboriginal Australian. This is an obvious feature of our daily life, and yet it poses a difficult question, one with a far from obvious answer: Why is it that Europeans came to replace most of the native population of North America and Australia, instead of Indians or native Australians replacing the original population of Europe?

JARED DIAMOND, THE ACCIDENTAL CONQUEROR

STRATEGIES FOR OPENINGS

To engage readers' interest, try one of the following strategies:

- Move from **general to specific** in your opening paragraph.
- Make a **striking assertion** in your opening.
- Add an **anecdote** that arouses your readers' curiosity.
- Grab their attention with an **interesting detail or quotation.**
- Ask a **provocative question** that can't be easily answered.

EDITING I: PRACTICE ━━━━━━━━━━━━━━━━━━━━━━━

Edit the following opening paragraph to make it more engaging. First assume you are writing a paper on economics for an economics class. Then edit the

paragraph again, assuming you are writing about economics for an audience of noneconomists. What should your opening achieve in each case? What goals are the same, and which ones differ?

> Dr. Ravi Batra, an economist at Southern Methodist University, has described a long-term cycle of economic indicators. Those indicators, he believes, forecast a depression in the next few years. The World Futurist Society also predicts a global economic collapse rivaling the Great Depression of the 1930s. Both predictions cite a rash of bank failures in recent years, implying that the first indication of wider economic troubles will be the downfall of financial institutions.

24 b Strengthening openings

Wanting to sound well informed and self-assured, writers sometimes lapse into misdirection, wordiness, overgeneralization, and cliché, which can be catastrophic in openings. Readers are more likely to keep reading when they see that each sentence, each word, is important to the purpose of the writing. To that end, edit any elements that may distract your readers.

1 Being direct

Ernie's draft starts on one topic and moves to another. Can you tell where his paper is headed?

> Isaac Asimov is among the first to have written about robotics. *I, Robot* is a collection of short stories on the subject, the earliest of which is from 1940. Even when going to the moon was science fiction, Asimov predicted that people would come to fear their own creation, a concept that dates back at least as far as Mary Shelly's Frankenstein.
>
> A movie that demonstrates the paranoia Asimov wrote about is *Terminator,* in which a computer takes control of machines, then attempts to eradicate the human race. This is the paranoia Asimov predicted: humanity the slave master has an innate fear of rebellion among its slaves.
>
> A robot is defined as "any mechanical device operated automatically, especially by remote control." The subject I will be addressing is the argument that robots are stealing jobs from humans, that painters, spot welders, machinists, skilled laborers of all kinds are being replaced by machines.

Ernie's problem is misdirection. Does he mean to focus on the workplace or the psyche? Keeping his literary examples as

context, Ernie edited a new opening to show his true position on the subject:

> The claim that robots are stealing jobs from humans is nothing new; it is an old fear in a new form. Many writers and filmmakers have explored the underlying anxiety.
>
> Isaac Asimov was among the first to write about robotics. . . .

Beware of *telling* the reader "My paper will be about. . . ." Edit phrases like these so that you jump right in and *show* the reader what you are going to discuss.

2 Sharpening focus

Too broad an opening can dull readers' interest. Try to limit opening generalizations so that readers understand your main idea right away, as Julie did in a reflective essay on the relations between men and women:

> Communication has become very important in our everyday lives. Without this ability to relate, friendships and marriages would fail. Furthermore, the different ways men and women communicate can result in serious problems at home and in the workplace.

Her draft sentences were too obvious, so Julie sharpened her focus. Her edited sentences outline the territory she plans to cover.

> Men and women have different ways of communicating that can create problems in marriages and work relationships. Overcoming these differences is essential to friendships and marriages alike.

3 Emphasizing the main idea

An opening should move quickly to establish the topic of your paper and tell readers what your point will be. Anything that slows their progress toward your main idea should be eliminated. In this draft, Dwayne intended to explore the morality of capital punishment, but he started with a dry definition likely to bore his readers:

> What exactly is capital punishment? According to the *Academic Encyclopedia*, capital punishment is the lawful imposition of the death penalty. In biblical times, the death penalty was prescribed for murder, kidnapping, and witchcraft. In England in the 1500s, major crimes such as treason, murder, larceny, burglary, rape, and arson carried the death penalty.

Between 1977 and 1991 in the United States alone, 2350 persons faced the death penalty, and at least 150 were executed. Although use of the death penalty has strict legal limitations, Americans have differing views on its value in protecting society. Is capital punishment right or wrong?

By asking the definition of a commonly known term, Dwayne wasted his opening words. When editing, he sharpened the question he planned to explore, moved the background information out of the way, and tightened everywhere.

Can capital punishment be morally justified?

Americans disagree about whether the death penalty protects society. Its supporters argue that the fear of death deters some criminals and that execution stops others from striking again. Opponents believe that even noble ends cannot justify such terrible means.

Lawful execution has been around since biblical times, when it was prescribed for murder, kidnapping, and witchcraft. . . .

EDITING 2: EXPLORATION

Read the following two paragraphs, which begin Ambrose Bierce's essay "Disintroductions." Consider the strategies Bierce has used to engage the reader's interest, and evaluate the effectiveness of this opening. Be prepared to discuss your views with other members of your class.

The devil is a citizen of every country, but only in our own are we in constant peril of an introduction to him. All men are equal; the devil is a man; therefore, the devil is equal. If that is not a good and sufficient syllogism I should be pleased to know what is the matter with it.

To write in riddles when one is not prophesying is too much trouble; what I am affirming is the horror of the characteristic American custom of promiscuous, unsought, and unauthorized introductions.

EDITING 3: PRACTICE

Read the following opening paragraph. What do you think are the writer's audience, purpose, and thesis? Generate at least two alternative versions of the paragraph. Evaluate your alternatives according to your understanding of audience, purpose, and thesis.

My research paper is on the clunker law and why people are in favor of it or opposed to it. The controversy exists between large corporations and individuals who own old cars. The law proposes that cars dated 1981 or

older that do not pass emission standards be destroyed or limited in their annual mileage. The law will affect the automobile industry and the economic welfare of the lower class. The clunker law is a short-term solution to the problem of pollution. I will state my own opinion about the clunker law. It's a fight between David and Goliath.

EDITING 4: EXPLORATION

Read several opening paragraphs by an author whose writing you admire, and select one that seems particularly effective to you. Jot down what you think were the writer's purpose, the intended audience, and the thesis or main idea. What techniques has the author used to engage your attention? How has the author focused your thoughts on the main idea? Which of these techniques can you use in your own writing?

EDITING 5: APPLICATION

Read the opening paragraph of a paper you are working on, and evaluate its effectiveness. Are you addressing your audience appropriately? Will it grab readers' attention? Have you focused attention on your central idea? Generate an alternative version with those questions in mind, and compare the alternative with the original. What are the strengths and weaknesses of each?

24 c Making conclusions satisfying

An effective conclusion leaves readers satisfied and gives them something to think about. Again, there is no magic formula for creating satisfying and memorable conclusions. Your conclusion should remind readers of your main idea, but it must go beyond a simple restatement.

Here are some strategies for driving your point home.

Rhetorical question

In closing an argument, one highly effective strategy is to end with a **rhetorical question,** one that is not meant to be answered but creates a situation in which the readers cannot help but agree with you.

> Drug violence will continue as long as citizens tolerate the easy availability of guns on the streets; as long as the public shells out money for violence glorified in television and film; as long as drug customers, deprived of effective treatment, pour money

VALID CONCLUSIONS

Here are some common pitfalls to avoid in conclusions:

- A conclusion that simply asserts your own belief—unsupported by evidence—is unlikely to persuade anyone not already disposed to agree with you.
- Last-minute appeals to beliefs or authority will not sway anyone who holds other beliefs or does not share your respect for your chosen authority.
- A conclusion that goes far beyond what your evidence will support also is unlikely to be persuasive.
- If you have not yet given readers an explicit statement of your main idea, you must do so in your conclusion.

into disadvantaged neighborhoods. How can society sit by and do nothing?

The reader isn't really expected to answer this question but rather is expected to respond by saying, "We must do something!"

2 Summary

Another strategy is a concise **summary** of your main points, followed by a *reflective* point about their meaning. This works well when your exploration has raised questions rather than provided firm answers, as in Teresa's exploration of the nature of death:

> Death is a reality we confront every day. Morticians tend to package death and sell it as interminable slumber. The military suggests that to be killed for a cause is an elevating experience that guarantees heroic stature. The medical profession struggles to preserve life beyond any reasonable hope for a significant future. One way or another, everyone has beliefs about an afterlife, but what happens beyond the grave, the world will never know. What happens lies beyond a door that one day each of us will unlock.

Teresa didn't want to say death was one thing and not another; she wanted her readers to ponder what death means to each of them.

3 Call to action

Consider concluding an argument with a *call to action*. What better purpose in marshaling all your powers of persuasion in the

paper if not to mobilize your readers on behalf of change? In so doing, you have to presume that your readers believe your argument
and are ready to leap up and help you change the world.

Media violence may not be the only cause of aggressive behavior, but it clearly has an adverse effect on viewers. Children are
most affected because they readily learn new behavior by imita-
tion. Their lessons are reenacted on playgrounds and on the
streets. As citizens and as parents, it's time we demanded better.

4 Speculation

You can also conclude with *speculation* about the future, showing your readers a better world—if they act as you have urged in
your argument. Anthropologist Margaret Mead ends her discussion
of capital punishment by presenting a vision of a better future:

The tasks are urgent and difficult. Realistically we know we
cannot abolish crime. But we can abolish crude and vengeful
treatment of crime. We can abolish—as a nation, not just state by
state—capital punishment. We can accept the fact that prisoners,
convicted criminals, are hostages to our own human failures to develop and support a decent way of living. And we can accept the
fact that we are responsible to them, as to all living beings, for the
protection of society, and especially responsible for those among
us who need protection for the sake of society.

MARGARET MEAD, "A LIFE FOR A LIFE"

STRATEGIES FOR CONCLUSIONS

Make your conclusions more satisfying by adopting one of the
following strategies:

- Ask a **rhetorical question,** one that does not need answering
  but will ring in the readers' ears.
- **Summarize** the important points of your paper, driving home any
  connections you want to make or any final overarching point that
  needs to be made.
- Sound a **call to action** when writing papers that argue for change;
  it's a good way to engage your readers in further thought.
- **Speculate** about the future, leaving your readers to weigh the outcome of the issues you have presented.

Edit the following conclusion to make it more satisfying. More than one edited version is possible. Be ready to explain your editing choices.

> Computers have already radically altered our society and will undoubtedly continue to do so. But how far will computers take us? Will we like our destination? From the banking and finance industries to recreation and art, every aspect of our lives has been affected by the ramifications of RAM and ROM. Much as the industrial revolution and the agricultural revolution did in past centuries, the computer revolution will fundamentally transform our culture in ways we cannot yet imagine. The three distinctive characteristics of computer transactions—speed of computation, ease of replication, and access through networking—are unremarkable in themselves, but when combined they change the very nature of information, the currency of our culture. No longer is knowledge accumulated over the centuries, unalterably fixed on pieces of paper and painstakingly consulted when needed. Today's information resembles a rushing torrent, always changing, impossible to contain or chart, and ready to sweep aside all limits or restrictions.

24 d Strengthening conclusions

An effective conclusion concisely summarizes, yet does not merely repeat, the whole message of the paper. This is your last chance to communicate with your readers. Given everything you've demonstrated, what is the strongest statement of your position that you can make? Focus on that statement and get everything else out of the way.

Broadening narrow conclusions

Take care not to limit your conclusion unnecessarily or to end by focusing on a point that is secondary to your overall intent. Mara originally drafted this conclusion arguing against religion's playing a formal role in public schools. When editing, Mara realized that she had ended on a minor point that made her conclusion seem narrower than the rest of her paper.

> Praying, reading from the Bible, and presenting the teachings of any one religion tend to exclude people who are not believers in

that religion. In the public school system, the prayers and beliefs of Christians would predominate and make non-Christians feel "different" and excluded. This is why religion should be kept out of the public schools and kept in the place of worship and the home. ~~However, I do think that holiday concerts and "Season's Greetings" decorations around Christmas and Hanukkah will continue.~~

2 Focusing conclusions

You may want to conclude by raising questions or making generalizations that follow from your discussion. Kyle's essay discussed his college's requirement that students acquire computers, explored the educational applications of computers, and touched on the problems students encountered using them. Yet his conclusion wandered far off into speculation. He eliminated that distraction and created a smooth transition.

With computers becoming as prevalent in college as they are in business, people are beginning to wonder where the computer age is taking us. Will computers become an integral part of every-

Exactly how they will change people's lives remains to be day life? ~~Will programmable machines make human minds obso-~~ *seen, but* *predicts changes more gradual than sweeping:* ~~lete?~~ One university official ~~seems to think not.~~ "When it comes to just plain living and thinking, the computer is not really much help."

3 Being direct

Wordiness saps the vitality of any conclusion, but worse, it undermines the credibility you have established in the rest of your paper. Transitional phrases such as *in conclusion, all in all,* or *to sum up* shouldn't normally be used to signal that a conclusion is approaching. The structure and language of your concluding paragraphs should show readers that you're winding up. Furthermore, a conclusion cluttered with unnecessary words or phrases makes you sound hesitant, unsure of yourself.

A **qualifying phrase** such as *I think* or *I believe* also can weaken your conclusion. Such a construction is entirely appropriate when you need to distinguish your conclusion from someone else's: *While Robinson concludes that the data clearly link low-frequency radiation to these illnesses, I would argue that the evidence is far from conclusive.* In most cases, however, readers will understand that the ideas expressed in the conclusion are your own.

In drafting her paper on sharks, Aliah concluded with a repetition of other people's opinions or facts, ones that she had carefully documented earlier. By qualifying them in the first person, her conclusion seemed to be merely her own opinion, not a carefully formulated conclusion based on research and analysis. When editing, Aliah removed the first-person references, and rather than telling what her conclusions would be, she simply stated them.

~~I can only hope that I have given some information to help~~
            Sharks
~~you see that sharks~~ are not the fearsome creatures humans
                        Millions of years old,
seem to think they are. They have their place in the scheme of
things like every other animal. The sooner we accept that the
oceans are their domain, the sooner we can learn to share the
oceans with them. ~~Sharks are millions of years old; I don't want
to be part of their destruction. I hope you too will consider helping to save humankind's ancient enemy, the shark.~~

EDITING 7: PRACTICE —————————————————————————

Edit the following conclusion to make it more satisfying. More than one edited version is possible. Be ready to explain your editing choices.

Everyone acknowledges that history is important, but there is a lot of debate over just what kind of history should be studied and taught. History matters. Some people mean different things when they say this, though. A form of social history that focuses on the lives and experiences of ordinary people has come into prominence in recent years. Traditionally, history was the study of "great men" and their wars. Economic conditions are also considered by some to be at the center of what we mean by "history." Issues of race and gender are now more prominent than they were before. There is no agreement. So where does that leave those of us who want to study history now? What model are we supposed to follow? There are so many

facts and ideas to learn in studying history. When you don't know what facts and ideas you are supposed to be learning, it makes the whole process overwhelming. You can't learn everything, can you? If historians rethink what their discipline is all about, maybe things will work themselves out. History is too important for this issue to be ignored.

EDITING 8: EXPLORATION

Select an essay that looks interesting to you because of its title but that you have not read before. First read only the opening paragraph. What can you tell about the essay from this paragraph alone? What is the topic of the essay? What will the author's position on this topic be? Think about the author's relation to the subject matter (expert, tourist, researcher, storyteller?). Who is the intended audience, and how does the author relate to that audience? What is the tone or mood of the essay?

Next read the conclusion. Compare your understanding of the audience, purpose, topic, position, and tone with your impressions of the opening. How are they different? Judging only from the opening and the conclusion, try to determine what were the important points made in the essay.

Last, read the entire essay and see how accurate your predictions were. How good were your guesses?

EDITING 9: APPLICATION

Find two essays that you have enjoyed recently and compare their conclusions. Then try rewriting the conclusions of the first essay in the style of the second (and vice versa). Compare the effectiveness of the new conclusions with that of the old. Does one seem better than the other? Why? You might try this exercise using essays representing different genres (an expository essay and a proposal, a reflective essay and an essay that seeks to explain a concept, etc.). Ask yourself whether some types of conclusions seem to work well in different kinds of writing while others do not. Think about why this might be the case.

25 Strengthening Sentence Structure

If each of your ideas stands alone in an individual sentence, the reader may see your statements as a string of isolated facts and fail to understand the connections you wish to make. By carefully combining ideas within sentences, you can show readers how those ideas are related.

Various *sentence structures* can express closely related ideas in different ways. Each technique of structuring sentences has specific uses.

Joining ideas through **coordination** emphasizes their equality.

> Give me liberty *or* give me death. [equal alternatives]
>
> PATRICK HENRY

Subordination creates a hierarchy of ideas, emphasizing one of greater importance.

> We should all be concerned about the future *because* we will have to spend the rest of our lives there.
>
> CHARLES KETTERING, "SEED FOR THOUGHT"

Parallelism—the repetition of a grammatical structure— suggests similarity between ideas in a way that can create symmetry, balance, and even elegance.

> No eye can see, no hand can touch, no tongue can name the devils that plague him.

25 a Using coordination

Elements joined by *coordination* must be in the same grammatical form—two or more independent clauses, dependent clauses, phrases, or words. Look for places where ideas of comparable

importance could be linked through coordination. By using coordination skillfully, you can suggest connections, avoid repetition, and enhance readability.

Coordinating conjunctions

Coordinate two or more sentences, or **independent clauses,** by joining them into a single **compound sentence** with a **coordinating conjunction** (*and, but, or, nor, so, for, yet*) and a comma or with just a semicolon. (For punctuation advice, see Chapter 33.) Choose the method of coordination carefully to express the relationship you intend between the two ideas.

> Gentlemen may cry peace, peace, *but* there is no peace. The war is actually begun!
>
> PATRICK HENRY

Henry states his opponents' objective, then with the contrasting conjunction but *tells them their hope for peace is in vain.*

Joining equivalent elements with *and* or with a semicolon implies continuation or addition.

> Nothing is illegal if one hundred businessmen decide to do it, *and* that's true anywhere in the world.
>
> ANDREW YOUNG

They were tired, lost, and hungry. ~~They~~ *, yet they* did not panic.

The conjunction yet *heightens the contrast between the situation and the response.*

Coordinate elements must have the same grammatical form. See 25e and 25f.

Correlative conjunctions

Another way to coordinate two independent clauses is by using a pair of correlative conjunctions such as *both . . . and, either . . . or,* or *not only . . . but also.*

not only
Lavar won high honors in mathematics and physics. ~~He~~ *, but he* was also recognized for his achievement in biology.

Conjunctive adverbs

A **conjunctive adverb** such as *however, moreover,* or *nevertheless* used with a semicolon can also join two independent clauses.

ESL **NOT ONLY . . . BUT ALSO**

If you join two sentences with *not only . . . but also,* you will need to change word order in the first clause.

- If the first clause has an auxiliary verb—*has, could, would, might*—or if the main verb is *be,* reverse the order of the subject and the auxiliary verb or *be.*

Not only *has the computer science department* added several new courses this year, but the faculty has also updated the curriculum.

Not only *is California* a large state geographically, but it also has many cities with large populations.

- If the first clause has no auxiliary, add an appropriate form of *do* before the subject. The verb must be in its base form. (See 34a.)

Not only *did the voters express* a lack of confidence in their governor, but they also showed concern about the effectiveness of the Congress.

If you join subjects with *both . . . and* or *neither . . . nor,* be sure to check for subject-verb agreement. (See 341.)

; however
An Advanced Placement Test score will be accepted. ~~However,~~ the
＾
test must be taken within the last year.

EDITING I: PRACTICE ————————————————

Edit the following passage, using coordination to relate ideas of equal importance. More than one edited version is possible. Be ready to explain your editing choices.

The workers were instructed to seal the oily rags in cans. They forgot to do it. At night the rags caught fire. The fire spread rapidly through the storage area. A smoke detector went off. No one noticed. The alarm was relayed to the fire station. Firefighters raced to the warehouse. Flames were already darting through the windows. Smoke poured through the ceiling. Glass

cracked in the heat. It shattered. The fire commander turned in a second alarm. Another company sped toward the scene.

COORDINATING CONJUNCTIONS, CORRELATIVE CONJUNCTIONS, CONJUNCTIVE ADVERBS

Relationship	Coordinating Conjunctions
addition	*and*
contrast	*but, yet*
choice	*or, nor*
effect	*so*
causation	*for*

Relationship	Correlative Conjunctions
addition	*both . . . and*
	not only . . . but also
choice	*either . . . or*
substitution	*not . . . but*
negation	*neither . . . nor*

Relationship	Conjunctive Adverbs
addition	*also, besides, furthermore, moreover*
contrast	*however, instead, nevertheless, otherwise*
comparison	*similarly, likewise*
effect	*accordingly, consequently, therefore, thus*
sequence	*first, meanwhile, next, then, finally*
emphasis	*indeed, certainly*

EDITING 2: EXPLORATION ━━━━━━━━━━━━━━━━━━━━━━━━━━━

Read the following passage from a personal narrative by N. Scott Momaday. How has Momaday used coordination? How many examples can you find of ideas joined by coordinating conjunctions? by semicolons? Could any of these ideas have been joined in other ways? If they had been, how would the effect of the passage have been different?

Once there was a lot of sound in my grandmother's house, a lot of coming and going, feasting and talk. The summers there were full of excitement and reunion. The Kiowas are a summer people; they abide the cold and keep to themselves, but when the season turns and the land becomes warm and vital they cannot hold still; an old love of going returns upon them. The

aged visitors who came to my grandmother's house when I was a child were made of lean and leather and they bore themselves upright. They wore great black hats and bright ample shirts that shook in the wind. They rubbed fat upon their hair and wound their braids with strips of colored cloth. Some of them painted their faces and carried the scars of old and cherished enmities.

N. SCOTT MOMADAY, THE WAY TO RAINY MOUNTAIN

25 b Using subordination

Like coordination, *subordination* joins ideas and implies a relationship between them. In addition, it focuses attention on certain ideas by de-emphasizing, or subordinating, others.

NO
SUBORDINATION Tom Peters has become a phenomenon among business writers. He focuses on excellence and quality.

SUBORDINATION Tom Peters, *who focuses on excellence and quality,* has become a phenomenon among business writers.

This construction emphasizes Peters's status as a phenomenon.

SUBORDINATION Tom Peters, *who has become a phenomenon among business writers,* focuses on excellence and quality.

This construction emphasizes the focus of Peters's writing.

A subordinate element may appear as a clause, a phrase, or a single word. The less important the element is grammatically, the less attention the reader pays to it.

NO
SUBORDINATION The committee selected a plan. It seemed to leave nothing to chance.

CLAUSE The plan *that the committee selected* seemed to leave nothing to chance.

PHRASE The plan *selected by the committee* seemed to leave nothing to chance.

WORD The plan *selected* seemed to leave nothing to chance.

A **dependent** or **subordinate clause**—one that contains a subject and a verb but cannot stand alone as a full sentence—is introduced by a subordinating conjunction or a relative pronoun.

EXPRESSING LOGICAL RELATIONSHIPS USING SUBORDINATION

Subordination can be useful to clarify logical relationships between ideas. As you edit, notice whether you rely heavily on coordinating conjunctions and conjunctive adverbs to express logical relationships. If you do, consider using subordinating conjunctions to indicate more clearly how ideas relate.

COORDINATING CONJUNCTION
Freud believed that our dreams reflect unconscious wishes, *but* today some psychologists disagree.

CONJUNCTIVE ADVERB
Freud believed that our dreams reflect unconscious wishes; *however,* today some psychologists disagree.

SUBORDINATING CONJUNCTION
Whereas Freud believed that our dreams reflect unconscious wishes, today some psychologists disagree.

The first two versions direct readers to what Freud thought, which is not where you are heading. Only the third version tells readers right away that you are writing about disagreement with Freud.

1 Subordinating conjunctions

A clause introduced by a **subordinating conjunction**—such as *although, because, if, since, whether,* or *while*—usually tells *when, where, why, how,* or *under what conditions.* Such clauses are called **adverb clauses.**

The plan has a chance of success. It requires the efforts of sev- ~, although it~
eral people. ~One~ person must be available to explain each course ~Because one~
offering to students. ~Many~ people are needed. ~, many~

2 Relative pronouns

A clause introduced by a **relative pronoun**—*that, what, which, who,* or *whom*—usually modifies a noun or pronoun. Such clauses are called **adjective clauses.** (See 36d.)

> **SUBORDINATING CONJUNCTIONS**
>
> | Relationship | Subordinating Conjunctions |
> |---|---|
> | cause/effect | *as, because, since, so that, in order that* |
> | condition | *if, even if, unless, if only* |
> | contrast | *although, even though, though* |
> | comparison | *than, as though, as if, whereas, while* |
> | choice | *whether, than, rather than* |
> | sequence | *after, as, as long as, as soon as, before, once, since, till, until, when, whenever, while* |
> | space | *where, wherever* |
> | time | *when, whenever* |

, which has been widening for more than twenty years,

The gap between rich and poor has caused great concern among

social thinkers. ~~The gap has been widening for over twenty~~

~~years.~~

who

I have interviewed several economists. ~~They~~ believe that the gap

will continue to grow.

3 Noun clauses

You can also subordinate a sentence by using it as a subject or
as an object. Such **noun clauses** can be introduced by *why, what,
that, where, whether,* or *how.*

What   *is*

~~There are a few basic facts~~ we know today about AIDS. ~~They are~~

the result of years of painstaking research.

in what Cate was discovering.

The entire department became interested. ~~Other teachers and~~

~~students wanted to learn about Cate's discoveries.~~

25 C Coordinating and subordinating effectively

Skillful coordination and subordination can prevent confusion.

1 Solving problems in logic

Avoid using coordination where the meaning of two sentences
is not related closely enough to warrant joining them.

so
I had eggs for breakfast, ~~and~~ I missed the bus.
        ^

If there is a connection between these two statements, it must be explained. Showing cause and effect, for example, is better done with subordination.

Because I took time to cook eggs for breakfast, I missed the bus.

Be sure to make an accurate connection between ideas.

so
The project was a huge undertaking, ~~yet~~ I was exhausted at
                    ^
the end.

The conjunction yet *implies a contrast, which is inappropriate. The conjunction* so *implies the proper cause-and-effect relationship.*

Careless subordination may suggest causal relationships that you do not intend, so be careful to check each of your subordinated structures.

Shortly after
~~When~~ Bush was elected president, the conflict in Macedonia
       ^
flared.

Do you mean a coincidence in time or causation?

EDITING 3: PRACTICE

Edit the following passage from a book review to strengthen coordination and subordination. More than one edited version is possible. Be ready to explain your editing choices.

At the start of *The Bridge Across Forever,* the narrator is a stunt pilot performing in small towns of the American Midwest, and the narrator and the author seem to have much in common. The author writes about flying, and the narrator takes people for rides in his plane, but he is bored with the routine, but he is convinced that he will find the perfect woman at one of these shows, so he keeps going. Disillusioned at last, he gives up flying to pursue his quest, and he encounters many women, but none of them is the soul mate he is seeking.

2 Avoiding excessive coordination or subordination

How much coordination or subordination is too much? Beware of an unintended pattern of similar sentences.

> The paper industry ~~is~~ notorious for its deep cyclical swings, ~~but~~
> *has been hit unusually hard by*
> this recession ~~has been unusually severe.~~ Prices have been cut
> sharply, but demand has dropped even faster.

The similarity of the original two sentences was not deliberate. Restructuring one of them solved the problem.

> Coordination can be overdone, and when it is used too much, it
> begins to sound repetitive. ~~and readers~~ *Readers* may begin to imagine the
> voice of a young child speaking in sentences that just go on and
> on, strung together with *and*. ~~and soon~~ *Soon* they may get tired or con-
> fused or bored. ~~and as~~ *As* a writer you should try to prevent that.

Too much subordination can make your writing sound insipid because every point seems to be qualified while nothing is said directly (as in this sentence). How much is too much depends partly on your audience, your purpose, and the level of formality you intend. To edit for proper coordination or subordination, scan your paper for common conjunctions (*and, or, but, because, if, although*) and relative pronouns (*who, which, that*) and evaluate your use of them; make such checking a part of your editing routine.

Careful repetition of *and*, however, can create a rhythmic effect. In a reflective essay on time and human mortality, E. B. White describes a circus bareback rider circling a ring on horseback again and again. The repetitive coordination emphasizes the rhythm of the scene's action.

> The rider's gaze, as she peered straight ahead, seemed to be circular, as though bent by force of circumstance; then time itself began running in circles, *and* so the beginning was where the end was, *and* the two were the same, *and* one thing ran into the next, *and* time went round and around *and* got nowhere. [Italics added.]
>
> E. B. WHITE, "THE RING OF TIME"

ESL USING SUBORDINATING CONJUNCTIONS

- When you use *whereas, while, although, though,* or *even though* in a dependent clause, do not use *but* before the independent clause.

    Although a smile shows happiness in most cultures, ~~but~~ in some it may be

    a sign of embarassment.

Alternatively, you could delete although *and keep* but.

- When you use *because* or *since* in a dependent clause, do not use *so* in the independent clause.

    Because Rudolf Nureyev defected from Russia, ~~so~~ for many years he

    could not return to dance in his native country.

You could also delete because *and keep* so.

- *Because* and *because of* are not interchangeable. *Because* is a conjunction—a word that introduces a clause containing both a subject and a verb.

    Because snow peas die in hot weather, you should plant them early in

    the spring.

- *Because of* is a two-word preposition, followed by a noun or pronoun.

    Because of the hot weather, the peas did not grow well.

EDITING 4: APPLICATION ─────────────────────────────

Try to edit out all the uses of *and* in a recent paper. You can use the search function on a computer to locate them. Replace each *and* with a more appropriate transition. Restore any uses of *and* that are necessary. What effect does this editing have on the paper?

EDITING 5: PRACTICE ─────────────────────────────

Edit the following passage to eliminate ineffective coordination and subordination. More than one edited version is possible. Be ready to explain your editing choices.

Last term I ended up with a low grade-point average, and my academic advisor thought that it was because I was taking too many difficult courses at the same time, so he recommended that I try to make a more sensible schedule this semester. I took his advice, yet I found myself with a much more manageable workload. I am taking calculus, which is difficult for me, and a photography course, which offers me different challenges, but I am finding the variety to be helpful. When I am tired of doing problem sets, I can go out and take pictures, so when the weather is bad, I can stay in and do math. I don't waste time the way I did last term. Because of this new sense of balance, right now I am doing much better in all my classes, so I hope the pattern will continue.

EDITING 6: PRACTICE

Edit the following passage from an analysis of director Oliver Stone's work to eliminate ineffective subordination. More than one edited version is possible. Be ready to explain your editing choices.

> The Doors completes what could be termed a '60s trilogy from Stone, since it differs greatly from Platoon and Born on the Fourth of July. Stone served in Vietnam, although that part of his work is grounded in personal experience. Because he did not experience the world of the Doors, Stone portrays it as he imagines it was, which makes his work in this film different from the others, although it is less effective and less compelling.

EDITING 7: EXPLORATION

The following passage from an essay argues that politics has influenced the decisions of art galleries such as the Corcoran Gallery of Art in Washington, D.C. How many examples of subordination can you find in the passage? Why has the author used subordination rather than coordination to join ideas?

> Whatever grave reservations regarding Congress may have motivated the directors of the Corcoran, they weakened the entire social fabric by yielding their freedom. Their decision should have been to show the work, whose merit they must have believed in to have scheduled the exhibition. Since then individual members of Congress have revealed themselves as enemies of freedom by letting their aesthetic attitudes corrupt their political integrity as custodians of the deepest values of a democratic society.
>
> ARTHUR C. DANTO, "ART AND TAXPAYERS"

25 d Eliminating choppy sentences

Too many separate sentences make a *choppy* passage that moves in baby steps. Using coordination and subordination can smooth your reader's path and make the connections needed to express the complexity of your thoughts.

In 1935, researchers ^who^ discovered the human sleep cycle. ~~They~~ found that sleep in humans is initiated by a hypnotic state. ~~This~~ hypnotic state affects brain waves of the neocortex, which ^~~These~~ are measured using a device called the electroencephalograph.

How long and how complicated you should make your sentences depends in part on how well you think readers will be able to follow.

EDITING 8: PRACTICE ─────────────────────

Edit the following passage, using subordination and coordination to clarify the relationships between ideas and to eliminate choppiness. More than one edited version is possible. Be prepared to explain your editing choices.

Sammy Sosa plays right field for the Chicago Cubs. He became famous for his 1998 home run race with Mark McGwire. By the standards of his native country, the Dominican Republic, he is fabulously wealthy. He is not among the most highly paid players in major league baseball. In Chicago he has bought baseball tickets for hundreds and hundreds of underprivileged children. In the Dominican Republic he has helped fund programs to update medical facilities and schools. For every home run he hit in 1998, he donated 40 computers to schools back home. He also organized a relief fund. It helped feed people and rebuild schools and homes after a major hurricane. For all his success, Sosa does not seem to be aloof or standoffish. People seem genuinely affectionate toward him.

25 e Using parallelism

Writers use *parallelism*—the repetition of a grammatical structure—to emphasize the similarity among ideas. Parallel structures are common in everyday speech as well as in formal writing.

It was the best of times, it was the worst of times.

CHARLES DICKENS, *A TALE OF TWO CITIES*

What goes around comes around.

I came, I saw, I conquered.

JULIUS CAESAR

To underscore the similarity of ideas, the elements of a parallel structure must balance grammatically: clauses paired with clauses, phrases with phrases, possessive nouns with possessive nouns, and so on.

CLAUSES Ask not what your country can do for you; ask what you can do for your country.

JOHN F. KENNEDY, INAUGURAL ADDRESS

PHRASES To die, to sleep; / To sleep: perchance to dream. . . .

WILLIAM SHAKESPEARE, *HAMLET*

WORDS Getting and spending, we lay waste our powers.

WILLIAM WORDSWORTH, "THE WORLD IS TOO MUCH WITH US"

⬛ **Compound elements**

Compound elements can be joined by a coordinating conjunction (*and, but, or, nor, so, for,* or *yet*) or by a pair of correlative conjunctions (*either . . . or, neither . . . nor, not only . . . but also, both . . . and, whether . . . or*). (See 25a.) When you edit, make sure that all compound elements are grammatically parallel.

He predicted that the day judgment would cause the earth to shake and the dead ~~would~~ to rise.

Most people think of the campus as a place to get an education, not ~~where you can~~ to exercise and get in shape.

He struggled not only with calculus, but chemistry ~~was hard~~ with too.

2 Comparisons

When elements are compared using *than* or *as*, they should be parallel in grammatical form because they are presented as equivalent alternatives.

He always believed that effective communication was more a matter of ~~clear~~ *clearly* thinking than ~~to try to write~~ *writing* well.

The weather is seldom as pleasant in Boston as *in* Miami's.

3 Lists

Elements presented in a series or list should be parallel in grammatical form.

Her favorite activities were painting, walking, and ~~she liked to visit~~ *visiting* museums.

EDITING 9: EXPLORATION

Coordinating conjunctions—*and, but, so, or, for, nor, yet*—and semicolons join grammatically equal elements, creating parallel constructions. Find each instance of coordinate or parallel construction in the following sentence from Thomas Jefferson's draft of the Declaration of Independence. Identify the individual elements of each use of coordination or parallelism. What is the effect of parallelism?

> We therefore, the representatives of the United States of America in General Congress assembled, in the name of and by the authority of the good people of these states reject and renounce all allegiance to the kings of Great Britain and all others who may hereafter claim by, through or under them; we utterly dissolve all political connection which may heretofore have subsisted between us and the people or parliament of Great Britain; and finally we do assert and declare these colonies to be free and independent states and that as free and independent states, they have full power to levy war, conclude peace, contract alliances, establish commerce, and do all other acts and things which independent states may of right do.

EDITING 10: EXPLORATION

The following passage by the black feminist Alice Walker discusses the position of African American women. Where has she used parallelism? What ideas are

emphasized through this use of parallelism? How is the passage as a whole strengthened?

> When we have pleaded for understanding, our character has been distorted; when we have asked for simple caring, we have been handed empty inspirational appellations, then stuck in the farthest corner. When we have asked for love, we have been given children. In short, even our plainer gifts, our labors of fidelity and love, have been knocked down our throats. To be an artist and a black woman, even today, lowers our status in many respects, rather than raises it: and yet, artists we will be.
>
> ALICE WALKER, "IN SEARCH OF OUR MOTHERS' GARDENS"

25 f Creating effective parallelism

Perhaps parallel structures are so common because they are so effective. However, when the words compared are not grammatically comparable, the ideas seem less similar, and the comparison becomes ambiguous.

To bring parallels into sharp focus, supply all necessary words. Words commonly omitted from parallel structures are prepositions (*to, for, at*), subordinating conjunctions (*although, since, because*), and relative pronouns (*who, which, that*).

The searchers tried to ensure that interviewees were representa-
   that
tive of the campus population and their opinions reflected those
                                ^
of the whole student body.

Without the second that, *it is unclear to whom the clause beginning with* their opinions reflected *refers.*

Few devices impart greater power, gravity, and impact than the formal, rhythmic, and forceful words of a well-constructed parallel. Consider using a parallel structure for emphasis.

With local leaders afraid of the "no-growth" label, the quality of

local decision making has clearly declined. The question facing
                 not   plan to have no growth but
towns like Abilene is whether they will do enough planning to
                       ^
whether they will face growth with no plan.
avoid uncontrolled development.
                              ^

If you employ complex forms of parallelism, match the elements of each structure carefully, and make sure the passage as a whole warrants the emphasis. Some writers use parallel structures inside other parallel structures, like sets of concentric circles. The effect is not only clarity but also the power, grace, and rhythm of a chant, useful on the most solemn of occasions.

> We can never be satisfied as long as our bodies, heavy with fatigue of travel, cannot gain lodging in the motels of the highways and the hotels of the cities. We cannot be satisfied as long as the Negro's basic mobility is from a smaller ghetto to a larger one.
>
> MARTIN LUTHER KING, JR., "I HAVE A DREAM"

STRATEGIES FOR STRENGTHENING SENTENCES

When editing, consider the following ways to clarify the relationships between your ideas:

- Use **coordination** for alternatives, comparisons, contrasts, and extensions.
- Use **subordination** to clarify logical relationships between ideas.
- **Combine** choppy sentences.
- Use **parallelism** for emphasis.

EDITING 11: PRACTICE _____

Strengthen sentence structures in the following paragraph from a record review by using parallelism and elliptical structures. More than one edited version is possible. Be ready to explain your editing choices.

> The first cut on *Hope Chest* by 10,000 Maniacs uses a reggae sound in the keyboard. It has an insistent bass line and a guitar that sounds like a swarm of mosquitoes. The vocals are so intricately woven that during the bridge, two sets of lyrics are being sung at once. That sound creates the effect of a breakdown. It also creates the impression of the dissolving of structure.

EDITING 12: PRACTICE _____

Edit the following paragraph from a personal narrative to correct faulty parallelism. More than one edited version is possible. Be ready to explain your editing choices.

First it rained, then hail was falling, and finally snow came down, As the temperature dropped, we moved our bedrolls closer to the fire, hung blankets over the windows, and more logs were added to the blaze. Nothing seemed to help. The thin walls seemed to invite the cold in. The wind whistled through cracks. The windows rattled in the wind. Snow was drifting under the door.

EDITING 13: PRACTICE _____

Edit the following passage—which analyzes the "Gonzo journalism" of Hunter S. Thompson—to strengthen sentence structure by using coordination, subordination, parallel structures, and elliptical structures as you think appropriate. Many edited versions are possible. Be ready to explain your editing choices.

Whether Hunter S. Thompson's world is reality or imagined, it makes for enjoyable reading. His humor arises from situations that are so frantic or such exaggerations as to be ludicrous. The writing moves from subject to subject, and it mimics the pattern of a drunken or drugged mind. His sentences ramble. His thoughts tumble. His subjects shift like colors in a hallucination. He somehow maintains a sense of reality. Each description and each phrase somehow contain a sharp shard of observation. The reader gets the feeling that his scenes could have happened. Many of them are completely far-fetched. He stretches our willingness to believe to the limit. This is the key to Thompson's style.

EDITING 14: APPLICATION _____

Select a page from a draft you are working on, and evaluate the sentence structures. First identify all examples of coordination by circling coordinating conjunctions and semicolons. Next identify all examples of subordination by drawing a line under subordinate elements. Are coordination and subordination used where they are most effective? Are there any places where two ideas would be better joined through another method? Is every conjunction or conjunctive adverb well chosen? Is either coordination or subordination overused? Then look for cases where you have used parallel structures. Are the words and ideas similar enough to be included in a parallel structure? Have you included all necessary words? Find places where you might consider using parallel structures. Edit the page by improving any weak sentence structure you find. How does the edited passage compare with the original?

26 Creating Emphasis and Variety

Effective writing focuses the reader's attention by emphasizing, or stressing, important ideas. You can establish *emphasis* by varying sentence structures and rhythms.

Variety not only keeps readers focused on your important ideas; it also ensures that you don't lose their attention altogether. A strong but varied rhythm carries the reader along without becoming predictable and monotonous.

When editing, decide what ideas you want to emphasize and where in your paper you might change the rhythm or sentence type to focus readers' attention.

26 a Using the emphatic first and final positions

If you want something to be noticed, place it at a beginning. The first words of a sentence, the first sentence of a paragraph, and the first paragraph of an essay all attract readers' attention.

> *I think that we're all mentally ill;* those of us outside the asylums only hide it a little better—and maybe not all that much better, after all. We've all known people who talk to themselves, people who sometimes squinch their faces into horrible grimaces when they believe no one is watching, people who have some hysterical fear—of snakes, the dark, the tight place, the long drop . . . and of course, those final worms and grubs that are waiting so patiently underground.
>
> STEPHEN KING, "WHY WE CRAVE HORROR MOVIES"

While first words immediately grab attention, those that come last can have an enduring impact. The last words of a sentence, a paragraph, or an entire essay resonate in the reader's mind, lingering to provoke further thought.

> Early civil rights bills nebulously state that other people shall have the same rights as "white people," indicating that there were "other people." But civil rights bills passed during and after the Civil War systematically excluded Indian people. . . . *Indians were America's captive people without any defined rights whatsoever.*
>
> VINE DELORIA, JR., "CUSTER DIED FOR YOUR SINS"

When editing, look for ways to use the emphatic first and final positions of each sentence, each paragraph, and each essay, especially in your opening and conclusion. (See Chapter 24.)

The costs
~~Whatever the rewards~~ of prohibition, ~~its costs~~ will always exceed
its rewards
~~them.~~ Users, who will always exist, are harmed not only by drugs but also by the law. The more effective the law, the more non-users are victimized by crimes committed for drug cash. The higher drug prices go, the more desperate and sophisticated drug gangs become. ~~With~~ *with* a stroke of a pen, ~~society~~ *Society* could eliminate drug profits and drug crime.

Editing the concluding paragraph of her argument, Darla phrased her first sentence more boldly. She then moved the phrase with the stroke of a pen *to the emphatic final position.*

EDITING I: APPLICATION ━━━━━━━━━━━━━

Select two pages from a paper you are working on. Underline the first and last sentence in each paragraph. Reading only these sentences, would a reader see the most important ideas in each paragraph? Edit each paragraph so that the most important idea is in either the first sentence or the last.

Next, on one of the edited pages, underline the most important element in each sentence, whether a thing, an action, or a description. How often does the most important element fall at the beginning or at the end of the sentence? How often is it buried somewhere in the middle? Edit each sentence, moving important elements to the emphatic first or final position within sentences wherever possible. Now, look for places where the flow of old information to new is reversed or interrupted. Edit to improve that flow.

FROM OLD TO NEW

As you edit for emphasis, consider what information you have already given your readers. Presenting information that readers already know—"old" information—before introducing "new" information helps readers see the connection to earlier ideas. This mental linking helps readers recognize the continuing thread of the discussion.

If the old-to-new pattern is not observed, the ideas are hard to follow, and the reader can't identify the main point.

Most artificial food colorings are synthetic chemicals.

new?

Hyperactivity in children was once thought to be increased by

old?

these colorings.

What is the main point that the writer will go on to explore? food colorings? hyperactivity? As it is written, we can't know.

See how much clearer the old-to-new pattern can be:

Most artificial food colorings are synthetic chemicals.

old   new

These colorings were once suspected of increasing hyperactivity in children.

Watch the flow of old information to new information from this masterful writer:

Big João was born near the sea, on a sugarcane plantation in Recôncavo, the owner of which, Sir Adalberto de Gumucio, was a great lover of horses. He boasted of possessing the most spirited sorrels and the mares with the most finely turned ankles in all of Bahia and of having produced these specimens of first-rate horseflesh without any need of English studs, thanks to astute matings which he himself supervised.

MARIO VARGAS LLOSA, *THE WAR OF THE END OF THE WORLD*

Compare the edited version with the original to determine which you prefer. Does strengthening emphasis help achieve your goals?

26 b Editing sentence length

Some writers write short sentences. They seldom use dependent clauses. They rarely use modifiers. Other writers never use simple sentences when elaborate ones, decorated with ribbons of dependent clauses, can be substituted, and thus they sometimes keep the reader waiting, hoping—perhaps even praying—eventually to find a period and, with it, a chance to pause for breath. (Whew!) Short sentences and long ones both have their uses, given a writer's purpose and intended audience. When you edit, vary sentence length to direct and focus readers' attention.

1 Short sentences

Short sentences pack power. They command full attention. They can show intense feelings, impressions, and events. In the following scene Richard Rodriguez describes distributing bread in a poor neighborhood in Tijuana. Notice how his brief sentences make his confrontation with hunger and need all the more chilling:

> Five or six children come forward. All goes well for less than a minute. The crowd has slowly turned away from the altar; the crowd advances zombie-like against the truck. I fear children will be crushed. Silent faces regard me with incomprehension. *Cuidado* [careful], damn it!
>
> RICHARD RODRIGUEZ, "ACROSS THE BORDERS OF HISTORY"

When you want to achieve such a dramatic effect—a critical scene in a personal narrative or in the summation of an argument—condense your ideas into as few words as possible and break up long sentences into shorter ones.

~~As soon as~~ I hit the ball and took ~~my first~~ step. ~~my~~ My knee collapsed, and I was on the ground ~~in~~ blinding pain. The pain was I heard my teammates yelling, "Get up! Run!" ~~but~~ I could no more run than ~~I could~~ fly.

2 Long sentences

Most academic writing requires that you elaborate on your ideas and show the connections between them. Long sentences give you the room to develop more complex thoughts and the structure to show the relationships between them. (See also Chapter 25.) If you find a patch of short sentences that say little and don't emphasize an important point, consider combining some sentences to emphasize the main ideas.

> Recent snows have renewed a problem in the town of Palmyra.
> , which are caused by water
> ~~The problem is~~ sinkholes. ~~Water~~ eroding underground limestone
> deposits ⊙ ~~causes them.~~ They are like huge potholes. *that* ~~They~~ appear
> quickly and grow rapidly. A few years ago a sinkhole opened in a
> car dealer's lot, swallowing a few cars. Last February a fuel truck
> , while another
> making a delivery ended up in a sinkhole. ~~Another~~ sinkhole swal-
> With heavy
> lowed a yard and threatened a house. ~~Heavy~~ snows ~~are~~ melting
> , we
> rapidly. ~~We~~ face the problem of a sinking town.

You can create emphasis by mixing both long and short sentences. Try changing abruptly from a long sentence to a sparsely worded, simple sentence that stresses one of your key points. The break in rhythm can stop readers in their tracks. Try it. It works.

EDITING 2: PRACTICE ────────────────────────

Edit the following passage, which appears just before the end of a personal narrative, varying the length of the sentences to improve emphasis and variety. More than one edited version is possible. Be ready to explain your editing choices.

> When I heard the mail drop through the slot in the door, my heart leapt. After I practically flew downstairs, I pounced on the mail that lay scattered on the floor. There, finally, was a letter for me from Iowa State University. "Today's the day," I said to myself, "the day that will seal my fate." At last I would have the answer to the all-important question of whether I had been accepted at the school of my choice. I wondered where I would spend the next four years. I wondered if I would be in Ames, Iowa, or at home in Deerfield, Illinois. After I took a deep breath and counted to three, I ripped open the envelope.

26 c Varying sentence types

Sentences can vary by *grammatical type*, by *rhetorical type*, or by *functional type*. (Also see Chapter 64.) Because readers' attention will be drawn to an atypical sentence—a question or command, for instance—varying sentence types provides another way to create emphasis.

Grammatical types

Varying grammatical sentence types usually means varying sentence lengths: short sentences are usually **simple sentences,** with a single independent clause, while long sentences are often **compound,** with more than one independent clause; **complex,** with at least one dependent clause; or **compound-complex,** with a dependent clause as well as at least two independent clauses. Each type has its own typical pattern and rhythm. If you have used too many sentences of one type, you may miss a chance to create emphasis and variety.

> A young-looking 43, he is a slim but strongly built man whose fast smile and self-deprecating patter convey the impression of relentless, perpetual movement. Talk slowly, or make a point twice, and an impatient glaze comes into his eyes. *He is restless in a designer suit.* But when I talked to him recently in his North London home, [British Prime Minister Tony] Blair was off duty, tousled and denim'd. He has always been a cheery rock-freak, a passionate father and a weekend slob. *And he has always been surprising.* [Italics added.]
>
> ANDREW MARR, "VANITY BLAIR"

Notice how the quick sentences keep the passage moving. The last sentence focuses attention forward, on what the writer finds "surprising."

Rhetorical types and word order

Within a sentence, should you put the main point first and the subordinate information later? Or should you first establish the context and then deliver the main message? Such decisions refer to rhetorical sentence types. The first strategy—placing the main idea first—results in a **cumulative sentence.**

GRAMMATICAL SENTENCE TYPES

- A **simple sentence** consists of a single independent clause:

  independent clause

  Pollution is a growing problem.

- A **compound sentence** consists of two or more independent clauses (joined by a comma and a coordinating conjunction or by a semicolon):

  independent clause   independent clause

  Pollution is a growing problem, and it affects every aspect of our lives.

- A **complex sentence** consists of one independent clause and one or more dependent clauses:

  dependent clause   independent clause

  Because clear-cut forests hold less water, water quality deteriorates.

- A **compound-complex sentence** contains at least two independent clauses and one or more dependent clauses:

  dependent clause   independent clause   independent clause

  When the rains stop, the ground dries out rapidly, and stream temperatures rise.

  (For more on sentence types, see Chapter 64.)

main point

Othello smothers the delicate Desdemona in a fit of an-

subordinate information   main point

guished passion and boiling fury. He kills the person

subordinate information

he loves most because he has trusted the lies of the vi-cious Iago.

The second strategy—which saves its punch for the end—results in a **periodic sentence.**

subordinate information

In a fit of anguished passion and boiling fury, Othello

main point

smothers the delicate Desdemona. Because he has

subordinate information   main point

trusted the lies of the vicious Iago, he kills the person he loves most.

Notice how the effects differ despite the very slight variation in the actual words used.

Cumulative sentences allow a writer to make a major point, then support it. Yet writing composed solely of cumulative sentences can be monotonous, so consider using a periodic sentence to emphasize a point.

A Small Place is an unsettling book. In it Jamaica Kincaid discloses shocking details about the tourist paradise Antigua, where she grew up. We see the poor condition of the school, the library, the hospital, and even the government, all problems she links to English and American imperialism. An American feels defensive and ashamed ⊙ When when confronted by the consequences of unthinking exploitation.

Alternatively, you can put important information first by using **inverted word order,** in which the verb precedes the subject: *Heavy hangs the head that wears the crown.* Although such inversion is uncommon, it can be used to strong effect in a special situation such as an opening or an ending.

3 Functional types

Most writing relies primarily on **declarative sentences**—
sentences that make statements. However, an occasional *question,
exclamation,* or *command* can grab the reader's attention. (Also
see 62a.)

> Yes, I love the church. *How could I do otherwise?* I am in the
> rather unique position of being the son, the grandson, and the
> great-grandson of preachers. Yes, I see the church as the body of
> Christ. *But, oh! How we have blemished and scarred that body
> through social neglect and through fear of being nonconformists.*
> [Italics added.]

> MARTIN LUTHER KING, JR., "LETTER FROM BIRMINGHAM JAIL"

*Notice how the emotional color of the paragraph changes as King
changes sentence types using questions and exclamations.*

> The church was a hub of Black children's social existence, and
> caring Black adults were buffers against the segregated and hostile
> world that told us we weren't important. But our parents said it
> wasn't so, our teachers said it wasn't so, and our preachers said it
> wasn't so. The message of my racially segregated childhood was
> clear: *let no man or woman look down on you, and look down on no
> man or woman.* [Italics added.]

> MARIAN WRIGHT EDELMAN, "A FAMILY LEGACY"

*Edelman stresses the message by putting it in a command, which the
reader can hear as Edelman heard it herself.*

EDITING 3: EXPLORATION ━━━━━━━━━━━━━━━━━━━

Extreme examples of periodic and cumulative sentences were much more
common in the past than now. Here are two excerpts from an essay by the
eighteenth-century writer Samuel Johnson in which he relates the demise of an
"adventurer in lotteries"—a gambler. What can you infer of Johnson's audience
and purpose? Which sentence is periodic, and which is cumulative? What effect
does each one have on you, the reader? Try to write sentences modeled
on these examples, following their general patterns and rhythms but using
different topics.

> As I have passed much of life in disquiet and suspense, and lost many op-
> portunities of advantage by a passion which I have reason to believe preva-
> lent in different degrees over a great part of mankind, I cannot but think
> myself well qualified to warn those, who are yet uncaptivated of the
> danger which they incur by placing themselves within its influence. . . .

ESL **REVERSING SUBJECTS AND VERBS FOR EMPHASIS**

In writing English, placing certain elements at the beginning of a sentence requires unusual word order. This unusual word order—reversing the position of the subject and the verb or part of the verb—creates emphasis.

These *introductory elements* create word order much like that of a question, with the verb or an auxiliary verb coming before the subject.

	auxiliary	base verb
introductory element	**subject**	

Under no circumstances did we wish to cut funding for this program.

These introductory elements require changing subject-verb order:

NEGATIVE ADVERBS	*Seldom* has a verdict created such an outrage among citizens.
OR ADVERB PHRASES	*In no way* should funding for this program be cut.
	(Others: *rarely, scarcely, hardly ever, only once, in no case, not until* [+ *time*], *not since* [+ *time*])
ADVERB OF EXTENT OR DEGREE	*So* intense was the hurricane that it destroyed much of the small town.
CONDITIONAL CLAUSES	*Only if* we take measures now will we rescue our city from urban blight.
	Only when there is justice will there be peace.

Certain other introductory elements require you to place the subject after both the auxiliary (if there is one) and the main verb.

ADVERB OF POSITION	*Beyond* the hedge stood a small shed.
COMPARATIVES	*More intriguing* than the main plot of the novel are several of the subplots.
PARTICIPLES WITH MODIFIERS	*Lying on my desk* should be a large sealed envelope.

My heart leaped at the thoughts of such an approach of sudden riches, which I considered myself, however contrarily to the laws of computation, as having missed by a single chance; and I could not forbear to revolve the consequences which such a bounteous allotment would have produced, if it had happened to me.

SAMUEL JOHNSON, "THE HISTORY OF AN ADVENTURER IN LOTTERIES"

26 d Varying sentence openings

Consider repositioning elements so that some sentences begin with elements other than the subject. Doing so will slightly emphasize that sentence.

Increasingly, doctors
~~Doctors~~ rely ~~increasingly~~ on advanced diagnostic equipment.

Overworked and often underpaid, single
~~Single~~ parents~~, who are overworked and often underpaid,~~ are among the most marginalized members of society.

Until researchers learned to translate its hieroglyphs, much
~~Much~~ of ancient Mayan culture remained a mystery ~~until researchers learned to translate its hieroglyphs.~~

EDITING 4: PRACTICE _____

To improve the emphasis and variety of the following passage, edit to begin some of the sentences with an element other than the subject. More than one edited version is possible. Be ready to explain your editing choices.

Chicken soup, a traditional remedy for colds, is a good food to eat in winter. It warms the body, as do other hot liquids. Chicken soup, not difficult to prepare, is made by boiling a whole chicken in about three quarts of water until the chicken is cooked fully and begins to come away from the bone. Be sure to add plenty of salt, which brings out the flavor, before you bring the chicken to a boil. Carrots, onions, and celery accentuate the flavor of the broth even more. Add these vegetables at the beginning. Remove the bones from the cooked chicken and dice it. Strain the broth. Cook noodles, peas, and diced carrots in the broth. Add the diced chicken when they are soft enough to eat with a fork.

26 e Using deliberate repetition

Deliberately repeating words, phrases, or sentence structures links the repeated elements and emphasizes them. (See 23c on repetition and paragraph coherence.) Repetition can also create powerful rhythms. A succession of similar phrases, falling on the reader's ear like the sound of waves striking the shore, can soothe or build to a strong climax. Getting just the right amount of repetition is difficult, however. When in doubt, err on the side of too little rather than too much. You can also use slight variations, or **synonyms,** rather than repeat the same word.

To use repetition effectively, look for words, phrases, or structures that are important to your meaning. Make sure that the element you have repeated deserves the emphasis and that the rhythmic effect you create is appropriate for your subject and audience. In this passage, Mark was trying to recreate the magic spell his mother cast by reading to him regularly:

~~When she~~ She read to me, I ~~could see~~ and saw faraway islands fringed with coconut palms. ~~With~~ She read to me, and with Jim Hawkins, I shivered in the apple barrel while the pirates plotted. She read to me, and I ran with Maori warriors to raid the villages of neighboring tribes. She read to me, and I saw Captain Cook slain on a beach of the Sandwich Isles. I saw the Tahitians welcome British sailors. I watched Fletcher Christian mutiny against Captain Bligh, and I marveled that Bligh reached safety in an open boat. I heard Ahab's peg leg thump on the deck overhead, and I marveled at the whiteness of the whale.

EDITING 5: EXPLORATION

In the following passage, identify instances of repetition. How does repetition contribute to the effectiveness of the passage? What ideas are emphasized?

His need for food stamps, quite obviously, is minimal now. But his need is not minimal for a reminder of those days when his father worked as a shipping clerk in a refrigerator plant and his mother stayed home to raise three children before she died so prematurely that her youngest son's heart still aches to think of it.

To reach the goal he has set for himself, to reach the level Sugar Ray Leonard once occupied at the top of boxing's craggy Mount Olympus, he must not lose a fight, but just as important, he must not lose his way.

He must avoid the normal pitfalls a fighter faces like the jabs to the nose and hooks to the liver, but this fighter must avoid more than that. He must avoid the eroding powers of money and fame, two things that build a man up and bring him crashing back to earth with the same swiftness.

RON BORGES, "A GOLDEN BOY WITH A PLATINUM PLAN"

26 f Omitting words deliberately

Sometimes, for the sake of brevity or to create a special rhythm, you can deliberately omit words that your reader will be able to supply mentally. Such an omission is called an **elliptical construction.** The omitted words are almost always dropped from the second part of a parallel construction after the idea has been introduced.

Her words suggested one thing, her actions ~~suggested~~ another.

Elliptical constructions work only when all the words you omit are identical to words that remain.

Of Shakespeare's female characters, Lady Macbeth is the most ruthless, Desdemona and Juliet *are* **the most loving, and Portia** *is* **the most resourceful.**

The omitted verbs must match exactly the verb that remains: is. *But the plural subject* Desdemona and Juliet *requires the verb* are, *so the omitted verbs had to be reinstated.*

Like repetition, elliptical construction affects rhythm and emphasis. It heightens rhythm by omitting unstressed words and leaving only the stressed words. But it also syncopates rhythm, so that a word occurs a beat or two sooner than expected. Read out loud any elliptical constructions you create, in the context of their sentences, to make sure that you have achieved the right rhythm.

✔ **STRATEGIES FOR ACHIEVING EMPHASIS AND VARIETY**

When editing to achieve emphasis and variety, try several of the following strategies; then choose ones that best suit your goals.

- Use the emphatic first and final positions.
- Edit sentence length.
- Vary sentence types.
- Vary sentence openings.
- Use deliberate repetition.
- Create elliptical constructions.

EDITING 6: EXPLORATION ─────────────────────────

The ways a writer achieves emphasis and variety are central to his or her writing style. Select a few pages of writing by one of your favorite authors and study the sentences for the techniques mentioned in this chapter. Does the author favor one technique more than the others? Which technique(s) do you think the author uses most effectively? Why? What does the author's use of variety and emphasis say about his or her style? Answers to these questions could tell you a great deal about why you like your favorite author's work.

EDITING 7: PRACTICE ─────────────────────────

Edit the following passage from a personal narrative for emphasis and variety. You will, of course, have to choose what to emphasize and which elements to preserve as you create variety. Think of at least two alternatives for each choice, and note the reasons for your decisions. If you have to make assumptions about audience or purpose, note them as well.

Sunday dinner at Grandma's house was about as appealing to me as a day without recess for me, an energetic nine-year-old. It meant leaving the other kids at the playing field at the bottom of the eighth inning. I had to take a bath in the middle of the day and wash behind my ears. The worst thing was that I had to put on my best clothes and try to keep them clean. For me to keep my clothes clean seemed beyond the realm of possibility in those days. My parents would look absolutely delighted as I emerged from the bath every week. I looked, frankly, nothing like myself. My father would exclaim, "She's as clean as a hound's tooth!" Yet I would arrive at

Grandma's week after week looking like Raggedy Ann, despite my parents' best efforts. My shirt would inevitably be stained; my stockings would inevitably be split; my shoes would inevitably be scuffed. My mother would look at me in disbelief as I climbed out of the car. She was amazed, no doubt, that such a metamorphosis could have occurred in a twenty-minute ride. My disheveled appearance, to be honest, never seemed to bother Grandma. She always exclaimed, "Don't you look nice!" I don't know to this day whether she was losing her eyesight or just being kind.

EDITING 8: APPLICATION

Select a passage from a paper you are working on and look for places that need emphasis or variety. Generate alternative versions using the various techniques discussed in this chapter—position, sentence length, sentence type, sentence openings, repetition, and ellipsis. Pick the version—alternative or original—that best suits your audience and purpose, and explain your choices.

27 Building Vital Sentences

What brings writing to life? Why does one writer's prose dull the senses while another's, on the same subject, rivets readers' attention? Sentence *vitality*—liveliness—helps create clear and compelling writing. By delighting the imagination, a vital sentence encourages readers to think and interact with your words. Clarity, appropriate descriptiveness, action, and specific examples all contribute to vitality.

In an argument paper, vitality means supporting your assertions with concrete evidence. In a reflective paper, it means providing candid insights into your perceptions and reactions. In a personal narrative, it means relating carefully observed detail in fresh, accurate language.

For example, most readers would find the first of these two descriptions dull and the second by Edward Abbey more vivid:

> The sky and the sunrise are reflected by the snow. There is a road in front of me that goes down the slope toward the stone formations.

> The snow-covered ground glimmers with a dull blue light, reflecting the sky and the approaching sunrise. Leading away from me the narrow dirt road, an alluring and primitive path into nowhere, meanders down the slope and toward the heart of the labyrinth of naked stone.

EDWARD ABBEY, *DESERT SOLITAIRE*

Why is the second passage more vital than the first? The first uses **general** nouns with few modifiers: *sunrise, road, stone formations*. The second uses **specific** nouns and modifiers that create tangible images: *alluring and primitive path, labyrinth of naked stone*. The first uses weak or **stative verbs**: *is, goes*. The second uses **dynamic verbs** that evoke actions readers can visualize: *meanders*. Finally, while the verb in the first passage is in the **passive**

voice (*are reflected*), the second passage uses a verb in the **active voice** (*glimmers*).

To improve the vitality of your writing, think of each sentence as a story. Like any story, a sentence has actors (nouns and pronouns) and actions (verbs). When you make each actor and action as vivid and as tangible as possible, readers can imagine the story unfolding before their eyes. When editing, use the following techniques to give your sentences immediacy and energy.

27 a Using concrete, specific nouns

If a sentence is to tell a story, your first task is to identify the actors in it so that readers can recognize them fully. Whether a character is a person, an object, or an idea, try to make that element come alive in readers' minds. Compare the mental pictures you get from the phrases *an old blue car* and *a rusted baby-blue '59 Buick Electra*. The first evokes images of a number of cars, the second a specific car.

As you edit, examine your choice of language. Is your language abstract or concrete? **Abstract** words refer to ideas and concepts that cannot be perceived by the senses: *transportation, wealth, childhood, nutrition.* **Concrete** words name things that can be seen, touched, heard, tasted, or smelled: *cars, dime, child, broccoli.*

Next, is your language general or specific? **General** words refer to categories and groups: *pets, stores, doctors.* **Specific** words identify individual objects or people: *Rover, the Reading Terminal Market, pediatrician Andrea McCoy.*

The terms *abstract* and *concrete* are not absolute. The same is true of the terms *general* and *specific.* Think of them as representing the ends of a continuum, with varying degrees of abstraction in between.

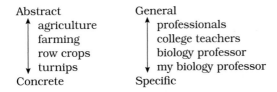

Abstract	General
agriculture	professionals
farming	college teachers
row crops	biology professor
turnips	my biology professor
Concrete	Specific

These two ways of characterizing words can overlap. *Music*, for example, is concrete in that you can hear it, but the word is also a general term embracing everything from Bartok to bagpipes to the Backstreet Boys.

Human thought depends on the ability to make connections between the general and the specific. Some kinds of thought require abstract terms: we could not think, speak, or write about *truth, insurance, constitutionality, political risk,* or *angular velocity* without using words developed for such concepts. Yet writing composed exclusively of abstractions can seem like nothing but "hot air." On the other hand, it may be hard to glean general truths from writing consisting only of details. Writers often err on the side of too many generalizations, so look for ways to enliven abstract terms with specifics.

We stand for a brighter future, a renewed hope, a better America.

Who doesn't want those things? How can you tell what this writer stands for?

We stand for a brighter future, a renewed hope, a better America, in which the unemployed find work, the sick receive health care, the old and the young are nurtured, and all of us are treated with respect.

What this writer means by a better America is clearer now, and the reader is free to agree or disagree with the specifics provided.

When writing about an abstract concept, provide a definition or example definition shortly after introducing it. Then make sure you ground the abstraction with clear, tangible examples so that it has meaning for your readers.

—money the government has borrowed in order to operate—
Concern about the national debt inspired efforts to balance the
∧
federal budget.

, like those that created the welfare system,
Liberal policies are bringing this country to ruin.
∧

, by slashing environmental protections, show they
Conservatives don't care about people, only business.
∧

When writing academic papers, you may want to use general statements in openings and conclusions. Make sure that elsewhere in the paper you have developed the specific and concrete details needed to support them. (See Chapter 24.)

27 b Choosing strong verbs

After you have clearly identified the actors in each sentence, describe their actions in equally vivid language by using strong verbs.

1 Replacing stative verbs

Verbs drive sentences the way an engine powers a car. *Dynamic verbs*—those that express motion or create vivid images—add horsepower to your writing. *Stative verbs*—verbs that simply show a state of being, such as *be, appear, become, seem, exist*—can leave your sentences underpowered. As you edit, look for stative verbs and consider replacing them with dynamic verbs.

Nothing ~~is more dangerous to~~ future economic stability than inflation.
<small>threatens</small> <small>more</small>

Even some forest-product corporations ~~have taken a stand against~~ deforestation, which is spreading rapidly.
<small>oppose</small>

Sometimes a form of *be* precedes a phrase or clause that may suggest or even contain a stronger verb that can become the main verb of the sentence.

The most effective writers ~~are those who~~ write as though they were simply talking.

Expletive constructions, those that begin with somewhat empty phrases like *there is/are* and *it is,* can frequently be replaced with stronger verbs.

~~There are several~~ moons ~~orbiting~~ Jupiter, Galileo found.
<small>Several</small> <small>orbit</small>

~~There are~~ several techniques ~~that researchers~~ employ to prevent self-selection in opinion surveys.
<small>Researchers</small>

~~There are many~~ people ~~who~~ still believe that Elvis Presley is alive, even though ~~it is~~ only tabloids ~~that~~ report such "news" seriously.
<small>Many</small>

2 Replacing weak dynamic verbs

Not all verbs that describe action spark clear images. Overuse has exhausted the image-making power of such verbs as *do, get, go, have, make,* and *think.* As you edit, watch for weak dynamic verbs and substitute stronger verbs that evoke clear images. (See 30b2.)

USING EXPLETIVE CONSTRUCTIONS

Expletive constructions such as *it is* and *there are* often serve useful functions. They can create emphasis by slightly delaying the subject of the sentence and by allowing opportunities for parallelism. (See 25e and 25f.)

It is a far, far better thing that I do, than I have ever done; it is a far, far better rest that I go to, than I have ever known.

CHARLES DICKENS, *A TALE OF TWO CITIES*

Expletives are also necessary in certain expressions about time and the weather.

There were showers this morning, but right now *it's* sunny outside.

It's five o'clock, sir; *it's* time to go.

owns
He ~~has~~ several antique cars.
     ^

      carves
She ~~does her carvings~~ with great skill.
            ^

       build
Beavers ~~make~~ dams that slow erosion.
         ^

Often a verb that relies on a modifier or other words for its descriptive power can be replaced. Choose the verb that best describes what you intend to convey.

       rushed
He ~~walked rapidly~~ out of the room.
          ^

     ran
He ~~walked rapidly~~ out of the room.
          ^

       scurried
He ~~walked rapidly~~ out of the room.
          ^

3 Turning nouns into verbs

The ease with which English words can be changed from one part of speech to another gives the language a marvelous flexibility. With the help of a suffix such as *-ance, -ment,* or *-ation,* verbs such as *deliver, announce,* or *tempt* can become useful nouns: *deliverance, announcement, temptation.*

Nouns thus made from verbs are called **nominalizations.** A nominalization can sometimes conceal the real action of a sentence

by requiring the use of a stative verb such as *do, have, make,* or *be.* If you have entombed the real action of your sentence in a nominalization, dig up the buried verb to give your prose new life.

>   *still fascinates*
> Pickett's Charge ~~has a continuing fascination for~~ historians of
>
> the Battle of Gettysburg.

Some nouns and verbs have the same form: *cause, dance, march, tie, love, hate.* If you use them as nouns, then you have to find new verbs, which are usually weaker. There is no reason to *perform a dance* when you can simply *dance,* no sense in *holding a march* when you can simply *march.*

> The signs told us to ~~make a~~ detour around the construction.

>   *meet*
> We plan to ~~hold a meeting~~ in two weeks.

Not every noun can be turned into a verb. Many grammarians object to using some nouns as verbs: instead of *Jay Leno* hosts *the Tonight Show,* they prefer *Jay Leno is the* host *of the Tonight Show.*

 CHANGING NOUNS TO VERBS

To enliven your writing, replace these common expressions with the dynamic verbs that are buried within them.

Expression	Buried Verb
put forth a proposal	propose
hold a discussion	discuss
formulate a plan	plan
reach a decision	decide
arrive at a conclusion	conclude
hammer out an agreement	agree
hold a meeting	meet
call a strike	strike
make a choice	choose

EDITING I: EXPLORATION

Read the following paragraph, which narrates one of the murders committed by Jack the Ripper. What verbs has Colin Wilson chosen to convey the action of

the scene? Are they effective? Wilson has used *be* as the main verb of a clause twice in this paragraph. Why do you think he does this?

> They tiptoed down the passageway, and crept into a corner of the yard by the fence. The man moved closer; she was not even aware of the knife he held in his left hand. A moment later she was dead; the first thrust had severed her windpipe. The man allowed her to slide down the fence. He slipped out of his dark overcoat, and bent over the woman.
>
> COLIN WILSON, "THE CRIMES OF JACK THE RIPPER"

EDITING 2: PRACTICE

Strengthen the verbs in the following sentences. Make any changes in wording that are necessary for smooth reading. More than one edited version is possible. Be ready to explain your editing choices.

1.　The first witness gave an adequate report of what he saw on the night of the murder.

2.　A police officer, he was the first person to arrive on the murder scene after the distress call.

3.　There was nobody standing or walking nearby, he said.

4.　The witness did a good job describing specifics, such as the knife and the severity of the wounds.

5.　He had a good memory and was very articulate, even when the defense attorney was asking him questions.

6.　When he was finished testifying, he was told he could leave the stand.

27 C Selecting active or passive voice

When a verb is in the **active voice,** the person or thing performing the action is the subject.

Donald *spent* the money.

Donald, the actor performing the action, is the subject of the sentence. *Money,* the recipient of the action, is the direct object.

When a verb is in the **passive voice,** things get turned around. The recipient of the action—*money*—becomes the grammatical subject, and *Donald* becomes the **agent** of the action in the prepositional phrase *by Donald.*

The money *was spent* by Donald.

Donald can appear as above or disappear entirely, depending on how important it is that the reader know who the agent of the action was: *The money was spent, and the club folded.* Perhaps there is no agent at all:

Mistakes *were made.*

1 Using the active voice to emphasize actors and actions

By making the actor the subject of the sentence, the active voice helps readers visualize the action of a sentence. Active-voice sentences usually use fewer words and proceed more directly than passive-voice sentences. If your writing situation requires vitality, editing for the active voice is a good strategy.

Manson and his followers planned the
~~The~~ Tate and LaBianca murders ~~were planned by Manson and his~~
They expected whites
~~followers~~ to incite a race war. ~~Whites were expected~~ to rise up in

alarm at the killings.

2 Using the passive voice for special purposes

The passive voice de-emphasizes the actor and highlights the recipient of the action. At times, this may be exactly what you want to do. Use the passive voice to accomplish the following special purposes:

- To stress the results of actions

  A constitutional amendment outlawing flag burning *was rejected* by the Senate.

- To leave the agent unstated

  According to investigators, the fire *was* deliberately *set.*

  By whom? No one knows at this point.

- To assert objectivity in research writing

  In the experiment, samples of food *were* first *contaminated* with bacteria. The samples *were* then *irradiated.* The samples *were tested* to see whether the bacteria survived.

  The passive voice de-emphasizes the role of an individual and suggests other researchers could produce similar results.

IMPROVING SENTENCE VITALITY

These two techniques can make sentences more vital.

1. Make the person or concept that performs the action of the sentence into the grammatical subject of the sentence.

WEAK	At the hearing by the selection committee, three sites were taken out of consideration, and the fourth was placed in further study.
STRONG	At the hearing, *the selection committee* took three sites out of consideration and said it would study the fourth.

In the original, the real subject—the selection committee—is hidden in a prepositional phrase.

2. Express the main action of the sentence in the main verb of the sentence.

STRONG	At the hearing, the selection committee *eliminated* three sites and *agreed to study* the fourth.

If you follow these two simple suggestions, your writing will spring to life.

• To strengthen flow between sentences

ACTIVE	Two crises threaten the economic security of the nation. Economists, business leaders, and politicians *have documented* the first crisis, the decay of manufacturing industries. They have all but ignored the second, however.
PASSIVE	Two crises threaten the economic security of the nation. The first crisis, the decay of manufacturing industries, *has been documented* by economists, business leaders, and politicians. They have all but ignored the second, however.

Notice how the change helps the sequence of topics flow from one sentence to the next.

• To take advantage of an emphatic position

**VERBS THAT CAN'T BE PASSIVE,
VERBS THAT CAN'T BE ACTIVE**

Most verbs in English can be either active or passive:

Charles Darwin *wrote* the famous book *The Origin of Species.* It *was written* after his expedition to the Galapagos Islands.

But not all English verbs have both active and passive forms. **Intransitive verbs,** verbs that do not take a direct object, can't be passive.

The improvement ~~was~~ resulted from his work with a tutor.

The baby ~~was~~ weighed seven pounds.

But weigh *used as a transitive verb can be used in the passive voice:* The baby was weighed *by the doctor.*

Certain other verbs, even though they may have objects, also cannot be used in the passive voice.

Do not use these verbs in the passive voice:

agree	disappear	live	sleep
arrive	exist	occur	stay
come	fall	rain	vanish
cry	go	result	walk
consist	happen	rise	weigh + amount
die	have	seem	

Do not use these verb phrases in the active voice:

be born	be killed	be made
be given	be located + preposition	

is located
The capital of the United States ~~locates~~ in Washington, D.C.

But locate *can be in the active voice when not followed immediately by a preposition:* Can you locate *Washington on the map?*

Two crises threaten the economic security of the nation. The first crisis, the decay of manufacturing industries, *has been documented* by economists, business leaders, and politicians. *The second*, however, *has* all but *been ignored*.

Using the passive moves the key word ignored *to the emphatic final position.*

EDITING 3: EXPLORATION

The following passage by James Baldwin makes extensive use of expletive constructions and the passive voice. Read it carefully, and try to decide why the author has used these techniques. Do they influence the meaning of the passage? its effect? Where do they focus your attention? Do they create a particular mood or atmosphere?

There is a custom in the village—I am told it is repeated in many villages—of "buying" African natives for the purpose of converting them to Christianity. There stands in the church all year round a small box with a slot for money, decorated with a black figurine, and into this box the villagers drop their francs. During the *carnival* which precedes Lent, two village children have their faces blackened—out of which bloodless darkness their blue eyes shine like ice—and fantastic horsehair wigs are placed on their blond heads; thus disguised, they solicit among the villagers for money for the missionaries in Africa. Between the box in the church and the blackened children, the village "bought" last year six or eight African natives.

JAMES BALDWIN, "STRANGER IN THE VILLAGE"

EDITING 4: PRACTICE

Edit the following paragraph from a paper arguing against pesticide use by substituting the active voice whenever you think it is effective. Make any changes in wording to make the passage flow better or have greater impact. More than one edited version is possible. Be ready to explain your editing choices.

We are all affected by pesticides. Hundreds of synthetic chemicals have been developed by scientists to destroy the insects and rodents that are called "pests" by farmers and Sunday gardeners. Once these deadly toxins are used, however, they are retained in the land for years sometimes. They are maintained in the environment, where our crops and water supply are contaminated and desirable species of birds and fish are killed off. Ironically, pesticides are even known not to work very well in the first place, since

usually a pest population that is resistant to the chemicals is created. And within a few years, the problem is as large as ever. The effect of pesticides on the environment and on our lives should be questioned. Perhaps even the right to use them at all should be questioned.

27 d Using vital modifiers

1 Using concrete, specific modifiers

Use the same considerations when selecting modifiers as you do for nouns: choose specific and concrete modifiers over abstract and vague terms. Some descriptive modifiers, such as *pretty, dull, dumb, nice, beautiful, good, bad, young,* and *old,* have become almost meaningless through overuse. They paint a very general picture. Rather than ask readers to accept your impression, give them the specific details so they can see things for themselves.

VAGUE	Everyone likes Alex.
SPECIFIC	Everyone likes witty Alex with his dimpled chin and big laugh.
VAGUE	A row of old brick houses stands along the street.
SPECIFIC	Dilapidated brick houses line the street, their shutters sagging and their windows boarded.
VAGUE	She played poorly.
SPECIFIC	She played hesitantly, making several jarring mistakes.

EDITING 5: PRACTICE _____

Edit the following paragraph by using concrete, specific nouns and modifiers. You may invent and add whatever details you think are necessary. Create one edited version. Then repeat the exercise, providing different details.

Our college library is really good. Not only does it have lots of books on all kinds of topics, but it also has plenty of periodicals. Many resources are available to help people with any research they might need to do, and the staff is always ready to give guidance. Research librarians are there to help answer all sorts of questions about library resources. Last year the library finally finished installing the new computer system. Now we can look up an item in the library from any of the remote computer terminals located all over campus. With just a few keystrokes, we can determine whether

the library owns the item and, if so, whether it it available or currently in circulation.

2 Untangling noun clusters

A remarkable quality of English is its use of nouns as modifiers. Instead of saying *a cabinet for files,* we can say *a file cabinet.* We can also string noun modifiers together. *A metal file cabinet* is far easier to say than *a cabinet of metal for files.*

ESL **ORDER OF ADJECTIVES**

Some types of adjectives typically occur before others. For example, an adjective describing size typically occurs before one describing color: *the large white house,* not *the white large house.* Shown below is the typical order of adjectives before nouns.

1.	Article	a, an, the
	Or possession	my, our, your, his, her, its, our, their
	Or demonstration	this, these, that, those
2.	Number	one, second, eleven, next, last, few, some, many
3.	Evaluation	good, pretty, ugly
4.	Size	big, small, tiny
5.	Shape	round, oblong, rectangular
6.	Condition	broken, shiny, rickety
7.	Age	old, young, new
8.	Color	blue, red, magenta
9.	Material	wooden, cotton, iron
10.	Noun as adjective	sports, flower, city

    1   2   6   7   10
He never forgot his first shiny new sports car.

   1 2 4 5   9
A few large round wooden containers were stacked on the floor.

Not all types of adjectives can be used together. For example, if you use an article, you shouldn't use a possessive: *the next project* or *my next project* but not *the my next project.* And generally, you should avoid long strings of adjectives.

Like any good thing, using nouns as modifiers can be done to excess. A long string of nouns used as modifiers is called a **noun cluster:** *do-it-yourself home improvement instruction videotape recordings.* Readers, upon finding a large noun cluster, must decide which nouns serve as modifiers and which is the "real" noun. Making readers struggle is unlikely to keep them reading. When editing, untangle noun clusters by moving some of the modifiers elsewhere.

Michael Graves' architecture attempts to revitalize a ~~building~~

of building forms

~~form~~ language that was lost during the heyday of International

Style modernism.

Sometimes writers are tempted to introduce a person with a long string of identifying modifiers in a special kind of noun cluster called a *false title.* Pick the elements about the person that you want to emphasize and move the other descriptive modifiers elsewhere.

Minnie Peppers, the

We met Texas-style chili cook-off champion ~~Minnie Peppers.~~

Carter McIlroy, who led the   *in*

The team signed 170-pound Big Ten Conference rushing and

kick-returns.

~~kick-return leader Carter McIlroy.~~

EDITING 6: EXPLORATION ────────────────────────

Read the following paragraph from Nancy Gibbs's description of modern American zoos. What choices has Gibbs made to give vitality to the passage?

> At some 150 American zoos . . . , the troubles are not very different. The sharks eat the angelfish. The Australian hairy-nosed wombat stays in its cave, and the South American smoky jungle frog hunkers down beneath a leaf, all tantalizingly hidden from the prying eyes of the roughly 110 million Americans who go to zoos every year. Visitors often complain that as a result of all the elaborate landscaping, they cannot find the animals. But this, like almost everything else that goes wrong these days, is a signal that America's zoos are doing something right.
>
> NANCY GIBBS, "THE NEW ZOO: A MODERN ARK"

EDITING 7: PRACTICE ────────────────────────

Edit the following paragraph to create vital sentences. You may invent and add any details you think are necessary. More than one edited version is possible. Be ready to explain your editing choices.

Most dog owners don't realize in advance how much time, money, and energy must be spent on a puppy. First, there is housebreaking the puppy and teaching it basic puppy obedience skills: how to accompany its owner while on a leash, how to respond to its name, how to stay near its owner. There are also other things—fetching, standing, and so on. And even when owners have the time for training, they probably don't have the necessary expertise. This means enrollment in expensive obedience school classes is required. Puppies create other expenses as well. Veterinarian visits, food and bedding, leashes and playthings, and grooming—a must for any well-bred dog—are all costly. And at least one nice rug or one pair of shoes must be replaced because a bad dog has chewed through them. Still, as any devoted dog owner will tell you, the expense is justified by the rewards: there's nothing like coming home from a hard day and being greeted by someone who loves you unconditionally and absolutely.

EDITING 8: APPLICATION

Read through a paper you are working on and pay close attention to the vitality of your sentences. Have you chosen specific, concrete nouns and modifiers wherever possible? Are your verbs precise? Do they convey action? If you have used the passive voice, do you have a good reason for doing so? Can you find any noun clusters? Consider the vitality of the language and sentence structure: keep the elements that you like and improve those that you don't like.

28 Being Concise

In most writing situations, the goal is to convey information clearly and efficiently. Vagueness, wordiness, and needless complexity can tire or annoy readers. Therefore, make your writing *direct:* express your ideas plainly. Be **concise:** use as few words as possible to achieve your purpose.

It is natural—indeed a good idea—to throw lots of ideas into your first draft just to get them all down; but when editing, strive to make your writing concise. Some writers call this process *boiling down,* referring to the cooking process that turns large quantities of thin broth into hearty, full-flavored soup. The drafts of this book required a lot of boiling down. The following is our original draft of a paragraph that appears later in this chapter:

> In a famous piece of advice, public speakers are urged, "Tell them what you're going to say, say it, then tell them what you said." In other words, say the message at least three times so that the audience will understand it clearly. This advice reflects the patterns of spoken language.

The second sentence seemed to do little more than rephrase the first, so we combined it with the third sentence.

> spoken language, repeating   will help
> In ~~other words, say~~ the message ~~at least three times so that~~ the
>   ^   ^
> audience ~~will~~ understand it clearly. ~~This advice reflects the pat-~~
> ~~terns of spoken language.~~

We edited further to eliminate other unnecessary words:

>   repetition helps listeners
> In spoken language, ~~repeating the message will help the audience~~
>   ⊙   ^
> understand ~~it clearly.~~
>   ^

At every step, we tested our results: we compared the new edited version both with the previous one and with our

understanding of what we were trying to say. We guarded against losing meaning, but we were willing to lose subtle shadings if we could state our point more clearly. If you polish relentlessly, your prose will begin to shine.

28 a Eliminating vague generalities

As we think and reason, we absorb specific information and experiences and then make associations to generalize about these data: *That radiator burned my hand when I touched it. Radiators can be dangerous.*

Writing that consists only of specific details may fail to convey broader ideas. On the other hand, writing with too many generalizations may omit useful details. Overly broad generalizations are called **generalities,** and they need editing.

It is our duty today to take responsibility for our actions.

When was it not everyone's duty to be responsible?

Some generalities attempt to make a point but result in circular reasoning: *During the harsh winters of the 1870s, the weather was very cold.* (A harsh winter is cold by definition.) Some don't really say anything at all: *Many factors played a part.* (What factors?)

Generalities don't advance discussion; the reader can only hope you will soon come to the point. Eliminating them will usually improve your writing.

Fetal alcohol syndrome affects one of every 750 newborn babies, ~~It is clearly not good for them,~~ causing coordination problems, malformed organs, small brains, short attention spans, and behavioral problems.

When you delete a generality, you may have to move some information from it to another sentence.

Is college worthwhile? ~~Whether or not to go to college is a decision that many eighteen-year-olds must face after graduating from high school.~~ Each graduate must decide according to his or

her finances, other career opportunities, and, most important, personal interests and goals.

Although unnecessary generalities can occur anywhere in a paper, carefully check your openings and conclusions, where you may be pushing for sweeping statements or impressive summaries. (See Chapter 24.)

28 b Removing idle words

Eliminate idle words. To determine whether a word is working hard enough, test it: if removing the word does not alter meaning, leave it out.

Condensing automatic and wordy phrases

The speech habit of embellishing sentences with unnecessary words too easily becomes a writing habit. It is a fact that most writers do it all the time. For example, in the previous sentence, *it is a fact that* adds no meaning. Phrases such as *it appears that* or *it has come to my attention that* merely preface what the writer is about to say, a sort of authorial "throat-clearing." Most sentences are better off without them.

Think of such phrases as **automatic phrases.** They often seem to write themselves, but when examined, they prove to add little if any meaning. Automatic phrases can appear anywhere in a sentence, but they appear most often at the beginning. When you find an automatic phrase, test it for meaning: if something seems missing without it, try inserting a condensed version of the phrase.

> *To*
> ~~In order to~~ understand the effects of the law, consider the following example.

> *Today* *often*
> ~~In this day and age,~~ children ~~in many instances~~ know more about dinosaurs than they know about American history.

Wordy phrases often can be condensed. Look for unnecesssary uses of the preposition *of* and for phrases containing *of* that can be reduced to a single word. Abstract nouns such as *area, aspect, factor, kind manner, nature, tendency, thing,* and *type* are imprecise and can create wordiness. Often you can delete them, condense them, or find more concrete substitutes. (See 27a.)

The author spent little time outside ~~of~~ his small circle of friends.

The architect had a specific ~~type of~~ construction method in mind.

2 Deleting useless modifiers

Modifiers such as *clearly, obviously, interestingly, undoubtedly, absolutely, fortunately, hopefully, really,* and *totally* are often used to intensify a whole sentence, making it sound more forceful or authoritative. Sometimes they add an important nuance that the writer intended, but more often they can be deleted. Always test for altered meaning.

The strike against General Motors ~~clearly~~ disrupted production on the Saturn assembly line. It was undoubtedly intended to do so.

Anna considered, but decided against, deleting undoubtedly, which tells the reader that the assessment is her own conclusion.

28 c Simplifying grammatical constructions

To fight wordiness another way, consider simplifying grammatical constructions. Changing a **passive-voice** sentence to the **active voice** usually shortens it slightly. (See 27c.) Eliminating **expletive constructions** such as *there were* and *it is* allows the use of strong verbs. (See 27b.)

Also consider shortening dependent clauses to phrases and phrases to single words. (For definitions, see 63e–f.) Look especially at **modifier clauses**—those that begin with a relative pronoun such as *which, that, who,* or *whom* or with a subordinating conjunction such as *because, before, when, where, while, if,* or *although.* To shorten a modifier clause to a phrase, try using just the past participle of the clause's main verb.

CLAUSE	The research project *that we were assigned to complete* involves a complex experiment.
PHRASE	The research project *assigned to us* involves a complex experiment.
WORD	*Our* research project involves a complex experiment.

FINDING UNNEEDED WORDS

Automatic phrases that "write themselves" and wordy phrases from informal speech can introduce unneeded words. Edit with a critical eye for words that do no work.

Delete	**Or Substitute**
it is a fact that	in fact
it is clear that	clearly
there is no question that	unquestionably, certainly
the reason is that	because
without a doubt	undoubtedly
beyond the shadow of a doubt	surely, certainly
it is my opinion that	I think

Wordy	**Concise**
most of the people	most people
all of the work	all the work
due to the fact that	since, because
despite the fact that	although
at that point in time	then
communicate to	tell
voice concern	say
in this day and age	today
in those days	then
in any case	anyway
in most instances	usually
in some instances	sometimes
subsequent to	after
in the event of	if
in the final analysis	finally

In some situations, using the fewest words may not be the best solution. Take care that you do not create an awkward cluster by simplifying too many constructions. (See 27d.)

ORIGINAL   The committee report listed sixteen international dealers, accusing them of illegally selling military weapons.

AWKWARD   The committee report listed sixteen alleged international illegal military-weapons dealers.

BETTER   The committee report listed sixteen alleged international dealers of illegal military weapons.

BETTER   The committee report alleged that sixteen international dealers illegally sold military weapons.

28 d Eliminating redundancy

In a famous piece of advice, public speakers are urged, "Tell them what you're going to say, say it, then tell them what you said." In spoken language, repetition helps listeners understand.

In writing, some repetition is important, even necessary, to provide continuity. (See 23c3.) Repeating a key word or phrase can also help you build a rhythmic pattern to emphasize an idea. (See 26e.) All that said, there is such a thing as too much repetition; it's called **redundancy.**

Exactly what constitutes redundancy remains for you to determine according to your purpose and your audience. Try testing each instance by omitting the repetition. Reread the passage, comparing it both to the earlier version and to what you want to say. Ask yourself whether the repetition helps link ideas, sustains rhythm, creates emphasis, or prevents confusion. If it serves none of these purposes, leave it out. Also consider having someone else read the passage for excessive repetition. Explain whom you are writing for and what you are trying to accomplish.

The most obvious redundancies arise from thoughtlessly using words that mean the same thing.

The ~~general~~ consensus ~~of opinion~~ among students was that the chancellor had exceeded her authority.

Consensus *means a general agreement.*

The raccoon warily circled ~~around~~ the tree.

Circled *means to go* around *something, so* around *should be omitted.*

An unnecessary definition is also usually easy to spot.

Foresters ~~who study trees~~ report that acid rain is damaging the state's population of hemlocks.

If you find yourself repeating the same word or a similar one, look for ways to eliminate one.

STRATEGIES FOR REDUCING CLAUSES

Here are some strategies for simplifying modifier clauses:

- A clause that starts with *which* or *that* often can be shortened by keeping only the past participle of the clause's main verb.

  His completed
  ~~The project, which he completed,~~ contained some intriguing conclusions.

- Look for clauses that contain *-ing* verbs.

  The child ~~who was~~ waiting at the bus stop seemed lost.

- If the important part of the clause is a noun or adjective, try finding a new place for it in the main part of the sentence. This strategy may take a little rewriting.

  Challenging courses
  ~~Courses that are challenging~~ tend to be more interesting.

  My problem courses
  ~~Courses that are a problem for me~~ include physics and algebra.

- Some clauses with only main verb cannot be shortened.

  The course that fulfills my science requirement has been canceled.

  That *cannot be taken out.*

- A clause that begins with *whose* usually cannot be shortened.

  The poet whose biography I read grew up in Haiti.

About ninety percent
~~A very high percentage~~ of the prison's inmates take advantage of the special education program, ~~about ninety percent.~~

As you edit your writing, be alert to possible redundancy. ~~One~~
such as
~~kind of redundancy is~~ an unnecessary repetition.

REDUNDANT PHRASES

first and foremost	refer back
full and complete	basic fundamentals
past history	initial preparation
round in shape	terrible tragedy
red in color	final result, end result
the general consensus of opinion	free gift
a faulty miscalculation	true facts
old and outdated	completely destroyed
first ever	circle around
cross over	irregardless

EDITING 1: EXPLORATION

Look for examples of generalities, idle words, and redundancies. Magazine articles and mass-market nonfiction books are often good sources. Collect two or three examples, and try editing them to make them more concise. You may want to bring your examples and edited versions to class to share with your classmates. Be ready to explain what you found wrong with the originals and how your editing improves them.

EDITING 2: PRACTICE

Edit the following passage to make it more concise by eliminating vague generalities, idle words, and redundancies and by simplifying grammatical constructions. More than one edited version is possible. Be ready to explain your editing choices.

Many languages have influenced the development of English. The first instance of important influence came from the north in the form of Viking invaders who spoke a Scandinavian language. It appears that when these Vikings settled down and became farmers and traders who were peaceful, they wanted to be able to communicate with and speak to their Anglo-Saxon neighbors. There were several factors involved. Both groups spoke Germanic languages with similar vocabularies but with systems of grammar and inflection that were somewhat different. Clearly the easiest of the ways to smooth communication was for each group to drop the elements of their language that gave the other group difficulty. This explains why it is the

case that modern English lacks the elaborate systems of verb endings and gender that characterize and distinguish other Indo-European languages.

28 **e** Avoiding pretentious language

Sometimes writers believe that in order to impress their readers, they need to use technical or obscure language. They write *institutionalized populations* instead of *people in prison*. Other writers overdecorate sentences: *In this sacrosanct institution of higher learning, we continually rededicate ourselves to the elevated principle that knowledge is empowering.* In most writing situations, it would be more effective to say *In this university, we believe that knowledge gives power.*

While professors do expect students to demonstrate familiarity with the technical terms of their discipline (see 30g), needlessly complex language is termed **pretentious.** A special class of pretentious language is called **bureaucratese** after the government functionaries who so often use it. Another kind of pretentious language uses **jargon**—the specialized vocabulary of a profession or a social group—when addressing people who are unfamilar with that vocabulary (see 30g). Pretentious language may overwhelm readers so much that they stop reading.

Pretentious language often avoids names and personal pronouns by using the third person and the passive voice. Editing it into plain English often requires you to choose subjects for verbs and find direct ways of addressing readers.

PRETENTIOUS   The range of services provided includes examinations to determine visual or auditory impairment and the

 PRETENTIOUS LANGUAGE

Pretentious	Direct
client populations	people served
voiced a concern	said, worried
range of selections	choice
minimizes expenditures	saves money
of crucial importance	important
institution of higher learning	college or university
have apprehension	fear

specification, provision, and instruction in the use of prosthetic devices including corrective lenses and auditory amplification devices.

EDITED   We can examine your eyes and ears, prescribe and sell glasses and hearing aids, and teach you to use them.

28 f Minimizing euphemism

A **euphemism** is a word chosen for its inoffensiveness to substitute for one considered harsh or indelicate. Social conventions make it difficult for us to speak of certain subjects, especially money, death, and the human body. For example, many people would consider it more delicate to say *I lost my grandmother last week* than *My grandmother died last week.*

Euphemisms are also used by writers or speakers who fear negative reaction to plain talk about bad news. This use is called **doublespeak,** a term coined by George Orwell in his novel about totalitarianism, *1984.* Someone reading of *unemployment compensation reductions* may not understand immediately that the meaning is *Workers without jobs will get less money from the government.*

Short of money,
~~As a result of the reordering of budget priorities,~~ the library ~~was~~
stopped buying books and maintaining its building.
~~forced to defer acquisitions and suspend maintenance activities.~~
                                                        ^

EDITING 3: EXPLORATION ─────────────────────────────

In the following passage, humorist Russell Baker lampoons contemporary rhetoric. How many examples of pretentious and euphemistic language can you find? Try editing the passage by replacing each example of pretentious language or euphemism with a more direct expression. Have you rescued "Little Red Riding Hood"?

Once upon a point in time, a small person named Little Red Riding Hood initiated plans for the preparation, delivery and transportation of foodstuffs to her grandmother, a senior citizen residing at a place of residence in a forest of indeterminate dimension.

In the process of implementing this program, her incursion into the forest was in mid-transportation process when it attained interface with an alleged perpetrator. This individual, a wolf, made inquiry as to the whereabouts of Little Red Riding Hood's goal as well as inferring that he was

TESTING EUPHEMISMS

In academic writing, your purpose is to inform, not to obscure or mislead, so if you push too far for a delicate phrase, you will obscure meaning. When editing euphemisms from your writing, select a more direct alternative. Then test—consider how comfortable you feel with the more direct wording and whether your audience will be offended by your directness. If in doubt, check with a peer or an instructor.

DRAFT   Some Republicans in Congress *held* the speaker of the House *responsible* for their party's *difficulties* in the election.

FIRST ALTERNATIVE   Some Republicans in Congress *blamed* the speaker of the House for their party's *poor showing* in the election.

SECOND ALTERNATIVE   Some Republicans in Congress *blamed* the speaker of the House for their party's defeat in the election.

Which is the best choice? Unless you have reason to soften your language, the second alternative is the most direct and therefore preferable.

EDITING FOR CONCISENESS AND DIRECTNESS

When editing for conciseness and directness, keep the following guidelines in mind:

- Eliminate vague generalities.
- Remove automatic or idle words.
- Simplify grammatical constructions.
- Eliminate redundant words or phrases.
- Avoid pretentious language.
- Minimize euphemism.

desirous of ascertaining the contents of Little Red Riding Hood's foodstuffs basket, and all that.

RUSSELL BAKER, "LITTLE RED RIDING HOOD REVISITED"

EDITING 4: PRACTICE

Edit the following passage to make it more concise and direct by eliminating pretentious language and euphemisms. More than one edited version is possible. Be ready to explain your editing choices.

We conducted employee reviews and maintained a high standard of objectivity. Despite high performance reviews for your department, however, we have decided to downsize the entire production staff by 40 percent. While we regret that this downsizing may inconvenience you in your relations with your subordinates, we know you, too, will understand our need to remain competitive in our market. Your continued loyalty—and that of your staff—will ensure that our company continues to set the standard of excellence for others to follow.

EDITING 5: PRACTICE

Edit the following passage from a paper for a history class. More than one edited version is possible. Be ready to explain your editing choices.

My great-grandfather emigrated from Poland when he was a young man. Several of his cousins already lived in small Pennsylvania mining towns. When my great-grandfather arrived in America, he joined his cousins and began working in the mines.

There were several things he found discouraging. The dirty work, which was also dangerous, was far different from the life of agricultural splendor he had expected to lead, but he refused to let these types of circumstances ruin his happiness. It eventually was the case that he brought two of his brothers over to this country, and together the three of them saved money that was sufficient to buy a good-sized farm. By the age of thirty-four my great-grandfather had once again started a new life: he moved into his farmhouse, married a local woman, and began raising a family that would eventually be blessed by the arrival of fourteen bundles of joy.

EDITING 6: APPLICATION ————————————————

Select a page from a paper you are working on. Examine each sentence carefully, looking for instances of wordy or indirect language. Using the checklists in this chapter, find euphemisms, pretentiousness, redundancy or any other problems, and draft alternatives. Working with a friend or a fellow student, compare versions and decide which most effectively suits your purpose.

29   Adjusting Tone

A speaker's tone of voice can express warmth, anger, confidence, hesitance, friendship, hostility, enthusiasm, regret. The **tone** of a piece of writing expresses the writer's attitude toward the subject and the audience. Do you sound hesitant or authoritative about your subject? enthusiastic? concerned? How do you address your audience? as friends? authority figures? Are you attempting to inform, persuade, or inspire them?

Tone isn't something you add to writing; it's already there as an important element of **voice,** which communicates a sense of the person who is writing. (See Chapter 6.) The tone of your writing should represent you accurately and appropriately. Just as you wouldn't lecture in a small, hesitant voice to an auditorium full of people, you won't want to use street slang or an overly casual tone in formal academic writing.

29   a   Making tone appropriate

In academic writing, your audience includes the instructor who assigned the paper and perhaps other students as well. Try to imagine them reading your paper, and adjust your tone if you think your readers might not get the right impression.

When you are describing personal experiences, your tone can be *informal,* as if you were capturing a conversation with a friend or addressing your audience—even the instructor—directly in a friendly manner. A reflective essay may strike a thoughtful, questioning, or contemplative tone as you explore the possible meanings of an experience or an event. (See Chapter 7.) You might use informal language when you want the audience to get to know something about yourself and your attitudes. However, some kinds of language interfere with an informal tone, so edit anything, such as colloquialisms, jargon, or excessive formality that muddies the writing.

My brother and I ~~grew acquainted with~~ the other kids who ~~at~~
met
~~tended~~ our elementary school; Tommy even ~~went so far as to ex~~
went to   swapped
~~change~~ his favorite slingshot ~~in return~~ for a pet frog.

To explain how something works or to interpret a work of literature, adopt a tone that assures readers of your confidence and expertise. (See Chapters 8 and 10.) Avoid unnecessary qualifications that make you sound hesitant, and edit out any informalities that weaken your authority.

The marooned students in Golding's *Lord of the Flies* are ~~probably~~ typical schoolboys, but they ~~somehow~~ degenerate into barbarism.

What is Title IX? ~~The original name of Beethoven's last sym~~
It
~~phony? No. Title IX~~ is part of the Educational Amendments of 1972 that gave women the same rights as men in all aspects of education, including athletics.

Use *formal* language when you want to downplay your personal involvement and emphasize facts, reports, or descriptions that can be verified or experienced by other observers. Research papers benefit from more formal language. (See Chapter 11.)

Three nineteenth-
~~In a search of the library, I found three 19th~~ century authors ~~who~~ discuss this aspect of Mill's theory of liberty.

When arguing a position, use a dispassionate tone to marshal evidence and appeal to readers' reason. Sometimes you can select language that appeals primarily to emotion to convince your readers, but make sure that any emotional appeals are not too strident. (See Chapter 9.)

EDITING 1: EXPLORATION _____

Read a few paragraphs aloud from your last three papers. First try to describe your tone in each paper. For whom were you writing, and what was your purpose? Does your tone vary greatly, or do you hear a similar tone throughout? Next try to picture the sort of person your readers would imagine as the writer of your papers, if they could judge only from the tone of the papers. Is that image accurate? Is it the one you want them to have? Finally, decide

DEVELOPING AN APPROPRIATE TONE FOR ACADEMIC WRITING

The tone of academic writing differs from that of other kinds of writing. For example, popular magazines tend to be informal and conversational, and advertising copy often relies more on emotional impact than on appeals to reason. Writing on the Internet often tries to portray the writer (and by extension, the reader) as well informed or "hip." To present yourself to an academic audience as an open-minded, careful researcher and thinker, avoid unnecessary slang and informal language. Guard against inflammatory language that might make you seem biased. (See Chapter 31.) Here are some strategies you can use:

- Pay attention to tone as you read texts of all kinds. Analyze how authors achieve different tones for different purposes.
- Collect a list of questions about tone to discuss with peers or your instructor. Discuss differences in tone you have observed between academic English and other kinds of writing.
- Read your writing aloud, or have a friend read it to you. Ask yourself what kind of tone you hear, and decide whether it is appropriate.
- Ask a friend to read your drafts and to comment on the tone.
- Flag any terms that are considered informal (*guy, kid*) or slang (*awesome, cool, rad*). Keep a list of such terms that crop up in your writing. When you edit for formal tone, use the list to remind you to evaluate them as you edit. Substitute alternatives and test for improvement in tone.

whether you would do anything to change your tone in these papers. Are there aspects of one paper's tone that you would like to use elsewhere?

29 b Selecting a point of view

A writer's **point of view** signals to the reader the writer's relation to the subject and the audience. One principal way in which a writer articulates a point of view is by selecting a **governing pronoun:** the first-person *I* or *we*, the second-person *you*, or the third-person *he, she, it,* or *they*.

Use the **first person** to relate personal reflection and personal experience. The first person is also appropriate in argument and research writing to describe your own observations or conclusions.

Everyone seemed a lot more upset than necessary about my Saturdays with Miss Dawson, which then made me really want to do it. I told my mother I was going to help the poor. She was disgusted, afraid of disease, toilet seats. I even knew that the poor in Chile had no toilet seats. My friends were shocked that I was going with Miss Dawson at all. They said she was a loony, a fanatic, and a lesbian, was I crazy or what?

LUCIA BERLIN, "GOOD AND BAD"

For about a month I spent most of each day either on the Peak or overlooking Melinda Valley. . . . Piece by piece, I began to form my first somewhat crude picture of chimpanzee life.

JANE GOODALL, *IN THE SHADOW OF MAN*

Using the **second person** can thrust your readers into the center of the scene or imply a close relationship between the writer and the reader. Address them directly using *you*.

Madrid—The window of the hotel is open and, as *you* lie in bed, *you* hear the firing in the front line seventeen blocks away. [Italics added.]

ERNEST HEMINGWAY, *BY-LINE: ERNEST HEMINGWAY*

The second person is appropriate for instructions such as formulas or recipes, which are often written as commands with the pronoun *you* omitted. (See 34f.)

To calculate the area of a rectangle, multiply its length by its width.

The subject of the verb multiply *is understood to be* you.

You in the sense of "people in general" is not acceptable in formal writing. Try replacing it with an impersonal construction or a more suitable noun or pronoun. (Also see 36c.)

Water can be separated
~~You can separate water~~ into its constituent elements by electrolysis by running an electric current through water and collecting the gases at the electrodes.

The **third-person** point of view focuses the writing directly on the subject rather than on the audience. It is the most widely used approach in formal academic writing.

One of the most important signs in the text is the color of Diane Chambers's hair. *She's* a blond, and blondness is a sign of considerable richness and meaning. America is a country where "gentlemen prefer blonds," and blond coloring is the most popular color sold. But what does blondness signify? [Italics added.]

ARTHUR ASA BERGER, "'HE'S EVERYTHING YOU'RE NOT. . . .';
A SEMIOLOGICAL ANALYSIS OF *CHEERS*"

Consider which point of view seems appropriate for your essay. In most cases, research papers and position or interpretive papers do not describe your personal experience but record what you as an investigator find and think. For these, the third-person point of view is best; it keeps the attention on the subject and supports your scholarly objectivity. (See Chapters 8–10.) If your essay is reflective or drawn from personal experience, the first person can convey a sense of immediacy and authenticity. (See Chapter 7 and 17b.)

29 C Achieving the right level of formality

The **level of formality** of writing, sometimes called the **register,** depends on word choice, sentence structure, and rhythm. Do you refer to your *home* or your *pad?* Are your sentences conversational in pattern or built of elaborate structures? As you edit, check that your level of formality is appropriate.

A *familiar tone* is common in everyday speech or in your personal journal but rare in academic writing. Familiar language includes slang, sentence fragments, and even vulgarity without regard to rules or conventions.

Really got into it with Jones today. The turkey can't see the value in anything. Thinks team sports make kids "aggressors" or some bull like that.

Familiar language also assumes that the audience already understands the context—who Jones is, for example.

An *informal tone* is appropriate in a letter to a friend or in a personal essay. Writing informally, you give readers a little more context than a purely familiar tone would allow. Complete your sentences and use language that omits slang but still allows your personal feelings to show through.

I had a real argument with Professor Jones in my behavioral psychology class. He was trying to tell us that team sports teach peo-

UNDERSTANDING FORMALITY

In academic writing, slang and inappropriate informality are likely to make your ideas appear less serious and committed than the work of others. An appropriate tone amounts to speaking responsibly to your fellow scholars.

Anyone who watches contemporary cartoons, such as ~~Just check out any of the cartoons today~~ *Beavis and Butthead, Ren &*

Stimpy, or *Mighty Morphin Power Rangers* ~~If you watch a whole show, you~~

^ *great deal*

~~can best believe you~~ will witness a ~~whole lot~~ of violence.

^

ple to be "aggressive" and "insensitive." He can't see the value in them at all.

Use a *formal tone* for a research paper, in which you focus not on emotion or conflict but on evidence and argument. Choose precise language that minimizes the personal aspects of the dispute. To establish a formal tone, write well-developed sentences, eliminate contractions, identify sources, and use language appropriate to academic readers.

Citing similarities between sports teams and primitive hunting bands, some scholars, including Professor Wilkin Jones in his writings on Aztec ball games, have suggested that competitive sports breed aggression. Other researchers, however, have found that team sports also foster self-discipline and cooperation.

Striking a level of formality appropriate to your purpose calls for judgment. Reflective essays, for example, are usually more formal than personal essays and less formal than research papers. Edit your writing so that it is neither too stiff nor too casual for the situation.

EDITING 2: EXPLORATION ─────────────

Read the following passage taken from Oliver Goldsmith's 1765 essay "On National Prejudice." Then rewrite the passage, adopting a more colloquial tone, one that you consider more appropriate for a modern

audience. Think about what changes you would make and why. Then compare the two passages. Has anything been lost in the translation?

> As I am one of the sauntering tribe of mortals, who spend the greatest part of their time in taverns, coffee houses, and other places of public resort, I have thereby an opportunity of observing an infinite variety of characters, which, to a person of a contemplative turn, is a much higher entertainment than a view of all the curiosities of art or nature. In one of these my late rambles, I accidentally fell into the company of half a dozen gentlemen, who were engaged in a warm dispute about some political affair; the decision of which, as they were equally divided in their sentiments, they thought proper to refer to me, which naturally drew me in for a share of the conversation.

> Amongst a multiplicity of other topics, we took occasion to talk of the different characters of the several nations of Europe; when one of the gentlemen, cocking his hat, and assuming such an air of importance as if he had possessed all the merit of the English nation in his own person, declared that the Dutch were a parcel of avaricious wretches; the French a set of flattering sycophants; that the Germans were drunken sots, and beastly gluttons; and the Spaniards proud, haughty and surly tyrants: but that in bravery, generosity, clemency, and in every other virtue, the English excelled all the world.

> This very learned and judicious remark was received with a general smile of approbation by all the company—all, I mean, but your humble servant.

EDITING 3: PRACTICE

Edit the following two paragraphs, adjusting the tone to the appropriate level of formality. The first paragraph is from a paper relating a personal experience; the second is from a formal research paper. More than one edited version of each paragraph is possible. Be ready to explain your editing choices.

PERSONAL EXPERIENCE ESSAY

> Who would find it credible that two adults would have trouble convincing one eight-pound feline that the time had come for his annual physical examination? Upon spotting his cage, the cat exits the room as quickly as he can. Under the bed, over the bed, up the staircase, down the staircase, he rushes with extreme celerity from one room to the next, ever eluding our grasp. When his outrageous behavior ceases and we have him cornered, I stealthily approach him and apprehend him. I loudly proclaim myself triumphant as I deposit him in his place of confinement and secure the top.

At the Dryden Correctional Center, the guys who run the education department try to prepare the inmates for living on the outside. That way criminals won't (they hope!) turn back to a life of crime. OK. Sounds like a good idea. But how do they do it? Well, they make sure that as soon as the criminals get tossed in the slammer they hit the books. This is so that they will have a better chance of getting jobs when they get out. The way they figure it is if the punks get jobs, they won't have to cross the line to make money. The educational programs are completely voluntary. Lots of the inmates take them, though.

29 d Maintaining consistent tone

An unnecessary shift in tone will throw your readers off balance; they won't know where your ideas are heading, and they may be reluctant to follow. Be alert to any language that suggests a shift in tone, level of formality, or point of view.

The assassinations of President Kennedy and Martin Luther King, Jr., the Vietnam War, the September 11 tragedy—each of these events shook public confidence in the nation and made it had gone mad.
seem that the world ~~was out of whack.~~

Some shifts are necessitated by content. A deliberate shift in tone can be appropriately humorous, moving, or even compelling. In the following passage, Stephen Jay Gould shifts from an amusing story, told in casual language, to an argument based on logic and hard evidence, written in a more formal tone:

> When Muhammad Ali flunked his army intelligence test, he quipped (with a wit that belied his performance on the exam): "I only said I was the greatest; I never said I was the smartest." In our metaphors and fairy tales, size and power are almost always balanced by a want of intelligence. Cunning is the refuge of the little guy. Think of Br'er Rabbit and Br'er Bear; David smiting Goliath with a slingshot; Jack chopping down the beanstalk. Slow wit is the tragic flaw of a giant.
>
> The discovery of dinosaurs in the nineteenth century provided, or so it appeared, a quintessential case for the negative correlation of size and smarts. With their pea brains and giant bodies, dinosaurs became a symbol of lumbering stupidity. Their extinction seemed only to confirm their flawed design.
>
> STEPHEN JAY GOULD, "WERE DINOSAURS DUMB?"

Using a deliberate shift is like telling a joke in front of a group of strangers: you have to be sure it's a good joke, and you have to deliver it smoothly and with expert timing.

 REFINING YOUR TONE

When editing for tone, ask yourself the following questions:

- Is the tone **appropriate to the audience** I am writing for **and for the goal** I want to accomplish? If not, you may need to adjust your point of view or level of formality.
- Have I chosen the **point of view** that best illustrates my relationship to my subject? Test other points of view and then choose the one that helps you succeed in your goals for the paper.
- Is the **level of formality** right for my intended audience? If not, go back and consider your presentation of ideas and choice of words throughout.
- Have I maintained a **consistent tone?** If not, you need to edit your writing to eliminate elements that are incompatible with the tone you want.

EDITING 4: PRACTICE _____

Edit the following passage from a formal literary interpretation, making sure to maintain a consistent, appropriate tone. More than one edited version is possible. Be ready to explain your editing choices.

You can really see the similarities between Shakespeare's *King Lear* and Jane Smiley's novel *A Thousand Acres*. Smiley makes you think of Shakespeare's play on purpose, and she expects you to be with it enough to catch on. You can see the parallels even in the names she gives to her characters. The three sisters in *A Thousand Acres* are named Ginny, Rose, and Caroline. These names make you think of Lear's daughters, Goneril, Regan, and Cordelia. Get it? (The first letters are the same.) In both the play and the novel, one really important idea is how parents and kids get along. In Smiley's story, Caroline, the youngest daughter, doesn't like her father's plan to retire and divide his huge farm among his three daughters, so he chills her. In *King Lear,* Cordelia, also the youngest, won't compete with her sisters in telling her old dad how crazy about him she is just so she can get the

largest part of his kingdom. In both works, the two older sisters tell their dad what he wants to hear, but the youngest stands up to him.

EDITING 5: APPLICATION

Read through a paper you are working on, paying close attention to its tone. How would you describe the tone? How do your choices of point of view, level of formality, and wording contribute to this tone? Given your subject and your purpose, is the tone appropriate? Have you maintained this tone throughout? If not, do your shifts in tone help the effectiveness of your paper or harm it? As you edit your paper pay full attention to its tone, keeping the aspects that you like and improving the aspects that you don't like.

30 Choosing the Right Word

Because English has a particularly rich vocabulary, writers can choose among many words with similar meanings. For example, the place you live could be called, in a formal manner, your *residence, domicile,* or *habitation;* less formally, it could be called your *house, quarters,* or *lodging.* Informally, it could be called your *home;* and most informally, your *shack, digs,* or *pad.* Not every word is appropriate or effective in every context. At every turn, you have to choose which word can best—given your purpose and audience—convey the shade of meaning you intend. Enlarge your vocabulary by reading widely and listening actively to the words others use. Make word lists to study; **paraphrase** new words right away and use them in sentences, and try to learn the meaning of unfamiliar words from context.

30 a Understanding the history of English

The special richness of the English vocabulary results from the merging of many languages. As waves of invasion and migration have swept over the British Isles during the past three thousand years, each group of new arrivals has brought a language that has blended with existing speech.

After the Romans arrived in the British Isles in 43 B.C., they conquered the Celtic-speaking inhabitants and ruled much of what is now England for nearly five hundred years. When the Romans retreated, the Celts kept a few Latin words, such as *plant, candle,* and *wine.*

In the fifth century A.D., Germanic peoples from northern Europe—the Jutes, Saxons, Frisians, and Angles (for whom England is named)—invaded Britain, bringing with them their Germanic language, the basis of modern English. In what is now England, the Celtic language was largely replaced by that of the newcomers as Celtic speakers were displaced to Cornwall, Wales,

and Scotland. Celtic words surviving in English include *clan, bin, gull,* and *crag.*

The invaders' early form of English, which became the dominant language for much of England, is called Old English. Many words in our modern vocabulary can be traced to this period: *work, bite, god, gold, hand, land, under, winter, word.*

Another wave of Latin began at the end of the sixth century with the arrival of missionaries sent from Rome to convert the Anglo-Saxons to Christianity. A flood of Latin religious and secular words gradually became part of English: *abbot, altar, Mass, acolyte, lily.*

In the eighth century, new invaders, known as Danes or Vikings, brought their Scandinavian language, Old Norse. Although they came as conquerors, many Danes settled alongside the Angles and Saxons. Words adopted from the Danes' conquest include *fellow, hit, law, rag, take, want,* and many words that begin with an *sk* sound (*scorch, scrape, scrub, skill, skirt, sky*).

In 1066 the Normans, from what is now western France, conquered England and brought with them their own language, Old French. Following the Norman Conquest, French became the language of the noble classes, the law, the monetary system, and learning. French words such as *parliament, justice, crime, marriage, money,* and *rent* seeped into common usage, as did *art, ornament, mansion, pleasure, joy,* and thousands more. English retains two sets of words for many things, an indication of the social divisions of Norman England. For example, farmers used the English words *pig, deer, sheep, cow,* and *calf,* but the ruling class, whose primary contact with these animals was consumption, used French names for their meat: *pork, venison, mutton, beef,* and *veal.* Eventually English became the predominant language among all classes, but by then French words had thoroughly infiltrated its vocabulary.

In the sixteenth century, a renewed interest in classical Greek and Latin learning—history, mythology, and science—brought into English a torrent of new words. From Greek came *democracy, hexagon, monogamy, physics, rhythm,* and *theory.* From Latin came *client, conviction, index, library, medicine, orbit,* and *recipe.* In the nineteenth and twentieth centuries, Greek and Latin roots have continued to provide a wealth of scientific and technical terms, many of which are invented words made up of ancient roots, prefixes, and suffixes: *cholesterol, cyanide, radioactive, telegraph, telephone, television.*

English also has absorbed words from many other languages as its speakers have spread across the globe and as many speakers of other languages have settled in English-speaking lands. Modern

American English includes words from dozens of languages, including Spanish (*canyon, mustang, poncho, rodeo*), Italian (*balcony, balloon, carnival, ghetto*), Arabic (*alcohol, algebra, candy, lemon*), Hindustani (*bungalow, cot, jungle, loot, shampoo*), Japanese (*kimono, samurai, zen, karate*), and various African languages (*banana, yam, voodoo, banjo*).

These linguistic riches place at your disposal an array of words with similar meanings. Is a particular man *male, manly, macho, virile,* or *masculine?* Does a particular woman have a *job,* a *profession,* a *vocation,* or a *calling?* The choice depends on the shade of meaning you desire and the effect you want your words to have on your readers.

EDITING I: PRACTICE ─────────────────────────

For each of the words below, think of as many synonyms and near synonyms as you can. Try to guess what language each word came from. Use a dictionary to check your guesses. You may want to compare your word lists with those of your classmates.

assist	chutney	hope	scream
calendar	good	name	truth
calculate	handle	number	vampire
cash	health	potlatch	verse
church	home	safari	warmth

`30` `b` **Using the dictionary and thesaurus**

Writers commonly rely on reference books to guide them in their use of language. The most widely used are a dictionary, a thesaurus, and a guide to usage.

▮ **The dictionary**

An *unabridged* dictionary offers information on word origins as well as definitions and usage samples. *Webster's Third New International Dictionary* (Springfield, MA: Merriam-Webster, 1993), which contains 470,000 words, is among the most widely used. The most comprehensive is the 616,500-word *Oxford English Dictionary,* 2nd edition, 20 vols. (Oxford: Clarendon University Press, 1989), which since 1928 has attempted to chronicle the first appearance and usage history of every word in the language. It is

available in a searchable edition on CD-ROM, as are many recently published dictionaries.

An *abridged* dictionary omits some less common words, so it may be easier to use than a huge unabridged volume. *Merriam-Webster's Collegiate Dictionary*, 10th edition (Springfield, MA: Merriam-Webster, 1996) offers 215,000 entries focused on contemporary usage. The Internet edition at <http://www.m-w.com/> includes the main A–Z listings of the print edition.

Bartleby.com
Great Books Online

| Reference | Verse | Fiction | Nonfiction |

Search | Dictionary ⬦ | | Go

Home | Subjects | Titles | Authors   Encyclopedia | Dictionary | Thesaurus | Quotations | English Usage

Reference > American Heritage® > Dictionary

‹ Langtry, Lillie   language arts ›

CONTENTS · INDEX · ILLUSTRATIONS · BIBLIOGRAPHIC RECORD

The American Heritage® Dictionary of the English Language: Fourth Edition. 2000.

language

SYLLABICATION: lan·guage

PRONUNCIATION: ◁ lăng′gwĭj

NOUN:
1a. Communication of thoughts and feelings through a system of arbitrary signals, such as voice sounds, gestures, or written symbols. **b.** Such a system including its rules for combining its components, such as words. **c.** Such a system as used by a nation, people, or other distinct community; often contrasted with *dialect*. **2a.** A system of signs, symbols, gestures, or rules used in communicating: *the language of algebra*. **b.** *Computer Science* A system of symbols and rules used for communication with or between computers. **3.** Body language; kinesics. **4.** The special vocabulary and usages of a scientific, professional, or other group: *"his total mastery of screen language—camera placement, editing—and his handling of actors"* (Jack Kroll). **5.** A characteristic style of speech or writing: *Shakespearean language.* **6.** A particular manner of expression: *profane language; persuasive language.* **7.** The manner or means of communication between living creatures other than humans: *the language of dolphins.* **8.** Verbal communication as a subject of study. **9.** The wording of a legal document or statute as distinct from the spirit.

ETYMOLOGY: Middle English, from Old French *langage*, from *langue*, tongue, language, from Latin *lingua*. See **dn̥ghū-** in Appendix I.

The American Heritage® Dictionary of the English Language, Fourth Edition. Copyright © 2000 by Houghton Mifflin Company. Published by the Houghton Mifflin Company. All rights reserved.

CONTENTS · INDEX · ILLUSTRATIONS · BIBLIOGRAPHIC RECORD

Another widely used abridged dictionary, *The American Heritage Dictionary of the English Language,* 4th edition (Boston: Houghton Mifflin, 2000), is available in print, on CD-ROM, and on the Internet at <http://www.bartleby.com/61/>. It offers tips on usage and includes new coinages such as *dot-com* and *soccer mom.* The annually updated *Random House Webster's College Dictionary* (New York: Random, 2000) lists more than 180,000 words, giving the most common definition first.

WHAT'S IN A DICTIONARY ENTRY?

Most dictionaries follow the format found in the tenth edition of *Merriam-Webster's Collegiate Dictionary* (Springfield, MA: Merriam-Webster, 1996).

① **entry word**   ② **pronunciation** ③ **part of speech label** ④ **inflected forms**

com·mu·ni·cate \ kə- ˈ myü-nə-kāt \ *vb* **-cat-ed; -cat-ing** [L *communications,* pp. of *communicare* to impart, participate, fr. *communis* common — more at MEAN] *vt* (1526) **1** *archaic* : SHARE **2 a** : to convey knowledge of or information about : make known <~ a story> **b** : to reveal by clear signs <his fear *communicated* itself to his friends> **3** : to cause to pass from one to another <some diseases are easily *communicated*> ~ *vi* **1** : to receive Communion **2** : to transmit information, thought, or feeling so that it is satisfactorily received or understood **3** : to open into each other : CONNECT <the rooms ~> — **com·mu· ni·ca·tee** \ -ˌ myü-ni-kə- ˈ tē \ *n* — **com·mu·ni·ca·tor** \ -ˈ myü-nə-ˌkā-tər \ *n*

⑤ **derivation**

⑥ **definitions**

1. The **entry word** appears in bold type. Bars, spaces, or dots between syllables show where the word may be hyphenated. If two spellings are shown, the first is more common, although both are acceptable. If two spellings are dissimilar, entries are cross-referenced: **gaol** (jal) *n. Brit. sp. of* JAIL. A superscript numeral before an entry indicates that two or more words have identical spellings.

2. Pronunciation is spelled phonetically, set in parentheses or between slashes. (The phonetic key is usually at the bottom of the page.) If two pronunciations are given, the first is more common, although both are acceptable.

(Continued)

3. Parts-of-speech labels are set in italic type. The abbreviations are *n* for noun, *vb* for verb, *vt* for transitive verb, and so forth.

4. Inflected forms are shown, including plurals for nouns and pronouns, comparatives and superlatives for adjectives and adverbs, and principal parts for verbs. Irregular spelling also appear here.

5. The **derivation** of the word from its roots in other languages is set between brackets or slashes. *OE* and *ME* = Old English and Middle English; *L* = Latin; *Gr* = Greek; *OFr* = Old French; *Fr* = French; *G* = German; and so on.

6. Definitions appear with major meanings numbered and arranged from the oldest to the most recent or from the most common to the least common. An example of the word's use may be enclosed in brackets.

- **Synonyms** or **antonyms** may be listed, often with comments on how the words are similar or different.
- **Usage labels** are used for nonstandard words or meanings.

  archaic: from a historic period; now used rarely if at all
  colloquial [coll.]: used informally in speech or writing
  dialect [dial.]: used only in some geographical areas
  obsolete [obs.]: no longer used, but may appear in old writings
  slang: highly informal, or an unusual usage
  substandard [substand.]: widely used but not accepted in formal usage
  British [Brit.], Irish, Scottish [Scot.] and so on: a word used primarily in an area other than the United States. Some dictionaries use an asterisk to mark Americanisms.

- **Usage notes** may follow definitions. They may also comment on acceptability or unacceptability.

2 The thesaurus

A **thesaurus** (the word comes from the Greek for "treasure") lists **synonyms**—words with similar meanings—for each entry. Many thesauruses list **antonyms**—words with opposite meanings—as well. *Roget's Thesaurus of English Words and Phrases*, the most popular, lists words in six major classifications and many related concepts. By contrast, *Roget's 21st Century Thesaurus* lists words in alphabetical order and contains a concept index.

A thesaurus can suggest words you can use to fit a particular context or level of formality. But be sure to check any unfamiliar words in a dictionary before using them. Some may be entirely

inappropriate to your situation or may have unwanted connotations. For example, if you are eagerly gathering information on a particular subject, you may be said to *assimilate* it, *absorb* it, *ingest* it, or perhaps *digest* it, but not *imbibe* it, since the last of these terms means "to drink."

Online thesauruses include *Merriam-Webster's Collegiate Thesaurus* at <http://www.m-w.com/>, *Lexico* at <http://www.thesaurus.com/>, and *Roget's Thesauri* at <http://www.bartleby.com/thesauri/>, where you'll find one thesaurus using Peter Roget's original scheme of classifying by subject and another organized alphabetically.

 WHAT'S IN A THESAURUS ENTRY?

① entry ② part of
word   speech   **synonyms and related words or phrases**

TOPIC—*N.*   topic, subject, matter, subject matter, motif, theme, leitmotif, thesis, text, business, affair, matter in hand, question, problem, issue, theorem, proposition, motion, resolution, case, point; moot point, point at issue, debatable point.

Adj.   Topical, local, limited, restricted, particular.

③ See also CONTENTS, INQUIRY, MEANING.

1. The entry word may appear in capital or bold letters.

2. Part-of-speech labels are followed by synonyms in the same part of speech. These synonyms are not defined, but they tend to be listed from most similar to least similar. A semicolon marks the beginning of a group of closely related synonyms from a special field or area of meaning.

3. *See also* refers you to related words or themes. These contain additional synonyms that might be useful.

---

3   **Guides to usage**

Should you use *appraise* or *apprise? Compose* or *comprise? Affect* or *effect? Much* or *many?* These are questions of **usage,** the choice of the appropriate word. A guide to usage offers what a thesaurus does not: advice on which word is appropriate or customary

in which context. Some choices include *A Dictionary of Modern American Usage* (Oxford: Oxford University Press, 1998); *Choose the Right Word,* 2nd edition (New York: HarperCollins, 1994); and *The American Heritage Book of English Usage* (Boston: Houghton Mifflin, 1996). For a quick reference, consult the Glossary of Usage at the back of this book.

4 Specialized dictionaries

Specialized dictionaries contain the vocabularies of various disciplines. For example, if you need terms for the architectural features of medieval cathedrals, consult the *Dictionary of Architecture and Construction.* There are also specialized dictionaries that cover the regional and cultural varieties of English, such as the *Dictionary of American Regional English.* The *New Dictionary of American Slang* lists words used in conversational (or colloquial) English. Some dictionaries focus on word origins, or **etymology.** Other dictionaries cover branches of the language, from Canadian to Jamaican and Bahamian English.

ESL BILINGUAL DICTIONARIES

If English is not your first language, a **bilingual dictionary**— sometimes called a **translating dictionary**—can be a great help. The most useful kind is one that translates both from English into your native language and vice versa, such as the *Oxford Spanish Dictionary: Spanish-English/English-Spanish* (Oxford: Oxford UP, 1994). A collection of basic bilingual dictionaries is available online at <http:// dictionaries.travlang.com/>. You can look up the English equivalent of a word in your first language, or you can look up the meaning of an English word you're not certain about. For academic writing, it's a good idea to consult a more comprehensive dictionary because abridged or pocket versions often offer several translations but provide no clue which one to choose.

EDITING 2: PRACTICE ———————————————————

Use a dictionary and a thesaurus to look up any words in the following passage that seem unfamiliar or that might be misused. Substitute more familiar words and correct any misuses but preserve the intended meaning. Be ready to explain your editing choices.

The role of Emma Woodhouse in Jane Austen's novel *Emma* often receives censure for her supercilious behavior. Many readers consider her attitude toward her neighbors to be unconscionable: she avoids calling on them whenever possible and suffers their visits with scarcely concealed ennui. And it's certainly true that Emma regards all social functions as opportunities to display her better charms and talents. Yet Emma may be understood as Austen's portrayal of an exceptional individual constrained by a mediocre society.

30 C Expanding your vocabulary

You can enlarge your tool kit of words, your **vocabulary,** in several ways. If you pay attention to the words others use, you will learn new words and usages. When you encounter a passage containing a new word, paraphrase it in familiar words; doing so will help fix the new word in your mind. Here are some other ways to improve your vocabulary.

1 Learning from context

You often can infer the meaning of words from the words around them, the **context.** Suppose you read the following:

> The integration deal means that customers will be able to plug Pipes' *middleware* directly into Sybases's message server, which provides wireless communications and transaction security. Combining both vendors' message systems gives users flexible *middleware* to bridge heterogeneous systems.

Even without knowing much about computers, you can guess that *middleware* is a computer device or program (*ware,* as in *software* and *hardware*) that connects different (*heterogeneous*) systems so users can send messages to each other.

2 Learning from roots, prefixes, and suffixes

You can find clues to a word's meaning by looking at roots, prefixes, and suffixes.

Roots

A **root** is a base word, the part of a word from which other words are formed. Sometimes words are formed with two roots, as in many scientific and technical terms. For example, the word

photograph is composed of the roots *photo*, from the Greek word meaning "light," and *graph*, meaning "writing." Other root words combined with *graph* make *telegraph*, meaning "distant writing"; *phonograph*, an instrument for recording sound; and *chronograph*, an instrument for recording time. This process works also in words like *software*, *shareware*, and *middleware*, all created by analogy with *hardware*.

One root may be spelled in several different ways, especially in words formed long ago. Thus *justice* and *jury* are both related to the Latin word *jus*, for "law." *Transcribe* and *manuscript*, as well as *inscription*, *conscript*, and *scripture*, share the Indo-European root *skeribh*, "to cut or incise," and hence, "to write."

Prefixes

A **prefix** is a group of letters attached to the beginning of a root to change its meaning. For example, the word *prefix* itself consists of a root, *fix*, meaning "attach," and a prefix, *pre-*, meaning "before." Changing a prefix can dramatically alter the meaning of a word. For example, *democracy* means "rule" (*-cracy*) "by the people" (*demos*); *autocracy* means "rule by one person"; *theocracy* means "rule by God or divine authority."

Suffixes

A **suffix** is a group of letters attached to the end of a root. Adding a suffix changes the meaning of the word and often changes the part of speech. For example, the verb *educate* means "to teach"; the noun *education* means "the process of teaching"; the adjective *educational* means "having to do with education or teaching."

Knowing some prefixes, suffixes, and roots can help you guess the meanings of words. For example, the words *antebellum*, *bellicose*, and *belligerent* share the same root *bellum*, Latin for "war." If you know that *belligerent* means "warlike or at war," you can guess that *bellicose* means "prone to war or fighting" and that *antebellum* means "before the [Civil] war." Be careful to check your guesses; sometimes words closely spelled have quite different meanings. *Disinterested* means "impartial or unbiased" while *uninterested* means "not interested or not concerned."

3 Keeping a word list

Reserve a page or two in your journal for a word list, and every time you encounter an unfamiliar word—whether in school or in a book—write it down. Write down your best guess of the word's

COMMON PREFIXES

Prefix	Meaning	Example
a-, an-	without	atheist, anhydrous
ante-	before	antecedent
anti-	against	antiwar
auto-	self	autopilot
co-	with	cohabit
com-, con-, cor-	with	compatriot
contra-	against	contradiction
de-	away from, off	deplane
	reverse, undo	defrost, decode
dis-	not	dislike
en-	put into	encode
ex-	out, outside	exoskeleton
	former	ex-president
extra-	beyond, more than	extraterrestrial
hetero-	different	heterogeneous
homo-	same	homogeneous
hyper-	more	hyperactive
hypo-	less than	hypobaric
il-, im-, in-, ir-	not, without	illogical, immoral, insensitive, irresponsible
in-	into	inject
inter-	between	intercollegiate
intra-	within	intravenous
macro-	very large	macroeconomics
micro-	very small	microscope
mono-	one	monomania
non-	not, without	nonsense
omni-	all, every	omnipotent
post-	after	postmodern, postmortem
pre-	before	preheat
pro-	forward	promote
sub-	under	submit
syn-	with, at the same time as	synchronize
trans-	across	transcontinental
tri-	three	triangle
un-	not	unloved
uni-	one	unicorn

COMMON SUFFIXES

NOUN SUFFIXES

Suffix	Meaning	Example
-ance, -ence,	act	adherence
-ation, -ion, -sion, -tion	act, state of being	abstention, pretension
-dom	place	kingdom
	state of being	wisdom
-er, -or	one who	pitcher, actor
-hood	state of being	childhood
-ism	act, practice	terrorism
-ist	one who	psychologist
-ment	act	containment
-ness	state of being	wildness
-ship	state of being	professorship
	quality	workmanship

VERB SUFFIXES

Suffix	Meaning	Example
-ate	to make	activate
-en	to make	broaden
-fy	to become	liquefy
-ize	to make into	crystallize

ADJECTIVE SUFFIXES

Suffix	Meaning	Example
-able, -ible	able to	acceptable
-al, -ial	pertaining to	musical
-ate	having, filled with	passionate
-ful	filled with	fanciful
-ish	resembling	devilish
-ive	having the nature of	votive, active
-less	without	shameless
-like	prone to, resembling	warlike
-ly	pertaining to	motherly
-ose, -ous	characterized by	morose

ADVERB SUFFIX

Suffix	Meaning	Example
-ly	in a manner characterized by	easily

meaning. Review the list regularly. Look up the words, and jot down the exact definitions. Immediately try out your new words in sentences in your journal and then in conversation.

30 d Considering connotations

The direct and literal meaning of a word is its **denotation.** For example, *fragrance, odor,* and *smell* all denote something detected by the sense of smell. But their associations differ: saying "You have a distinctive fragrance" is quite different from saying "You have a distinctive odor." The indirect meaning, based on such associations, is a word's **connotation.** As you edit, pay attention to the connotations of your words because they will affect the meaning you convey.

Some words have such strong connotations that using them will make you sound **biased.** (See Chapter 31.) Calling someone's hobby a *fixation* or *obsession* rather than just a *pastime* implies that the person is mentally unstable, a judgment that will seem unfair unless you can support the implication with evidence. When you find words that make your writing seem biased, replace them with more balanced alternatives.

Another way in which connotations differ is in **level of formality.** (See 29c.) Some words are appropriate for informal contexts such as writing about personal experience, while others are appropriate for formal academic writing. Deciding whether you refer to an instructor as a *prof,* a *teacher,* a *professor,* an *educator,* or a *pedagogue* is partly a choice among increasing levels of formality.

EDITING 3: PRACTICE

Here's a way to have some fun with connotations. Pick an adjective and "conjugate" it as follows: *I am firm, you are obstinate, she is stubborn* or *I am thrifty, you are tight, he's an old skinflint.* Try it with these modifiers:

aging gracefully	adventurous	thoughtful
prudent	charming	sophisticated
bold	delicate	mature

EDITING 4: PRACTICE

Complete the following passage from a personal narrative, choosing one of the two words in each set of parentheses. Be sure the words you choose have the connotations you want. More than one version is possible for some sentences. Be ready to explain your choices.

As a girl, my grandmother worked in a textile mill. Recently she (*revealed to/told*) me what it was like. Every morning she had to feed her (*younger/youthful*) sister breakfast and then take her to the house of Cousin Sophia, who looked after them. My grandmother was at the (*gates/portal*) of the factory by 5:25 A.M. An employee who was late would (*forfeit/lose*) half a day's pay. The work was (*drab/tedious*). My grandmother had to (*patrol/watch*) the same machine for hours on end, with nothing to (*distract/entertain*) her but the whirring and clanking of the engines.

30 e Distinguishing among frequently confused words

Homonyms, words with the same sound but different spellings and meanings, frequently create confusion. Even experienced writers sometimes use *their* when they mean *there* or *they're*, or confuse *write, right,* and *rite; its* and *it's;* or *principle* and *principal.*

Sometimes the confusion arises from spelling errors. If you drop a letter from *two* or *too,* you may write *to,* and your computer spell checker won't notice either. As you edit, be aware of potentially confusing words and examine each word to be sure it is used correctly. A list of problem homonyms appears in 45a.

30 f Using prepositions and particles idiomatically

Idioms are expressions or speech patterns that cannot necessarily be understood or predicted by rules of logic or grammar. Why do we ride *in* a car but *on* a train? Why do we *take* a picture but *make* a recording? Why do Americans stay *in school* but not *in hospital* as the British do? In each case the correct word is determined by what is conventional and customary, or idiomatic.

Idiomatic expressions can cause problems even for native speakers; prepositions, for example, are often used in unexpected ways. We know that a **preposition**—*at, by, for, out, to, with*—shows a relationship between a noun or a pronoun and other words in the sentence. The only guide to the correct use of prepositions with nouns and verbs is to learn the conventional idioms.

This novel shows a great similarity *to* that one. The similarity *between* the stories is remarkable.

I will meet *with* you *in* the morning *at* the office.

VERBS THAT ARE OFTEN CONFUSED

Several pairs of verbs are similar in form but very different in meaning. You'll want to memorize them and edit for them when checking word choice.

SIT AND SET

Sit means "to be seated."	Neighbors *sit* on their screened porches every night.
Set means "to put or place."	I *set* a bowl of milk on the porch for our cat.

LIE AND LAY

Lie means "to recline."	She *lies* down every day and meditates.
Lay means "to put or place."	He *lays* the paper on the table every morning.

AFFECT AND EFFECT

Affect is almost always a verb; *effect* is usually a noun, although it has some uses as a verb.

Affect means "to produce an effect."	Raising prices could *affect* sales volume.
Effect, as a noun, means "the result of a change or action."	Higher prices could have a bad *effect* on sales.
Effect, as a verb, means "to make happen."	She was able to *effect* a change in policy.

COMPOSE AND COMPRISE

Compose means "to form."	Fifty states *compose* the United States.
Comprise means "consist of" or "include."	The United States *comprises* fifty states.

Other problem pairs are listed in the Glossary of Usage.

Phrasal verbs are **two-word verbs,** verbs that need another word to complete their meanings. These extra words, called **particles,** look like prepositions (*up, down, out, in, off,* and so on) and function with the verb to convey the full meaning, which may be quite different from the meaning of the verb alone. The meanings of

slang sexual term; and *jeep*, from the World War II general purpose or "g.p." vehicle.

Regionalisms are expressions used in one part of the country but not standard nationwide. The generic word for *carbonated beverage*, for example, varies by region from *pop* to *soda* to *soft drink* to *seltzer*. Some expressions from regional dialects are regarded as substandard, not acceptable in formal writing.

A **colloquialism** is an expression common in spoken language but not usually used in formal writing. For example, the noun *pot* can refer not only to a cooking vessel but also to an illegal drug, the amount of money bet on a hand of cards, and ruination (*go to pot*).

Use slang, regionalisms, and colloquialisms sparingly, if at all. Such words may not be understood by everyone, and for academic writing they are usually too informal. In descriptions and dialogue, however, they can convey immediacy, authenticity, and unpretentiousness, and in some informal contexts—personal experience essays, for example—they may be effective.

Specialized language particular to a field or discipline is called **jargon.** Each discipline develops special terms to express its ideas. Studying biology would be impossible without terms such as *chromosomes* and *osmosis*. Literary criticism employs such words as *climax* and *dénouement*. Politics has generated such terms as *spin*, *sound bite*, and *PAC* (political action committee). Unlike slang, jargon is often highly formal. Of course, a group's jargon may be unintelligible outside that group.

As you edit, you must decide whether the special terms you have used are appropriate for your audience. For example, a general audience would understand *thigh bone*, but an instructor reading a paper on a medical subject would expect you to use the technical term *femur*. To a specialized audience, correct and conventional use of technical language helps demonstrate your mastery of a subject and enhances your credibility. Less technical terms are better for a general audience.

If you adopt jargon for its own sake, however, you may sound stilted or pretentious. (See 28e.) As you edit, decide which special terms are essential to your meaning and which are merely for show.

JARGON	It is incumbent on us to challenge the prevailing proposition that critical-theoretical approaches are the most enlightened ways of introducing students to literary experience.
EDITED	We should question the widely held idea that using theories of criticism provides the best way to introduce students to literature.

Sometimes the most direct language cannot communicate a complex concept—you need a technical term. Introducing it in a certain context can help the reader grasp its meaning. An explicit definition can help too. The following passage was written for car enthusiasts but not for mechanical engineers, so the writer had to explain clearly the terms *lean* and *stoichiometric:*

> Running an engine *lean* means that there is less fuel in the cylinders than is needed to completely burn all of the available air. With gasoline, 14.7 pounds of air are required to burn 1 pound of fuel. This air–fuel ratio is referred to as *stoichiometric.*
>
> FRANK MARKUS, "LEAN-BURN ENGINES"

EDITING 6: PRACTICE

Edit the following paragraph from a paper describing computer enthusiasts to a general readership. Try a couple of versions, one minimizing jargon as much as possible and the other making the jargon reader friendly. What do you have to assume about your audience in either case?

> Virtually all the members of the campus Internet users group regard their computers as indispensable. These people spend most of their time logged on, cruising the net, swapping MP3s by e-mail, chatting online, or waging virtual combat in a multiuser dungeon. Word processing? spreadsheets? Old hat in this crowd! We're talking major modem traffic, personal Web sites, and Java scripts. The more adventurous of these folks speak UNIX like natives and are hacking around in mainframes that are supposed to be safe behind firewalls.

30 h Using figurative language

Figurative language, which likens one thing to another in an imaginative or fanciful way, can enliven your writing. Too much literal language can shackle your prose to the hard, dull ground. Figurative language can unchain your thoughts, allowing an occasional leap of the imagination.

Figurative language makes connections through metaphor or analogy. This process is so deeply embedded in our language that we often overlook it. For example, the verb *overlook* in the previous sentence suggests we can fail to see a process or idea in the same way that we can fail to see a physical object. Figurative language should be fresh, not hackneyed. Take care to use it effectively, not

TYPES OF FIGURATIVE LANGUAGE

- A **simile** is a direct comparison that expresses a resemblance between two essentially unlike things, using *like, than,* or *as.*

German submarines swam the seas like sharks, suddenly seizing their prey without warning.

- A **metaphor** implicitly equates one thing with another.

Her life became a whirlwind of design meetings, client conferences, production huddles, and last-minute decisions.

- An **analogy** uses an extended comparison to show similarities in structure or process.

The course catalog at a large university resembles a smorgasbord. Courses range from differential calculus to American film, from Confucianism to liberation theology. Students receive little advice as to which classes are the salads, which the desserts, and which the entrees of a college education. Even amid this feast, without guidance a student may risk intellectual malnutrition.

- **Personification** is the technique of attributing human qualities or behavior to a nonhuman event or phenomenon.

This ship sailed into the teeth of the hurricane.

- Deliberate exaggeration is called **hyperbole.**

No book in the world is more difficult than this economics text. Reading it is absolute torture.

- The opposite of hyperbole is deliberate **understatement.**

With temperatures remaining below zero all day, it will seem just a bit chilly outside tomorrow.

- **Irony** is an unexpected result, especially a humorous or tragic one, usually resulting from a change or a contrast.

Ishmael, the only man aboard Ahab's ship who has shown the slightest concern for any other human being, is the sole survivor. He is found floating in the sea, clinging to the coffin made for his friend Queequeg.

A special case of irony is **sarcasm,** in which words are used to mean the opposite of what they literally say.

"House guests for three weeks? Terrific!"

- A **paradox** contains a deliberately created contradiction.

For a moment after she spoke, the silence was deafening. Then the audience erupted in cheers.

for ornament or embellishment, but to help readers understand your meaning.

A **mixed metaphor** combines two or more unrelated images, occasionally with unintended effects. If you find a mixed metaphor, consider eliminating the weaker image and extending the stronger.

> He was ~~sitting on the fence~~ about the election; he liked the chal-
> _{undecided}
> lenger better than the incumbent but didn't want to change horses in midstream.

EDITING 7: PRACTICE

Edit the following paragraph from a paper defending a popular TV show to improve its use of figurative language. More than one edited version is possible. Be ready to explain your editing choices.

> Many people object to the television cartoon *The Simpsons* because they say it is over the top, but millions of children watch it with bated breath every week. Critics say shows like this are causing the American family to disintegrate and are teaching children that it is OK not to hit the books. They think that young people want to be like Bart Simpson, who is as proud as a peacock of being a bad student, and that the show is a stumbling block for students who want to be above par. I think it's crystal clear that children can tell the difference between television and reality. When they laugh at Bart talking back to his parents, they are just letting off steam because adults are always laying down the law.

`30` `i` Eliminating clichés

An overused expression or figure of speech is called a **cliché.** The word itself, interestingly, is a metaphor. Cliché is a French word for the sound a stamping press makes in a process of making multiple identical images. In other words, some-

thing has become a cliché if it is ordinary, run-of-the-mill, like the following:

the last straw	needle in a haystack
strong as an ox	handwriting on the wall
better late than never	tried and true
lay the cards on the table	hit the nail on the head

To edit a cliché, try improving upon it. Go back to the original image and describe it in new words, add fresh detail, or introduce a play on the too-familiar words.

keened

Outside, the wind ~~howled~~.

If you cannot revive the cliché, replace it, striving for directness.

so   that we waited in vain for our eyes to adjust

It was dark ~~as night~~ inside the cave.

EDITING 8: PRACTICE ━━━━━━━━━━━━━━━━━━━━━━━━

Edit the following passage for an academic audience, examining word choice. More than one edited version is possible. Be ready to explain your editing choices.

> If this has been a golden era for home shopping channels, it has also been one for mail-order catalogs. In the past five years the number of catalogs delivered to American homes has tripled. Vendors compose not only old favorites such as L.L. Bean and discount electronics distributors but also newer outfits that have been created merely to take advantage of this trend. According to one survey, the average mail-order catalog junkie receives ten garb catalogs, nine catalogs for housewares and garden equipment, five catalogs for his or her favorite hobby, and six gift catalogs each month. Mail-order companies sell each other their lists of suckers, so once a consumer receives one catalog, chances are that he or she will be receiving catalogs to life.

EDITING 9: APPLICATION ━━━━━━━━━━━━━━━━━━━━━━━

Select one page from a paper you are working on. Remembering the purpose of the paper and its intended audience, examine your choice of words. Use the dictionary and thesaurus to check any word about which you are not sure. Does each word convey the precise meaning you intended? Do any words have

connotations that are inappropriate in context? Have you misused any frequently confused words? Have you used prepositions and particles conventionally? Are your expressions idiomatically worded? Have you used any slang, regionalisms, colloquialisms or jargon? If so, why? Edit the page to improve word choices as necessary, and pay close attention to word choice as you edit the rest of the paper.

31 Eliminating Biased Language

Generalization means summarizing experience or observations: *Canada geese fly south for the winter.* From individual facts, we can make broad conclusions. Generalizing offers a powerful tool to understand patterns or anticipate future events. But relying too greatly on generalization can lead to error. Indeed, many but not all Canada geese are migratory; an increasing number stay put all winter in temperate regions.

Using a generalization about a group of people to predict the behavior or characteristics of an individual is particularly risky. Careless or unexamined generalizations, such as those based on race, ethnicity, cultural background, age, or lifestyle, are called **stereotypes.**

Writing that relies on stereotypes—*sleepy Southern town, typical New York attitude*—as shorthand for description, rather than providing specifics, reflects mental laziness. Appealing to prejudice to invoke what an audience "knows" about a group—*liberal politicians, religious fundamendalists*—or to provoke an emotional reaction is no substitute for reasoned academic discourse. Such writing is called **biased.** From your own experience as a reader, you know your audience is likely to mistrust any writer who relies on stereotypes rather than on specifics, evidence, and reason.

31 a Eliminating stereotypes

The danger of using a negative stereotype is obvious. But a positive stereotype—such as assuming that someone's ethnic background implies skill at mathematics—can be demeaning too if it substitutes a simplistic formula for appreciation of an individual.

To edit out stereotypes, consider qualifying a broad generalization or replacing sweeping statements with specific, relevant details. Some stereotypes simply need to be deleted.

EDITING STEREOTYPES AND GENERALIZATIONS

As you edit your writing, look for stereotypes and generalizations. Ask yourself these questions:

- **Am I relying on stereotypes to make my point?** A stereotype such as *soccer moms* or *computer nerds* is a shorthand way of saying to readers, "You know what I mean." But readers may not know, or they may disagree. Show them specifics instead.

- **Does this generalization follow logically from factual evidence?** Two facts together don't imply that either one caused the other. That one Scot likes finnan haddock does not mean that all Scots like finnan haddock any more than it means that if you like finnan haddock, you must be from Scotland.

- **Am I generalizing responsibly?** Generalizations about a group, even valid ones, cannot predict the knowledge, abilities, attitudes, beliefs, or behavior of an individual. For example, anthropologists have suggested that Japanese culture emphasizes group values over individuality, but that does not support an automatic characterization of any one individual.

- **Does a positive description mask a stereotype?** Even a positive stereotype can be a slur in disguise, as when someone praises a woman for being an asset to her husband as if being a wife were her defining role in life.

Frank Peters, stooped from years in the woods ~~but still alert,~~ re-members the hot, dry summer of the Tillamook Burn.

The assumption that a man of Peters' age would not be alert is a stereotype.

I need someone who can understand my questions, so I hope my next course adviser will be a woman.

Someone's gender does not guarantee empathy. Does the following alternative raise the same issue?

I would feel more comfortable discussing my questions with a woman.

Read the terms on the following list. Write down your reactions to each, and note what images and ideas spring to mind.

BMW drivers	African Americans	Arabs
baby boomers	whites	Jews
lawyers	Asians	career politicians
Generation X	bureaucrats	atheists
conservatives	liberals	religious fundamentalists

Now ask yourself the questions from the "Editing Stereotypes and Generalizations" box on page 453. Are any of your responses based on stereotypes? How many people do you know in each category? Are your reactions based on your own experience, or do they come from what you have heard or read of other people's attitudes? Do you have similar impressions of everyone you have met in the group, or have you noticed variations? If you find yourself harboring stereotypes, remember to try to counterbalance them when you write.

31 b Using labels carefully

Everyone who communicates uses labels to identify groups: *whites, females, Democrats, psychiatrists, Taiwanese.* But labels inevitably focus on a single feature and have the potential to offend those who do not want to be characterized in one particular way. Also, some labels are considered derogatory; that is, they go beyond simple identification and evoke stereotypes. Here are some ways to judge how to use labels in your writing.

Using a group's own labels

Whenever possible, refer to a group of people by the label its members themselves prefer. Sometimes this is easy: members of the Rotary Club call themselves *Rotarians;* members of the Ancient Free and Accepted Masons are *Masons.*

With ethnic, racial, national, cultural, sexual, or gender labels, your choices become more difficult. Sometimes even those who belong to a group do not agree on what they should be called.

Designations of race, ethnicity, and nationality

Today some Americans whose birthplace or ancestry is in Spanish-speaking countries of South or Central America or Mexico refer to themselves as *Hispanics* while others prefer *Latino* and *Latina.* Some Mexican Americans prefer *Chicano* and *Chicana.* The term *Spanish Americans,* however, properly refers only to

Americans whose country of birth or ancestry is Spain. Many *Native Americans* prefer that term to *Indian* or *American Indian*, but using the name of the tribe or nation is often a better choice: *Navaho, Lakota Sioux,* or *Seneca.* Some *Inuit* prefer that term to *Eskimo.* Some people use a term that indicates both their ethnic or national heritage and their American identity: *Chinese American, German American.*

Naming the specific country of someone's origin is always correct and worth the trouble: *Japanese, Vietnamese, Dominican, Chilean, Bosnian, Palestinian, Iraqi,* and so on. In some cases, you may need to identify people by ethnic origin as well as nationality: *Bosnian Serbs, German-speaking Poles, Israeli Arabs.*

The terms *black* and *African American* and the more general *people of color,* usually used to include Native Americans and Asians, are generally accepted, while *Negro* and *colored* are no longer acceptable. The phrase *people of color* is acceptable, especially in referring to people of various origins.

If the religion of a particular group has a specific relevance in your writing, use the preferred terms: for example, a follower of Islam is a *Muslim.*

ESL **USING LABELS DERIVED FROM ADJECTIVES**

Many labels that describe groups are derived from adjectives: *the rich, the poor, the homeless.* Take care to use such collective nouns correctly.

- Always use the definite article *the* before the labeling noun.

  the
  The legislature passed a law to assist ^homeless.

- Use a plural verb when the collective noun is the subject.

  are
  The poor ~~is~~ ^always with us.

- A collective noun cannot refer to an individual. If you refer to one person in a group, use an adjective-plus-noun construction.

  woman
  We spoke to a homeless ^about her search for a job.

Designations of gender and sexual orientation

Most adult females prefer to be called *women* rather than *girls* or *ladies*.

When writing about sexual orientation, keep in mind that people have widely different views about the role of sexuality in public and private life. Not everyone may share your perspective. The terms *homosexual, heterosexual, gay, straight, lesbian, bisexual,* and *transgendered* are all generally acceptable.

2 Checking labels for negative connotations

Labels that seem neutral can hide negative connotations. For example, the term *AIDS victims* implies that such people are blameless, which you may intend, but also that they are helpless, which you may not.

As you edit, watch for unnecessary or unintended negative connotations, and substitute more neutral alternatives. Focus whenever possible on people's strengths, referring to people as *living with cancer* or as *cancer survivors* rather than *suffering from cancer*. Focus on individuals first and their characteristics second: *a woman with quadriplegia* rather than *a quadriplegic*.

People's preferences for certain labels change frequently as connotations change. People with physical limitations often, but not universally, prefer *disabled* to *handicapped*, and the latter term one time seemed more neutral than *crippled*. The continuing attempt to avoid negative connotations has resulted in the use of *visually impaired* or *hearing impaired* for *blind* and *deaf* and in such constructions as *differently abled* for *disabled*. Such terms are easily lampooned as an excess of "political correctness," but you must balance the need for directness against the need for sensitivity. Sometimes the solution is not to label at all.

He was a fascinating ~~old~~ man with a lifelong passion for rare books and fine cognac.

EDITING 2: PRACTICE ———————————————————————

Identify stereotypes in the following passages and describe the ways in which they may be thoughtless or offensive. If there is any useful information in the particular passage, edit it to communicate the information in a way that is not offensive. Be ready to explain your editing choices.

1. In order to achieve more diversity on college campuses, admissions officers all over the country are eager to accept foreigners, especially from poor countries.

2. Because of policies like this, during my freshman year I found myself living with an Oriental guy as well as with a Jew from New York City.

3. Since I had trouble in math and science, I asked my Vietnamese roommate to help me in calculus and physics; I also asked him to show me some karate.

4. My other roommate, not surprisingly, was majoring in business.

5. All in all, I enjoyed the chance to live with a couple of minorities; it taught me a lot about how different people view things differently.

31 c Using nonsexist language

If you use words that embody gender stereotypes—also called sexist language—you risk alienating half your potential audience (or more). Several kinds of gender bias arise from unexamined habits of thought and language.

In generic pronouns

Until recently, writers and readers alike accepted use of the pronouns *he, him,* and *his* in a generic sense when gender was unspecified or irrelevant: *Anyone who believes those promises should have* his *head examined.* The "generic *he*" was understood to refer to females as well as males.

As acceptance of this convention wanes, some speakers substitute plural pronouns: *Everyone had fun on their vacation.* This is grammatically incorrect, since *everyone* is singular and thus requires a singular pronoun. However, English has no singular personal pronoun of indefinite gender, only *he* or *she, him* or *her, his* or *hers.* In formal writing, you have to find ways around this dilemma.

Every nun has ~~their~~ own room.
       ^her

Nuns are women, so you can substitute her.

All attorneys have their specialties.
~~Every attorney has his~~ own legal ~~specialty.~~

If you switch to the plural, watch for other agreement problems.

(For a complete discussion of gender agreement and avoiding the generic *he,* see 36j.)

2 In universal terms

The use of *man* and *mankind* to refer to the whole of humanity has fallen into disfavor because those terms seem to exclude or diminish the female half of the species. Substitute *humanity, the human race, humankind,* or *people.*

3 In occupational terms

In terms for a person's occupation, focus on the occupation, not the person's gender. Otherwise you risk suggesting that gender is a person's most important attribute or that some jobs are "naturally" held by either men or women.

Many occupational terms have a feminine form consisting of the neutral base form and a suffix that indicates the female gender: *actor/actress, author/authoress, poet/poetess.* Avoid the feminine forms; use gender-neutral alternatives: for *stewardess,* use *flight attendant;* for *waitress,* use *server;* for *actress, actor.*

Occupational terms that end in *-man* imply that everyone who engages in that profession is a man. Sex-neutral substitutes for many occupations are readily available.

BIASED	NEUTRAL
statesman	diplomat, national leader
congressman	representative to Congress, congressional representative
mailman	letter carrier, mail carrier
policeman	police officer
fireman	firefighter
businessman	executive, businessperson
chairman	chair, head, chairperson

Similarly, do not use language that implicitly assumes that an occupation determines a person's gender—that all nurses, secretaries, or teachers are female or that all airline pilots, business executives, or bronco busters are male.

The physician was assisted by a ~~male~~ nurse.

4 In descriptions

Treat the sexes equally. As you edit, notice comments about a woman's appearance or family life. If you would not have made similar comments about a man, delete them.

Dr. Jones, ~~mother of three,~~ was named to the hospital's peer review board.

5 In comparisons

Whenever you use a pair of terms for male and female, make sure that the terms are directly comparable. The phrase *man and wife,* for example, identifies one partner as independent (*man*) and the other in terms of her relation to him (*wife*). Edit it as *man and woman* or *husband and wife.*

Her essay contrasted the novelists Dickens and ~~Jane~~ Austen.

6 In addressing your audience

Do not address a general audience as if it were made up of people of a single gender.

you
When you buy a house, ~~your wife~~ will have to get used to a
∧
new kitchen.

EDITING 3: EXPLORATION ━━━━━━━━━━━━━━━━━━━━━━

The following are excerpts from three political statements from earlier centuries, when ideas about the roles of the sexes and sexism in language were very different. To whom do you think Jefferson is referring? How about Lincoln? Is either statement ambiguous or open to more than one interpretation? How do you think Stanton interpreted Jefferson's text? In what ways is her use of male and female terms different from Jefferson's? In what ways is it similar to Jefferson's?

> When in the course of human events it becomes necessary for one people to dissolve the political bands which have connected them with another, . . . a decent respect to the opinions of mankind requires that they should declare the causes which impel them to the separation.
> We hold these truths to be self-evident, that all men are created equal, that they are endowed by their Creator with certain unalienable Rights. . . . That to secure these rights, Governments are instituted among Men deriving their just powers from the consent of the governed.
>
> THOMAS JEFFERSON, DECLARATION OF INDEPENDENCE (1776)

Four score and seven years ago, our fathers brought forth on this continent a new nation, conceived in liberty and dedicated to the proposition that all men are created equal.

ABRAHAM LINCOLN, GETTYSBURG ADDRESS (1863)

When in the course of human events it becomes necessary for one portion of the family of man to assume among the people of the earth a position different from that which they have hitherto occupied, . . . a decent respect to the opinions of mankind requires that they should declare the causes that impel them to such a course.

"We hold these truths to be self-evident: that all men and women are created equal; that they are endowed by their Creator with certain inalienable rights; . . . that to secure these rights governments are instituted, deriving their just powers from the consent of the governed."

ELIZABETH CADY STANTON, DECLARATION OF SENTIMENTS (1848)

EDITING 4: PRACTICE

Edit the following passage, eliminating any biased language that may be offensive to readers. More than one edited version is possible. Be ready to explain your editing choices.

All of the old people at White Pines Residence agree that there couldn't be a better place for them to live. The modern residence has been designed to meet their every need, and in some ways it resembles a spa more than an old-folks' home. For one thing, the food is terrific. Every meal offers at least one exotic dish, always cooked to perfection. This isn't surprising, considering that the chef was born in Paris. In the medical area, facilities and services are first rate. A doctor is on call around the clock to provide care to all of the residents, many of whom suffer from cancer. With the handicapped in mind, doorways have been built that are wide enough for a cripple's wheelchair to pass through, and ramps are familiar sights, both inside and outside. Staff members have been carefully chosen for both their experience with old people and their personalities. They are all extremely popular with the residents. One of the best loved is a male nurse who always makes time in his busy schedule to read to the blind residents. Another nurse is a former actress; she has arranged for a local theater group to perform regularly at the residence. In addition, volunteers from the local college visit with the residents, providing them with companionship and friendship. Like so many old people, the residents at White Pines enjoy spending time with young people and telling stories about their

youth. State-of-the-art facilities are not cheap, however, and White Pines is no exception; the cost of the facility may explain the high percentage of Jewish residents. To judge from the level of satisfaction among the residents, however, it is money well spent.

EDITING 5: APPLICATION

Read through a paper you are working on, looking for examples of biased language. Are there any characterizations that might be considered stereotypical? If so, can you supply specific details to support your use of the stereotypes? Or should they be eliminated? Have you used any labels to describe groups of people? Would these labels be acceptable to the people themselves? Have you used male pronouns to refer to both genders? Can you find any other examples of sexist language? If you discover such stereotypes or biased language in your paper, consider carefully why you might have written that way in the first place and how you can avoid doing so in the future. Then edit the relevant passages to eliminate the biased language. How does the edited version compare with the original?

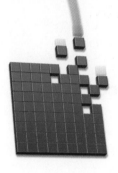

EDITING SECTION
Editing Grammar

32 Eliminating Sentence Fragments

Does every sentence "start with a capital letter and end with a period"? As a character in *Porgy and Bess* says, "It ain't necessarily so." A group of words punctuated as a sentence that is not grammatically complete is called a **fragment.**

> There are several ways to select text with the mouse. *A few of which may be known to you.*

One kind of fragment lacks a subject, a verb, or both. Another type has a subject and a verb but begins with an element such as *because* or *when* that makes it impossible for it to stand alone. While skilled writers sometimes deliberately use fragments for effect, less experienced writers tend to use them inadvertently.

In academic writing, most instructors regard sentence fragments as errors. The problem with a fragment is its incompleteness. A sentence expresses a complete idea, but a fragment neglects to tell the reader either what it is about (the subject) or what happened (the verb). Fortunately, fragments can usually be corrected by a simple change.

32 a Editing fragments lacking subjects or verbs

You can identify fragments by searching your sentences for subjects and verbs. A complete sentence—or **independent clause**—has a subject and a verb, but if one or the other is missing, you have found a fragment. You need to edit these fragments to create complete sentences. First, decide which element is missing. Then try one of the following editing solutions:

Adding missing elements

It is simple enough to fill in the missing sentence element.

rocked
A fleet of colorful fishing boats at anchor in the bay.
          ^

The fragment is easily repaired by supplying a verb.

RECOGNIZING FRAGMENTS

A group of words can fail to form a complete sentence (or an independent clause) because of a missing verb, subject, or both. But remember that a group of words containing a verb and a subject may also contain a subordinating word or phrase, which turns the whole into a dependent clause. If you're unsure whether a group of words is a fragment, ask yourself the following questions:

- **Does it contain a verb?** If not, it is a fragment. (See 32a.)

   ran by
   A middle-aged jogger in beat-up Nikes.
             ^

- **Does it contain a subject?** If not, it is a fragment. (See 32a.)

       ,   *and*
   During the night the protesters talked quietly and slept. ~~And~~ prayed.
                         ^

   Certain sentences in the imperative mood (commands, orders, and requests) do not require explicit subjects: *Come at noon.* When the subject is understood to be *you* though it is not stated, the sentence is an **imperative sentence** and is not considered a fragment. (See 34f.)

- **If it has a subject and a verb, does it contain a subordinating word or phrase?** A clause introduced by a subordinating conjunction (*until, because, after, although*) or a relative pronoun (*who, that, which*) cannot stand alone as a complete sentence. (See 32b.)

                                         because
   None of the research was completed before the deadline. ~~Because~~ of
                         ^
   the delay in preparing the samples.

Out of control, the careening truck hit the guardrail. Then *it* spilled chickens and feathers halfway across the landscape.

Adding a subject completes the sentence.

My uncle was singing to his new baby. *She was cooing* ~~Cooing~~ back with happy sounds of her own.

Adding a subject and completing the verb repairs the sentence.

2 Joining the fragment

Another solution is to incorporate the fragment into a nearby sentence. There may be several ways to do that.

Symbolism is important in Alice Walker's "Everyday Use*,*" ~~A~~ *a* story that shows cultural differences between generations.

I was in the library when I saw him*, the* ~~The~~ new student from Hong Kong. He was looking up something in the card catalog.

The phrase the new student from Hong Kong *restates* him, *so it can be punctuated as part of the preceding sentence.*

I was in the library when I saw him. The new student from Hong Kong. He was looking up something in the card catalog.

The fragment has become the subject of the following sentence.

Few employees interviewed held the company president in high regard. *or* ~~Or~~ believed he could bring the business back to profitability.

Repunctuating the sentence provides a subject for believed.

Join a fragment that is a list or set of examples to an introductory statement.

Taking the boat out alone for the first time, I tried to think of everything my father had shown me*: centerboard,* ~~Centerboard,~~ halyards, jib sheets, main sheet, tiller, and telltales.

Note: Following a colon, the first word of a list that is not a complete sentence is not capitalized. (See 41b.)

EDITING 1: PRACTICE

Edit the following passage to eliminate any fragments, making any changes in wording or punctuation that are necessary for smooth reading. More than one edited version is possible. Be ready to explain your editing choices.

> There he stood. In the middle of the public square. Speaking at the top of his lungs about the end of the world. After two or three hours in the hot sun, he rested. Sat down in the shade of the clock tower. He opened his satchel and took out his lunch. A banana. A small can of apple juice. Three cookies and a wedge of cheese. I walked over to talk to him. He looked me right in the eye. For a long moment. Then spoke: "Have a cookie."

ESL

PREPOSITION FRAGMENTS: MULTIPLE-WORD PREPOSITIONS

Fragments introduced by multiple-word prepositions can be more difficult to spot than those introduced by one-word prepositions. Here is a list of common multiple-word prepositions:

according to	for the sake of
along with	in contrast with
as a result of	in favor of
as compared with	in spite of
as for	instead of
aside from	on account of
as well as	regardless of
because of	relative to
contrary to	up until
due to	with respect to
except for	with the exception of

Whenever you use one of these prepositions in your writing, make sure the phrase it introduces is attached to an independent clause.

> Our debate team was not invited to participate~~,~~ ^in^ ~~In~~ spite of our
>
> winning record.

32 b Editing dependent clause fragments

A **dependent clause** is a clause introduced by a **subordinating conjunction** (such as *after, although, since, because, when, where, whether*) or a **relative pronoun** (such as *who, which, that*). Even though it has a subject and a verb, a dependent clause such as *that extended from before dawn until long past dark* cannot stand alone as a sentence. (See 25c, 25d.)

If you find a dependent clause punctuated as a sentence, try attaching it to a nearby independent clause that completes the thought.

Contemporary accounts describe a battle. ~~That~~ extended from before dawn until long past dark.

[insertion above: that]

Tests isolated the virus. ~~Which~~ can be deadly.

[insertion above: , which]

You might also remove the subordinating element so that the clause can stand alone.

~~After the~~ leaves had all fallen. The trees stood bare.

[insertion above: The]

On occasion, a fragment could be attached to either the preceding or following sentence. In such a case, you will have to choose which nearby sentence should take in the dependent clause. Edit the sentence to clarify your meaning.

It sounds like an excellent opportunity. ~~Although~~ the starting pay is barely minimum wage. It provides more training than many entry-level jobs.

[insertion above: , although]

The value of the opportunity is qualified.

It sounds like an excellent opportunity. Although the starting pay is barely minimum wage. ~~It~~ provides more training than many entry-level jobs.

[insertion above: , it]

The value of the training provided is stressed.

(See 39b and 39c for punctuation of dependent clauses.)

Edit the following paragraph to eliminate dependent clause fragments. More than one edited version is possible. Be ready to explain your editing choices.

> Despite the fact that doctors take an oath to protect life. Many physicians believe they should be allowed to help patients who want to commit suicide. They want to do whatever they can to ease the pain of death for those who are suffering. Because they believe people should be able to die with dignity. Although euthanasia is not legal in most of Europe, it is becoming more accepted in some countries. Especially in the Netherlands. Which has one of the most liberal policies in the world. There, specific guidelines allow a doctor to assist in the suicide of a patient who is terminally ill. As long as the patient requests it.

32 C Using sentence fragments for special effects

Man is the only animal that blushes. Or needs to.

MARK TWAIN

Writers occasionally use fragments on purpose. Because a fragment provides a dramatic break in rhythm, it can create dramatic emphasis. For this reason, fragments abound in advertising.

> The sun's harsh rays can wrinkle your skin. Even cause cancer. Introducing the ultraviolet protection of new No-ray Oil. A fluid that blends smoothly with your skin, penetrating and softening. To soothe and protect.

Here essayist Joan Didion uses fragments to underscore a major point:

> I knew that I was no legitimate resident in any world of ideas. I knew I couldn't think. All I knew then was what I couldn't do. All I knew then was what I wasn't, and it took me some years to discover what I was.
>
> Which was a writer.
>
> By which I mean not a "good" writer or a "bad" writer, but simply a writer, a person whose most absorbed and passionate hours are spent arranging words on pieces of paper.
>
> JOAN DIDION, "WHY I WRITE"

Because fragments are used infrequently in academic writing, you should consider carefully before using one deliberately. Will it

be seen as an effective stylistic device or as just a grammatical error? Make sure it seems intentional, not inadvertent. When your point warrants disrupting readers' expectations, a fragment may be in order. If it works.

EDITING 3: EXPLORATION

Look through popular magazines, essay collections, and other publications written for a general audience and note the use of intentional fragments. In each case, what effect does the fragment have on you, the reader? Defend or criticize the effectiveness of each fragment you find.

EDITING 4: PRACTICE

Read the following passage, which includes a number of intentional fragments. Identify each fragment and consider its overall effect. What do you think the writer was trying to achieve? Do you think the fragments are effective? To determine the overall effectiveness of the passage, edit it to eliminate fragments and then compare your edited version with the original.

> There never was any question whether we would finish. Just how soon. It seemed every time we got ready to close up, another busload would come in. Tired and hungry. And the boss would say, "Can't turn away money," so we'd pour more coffee. Burn more toast. Crack more eggs. Over and over again. Because we needed the money too.

EDITING 5: PRACTICE

Edit the following passage to eliminate sentence fragments. Make any changes in wording that are needed for smooth reading. More than one edited version is possible. Be ready to explain your editing choices.

> Ferdinand le Menthe Morton was born in New Orleans to a Creole family. Although he took classical piano lessons, he fell in love with another kind of music. Jazz and blues. Which he heard in the part of town called Storyville. In Chicago in the 1920s, he got a recording contract with RCA. He made some records and began calling himself "Jelly Roll." He claimed to have invented jazz. By himself. George G. Wolfe wrote a musical about his life. Called *Jelly's Last Jam* and written as though looking back from the moment of his death. At the end of his life, Morton had to acknowledge the contributions of other blacks to jazz. Which he had denied all his life. He came to recognize the heritage he shared with other black musicians. To

accept and understand them. Although he had always thought of himself, a Creole, as different from blacks.

EDITING 6: APPLICATION ─────────────────────

Examine your recent writings for sentence fragments. Do you write one kind of fragment frequently? If so, can you explain why you might tend to make this particular mistake? Practice editing any fragments you find by correcting each one in two or three different ways. Then decide which edited version of each sentence works best in your paper.

33   Correcting Fused Sentences and Comma Splices

An **independent clause,** one that includes a subject and a predicate and constitutes one complete idea, can stand alone as a complete sentence.

     subject   predicate

Professional athletes can earn huge salaries.

Two or more independent clauses within a single sentence must be joined in one of four ways: with a comma and a coordinating conjunction, with a semicolon alone, with a semicolon and a conjunctive adverb or transitional phrase, or with a colon. These markers tell readers that a new idea is about to be presented and clarify the relationship between the ideas.

          independent clause   independent

Professional athletes can earn huge salaries, yet some of them

    clause

want still more.

In this example the comma and the conjunction *yet* mark the beginning of a new idea, a new independent clause. They help prevent misreading by limiting the number of possible ways the sentence can proceed from that point.

Two independent clauses joined without such a marker make a **fused sentence** (also called a *run-on sentence*). Readers get no warning when one independent clause ends and another begins.

              independent clause

FUSED SENTENCE Professional athletes can earn huge salaries some are

            independent clause

paid millions of dollars per year.

Two independent clauses joined (or "spliced together") by only a comma make up a **comma splice.**

COMMA SPLICE   Professional athletes can earn huge salaries, some are paid millions of dollars per year.

RECOGNIZING COMMON CAUSES OF SENTENCE ERRORS

Comma splices and fused sentences, sometimes called *sentence errors,* often occur when two clauses express ideas closely linked in the writer's mind. Understanding why sentence errors occur can help you recognize them in your own writing. Here are some common situations that can lead to sentence errors:

• **Additional information.** The second clause explains, elaborates on, or illustrates the first.

Every summer the tribes gathered along the banks of the river, ~~they~~ to

fish~~ed~~ and hunt~~ed~~ and pick~~ed~~ berries.

• **Contrast.** The meaning of the second clause contrasts with the meaning of the first.

but
The Security Council supported the resolution, the United States

vetoed it.

• **Same or similar subjects.** The subject of the second clause renames the subject of the first clause.

⊙He
The professor asked us to write our thoughts down, he said just to write

whatever came to mind as fast as we could

• **Incorrect use of conjunction or transition.** A conjunctive adverb or transitional phrase is incorrectly used to join two sentences.

⊙
Congressional offices once were completely contained in the Capitol
In   ,
~~in~~ fact the Supreme Court also had space there.

Seeing a comma without a conjunction, readers expect what follows to be part of the first clause rather than the beginning of a new clause. So that the reader will not need to stop and go back for clarity, edit out any comma splices.

REVISED   Professional athletes can earn huge salaries; some are paid millions of dollars per year.

33 a Using a comma and a coordinating conjunction

The **coordinating conjunctions** *and, but, yet, so, for, or,* and *nor* join equal grammatical elements and specify a relationship between them, such as addition (*and*), contrast (*but, yet*), causation (*so, for*), or choice (*or, nor*). (See Chapter 25.) If the ideas in two independent clauses are equally important, you can join them with a coordinating conjunction preceded by a comma. (See 39a.)

, and

The cyclone was especially savage it struck a particularly vulnerable area.

but

Maya Angelou has worked as an actress and director, her greatest success has come as an autobiographer and poet.

EDITING I: PRACTICE ———————————————————

Edit each fused sentence or comma splice by using a comma and a coordinating conjunction. More than one editing option is available to you. Be ready to explain your editing choices.

1. The praise that David Halberstam has received for his nonfiction writing is due in large part to his blunt style he always says what he means.
2. He was critical of the media's involvement in the 1988 presidential election, he said so openly.
3. In his writing he not only identifies his main points he also solidifies and clarifies them.
4. He leads the reader through his thought processes, rarely is any point unsubstantiated.
5. He feels strongly about his subjects he seems to become very involved with them.

33 b Adding a semicolon

Another way to join two independent clauses is to add a **semicolon** between the clauses to signify their equality.

Semicolon alone

Use a semicolon alone only when the clauses are closely and clearly related. (See 40a.) If they are not closely related, make them separate sentences. (See 33d.) If the relationship is unclear, use a conjunction to clarify it.

> For years, free-market proponents have advocated legislation to allow competitive auctions for broadcast licenses ; so far Congress has refused.

Note: The second independent clause does not begin with a capital letter.

Semicolons are useful in sentences that contain more than two independent clauses, particularly when one or more items in a series have internal commas.

> The sculpture, a poor imitation of the work of Dresner, was monstrous ; its surface was rough and pitted ; and its colors, ranging from fuschia to lime, were garish.

When two or more independent clauses are short, closely related, and parallel in form, some writers use only a comma. However, the effect is somewhat informal.

> I washed the clothes, I dusted the furniture, I fed the children.

But a semicolon is necessary when the sentence becomes more complicated.

> He dovetailed the joints of the drawers ; he sanded, stained, and varnished.

A semicolon is not needed before a **tag question.**

> A semicolon would look odd here, wouldn't it?

✓ CONJUNCTIVE ADVERBS

accordingly	incidentally	now
also	indeed	otherwise
anyway	instead	similarly
besides	likewise	still
certainly	meanwhile	subsequently
consequently	moreover	then
conversely	namely	therefore
finally	nevertheless	thus
furthermore	next	undoubtedly
hence	nonetheless	whereas
however		

---

2 Semicolon with a conjunctive adverb or transitional expression

Conjunctive adverbs, such as *finally, however,* and *therefore,* cannot be used with a comma to join two independent clauses. Neither can phrases such as *in fact* or *for example,* which are called **transitional expressions.** Use a semicolon instead. (See the list of conjunctive adverbs above; see 23c2 for a list of transitional expressions.)

The rebel forces were never completely defeated⨟ moreover, they still control several strategic highland passes.

EDITING 2: PRACTICE ━━━━━━━━━━━━━━━━━━━━━━

Edit each fused sentence or comma splice by using either a semicolon alone or a semicolon with a conjunctive adverb or transitional expression. More than one editing option is available. Be ready to explain your editing choices.

1. Michael Crichton's *Jurassic Park* explores the disastrous consequences of disturbing the balance of nature, it presents what could happen if scientists bring dinosaurs back from extinction.

2. Crichton does not preach about environmental issues, he uses them to create an engaging, fast-paced story.

3. Alan Grant, the main character, is an expert in dinosaurs no one else knows as much about velociraptors as he does.

4. Grant questions the safety of the theme park, for example, having rides in the park disturbs him.

5.   Crichton's characters, especially Grant, are realistic their words, thoughts, and actions are believable and true to life.

---

3 3 c Adding a colon

When the second clause of two independent clauses explains, elaborates, or illustrates the first, you can use a **colon** to join the clauses.

> This year's team is surprisingly inexperienced, seven of the play-
>
> ers are juniors, and six are sophomores.

When the second independent clause conveys the main point of the sentence, some writers capitalize the first word after the colon.

> My mother gave me one important piece of advice: Never wear plaids with stripes.

Such capitalization is optional; a lowercase letter after the colon is always correct. (See Chapters 41 and 46a.)

EDITING 3: PRACTICE ———————————————

Edit each fused sentence or comma splice by using a colon.

1.   The first recorded outbreak of the ebola virus, which occurred in Zaire in 1976, took a heavy toll in human life more than 340 people died.

2.   Medical researchers know very little about the disease, they have only a vague idea of where the virus originated.

3.   Many people have compared ebola to AIDS because of its severity, but there is one important difference unlike AIDS ebola can kill a person in a few days.

4.   Between epidemics the virus appears to go dormant many years might pass without a reported case.

5.   We cannot afford to wait until the next epidemic before taking action, we must find a cure as soon as we can.

---

3 3 d Writing separate sentences

A comma-spliced or fused sentence may read better as two sep-arate sentences, especially when one clause is much longer than

the other or when the two clauses are dissimilar in structure
or meaning.

> The president outlined his administration's new economic
> strategy on the same day that war broke out in the Middle East, ⊙
> ~~Almost~~
> ~~almost~~ no one noticed his announcement.
>   ^

Forming two sentences often increases emphasis on the second clause.

33 e Subordinating one clause to the other

To emphasize one of the two ideas in a fused or spliced sentence, put the less important idea in a **subordinate clause.** Subordinating one clause to the other will make it dependent—no longer
able to stand on its own. (See 25b.) The effect is to bring important
information into the foreground while leaving other information in
the background.

Dependent clauses are introduced by a **subordinating conjunction** such as *after, although, as, because, if, than, whenever,* or
while or by a **relative pronoun** such as *who, which,* or *that.*
Choose the subordinating conjunction or relative pronoun that
best describes the relationship you want to establish.

> Because the   ,
> ~~The~~ rain froze as it hit the ground the streets were icy.
>   ^   ^

>   that
> The committee studied the issue ~~it~~ decided to recommend allow-
>   ^
> ing the group to participate.

33 f Creating one independent clause

When two independent clauses are closely related, often you
can collapse them into one clause.

>   and
> This book held my attention, ~~it~~ gave a lot of information about the
>   /   ^
> colonial period.

Since book *and* it *are the same subject, it can be dropped.*

You can also turn one clause into a modifier phrase.

The huge chestnut oak cast a heavy blanket of shadow on the
ground beneath it, ~~it dwarfed~~ a few saplings.
dwarfing ^

, my favorite author,
Bobbie Ann Mason writes interesting stories about offbeat char-
^
acters. ~~She is my favorite author.~~

EDITING 4: PRACTICE ─────────────────────────────

Edit each fused sentence or comma splice in the following passage by creating a
single sentence or separate sentences. More than one edited version is possible.
Be ready to explain your editing choices.

The weather report was over, we knew the storm was rapidly approaching.
We were all very nervous hurricanes had struck our town many times before they did a lot of damage. My father came back from the hardware
store with several rolls of masking tape, he gave each of us a roll and told
us to tape the windows to keep the glass from shattering if hit by debris.
Then mom sent me to check on our next-door neighbor he is extremely
scared of storms. He still remembers the violent storms of his childhood,
he was born in Texas. He returned with me to our house, we all waited in
the basement we played cards and we listened to the radio. Fortunately,
the storm dissipated when it hit the coast south of us, all the excitement
was for nothing.

EDITING 5: PRACTICE ─────────────────────────────

Edit the following passage to eliminate fused sentences and comma splices,
using any strategy discussed in this chapter. Be ready to discuss your editing changes.

Expanding the airport will generate more flights, more flights will bring
more travelers and money into the region. Each traveler spends an average
of $7 in the airport on goods and services, when parking and ground
transportation are added, the total approaches $25. The report said that
developing the local economy would benefit the area, it said that air travel
would make traffic problems worse on roads around the airport. According to the report, expanding the airport offers many advantages, including
providing jobs, making travel more convenient, and boosting the economy.
However, the expansion plan faces some problems, it would cost $17 mil-
lion and it would have to be built on land that might be valuable as wetlands. Opponents of the airport expansion appeared before the port

EDITING COMMA SPLICES AND FUSED SENTENCES

As you edit your work, watch for sentences that contain two independent clauses; check to see that you have joined them in an acceptable way. There are several ways to correct fused sentences and comma splices:

- **Use a comma and coordinating conjunction** to specify the relationship between clauses.

    > Columbus believed he would reach Asia, *but* his sailors had much
    >
    > less confidence.

- **Insert a semicolon** to signal the clear, close relationship of the clauses.

    > He did not prove the world was round*;* he discovered the New World.

- **Precede a conjunctive adverb or transitional phrase with a semicolon.**

    > Columbus continued to believe he had reached Asia*; in fact,* he did not realize
    >
    > he had discovered a "New World" until he found the mouth of the
    >
    > Orinoco River during his third voyage.

- **Use a colon when the second clause illustrates the first.**

    > Columbus really did not know where he was*:* he insisted the islands he
    >
    > found were near Asia.

    Other methods of correcting sentence errors involve greater changes.

- **Divide the sentence into two sentences**

(Continued)

                             ○The
Columbus never set foot in North America, ~~the~~ closest he came to discovering "America" was landing in what is now Puerto Rico.

- **Subordinate one clause to the other.**

  Although
  Columbus believed he would reach Asia, his sailors had much less confidence.

- **Rewrite the sentence as one independent clause.**

  On Hispaniola, Columbus established a settlement called Isabella, ~~it was~~ the first European colony in the New World.

  Your choice should depend on the meaning you wish to convey, the length of the sentence, and the rhythm and wording of surrounding sentences.

commission, saying that new runways would endanger the nesting grounds of several rare migratory birds. The Department of Environmental Quality studied the bird migration patterns it said that the fifteen acres of wetlands in question were home to at least nineteen different species. The Southeast Region Chamber of Commerce has supported the airport expansion, claiming that the plan could create dozens of new jobs, the chamber president called those jobs more important than a few ducks.

EDITING 6: APPLICATION

Examine your own recent writing for fused sentences and comma splices. If you have used any, is there a pattern to your errors? Can you see why you made these mistakes? Edit any fused sentences and comma splices you found, and think about how best to correct or avoid these errors in the future.

34 Using Verbs Correctly

Effective writing uses strong verbs that show action. Verbs convey a great deal of other information as well. They help show *who* performed the action by changing form according to **person:** *I talk. He talks.* They show *how many* people performed the action by changing **number:** *She sings. They sing.* They show *when* it occurred by changing **tense:** *He thinks. He thought.* They show the speaker's *attitude* toward or *relation* to the action by changing **mood:** *You are an honors student. Be an honors student.* They also show whether the subject of the sentence acts or is acted upon by changing **voice:** *She took the picture. The picture was taken.*

Using verbs correctly in all these ways is not as difficult as it may seem. If you speak English fluently, you have been using the right person, number, tense, mood, and voice most of the time without thinking about it. In conversation, however, people often ignore the subtleties of correct usage. Additionally, what is "correct" varies from community to community. People who grew up speaking a dialect may find their use of verbs is considered nonstandard in formal academic writing.

This chapter gives an overview of verb forms, tense, and mood. The uses of the active and passive voice are discussed in Chapter 27. For questions of agreement between verbs and subjects, see 34h–34u. **Verbals,** verb forms that are used as nouns or adjectives, do not change form to show person or number. (See 62c.)

VERB FORMS

34 a Understanding the five verb forms

Except for the verb *be*, all English verbs have five forms.

Two forms express action occurring now: the **base form** and the **-s form.** The base form, also called the *plain form* or

TERMS USED TO DESCRIBE VERBS

Knowing the terms used to describe verbs isn't a prerequisite for writing good English. Nevertheless, the terms given here are useful for describing verb problems and their solutions.

- **Person** indicates who or what performs an action. (See 34a–34b.)

first person	the one speaking	*I read.*
second person	the one spoken to	*You read.*
third person	the one spoken about	*He reads.*

- **Number** indicates how many people or things perform the action. (See 34a–34b.)

singular	one	*I think.*
plural	more than one	*We think.*

- **Tense** indicates the time of the action. (See 34d–34e.)

present	at this time	*I learn.*
past	before this time	*I learned.*
future	after this time	*I will learn.*

- **Mood** indicates the speaker's attitude toward or relation to the action. (See 34f–34g.)

indicative	speaker states a fact or asks a question	*You are happy.* *Are you happy?*
imperative	speaker gives a command or direction	*Be quiet!*
subjunctive	speaker expresses desire, wish, or requirement or states a condition contrary to fact	*I would be happier if you were quiet.*

- **Voice** indicates whether the grammatical subject of the sentence performs the action or is acted upon. (See 27c.)

active	the subject acts	*She read the book.*
passive	the subject is acted upon	*The book was read by her.*

THE FIVE VERB FORMS

The five principal forms of English verbs are the base form, the -s form, the past tense, the past participle, and the present participle. Regular verbs add -d or -ed to form the past tense and past participle. Irregular verbs follow some other pattern. (The verb be has more than five forms. It is the most irregular verb in the English language. See 34b4.)

	Base Form	-s Form	Past Tense	Past Participle	Present Participle
REGULAR	act	acts	acted	acted	acting
	seem	seems	seemed	seemed	seeming
IRREGULAR	know	knows	knew	known	knowing
	eat	eats	ate	eaten	eating
	hit	hits	hit	hit	hitting

simple form, is used for present-tense action performed by *I, we, you,* or *they: I walk, you walk, they walk.* The -s form is used for *he, she,* or *it* (third-person singular): *he walks, she walks, it walks.*

Two verb forms express action that occurred in the past: the **past tense** and **past participle.** For **regular verbs,** the past tense and past participle are formed by adding -d or -ed to the base form: *I walked. I have walked.* Verbs that form the past tense and past participle in other ways are called **irregular verbs.** Often the two past forms of an irregular verb differ from each other: *I knew. I have known.* The past tense and the past participle do not change to reflect who performed the action: *I tried. She tried. They tried.*

The fifth verb form, the **present participle,** is formed by adding -ing to the base form: *know, knowing.* It expresses continuing action in the present or past. Like the past tense and past participle, it does not change according to person and number, and to serve as the main verb of a sentence it must be used with a form of *be: She is sleeping.* (See 34c.)

(For a discussion of the verb *be,* see 34b4; for more on other irregular verbs, see 34b2.)

34 b Using standard verb forms

1 Using -s and -ed forms correctly

The *third-person singular form*, used when *he, she, it,* or any singular noun is the subject, is formed for all present-tense verbs by adding -s or -es to the base form: *I go; she goes.* (The only exceptions are *be* and *have: I am; he is* and *I have; she has.*) The past tense of regular verbs is created by adding -d or -ed to the base form.

Speakers of some dialects do not use the -s and -ed endings, but such usage is considered nonstandard in formal writing. As you edit your work, watch for missing -s and -ed endings.

He ~~want~~ very much to go to the basketball game.
wants

The waiter ~~ask~~ me how I ~~like~~ the food at Al's Barbecue.
asked *liked*

2 Using irregular forms correctly

Irregular verbs, unlike regular verbs, do not add -d or -ed to form the past tense or past participle. The past tense of *have,* for example, is not *haved* but *had.* The past participle of *eat* is not *eated* but *eaten.*

There are some patterns that appear among irregular verbs. For example, some verbs, such as *bet, bid, burst, cast, cut, hit,* and *quit,* do not change form for the past tense or past participle. Certain vowel changes provide another pattern: *ring, rang, rung; sing, sang, sung; drink, drank, drunk.* But these patterns are not reliable enough to predict. The past tense of *think* is not *thank,* nor is its past participle *thunk;* both the past and past participle are *thought.*

Since irregular verbs cannot easily be predicted, you need to try to memorize them. Whenever necessary, consult a dictionary that lists the forms of irregular verbs. Be sure to edit your papers carefully for the correct verb forms. (See the examples on pp. 486–488.)

She ~~seen~~ her mistake immediately.
saw

I've ~~knowed~~ all along that she would.
known

IRREGULAR VERBS

Base Form	Past Tense	Past Participle
arise	arose	arisen
awake	awoke, awaked	awaked, awoken
be	was, were	been
beat	beat	beaten, beat
become	became	become
begin	began	begun
bend	bent	bent
bet	bet	bet
bind	bound	bound
bite	bit	bitten, bit
blow	blew	blown
break	broke	broken
bring	brought	brought
broadcast	broadcast	broadcast
build	built	built
burst	burst	burst
buy	bought	bought
catch	caught	caught
choose	chose	chosen
cling	clung	clung
come	came	come
cost	cost	cost
creep	crept	crept
deal	dealt	dealt
dig	dug	dug
dive	dived, dove	dived
do	did	done
draw	drew	drawn
drink	drank	drunk
drive	drove	driven
eat	ate	eaten
fall	fell	fallen
feed	fed	fed
feel	felt	felt
fight	fought	fought
find	found	found
flee	fled	fled
fly	flew	flown
forbid	forbade	forbidden

(Continued)

forget	forgot	forgotten, forgot
forgive	forgave	forgiven
freeze	froze	frozen
get	got	gotten, got
give	gave	given
go	went	gone
grow	grew	grown
hang (suspend)	hung	hung
hang (execute)	hanged	hanged
have	had	had
hear	heard	heard
hide	hid	hidden
hold	held	held
hurt	hurt	hurt
keep	kept	kept
know	knew	known
lay (put)	laid	laid
lead	led	led
leap	leapt, leaped	leapt, leaped
leave	left	left
lend	lent	lent
let (allow)	let	let
lie (recline)	lay	lain
light	lit, lighted	lit, lighted
lose	lost	lost
make	made	made
mean	meant	meant
meet	met	met
mistake	mistook	mistaken
pay	paid	paid
prove	proved	proved, proven
quit	quit	quit
read	read	read
rid	rid	rid
ride	rode	ridden
ring	rang	rung
rise	rose	risen
run	ran	run
say	said	said
see	saw	seen
seek	sought	sought
sell	sold	sold

(Continued)

send	sent	sent
set	set	set
shake	shook	shaken
shoot	shot	shot
show	showed	shown, showed
shrink	shrank	shrunk
sing	sang	sung
sink	sank	sunk
sit	sat	sat
sleep	slept	slept
speak	spoke	spoken
spend	spent	spent
spin	spun	spun
spit	spit, spat	spit, spat
spring	sprang	sprung
stand	stood	stood
steal	stole	stolen
stick	stuck	stuck
sting	stung	stung
stink	stank, stunk	stunk
strike	struck	struck, stricken
swear	swore	sworn
swim	swam	swum
swing	swung	swung
take	took	taken
teach	taught	taught
tear	tore	torn
tell	told	told
think	thought	thought
throw	threw	thrown
wake	woke, waked	woken, waked
wear	wore	worn
win	won	won
write	wrote	written

3 **Using *sit* and *set* and *lie* and *lay* correctly**

Sit and *set* and *lie* and *lay* cause confusion because of their similar sounds and meanings. To distinguish them, remember that *sit* and *lie* never take direct objects (the ones with an *i* in them are **intransitive verbs**), while *set* and *lay* always take direct objects (they are **transitive verbs**). *Sit* means "to be seated"; *set*

SIT/SET AND LIE/LAY

Base Form	Past Tense	Past Participle	Present Participle
sit (to be seated)	sat	sat	sitting
set (to put or place)	set	set	setting
lie (to recline)	lay	lain	lying
lay (to put or place)	laid	laid	laying
lie (to tell a falsehood)	lied	lied	lying

SURE AND, TRY AND, GOT TO, HAVE GOT, COULD OF

The expressions *be sure and, try and,* and *got to* are colloquial and should be avoided in formal writing. The correct equivalents are *be sure to, try to,* and *must.*

Be sure ~~and~~ get there on time.
^ to

He promised to try ~~and not~~ be late.
^ not to

You ~~have got to~~ finish by Friday.
^ must

In formal writing, use a form of *have* in place of *has got* to indicate possession.

He's ~~got~~ a huge collection of fishing flies.
^ has

Do not use *could of, must of,* or *should of* in place of *could have, must have,* or *should have.*

She should ~~of~~ finished by now.
^ have

means "to put or place." *Lie* means "to recline"; *lay* means "to put or place."

INTRANSITIVE People *sit* outside when it's warm.

I always *lie* down after lunch.

TRANSITIVE   We *set* the books on the table.

Every morning I *lay* the mail on her desk.

4 Using *be* correctly

The verb *be* is an irregular verb that has many different forms. Every other English verb uses only two forms in the present tense: the base form and the *-s* (or *-es*) form: *I work, you work, we work, they work, she works.* The verb *be*, however, has three present-tense forms, all different from the base form: *I am, you are, we are, they are, he is.* Take special care to use the correct form.

are
These books ~~is~~ due back at the library next week.
      ^

Some speakers use the base form of *be* instead of the correct present-tense form, and others drop the verb entirely. Such usage is regarded as nonstandard in formal writing.

is
He ~~be~~ happy watching television.
   ^

are
We on our way over.
^

THE FORMS OF *BE*

The most irregular verb in English is *be*, which has three forms in the present tense and two forms in the past tense.

	Singular	Plural
PRESENT	I am	we are
	you are	you are
	he, she, it is	they are
PAST	I was	we were
	you were	you were
	he, she, it was	they were

These are the principal parts of *be:*

Base Form	*-s* Form	Past Tense	Past Participle	Present Participle
be	is	was, were	been	being

The three **simple tenses** place action in the present, past, or future. Notice that the future tense is expressed with the use of a modal auxiliary, *will.*

PRESENT   He *looks* happy today.

PAST   He *looked* a little depressed yesterday.

FUTURE   He *will look* different ten years from now.

The three **perfect tenses** indicate *action completed by a specific time.* They also are divided into present, past, and future.

The *present perfect tense* indicates action that was completed in the past or a completed action that has some relationship to the present.

PERFECT PRESENT She *has looked* for the file already.

       She *has looked* for it every day this week.

The *past perfect tense* indicates action completed before another past action took place.

PAST PERFECT She *had looked* for the file several times before she *found* it.

The *future perfect tense* indicates action that will be completed before some specific time in the future.

FUTURE PERFECT After she checks the computer room, she *will have looked* everywhere.

The three *progressive tenses* describe *continuing action in the present, past, or future.*

The *present progressive tense* describes continuous, temporary, or ongoing action in the present.

PRESENT   She is *anticipating* the holidays.
PROGRESSIVE

The *past progressive tense* describes continuous or ongoing action in the past, although not always with a specified conclusion.

PAST   Before her father's illness, she *was anticipating*
PROGRESSIVE the holidays.

The *future progressive tense* describes continuous or ongoing action in the future, often dependent on some other action or condition.

FUTURE
PROGRESSIVE
Once her father is better, she *will be looking* forward to the holidays again.

The three **perfect progressive tenses** describe *action continuing up to a specific time of completion in the present, past or future.*

The *present perfect progressive tense* describes ongoing action that began in the past and continues in the present.

PRESENT PERFECT
PROGRESSIVE
He *has been looking* for a job since August.

The *past perfect progressive tense* describes continuing action that was completed before some other action.

PAST PERFECT
PROGRESSIVE
Before he found work, he *had been looking* for a job since August.

The *future perfect progressive tense* describes continuous action that will be completed at some future time.

FUTURE PERFECT
PROGRESSIVE
Come August, he *will have been looking* for a job for six months.

VERBS THAT DO NOT HAVE A PROGRESSIVE FORM

Verbs that express actions, processes, or events can usually be used in a progressive *-ing* form to indicate that something is in progress: *She is writing lyrics for the new musical.* These verbs are called **dynamic verbs.** Most verbs fit into this category.

Other verbs express attitudes, conditions, or relationships. These verbs, called **stative verbs,** cannot be used in a progressive *-ing* form.

> believe
> I ~~am believing~~ your story.
>   ^

Here are some common stative verbs that are generally not used with *-ing* forms:

admire	cost	like	prefer
agree	disagree	love	seem
appear	dislike	need	sound
believe	hate	own	understand
belong	know	possess	want
contain			

EDITING 3: PRACTICE ────────────────────────

Edit the following passage twice, changing the verbs first to the present tense and then to the future tense.

> For one week at the beginning of each semester, sororities opened their houses to prospective members. The women wore their best dresses and carefully put on their makeup. Along with frozen hair went frozen smiles. Hundreds of young women moved from house to house, where they were looked over and judged. For some women this was an exciting time; for others it was humiliating and degrading.

34 e Using verb tenses in appropriate sequence

The *dominant* or **governing verb tense** in a piece of writing affects the choice of tense for nearly every verb. "If a melody in a major key is transposed into a minor key," Theodore M. Bernstein writes in *The Careful Writer*, "it is not just the first few notes that are modified; almost every phrase that follows undergoes change." In other words, all the verbs throughout a passage must relate logically to the governing tense. This logical relation is called the **sequence of tenses.**

Within a single sentence, the tense of the main clause limits what tenses make sense in a dependent clause. For example, the present-tense sentence *I think that I am lost* becomes *I thought that I was lost* in the past tense. It would make no sense to say *I thought that I am lost.* Still, many combinations of tenses are possible.

present   present
I think that you like foreign films.

present   past
I think that you misunderstood me.

present   future
I think that you will enjoy this movie.

Changing the tense of any verb in a sentence can change the meaning of the sentence. As you edit, check to make sure that all your choices make sense.

Sequence with habitual actions and universal truths

When a dependent clause expresses a habitual action or a universal truth, the verb in the dependent clause remains in the present tense regardless of the tense in the main clause.

He *told* me that he *works* for Teledyne.

Copernicus *showed* that the earth *revolves* around the sun.

Notice that this use of the present tense distinguishes between statements accepted as true and assertions that may or may not be true.

He *told* me he *worked* for IBM, but I *learned* later that he *works* for Teledyne.

Only the second dependent clause uses the present tense works *because only it expresses a habitual action.*

Sequence with direct and indirect quotation

Verbs in a direct quotation are not affected by the tense of other verbs in the sentence. The words within quotation marks should be precisely the words used by the speaker.

Nancy *said,* "My dog *is* chasing a squirrel!"

However, when you express someone else's words using indirect quotation, or indirect discourse, you should paraphrase, changing person and tense to make the quotation grammatically compatible with the rest of the sentence. (See 16d, 37a5.)

Nancy said that her dog ~~is~~ chasing a squirrel.
_{was}

Sequence with infinitives and participles

The tense of an infinitive or a participle is affected by the tense of a main verb. The base form of a verb preceded by *to* is the *present infinitive* (*to know*), sometimes called simply the infinitive. Use the present infinitive to show action occurring at the same time as or later than the action of the main verb.

PRESENT
INFINITIVE   Many children like *to play* video games.

The liking *and the* playing *take place at the same time.*

The professor wants to conduct a seminar for poets.

The seminar is in the future.

The *perfect infinitive* consists of the past participle preceded by *to have: to have known.* Use the perfect infinitive to indicate action that occurred before the action of the main verb.

PERFECT
INFINITIVE
The mayor *appears to have decided* not to seek reelection.

The deciding has already taken place.

Use the *present participle,* the *-ing* form of the verb, to show action taking place at the same time as the action of the main verb.

PRESENT
PARTICIPLE
Writing feverishly, he *worked* late into the night.

The writing *and the* working *take place at the same time.*

Use the *present perfect participle—having* plus the past participle—to show action completed before that of the main verb.

PRESENT PERFECT
PARTICIPLE
Having worked hard on the performance, she *was pleased* by the reviews.

She worked hard *before* being pleased *by the reviews.*

Use the *past participle* to show action taking place at the same time as or completed before the action of the main verb.

PAST PARTICLE
Guided by instinct, the swallows *returned* to Capistrano as usual on March 19.

The guiding *and the* returning *take place at the same time.*

John F. Kennedy, *born* in 1917, became the nation's youngest president in 1961.

Kennedy was born before he became president.

EDITING 4: PRACTICE

Edit the following passage, using appropriate verb tenses and putting them in a logical sequence. More than one edited version is possible. Be ready to explain your editing choices.

Many people thought that it will never happen, but Los Angeles finally opened a subway system. Perhaps you imagine that the name L.A. will

never be associated with public transit, because it was practically synonymous with the word *automobile*. When questioned, some people say that the new system, although it is modest so far, was a turning point for the city. If you have visited New York, which has more than 450 stations and hundreds of miles of tracks, you realize that the new system is quite small. On opening day, supporters of the new system had said that they hoped to have put the city's dollars toward building stations rather than freeways.

VERB MOOD

34 **f** **Understanding verb mood**

The **mood** of a verb expresses the speaker's attitude toward or relation to the action described.

- The **indicative mood** is used for statements of fact and opinion and for questions—for things that have happened or will happen.

  He *believes* that the theory *is* valid.

  When *did* she *graduate*?

- The **imperative mood** is used to give commands, orders, or directions. It consists of the base form of the verb and usually omits the subject, which is understood to be *you*.

  Open your exam book and *read* the instructions.

  Mix the eggs, milk, and vanilla and *fold* them into the dry ingredients.

- The **subjunctive mood** expresses wishes, desires, requirements, or conditions that the speaker knows not to be factual.

  The *present subjunctive* is simply the base form of the verb for all persons and numbers.

  I asked that she *leave* early to avoid traffic.

  The *past subjunctive* is the same form as the simple past tense for all verbs except *be*, which uses *were* for both singular and plural subjects. The time implied, however, is present or future.

  Even if I *had* time, I would not take up golf.

  If she *were* rich, would she be different?

The *perfect subjunctive* uses the past perfect tense form (*had* with the past participle) to show that the statement is not factual.

Had he *caught* the bear, he would have been very sorry.

For correct use of *could* and *would,* see 34g3.

`34` `g` Using the subjunctive mood

▌ In standard idiomatic expressions

The subjunctive appears in some idiomatic expressions such as *if I were you, as it were,* and *far be it from me.* As with other idioms, take care to word these phrases in the customary way.

Long live the Queen!

If he were to arrive on time, then all would go smoothly.

▌ After *as if, as though,* or *if*

In clauses beginning with *asj if* or *as though,* which always specify conditions that are not factual, use the past or perfect subjunctive.

He screamed as though the house ~~was~~ on fire. *[were]*

When a dependent clause beginning with *if* describes a condition contrary to fact, use the past or perfect subjunctive.

If only it ~~was~~ sunny, he would be happy. *[were]*

Note: When the *if* clause expresses an actual condition, the subjunctive is not needed.

If it was sunny, he was happy.

To suggest that the *if* clause expresses something uncertain rather than untrue, use the indicative rather than the subjunctive.

If she ~~were~~ awake, she should have heard the doorbell. *[was]*

▌ With *might, could, should,* and *would*

When one of the modal auxiliaries that express conditionality—*might, could, should, would*—is used in an independent clause, the

verb in the dependent clause can be either a subjunctive verb (*I would go if they invited me*) or an indicative (*I would go if they invite me*). However, if the dependent clause verb is a form of *be*, use the subjunctive.

were
I would go if there ~~would be~~ a good reason.
              ^

With *might have, could have, should have,* or *would have* (the conditional perfect) in the independent clause, use the perfect subjunctive, not another conditional modal auxiliary, in the dependent clause.

had
The president could have won if he ~~would have~~ fought harder.
                                    ^

4 **To express a wish, a requirement, or a request**

Use the past or perfect subjunctive in dependent clauses expressing wishes, which are usually contrary to fact.

had been
I wished there ~~was~~ some way to help them.
               ^

Dependent clauses following verbs stating requirements—such as *demand, insist, recommend, request, specify,* and *ask*—should use the present subjunctive.

dress
Courtesy requires that he ~~dresses~~ formally.
                          ^

go
Barbara insisted that she ~~goes~~ alone.
                          ^

The subjunctive makes a request sound a little more formal, and therefore perhaps a little more polite, than the indicative or the imperative.

SUBJUNCTIVE   We ask that you *be* seated.

INDICATIVE   We ask you *to be* seated.

IMPERATIVE   *Be* seated.

EDITING 5: PRACTICE ————————————————

Edit the following passage, using subjunctive verb forms wherever appropriate.

I was driving on the expressway when the earthquake occurred. The whole car began to shake as if the engine was about to stall. But quickly I realized what was happening. The drivers around me panicked, their faces contorted in fear. They swerved their cars, as though switching lanes save them.

If only I stayed home! If I was home, I thought, I can find shelter in the basement. In seconds, the cars ahead of me collided, blocking all traffic. The situation demanded that I acted quickly. I slammed on the brakes.

EDITING 6: PRACTICE

Edit the following passage, using the correct form, tense, and mood of each
verb. More than one edited version is possible. Be ready to explain your
editing choices.

Until the early years of this century, the Constitution does not extend to
women the right to vote. Suffragists wished that every woman citizen was
able to vote and they strived to amend the Constitution so that no state
can deny any citizen the right to vote on account of sex. For this to happen,
the Constitution required that three-quarters of the states were in favor of
the amendment. Many of the arguments against women's suffrage struck us
as absurd now. Some people argued that women do not understand the
business world; others said that the cost of elections will go up. If women
would get the vote, some worried, next they would want to hold office.
Some felt that a woman is represented by her husband and that when he
voted it was as though she is voting. Some also fear that a vote for women
will be a step toward feminism, which many people consider a radical and
dangerous idea.

EDITING 7: APPLICATION

Examine your recent writing for misused verb forms, tenses, and moods. Is there
one kind of verb error that you make most often? If so, think about how best to
identify your verb errors when you edit your work. Practice editing sentences
with incorrect verbs.

SUBJECT–VERB AGREEMENT

34 h Making subjects and verbs agree

Verbs and their subjects must **agree,** or correspond, in **person**
and in **number.** A singular subject requires a singular verb; a
plural subject requires a plural verb. The first-person pronoun *I* requires a different verb form from a third-person subject. Such
agreement, especially in a long sentence like this one in which
many words separate the subject from the main verb, helps readers
see relations between parts of the sentence. After seeing a singular

subject, such as *agreement* in the previous sentence, readers look for a singular verb, in this case *helps*, as the main verb of the sentence.

To solve agreement problems, first identify the subject. (See 62a.) Next, determine whether the subject is singular or plural. Then use the appropriate verb form.

Matters of agreement often come down to a single letter: *s*. Most English nouns form plurals by adding *-s* or *-es*.

SINGULAR	PLURAL
house	houses
rock	rocks
box	boxes

Most present-tense, third-person singular verbs end in *-s* or *-es*.

$$\left.\begin{matrix} \text{I} \\ \text{you} \\ \text{we} \\ \text{they} \end{matrix}\right\} \text{think} \qquad \left.\begin{matrix} \text{he} \\ \text{she} \\ \text{it} \end{matrix}\right\} \text{thinks}$$

A simple rule can guide you through many agreement problems: If the subject ends in *-s* or *-es* (is plural), the verb probably shouldn't; if the verb ends in *-s* or *-es* (is singular), the subject probably shouldn't.

The *road winds* through the mountains.

The *roads wind* through the mountains.

Irregular plurals such as *children* and *men* provide an exception to this rule. These plural nouns still require a verb without an *-s* or *-es*: *The children walk home.* Another exception is nouns that end in *-s* but are singular: *Economics is called "the dismal science."*

34 i Ignoring words between subject and verb

When a verb follows its subject immediately, it is usually easy to tell whether the verb should be singular or plural. When a word or words come between the subject and the verb, however, confusion can arise. Restating the sentence in its simplest form—just subject and verb—can help clarify your choice.

People interested in helping reelect an incumbent representative typically (*volunteer/volunteers*) time as well as money.

Reduced to subject and verb, the sentence reads People volunteer; *both subject and verb are clearly plural.*

Often, the intervening words are **prepositional phrases,** groups of words introduced by a preposition such as *of* or *with.*

The bowl of apples (*is*/*are*) very tempting.

Is the subject of the verb the singular bowl or the plural apples? Here, of apples *is a prepositional phrase.* Bowl *clearly is the subject, so the verb should be singular:* The *bowl* of apples *is* very tempting.

Intervening phrases that begin with such words as *including, as well as, along with, together with,* and *in addition to* are not part of a compound subject. (See 341.) You should ignore them in making decisions about subject–verb agreement. Try to think of them as parenthetical asides.

The president, along with many members of his party, ~~support~~ *supports*

stringent reforms.

34 **j** Finding the subject when it follows the verb

In some sentences the subject follows the verb.

Underneath the freeway overpasses (*huddle*/*huddles*) a ramshackle collection of cardboard shelters.

Mentally restoring normal word order to the sentence can help you find the subject.

A ramshackle *collection* of cardboard shelters *huddles* underneath the freeway overpasses.

The subject is collection, *which is singular, so* huddles *is correct.*

In a question, part of the verb almost always precedes the subject. As you edit, look for the subject after the verb, and make sure the verb agrees with it.

Are those *seats* next to you empty?

With so many chores, *is Juan* able to finish on time?

Expletives are words such as *it, here,* and *there* that begin a sentence with inverted word order. *Here* and *there* are never subjects, so look for the subject elsewhere in the sentence.

There *are* a million *stories* in the Naked City.

There *was* a *chance* that Marlin would catch Gordon.

However, when *it* is used in an expletive construction, it is considered the grammatical subject of the sentence. Because *it* is singular, it is always followed by a singular verb.

It is administrators who want this change, not students.

The constructions *there is, there are,* and *it is* are usually considered weak; for stronger alternatives, see 27b1.

34 k Creating agreement with linking verbs

Linking verbs include *be, become,* and *seem* and the sensory verbs *appear, look, feel, taste, smell,* and *sound.* They link the subject of a sentence to an element, called a **subject complement,** that renames or identifies the subject. Think of a linking verb as an equal sign between two equivalent terms.

Angela is captain.   Angela = captain
That looks difficult.   that = difficult

The term to the left of the equal sign is the subject; the term on the right of the equal sign is the subject complement.

Subject   Subject Complement

My paper's title is "Eliot's Rite of Spring."

      Subject   Subject Complement

"Eliot's Rite of Spring" is my paper's title.

The verb in such a sentence should always agree with the subject, not necessarily with the complement.

                         is
The thing that keeps him going ~~are~~ his hobbies.

Thing *is the subject;* hobbies *is the complement.*

EDITING 8: PRACTICE

Edit the following passage to make verbs agree with their subjects. Take special care in identifying the subject.

Throughout its history, the National Aeronautics and Space Administration (NASA) have been at the center of both controversy and praise. The exploration of the solar system, along with the research conducted by space shuttle crews, are hailed as significant human endeavors. The costs of these achievements, though, often becomes the subjects of newspaper headlines. Currently, there are many who think that federal government allocate too much money to NASA. Supporters, however, who credit the agency for spearheading developments in the aeronautics industry, points out that NASA's budget is the smallest of all major governmental agencies. Moreover, they say that the agency generate more revenue nationwide than it consume because of the new industries built upon space-exploration technology. Aeronautics, personal computers, telecommunications, and even weather forecasting depends on this technology, and these industries employ millions of Americans. Behind some of the most significant technological advances in American society are the team of researchers, engineers, and scientists working for NASA. Without them and the technology they have developed over the years, some entire industries today would not exist.

34 I Making verbs agree with subjects joined by *and*

When the conjunction *and* links two or more parts of a subject, it creates a **compound subject.** (Also see 36g.) Such a subject is almost always considered plural and thus requires a plural verb.

Peter and Patrick *appear* in the first act.

This rule has several exceptions. When the two elements joined by *and* are regarded as a single entity, the subject is considered singular and requires a singular verb.

is
Hare and hounds ~~are~~ my favorite game.
            ^

If all parts of a compound subject refer to the same person or thing, a singular verb is appropriate.

> has
> My friend, my partner, and my mentor ~~have~~ brought wisdom and
> ^
> courage to this firm.

The writer is referring to one person who is all three things.

When singular elements joined by *and* are preceded by *each* or
every, use the singular.

> has
> Each river, brook, and stream in the county ~~have~~ suffered
> ^
> pollution.

However, when *each* comes after a *compound subject* rather than
before it, the subject is plural.

> *deserve*
> Government and industry each ~~deserves~~ credit for the success of
> ^
> cleanup efforts.

---

34 m Making verbs agree with subjects joined by *or* and *nor*

The conjunctions *or, nor, either . . . or, not only . . . but also,* and
neither . . . nor also create compound subjects by linking two or
more elements. When one element of the subject is singular and
another is plural, convention dictates that the verb agree with the
part of the subject closer to it.

> Neither the senator nor the witnesses *are* ready for the hearing.
> Neither the witnesses nor the senator *is* ready for the hearing.

If a singular verb sounds awkward, try rearranging the subject to
put the plural part closer to the verb.

> One   or two crabs make
> ~~Two crabs or one~~ lobster ~~makes~~ an excellent dinner.
> ^   ^

EDITING 9: PRACTICE ———————————————————————

Edit the following sentences to make verbs agree with their compound subjects.
Circle the number of any sentence that is correct.

1. Neither the police officers nor the detectives knows how the intruder entered or
    left the house.

2. Each window and door are locked securely.

3. In addition, the outside security system and inside motion sensors shows nothing unusual last night.

4. Nonetheless both the house and the safe was broken into and all the money taken.

5. On the living room sofa, the banker and his wife sits weeping, lamenting their loss.

6. Not only their savings bonds but also their expensive jewelry was gone forever.

7. Police and specially trained dogs scours the grounds of the estate for clues, but not a single footprint or trace of evidence can be found.

8. Finally, the detectives and the police discover and nab the perpetrator, who were hiding in a broom closet.

34 n Making verbs agree with collective nouns

Collective nouns refer to groups of people or things: *couple, flock, crowd, herd, committee.* They can cause confusion because the words themselves have a singular form even though they refer to several individuals. Whether a collective noun takes a singular or plural verb depends on whether the members of the group are acting as individuals or as one unit. If the members of a group act individually, use a plural verb.

The jury *have* returned to their homes.

If such a construction sounds awkward to you, try replacing the subject with one that is clearly plural.

The members of the jury *have* returned to their homes.

If an action is taken by an entire group together as a unit, use a singular verb.

The jury *has* reached a verdict.

The collective noun *the number* refers to a group as a single unit, so it needs a singular verb.

The number of tourists *has* declined in recent years.

However, the expression *a number of* means "several" or "more than one," so it needs a plural verb.

VERB AGREEMENT WITH NONCOUNT NOUNS

Count nouns name persons, places, or things that can be counted: *one apple, two oranges*. **Noncount nouns** refer to things that can't be quantified, such as abstract concepts, emotions, and qualities. Sports and games, chemical elements, and weather are other categories that include noncount nouns.

Mass Nouns	Abstract Concepts	Emotions	Qualities	Food
equipment	behavior	anger	confidence	butter
furniture	education	happiness	honesty	rice
homework	health	love	integrity	outmeal
money	knowledge	surprise	sincerity	

Noncount nouns are usually used only with singular verbs. In English these words usually have no plural form.

>   *equipment makes*
> Good ~~equipments makes~~ the job easier.
>   ^
>
> *This information*   *is*
> ~~These informations~~ about subject–verb agreement ~~are~~ intended to help
>   ^
> you with your editing.

For information on using articles (*a, an, the*) with nouns, see the box in 35a.

A number of visitors *have* complimented the park management on the new trail markers.

34 o Making verbs agree with indefinite pronouns

Whether a pronoun is singular or plural usually depends on whether the word or words it refers to are singular or plural. In the sentence *My uncle enjoys fishing, and he often goes on fishing trips,* the pronoun *he* is singular (and takes a singular verb, *goes*) because it refers to a singular noun, *uncle.*

However, an **indefinite pronoun,** such as *someone, some, few, everyone, each, or one,* often does not refer to a specific person or thing. Most indefinite pronouns are either always singular or always plural.

SINGULAR   Everybody *has* heard that old joke already.

PLURAL   Luckily, few of the passengers *were* injured.

Although pronouns such as *everybody* and *someone* are singular, many people in everyday speech treat them as if they were plural in order to avoid sexist language: *Everybody has their mind made up.* In formal writing, this usage is considered incorrect. (See 31c for alternatives in formal writing.)

Some, any, all, more, most, what, and *none* can be either singular or plural depending on what they refer to.

Of the *time* that remained, more *was* spent in arguing than in making decisions.

Of the *hours* that remained, more *were* spent in arguing than in making decisions.

As you edit, try mentally recasting the sentence without the indefinite pronoun, using *it* or *they* if necessary to determine whether the pronoun is singular or plural.

Some of the children (*is/are*) eager to leave.

They are eager to leave.

All is plural when it means the total number in a group; it is singular when it means "everything" or "the only thing."

All of us *are* preparing for the examination.

All I have *is* twenty dollars.

None standing alone is always singular: *None was injured.* Followed by a prepositional phrase, *none* can be singular or plural, depending on the phrase.

None of the information *was* missing.

None of the players *were* gone.

Be aware that some experts argue that because *none* means "not one" or "no one," only the singular is strictly correct: *None of the players was gone.*

COMMON INDEFINITE PRONOUNS

ALWAYS SINGULAR

someone	anyone	no one	every	either
somebody	anybody	nobody	everyone	neither
something	anything	nothing	everybody	each
			everything	one
			much	

EITHER SINGULAR OR PLURAL

some	any	none	all	more
			most	what

ALWAYS PLURAL

few	both	several	many

ESL

VERB AGREEMENT WITH QUANTIFIERS

- *Few and a few*

  Few means "not many." *A few* means "some," "several," or "a small number." *Few* and *a few* take plural verbs.

Many law students are taking the bar exam today. *A few* have taken it in other states.

Few have failed it more than once.

- *Little and a little*

  Little means "not much." *A little* means "some" or "a small amount." *Little* and *a little* take singular verbs.

Doctors have done considerable research on heart disease. However, *little has been done* with women as subjects.

Be careful pouring that hot sesame oil. *A little goes* a long way.

- *Most of the and most*

Most of the (or *most of*) means "the majority of"; it takes a plural verb when it is followed by a plural noun or pronoun and a singular verb when it is followed by a noncount noun or a singular pronoun.

PLURAL   *Most of the dogs* in the neighborhood *bark* in the morning.

(Continued)

PLURAL	*Most dogs are* tied while their owners are at work [adjective *most* modifying plural *dogs*]
SINGULAR	*Most of the violence* on TV *is* unnecessary.
SINGULAR	*Most is* treated as harmless by TV producers. [pronoun *most* referring to *most of the violence*]

34 p Making verbs agree with *who, which,* and *that*

To decide whether a verb following the **relative pronouns** *who, which,* or *that* should be singular or plural, find the word for which the pronoun stands (its **antecedent**).

are
The dean and the department head, who ~~is~~ working on the search
                                              ^
committee, will meet with the candidates.

If the dean and the department head are both on the committee, the verb should be plural.

slips
A bale of shingles that ~~slip~~ off the roof could hurt someone.
                          ^

That refers to bale, so slips *is singular.*

Relative pronouns can be troublesome when they follow the construction *one of the* or *the only one of the.* If the relative pronoun refers to *one,* it is singular.

The only *one* of the experiments that *works* is mine.

If the relative pronoun refers to whatever comes after *one of the* or *the only one of the,* it is plural.

One of the areas that *were* cut most heavily *is* social spending.

EDITING 10: PRACTICE ⎯⎯⎯⎯⎯⎯⎯⎯⎯⎯⎯⎯⎯⎯

Edit the following sentences to make verbs agree with collective noun subjects, indefinite pronoun subjects, and relative pronoun subjects. Circle the number of any sentence that is correct.

1. The pictures in the exhibit, which are open every night, feature children from Third World countries.
2. Many of the children photographed in Mexico was casualties of the earthquake.
3. Most people think that the look of sadness on their faces are most moving.
4. The best of the photographers, who spend three months every year in Southeast Asia, has won numerous awards.
5. Adding photography exhibits to the museum was one of many good ideas of the curator, who is herself a photographer.

34 q Making verbs agree with subjects that refer to amounts

Words that describe amounts of time, money, distance, measurement, or percentage can take singular or plural verbs. As with collective nouns, the number depends on whether the subject is considered as a group of individuals (plural) or as a single unit or sum (singular).

Four *hours have* passed since we saw each other last.

The hours pass one at a time, individually.

Fifteen *minutes is* too long to keep the boss waiting.

The minutes here are a block of time, a unit.

34 r Using noun phrases and noun clauses

Noun phrases and **noun clauses** are groups of related words that function as a subject, object, or complement in a sentence. A *noun phrase* often lacks a subject or a predicate or both; a *noun clause* has both a subject and a predicate. All noun phrases and noun clauses are singular.

NOUN PHRASE   *Planning to write* is easy; actually writing is harder.

NOUN CLAUSE   *That he would not listen to us* was surprising.

34 s Using singular verbs with titles and with words used as words

Titles of books, plays, and movies are treated as singular even if they are plural in form. The name of a company is also singular.

Happy Days was a popular TV series.

General Motors is an important employer in Michigan.

In discussing a word itself, use a singular verb even if the word is plural.

"Hyenas" *was* what my father lovingly called us children.

34 t Recognizing singular subjects that end in *-s*

Although words such as *statistics, politics, economics, athletics, acoustics,* and *aesthetics* seem to be plural because they end in -s, they take singular verbs when used in a general sense to mean a field of study, a body of ideas, or a profession. However, some of these words can be plural when referring to specific instances, activities, or characteristics.

Economics *is* a field that relies on statistics.

The economics of the project *make* no sense.

Words that refer to an ailment such as AIDS or measles are usually singular. So is the word *news*.

34 u Recognizing troublesome plurals

Words such as *media* and *data* look like singular words in English, but they are Latin plurals and should take plural verbs. The corresponding singular forms are *medium* and *datum.* Look out, too, for *curriculum* and *curricula, criterion* and *criteria, phenomenon* and *phenomena.* The use of *data* as singular is gaining ground, especially in reference to computers, but you should avoid it in writing.

love
The media ~~loves~~ a political scandal.

ESL

SOME COLLECTIVE NOUNS THAT REQUIRE PLURAL VERBS

Some collective nouns are derived from adjectives and refer to a group of people: *the wealthy, the homeless, the elderly.* These nouns are considered plural and take plural verbs.

The *young* often *ignore* the advice of their elders.

The collective nouns *people* and *police* are always plural. The singular forms are *person* and *police officer.* The article *a* or the adjective *one* may be used before *people* to refer to a national or ethnic group, but the word is still plural. *A* is not used before *police.*

One people who *are* proud of their language *are* the French.

People are wondering who will be the next governor.

That *person is* wondering when to register to vote.

Police have been stationed in front of the house all afternoon.

A *police officer is* always on duty inside the courthouse.

support
The experimental data ~~supports~~ the theory you advanced.

Dictionaries list the preferred plural and singular forms of these and other words of foreign origin; some, like *stadium*, have lost their original plural forms completely.

Some nouns, such as *pants, sunglasses, binoculars,* and *scissors,* refer to single objects but take plural verbs.

The scissors *are* no longer sharp.

When the construction *pair of* is used, the verb is singular.

This pair of scissors *is* sharper.

EDITING 11: PRACTICE ───────────────────────────

Edit the following sentences by making verbs agree with their noun phrase or noun clause subjects, subjects that are titles or words used as words, or troublesome singular or plural subjects. Circle the number of any sentence that is correct.

EDITING FOR SUBJECT–VERB AGREEMENT

> To solve problems of agreement, first identify the subject. Next determine whether it is singular or plural. Then use the corresponding verb form. Remember the following tips as you edit.

- Ignore words between the subject and the verb.
- Identify the subject even when it follows the verb.
- Identify the subject of a linking verb.
- Determine whether subjects joined by *and* are singular or plural.
- Determine whether subjects joined by *or* or *nor* are singular or plural.
- Determine whether collective nouns are singular or plural.
- Determine whether indefinite pronouns such as *everything* and *some* are singular or plural.
- Determine whether relative pronouns such as *who, which,* and *that* are singular or plural.
- Determine whether subjects that refer to amounts are singular or plural.
- Use singular verbs with noun phrases and noun clauses.
- Use singular verbs with titles and with words used as words.
- Identify singular subjects that end in *-s*.
- Use plural verbs with troublesome plurals.

1. Although a course in statistics often baffle college students, studying aesthetics is also challenging, particularly in courses that compares the arts.

2. Sometimes one artistic medium, like painting and sculpture, tell us something new about a novel, for instance.

3. This semester we read *Pride and Prejudice,* which were written by Jane Austen, but we also examined paintings of country houses.

4. Comparing the novel with the paintings provide a clearer picture of Austen's descriptions.

5. Preparing for exams for my interarts classes sometimes seem difficult because we cover a lot of material.

EDITING 12: PRACTICE _____

Edit the following passage to make verbs agree with their subjects. More than one edited version is possible. Be ready to explain your editing choices.

The county employees and volunteers who run the prison education program focuses on illiteracy. Statistics shows that among prison inmates nationwide, some 60 percent is illiterate, and neither substance abuse programs nor vocational training seem as effective as literacy education in limiting the return of repeat offenders. The core of the program, therefore, are reading and writing skills. Each employee and volunteer go through a three-week training program in literacy education. If they can demonstrate sufficiently high reading levels, inmates may also train to become tutors.

EDITING 13: APPLICATION ─────────────────────────────

Examine a paper you are working on to find any verbs that do not agree with their subjects. What kinds of mistakes did you make? Do you make one kind of mistake more than others? If so, why do you think you do?

35   Using Modifiers Correctly

Adjectives and adverbs *modify* other words—that is, they describe, specify, or limit the meanings of other words. **Modifiers** can enrich description, changing a simple sentence like *The explorers were lost* into an expressive one like *The polar explorers were thoroughly, hopelessly, horribly lost.* To be effective, modifiers must be used carefully and according to convention.

35   a   Choosing adjectives or adverbs

Adjectives modify nouns and pronouns.

> noun   noun
> Many *deciduous* trees in the *mid-Atlantic* states are subject to

> noun
> attack by *voracious* insects.

> pronoun
> They are especially *vulnerable* during a drought.

Adverbs modify verbs, adjectives, or other adverbs.

> verb
> Drought *rapidly* weakens the trees' natural defenses, sometimes

> adjective
> with *truly* devasting consequences.

Many adjectives and adverbs are formed by adding **suffixes,** or endings to other words. (See 30c.) Adjectives are often formed by adding *-able, -ful, -ish,* and other endings to nouns or

521

USING ARTICLES WITH NOUNS

An **article** (*a, an, the*) is a special kind of adjective. Which one you select depends on the context and on the type of noun it precedes.

- Use the **indefinite article** *a* or *an* when you first mention a noun. At that point, its meaning is indefinite, not yet specified.

There is *a problem* with his approach. [an unspecified problem]

- Before unspecified singular nouns, you may also use *one* or a personal pronoun.

one person   our child

- Don't use an article before an unspecified plural noun.

Geese can be aggressive.

- Don't use an article before a noncount noun. (For a definition of noncount nouns, see 61a.)

The refugees demand *justice.*

- Before a plural or noncount noun, you may use *some* (or, in a negative sentence, *any*).

They want *some answers.* [plural]

They have not been given *any information.* [noncount, negative]

- Once the noun has been mentioned, use the **definite article,** *the.*

The problem begins in his assumptions. [the problem just mentioned]

- Use the definite article if the noun is made specific by context.

The premises that support his argument should not be accepted without question. [The premises are immediately specified.]

- Use the definite article when referring to a unique person, place, or thing.

The moon was setting as we awoke.

ARTICLES WITH PROPER NOUNS

Most proper nouns have no articles, but there are some exceptions. Ignore *The* as part of the formal name of an organization unless

(Continued)

> that organization is an important part of your audience, as in a job ap-
> plication to *The New York Times* or an admission letter to *The Ohio
> State University*.
>
> Britain   (*but* the United Kingdom)
> America   (*but* the United States—singular)
> Lake Michigan   (*but* the Mississippi River)
> Hawaii   (*but* the Hawaiian Islands)
> Roger Smith   (*but* the Smiths—plural)
> Second Street   (*but* the second street from here—common
>   noun)

verbs: *acceptable, beautiful, foolish.* Many adverbs are formed by
adding *-ly* to an adjective: *nearly, amazingly, brilliantly.*

In speaking, some people substitute adjectives for adverbs: *It
worked real well* rather than *It worked really well.* If this is a
speech habit of yours, edit your writing carefully to use only adverbs to modify verbs, adjectives, or other adverbs. Use adjectives
only to modify nouns and pronouns.

       badly
We played ~~bad~~ in the first inning.
       ^

An *-ly* suffix does not always mean that a word is an adverb:
brotherly, friendly, and *lovely,* for example, are adjectives. Also,
many adverbs do not end in *-ly: often, always, later.* Still other
words can be used as either adjectives or adverbs, such as *hard* or
fast. To be sure of the correct form, consult a dictionary. (Also
see 35c.)

EDITING 1: PRACTICE _____

Edit the following sentences, using adjectives and adverbs in the proper places.

1.   When I first started running competitive, I had all kinds of physical problems.

2.   My track coach told me that breathing too heavy was causing my painful
cramps.

3.   He suggested I take short, even breaths to help me run smooth.

4.   But once I perfected my breathing, my feet began to hurt real bad.

5.   I found out, to my great surprise, that I was pigeon-toed and that my shoes
did not fit correct.

6.   After a lot of looking, I found special track shoe.

35 b Using adjectives after linking verbs

Confusion about whether to use an adjective or an adverb arises occasionally with **linking verbs,** such as *be, become, feel, seem, appear, look, smell, taste,* and *sound.* A modifier after a linking verb usually modifies the subject of the verb, not the verb itself, so the modifier should be an adjective, not an adverb.

      bad
I felt ~~badly~~ about not being able to help.
      ^

Some of these verbs can also express action, in which case they do not function as linking verbs.

LINKING VERB   The ghost of Hamlet's father *appears* anxious.

Anxious *is an adjective modifying the noun* ghost.

ACTION VERB   The ghost of Hamlet's father *appears* suddenly.

Suddenly *is an adverb modifying the verb* appears.

EDITING 2: PRACTICE ─────────────────────────

Edit the following sentences, using adjectives and adverbs correctly after linking verbs. Circle the number of any sentence that is correct.

1.   One day, when Shelly first woke up, she seemed deliriously.
2.   She started talking, but her voice sounded harshly and raspy.
3.   I walked across the room and saw that she was pale and that her forehead was splotchy.
4.   I put my hand on it and, sure enough, her brow felt coldly and clammy.
5.   Fortunately one of our neighbors was a doctor, and she came over to see us.
6.   After she gave her some antibiotics, Shelly was able to sleep, and a few days later, she felt strongly and healthy again.

35 c Choosing between commonly confused modifiers

Several pairs of modifiers are commonly confused in everyday speech.

Bad and badly

In standard English, *bad* is always an adjective, *badly* always an adverb. Be sure to use them correctly, especially after linking verbs.

       bad   badly
She felt ~~badly~~ about doing ~~bad~~ on the test.

Good and well

Good and *well* share the same comparative and superlative forms: *good, better, best; well, better, best.* (See 35e.) *Good* is always an adjective. *Well* can be either an adjective or an adverb. As an adjective, *well* means "healthy," the opposite of *ill.* As an adverb, *well* means, among other things, "satisfactorily" or "skillfully." Do not use *good* as an adverb or *well* as an adjective meaning "satisfactory."

            well
She read ~~good~~ enough to get the part.

               good
My hat looked ~~well~~ on my mother.

Real and really

Real is properly used as an adjective meaning "genuine, true, not illusory": *They wondered whether the ghost was real. Really* is an adverb meaning "truly" or "very." Even if you sometimes use *real* as an adverb in speech, be careful as you edit to use *really* to modify adjectives and adverbs.

          really
He talks ~~real~~ fast.

Less and fewer

Use *less* to describe something considered as a whole unit: *less hope, less misery, less money.* Use *fewer* for quantities that can be counted: *fewer dreams, fewer problems, fewer dollars.*

                                 fewer
The house would lose less heat if ~~less~~ windows were open.

Few is always an adjective, but *less* can be used as an adverb.

Ventilation makes the heating system *less* efficient.

35 d Avoiding double negatives

In English, one negative modifier (*no, not, never, none*) is sufficient to change the meaning of a sentence. Although double negatives are common in some dialects, particularly when one of the negatives is a contraction, be sure in editing to make negative statements with only one negative modifier.

He didn't want ~~no~~ *any* dinner.

He ~~didn't have~~ *had* no money.

Using *no* or *not* with an adverb such as *hardly, barely,* or *scarcely* creates a double negative.

She ~~didn't~~ hardly ~~have~~ *had* time to catch her breath.

Sometimes you need a double negative to make a *positive* statement.

The issue was *not* that he had *no* money; he simply did not want to spend it.

He had money.

One acceptable double negative is *not without.*

The Curies' research on radium was *not without* risk, but the hazards of radiation were not yet understood.

EDITING 3: PRACTICE

Edit the following passage, using the correct form of any commonly confused modifiers and correcting any double negatives. More than one editing choice is possible.

Alan whispered to me one day in class that he was real hungry. I told him that I didn't have no food with me. He started mumbling something about how he couldn't be expected to do good on a chemistry exam when his stomach felt so badly. I couldn't see hardly no reason for him to complain so much. Everybody knew that he always brought lunches to school with him. In fact, the more I thought about it, the more I realized that nobody had less reasons to complain about being hungry than Alan. What made me even angrier, though, was that now he had made me want a snack.

USING NEGATIVES: *NOT* VS. *NO*

- Use *not* in a negative verb phrase.

I *do not* agree with the author's opinion

The professor *did not assign any* homework.

Use any with the object of a negative verb. (See 35d.)

- Use *no* or *not one* with nouns.

The professor assigned *no homework.*

There are *no places* to sit in the theater.

There is *not one* empty seat.

Use not one only with a count noun.

- These negative adverbs can be used in verb phrases:

never   almost never
rarely   hardly ever
seldom   scarcely ever

We *seldom* agree.

Rarely do I cook for myself.

Starting a sentence with one of these negative adverbs calls for inverted word order.

- Note the difference in the meanings of these negated pronouns:

No one can solve that problem.

It cannot be solved.

Not everyone can solve that problem.

Some people can solve the problem, but others cannot.

- Note the difference in the meanings of the negated pronoun and the negated verb in the following examples:

Not everyone is here yet.

Some are here, but not all.

(Continued)

Everyone is *not* here yet.

No one is here yet.

- To emphasize negation, negate a noun with *no* instead of negating the verb with *not.*

NEGATIVE   *I do not see any reason to assume he is lying.*

EMPHATIC   *I see no reason to assume he is lying.*

---

35 e Using comparatives and superlatives

The basic or **positive form** of an adjective or adverb describes a quality or property: *large, delicious, late, graciously.* The **comparative form,** which usually ends in *-er* or is preceded by *more,* compares two people or things.

She arrived *later* than I did but was greeted *more graciously.*

The **superlative form,** usually ending in *-est* or preceded by *most,* makes a comparison among three or more people or things.

Of all their guests, she always arrived *latest* and was greeted *most graciously.*

Your choice of a comparative or a superlative modifier gives readers an important clue about the nature of the comparison.

Of the brothers, Joe was the *stronger* athlete.

Of the brothers, Joe was the *strongest* athlete.

The first sentence says that there are only two brothers, while the second indicates that there are at least three brothers.

Forming regular comparatives and superlatives

Most one-syllable adjectives and adverbs add *-er* and *-est* to form comparatives and superlatives: *smarter, closest.* There are exceptions such as *wrong, more wrong,* not *wronger.* Adjectives of three or more syllables, adjectives ending in *-ful,* adverbs of two or more syllables, and most adverbs ending in *-ly* generally use *more* and *most: more impressive, most hopeful, most often, most sharply.*

ARTICLES WITH COMPARATIVES AND SUPERLATIVES

When a comparative adjective (*warmer, easier*) is used by itself, do not use an article (*a, an,* or *the*).

This house is ~~the~~ *larger* than the other one.

DEFINITE ARTICLE *THE*

Use *the* when a comparative or superlative adjective is followed by a specific noun or by a pronoun renaming a specific noun.

This house is *the larger* one.

This house is *the largest* one.

The use of *the* is optional when the comparative or superlative adjective is used without a noun but the noun is implied.

Of the two houses, which one is *the larger?* [implied; *the larger* house]

Of the two houses, which one is *larger?*

INDEFINITE ARTICLES *A/AN*

Use *a* or *an* with comparative adjectives modfying a noun that is not specific.

I've never seen *a larger* grapefruit.

The grapefruit mentioned is any grapefruit, not a specific grapefruit.

Use *a* or *an* with superlative adjectives only if the superlative has the meaning "very."

That was *a most refreshing* glass of grapefruit juice.

The meaning is "very refreshing."

For more about article usage, see the box in 35a.

With many two-syllable adjectives, the choice is yours (*happiest, most happy; luckiest, most lucky*), although the *-er* and *-est* endings are more common.

Negative comparisons are formed using *less* for comparatives and *least* for superlatives: *less often, least hopeful.*

2 Avoiding double comparatives and superlatives

Use either -er or *more*, not both. Use either -est or *most*, not both.

Eating made him feel ~~more~~ better.

3 Forming irregular comparatives and superlatives

A few adjectives and adverbs form comparatives and superlatives in irregular ways. Take care to memorize them, especially if English is not your first language.

better
Paul did ~~gooder~~ on the test than I did.
^

better
She said she felt ~~weller~~ today.
^

4 Using only the positive form of absolute modifiers

Some modifiers, called **absolutes,** do not logically form comparatives or superlatives because their meaning suggests comparison is inappropriate. Words such as *perfect, unique, equal, essential, final, total,* and *absolute* should not be intensified. As you edit, make sure that you have not used *more* or *most* with such words.

The turbo engine makes this car ~~even more~~ unique.

  IRREGULAR ADJECTIVES AND ADVERBS

Positive	Comparative	Superlative
good	better	best
well	better	best
bad	worse	worst
badly	worse	worst
ill	worse	worst
many	more	most
much	more	most
some	more	most
little*	less	least

*Little in the sense of "not much" is irregular. Little in the sense of "small" is regular: She wanted a little dog, but mine is littler than hers, and my cousin's is littlest of all.

CHOOSING THE RIGHT MODIFIER

As you edit, examine your adjectives and adverbs carefully and make sure to do the following:

- Choose an adjective or adverb according to the part of speech that it modifies.
- Use adjectives after linking verbs.
- Choose correctly between commonly confused modifiers.
- Avoid double negatives.
- Use comparatives and superlatives correctly.

EDITING 4: PRACTICE _____

Edit the following passage, using the correct comparative and superlative forms of adjectives and adverbs. More than one edited version is possible. Be ready to explain your editing choices.

Do students from other countries perform better or worser than American students? Over the past decade, American scores on standardized tests have been declining steadilier in the United States than in other countries. Scores in Japan and Germany are often much more strong. Of those two countries, Japan's scores are usually highest. U.S. educators need to take a more closer look at preparing students for the challenges of an international labor market. Traditional methods of teaching may not be the most perfect. The most new methods and may help students learn gooder.

EDITING 5: PRACTICE _____

Edit the following passage, using adjectives and adverbs correctly. More than one edited version is possible. Be ready to explain your editing choices.

The "guru of alternative medicine," Andrew Weil, M.D., has harshly criticism for mainstream doctors and their methods. He draws his ideas various from traditional Asian methods, Native American traditions, and more new disciplines such as hypnosis, magnetism therapy, and feedback control. He argues that mainstream medicine relies too heavy on scientific methods, ignoring the important role of the mind in controlling disease, which he believes is real important. To Weil, much diseases can be best understood in terms of the mind's relationship to the body. To his critics, Weil's work

shows few evidence of the kind of careful collected data that mainstream medicine relies on to evaluate its methods. Those critics, including Arnold S. Relman, editor-in-chief emeritus of the *New England Journal of Medicine*, claim Weil's ideas need to be tested thorougher in the same ways that new surgical techniques or pharmaceutical products receive routinely evaluation.

EDITING 6: APPLICATION _____

Take a few moments to reflect on the difficulties you most commonly have with the correct use of adjectives and adverbs. Now examine a piece of your own writing to see whether you have incorrectly used any. Do you see any patterns in the kinds of mistakes you make most often? Did you accurately predict where your problem areas would be? Edit any sentences that contain mistakes.

35 f Placing modifiers correctly

In English, word order affects meaning: *The man ate the fish* does not mean the same thing as *The fish ate the man.* Word order problems in writing often involve **modifiers.** If a modifier's placement does not make clear what it modifies, readers may misinterpret the sentence. *They want only her to sing this song* means something different from *They want her to sing only this song.*

Because readers usually assume that a modifier modifies the nearest grammatically acceptable element, a **misplaced modifier** may seem to modify the wrong element, not the one the writer intended. When editing, move the modifier close to the word modified.

We wanted our ordeal to end desperately.

Unless the writer intended things to turn out badly, the adverb desperately *is misplaced.*

in a glass jar
He took a frog to biology class ~~in a glass jar.~~

It seems unlikely that the biology class was held in a glass jar.

Modifiers such as *almost, even, hardly, just, merely, nearly, only, scarcely,* and *simply* are called **limiting modifiers.** They create an implicit contrast: to say that *only A is true* implies that *B* and *C* are not true. Readers understand a limiting modifier to modify the sentence element that directly follows it. Consider the differ-

ence in meaning created in the following sentences by moving the limiting modifier *just*:

> *Just* the children applauded the conductor.
>
> *Only the children, not the adults, applauded.*
>
> The children *just* applauded the conductor.
>
> *They applauded but did nothing else.*
>
> The children applauded *just* the conductor.
>
> *The children applauded the conductor and no one else.*

A **squinting modifier,** one that seems to modify two things at once, appears between two sentence elements that it might modify—and seems to look in both directions at once.

> Students who follow directions *consistently* score well on standard-
>
> ized tests.
>
> *What occurs consistently, the following of directions or the scoring well on tests?*

To edit a squinting modifier, decide which sentence element you want it to modify, and then reposition it or otherwise rearrange the sentence so that no other interpretation is possible.

> consistently
> **Students who follow directions ~~consistently~~ score well on stan-**
> **dardized tests.**

> consistently
> **Students who follow directions ~~consistently~~ score well on stan-**
> **dardized tests.**

EDITING 7: PRACTICE ───────────

Edit the following passage, moving any misplaced modifiers. More than one edited version is possible. Be ready to explain your editing choices.

> Most people assume that black bears hibernate incorrectly all winter. During the winter, although sleeping deeply, a true state of hibernation is not achieved by black bears. Their body temperature only drops a little, and one can wake up a black bear with just a little effort. Preparing to sleep for

several months, a very large amount of food is eaten by the bears. This way, they can store fat and feed off it all winter while they are sleeping. The female surprisingly gives birth to her young at this time.

35 g Eliminating dangling modifiers

A **dangling modifier** cannot be attached logically to anything in the sentence. Either the element that the modifier is intended to modify does not appear in the sentence, or it does not appear in a grammatically appropriate form. Readers interpret a dangling modifier as modifying the nearest grammatically acceptable element, which may not be what the writer had in mind. Often a dangling modifier consists of a prepositional phrase or verbal phrase at the beginning of a sentence.

Running through the rain, our clothes got soaked.

Clearly, it was we who were running through the rain, not our clothes. But we does not appear in the sentence, only our, which cannot be modified by the phrase Running through the rain.

In a sense, it is the reader who is left dangling, wondering what the writer meant. When editing a dangling modifier, introduce an element that logically can be modified, or change the form of an existing element. Then place it directly after the modifier.

she earned an A on
Having done well on her research, the paper ~~earned her an A.~~

When her *becomes* she *and is inserted after the modifying phrase, the sentence makes sense.*

When the main clause is in the passive voice, an introductory phrase often has no subject to modify. One solution is to place the sentence in the active voice. (See 27c.)

we fixed
Preparing for the experiment, several slides ~~were fixed~~ with dye.

Who was preparing? The sentence doesn't say, so insert a subject.

researchers have forced
To study the effects of cigarette smoking, monkeys ~~have been forced~~ to inhale the equivalent of a hundred cigarettes a day.

Clearly, the monkeys are not conducting the research.

Edit the following passage, clarifying squinting modifiers and eliminating dangling modifiers. More than one edited version is possible. Be ready to discuss your editing choices.

> Examining the patient death rates of more than fifty doctors, the results were compared by a panel to a statistical average. Having a better than average rate, a minus score was entered for those doctors. A positive score was entered for those who had worse than average rates. Consisting of only the doctors with positive scores, the panel released a list of names to a local newspaper. After reading the article, a protest was lodged by the county medical society. Doctors who criticized the study strongly argued that the scoring was biased.

35 h Moving disruptive modifiers

A modifier that disrupts the flow of a sentence may confuse readers or distract, inadvertently, their attention from your meaning. In the previous sentence, for example, there are several better places for *inadvertently*. **Disruptive modifiers** include those that split an infinitive, those that divide verb phrase, and those that needlessly separate major sentence elements.

Modifiers that split infinitives

An infinitive consists of the base form of a verb preceded by *to: to fly, to grow, to achieve.* Whenever possible, avoid placing modifiers between *to* and the verb, which is called **splitting an infinitive.** Many instructors and readers regard this construction as a mark of careless writing.

> smoothly.
> He attempted to ~~smoothly~~ mix the ingredients.

Many instructors will not object to a split infinitive if it is difficult to find a natural-sounding alternative.

> The snow was just enough *to lightly dust* the city, which twinkled in the evening light.

> *The alternatives* lightly to dust the city *or* to dust the city lightly, which twinkled *both sound forced.*

However, do not split an infinitive with a lengthy modifier.

ESL **PLACING FREQUENCY ADVERBS WITHIN VERB PHRASES**

When an adverb is used between elements of a verb phrase—such as *has been happening* or *will remember*—it usually appears after the first auxiliary verb.

Our baseball stadium has *rarely* been filled to capacity this season.

In questions, the adverb appears after the first auxiliary verb and the subject and before the other parts of the verb.

In the past, have you *usually* found yourself writing a paper the day before it's due?

When *not* is used to negate another adverb, it should appear directly after the first auxiliary verb and before the other adverb.

This newspaper does *not usually* put sports news on the front page.

Not *negates* usually; not usually *means "seldom."*

Not should appear after the adverb when being used to negate the action expressed by the main verb.

The senators have *often not* paid much attention to those who elected them.

Not *negates* paid.

She wanted to ~~as soon as possible~~ try rock climbing. as soon as possible.

You can also edit the sentence to eliminate the infinitive altogether.

The director ~~wanted to vividly re-create~~ a bullfight for the theater audience. wanted a vivid re-creation of

2 Modifiers that split verb phrases

A **verb phrase** consists of one or more auxiliary verbs, such as a form of *be* or *have,* and a participle or base form: *had been formed, does happen.* Most instructors will accept a single adverb (or *not* plus another adverb) placed between the elements of a verb phrase.

Some early settlements in the New World have *inexplicably* vanished without a trace.

However, an intervening phrase or clause will be considered disruptive, so rewrite the sentence.

~~The Roanoke colony had, by~~ By the time a supply ship arrived four
the Roanoke colony had
years later, disappeared without a trace.

3 Modifiers that separate major sentence elements

Placing modifiers often means balancing conflicting goals. On the one hand, placing major sentence elements such as subjects, verbs, objects, and complements near each other helps make their relationships clear. On the other hand, any word modifying one of those elements needs to be close to that element and thus risks disrupting one of those primary relationships, causing readers to forget where the sentence was originally heading. When deciding where to put a modifier clause or phrase, try to minimize disruption and yet place the modifier so that what it modifies is clear.

Because of her great popularity with audiences,
Mary Pickford, ~~because of her great popularity with audiences,~~ became the first silent film actor to be publicized by name.

never a stronghold of slavery.
Kentucky was, even though it had residents who fought for the Confederacy during the Civil War, ~~never a stronghold of slavery.~~

POSITIONING MODIFIERS APPROPRIATELY

When editing to position modifiers appropriately, do the following, consulting this chapter as necessary:

- Reposition misplaced modifiers close to the word modified.
- Clarify which element is modified by a squinting modifier and move it.
- Eliminate dangling modifiers by adding the elements they should modify.
- Find a better position for any modifier that disrupts the sentence flow.

EDITING 9: PRACTICE

Edit the following passage, moving disruptive modifiers for easier reading. More than one edited version is possible. Be ready to discuss your editing choices. What effect do the many disruptions have on you as a reader?

> To persuasively write, one must keep always in mind one's audience. An effective argument requires, because one cannot assume that a potential reader knows as much about the topic as the writer, a good introduction. In addition, an argument essay should, for the sake of clarity, explain any unfamiliar terms or technical language it employs. The most important point to remember though, is to clearly articulate one's thesis early in the essay. The thesis statement, because we want our readers to concentrate on the arguments we make to support our position and to not have to needlessly struggle to figure out what that position might be, must be direct and unambiguous. If the thesis is strong, key terms are defined, and sufficient background is provided, the writer of a persuasive essay should feel confident that the reader will impartially consider the merits of the writer's argument.

EDITING 10: PRACTICE

Edit the following passage for correct use of modifiers. More than one edited version is possible. Be ready to explain your editing choices.

> Striking millions of Americans, some people only are afflicted by insomnia occasionally, while other people live with it for several years. Having experienced mild, occasional sleeplessness, your insomnia shouldn't be considered a major concern. The causes from which it stems most often are quite simple. Having something troubling or exciting on your mind, exerting too much physical or mental activity before bedtime, having a mild fever, drinking too much caffeine, or eating a heavy meal, sleeplessness might occur. Changing your schedule or surroundings, insomnia can also result. The way to best ensure a good night's sleep is to consistently follow a few simple steps. Try to go to bed at the same time every night. Sleep on a comfortable bed in a dark room. Realizing that it is still, after twenty minutes, hard to fall asleep, it is helpful for you to get up and do something, such as read, until you feel drowsy. And remember to always avoid caffeine and heavy foods as well as strenuous activity before bedtime.

EDITING II: APPLICATION

Take a few moments to reflect on any difficulties you have with misplaced, squinting, or dangling modifiers. Now examine a paper you are working on and see whether you have positioned modifiers correctly. Do you notice any patterns of error? Edit any sentences that need correction.

36   Using Pronouns Correctly

Pronouns serve as stand-ins for nouns, noun phrases, or other pronouns. Unless readers can tell what word a pronoun such as *she* refers to, they may find themselves asking, "She who?" Readers should know that you are talking about Maya Angelou or Joan of Arc or whomever.

The word for which a pronoun substitutes is called its **antecedent** (from Latin roots meaning "to go before"). Although antecedents normally appear before pronouns that refer to them, sometimes they follow the pronouns. In either case, there must be no conflicting choices to confuse readers. This chapter focuses on clarifying pronoun reference, on ensuring that pronouns agree with their antecedents, and on choosing the correct pronoun case. (See 61b for a complete list of the various types of pronouns.)

PRONOUN REFERENCE

36   a   Establishing a clear antecedent

A pronoun with more than one possible antecedent can create confusion.

> Vice President Cheney met with President Bush after *he* returned to Washington.

Who was returning, Bush or Cheney? Because *he* could refer to either, the meaning is unclear. Edit such a sentence so that the pronoun has only one possible antecedent. You can eliminate the pronoun if the result does not seem awkward.

>   *Cheney*
> Vice President Cheney met with President Bush after ~~he~~ returned to Washington.

You can also place the pronoun so that confusion is less likely.

After
Vice President Cheney met with President Bush after he returned
to Washington. , he

You can use *the former* or *the latter* instead of a pronoun.

the former
Vice President Cheney met with President Bush after he returned
to Washington.

Paraphrasing a direct quotation can sometimes create confusion about antecedents. Using the direct quotation can sometimes avoid the problem.

, "You   "
Peter told Patrick that he had passed the test.

The closer a pronoun and its antecedent appear to each other, the more easily readers can spot the relationship between them. If many words intervene, the reader may lose the connection. In the following passage, by the time readers get to *he* in the fourth sentence, they may have forgotten *Galileo* is the antecedent. Find a place to introduce the pronoun earlier, or use the antecedent again.

In the seventeeth century, the Italian scientist Galileo Galilei upset the Catholic church by publishing a scientific paper asserting that the Earth revolved around the sun. That assertion contradicted contemporary church belief, which held that the Earth was the center of the universe. The paper also violated a papal order
that Galileo had accepted
of sixteen years earlier not to "hold, teach, or defend" such a doc-
Galileo
trine. Under pressure from the church, he recanted his theory of
Galileo
the Earth's motion, but even as he recanted, he is said to have
whispered, "Eppur si muove" ("Nonetheless it moves").

EDITING 1: PRACTICE ────────────────────────────

Edit the following passage by making each pronoun refer clearly to a single antecedent. More than one edited version is possible. Be ready to explain your editing choices.

Diane spotted Laura as she was beginning her regimen of stretching exercises. It was twenty minutes before the race was due to begin. Diane told Laura that she thought she would win the race. She was just plain faster. Laura responded that she had a good chance but that she was going to be tough to beat. Nodding in agreement, Diane shook hands with Laura. "Good luck," she said. "Have a good race."

36 b Providing explicit antecedents

Most pronouns need explicit antecedents. (Indefinite pronouns, such as *somebody, everybody,* and *no one,* are exceptions. See 36j.) A pronoun whose antecedent is merely implied may confuse readers.

Interviews with several computer programmers made *it* seem like a fascinating career.

What does *it* stand for? A reader might guess that *it* stands for *computer programming,* since this is a possible career, but *computer programming* does not appear in the sentence. To edit such a sentence, substitute a noun for the pronoun, use another pronoun that can refer to something already explicit in the sentence, or provide a clear antecedent for the pronoun.

Interviews with several computer programmers made ~~it~~ programming seem like a fascinating career.

Interviews with several computer programmers made ~~it~~ theirs seem like a fascinating career.

Interviews with several ~~computer programmers~~ people in programming made it seem like a fascinating career.

Providing grammatically acceptable antecedents

An antecedent must be a noun, a noun phrase, or another pronoun. Usually, it cannot be the possessive form of a noun or an adjective or other modifier. As you edit, make sure that any pronoun refers to a grammatically acceptable antecedent.

among the committee members
The ~~committee's~~ bitter argument reflected badly on all of *them*.

A possessive form of a noun or pronoun can be an antecedent, however, if the pronoun that refers to it is also possessive.

The *committee's* argument reflected badly on all of *its* members.

2 Supplying explicit antecedents for *this, that,* and *which*

Confusion can arise when *this, that,* or *which* has two possible antecedents.

No one has suggested taxing health care. *This* is unlikely.

What is unlikely, the taxing of health care or the chance that anyone would suggest it? You can usually clarify the reference by restating the antecedent that you intend.

tax
No one has suggested taxing health care. This is unlikely.

When *which* and *that* (and *who* and *whom*) introduce clauses, they are called **relative pronouns.** Usually, a relative pronoun introduces a clause that immediately follows the pronoun's antecedent.

This book, *which I heartily recommend,* is out of print.

If other elements intervene or if the relative pronoun has more than one possible antecedent, confusion can result. To clarify, you can provide an unambiguous antecedent, or you can replace *which* or *that* with another construction.

a response that
She took the situation seriously, ~~which~~ I found laughable.
though   it
She took the situation seriously, ~~which~~ I found laughable.

EDITING 2: PRACTICE

Edit the following passage by making all pronouns refer to explicit antecedents. More than one edited version is possible. Be ready to explain your editing choices.

Thank you for giving me the chance to tour your videotape recycling facility. It gave me an excellent glimpse of what it is all about. I especially

USING *THIS* AND *THAT*

> The demonstrative adjectives *this* and *that* mean "near" and "far," respectively. This concept of distance can apply to space or time.
>
> *This* vase right here is a better choice than *that* one in the back of the store.
>
> *That* article I showed you last week was very technical.
>
> *This* book I just found is more readable.
>
> She has been very happy from *that* day to *this.*

enjoyed the knowledge and wit of Bob Jones, our tour guide, which kept everyone in our group interested in the process. Bob showed us examples of tapes before and after they are refurbished, and that was incredible. Before processing, the tapes are scuffed and covered with labels, and after the workers finish their efforts, they look brand new. I know some people are skeptical about recycled videotapes, which I find somewhat understandable. But your recycling lines help the environment, even if in a small way. Each year corporations throw thousands of videotapes away, which pollute the environment. We need to recycle not just cans, paper, and bottles, but everything we can. He made this clear to us before we left it.

36 c Replacing a vague *it, they,* or *you*

In casual speech, people often use *it, they,* and *you* with no definite antecedent. In academic writing, however, indefinite uses of *it, they,* and *you* should be avoided in favor of more specific constructions.

      The   report   said
~~It said on the~~ news this morning that the game was canceled.

The police
~~They~~ tow away any car that is illegally parked.

                       local residents
If the weather doesn't clear, ~~you~~ could see flooding.

You may be used to address the reader directly (as in *You should use specific nouns whenever possible*), but in academic writing, do not use *you* to mean "people in general." One way to avoid

reliance on *you* is to use indefinite pronouns such as *one* or *someone* that refer to an unspecified third person.

The pronoun *it* has three common uses. First, *it* can function as a personal pronoun: *I want to read the book, but Shana won't let me borrow* it. Second, *it* can be used to introduce a sentence in which the subject and verb are inverted: It *is necessary to apologize.* (See 34j.) Third, *it* appears in idiomatic constructions about time, weather, and distance: It *is ten past twelve.* In speech, few people notice if these senses of *it* are mixed. In writing, however, you should avoid using the same word in different senses in the same sentence.

Remember
~~It is important to remember~~ that once the exam begins, it will be
two hours before ~~it breaks for~~ intermission.

EDITING 3: PRACTICE

Edit the following passage by clarifying all uses of the pronouns *it, they,* and *you.* Make any changes in wording needed for smooth reading. More than one edited version is possible. Be ready to explain your editing choices.

They say that you shouldn't believe everything you read in the newspaper. It is foolish to assume that it is possible for it to report the news accurately all of the time. You can't expect that reporters and editors will never make mistakes. Sometimes they receive late-breaking stories and have to rush to edit them before it goes to press. Occasionally you even can see contradictions between two articles on the same topic. It will say one thing in one article and then it will say something different in the other. It is when this happens that it is hard for you to know which article you should believe.

36 d Choosing *who, which,* or *that*

In general, *who* is used for people or animals with names; *which* and *that* are used for objects, ideas, unnamed animals, and anonymous people or groups of people.

Black Beauty is a fictional horse *who* lives in a world that has now disappeared.

Jake tried to rope the last steer, *which* twisted to avoid him.

This is the policy *that* the administration wants to enforce.

The tribes *that* built these cities have long since vanished.

(The difference between *who, whom,* and *whose* is one of case. See 36q.)

Most writers avoid using *which* to refer to people.

whom
I have met many actors, of ~~which~~ Jim Carrey is the funniest.
^

If using *of which* to refer to an inanimate object results in an awkward construction, substitute *whose.*

whose
This is an idea ~~the~~ time ~~of which~~ has come.
^

CHOOSING BETWEEN *WHICH* AND *THAT*

How can you tell whether to use *which* or *that?* The choice often depends on whether the modifier to be introduced is restrictive or nonrestrictive

- A **restrictive modifier** is one that is necessary to identify what it modifies. It restricts, or limits, what it modifies in such a way that it is essential to the meaning of the sentence. It can be introduced by either *which* or *that* and is never set off by commas.

All the courses *that are offered free of charge* are held in the evenings.

The modifier that are offered free of charge *restricts (limits) the larger entity. All the courses* to those held in the evening. The implication is that there may be other courses that are not free.

- By contrast, a **nonrestrictive modifier** merely adds more information, not affecting the meaning of the sentence. It is introduced only by *which* (not by *that*) and is set off by commas.

All the courses, which are offered free of charge, are listed in the catalog.

All the courses are listed. The commas indicate that which are offered free of charge *doesn't limit or help identify the subject.*

- Although some people prefer *that* for all restrictive modifiers, *which* is acceptable as well.

When in the course of human events it becomes necessary for one people to dissolve the political bands *which* have connected them with another . . . a decent respect for the opinions of mankind requires that they should declare the reasons *which* impel them to the separation.[Italics added]

DECLARATION OF INDEPENDENCE

(Continued)

• *Who* may introduce either restrictive or nonrestrictive modifiers.

NONRESTRICTIVE Americans, *who* tend to eat a richer diet than Europeans, have rising rates of heart disease.

The nonrestrictive who *clause adds information about Americans in general.*

RESTRICTIVE Americans *who* curb their appetites for rich foods may live longer than those *who* don't.

The restrictive who *clause is necessary to identify the subject fully—in this case, just certain Americans.*

For more on restrictive and nonrestrictive clauses, see 39c.

 STRATEGIES FOR CLARIFYING PRONOUN REFERENCE

To clarify pronoun reference, edit your sentence using the following strategies.

• Make sure a pronoun clearly refers to a single antecedent.
• Place a pronoun close to its antecedent.
• Provide an explicit antecedent.
• Use *it, they,* and *you* appropriately.
• Avoid overusing *it.*
• Choose *who, which,* or *that* according to the antecedent.
• Eliminate unneeded pronouns.

EDITING 4: PRACTICE _____

Complete the following passage, filling in the blanks with the correct pronoun: *who, whom, which,* or *that.*

None of the carpenters _____ works here has any use for imported nails. They swear that American-made nails are the only ones _____ are worth using. A nail _____ bends when it is driven in was probably made in Canada, they say. One box of nails, _____ they got from Japan, had heads _____ broke off if they tried to pull them out. There are problems every time the contractor brings them boxes _____ are imported. These men, every one of _____ works with nails every day, believe that

they can tell where a nail comes from as soon as they hit it with a hammer. One thing is certain: a nail never bends because a carpenter hit it crooked.

36 e Eliminating unneeded pronouns

Speakers of some dialects use a pronoun immediately following its antecedent.

After the shot, the deer it~~ just took off.

EDITING 5: PRACTICE

Edit the following passage by making sure that all pronoun references are clear and that all pronouns are used appropriately. More than one edited version is possible. Be ready to explain your editing choices.

Studies have shown that alcoholism is a major problem in this city, that has a high percentage of unemployed and homeless people. This is true in other metropolitan areas as well. However, it affects not only the down-and-out but also working people, the elderly, and teenagers which have begun to experiment with drinking. We interviewed some social workers, which said that being homeless caused some people to drink.

We learned from interviewing homeless people, though, that many of those which are homeless now say they were drinking before they were on the street. Excessive drinking may force you to lose your home, if you're not careful, it seems from their experience.

EDITING 6: APPLICATION

Read through a paper you are working on. Are pronoun references unclear? Can you see any pattern to the problems? Edit any sentences in which you found pronoun reference problems, and think about how best to identify and correct these mistakes in your future editing.

PRONOUN–ANTECEDENT AGREEMENT

36 f Making pronouns and antecedents agree

To be clear and correct, personal pronouns should **agree** with, or correspond to, their antecedents in number, person, and gender.

GENDER OF POSSESSIVE PRONOUNS

> In my language, the gender of a noun determines the gender of any element that modifies it. In French, for example, the word *mère* (mother) is feminine, so any word modifying it must be feminine as well, including possessive pronouns.

> his mother   *sa mère*
> her mother   *sa mère*

> In English, however, the gender of a possessive personal pronoun must match the gender of its antecedent, not that of the word it modifies.

> her mother   her father
> his mother   his father

- Personal pronouns should agree with their antecedents in **number**—singular or plural. Most agreement problems involve confusion about number.

  A *pronoun* is singular if *it* has a singular antecedent.

  Pronouns are plural if *they* have plural antecedents.

- Personal pronouns should agree with their antecedents in **person**—first (*I, we, my, our*), second (*you, your*), or third (*he, she, it, they, his, her, its, their*).

  I write in *my* journal at least once a week.

  Robert writes in *his* journal every day.

- Singular personal pronouns should agree with their antecedents in **gender**—feminine, masculine, or neuter.

  Rosanna finds that writing in *her* journal helps *her* clarify *her* thoughts. Jimmy says *it* helps *him* analyze *his* research.

36 g Making pronouns agree with antecedents joined by *and*

A **compound antecedent** is one in which two or more parts are joined by a conjunction such as *and, or,* or, *nor: you* and *I, ducks or geese, neither rain nor snow.* When *and* links elements, the resulting grouping is usually considered plural, so a pronoun that refers to a compound antecedent joined by *and* should be plural as well.

Wind energy and solar power should soon take *their* place as major energy sources.

There are a few exceptions. A compound antecedent preceded by *each* or *every* takes a singular pronoun (Also see 34o.)

Each leaf and twig was put in *its* own envelope.

When the parts of a compound antecedent refer to the same person or thing, the pronoun should be singular.

As *the systems manager and my immediate supervisor, she* oversees my work.

Also when the elements linked by *and* constitute a single entity, use a singular pronoun.

Hansel and Gretel is a chilling fairy tale. Like *Cinderella, it* offers an archetype of conflict between children and stepparents.

36 h Making pronouns agree with antecedents joined by *or* and *nor*

The conjunctions *or* and *nor* can also be used to form a compound antecedent. When both elements are singular, a pronoun that refer to the compound antecedent is singular.

Either *hunger* or bad *weather* will take *its* toll on the soldiers.

When one element of a compound antecedent is singular and the other is plural, a pronoun clearly cannot agree with both of them. The convention is that the pronoun agree with the antecedent closer to it.

Either the supply problems or the *weather* will take *its* toll.

If following this convention seems awkward in a particular sentence, try putting the plural part of the antecedent nearer to the pronoun

Either the weather or the supply *problems* will take *their* toll.

---

36 i Making pronouns agree with collective nouns

Collective nouns, such as *couple, flock, crowd, herd,* and *committee,* often cause agreement problems because they are singular in form yet they refer to groups or collections that can be regarded as plural. Take your cue from the intended meaning of the sentence. Use a plural pronoun if members of the group are acting separately.

The *crew* gather *their* belongings and prepare to leave the ship.

Use a singular pronoun if the group acts as a unit.

The *flock* arose in flight and made *its* way to the shelter of the trees.

EDITING 7: PRACTICE _____

Edit the following passage by making pronouns and antecedents agree. Be especially careful about compound and collective antecedents.

Often conflict at the workplace is inevitable, especially when an employee cannot agree with their supervisor's decisions. Sam experienced this conflict firsthand. Both he and his supervisor are unhappy with his relationship

with each other. They disagree about how each regular task and special assignment should be performed, and the supervisor tinks that Sam takes too much time to complete them. The supervisor makes Sam write memos about his many overtime hours to justify it. Sam believes his boss works him too hard because she doesn't like them. Neither the personnel director nor Alicia, Sam's closest friend at work, can use their influence to help Sam transfer because the staff unanimously gives their support to the supervisor.

36 j Making pronouns agree with indefinite antecedents

An **indefinite pronoun**—such as *anyone, everyone, someone, nothing, everything*—does not require an explicit antecedent. You can write *Everyone likes ice cream* without further identifying your subject.

Agreement problems can arise when other pronouns have indefinite pronouns as their antecedents. It can be difficult to determine whether a pronoun that refers to an indefinite pronoun should be singular or plural.

Most indefinite pronouns are always singular: *anyone, everyone, someone, anybody, everybody, somebody, anything, everything, something, either, neither, each, nothing, much, one, no one.*

Each of the samples was placed in *its* own petri dish.

Neither of the Boy Scouts had brought *his* compass.

These singular indefinite pronouns also raise problems of gender agreement.

Someone has lost *his or her* briefcase.

In conversation, many people would say *Someone has lost their briefcase.* But this is incorrect in formal writing, since *anyone* is singular. Using *his or her* avoids the implication that you're ignoring females, but that construction quickly becomes awkward. Using *he* or *his* in a generic sense when gender is unspecified was once acceptable but is today considered sexist. (For alternatives to the generic *he*, see the box on the next page. For other tips on avoiding sexist language, see 31c.)

AVOIDING THE GENERIC *HE*

Here are four ways to avoid the generic *he:*

- If there is no doubt about the gender of the antecedent, you can use the pronoun of the same gender.

  her
  Anyone who wants to be an operatic soprano must train ~~their~~
  voice carefully.

- You can make the antecedent plural and edit any other agreement problems.

  All attorneys have their   specialties
  ~~Every attorney has his~~ own legal ~~specialty.~~

- Use *his or her.* Use this strategy sparingly because *his or her* becomes monotonous with repetition.

  or her
  A lawyer is only as good as his preparation.

- Restructure the sentence to eliminate the pronoun. This strategy is often the most effective because it simply avoids the potential problem.

  All writers wrestle   ⊙
  ~~Everyone wrestles~~ with this problem ~~in his own writing.~~

Because the word *none* is derived from *no one,* some authorities say it should always be singular. Others allow the use of a plural verb and a plural pronoun to agree with *none* if it is followed by a plural noun.

None of the *puppies have* had *their* shots.

However, the treatment of *none* as singular is always acceptable.

has   its
None of the puppies ~~have~~ had ~~their~~ shots.

Some indefinite pronouns are always plural: *few, many, both, several.*

Hundreds of baby turtles climb out of the sand and crawl toward the sea. *Few* survive *their* first week.

Still other indefinite pronouns can be singular or plural depending on context: *any, all, more, most, some.*

Most of the work *was* tedious because *it* was so repetitious.

Most *refers to* work, *which is singular, so* it *is singular.*

Most of the fans *have* left *their* seats and headed for *their* cars.

Most *refers to* fans, *which is plural, so* their *is plural.*

EDITING 8: PRACTICE ————————————————————

Edit the following passage by making pronouns and antecedents agree. More than one edited version is possible. Be ready to explain your editing choices.

> Most people make many pronoun agreement mistakes in his or her speech because spoken English is much more informal than written English. Almost everyone knows that they shouldn't say "they" when they're talking about one person, but often they do so anyway when speaking. In conversation, even a professor, a freelance writer, or anyone else who works with words professionally won't always make a pronoun agree with the noun they refer to. But when someone writes, they should make sure that "something" is an "it" and not a "they." Otherwise, the reader will think the writer doesn't know what they are doing.

EDITING 9: PRACTICE ————————————————————

Edit the following passage for agreement. (You may have to change some verbs and nouns as well.) More than one edited version is possible. Be ready to explain your editing choices.

> Changes in facial hair, a higher or a lower voice, and a decreased sex drive: this is some of the side effects of taking steroids. Yet many continue using this dangerous drug to improve their performance. Athletics is ever more

competitive, and athletes are always striving to be the best he or she can be. In a race, mere seconds are a long time to an athlete when they mean the difference between a gold and a silver medal. Perhaps the athlete does not know what harm they are doing to their bodies. Someone cannot be physically addicted to steroids; any addiction to it is psychological and based on the fact that athletes like what they see. Unfortunately, the athlete cannot always see what lies ahead for them. Ben Johnson and some others should count himself lucky. All Johnson lost was a gold medal and the chance to compete again. Benjamin Ramirez was not so lucky. Nor were the many like him who lost his life.

EDITING 10: APPLICATION ─────────────────────────────

Read through a paper you are working on to find pronouns that do not agree with their antecedents. Can you see why you made mistakes? Edit any sentences with agreement problems, and think about how best to avoid them. Write a brief set of guidelines to help yourself in the future.

PRONOUN CASE

36 k Choosing pronoun case

In speaking, we automatically choose among the pronouns *I* or *me* or *my*, *he* or *him* or *his*. We say *I saw him* rather than *me saw he*, or *my car* rather than *I car*. These changes of form, the grammatical property of nouns and pronouns called **case,** help indicate a word's role in a sentence. The **subjective case** (*I, he, she,* or *they,* for example) serves grammatically as a subject—the person or thing that performs the action of a sentence or a clause. The **objective case** (*me, him, her, them*) is used for an object—the person or thing that receives the action. The **possessive case** (*my, mine, your, yours, his, hers*) shows possession or ownership.

Most problems with case arise from the choice between subjective and objective pronouns: *I* or *me*, *we* or *us*, *she* or *her*, *who* or *whom.* Often the difficulty arises because nonstandard usages that are acceptable in everyday speech (*It's me!*) are inappropriate in formal writing (in which you would write *It is I*). The key to choosing correct case is to analyze whether the pronoun in question is serving as a subject or as an object or is indicating possession.

DETERMINING PRONOUN CASE

PERSONAL PRONOUNS

SINGULAR	Subjective	Objective	Possessive
First person	I	me	my/mine
Second person	you	you	your/yours
Third person			
Masculine	he	him	his
Feminine	she	her	her/hers
Neuter	it	it	its

PLURAL			
First person	we	us	our/ours
Second person	you	you	your/yours
Third person	they	them	their/theirs

INTERROGATIVE OR RELATIVE PRONOUNS*

	Subjective	Objective	Possessive
	who	whom	whose
	whoever	whomever	—

*These pronouns are called **interrogative pronouns** when used to ask questions: Whose *book is that?* They are called **relative pronouns** when used to introduce dependent clauses: *The writer* whose *book we read visited the university.*

36 I **Choosing case after elements joined by**
and, or, **and** *nor*

Joining two or more words by *and, or,* or *nor,* and thus creating a compound element, does not affect their case. One test for correctness is to take out one word and the *and* or *or* and see how the sentence reads.

Joe and ~~me~~ talked to him.

If you mentally remove *Joe and,* you are left with *me talked to him.* Some people, trying to avoid this mistake, assume that *and me* is always wrong and thus make errors such as *He talked to Joe and I.* But we say *He talked to me,* not *He talked to I,* so we should also say *He talked to Joe and me.*

▌ Subjective case for subjects

A subject that has two or more parts joined by *and, or,* or *nor* is a **compound subject.** Use the subjective case for each part of a compound subject. When one part of a compound subject is in the first person (*I*), put that part last.

> and I
> ~~Me and~~ Sandy found five lost lottery tickets.
> ⌃

▌ Objective case for objects

With **compound objects,** as with compound subjects, case is not affected by *and, or,* or *nor.* Use the objective case for each part of a compound object, whether it is the object of a verb or of a preposition.

> him   me.
> The judges chose neither ~~he~~ nor ~~I.~~
>   ⌃   ⌃

> them
> I spoke to Olga and ~~they~~ about the competition.
>   ⌃

To clarify the correct choice, mentally drop all but one pronoun from the compound object: *The judges chose him. The judges chose me. I spoke to them.*

The preposition *between* is used with two things, *among* with three or more. As with any preposition, the objects should be in the objective case.

> me
> Between Jack and ~~I,~~ we sold more than four dozen souvenir T-
>   ⌃   among   me.
> shirts. We divided the money ~~between~~ him, Janet, and ~~I.~~
>   ⌃   ⌃

▌ Subjective case following linking verbs

A **linking verb**—such as *be, become, seem, appear*—links its subject to a **complement** that follows the verb and renames the subject. In writing, both the subject and the complement should be in the subjective case.

> I
> The first contestants were Laura and ~~me.~~
>   ⌃

If you have trouble choosing case following a linking verb, try turning the sentence around and simplifying the compound structure to a single pronoun: *I was the first contestant.*

USING THE PRONOUN CASES

SUBJECTIVE CASE

Use the subjective case (*I, you, he, she, it, we, they, who, whoever*) for the subject of a sentence or of a dependent clause.

She researched the origins of the tune.

James knew *who* would answer.

Also use the subjective case for a subject complement, which follows a linking verb (*be, seem, become, appear*) and renames the subject.

It is *they* who will benefit most.

OBJECTIVE CASE

Use the objective case (*me, you, him, her, it, us, them, whom, whomever*) for the object of a verb or of a preposition.

The judges chose *her* first.

They awarded the prize to *us*.

USING THE OBJECTIVE CASE WITH *MAKE, LET,* AND *HAVE*

Use objective case pronouns when infinitives follow *make, let,* and *have* even though these infinitives do not have the form *to* in front of them.

He let *us* retake the exam.

We made *him* tell us the secret recipe.

She had *me* turn the computer on.

POSSESSIVE CASE

Use the possessive case to show ownership, possession, or connection. The adjective form (*my, your, his, her, its, our, their, whose*) is used before a noun.

I wrote in *my* journal.

We heard the singer *whose* songs we liked.

The noun form (*mine, yours, his, hers, ours, theirs*) can stand alone, without a noun.

The black coat is *hers*.

His is the plaid one.

Edit the following sentences, using the appropriate pronoun case for compound subjects and objects.

1. To him and I they provide hours of entertainment and neither he nor me ever seems to tire of them.
2. I don't remember whether it was him or me who first started watching them.
3. Others may not appreciate our passion for these shows, but they never seem boring to either he or I.
4. The best ones make me and him laugh every time we see them, and, thanks to the invention of the VCR, him and I can see them over and over.
5. Me and him have seen some shows so often that we have practically memorized them.

36 m Choosing case for appositive pronouns

An **appositive** is a noun or pronoun that renames a preceding noun. (See 39c.) Pronouns used as appositives must be in the same case as the nouns they rename.

The losers—Tomoko, Rodney, and ~~me~~ I—all wanted a rematch.

The appositive renames the subject, losers, *so the pronoun is in the subjective case.*

It was her sons, Paul and ~~him~~ he, who missed their mother most.

The appositive renames the subject complement, sons, *so it is in the subjective case.*

They asked the medalists, Katya and ~~I~~ me, to pose for a picture.

The appositive renames medalists, *the object of the verb* asked, *so it is in the objective case.*

To decide between the subjective and objective case in such sentences, simplify the construction: *They asked me to pose for a picture.*

36 n Choosing *us* or *we* before a noun

Pronouns immediately followed by nouns can cause confusion, but the correct case again depends on whether the pronoun is a subject or an object. (The noun following the pronoun is an appositive renaming the pronoun. See 39c.)

> We
> ~~Us~~ bikers were worried about the weather.

The pronoun is the subject, so the subjective case is correct.

> us
> They told ~~we~~ bikers not to worry about the weather.

The pronoun is an object, so the objective case is correct.

Mentally dropping the noun following *us* or *we* can make the choice clearer: *We were worried about the weather. They told us not to worry about the weather.*

EDITING 12: PRACTICE ———————————————

Edit the following paragraph for pronoun case.

> Fishing with our dad, Charley and me hadn't caught any fish all week. We decided it was up to the two of us, him and I, to find some way to catch something. Us two kids borrowed a rowboat and, with him and me rowing, went way out in the middle of the pond. We dropped anchor and began fishing, him out of one side of the boat and I out of the other side. Charley asked me if I was sleepy and I said, "Not me," but then a splash of water woke me, and the boat was rocking. Charley was pulling madly on his rod, and it seemed as if his catch would tip the boat over and he and I with it. It took ten minutes for us, Charley and I, to get that catfish on board. Dad said it was turning out that the real fishers in the family were Charley and me. Dad made both Charley and I feel really proud.

36 o Choosing case with verbals

Participles, gerunds, and infinitives are called **verbals** because they are derived from verbs. However, they cannot function by themselves as verbs in sentences. A **past participle** (*worked, eaten, brought*) or present participle (*working, eating, bringing*) without an auxiliary verb can be used as a modifier. A **gerund** is

the *-ing* form of the verb used as a noun. An **infinitive** is the base form of the verb, usually preceded by *to.*

PRESENT PARTICIPLE	A person *waking* at that hour is often groggy.
PAST PARTICIPLE	He seemed *tired.*
GERUND	*Waking* at that hour can ruin my day.
INFINITIVE	I hate to *wake* so early.

1 Objective case for objects of verbals

Verbals can have objects. In the sentence *I like to read books,* for example, the object of the infinitive *to read* is *books.* Choose the objective case for a pronoun that is the object of a verbal.

Watching *her* was fascinating.

He hadn't intended to lose *them.*

2 Objective or possessive case before *-ing* verbals

The choice of pronoun case before an *-ing* verbal depends on whether the verbal is used as a noun or as a modifier. Which of these sentences is correct? Either could be correct depending on the intended meaning.

He heard their shouting.

What did he hear? He heard shouting.

He heard them shouting.

What did he hear? He heard them.

My
~~Me~~ leaving made them all sad.

me
He heard ~~my~~ leaving just before midnight.

3 Objective case before infinitives

A pronoun that immediately precedes an infinitive should be in the objective case.

The study group asked *her* to stay.

36 P Choosing case after *than* or *as*

The subordinating conjunctions *than* and *as* often appear in **elliptical constructions**—clauses that have one or more words intentionally omitted. Understanding exactly what is omitted is the key to choosing the correct case for a pronoun that follows *than* or *as*.

> Alex is as strong as (*I/me*).

Restore the omitted word *am* at the end of the sentence, and it is easy to choose the correct pronoun: *Alex is as strong as I am.*

Sometimes the omitted words will call for the possessive case.

> Jen's luggage weighs as much as *mine* [my luggage].

The subjective case could also be meaningful in this sentence:

> The Jen's luggage weighs as much as *I* [weigh].
>
> *The objective case, me, would not be correct in any sense here.*

By using the correct case, you can help the reader understand sentences that offer more than one possibility for omitted words.

> My sister has more respect for her friends than *I* [have].
>
> My sister has more respect for her friends than [she has for] *me.*

EDITING 13: PRACTICE ───────────────

Edit the following sentences, using the correct pronoun case after *than* or *as*. Circle the number of any sentence that is correct.

1. We're both columnists, but I think my columns are consistently better than her.
2. Our fellow writers consider I as funny as she.
3. But apparently our readers find she funnier.
4. Maybe I just have different taste than them.
5. Someday I know my writing will become more popular than her.

36 **q** Choosing *who* or *whom*

The distinction between *who* and *whom* and between *whoever* and *whomever* has all but disappeared from everyday speech, so your "ear" for the correct form may be of little help. Yet in formal writing, making the wrong choice is considered an error. When you encounter one of these pronouns, remember to use *who* and *whoever* only for subjects, *whom* and *whomever* for objects.

As a test, answer a question posed by *who* or *whom* with a sentence using *he* or *him.*

(*Who*/*Whom*) got here first? *He* got here first.

Who *and* he *are both subjective, so use* who.

(*Who*/*Whom*) do you trust? I trust *him.*

Whom *and* him *are both objective, so use* whom.

Use *who* when the answer uses *he;* use *whom* when it uses *him.*

▍ **To introduce questions**

Who, whom, whoever, and *whomever* can introduce questions; when they do, they are **interrogative pronouns.** If the pronoun is the subject of the question, use *who* or *whoever: Who is going? Whoever could be calling at this hour?*

When the pronoun is the object of the verb, use *whom* or *whomever: Whom did you see? Whomever did he want?*

Also use *whom* or *whomever* when the pronoun is the object of a preposition: *To whom are you speaking?*

Who
~~Whom~~ had the authority to enter the building at night?
  ^

Test: He *had the authority. Use* who.

Whom
~~Who~~ did you admit to the building?
  ^

Test: You *did admit* him. *Use* whom.

whom
To ~~who~~ did you give authority to enter the building?
   ^

Test: You *did give authority to* him. *Use* whom.

Don't be fooled by other clauses inserted nearby.

Who
~~Whom~~, may I ask, is calling?
^

Drop out may I ask *and the correct choice is clear*

who
He was a student ~~whom~~ people thought would succeed.
^

Test: People thought he *would succeed, so use* who.

Be particularly careful when a preposition is left at the end of a question. Pronouns that are objects of such prepositions still need to be in the objective case.

Whom did you give it to?

Moving the preposition so that it appears just before its object can make the choice clear.

To whom did you give it?

2 In dependent clauses

Who, whom, whoever, and *whomever* are *relative pronouns* when they introduce dependent clauses, but the same rules about case apply. Use *who* and *whoever* when the pronoun is the subject of its clause, *whom* and *whomever* when it is the object of its clause. The case of a relative pronoun is determined by its role in the dependent clause, not by anything in the surrounding sentence.

The man *who* lives next door is a rock climber.

Who is the subject of the clause who lives next door.

The fellow *whom* I met last week is also a rock climber.

Whom is the object of met.

As with interrogative pronouns, the question test can help you choose the right case. Turn the dependent clause into a question introduced by the pronoun, and then answer that question with *he* or *him.* If the answer uses *he* (subjective case), then *who* is correct. If the answer uses *him* (objective case), then *whom* is correct.

who
I want a list of everyone ~~whom~~ visited the plant today.
^

Test: Who/Whom *visited the plant?* He *did, so use* who.

The police will interrogate ~~whoever~~ the foreman accuses.
                                  whomever

Test: Who/Whom *does the foreman accuse? The foreman accuses* him, *so use* whomever.

EDITING 14: PRACTICE ─────────────────────────

Edit the following passage, using *who, whom, whoever,* and *whomever* correctly.

Whomever took the last piece of German chocolate cake has caused an uproar in our household. Dad had vowed vengeance on whomever touched it. But this afternoon it was gone. Only a crumb-filled plate remained. Mom said she would not defend whoever Dad suspected. Dad fumed and fussed and brooded and interrogated whoever looked guilty. None of my brothers and sisters confessed to the crime, even when he threatened whoever the guilty party was helped by. In the end, though, we learned that the culprit was Mom, whom had made the cake for his birthday and said she just wanted a midafternoon snack. What could Dad say? If he complained too much, she wouldn't bake for him anymore.

36 **r** **Using reflexive pronouns**

The pronouns *myself, yourself, himself, herself, itself, ourselves, yourselves,* and *themselves* are called **reflexive pronouns.** A reflexive pronoun reflects the action of the verb back toward its subject, making it clear that the object and the subject of the verb are one and the same: *I looked at* myself *in the mirror.* These pronouns are called **intensive** when they are used to rename and emphasize an element appearing earlier in the sentence: *He did it* himself.

Never use a reflexive pronoun as a subject. This error is most common when the subject should be *I* or *me.*

                        I

My friend and ~~myself~~ plan to attend.

When the subject and the object of a verb refer to the same person or persons, use a reflexive pronoun for the object.

               himself

John cut ~~him~~ with the scissors.

Himself makes it clear that the person who has been cut is the same as the person who did the cutting.

John cut ~~myself~~ *me* with the scissors when he handed them to me.

The words myself *and* John *do not name the same person, so* myself *is incorrect.*

A reflexive pronoun should be used as the object of a preposition only when it and an earlier noun or pronoun in the sentence name the same person or persons.

EDITING FOR CORRECT PRONOUN CASE

To edit for pronoun case, do the following:

- Check pronoun case in elements joined by *and, or,* or *nor.*
- Check the case of pronouns used as appositives.
- Determine whether you need *us* or *we* before a noun.
- Check the case of pronouns used with verbals.
- Check the case of pronouns after *than* or *as.*
- Choose between *who* or *whom, whoever* or *whomever.*
- Use reflexive pronouns only as objects, only when necessary.

I speak only for ~~me,~~ *myself,* not for my roommate.

Myself *is correct because* I *precedes it in the sentence.*

As for Carlos and ~~myself,~~ *me,* we want to work in software design.

Myself *is incorrect because* I *does not precede it.*

EDITING 15: PRACTICE

Edit the following passage, using the appropriate pronoun case throughout.

In the memories of my siblings and myself, our house used to be surrounded by a forest on three sides. Us children—my three brothers and me—used to hunt for snakes and salamanders in the woods by overturning the rocks that they lived under. One of the best hunting grounds for ourselves was the land to the south of our yard. When I was eight years old, I saw a garter snake catch a frog and devour it whole. It eating the frog

upset my brothers and I terribly. Us, with our childish minds, thought that snakes were nasty, cruel creatures and that frogs were clearly nicer than them. Now that I am grown up, I realize that the snake eating the frog was not an act of cruelty. Each creature on earth lives and dies according to the natural order of things.

EDITING 16: APPLICATION ————————————————————————

Examine a paper you are working on to see if you have used inappropriate pronoun case. Do you make one kind of error more than others? Think of ways to avoid such errors. Edit your work.

37 Making Sentences Consistent and Complete

Like bus riders, readers like to know where they are being taken. A good writer respects readers' expectations the same way that a good driver keeps passengers comfortable: by avoiding needless detours and sudden changes in destination. As you edit, make sure that you have not taken any detours that will confuse your readers.

37 a Avoiding unnecessary shifts

Readers generally expect continuity in point of view and in references to time throughout a piece of writing. Within sentences, readers expect a logical consistency in the person and number of subjects (see 34h–34u), in the forms of verbs (see 34a–34c), and in the way quotations are reproduced. A change in any of these elements is called a **shift.** Often a writer's meaning does require a shift, such as a change of subject from third person to first person or from singular to plural.

As *Bonds* rounded the bases, *we* in the stands erupted in a frenzy of cheers and applause.

However, a shift in verb tense in the same sentence would be unnecessary and confusing: *As Bonds rounded the bases, we in the stands erupt in a frenzy of cheers and applause.* Such unnecessary shifts disrupt effective communication.

Shifts in person and number

We refer to ourselves in the **first person** (*I, we*), to our audience in the **second person** (*you*), and to other subjects in the **third person** (*he, she, it, one, they*). Unnecessary shifts in **person** often arise in sentences about groups or about unidentified people. Some writers shift unnecessarily to the second person, particularly when

trying to make a comprehensive statement. To avoid unnecessary shifts to the second person, use *you* in formal writing only when referring to the reader. (See 36c.)

they
The chemistry students learned that ~~you~~ had to be careful.

one sees
As one enters the building, ~~you see~~ little evidence of fire.

Unnecessary shifts in **number**—from singular to plural and vice versa—generally occur when a writer has used a singular noun or pronoun of indeterminate gender (*student, one*) and then uses a plural pronoun to refer to it, perhaps to avoid the appearance of sexism. (See 31c and 36c.) You can avoid such shifts by making the antecedent plural or by substituting a singular pronoun.

Students   *s*
~~Every student~~ makes their own schedule.

his or her
Each student is responsible for ~~their~~ own work.

The first-person plural—*we*—has many uses. Some writers use *we* to speak inclusively of themselves and their audience: *We all use informal constructions in everyday speech.* Other writers use *we* to refer to themselves (the **editorial *we***) even when only one person is writing: *We have shown that most colloids are stable only within a limited range of temperatures.* Be careful not to mix different senses of *we*.

Americans'
We asked a dozen people to share their opinions about ~~our~~ apparent national obsession with politicians' personal lives.

2 Shifts in tense

Tense places the action of the verb in time: *Today I go. Yesterday I went. Tomorrow I will go.* Different verbs in a sentence or paragraph may logically use different tenses to reflect actions occurring at different times. (See 34d–34e.)

We *will play* tennis before we *eat* breakfast but after we *have had* our coffee.

The tense you select to describe most of the actions in your paper is called the **governing tense.** Once you establish it, do not use another tense without a good reason.

When the contract was finished, it ~~sets~~ a firm deadline.
^ *set*

The **literary present tense** is used to describe literature or art. (See 34d.) If you use it, do so consistently.

In *The Glass Menagerie*, Tom realizes how trapped he is after the Gentleman Caller ~~departed~~.
^ *departs*

 SHIFTING TENSE WITHIN A PARAGRAPH

Sometimes verb tense shifting within a paragraph is necessary when you support or comment on an idea. Following are some acceptable reasons for shifting tense.

SHIFTING FROM PRESENT TENSE TO PAST TENSE

- To provide background information
- To support a claim with an example from the past
- To compare a present situation with a past one

Truly dedicated writers *find* time to write regardless of the circumstances. Austen *wrote* most of her novels in short bursts of activity between receiving visitors and taking care of household duties.

SHIFTING FROM PAST TENSE TO PRESENT TENSE

- To express a comment, opinion, or evaluation

On May 6, the town council *voted* against the school bond. Their decision *is* unfortunate.

 Shifts in mood

English verbs are used in one of three **moods.** The **indicative mood** is used for statements and questions: *Rain fell, Did you hear it?* The **imperative mood** expresses commands, orders, or directions: *Close the door.* Unnecessary shifts from the imperative to the indicative mood commonly occur in instructions.

First cover your work surface with newspapers, and then ~~you~~ make sure your materials are within easy reach.

By contrast, the **subjunctive mood** expresses wishes or statements that are known to be not factual: *He wishes chocolate* were *not fattening. If he were a millionaire, he'd be happy without it.* (See 34f–34g.) Often, you will find that using the subjunctive mood and the indicative mood in the same sentence is appropriate. In the next two examples, the verbs in the independent clauses (*wishes* and *would be*) are in the indicative, while the verbs in the dependent clauses (*were* in both cases) are in the subjunctive.

My professor *wishes* that I *were* more diligent.

The world *would be* nicer if everyone *were* as kind as you.

Avoid unnecessary shifts from the subjunctive to the indicative or to the imperative.

The contract requires that you be in Denver on July 1 and that you ~~will~~ be in Houston on August 1.

4 Shifts in voice and subject

The subject of an **active-voice** verb performs the verb's action: *He hit the ball.* The subject of a **passive-voice** verb is acted upon: *The ball was hit by him.* (See 27c.) If a sentence has two verbs with the same subject, a shift of voice can be acceptable.

The students *completed* the project and *were given* first prize.

The verbs shift from active (completed) *to passive* (were given) *but have the same subject,* students. *The shift is acceptable because it keeps the focus on the subject.*

A shift from the active to the passive voice (or vice versa) can be distracting and unnecessary, however, when it requires a shift in subject as well.

we saw

As we peered out of the tent, the waning moon ~~was seen~~ through the trees.

5 Shifts between direct and indirect quotation

Direct quotation, sometimes called *direct discourse,* reproduces someones's exact words, which are enclosed in quotation marks.

> "I love my work," he insisted.

Indirect quotation, or *indirect discourse,* is a paraphrase of someone else's words; it is not placed in quotation marks. (See Chapter 16.)

> He insisted that he loved his work.

As you edit, watch for shifts from indirect to direct quotation that are not clearly needed. Either use indirect quotation consistently, or rewrite the sentence so that the direct quotation is introduced by a new verb and is enclosed in quotation marks.

> ~~wondered~~   ~~was~~
> He loved his work and why ~~was~~ the job being eliminated?
>
> ~~asked, "Why~~   ~~"~~
> He loved his work and ~~why~~ is the job being eliminated?

Now you know that he didn't just ask such a question but that these were his exact words.

Avoid using one verb (such as *said*) to introduce both an indirect quotation and a complete sentence of direct quotation. You have three editing choices: use indirect quotation in both instances, quote less than the full sentence directly, or start a new sentence.

> Dr. Ryan claims that the play was composed before 1600 and "It
> that it was certainly written by
> ~~shows the clear hand of~~ Shakespeare."
>
> Dr. Ryan claims that the play was composed before 1600 and "It
> a"shows the clear hand of Shakespeare."
>
>   He says, "It
> Dr. Ryan claims that the play was composed before 1600 ~~and "It~~
> shows the clear hand of Shakespeare."

TRANSFORMING DIRECT QUOTATIONS TO INDIRECT QUOTATIONS

You must make certain changes when you transform a direct quotation into an indirect quotation.

VERBS

You must often change the tense of verbs in a direct quotation to be consistent with the rest of the sentence and avoid confusing shifts.

Direct Quotation	**Indirect Quotation**
Present tense	**Past tense**
He said, "They *are* tired."	He said that they *were* tired.
Past tense	**Past perfect tense**
She said, "They *lost* their keys."	She said that they *had lost* their keys.
Present perfect tense	**Past perfect tense**
He said, "She *has written* a great short story."	He said that she *had written* a great short story.

Some auxilliary verbs change from present to past tense.

Direct Quotation	**Indirect Quotation**
can	could
may	might
must, have to	had to
will	would
He said, "They *can* watch television."	He said that they *could* watch television.

PRONOUNS

In some cases, you may have to change pronouns when you transform a direct quotation into an indirect quotation. Pay attention to meaning when considering these changes.

Direct Quotation	**Indirect Quotation**
She said, "*I* was wrong."	She said that *she* was wrong.
She said to me, "*You* can sing."	She said that *I* could sing.
She said to them, "*You* can sing."	She said that *they* could sing.

(Continued)

FOR QUESTIONS

When a direct quotation is a question, you may need to change the word order or add a word such as *if* or *whether* when transforming it into an indirect quotation.

Direct Quotation
She asked, "*What is the answer?*"

Indirect Quotation
She asked *what the answer was.*

He asked, "*Is this correct?*"

He asked *If that was correct.*

FOR COMMANDS AND REQUESTS

When a direct quotation that is a command or a request is transformed into an indirect quotation, it should be introduced with a verb such as *tell, order,* or *ask* and should contain an infinitive. It may also need to specify who was given the command or request.

Direct Quotation
I said, "*Don't* get up."
She said, "*Please* leave."

Indirect Quotation
I *told him not to* get up.
She asked *him* to leave.

EDITING 1: EXPLORATION

Throughout the following excerpt from his essay "Computers," Lewis Thomas uses the pronouns *you* and *we* inconsistently. Consider what effect Thomas hoped to achieve with this unconventional use of pronouns. Do you think he was effective?

It would be nice to have better ways of monitoring what we're up to so that we could recognize change while it is occurring, instead of waking up as we do now to the astonished realization that the whole century just past wasn't what we thought it was, at all. Maybe computers can be used to help in this, although I rather doubt it. You can make simulation models of cities, but what you learn is that they seem to be beyond the reach of intelligent analysis; if you try to use common sense to make predictions, things get more botched up than ever. This is interesting, since a city is the most concentrated aggregation of humans, all exerting whatever influence they can bring to bear. The city seems to have a life of its own. If we cannot understand how this works, we are not likely to get very far with human society at large.

EDITING 2: PRACTICE ────────────────────────

Edit the following sentences to avoid distracting or awkward shifts. Some sentences have more than one possible answer. Be ready to explain your editing choices. Circle the number of any sentence that is correct.

1. Last night, Karen reminded me about the time of the exam and says, "You had better not be late this time."

2. Fortunately, this morning she also gave me a wake-up call; she says she knew that I would oversleep.

3. I arrived at the examination room about five minutes early and was given an answer booklet and a seating assignment by the proctor.

4. We were allowed one hour for the examination, and do not use any books.

5. When it was time to begin, we were told first to review, and then you can begin to answer the questions.

6. As I turn to the first section, though, I saw a truly horrible sight.

7. My test dealt with second-year organic chemistry, but I was enrolled in American history.

8. I start sweating, and then, when I looked next to me, I saw another student busily scribbling in their answer book.

9. Suddenly, it dawns on me that I don't recognize anyone in the room, and I began to panic.

10. Just then the phone rang, and I hear Karen saying "Get up!" and telling me that she knew I would oversleep.

37 b Eliminating mixed constructions

The term **mixed construction** applies to a sentence that begins one way and then takes a sudden, unexpected turn, so that readers are unsure what it means. One kind of mixed construction uses a grammatically unacceptable element as a subject or predicate. Another kind of mixed construction links subject and verb in an illogical way.

Making subjects and predicates grammatically compatible

In English, a prepositional phrase cannot be the subject of a sentence.

~~By listening~~ Listening closely and paying attention to nonverbal signals

helps a doctor make a fuller diagnosis.

The prepositional phrase is converted into something that can be a subject.

A doctor can make a fuller diagnosis by

~~By~~ listening closely and paying attention to nonverbal signals

~~helps a doctor make a fuller diagnosis.~~

A completely new subject is created.

A modifier clause also cannot be the subject of a sentence. A modifier clause begins with a subordinating conjunction such as *after, before, when, where, while, because, if, although,* and *unless.* To edit such a sentence, provide a new subject for the sentence.

The doctor's status as

~~Because the doctor is~~ an expert does not mean a patient should

never question a diagnosis.

The subject is now status *rather than the clause beginning with* Because.

Another kind of grammatically mixed sentence uses an inappropriate element as a predicate. A dependent clause cannot contain the main verb of a sentence.

The fact that most patients are afraid to ask questions, ~~which~~

gives doctors complete control.

Removing which *turns* gives *into the main verb.*

2 Making subjects and predicates logically compatible

Sometimes a sentence combines elements that logically do not fit. Although the intent is usually clear, something is wrong at the level of literal meaning. If you sense that some elements do not work together, reduce your sentence to its most basic elements—subject and verb—to see where the problem lies.

Most

~~The opinion of most~~ people believe that dogs make better pets

than cats.

Reduce the sentence to subject and verb: The opinion *cannot* believe; people *can. So* people *makes a more logical subject.*

~~The increase in the~~ ^The^ number of cat owners in the United States has doubled since 1960.

The increase hasn't doubled; the number of cat owners has doubled.

Repeat offenders whose licenses have already been suspended for drunk driving will ~~be~~ ^have their licenses^ revoked.

It is not offenders who will be revoked but rather their licenses.

A subject complement must rename the subject in a logical way.

My father's favorite kitchen appliance is ~~using~~ our microwave.

Using is not an appliance. When oven *functions as the subject complement renaming* appliance, *the sentence makes sense.*

3 Eliminating faulty predication

A type of mixed construction called **faulty predication** is both ungrammatical and illogical. Sentences with faulty predication use a modifier clause starting with *when, where,* or *because* to rename the subject. Some contain the phrase *The reason is because.*

A stalemate is ~~where neither player can~~ ^the inability of either player to^ win.

~~Pop art is where~~ ^In pop art^ an artist reproduces images from commercial products and the popular media.

Such constructions are ungrammatical because a modifier cannot rename a subject. They are illogical because a person or thing (the subject) cannot be a *when, where,* or *because.*

Reserve *when* and *where* clauses to modifiers specifying time and place. Whenever you see *the reason is because,* substitute the *reason is that* or restate the subject.

The reason little has been done to solve the problem is ~~because~~ ^that^ the committee is deadlocked.

> Little
> ~~The reason little~~ has been done to solve the problem ~~is~~ because
>   ^
> the committee is deadlocked.

EDITING 3: PRACTICE ─────────────────────────

Edit the following passage by eliminating mixed constructions. More than one edited version is possible. Be ready to explain your editing choices.

> The reason some readers feel that Ernest Hemingway's fiction is overrated is because his style seems so simple and repetitive. By focusing on the subtleties of his language, though, can tell us a great deal about the psychology of his characters. In "The Big Two-Hearted River," for example, the intention of Hemingway tries to give the reader a sense of Nick Adams's struggle to maintain some degree of emotional stability by focusing on the minute details of a trout-fishing excursion. By repeatedly reminding himself that he had made a "good camp" shows that Nick feels a sense of anxiety on some other, subconscious level. In an example like this, then, we can see that Hemingway's unique style is using small details to offer deeper insights into his characters' minds.

37 C Inserting missing words

Sentences can be incomplete because of inadvertently omitted words, faulty elliptical constructions, or ambiguous comparisons.

1 Checking for omitted words

Little words like *the, a, an, is, was, in, at, to,* and *that* are easy to omit, either in haste or in the interest of brevity. As you edit, check that you have not omitted necessary words.

>   to   was
> When she told me meet her at the office, I sure she meant
>   ^   ^
> her office.

When you read silently, your eye has a tendency to "fill in" what it expects to see; therefore, a good way to check for missing words is to read your writing aloud.

2 Completing elliptical constructions

In **elliptical constructions,** words are intentionally omitted that readers can be expected to understand. Elliptical structures

are usually used in parallel constructions. For example, in the sentence *The sky seemed gray and the day gloomy,* the verb *seemed* has been omitted before *gloomy.* (See 25e–25f, 26f.)

When you use an elliptical construction, make sure that the words omitted are identical to the words already used in the other part of the parallel. Otherwise readers may be confused about your meaning.

> were
> **The sun shone brilliantly and the clouds ᴧ radiant.**

The second clause requires a different verb from the verb in the first clause, shone, *so the second verb cannot be omitted.*

For the sake of clarity, consider repeating conjunctions and prepositions, especially in long parallel structures.

> **The project was designed to measure how drinking alters metab-**
> how
> **olism and it affects a person's body chemistry.**
> ᴧ

> in
> **Little words are easy to omit, either in haste or ᴧ the interest**
> **of brevity.**

3 Making comparisons complete

Comparisons may be incomplete or illogical if a writer leaves out words that are necessary for reader understanding. Comparisons must be complete and explicit. Beware of inadvertently equating a person with a thing.

> Cooper's⊙
> **Many of Melville's novels are superior to ~~Cooper.~~**
> ᴧ

Novels cannot be compared with Cooper; *they must be compared with* Cooper's *novels.*

Do not leave readers in doubt about what you are comparing.

> she likes
> **It seems that Goodall likes apes more than ᴧ other people.**

Does she like apes more than she likes *other people, or* more than other people do? *Rather than make readers choose, make the comparison clear and complete.*

(For more on comparisons, see 35e, 36p.)

COMPOSING CONSISTENT AND COMPLETE SENTENCES

As you edit, check to make sure that your sentences are consistent and complete by doing the following:

- Make sure sentences include no unnecessary or distracting shifts.
- Make subjects and predicates relate to one another grammatically and logically.
- Make sure each sentence omits no words necessary to express its ideas clearly.

EDITING 4: PRACTICE

Edit the following passage by adding any necessary words, making all comparisons complete. More than one edited version is possible. Be ready to explain your editing choices.

It's important to keep in mind that the children at the community center are individuals. No child's problems are the same as another. Change is difficult for everyone, children more so. Some of the children here are severely emotionally disturbed. The goal of the center is assess each child's needs to discover those who need a lot of attention and those who need less attention. For youths who are severely emotionally disturbed, their disturbance has an invisible handicap and becomes more apparent at stressful times. The behavior ranges of emotionally disturbed children are wider than adults. The social workers give the children's lives a sense of structure, the schedule stability.

EDITING 5: PRACTICE

Edit the following passage, making all of the sentences consistent and complete. More than one edited version is possible. Be ready to explain your editing choices.

I'll bet that most people sit down to their dinner between six and seven o'clock each night. You can tell because that's when the infuriating salespeople from the local paper call. He pretends that I already have a subscription, and then he'll ask you, "Was your paper delivered on time today?" or whether it was late. It is especially annoying is where they ask the same question every time. And they think that if you say, "No, I'm not a

subscriber," somehow I will agree to listen to their sales pitch. What makes it even worse is a terrible newspaper. If they were trying to sell me *The New York Times* would be a different story.

EDITING 6: APPLICATION ━━━━━━━━━━━━━━━━━━━━━━━━━━━━

Examine a paper you are working on, and see whether you have written any sentences that are inconsistent or incomplete. Is there one kind of mistake that you make frequently? Can you see why you might have made this mistake? Edit those sentences, and think about how best to avoid these problems in the future.

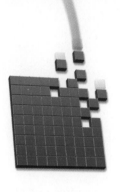

EDITING SECTION
Editing Punctuation

38   End Punctuation

The full stop at the end of every written sentence requires one of three marks of **end punctuation:** a *period, a question mark,* or an *exclamation point.* Sometimes the only clue to the meaning of a sentence is the end punctuation: *They won. They won? They won!* Periods are also used with abbreviations, and question marks are sometimes used in parentheses to indicate uncertainty.

As you edit, be aware of the conventional uses of end punctuation.

38   a   Using periods

Use a period at the end of a statement, a mild command, or a polite request.

> The administration has canceled classes.

> Do not attempt to drive to school this morning.

> Please forward an application to the address above.

Also use a period after an indirect question (one that is reported, not asked directly). (See 37a5 and 38b.)

> I wonder who made the decision?

Use a period in most conventional abbreviations. Do not put a space between the parts of an abbreviation (*U.S.*), except for the initials used for a person's name (*S. E. Hinton*).

Mr., Mrs., Ms.	A.M., P.M.	U.S., U.K.
Dr., Rev., Msgr.	sec., min., hr.	B.C., B.C.E., A.D.
Gov., Sen.	wk., mo., yr.	etc., e.g., i.e., vs., ca.
B.A., M.A., Ph.D.	in., ft., yd., mi.	p., para., fig., vol.

R.N., M.D.	Mon., Tues., Wed.	St., Ave., Blvd.
Jr., Sr.	Jan., Feb., Mar.	

When an abbreviation containing a period falls at the end of a sentence, use a single period to end the sentence.

> **The Athenian empire ended in 404 B.C.**✓

Note that the names of government agencies, organizations, corporations, and other such entities are generally abbreviated without periods: *FBI, NCAA, CBS, SAT.* Many other familiar initial abbreviations are also written without periods: *VCR, CD, RFD.* Periods are also not used with most shortened forms of words: *lab, grad, premed, champ.* Periods are never used in **acronyms,** which are abbreviations made up of initials and pronounced as words: *NASA, NATO, HUD.* (See Chapter 49 for more on abbreviations and acronyms.)

EDITING 1: PRACTICE ⎯⎯⎯⎯⎯⎯⎯⎯⎯⎯⎯⎯⎯⎯⎯⎯⎯⎯⎯⎯⎯⎯⎯⎯⎯⎯

Edit the following sentences by using periods correctly.

1. Sandra Booker, MD, is a role model for our community.
2. Dr Booker focuses her practice on pediatric care for homeless children, beginning her day as early as 5:00 A.M..
3. She volunteers two days a week at an A.I.D.S. clinic.
4. She has worked with the US. Department of Housing and Urban Development (H.U.D.) to develop programs for at-risk families.
5. She even conducts a learning lab, for high school students who are considering becoming doctors.
6. I wonder who else in the community does so much?

---

38 b Using question marks

Use a question mark at the end of every **direct question.** Direct questions are usually signaled either by an interrogative pronoun such as *what, where, or why,* or by inverted word order, with part of the verb before the subject.

Where is Times Square?	*How* can I get there?
Can I take the subway?	*Do you* know the fare?

A sentence that ends with a **tag question** also takes a question mark. (See 39e for the use of commas with tag questions.)

This train goes to Times Square, doesn't it?

Direct questions in a series may each be followed by a question mark, even if they are not all complete sentences (See 46a for advice on capitalizing fragmentary questions.)

Where did Mario go? Did he go to the library? the cafeteria?

When a quotation is itself a question, put the question mark inside the quotation marks. No additional comma or period is needed.

I asked, "should I go?"

Gertrude Stein was reportedly asked on her deathbed, "What is the answer?" "What is the question?" she replied.

When a quotation that is not a question appears in a sentence that is a question, put the question mark outside the quotation marks.

Did you say, "I should go"?

When both the sentence and the quotation it contains are questions, use a question mark inside the quotation marks.

Did you say, "May I go too?"

The same rules apply to exclamation points (see 38c).

Writers sometimes phrase questions in normal word order, as if they were statements; a question mark indicates that they should be read as questions.

Sylvester Stallone will play Hamlet next year? Don't count on it.

On the other hand, a polite request can be phrased as a direct question and written with a period instead of a question mark, especially when compliance is expected: *Would you join us in the conference room at 10:00.*

Remember that unlike direct questions, **indirect questions**—ones that are reported rather than asked directly—are not followed

by question marks. In other words, if the independent clause in a sentence is a question, then use a question mark. If the independent clause is not a question, don't use a question mark.

Independent Clause	Dependent Clause

Are you asking me which subway you should take?

Independent Clause	Dependent Clause

He wants to know how he can get to Times Square.

(For more on indirect questions, see 37a5.)

Use a question mark in parentheses to indicate uncertainty about a specific fact such as a date or the correct spelling of a word.

The plays of Francis Beaumont, 1584–1616, were as popular in
(?)
∧

their day as Shakespeare's.

Do not use question marks in parentheses to suggest sarcasm or irony.

Some people think it is funny ~~(?)~~ to humiliate others.

EDITING 2: PRACTICE _____

Edit the following sentences by using question marks correctly.

1. "You say that by learning another language a person can learn a lot about another culture," I asked.
2. I wonder how long it takes to be able to think in a different language?
3. What is the best way for me to learn to speak French, converse with my friends, go to the language lab, go to France?
4. The best way to learn to speak another language is to speak it as often as possible, isn't it.
5. Some students think it's entertaining (?) when classmates make mistakes.
6. Don't you know that we learn by making mistakes.

38 c Using exclamation points

Use an exclamation point to convey emphasis or strong emotion in exclamations, forceful commands, interjections, and statements or questions that require special intensity.

What a mess!   Wow! It's getting late!
Stop the train!   Was that train fast!

When the words in a direct quotation are an exclamation, put an exclamation point within the quotation marks.

"Ouch" ⁀**my brother cried. "That hurts!"**

If a sentence that requires an exclamation point ends with a quotation that does not, put the exclamation point outside the quotation marks.

Don't call it "Frisco!"

If both the sentence and the quotation within it are exclamations, put an exclamation point inside the quotation marks.

Quick, yell "Fire!"

Do not use an exclamation point, even in parentheses, to indicate amazement or sarcasm. Do not use more than one exclamation point or a combination of exclamation points and question marks to indicate amazement.

The judges selected Carl (!) to represent us in the regional competition.

Can you believe that the baby slept through the night!!?!

Because exclamation points signal emphasis, they make demands on readers' attention and energy. Your writing will lose effectiveness if you use too many of them. Use only one or two in a passage; pick the most important exclamation point and replace the others with periods.

EDITING 3: EXPLORATION

Find four or five examples of popular writing that overuse exclamation points. A good place to start your search is in advertising and comic strips in newspapers or magazines. What effect do the exclamation points have?

EDITING 4: PRACTICE

Edit the following sentences by using exclamation points correctly. Some sentences have more than one possible answer. Be ready to discuss your editing choices.

1.   Our mother told us to be careful! not to slip on the ice when we were running for the bus.
2.   "Be careful," she called out as we hurried down the icy driveway.
3.   "Oh! No! Here comes the bus now. Hurry up."
4.   "Too late. Now we'll have to walk to school."
5.   "Are you crazy!? It's a four-mile walk to school."
6.   "Don't tell me you can't walk four miles?" I exclaimed.

EDITING 5: PRACTICE _____

Edit the following by using all end punctuation correctly. More than one edited version is possible. Be ready to explain your editing choices.

Have you always assumed eating sugar will make you gain weight. This fact (?) is increasingly subject to debate. According to recent research, the main problem with sugar is that it usually accompanies fat in a diet Dr Adam Berg, a nutritionist, wondered what makes some people gain weight more than others? His research has led him to believe that excess fat is actually more likely than sugar to cause problems with weight and health! A study by the US Food and Drug Administration shows that the average American eats about two ounces of sugar a day. According to Berg, the level of sugar consumption found by the F.D.A. applies to both moderately overweight and obese people. Does the difference lie in amount of exercise? genetic makeup. calorie intake. Berg believes it is a combination of these, but he notes specifically that the eating patterns of obese people reflect a particularly high consumption of fatty foods. He suggests cutting out the doughnuts (!) and eating low-fat sweets instead. If only it could be so easy.

EDITING 6: APPLICATION _____

What difficulties do you have with end punctuation (periods, question marks, exclamation points)? Examine a paper you are working on to see if you have misused punctuation in any way. Were you able to identify your trouble spots? See if you can detect any patterns in your mistakes. Edit any sentences that have incorrect end punctuation.

39   Commas

The *comma* is the most frequently used mark of punctuation in English. Commas shape the phrasing of written sentences in the same way that brief pauses shape the phrasing of spoken sentences. Commas can indicate that a sentence is divided into distinct grammatical parts. By showing which words go together and which should be separated, commas help readers understand a sentence's meaning.

Consider, for example, how difficult it is to understand the meaning of the following sentence, from which all commas have been deleted:

> A quarter of a century after the introduction of television into American society a period that has seen the medium become so deeply ingrained in American life that in at least one state the television set has attained the rank of a legal necessity safe from repossession in case of debt along with clothes cooking utensils and the like television viewing has become an inevitable and ordinary part of daily life.

With its commas restored, however, this complex sentence is actually quite clear:

> A quarter of a century after the introduction of television into American society, a period that has seen the medium become so deeply ingrained in American life that in at least one state the television set has attained the rank of a legal necessity, safe from repossession in case of debt along with clothes, cooking utensils, and the like, television viewing has become an inevitable and ordinary part of daily life.
>
> MARIE WINN, "THE PLUG-IN DRUG"

An **independent clause** is a group of words that contains a subject and a predicate and that can stand alone as a complete sentence. A **compound sentence** contains two or more independent clauses. If those clauses are joined with a **coordinating conjunction** (*and, or, but, for, nor, yet, so*), use a comma before the coordinating conjunction.

> Campaign workers distributed leaflets, and posters lauding the candidates were hung throughout the hall.

When two short independent clauses are related in meaning or parallel in structure and there is no chance of misreading, the comma between them may be omitted.

> The sun rose and the fog lifted.

To prevent misreading of a compound sentence when the independent clauses contain internal commas, you may use a semicolon rather than a comma before the coordinating conjunction that joins the independent clauses.

> Cruise passengers may disembark to shop, tour the island, or snorkel, or, if they wish, they may swim, view a movie, or just relax on the ship.

Do not use a comma without a coordinating conjunction to join independent clauses. If you do, the result is an error known as a **comma splice.** (See Chapter 33.)

> *and*
> His hobby is raising geese, he proudly displays the blue ribbons he has won at the state fair.

Do not use a comma before a coordinating conjunction joining two dependent clauses.

> When the board meets and when the vote is officially recorded, the decision will be final.

Also do not use commas between other compound elements, such as compound subjects and compound verbs. (See 39j2.)

EDITING I: PRACTICE _____

Edit the following sentences, using commas correctly with coordinating conjunctions joining independent clauses. Circle the number of any sentence that is correct.

1.   The highway department sets speed limits on state roads and highways and it determines standards for intersecting roads.

2.   Every new business or residence along a highway needs an access road but first the highway department must approve its design and location.

3.   The developer of a new housing development or commercial center must complete an application, and must submit it for the highway department's review.

4.   The regulations set standards for sight distances and markings so a developer can tell whether a driveway is acceptable.

5.   The minimum sight distances vary with the speed limit and the grade of the road and the standards for driveway construction vary with the expected volume of traffic.

6.   The highway department does not have to permit a driveway that does not meet its standards or that would require modifications to the roadway.

39 b Using commas after introductory elements

An **introductory element** is a dependent clause, phrase, or word that precedes and introduces an independent clause. In most cases, a comma should separate the introductory element from the independent clause.

DEPENDENT CLAUSE	*When Elizabeth I assumed the throne of England in 1558,* the country was in turmoil.
PREPOSITIONAL PHRASE	*In every taste test,* the subjects chose the new flavor over the old.
INFINITIVE PHRASE	*To do the job properly,* they need more time.
PARTICIPIAL PHRASES	*Praised by all the critics,* the movie was still not a hit.
	Barking furiously, the little dog lunged at me.
ABSOLUTE PHRASE	*His dream of glory destroyed,* the boxer died an embittered man.

Some writers do not use a comma when the phrase is only two or three words and there is no possibility of confusion. This is particularly true with short prepositional phrases: *In 1963 an assasin's bullet shocked the world.* However, a comma is always correct in these situations and may be preferred by some instructors.

Do not use a comma after an introductory phrase when the word order of the sentence is inverted so that the verb precedes its subject.

> **In the back of the closet/ was an old box.**
>
> *In this sentence,* box *is the subject and* was *is the verb.*

Do not use a comma after a phrase that functions as the subject of the sentence rather than as a modifier.

> **Hearing that song/ evokes warm memories.**
>
> *In this sentence,* hearing that song *is the subject.*

Introductory words should generally be separated from an independent clause by a comma.

> *Together,* we are a great team.
>
> *Nervously,* I waited for my name to be called.

Conjunctive adverbs, transitional expressions, and interjections are set off no matter where they fall in a sentence.

CONJUNCTIVE ADVERB	*However,* taxes must be raised.
TRANSITIONAL EXPRESSION	*First,* remove the plastic wrapper. *Then,* unfold the bag.
INTERJECTION	*Yes,* we need to improve our parks.

(See 39d and 39e. See 23c and 33b for more examples of transitional expressions and conjunctive adverbs.)

EDITING 2: PRACTICE _____

Edit the following passage, using commas after introductory elements.

> Despite his own admission that he had lived a life full of failings Mickey Mantle died a hero to many Americans. During the 1950s and 1960s Mantle was the most popular player on the New York Yankees. Because of that team's unsurpassed success on the baseball diamond Mantle's personal

achievements took on an even greater luster than they otherwise might have. However it was not just his skills as a player that made him beloved. In fact Mantle's warmth as a human being endeared him to fans and sportswriters more than did any other trait. When Mantle died in 1995 his passing was felt deeply by many who had seen him play. Although years separated them from their childhood days at the ballpark many older Americans took time to cherish their memories of watching "the Mick" play. To many he was the symbol of a less cynical and materialistic era.

39 **C** **Using commas to set off nonrestrictive elements**

A modifier is **restrictive** if it provides information that readers must have in order to understand the meaning of the word or words modified. It "restricts" or limits the meaning from a general group to a more specific one.

Students *who are late* will be prohibited from taking the exam.

The modifier who are late *is restrictive because it limits the meaning to a specific group of students—those who are late.*

A modifier is **nonrestrictive** if it provides additional information but is not essential to the meaning of the word or words it modifies.

Qualified doctors, *who must be licensed,* are in short supply.

The modifier who must be licensed *tells the reader more about doctors but does not restrict the meaning to a specific group of doctors.*

When something or someone is identified by name, its meaning cannot be further specified; therefore, any modifier is nonrestrictive.

Ernesto Seguerra, *who used to run a hardware business,* is now running for mayor.

Use commas to set off nonrestrictive modifiers but not restrictive ones. Often, the only clue to whether a modifier is restrictive or nonrestrictive—and to the writer's meaning—is how the sentence is punctuated.

Company employees *who receive generous benefits* should not complain.

Company employees, *who receive generous benefits,* should not complain.

The restrictive modifier in the first sentence limits the meaning to a specific group of employees, implying that not all employees *of the company receive generous benefits. The nonrestrictive modifier in the second sentence says something different: by not specifying a specific group, it implies that* all employees *receive generous benefits.*

To determine whether a modifier is restrictive or nonrestrictive, try omitting it. Omitting a nonrestrictive modifier usually will not change the basic meaning of a sentence, but omitting a restrictive one will.

RESTRICTIVE   Athletes who take steroids want a shortcut.

Athletes want a shortcut.

These two sentences have very different meanings; the modifier is restrictive.

NONRESTRICTIVE   Olympic athletes, who all have trained intensely, are usually in top physical shape.

Olympic athletes are usually in top physical shape.

These two sentences mean about the same thing; the modifier is nonrestrictive.

Another way to see whether a modifier is restrictive or nonrestrictive is to ask a question about the identity of the subject. If the answer requires the information contained in the modifier, the modifier is restrictive.

RESTRICTIVE   A cat that neglects to groom itself will have matted fur.

What will have matted fur? A cat that neglects to groom itself.

NONRESTRICTIVE   A cat, a nocturnal mammal, hunts small rodents.

What hunts small rodents? A cat.

Adjective and adverb clauses

Adjective clauses—clauses that begin with *that, where, which, who, whom,* and *whose*—can be either restrictive or non-restrictive. *That* is used only in restrictive clauses. *Which* is used for nonrestrictive clauses, but it can be used for restrictive as well. (For more information on *that* and *which,* see 36d.) Restrictive clauses are not set off by commas because they are necessary to the meaning of the sentence; nonrestrictive clauses are set off by commas.

RESTRICTIVE   Anyone *who visits the National Air and Space Museum* can touch a piece of the moon.

Note that a clause modifying an indefinite pronoun, such as anyone, *is usually restrictive.*

NONRESTRICTIVE The festival will honor Spike Lee, *who directed Malcolm X.*

Note that a clause modifying a proper noun, such as Spike Lee, *is almost always nonrestrictive.*

Adverb clauses—those that begin with subordinating conjunctions such as *because, when,* and *before*—are usually restrictive, needing no commas.

I usually do well on tests *when I am prepared.*

When an adverb clause introduces a sentence, however, a comma is requried.

When I am prepared, I do well on tests.

2 Appositives

An **appositive** is a noun or noun phrase that immediately follows another noun and renames it. An appositive is restrictive only when it is more specific than the noun it renames. (See 36m.)

RESTRICTIVE   Poet *Gary Soto* has written several novels for young adults.

His poem *"Oranges"* is about having a crush on someone.

Gary Soto *is more specific than* poet. "Oranges" *specifies which of many poems.*

NONRESTRICTIVE Gary Soto, *a popular poet,* writes novels for young adults.

"Oranges," *my favorite of his poems,* seems autobiographical.

A popular poet *is less specific than* Gary Soto. My favorite of his poems *is not more specific than* "Oranges."

EDITING 3: PRACTICE

Edit the following passage, using commas correctly.

Anger an emotion all of us experience at one time or another generally arises, when we feel we can't control a situation or we don't get what we want. Anger may be natural but researchers say that people, who get angry often, may be giving in to a learned response. Such uncontrolled fits of anger which can actually kill a person may be controlled if people, can learn to deal with their anger, in a positive way. C. Mack Amick a counselor from North Carolina advises people to ask themselves three questions when they get angry. The first question, recommended by Amick, is "Is this really important to me?" The answer well may be "no" which means it's time to cool off. The second question that he recommends is "Is this the right time to get angry?" The final question designed specifically to help one gain control is "Do I have an effective response?" Finding a response, that is assertive but not aggressive, is the key to controlling one's anger.

---

39 d Using commas to set off parenthetical expressions and elements of contrast

Parenthetical expressions are words and phrases that interrupt the flow of a sentence to offer a comment, a supplemental explanation, or a transition. In many cases, **transitional expressions** and **conjunctive adverbs** (such as *furthermore, for example, as a result, therefore, however,* and *meanwhile*) serve as parenthetical expressions and are set off with commas. Other conventional parenthetical expressions include *in fact, of course, without a doubt, by the way,* and *to be honest.* Phrases that begin with *according to, such as,* and so forth are also parenthetical expressions.

One Saturday, *for example,* we had marshmallows for breakfast.

Parenthetical expressions can often be moved within a sentence without affecting its meaning. No matter where they appear in a sentence, they are generally set off with commas.

The commissioner was not amused by the report, *however.*

The commissioner, *however,* was not amused by the report.

However, the commissioner was not amused by the report.

Note that if a conjunctive adverb is being used to join two independent clauses, you must use a semicolon rather than a comma before it. Otherwise, you will create a **comma splice.** (See Chapter 33 and 40a.) A conjunctive adverb at the beginning of a sentence must be followed by a comma. (See 40a.)

Commas may also be used to set off **elements of contrast**—words, phrases, or clauses that emphasize a point by describing what it is not or by citing an opposite condition.

> The experience was illuminating, but unnerving, for everyone.

> The article mentioned where he obtained his degree, not when he received it.

EDITING 4: PRACTICE _____

Edit the following sentences, using commas correctly. Circle the number of any sentence that is correct.

1. Soothing music it seems is effective for reducing stress.
2. Many physicians in fact are recommending relaxing music not tranquilizers to patients with high levels of stress.
3. One Boston doctor surprisingly enough has produced a recording of music that according to him uses the rhythms of a healthy heartbeat.
4. He believes exposure to such rhythms can promote a slower and more regular heartbeat in patients.
5. Other physicians however suggest that patients should select their own favored music not a doctor's prescription.
6. A Phoenix psychologist for example advises patients to start with music that is the same as not calmer than their energy level; they can later switch to music of a lower intensity.

---

39 **e** **Using commas to set off tag sentences, direct address, and interjections**

Use commas to set off nonessential elements such as tag sentences, direct address, and some interjections.

⬛ Tag sentences

Use a comma before **tag sentences**—short statements or questions at the ends of sentences that express or elicit an opinion.

You received my application in time, *I hope.*

We are not so trusting of strangers these days, *are we?*

2 Direct address

Use a comma or commas to set off words of **direct address—** words that name the person or group to whom a sentence is directed.

Lilith, I hope you are well.

That, *my friends,* is not the end of the story.

We appreciate your generous contribution, *Dr. Collins.*

3 Interjections

Use a comma or commas to set off mild **interjections,** expressions of emotion. (Set off a stronger interjection by treating it like a separate sentence: *Hooray! I got an A on my exam!*)

Oh, what good times we had together.

The replacement players, *alas,* were doomed from the start.

Yes and *no* are treated similarly.

Yes, I enjoyed the party, but *no,* my date didn't.

A comma is not required before no *in this sentence because the interruption is so brief.*

EDITING 5: PRACTICE ───────────────────

Edit the following sentences, using commas correctly. Circle the number of any sentence that is correct.

1. Oh the promises politicians make.
2. They always begin with something like, "My fellow citizens it is my goal to follow the will of the people."
3. Then they tell us, "You realize that my first concern is my constituents I hope."
4. They can't really expect us to believe their promises can they?
5. Ah we're just disillusioned with politicians these days my friends, so no wonder turnout on election day gets lower every year don't you think?

39 f Using commas between items in a series and between coordinate adjectives

1 Items in a series

A **series** consists of three or more words, phrases, or clauses that are equal in grammatical form and in importance. A coordinating conjunction—*and, or, but, nor, so, for, yet*—usually precedes the final item in the series. Use a comma after each item in the series except the last.

> He studied all of the notes, memos, letters, and reports.

> To accelerate smoothly, to stop without jerking, and to make complete turns can require many hours of driving practice.

Sometimes, the **serial comma,** the one that would normally precede the coordinating conjunction, is omitted: *Participants in the peace talks included Israelis, Palestinians and Syrians.* This style is common in newspapers. In academic writing, however, using the final comma is generally preferred.

Unless a comma is required by another rule, do not use one before the first item or after the last item of a series.

> The primary colors are, red, yellow, and blue.

> They visited Nevada, Utah, and Arizona, on their trip west.

When individual items of a series include commas, you can help readers avoid confusion by separating the elements with semicolons instead of commas. (See 40b.)

2 Coordinate adjectives

Coordinate adjectives are two or more adjectives that modify the same noun: *warm, sunny day.* Coordinate adjectives are independent of each other in meaning and in their relationship to the noun. Use commas to separate coordinate adjectives.

To see whether adjectives are coordinate, try inserting *and* between them or reversing their order. If the resulting sentence still makes sense, the adjectives are coordinate and require commas. If the adjectives are not coordinate, do not separate them with a comma. Such adjective combinations, called **cumulative adjectives,** build on one another and together modify a noun.

COORDINATE ADJECTIVES

YES He put on a *clean, pressed* shirt.

YES He put on a clean and pressed shirt.

YES He put on a pressed, clean shirt.

CUMULATIVE ADJECTIVES

YES I found *five copper* coins.

NO I found five and copper coins.

NO I found copper five coins.

Do not use a comma between the last adjective and the noun it modifies, whether the adjectives are coordinate adjectives or not.

They walked with delicate, deliberate, steps across the ice.

(See the ESL box in 27d2.)

EDITING 6: PRACTICE ─────────────────────────

Edit the following sentences, using commas correctly. Circle the number of any sentence that is correct.

1. Burlington International Airport, like any other airport, has a tower, a radar room and many safety devices.
2. Inside the airport are a comfortable spacious lounge, three departure gates, and a restaurant.
3. The airport leases the space to a number of customers, including airlines car rental agencies food concessions and gift shops.
4. The airport's representative explained that the airport is run like larger airports that it leases out its buildings and that it takes a percentage of the profits made by the independent businesses.
5. The majority of air travel at the airport is between Boston Newark and Chicago, although travel is by no means limited to these three, major cities.
6. Over the next ten years, the airport hopes to replace the few, remaining pre-1950s buildings with large modern facilities.

39 g Using commas with quotations

Direct quotations are often accompanied by **attributory words,** which identify the source of the quotation. In general, use

commas to set off attributory words, whether they appear before, after, or in the middle of the quotation.

> In 1948 Jack Kerouac first declared, "We're a beat generation."

A comma before attributory words goes *inside* the quotation marks.

> "Scratch a lover," according to Dorothy Parker, "and find a foe."

When an attributory phrase appears between two complete quoted sentences, it is followed by a period. If the quotation ends with a question mark or exclamation point, do not add a comma.

> **"Dead, did I say?⸜," Chief Seattle concludes. "There is no death, only a change of worlds."**

Do not use a comma before a partial quotation preceded by *that* or when there is no true attributory phrase.

> **He closed by saying that⸝ "time will prove us right."**

> **According to one critic, the program is⸝ "a sinkhole for public dollars."**

> **The slogan⸝ "You deserve a break today⸝" was particularly successful.**

In general, do not use a comma before indirect quotations.

> **Jones claimed⸝ he had not yet begun to fight.**

A comma may, however, follow an introductory phrase before indirect quotation.

> According to Jones, he has not yet begun to fight.

(See Chapter 43 for more on punctuating quotations.)

EDITING 7: PRACTICE ─────────────────────────

Edit the following sentences, using commas correctly.

1. "Love looks not with the eyes" according to Shakespeare "but with the mind."

2.   In her novel *Jacques,* George Sand writes "No human creature can give orders to love."

3.   "How do I love Thee?," asked Elizabeth Barrett Browning. "Let me count the ways."

4.   "Man must evolve for all human conflict a method which rejects revenge, aggression, and retaliation" said Martin Luther King, "The foundation of such a method is love."

5.   Dr. King also said "I believe that unarmed truth and unconditional love will have the final word in reality."

6.   "Love is heaven" wrote Walter Scott "and heaven is love."

---

39 **h** **Using commas with numbers, dates, names, places, and addresses**

Various rules and conventions govern the use of commas with numbers, dates, names, places, and addresses.

Numbers

For numbers of five digits or more, use a comma before every three digits, counting from the right. In four-digit numbers, the comma is optional.

2700 (*or* 2,700)   79,087   1,654,220

Do not use a comma in years or page numbers of four digits or with numbers in addresses.

That example is found on page 1269.

In 1990, our address was 21001 South Street, Lodi, Ohio 43042.

Dates

Always use a comma between the words for the day and month and between the numbers for the date and year.

Friday, March 22   June 10, 1999

Also use a comma after the year when a date giving month, day, and year is part of a sentence.

Our family reunion was held on July 22, 2001, in Chicago.

Don't use commas when only the month and year are given in a date or when the month separates the date and year. (The day,

month, year order is more common in British English than in American English.)

> The war broke out in *August 1914* and ended on *11 November 1918*.

3 Names

Use commas to set off an abbreviation or title following a name.

> Joyce B. *Wong, M.D.,* supervised the CPR training session.

> Renee *Dafoe, vice president,* welcomed the new members.

> Edwin M. *Green, Jr.,* was the first speaker.

Do not use commas to set off roman numerals following a name.

> Frank T. Winters III

4 Places and addresses

Use a comma before and after the state when naming a city and state in a sentence.

> She was born in *Lexington, Kentucky,* and raised in New York.

When a full address is given in a sentence, use a comma to separate each element except the postal code, which should have no comma before or after it.

> My address is *169 Elm Street, Apartment 4, Boston, Massachusetts 02116* through the end of June.

For an address in block form, as on the front of an envelope, do not use a comma at the end of each line.

EDITING 8: PRACTICE ───────────────────────────────

Edit the following sentences, using commas correctly.

1. In the week before Christmas, the mail order company where I worked filled 84567 orders.
2. I started my job in February, 1998, and the last day I worked was January 15 1999.
3. During that time, I answered 3456 calls and sold merchandise worth more than $200000.

4.   The worst customers are the ones with names like Jane Jones Ph.D. or John Johnson, III, who insist on having their titles appear on all their mail.

5.   You may write to my former employer at this address: National Mail Order Products, 19123 Fifth Avenue New York New York 10001.

6.   With $1500 in my savings account, I did not need to worry about getting another job until March 1999.

39 i Using commas to prevent misreading

Commas may occasionally be used, even when they are not required by any specific rule, to prevent misreading.

We will all pitch in, in the event of a problem.

I believed, once I had seen the evidence.

Those of us who can, preserve the memories fondly.

They found that in 1990, 256 people were infected.

If a clause that begins with *because* follows the main clause but could modify more than one element in the sentence, a comma can help clarify the meaning.

We knew that she called her brother because her mother asked her to do so.

We knew that she called her brother, because we saw the phone bill.

Usually a modifier modifies the closest suitable element. If that's not the case, the comma helps alert the reader.

EDITING 9: EXPLORATION

Make up sentences that are awkward, confusing, or humorous without commas. Read them to your classmates to see if they are able to understand them. Examples:

In the winter time seems to stand still.
I dressed and fed my cats.

✔ GUIDELINES FOR USING COMMAS

As you edit use the following guidelines for placing commas in your paper:

- Before a coordinating conjunction that joins independent clauses. (See 39a.)

[Independent Clause],   [Independent Clause]

I had studied for hours, but I still found the exam difficult.

- To set off an introductory element (See 39b.)

[Introductory Element],   [Main Clause]

Concentrating intensely, I completed the exam in twenty minutes.

- To set off any nonrestrictive element. (See 39c.)

[Main Clause],   [Nonrestrictive Element]

They toured the *Balclutha*, which was moored near Fisherman's Wharf.

[Nonrestrictive Element]

Dr. Parke-Cookson, our chemistry professor, gives exams weekly.

- To set off parenthetical expressions and elements of contrast, (See 39d.)
- To set off interjections, tag sentences, and direct address. (See 39e.)
- Between items in a series. (See 39f1.)

[Item],   [Item],   [Item]

English, history, and philosophy are my favorite subjects.

- Between coordinate adjectives. (See 39f2.)

[Coordinate Adjective],   [Coordinate Adjective],   [Noun]

Well-written, well-researched papers receive the best grades.

- Between quotations and attributory phrases. (See 39g.)
- With numbers, dates, names, and addresses. (See 39h.)
- To prevent misreading. (See 39i.)

39 **j** Editing misused commas

Failing to include commas where they are conventionally expected can confuse readers and undercut your authority as a writer. It can be equally distracting, however, to use commas where they are not required.

Misuses of commas already discussed in this chapter are summarized in the box on page 611. This section covers several other common misuses.

 Avoid putting single commas between subjects and verbs, verbs and objects or complements, or objects and complements.

Subject and verb

A *season* of drought, *worried* the farmers.

Verb and object

The agreement *entails, training* for part-time staff.

Verb and complement

The laid-off workers *seem,* surprisingly *understanding.*

Object and complement

The extra pay made *him,* quite *happy.*

However, a pair of commas, such as those used to set off nonessential elements, may separate subjects from verbs.

David *Hill, the chief researcher,* developed the method.

2 **Avoid putting commas between two compound elements.**

Compound subject

The *members* of the senior class, and their *parents* were invited.

COMMA TROUBLESHOOTING

When editing your papers for correct use of commas, pay special attention to the commas that help readers understand your ideas. (From a reader's point of view, some commas are more important than others.)

- As an editing strategy, put brackets around structures that need commas so that you can easily identify where phrases or clauses begin and end.

    My English teacher [who is new this year] just graduated from Stanford.

    [If we consider the source of humor for this joke] we see that it depends on something that is contrary to our expectations.

- Check for commas following all adverb clauses (*because, although, when,* etc.) that begin sentences. Find the end of the clause and add a comma if necessary.

    Because the library was closed I studied at home.

- When using *that* as a relative pronoun, make sure that you have not set it off by commas. (See 39j3.)

    In the library, we found the materials, that we needed to complete the project.

- If you have listed three or more items in a series, make sure that you have put a comma and the word *and* or another coordinating conjunction before the last item. (See 39f.)

    , and
    We studied similies, metaphors analogies.

CHECKING FOR COMMAS THAT OCCUR IN PAIRS

- Always make sure to use a pair of commas to set off the following when they appear in the middle of a sentence: **nonrestrictive modifiers** and **appositives** (39c); **parenthetical elements** and **elements of contrast** (39d); **interjections** and **words of direct address** (39e); and **years in full dates, titles, abbreviations after names,** and **state names preceded by city names** (39h).

> This book ‸, which he had read three times, was quite tattered.

> The instructors ‸, rather than the students, are being tested.

> I bought it from a Joplin, Missouri ‸, publisher.

> It will be January 3, 2004 ‸, before I receive my degree.

- Delete single commas that separate the subject from the verb, no matter how many words make up the subject (unless it has phrases or clauses after it that need commas). (See 39b and 39jl.)

> The city in the southern United States that I like the most͵ is New Orleans.

Compound verb

Maria quickly *turned off* the lights͵ and *locked* the door.

Compound object

Sean put the *books* on the shelf͵ and the *pens* in the drawer.

Compound complement

He found the work *easy to learn͵* but *hard to continue.*

Commas are used to separate the independent clauses of a compound sentence. (See 39a.)

> The rain finally stopped and then the sun came out.

3 Avoid putting commas following a relative pronoun or subordinating conjunction.

> The map *that* we requested turned out to be incorrect.

> Our legislators have no idea how to proceed *because we have not come to a consensus.*

A pair of commas, such as those used to set off parenthetical elements, may separate these elements.

> We found that, according to the latest data, the population had doubled.

(See 39g for uses of commas with quotations.)

EDITING 10: PRACTICE ———————————————

Edit the following passage for correct comma use.

> More kids than ever before are playing video games, to fill up their leisure time. Some popular, video games have inspired movies that became a huge, financial success. Playing such a game, is thought by some to have a negative influence on behavior, though. Some, recent studies suggest that children, witnessing simulations of extreme violence, are more likely, than others, to behave violently, themselves. On the other hand, many others argue that video games are a harmless way for people, to relieve stress, and aggression. In their view, human beings are naturally prone to violence, and to claim that the elimination of a single, video game would make a difference, is sheer fantasy.

EDITING 11: PRACTICE ———————————————

Edit the following passage for correct comma use.

> In two, recent scientific studies researchers have found what might be called, an "excitability gene." This genetic variation as it is called is found in people who crave, excitement, thrills and new experiences. They are also

EDITING UNNEEDED COMMAS

Do not use a comma for the following:

- To join independent clauses without a coordinating conjunction. (See 39a and Chapter 40.)

  We won the game ; it was the first of many victories.

- After an introductory phrase when the verb precedes the subject in a sentence. (See 39b.)

  Along with every challenge comes an opportunity for success.

- After a phrase that is the subject of the sentences (See 39b.)

  Eating sensibly and exercising regularly improved my health.

- To set off restrictive elements. (See 39c.)

  The materials that you requested have arrived.

  A bird with only one wing has little chance of survival.

  Singer and guitarist John Hall will appear at the benefit.

- Before the first element or after the last element of a series, unless required by another rule. (See 39f1.)

  We contributed to United Way, World Watch, and the Red Cross last year.

  Rice, beans, and peppers provide the basis for many local dishes.

- Between adjectives that are not coordinate. (See 39f2.)

  There are three different patterns of male baldness.

themselves excitable, and prone to temper flare-ups. If the discovery holds up after further research it will represent the first link ever discovered between a gene and normal nonpathological behavior. "Success in mapping genes for a normal personality trait may signal a fruitful way to map genes for psychopathology" according to one of the researchers C. Robert Cloninger M.D. Cloninger who is on the staff of Washington University, proposed the hypothesis that, people's need for excitement is related to how dopamine a neural chemical is processed by the brain. This process is governed by a specific gene that in fact occurs in two variant forms, as a series of seven sequences or a series of four. What researchers discovered was that people, who could be called "novelty-seekers," generally had the longer seven-sequence version of the gene. This does not mean however, that the behavioral trait is governed solely by this single gene and researchers caution that other factors such as personal experience come into play.

EDITING 12: APPLICATION ━━━━━━━━━━━━━━━━━━━

Take a few moments to reflect on the difficulties you most commonly have in using commas. Make a brief list that ranks your problems in order from greatest to least amount of difficulty. Now examine a paper you are working on and look for any examples of misused or omitted commas. Do you notice consistent patterns? How accurate was your initial prediction of where your difficulties would lie? Edit any sentences in which you have misused or omitted commas.

40 Semicolons

While a comma marks a pause within a sentence, a *semicolon* marks a stop within a sentence, telling readers that what precedes it is complete and that what follows is also complete and closely related. The semicolon always comes between sentence elements of equal rank; it is not used to introduce, enclose, or end a statement.

Although using a period or a comma is often mandatory, using a semicolon is usually a choice; in certain situations it may be an alternative to a period, and in other circumstances, it may replace a comma.

40 a Using semicolons between independent clauses

An **independent clause** is a group of words that contains a subject and a predicate and that can stand alone as a complete sentence. Two or more such clauses may be joined with a semicolon to indicate that the clauses are closely related.

The storm raged all night; most of us slept fitfully, if at all.

A semicolon can emphasize contrast or contradiction.

Most dogs aim to please their owners; cats are more independent.

A semicolon must be used between independent clauses joined with a **conjunctive adverb** (*however, furthermore, therefore*) or a **transitional expression** (*for example, on the other hand*). (See 25a3, 33b2.)

Many in the community were angry; however, they lacked an articulate leader.

The contract was approved; indeed, no one questioned the restrictions.

Do not use both a coordinating conjunction and a semicolon to join simple independent clauses. Either delete the conjunction, or replace the semicolon with a comma.

> **Hundreds of volunteers assisted in the cleanup effort; and̶ many worked from dawn to dusk.**

> **To feel compassion is natural; but to help someone is truly virtuous.**

You may use a semicolon with a coordinating conjunction to join complex or lengthy independent clauses, particularly if they contain commas.

> If the weather clears, we plan to leave for our camping trip at dawn; and if it doesn't, given the dangerous trail conditions, we'll pack up and go home.

(For more on joining independent clauses, see Chapter 25.)
Eliminate any semicolon between an independent clause and a dependent clause. If the dependent clause precedes the independent clause, use a comma. (See 39b.) No punctuation is needed if the independent clause is first unless punctuation is required by another rule or convention.

> **Torrential rains fell every day; when we visited Florida last summer.**

> **As soon as the rain stopped; the mosquitos came out.**

EDITING I: PRACTICE ————————————————

Edit the following sentences, using semicolons as necessary to join independent clauses.

1. The amount of crime shown on television has been criticized for inciting aggression in viewers, in fact, it may be equally criticized for unreasonably raising viewers' fears.

2. Some experts estimate that 55 percent of prime-time characters experience a violent confrontation in the course of a week, the actual figure in life is less than 1 percent.

USING SEMICOLONS SPARINGLY

As a stylistic device, the semicolon can be overused, creating a monotony of rhythm and sentence structure. Save the semicolon for the sentences in which it is most effective.

⊙For
Tax incentives can distort the economy; ~~for~~ example, real estate tax shelters helped create the glut of empty office buildings that forced developers into bankruptcy and caused a banking crisis due to defaults on loans.
⊙They
More tax breaks are not the answer; ~~they~~ would only create more distortion. Politicians, however, compete to think up special tax cuts; it must be an election year.

The editing reserves the semicolon to set up the statement that requires the most emphasis.

3.   Studies have found that frequent viewers of television are likely to overestimate the statistical chance of violence in their lives, no matter what their gender, educational level, or neighborhood, and, moreover, fear, mistrust, and even paranoia can be the result.

4.   For example, among city dwellers almost half of those identified as frequent viewers see crime as a very serious problem, only a quarter of infrequent viewers do.

5.   Many Americans today rate crime as the country's number one problem, in fact, only a small segment of the population is likely to experience a violent crime.

6.   Television-related misconceptions about crime may lead citizens to clamor for more protection, local governments to request additional funding, and politicians to raise taxes, and, worse, they may also contribute to increasing social mistrust.

40 **b** Using semicolons in a series containing commas

Items in a series are generally separated by commas. (See 39f1.) In some situations, however, you can use semicolons instead.

Use a semicolon between elements in a series if any element of the series includes a comma.

> The candidates for the award are Maria, the winner of the essay competition; Elanie, the top debater; and Shelby, the director of the senior play.

Some writers use a semicolon to separate a series of long phrases or clauses, even when they contain no internal commas.

> As a nation, we need to understand why these regional conflicts occur; how they are rooted in the power vacuum that followed the fall of the Soviet Union; and what kinds of responses we can offer in settling them.

As with commas, a series should not be preceded or followed by a semicolon unless another rule requires it.

Use a colon, not a semicolon, when an independent clause introduces a list. (See 41a.)

> **It was a fine old house, but it needed work; plastering, repainting, rewiring, and a thorough cleaning.**

WHEN IS A SEMICOLON NEEDED?

- To separate two independent clauses
- In a series to separate items containing commas

EDITING 2: PRACTICE _____

Edit the following sentences, using semicolons as necessary. Circle the number of any sentence that does not need semicolons.

1. Our vacation to New England included trips to Mystic, Connecticut, Ogunquit, Maine, Boston, Massachusetts, and Keene, New Hampshire.

2. Several different craft can be seen on the Charles River; including sculls rowed by students from the universities in the area, canoes, rowboats that can be rented for a small fee, and motorboats.

3. To learn about a new place quickly, obtain a detailed map of the area you plan to visit, walk to as many places as possible, always wearing shoes with goods soles, and talk to the residents, provided they look friendly.

4. If you go to Boston's Museum of Fine Arts, don't miss the Paul Revere silver, the Egyptian mummies, the Athenian vases, and the terrific collection of paintings, including works by Gauguin, Degas, Monet, van Gogh, and Whistler.

5. In addition to its art collection, New England has been home to some of the greatest writers in America: Henry David Thoreau, who wrote *Walden*, Henry Wadsworth Longfellow, whose house on Brattle Street in Cambridge is a historic landmark, and Nathaniel Hawthorne, a resident of Salem, Massachusetts, and author of *The Scarlet Letter*.

EDITING 3: PRACTICE —————————————————————

Edit the following sentences by replacing any incorrectly used semicolons with the correct mark of punctuation or by rewording the sentence. Some sentences can be edited in more than one way. Circle the number of any sentence that is correct. Be ready to explain your editing choices.

1. Farley Mowat's books are not depressing though, they make one think about the role of humans in the universe.

2. His writing abounds with examples of the greedy nature of human beings; however, it does not convey a sense of helplessness.

3. Mowat clings to a spark of hope that it is not too late for humans to develop a respectful attitude toward our planet and the animals that inhabit it; although he regards humans as covetous.

4. A self-designated advocate for nonhuman animals, Mowat reveals the precariousness of the relationship between humans and animals; with unforgiving honesty for the most part.

5. He can be delightfully witty when he describes a positive, healthy relationship but also merciless when he condemns one; especially when it is destructive and exploitative.

6. After describing the harsh conditions in the village of Burgeo in the north of Newfoundland, he reveals the paradoxical lure of the place; abundant fish, seals, dolphins, and whales.

EDITING 4: PRACTICE —————————————————————

Edit the following passage, using semicolons correctly. More than one edited version is possible. Be ready to explain your editing choices.

Often students will not use the semicolon because they are unsure how to use it. They find the rules confusing; or hard to follow, or they have trouble

applying the examples from textbooks to their own writing. Consequently, they avoid using semicolons whenever possible. A person does not have to be a professional writer, however, to use semicolons correctly. The following three rules might help; use semicolons between independent clauses when they are closely related, use semicolons to separate items in a complex series, and finally, do not use semicolons too often or your reader will think you don't know what you're doing—an important consideration; especially if you are writing for an instructor.

EDITING 5: APPLICATION _____

Examine a paper you are working on to see whether you have overused semicolons or overlooked opportunities to use them effectively. Is there one kind of mistake you consistently make? If so, think about how best to identify misused semicolons and about places where you might use them effectively when you edit your work. Edit any sentences in which you need to improve the use of semicolons.

41   Colons

Like the semicolon, the *colon* indicates a stop within a sentence. As a mark of introduction, the colon alerts the reader that the information preceding it is illustrated by what follows. The colon is also required as a mark of separation in certain other situations, such as in writing the time of day in numerals.

The colon is a strong and rather formal mark of punctuation. Be careful not to overuse it.

41 a   Using colons as marks of introduction

Use a colon to introduce an example, explanation, list, or quotation. The colon must be preceded by an **independent clause,** one that contains a subject and a verb and can stand alone as a complete sentence.

An example or explanation can be a single word, a phrase, or a clause.

He has but one objective: success.

Much remains to be done: updating our computers, for example.

The budget agreement erected a wall between health care and education: no money was to be transferred between the two.

Capitalizing the first word of an independent clause following a colon is optional, but be consistent throughout a paper.

Use a colon to introduce a list that follows an independent clause. Frequently, an independent clause before a list will contain an expression such as *the following* or *as follows.*

Almost everything you buy travels to you by truck: paper products, food, medicine, even pickup trucks.

To complete the dish, proceed as follows: transfer the meat to a warm platter, arrange the cooked vegetables around it, ladle on some of the sauce, and sprinkle with chopped parsley.

A colon is used to introduce a quotation that is preceded by an independent clause.

> As he left, he quoted Puck's final lines from *A Midsummer Night's Dream:* "Give me your hands, if we be friends, / And Robin shall restore amends."

However, use a comma, not a colon, before a quotation if the words preceding it do not constitute an independent clause.

EDITING MISUSED COLONS

In most sentences, a colon should follow only an independent clause. Otherwise, use other punctuation conventions.

- Eliminate a colon that comes between a verb and its object or complement.

  For lunch, he usually eats: fruit, salad, or yogurt.

  My favorite fruits are: peaches, grapes, and bananas.

- Delete any colon between a preposition and its object.

  She has traveled to: New Orleans, San Francisco, and Boston.

- Eliminate any colon that follows an introductory expression (*including, such as, like, for example,* etc.).

  The show displayed several unusual pets, including: iguanas, raccoons, a civet, and a black widow spider.

- Do not use more than one colon in a sentence.

  Wesley's visits always meant gifts; records, magazines, and books: *of* pirate tales, mystery stories, and epic sagas.

As the song from *South Pacific* puts it, "You've got to be carefully taught."

(See Chapter 43 for more on punctuating quotations.)

A long quotation set off from the main text in block format may also be preceded by a colon. (See 43a2.)

41 b Using colons as marks of separation

Between numerals expressing hours, minutes, and seconds

The winning car's official elapsed time was 2:45:56.

Between a main title and a subtitle

Blue Highways: A Journey into America

"A Deep Darkness: A Review of *Out of Africa*"

Between chapter and verse numbers in biblical citations

Isaiah 14:10–11

After business letter salutations and in memo headings

Dear Mr. Nader:

To: Alex DiGiovanni
From: Paul Gallerelli
Subject: 2004 budget

USES FOR COLONS

- **Use colons as marks of introduction:** explanations, examples, lists, quotations.
- **Use colons to separate elements:** time, titles, biblical citations, salutations in letters and memos.

Colons are also used to separate elements in bibliographies and reference lists in research papers. (See Part Eight.)

EDITING 1: PRACTICE

Edit the following sentences, using colons correctly.

1. One thing is certain, the new crewmate on a whale watch always has to do the worst chores.

2. Given the terrible weather of the last few days, I was relieved by what I saw out in the distance, a nice, calm ocean.

3. I stepped on the deck and spoke these words from Melville's *Moby-Dick*, "Call me Ishmael."

4. The sight of my first whale made me think of Jonah 1.17–2.10.

5. Finally, I began the job I had been hired to do, preparing snacks and beverages in the galley.

6. We spotted various kinds of whales on the excursion, right whales, humpback whales, finback whales, and minke whales.

7. There is one thing whale watch enthusiasts should always remember to do, wear rubber-soled shoes.

8. The people on the deck wore clothes to keep them dry ponchos and garbage bags.

9. When we returned to land at 6.00, I wanted nothing more than to go home and sleep.

10. One more chore awaited me, however, scrubbing the slime off the sides of the boat.

EDITING 2: APPLICATION

Examine your use of colons in a recent paper. Do you use colons very often? If so, is there any colon mistake that you often make? If you do not use colons, can you identify any places where they might have been useful? Then edit your paper, fixing colons that are misused and inserting others where they are appropriate.

42 Apostrophes

The *apostrophe*, used primarily to form the possessive of a noun or an indefinite pronoun, also indicates certain unusual plural forms and shows where a letter has been dropped in a contraction. (For this symbol's use as a single quotation mark, see Chapter 43.)

42 a Using apostrophes to form the possessive case of nouns and indefinite pronouns

The **possessive case** of a noun or pronoun shows ownership or an association between that noun or pronoun and another word: *Sarah's book.*

Singular nouns

To form the possessive of any singular noun that does not end in *-s*, use an apostrophe and *-s*.

Denzel Washington's new movie is one of his best.

The *camera's* shutter speed is fixed.

For singular nouns ending in *-s*, it is always correct to form the possessive by adding both an apostrophe and *-s*. However, if pronouncing the additional syllable is awkward—as with last names that sound like plurals—some writers add only an apostrophe.

Don't waste the *class's* time.

John Adams' [or *Adams's*] presidency was marked by crisis and conflict.

Plural nouns

For plural nouns ending in *-s*, add only an apostrophe to form the possessive.

They examined the structure of several *moths'* wings.

The *Mertzes'* apartment was beneath the *Ricardos'*.

For irregular plural nouns not ending in -*s*, form the possessive by adding an apostrophe and -*s*.

We studied the *media's* coverage of *children's* issues.

Compound nouns

Use an apostrophe and -*s* on only the last word to form the possessive of a hyphenated or unhyphenated compound noun.

He borrowed his *mother-in-law's* car.

The *secretary of state's* office certified the election results.

USING APOSTROPHES WITH PROPER NOUNS

Sometimes writers use apostrophes incorrectly with proper nouns. One common problem is the use of 's to form the plural of family names. Edit your papers to eliminate any apostrophes used to form nonpossessive plural nouns.

For more than forty years, the Kennedy's have fascinated the American public.

Thomases
The ~~Thomas's~~ live on Maple Street.

An apostrophe may seem to be called for in the names of certain companies, organizations, and publications that appear to include the possessive form of a noun. Check these names in a directory or in a copy of the publication in question to find out whether to use an apostrophe and, if one is required, whether the possessive noun is singular or plural. The following are a few examples of different treatments of the issue of possessive forms in proper names:

Bloomingdale's
Publishers Weekly
Reader's Digest
Saks Fifth Avenue
Service Employees International Union

Two or more nouns

When nouns joined by *and* are considered a unit and are jointly in possession, add an apostrophe and *-s* to only the last noun.

My *aunt and uncle's* anniversary party was a disaster.

When nouns joined by *and* are considered individuals in separate possession, add an apostrophe and *-s* to each noun.

The documentary compared *Aretha Franklin's* and *Diana Ross's* early careers.

Indefinite pronouns

An **indefinite pronoun** is a pronoun that does not refer to any specific person or thing, *someone, anybody, no one, one, another.* Use an apostrophe and *-s* to form the possessive case of some indefinite pronouns.

Someone's umbrella was left in the assembly hall.

It is *no one's* business but mine.

Do not use an apostrophe and *-s* to form the possessive of the indefinite pronouns *all, any, both, each, few, many, most, much, several, some,* and *such.* Indicate the possessive by using a preposition such as *of,* or use a pronoun that has a possessive form.

For the Dickinson and Crane seminar, we must read ~~both's~~ complete works, *of both.*

Unfortunately, we cannot respond to ~~each's~~ questions. *everyone's*

EDITING 1: PRACTICE ⸻

Edit the following sentences, using apostrophes correctly to form the possessive forms of nouns and indefinite pronouns. Circle the number of any sentence that is correct.

1. Some people believe that students' test scores have fallen in recent years.
2. In fact, high school juniors and seniors scores on many commercial achievement tests are higher than they have ever been.
3. It seems that the medias need to report negative news is a large factor in leading people to believe that young peoples' knowledge today is not as great as it was in the past.

4.   What older people do not always realize is that no ones knowledge of the world at eighteen is as comprehensive as it will be after another ten or twenty or thirty year's worth of learning.

5.   Many also do not consider that student's work today is generally more advanced than in the past, particularly in the sciences.

6.   Todays' high school biology textbooks, for example, include lessons on DNA, RNA, gene splicing, and biochemical engineering.

7.   During my mother and father's high school years, such subjects were reserved for college or even graduate school.

8.   Even in terms of history and geography, areas in which the current generations knowledge has been shown to be weak, critic's reports of declining standards seem to be exaggerated.

9.   A 1943 survey of college freshmen found that even elite students knew nothing at all about Thomas Jefferson and Abraham Lincoln's presidencies and could not identify the Mississippi River's location on a map!

42 b Forming plurals of words used as words, letters, numbers, and symbols

Use an apostrophe and -s to form the plural of a word used as a word.

Analysis reveals more *the*'s than *and*'s in most writing.

Also use an apostrophe and an -s to form the plural of letters, numerals, and symbols.

Tic-tac-toe is played on a grid with *x*'s and *o*'s.

We have no size *8*'s in that style but five size *10*'s.

Today most telephone dial pads include #'s and *'s.

A word, number, or letter used this way is usually set off by italics or underlining. (See 48d.) However, note that the apostrophe and the -s in the plural form are not italicized or underlined.

To form the plural of centuries and decades, you may use an apostrophe and -s or an -s alone, as long as you are consistent within a paper. (The Modern Language Association prefers an -s alone.) Do not use an apostrophe when the century or decade is expressed in words.

the 1800s (*or* the 1800's)

the '60s (*or* the '60's) *but* the sixties

(See 42c2 for the use of the apostrophe to indicate omitted digits in a year.)

For plurals of abbreviations ending with periods, use an apostrophe and -s. Use -s alone for abbreviations without periods.

My science professor has earned two Ph.D.'s.

Like all politicians, she has some IOUs.

(See Chapter 49 for more on abbreviations.)

42 c Using apostrophes to show the omission of letters

1 Contractions

Apostrophes can be used to indicate that letters have been omitted from a word. A **contraction** joins two words into one by replacing one or more letters with an apostrophe. The following list shows the correct use of the apostrophe in some common contractions:

cannot	can't	will not	won't
do not	don't	would not	wouldn't
does not	doesn't	was not	wasn't
she would	she'd	it is	it's
who is	who's	you are	you're
I am	I'm	they are	they're
let us	let's	we have	we've
there is	there's	he has	he's

Because they are conversational, contractions help to create a friendly, accessible tone (which is why we have used contractions in writing this book). But because of their informality, contractions tend not to be appropriate for most academic writing.

2 Omitted letters in colloquial expressions and digits in a year

Apostrophes can also be used to indicate omitted letters in certain colloquial expressions and omitted digits in a year.

spic 'n' span   rock 'n' roll   the class of '99

An apostrophe is not used, however, when digits are omitted from the second year in a range of years: *Rembrandt van Rijn (1606–69).*

PRONOUNS AND APOSTROPHES

Most pronouns—personal, relative, interrogative, demonstrative, or reflexive—show possession by using the preposition *of* (*of himself, of which*) or by changing form (see 36k and 62b2), but pronouns do not use apostrophes—as nouns do—in the possessive form. For example, the possessive of *she* is *hers* (not *her's*), and the possessive of *they* is *theirs* (not *their's*).

When pronouns appear with apostrophes, they form contractions, such as *it's* for *it is* and *I'll* for *I will*. If you want to use a contraction, remember to include the apostrophe, or you may produce a totally different word from the one you intend. For example, *I'll* becomes *Ill* without the apostrophe.

The possessive pronouns *its, whose, your,* and *their* sound like the contractions *it's, who's, you're,* and *they're,* so be especially careful to choose the form that expresses your intended meaning.

A good test is to substitute the spelled-out form of the word whenever you see a pronoun with an apostrophe in your writing. (Consider using the search function on your computer to locate apostrophes.) If the result makes no sense, then you have incorrectly used a contraction.

The storm was brief, but ~~it's~~ *its* [it is] effects were devastating.

She is the candidate ~~who's~~ *whose* [who is] views most reflect my own.

3 Letters omitted to show pronunciation

Writers sometimes use apostrophes in dialogue to indicate letters omitted from certain words, suggesting the speaker's pronunciation.

"Courtin' was diff'rent in my day," the old man said.

EDITING 2: PRACTICE

Edit the following sentences, using apostrophes correctly to form contractions.

1.   If your a fan of the outdoors, youll enjoy exploring the Hudson River Valley, which isnt far from New York City.

PLURAL AND POSSESSIVE FORMS

Singular	Singular Possessive	Plural	Plural Possessive
school	school's	schools	schools'
box	box's	boxes	boxes'
class	class's	classes	classes'
Duvalier	Duvalier's	Duvaliers	Duvaliers'
Jones	Jones's	Joneses	Joneses'

When spoken, the plural, the singular possessive, and the plural possessive sound the same for most words. In writing, the spelling and the placement of the apostrophe help readers distinguish among the three forms.

APOSTROPHE OR NO APOSTROPHE?

What needs an apostrophe?

- Possessive cases of nouns or indefinite pronouns: *Janey's* book, *somebody's* dog.
- Plurals of words used as words, numbers, letters, symbols: *if's, Ph.D.'s, A's, $'s.*
- Contractions: *Who's* coming? *We're* late. *It's* raining.

What can't have an apostrophe?

- Personal pronouns: *you, yours; she, hers; he, his; it, its; we, ours; they, theirs.*
- Relative pronouns: *that, which, who, whose.*
- Interrogative pronouns: *Whose* are these?
- Demonstrative pronouns: *this, these, that, those.*
- Reflexive pronouns: The hunters found *themselves* lost in the fog. I consider *myself* honest.

2. In the summer, a boat will take passengers from the city to Bear Mountain, where hiking enthusiasts wont be disappointed.

3. The views from the mountain's 1300-foot summit cant be surpassed; youll see wilderness stretching out before your eyes in every direction.

4.   A trip to the country wouldnt be complete without a stop at Buddy's Café n Deli.

5.   Similarly, you shouldnt visit Hyde Park without stopping by FDR's country home, which has been preserved as it was when he died in 45.

6.   Both the Hudson River Valley and New York City offer plenty to do for the outdoor buff whos interested in stunning scenery, fine hiking, and rich history.

EDITING 3: PRACTICE ─────────────────────

Edit the following sentences, being careful to distinguish plurals, contractions, and possessives.

1.   Charles Dicken's brief experience of a debtor's prison with it's deplorable conditions had a profound effect on him.

2.   Its perhaps surprising to learn that Dickens didn't start out as a novelist; instead, he trained as a lawyer's clerk.

3.   The author, who's literary career began during the 1830s, started out writing for magazines' under the pseudonym "Boz."

4.   Society's evil, corruption, and crime were concerns to Dickens, and their frequently found as themes throughout his novel's.

5.   They're style and structure were affected by the fact that Dickens wrote his novel's for publication in monthly installments.

6.   Dickens's first novel, *Pickwick Papers,* was illustrated by a popular artist, who's plates contributed to the success of the work.

EDITING 4: EXPLORATION ─────────────────────

During the next week, keep your eye out for what you consider mistakes in the use of apostrophes, and write down any that you find. Look in newspapers, in magazines, on billboards, on the sides of commercial vehicles, on storefronts, and in television advertising. Do these mistakes make any difference in how the words are read and understood? What would be the advantages or disadvantages of leaving out apostrophes?

EDITING 5: PRACTICE ─────────────────────

Edit the following passage, using apostrophes correctly.

The computer industrys' most important "enhancement" these days may be many software companies expansion of they're call-in help desks. With the enormous growth in the number of computer owners' over the past five years has come a corresponding growth in those owners need for

truly helpful technical support, particularly considering that the average first-time buyer of a computer today has very little understanding of it's operation or functions. Just a few years ago, most companies technical support staff's consisted only of technicians and computer experts, who's attitude often suggested that a customers' questions were too stupid to be taken seriously, implying that "the problem is yours' not our's." Worse, their advice could be so technical that it's usefulness to customers was almost nonexistent. Today, however, companies are beginning to realize that ones success in an increasingly competitive market will depend on good customer service. Now when all those *Es* for "Error" appear on a users' screen, real help will be only a telephone call away.

EDITING 6: APPLICATION

Examine one of your past papers for misused or omitted apostrophes. Do you consistently make one kind of mistake in using apostrophes? Which kinds of mistakes are the most difficult to spot? Why? As you review your paper, think about how best to identify misused apostrophes or places where you tend to omit apostrophes. When you're finished, write down, in your own words, a set of guidelines for using apostrophes correctly. Then, as a final test, apply these guidelines to a different paper. Do the guidelines help? Correct any mistakes that you find.

43 Quotation Marks

Quotation can be a powerful tool. By using quotations, you can document exactly what was said at a crucial time, portray people speaking to each other, or enlist an expert's support for your argument.

Using another person's exact words is called **direct quotation.** When you quote directly, you must tell readers you are doing so by indicating the source and by enclosing the person's exact words in quotation marks (or by setting off long quotations). Restating someone else's idea in your own words is called **paraphrasing** or **indirect quotation.** When quoting indirectly, you still must identify the source, but do not use quotation marks.

Quotation marks are also used to distinguish certain words, such as titles, from the main body of the text. Italics are used for this purpose as well. (See 48a.)

The guidelines for presenting quotations vary somewhat from discipline to discipline. This chapter follows the conventions of the Modern Language Association, the style for papers written in the

---

 USING QUOTATION MARKS

Quotation marks are like shoes: use them in pairs. In written American English, there are two types of quotation marks: **double quotation marks** (" ") which identify quotations, titles, and so on, and **single quotation marks** (' ') which identify quotations within quotations (or titles within titles). In print and in handwriting, a distinction is made in the direction of the curve between an opening quotation mark (") and a closing quotation mark ("). Many word processing programs automatically set opening and closing quotation marks using the same key. However, most typewriters use the same straight quotation mark or marks at both ends of a quotation.

---

languages and literature. (For information on this and other disciplinary styles, see Chapters 54–61.)

43 a Using quotation marks for direct quotations

The conventions are different for using quotation marks when quoting short passages and long ones. (See examples in Chapter 18.)

1 Short passages

Use quotation marks to enclose brief quotations, those from one word up to four typed lines of prose or three lines of poetry. If a parenthetical citation of the source is provided, place it after the closing quotation marks but before the period or other punctuation. (See 43e for advice about using other punctuation marks with quotation marks.)

> Boswell calls this relationship a "collateral adoption," a
> term other experts do not use (97).

> In *Lives Under Siege,* Ratzenburger argues that "most
> adolescents are far too worried about the next six months
> and far too unconcerned about the next sixty years" (84).

When quoting poetry, use a slash preceded and followed by a single space to indicate line breaks. (See 44e.)

> Shakespeare concludes Sonnet 18 with this couplet: "So
> long as men can breathe or eyes can see, / So long lives
> this, and this gives life to thee."

Forgetting the quotation marks at the end of a quotation is a common typographical error, so check for these carefully as you edit.

2 Long passages

Longer direct quotations are set off from the main text in **block format.** Start a new line for the quotation; indent all lines of the quotation one inch or ten spaces, and do not use quotation marks.

If the words introducing a block quotation form a complete sentence, they are usually followed by a colon, although a period is also acceptable. (See 41a.) If the introductory words do not constitute a complete sentence, a comma or no punctuation at all is used, depending on context. If a parenthetical citation of the source is provided, place it two spaces after the final punctuation.

> A recent editorial describes the problem:
>
>> In countries like the United States, breastfeeding,
>> though always desirable, doesn't mean the
>> difference between good and poor nutrition—or life
>> and death. But it does in developing countries,
>> where for decades infant food manufacturers have
>> been distributing free samples of infant formulas to
>> hospitals and birthing centers. (<u>Daily Times</u> 17)
>
> The editorial goes on to argue that the samples last only
> long enough for the mothers' own milk to dry up; then the
> mothers find they cannot afford to buy the formula.

A single paragraph or part of a paragraph in block format does not use a paragraph indent. For two or more quoted paragraphs, the first line of each new paragraph after the first is indented three additional spaces.

When quoting poetry, reproduce as precisely as possible the line breaks, indents, spacing, and capitalization of the original.

> Lawrence Ferlinghetti's poem opens with a striking image
> of the poet's work:
>
>> Constantly risking absurdity
>>> and death
>> whenever he performs
>>> above the heads
>>>> of his audience
>> the poet like an acrobat
>>> climbs on rime
>>>> to a high wire of his own making

If a quotation appears within a quotation, use single quotation marks for the inner quotation.

> After the election, the incumbent said, "My opponent will
>
> soon learn, as someone once said, 'You can't fool all of the
>
> people all of the time.'"

If a quotation appears within a quotation that is displayed in block format, and that therefore is not within quotation marks, use double quotation marks for the inner quotation.

`43` **b** Using quotation marks for dialogue

Use quotation marks when reproducing dialogue, whether real or fictional. Start a new paragraph to show every change of speaker. Once the pattern is established, readers can tell who is speaking even if not every quotation has attributory words.

> "Early parole is not the solution to overcrowding," the prose-cutor said. "We need a new jail."
>
> The chairman of the county commission asked, "How do you propose we pay for it?"
>
> "Increase taxes if you must, but whatever you do, act quickly."

If one speaker's words continue for more than a single paragraph, use quotation marks at the beginning of each new paragraph but at the end of only the last paragraph.

(See 39g for advice about using commas to set off attributions.)

EDITING 1: PRACTICE ────────────────────────

Edit the following sentences, using quotation marks correctly with brief direct quotations.

1. Remembering a trip with her parents in 1947, black American poet Audre Lorde writes in her memoir, *Zami,* The first time I went to Washington, D.C., was on the edge of the summer when I was supposed to stop being a child.

2. "Preparations were in the air around our house before school was even over, she recalls. We packed for a week."

3. Once in Washington, Lorde remembers, I spent the whole next day after Mass squinting up at the Lincoln Memorial where Marian Anderson had sung

after the D.A.R. refused to allow her to sing in their auditorium because she was Black. Or because she was "Colored," my father said as he told me the story. Except that what he probably said was "Negro," because for his times, my father was quite progressive.

4.   Lorde goes on to observe that later in the evening, "The family stopped for a dish of vanilla ice cream at a Breyer's ice cream and soda fountain.

5.   When the waitress first spoke, they didn't understand her, so then, writes Lorde, "The waitress moved along the line of us closer to my father and spoke again. 'I said I kin give you to take out, but you can't eat here. Sorry.'"

6.   The young Lorde's feelings about this casual racism in the nation's capital seems to be summarized by the first lines of a poem she wrote many years later: There are so many roots to the tree of anger / that sometimes the branches shatter / before they bear.

EDITING 2: APPLICATION ─────────────────────────────

Look through some of your recent papers and locate a passage that could have been written in dialogue. Edit the passage to turn it into dialogue, following the guidelines described in this section.

---

43 C Using quotation marks for certain titles

Use quotation marks for titles of brief poems, short stories, essays, book chapters and parts, magazine and journal articles, episodes of television series, and songs. (Italics are used to indicate titles of longer works such as books, magazines, journals, television series, recordings, films and plays. See 48a.)

"Araby" is the third story in James Joyce's book *Dubliners.*

This chart appeared with the article "Will Your Telephone Last?" in November's *Consumer Reports.*

In my favorite episode of *I Love Lucy,* "Job Switching," Lucy and Ethel work in a chocolate factory.

"Tub Thumping" was a hit single from Chumbawamba's album *Tub Thumper.*

If the title of a part of a work or series is generic rather than specific—for example, Chapter 8—do not use either quotation marks or italics.

Use single quotation marks to indicate quoted material that is part of a title enclosed in double quotation marks.

We read "'This Is the End of the World': The Black Death" by historian Barbara Tuchman.

Titles are indicated by quotation marks only in text, so do not put quotation marks around the title at the beginning of your own essay, poem, or story. However, use quotation marks wherever your title includes a quotation or title.

An Analysis of the "My Turn" Column in *Newsweek*

TITLES WITHIN TITLES

Use the following models when presenting titles within other titles. These same guidelines apply to other words that normally are indicated by quotation marks or italics (such as foreign words or quotations) when they appear in titles.

- A title enclosed in quotation marks within an italicized title

"A Curtain of Green" and Other Stories

- An italicized title within a title enclosed in quotation marks

"Morality in *Death of a Salesman*"

- A title enclosed in quotation marks within another title enclosed in quotation marks

"Symbolism in 'Everyday Use'"

- An italicized title within another italicized title

Modern Critics on Hamlet *and Other Plays*

(For more on using italics, see Chapter 48.)

EDITING 3: PRACTICE _____

Edit the following sentences, using quotation marks correctly with titles. Circle the number of any sentence that is correct.

1. Jeff read a review of *Sunset Boulevard* in The Theater, a column in *The New Yorker* magazine, and he wants to see the play tonight.

2. Jan prefers to stay at home and finish reading *A View from the Woods,* one of the stories in Flannery O'Connor's *Everything That Rises Must Converge.*

3. As usual, Kim will be watching *Star Trek* reruns on television. Her favorite episode is Who Mourns for Adonis?

4. Erik will spend the evening reading "Why I Write," an essay that Orwell wrote the year after he published his novel *Animal Farm.*

5. Alan wants to stay home and study Thomas Hardy's poem *At the Word "Farewell."*

6. Jeff decides to stay at home and listen to his jazz records. He always turns up the volume when the song *Basin Street Blues* comes on.

43 d Using quotation marks for translations, specialized terms, ironic usages, and nicknames

1 Translations

When a word or phrase from another language is translated into English, the translation may be enclosed in quotation marks. The original word or phrase is italicized. (See 48d.)

I've always called Antonio *fratellino,* or "little brother," because he is twelve years younger than I.

2 Specialized terms

A specialized term or new coinage is often introduced in quotation marks when it is first defined.

The ecology of this "chryocore"—a region of perpetual ice and snow—has been studied very little.

3 Irony

You may indicate that you are using a word in an **ironic** sense—that is, with a meaning opposed to its literal one—by putting the word in quotation marks; but use this technique sparingly in academic writing.

Jonathan Swift's essay "A Modest Proposal" offers a quick "solution" to Ireland's poverty and overpopulation: eat the children.

4 Nicknames

An unusual nickname may be enclosed in quotation marks at first mention, particularly when it is introduced as part of the full name.

When I joined the firm, the president was a man named Garnett E. "Ding" Cannon.

43 e Using other punctuation with quotation marks

1 Periods and commas

Periods and commas go inside quotation marks.

Juliet Schor refers to "the rise of what some have called 'post-materialist values.'"

Note that the period or comma goes inside both single and double quotation marks.

2 Colons and semicolons

Colons and semicolons go outside quotation marks.

The sign read "Closed": there would be no sodas for us.

Willie Nelson wrote "Crazy"; Patsy Cline made the most famous recording of it.

3 Question marks, exclamation points, and dashes

Question marks, exclamation points, and dashes go inside the quotation marks if they are part of the quotation or title.

Dr. King asked, "How does one determine whether a law is just or unjust?"

Robert Frost's famous poem "Out, Out—" was published in 1916.

When they are not part of the quotation or title but rather apply to the whole sentence, these marks go outside the quotation marks.

Who invented the expression "Have a nice day"?

To make matters worse, from the altar the bride sang "I Got You, Babe"!

When both the quoted material and the sentence as a whole require one of these marks, use only the question mark or exclamation point inside the quotation marks. (See 38b, 38c.)

Was it Rodney King who asked, "Why can't we all just get along?"

If the logic of a sentence dictates that a quotation end with a question mark or an exclamation point but sentence grammar calls for a period or comma as well, use the stronger mark (the question mark or exclamation point) and delete the weaker one (the period or comma).

As soon as we heard someone shout "Fire!", we began to run for the exit.

4 Parentheses and brackets

Parentheses and brackets can be used to indicate comments on or alterations to a quotation. Words that are not part of the quotation are set off in parentheses when they are *outside* the quotation marks and in brackets when they are *within* the quotation marks.

For example, you may add italics for emphasis in a quotation, but always indicate that you have done so by enclosing the phrase "italics added" in brackets at the end of the passage, after the closing quotation mark but before the period.

According to this study, in 1992 "the *average* major league baseball player earned more than $1 million a year" [italics added].

(For examples of bracketed material within quotations, see 44d.)

EDITING 4: PRACTICE _____

Edit the following sentences, adding quotation marks as needed and making sure that they, as well as other punctuation marks, are used correctly.

1. No matter how many times you say it, Christie, Malcolm said, I still can't accept the idea that international law should have no bearing on how nations act.
2. "Wait a minute"! she retorted. That's not what I said at all.
3. Well, what did you say, then? Malcolm asked.
4. "My point, Christie said, is that a government can't allow itself to be constrained from acting to preserve its interests without some kind of guarantee that other countries won't take advantage of the opportunity".

5.   But that's what international law is designed to do, isn't it? Clearly, there's an element of self-interest in any collective security arrangement, he argued, but that doesn't mean that there are no restraints on that interest.

6.   "That's true", she replied, wearily. "But sometimes"—wait, let me finish"—governments use international law as a smokescreen. Besides, she continued, you have to admit that powerful countries are more likely to get what they want in the United Nations or the World Court."

7.   I'm not so sure, Malcolm mused, grinning. I guess I'm just not as cynical as you are.

8.   "Spare me, she replied, and will you stop jabbering and help me fix this flat"?

EDITING 5: PRACTICE

Edit the following passage to make sure that quotation marks and related punctuation are used correctly.

Tennessee Williams's play "The Glass Menagerie" opens with the character Tom speaking directly to the audience: "Yes, I have tricks in my pocket, I have things up my sleeve." "But I am the opposite of a stage magician." This opening monologue serves to set the stage for the story to come. "I am the narrator of the play, continues Tom, "and also a character in it. The other characters are my mother, Amanda, my sister, Laura, and a gentleman caller who appears in the final scenes." Amanda is an aging "Southern belle" living with her two adult children in a dingy St. Louis apartment and desperate to find a match for her daughter. Crippled and painfully shy, Laura often retreats to a fantasy world of glass animal figurines and old songs like Dardanella and La Golondrina played on a scratchy Victrola. When asked by Amanda how many gentleman callers are expected one afternoon, Laura replies "I don't believe we're going to receive any, Mother. "Not one gentleman caller?, Amanda exclaims. "It can't be true! There must be a flood, there must have been a tornado"! When Amanda enlists Tom to bring home a potential "beau" for Laura, the gentleman caller turns out to be a former high school classmate, Jim, whose nickname for Laura was Blue Roses. "Whenever he saw me, Laura recalls at one point, he'd holler, "Hello, Blue Roses!" Jim is already engaged, however, a situation that leads to a climactic confrontation between Amanda and Tom.

EDITING 6: APPLICATION

Examine a paper you are working on to see if you have incorrectly punctuated any quotations. Is there one kind of mistake in punctuating quotations that you

consistently make? If so, think about how best to identify misused quotation marks or places where you have omitted quotation marks when you edit your work. Edit any sentences in which you have incorrectly punctuated quotations. To ensure you are using quotation marks in pairs, have your computer search for opening quotation marks. Then each time, move the cursor through the quotation until you reach the closing quotation mark. If you can't find one, insert one at the appropriate place.

44 **Other Punctuation**

Parentheses, dashes, ellipsis points, brackets, and slashes each have specific functions in sentences, and using them appropriately can bring extra polish to your writing. Use them sparingly, however, and for specific purposes. (For the correct use of hyphens, see Chapter 47.)

<hr>

44 **a** **Using parentheses**

Parentheses can enclose **parenthetical expressions,** elements that would otherwise interrupt a sentence: explanations, examples, asides, and supplementary information. They are also used to set off cross-references, citations, and numbers in a list.

Enclosing explanations, examples, and asides

In setting off explanations, examples, and asides, writers often have the choice using commas, parentheses, or dashes. (For a comparison, see the box in 44b.) Because parentheses tend to de-emphasize what they enclose, use them for material that is not essential to the meaning of the sentence or to the point being made.

Current Hollywood stars whose parents were stars include Anjelica Houston (daughter of John) and Michael Douglas (son of Kirk).

Speaking little English (he had immigrated to the United States only a few months earlier), my grandfather found his first job in a tuna-packing factory.

Parentheses may also be used to enclose dates, a brief translation, abbreviations, or initials.

The Oxford English Dictionary was first published under the editorship of James A. H. Murray (1888–1933).

English also borrowed the Dutch word *koekje* ("cookie").

The North American Free Trade Agreement (NAFTA) continues to spark controversy.

2 Enclosing cross-references and citations

Use parentheses to enclose cross-references to other parts of your paper and to identify references and sources for quotations.

The map (p. 4) shows the areas of heaviest rainfall.

Nick Carraway felt unsettled to see Gatsby at the end of his dock beckoning in the direction of a "single green light" (21).

(See 43a and Chapters 54–60 for more about citing sources for quotations.)

3 Enclosing numbers or letters in a list

Use parentheses to enclose numbers or letters that introduce items in a list within a sentence.

The dictionary provides (1) pronunciation, (2) etymology, (3) past meanings, and (4) usage citations for almost 300,000 words.

4 Using other punctuation with parentheses

When information within parentheses is not a complete sentence, end punctuation appears outside the final parenthesis, thereby punctuating the sentence as a whole.

The strikers protested the company's practice of buying parts from other companies (outsourcing).

When one complete sentence is enclosed in parentheses but stands alone, the end punctuation is placed inside the final parenthesis, and the first word is capitalized.

The damage caused by the storm is estimated at $1.5 million. (This figure does not include the costs of emergency medical aid.)

When a complete sentence enclosed by parentheses falls within another sentence, the first word is not capitalized, and no period is used. A question mark or exclamation mark may be used for effect.

The damage caused by the storm (estimates run as high as $1.5 million) was the worst in more than three decades.

After a visit to Buffalo (how can people there stand the cold weather?), it was a relief to return to the South.

A comma never comes directly before a set of parentheses. If a comma is required by the sentence structure, place it directly after the parentheses.

Working for the minimum wage ($2.30 an hour at the time)' I had very little money to spare.

(For the use of brackets with direct quotations, see 43e4.)

EDITING I: PRACTICE ━━━━━━━━━━━━━━━━━━━

Edit the following sentences, inserting parentheses where appropriate, deleting unnecessary parentheses, and correcting any nonstandard use of other punctuation with parentheses. (You may need to make other changes in punctuation.) Some sentences can be edited in more than one way. Be ready to explain the changes you made.

1. Buddhism is a religion and philosophy that was founded in India around 535 B.C.E. by Siddhartha Gautama, who is called Buddha "the Enlightened One".
2. Other names for Buddha are the Tathagata, "he who has come thus," Bhagavat, "the Lord," and Sugata, "well-gone."
3. Tradition has it that Gautama, also spelled Gotama, was born a prince but renounced the world at age twenty-nine to seek to understand the inevitability of human suffering.
4. Eventual spiritual enlightenment led him to the "four noble truths" of Buddhism: 1 existence is suffering; 2 suffering is caused by attachment to the physical world; 3 the suffering humans experience can cease; 4 the path to release from suffering involves eight stages of thinking and behavior.
5. For the next forty-five years, (He was thirty-five when he reached enlightenment.) Buddha traveled and taught his doctrine to a growing number of disciples.
6. Central to the practice of Buddhism are meditation (and adherence to a set of clearly defined moral precepts).
7. These moral precepts, for example, injunctions against taking life, stealing, and dishonesty, continue to provide a primary basis of Buddhist practice.

Using dashes

Dashes serve many of the same purposes as parentheses—that is, they set off explanations, examples, asides, and supplementary information that would otherwise interrupt the meaning of the sentence. However, dashes tend to emphasize the material they set off rather than subordinate it, as parentheses do. Dashes can also be used to highlight contrast and to indicate interruptions and changes in tone. Because dashes break the flow of a sentence, use them sparingly.

In word processing, use two hyphens with no space on either side to create a dash.

> A dash--when you use one--should look like this.

Note that unlike a single parenthesis, a dash can be used singly to set off material at the end of a sentence.

Dashes for explanations, examples, and asides

She donates a considerable sum to Georgetown University—her alma mater—every year.

At first we did not notice the rain—it began so softly—but soon we were soaked through.

Of all the oddities in Richard's apartment, the contents of the bathtub—transistors, resistors, circuit boards, and odd bits of wire—were the strangest of all.

Dashes to emphasize contrast

The restaurant is known for its excellent food—and its astronomical prices.

Dashes to indicate a pause, interruption, or change of tone

"Well, I guess I was a little late—OK, an hour late," I admitted.

"Hold on," she shouted, "while I grab this—"

Dashes with other marks of punctuation

If the words enclosed by dashes within a sentence form a sentence, do not capitalize the first word of the inner sentence or use a period. If the enclosed sentence is a question or an exclamation,

you may use a question mark or an exclamation point, but do not capitalize the first word.

> Ward and June Cleaver—who can forget their orderly world?—never once question their roles in life.

Do not use a comma or a period immediately before or after a dash.

> My cousin Eileen—she is from Ireland,—brought a strange flute with her when she came to visit.

> With so many things happening at once—graduation, a new job—,Marcelle felt she had become a different person.

Avoid using more than two dashes in a sentence.

> He never told his father about his dreams—he couldn't explain them—but silently began to make plans—plans that would one day lead him away from this small town.

 CHOOSING COMMAS, PARENTHESES, OR DASHES

Commas, parentheses, and dashes can all be used to set off nonessential material within a sentence.

- Use **commas** when the material being set off is closely related to the rest of the sentence. (See Chapter 39.)

A dusty plow**,** the kind the early Amish settlers used**,** hung on the wall of the old barn.

- Use **parentheses** when the material being set off is not closely related to the main sentence and when you want to de-emphasize it. (See 44a.)

Two young boys found an old plow **(**perhaps as old as the first Amish settlement**)** hidden in an unused corner of the barn.

- Use **dashes** when material being set off is not closely related to the main sentence but you want to emphasize it. (See 44b.)

The old plow—one his great-grandfather had used—was still in good working order.

EDITING 2: PRACTICE ━━━━━━━━━━━━━━━━━━━━━━━━

Edit the following passage, deleting dashes where they are not effective. More than one edited version is possible. Be ready to explain your editing choices.

> Jamaica Kincaid's most openly opinionated—and, to my mind, best—book—*A Small Place*—is a social critique of her home island—Antigua. In this book, her voice—humble yet strong, and sometimes filled with anger—speaks for her people. Her feelings—stemming from years of living in Antigua in the aftermath of British imperialism—are expressed in a simple—yet beautiful—manner.

44 c Using ellipsis points

Ellipsis points are three periods, each preceded and followed by a space. They are used to mark an **ellipsis,** any deliberate omission of words from a direct quotation. Quotations are often shortened either to make a passage more emphatic or to achieve a usable length, but writers must be careful, when deleting portions of quotations, not to change the original passage's meaning. (See 16d.)

Consider the following paragraph from Betty Edwards's *Drawing on the Right Side of the Brain:*

> Drawing is not really very difficult. *Seeing* is the problem, or, to be more specific, *shifting to a particular way of seeing.* You may not believe me at this moment. You may feel that you are seeing things just fine and that it's the drawing that is hard. But the opposite is true, and the exercises in this book are designed to help you make the mental shift and gain a twofold advantage: first, to open access by *conscious volition* to the right side of your brain in order to experience a slightly altered mode of awareness; second, to see things in a different way. Both will enable you to draw well.

Use ellipsis points to indicate an omission within a sentence.

> Edwards tells the reader, "You may feel . . . that it's the drawing that is hard."

If an omission comes at the end of a complete sentence, include the period or other end punctuation before the ellipsis points.

> Edwards addresses the reader directly with a provocative assertion: "Drawing is not really very difficult. . . . You may not believe me at this moment."

Likewise, if you end the quotation before the end of the original sentence, include a period before the ellipsis. (Note that in such cases, there is no space between the last quoted word and the period or between the final ellipsis point and the closing quotation mark.)

> In Edwards's view, "Drawing is not really very difficult. *Seeing* is the problem. . . ."

However, when parenthetical documentation is included after a quote ending with an ellipsis, the period follows the parentheses.

> Betty Edwards writes, "Drawing is not really very difficult. *Seeing* is the problem . . ." (2).

Ellipsis points are not necessary when what you quote is obviously not a complete sentence.

> Edwards offers the reader paths to "a slightly altered mode of awareness."

If you omit a whole line or more when quoting poetry, indicate the omission by using ellipsis points for the length of a line.

> She walks in beauty, like the night
> . . . .
> And all that's best of dark and bright
> Meet in her aspect and her eyes.

In dialogue, ellipsis points can indicate a hesitation or a trailing off of speech, and in informal writing they may be used to create a pause for dramatic effect.

> I could only stammer, "What I mean is . . . well. . . ."

> For a moment there was silence . . . followed by a rush as the cat bolted from the underbrush.

EDITING 3: PRACTICE ─────────────────────────────

Using ellipsis points, edit the following paragraph to shorten it for a paper on racism. More than one edited version is possible. Be ready to explain your editing choices.

> Until we label an out-group it does not clearly exist in our minds. Take the curiously vague situation that we often meet when a person wishes to locate responsibility on the shoulders of some out-group whose nature he cannot specify. In such a case he usually employs the pronoun "they"

without an antecedent. "Why don't they make these sidewalks wider?" "I hear they are going to build a factory in this town and hire a lot of foreigners." "I won't pay this tax bill; they can just whistle for their money." If asked "who?" the speaker is likely to grow confused and embarrassed. The common use of the orphaned pronoun they teaches us that people often want and need to designate out-groups (usually for the purpose of venting hostility) even when they have no clear conception of the out-group in question. And so long as the target of wrath remains vague and ill-defined specific prejudice cannot crystallize around it. To have enemies we need labels.

GORDON ALLPORT, "THE LANGUAGE OF PREJUDICE"

44 d Using brackets

Brackets are used to enclose words that are added to or changed within direct quotations. (See 16d1.) They can also enclose comments about quotations and about material that is already inside parentheses. (If your typewriter or word processor does not have brackets, you can write them in by hand.)

Consider this passage from an article titled "Interview with a Sparrow" by E. B. White:

> As yet the onset of Spring is largely gossip among the sparrows. Any noon, in Madison Square, you may see one pick up a straw in his beak, put on an air of great business, twisting his head and glancing at the sky. Nothing comes of it. He hops three or four times and drops both the straw and the incident.

In quoting from this passage, it would be permissible to make small changes in order to clarify a pronoun reference, to add an explanatory phrase, or to make the quoted words read correctly within the context of the new sentence.

> E. B. White describes just such a spring day: "Any noon, in Madison Square, you may see [a sparrow] pick up a straw in his beak, [and] put on an air of great business, twisting his head and glancing at the sky."

> E. B. White describes a sparrow on a spring day: "Any noon, in Madison Square [in New York City], you may see one pick up a straw in his beak, [and] put on an air of great business, twisting his head and glancing at the sky."

> White concludes by noting that the bird "[hopped] three or four times and [dropped] both the straw and the incident."

ESL PLACEMENT OF PUNCTUATION

Only a few kinds of punctuation can begin a line of text in English.

Ellipsis points: . . .
Opening quotation mark: "
Opening parenthesis: (
Opening bracket: [

All other types of punctuation should be placed within or at the end of a line. However, an opening quotation mark, an opening parenthesis, or an opening bracket may not be placed at the end of a line.

If you are using a word processing program, it will avoid most problems for you automatically, as long as you have not incorrectly inserted a space before or after a mark of punctuation.

Brackets are also used to change capitalization in the original quotation to make it correct in the new sentence.

The fact that "[n]othing comes of it" is, for White, what makes the sparrow's activity worth noting.

Brackets can be used to indicate a spelling or punctuation error in quoted material that was present in the original. By enclosing the word *sic* (Latin for "such") in brackets directly after the error, you inform the reader that you see the error but are not responsible for it.

In its statement, the commission said that its new health insurance program "will not effect [sic] the quality of medical care for county employees."

Within parentheses, use brackets to avoid double parentheses.

(These findings are summarized in Table C [p. 12].)

EDITING 4: PRACTICE

Edit the following passage, using brackets correctly.

According to the findings of a new study, people who smoke may be hurting not only themselves. "It (tobacco smoke) can be just as detrimental to nonsmokers as to smokers," a spokesperson for the study told reporters.

"In fact, secondhand smoke may be even more dangerous," she added, "since they (nonsmokers) are inhaling it without a filter." This latest finding adds to the growing list of the dangers of cigarette smoking. (See related article on the effects of smoking on fetal development (p. 14).)

44 e Using slashes

A *slash* (/) is a slanted line, also known as a *solidus* or *virgule*. Use a slash, preceded and followed by a space, to mark the end of a line of poetry incorporated in text.

> Shakespeare opens *The Passionate Pilgrim* with a seeming paradox: "When my love swears that she is made of truth, / I do believe her, though I know she lies."

(See 43a for more on quoting poetry.)

Use a slash with no space before or after it in some common expressions indicating alternatives.

either/or proposition   pass/fail system   true/false test

When possible, however, in most formal writing use a conjunction and hyphens between the alternatives rather than a slash.

                win-or-lose
A small business can be a ~~win/lose~~ investment.
                        ^

In particular, the slashed alternatives *and/or, he/she,* and *s/he* are considered inappropriate for writing in the humanities.

Also use a slash without spaces to separate numerals when they represent the parts of a date (*1/3/02*) and the numerator and denominator in a fraction (*1/2*). (In typescript, use a hyphen to separate a whole number from its fraction: *2-1/2*) Some word processing programs recognize 1/2 as a fraction and set a special character: $\frac{1}{2}$.

EDITING 5: PRACTICE ─────────────────────────

Edit the following paragraph, using parentheses, dashes, and brackets correctly. (You may have to alter some other punctuation.) More than one edited version is possible. Be ready to discuss your editing choices.

> One of my biggest pleasures when I am out driving is reading other drivers'
> bumper stickers. These little messages, often provocative, always revealing

of the people who stick them so proudly on the backs of their cars, serve a number of functions. They allow people to express their views on politicians, "Impeach whoever happens to be in office," for example, or "Vote for Nobody," as well as their views on political issues more generally, "Visualize World Peace" and "Who Needs the Whales?" They work as advertisements, "Ask me about Avon," and as personal statements, "I live to fish." They even give parents a chance to show their pride in their children, "My child is an honor student at Pineview School," or to display their ignorance, "My child can beat up you're (sic) honor student." I don't have a bumper sticker myself, but I definitely will once an "I Love Bumper Stickers" version appears on the market!

EDITING 6: APPLICATION ━━━━━━━━━━━━━━━━━━━━━━━━━━━

Examine a paper you are working on for misused or omitted parentheses, dashes, ellipsis points, brackets, and slashes. Do you make one kind of error often? Which of these marks seems the most difficult to use? In your own words, write a brief set of guidelines for using each of these marks correctly. Now reread your paper and see if you can find opportunities for using any of these marks that you have not used before. Also edit sentences in which you have misused any punctuation marks.

EDITING SECTION
Editing Mechanics

45 Spelling

The spelling of English words seems sometimes to defy reason. Some words sound exactly the same even though they are spelled differently (*their, there, they're*), and the same sound may be represented by different letters or letter combinations—as with the long *e* sound in *meet, seat, concrete, petite, conceit,* and *piece*. Conversely, the same letter or letter combinations can represent different sounds—such as the *a*'s in *amaze;* the *g*'s in *gorgeous;* and the *ough* in *tough, though,* and *through.*

English spelling reflects the language's many etymological sources. As English has absorbed words from other languages, it has assumed or adapted their spellings; thus the spelling of a word in English often cannot be determined simply by its pronunciation. (See 30a for more on the history of the English language.)

Misspellings can seriously undermine your credibility and, in some cases, can lead readers to misunderstand. Always edit carefully for spelling, keeping in mind the guidelines that follow.

45 a Checking for commonly confused words

Distinguishing between homonyms

Homonyms are words with the same sound but different meanings: *great, grate; fair, fare.* When you are drafting and revising, it is easy to confuse homonyms, writing *their* instead of *there,* for example, or *rite* instead of *write.* As you edit, check carefully to make sure you've chosen the correct word in every case.

Memory aids can help you distinguish between some homonyms. For example, *piece,* what you slice a pie into, has a *pie* in it, whereas *peace* does not. Knowing word origins or related words can also help. *Rite* is related to *ritual,* in the sense of ceremony. *Write* is descended from an Old English word, *writan,* meaning "to scratch, draw, or engrave." Sometimes examining roots,

prefixes, and suffixes is helpful. For example, *migrate* ("to move from one place to another") serves as the root for both *emigrate* and *immigrate*. The prefix *e-* means "out of" or "away from," so to *emigrate* is to leave one place for another: *Many Soviet Jews emigrated to Israel in search of a better life.* The prefix *im-*, on the other hand, means "into" or "toward," so to *immigrate* is to come into one place from another: *Many nineteenth-century immigrants came to this country seeking economic opportunity or fleeing political upheaval.*

 HOMONYMS AND SIMILAR-SOUNDING WORDS

accept (receive)
except (leave out)

access (approach)
excess (too much)

adapt (change)
adopt (choose)

advice (suggestion)
advise (suggest)

affect (influence)
effect (result)

allude (refer)
elude (escape)

allusion (reference)
illusion (deception)

altar (church table)
alter (change)

antidote (poison remedy)
anecdote (brief story)

ascent (climb)
assent (agree)

bare (uncovered)
bear (carry; the animal)

bazaar (market)
bizarre (weird)

birth (childbearing)
berth (place of rest)

board (plank; food)
bored (drilled; uninterested)

born (given birth to)
borne (carried)

break (smash, split)
brake (stopping device)

canvas (fabric)
canvass (examine)

capital (city; wealth)
capitol (building)

censor (prohibit)
sensor (measuring device)

cent (money)
scent (fragrance)
sent (past of send)

cite (mention)
site (place)
sight (vision)

coarse (rough)
course (way, path)

complement (make complete)
compliment (praise)

(Continued)

conscience (moral sense)
conscious (aware)

cursor (computer marker)
curser (swearer)

council (committee)
counsel (advise; adviser)

dairy (milk-producing farm)
diary (daily book)

dessert (sweet food)
desert (abandon)

dissent (disagreement)
descent (movement downward)
decent (proper)

dual (having two parts)
duel (fight between two
    people)

dye (color)
die (perish)

elicit (draw forth)
illicit (improper)

eminent (noteworthy)
imminent (impending)

ensure (make certain)
insure (indemnify)

exercise (activity)
exorcise (drive out)

fair (just)
fare (food; fee)

faze (disturb)
phase (stage)

formerly (at an earlier time)
formally (according to a
    pattern)

forth (forward)
fourth (follows *third*)

forward (to the front)
foreword (preface)

gorilla (ape)
guerrilla (fighter)

hear (perceive)
hear (in this place)

heard (perceived)
herd (group of animals)

heroin (drug)
heroine (principal female
    character)

hole (opening)
whole (entire)

holy (sacred)
wholly (entirely)

immigrate (come in)
emigrate (leave)

incidents (events).
incidence (frequency of
    occurrence)
instance (example)

its (possessive of *it*)
it's (contraction of *it is*)

know (be aware)
no (negative, not yes)

lead (to guide; metal)
led (guided)

lesson (instruction)
lessen (reduce)

lightning (electric flash)
lightening (making less heavy)

loose (opposite of *tight*)
lose (opposite of *find* or *win*)

meat (food)
meet (encounter)

(Continued)

miner (excavator)
minor (person under a given
  age)

pair (two)
pear (fruit)
pare (peel; reduce)

passed (went by)
past (an earlier time)

peace (absence of war)
piece (part; portion)

peer (look; equal)
pier (pillar)

plain (simple; flat land)
plane (flat surface; smooth off;
  aircraft)

pray (ask, implore)
prey (hunt down; what is
  hunted)

principle (rule)
principal (chief person; sum
  of money)

quiet (silent)
quite (really, positively,
  very much)

rain (precipitation)
reign (rule)

right (correct)
rite (ritual)
write (inscribe)

road (path)
rode (past of ride)

scene (setting, stage setting)
seen (perceived)

sense (perception)
since (from that time)

shone (past of shine)
shown (past of show)

stationary (not moving)
stationery (writing paper)

straight (not curved)
strait (narrow place)

tack (angle of approach)
tact (sensitivity; diplomacy)

taut (tight)
taught (past of teach)

than (word of comparison)
then (at that time)

their (possessive of them)
there (in that place)
they're (contraction of they are)

threw (past of throw)
through (by way of)

to (in the direction of)
too (also)
two (the number)

waist (middle of the torso)
waste (squander)

weak (feeble)
week (seven days)

wear (carry on the body)
where (in what place)

weather (atmospheric
  conditions)
whether (if, in case)

which (what one)
witch (sorceress)

whose (possessive of who)
who's (contraction of who is)

yore (past time)
your (possessive of you)
you're (contraction of you are)

2 Distinguishing between expressions written as one or two words

Some words can be written either as one word or two: *We'll go there sometime. We spent some time there.* In almost all cases, the two spellings have two different meanings.

all ready (completely prepared)   already (previously)
all together (all in one place)   altogether (thoroughly)
all ways (all methods)   always (at all times)
a lot (a large amount)   allot (distribute, assign)
every day (each day)   everyday (ordinary)
may be (could be)   maybe (perhaps)
some time (an amount of time)   sometime (at some unspecified time)

Remember that *cannot* is always spelled as one word and that most dictionaries suggest spelling *all right* as two words.

A computer spell checker won't help you find **errors in meaning**—that is, when you want *affect* instead of *effect*; or *you're*, not *your*; or *dinner*, not *diner*. It's up to you as a writer and careful proofreader to catch these problems.

3 Distinguishing between words with similar spellings and meanings

Misspellings often occur with words that are closely related in meaning and spelled and pronounced similarly. The following pairs of words can be confusing because their meanings are related and the spelling in each case differs by only a single letter.

advice (noun)   advise (verb)
breath (noun)   breathe (verb)
chose (past tense)   choose (present tense)
cloths (fabrics)   clothes (garments)
device (noun)   devise (verb)
envelope (noun)   envelop (verb)
later (after more time)   latter (in the final position)
prophecy (noun)   prophesy (verb)

Similar problems can occur where the only spelling difference is in the prefix or suffix: *perspective, prospective; personal, personnel.* If you have trouble with words like these, remembering differences in pronunciation can help you distinguish the correct spelling of the word you intend.

Watch out for confusion between contractions of pronouns and verbs and the possessive forms of the same pronouns. Remember: a pronoun with an apostrophe is a contraction; a pronoun without an apostrophe is possessive. (See the box in 42c.)

CONTRACTIONS	POSSESSIVE PRONOUNS
it's (it is, it has)	its (belonging to it)
they're (they are)	their (belonging to them)
who's (who is, who has)	whose (belonging to whom)
you're (you are)	your (belonging to you)

EDITING I: PRACTICE _____

Edit the following passage, looking for commonly confused words and for words misspelled because of how they may be pronounced.

"Were just about to have our desert. Would you care to join us?"

"Thanks allot, but no. I've all ready eaten—a fore-coarse meal."

"Oh, just have one small peace of pie. You can have it plane, without any topping."

"It looks extrordinary, but to tell you the truth, I'm a little afraid of the affect it'll have on my waste. I've been trying to loose wait; my cloths are getting so tight that I can hardly breath."

"Are you getting any exorcise? Their is probly no better way to lose weight."

ESL **RECOGNIZING BRITISH SPELLINGS**

For some words, British spelling—also used widely in other countries, including Australia, Canada, and India—differs from the preferred American spelling: *centre* rather than *center, labour* rather than *labor*. In general, writers in the United States are expected to conform to American spellings, so if you've learned British spellings, you'll need to take note of such differences and edit your work accordingly. Also check the spelling of proper nouns that include these words: *New York State Theater* at Lincoln Center but *Helen Hayes Theatre*.

PRONUNCIATION AND SPELLING

Careless pronunciation can throw off your spelling. If you spell the following words the way you often hear them, you will probably misspell some of them. Pronounce each of these words, paying careful attention to the italicized letters that many people drop or mispronounce. As you edit, check each of these words carefully.

accident*al*ly | mathematics | recognize
arctic | meme*n*to | re*l*evant
arithmetic | mischie*v*ous | roommate
a*th*lete | nu*c*lear | sandwich
can*d*idate | possi*b*ly | sim*i*lar
envir*o*nment | prejudice | surprise
extra*o*rdinary | (noun) | temperature
February | prejudice*d* | tentative
gover*n*ment | (adjective) | use*d* to
interference | prob*a*bly | usu*a*lly
laboratory | pronunciation | veteran
library | quantity | We*d*nesday
literature | rea*l*tor | win*t*ry

"Well, I never was much of an athalete, as you know. I have a stationery bike, but I just can not seem to motivate myself to workout. I always seem to find an excuse to put it off until latter."

45 b Using spelling rules

Remembering the *ie/ei* rule and its exceptions

You may already be familiar with the rule about using "*i* before *e*": Put *i* before *e* except after *c,* or when it sounds like "ay" as in *neighbor* and *weigh.* In most cases the rule holds true:

i before e: belief, field, friend, mischief, niece, patience, piece, priest, review, shield, view

ei after c: ceiling, conceit, conceive, deceit, deceive, receipt

ei sounding like "ay": eight, feign, freight, sleigh

There are, however, several common exceptions to remember.

ie *after* *c*: *ancient, conscience, financier, science, species*

ei *not after* *c* *or sounding like* "*ay*": *caffeine, codeine, counterfeit,
either, feisty, foreign, forfeit, height, leisure, neither, seize, weird*

2 Adding suffixes according to spelling rules

A **suffix** is a syllable or group of letters attached to the end of a
word to change its meaning and, sometimes, its part of speech:
tap + *ed* = *tapped, reverse* (verb) + *-ible* = *reversible* (adjective).
(See 30c2.) Adding a suffix can sometimes change the spelling
of the base word. In addition, remember to watch for similar-
sounding suffixes that are commonly confused with one another.
Adding a **prefix,** a syllable attached to the beginning of a word, almost never causes a spelling change in the base word. However,
some prefixes require hyphens. (See 47b.)

Suffixes after words ending in *y*

If the letter before the final *y* is a consonant, the *y* changes to *i*
when a suffix is added, *unless* the suffix itself begins with *i*.

CONSONANT
BEFORE *y*

friendly + -er = friendlier
happy + -ly   = happily
apply + -ing = applying
baby + -ish   = babyish

If the letter before the *y* is a vowel, the *y* doesn't change to *i*.

VOWEL
BEFORE *y*

convey + -ed   = conveyed
annoy + -ance = annoyance
pay + -ment   = payment

The few exceptions to these rules include (1) some short words
ending in *-y* when the suffix begins with a consonant (*dryness,*

 USING *-CEDE, -CEED,* AND *-SEDE*

Because they have identical sounds, the syllables *-cede, -ceed,* and
-sede are often confused. The most common is *-cede,* as in *accede, con-
cede, intercede, precede, recede,* and *secede.* *-Ceed* appears in the
words *exceed, proceed,* and *succeed.* *-Sede* appears only in the
word *supersede.*

shyly): (2) the adverb form of very short words ending in *-ay* (*daily, gaily*); and (3) the past tense of three irregular verbs ending in *-ay* (*laid, paid, said*).

Proper nouns ending in *-y* generally do not change spellings when suffixes are added (for example, *McCarthyism, Kennedyesque*).

(See 45b3 for rules about plurals of words ending in *y*.)

Suffixes after words ending in *e*

If the suffix begins with a consonant, keep the final *e* of the base word.

SUFFIX STARTING
WITH
CONSONANT

hate + -ful	= hateful
polite + -ness	= politeness
state + -ment	= statement
sure + -ly	= surely

There are a few exceptions to this rule, which you should memorize: *acknowledgment, argument, judgment, duly, truly, wholly, awful, ninth.*

If the suffix begins with a vowel, usually drop the final *e* of the base word.

SUFFIX STARTING
WITH VOWEL

admire + -able	= admirable
dance + -er	= dancer
insure + -ing	= insuring
use + -able	= usable (but *useable* is an acceptable alternative spelling)

But keep the *e* if it is necessary to prevent misreading: *dye + -ing = dyeing* (not *dying*); *canoe + -ing = canoeing* (not *canoing*). In addition, keep the *e* when it follows a soft *c* (one that sounds like *s*, not *k*) or a soft *g* (one that sounds like *j* or *jh*) and the suffix starts with *a* or *o*; dropping the *e* in such cases would give the *c* or *g* a hard pronunciation.

BASE WORD WITH
SOFT C OR G

enforce + -able	= enforceable
outrage + -ous	= outrageous

Suffixes after words ending in a consonant

If a suffix begins with a consonant and is added to a word that ends in a consonant, simply add the suffix, even if doing so results in a double consonant.

SUFFIX STARTS WITH CONSONANT	cup + -ful	= cupful
	defer + -ment	= deferment
	girl + -like	= girllike
	open + -ness	= openness

If a suffix beginning with a vowel is added to a word ending in a consonant, you may be unsure whether to double the final consonant of the base word. The rules are simple. Double the final consonant only if (1) the base word is one syllable or the stress in the base word is on the last syllable *and* (2) the final consonant is preceded by a single vowel.

abet + -or	= abettor	refer + -al	= referral
admit + -ing	= admitting	slap + -ed	= slapped
hop + -ing	= hopping	star + -ing	= starring (not to
occur + -ence	= occurrence		be confused with stare +
			-ing = staring)

If the stress in the base word is not on the last syllable, or if the final consonant is preceded by a consonant or two vowels, do not double the final consonant.

STRESS NOT ON FINAL SYLLABLE	barter + -ing	= bartering
	danger + -ous	= dangerous
	envelop + -ed	= enveloped

FINAL CONSONANT FOLLOWS CONSONANT	hurt + -ing	= hurting
	doubt + -able	= doubtable
	enact + -ed	= enacted

FINAL CONSONANT FOLLOWS TWO VOWELS	fuel + -ing	= fueling
	repeat + -ed	= repeated
	sweep + -er	= sweeper

Two exceptions to this rule are *format* (*formatted, formatting*) and *program* (*programmed, programming*). In addition, if the base word is stressed on the last syllable but adding the suffix changes the pronunciation so the stress of the base word is no longer on that syllable, do not double the final consonant: *refer + -ence* = reference.

-ly or -ally

The suffix *-ly* or *-ally* turns a noun into an adjective or an adjective into an adverb. Add *-ally* to words that end in *-ic.* (An exception is *publicly.*)

automatically	characteristically
basically	dynamically

Add -*ly* to words that do not end in -*ic.*

absolutely	instantly
differently	interestingly

Most other words that end in -*ally* are formed by adding -*ly* to the adjective suffix -*al: nation, national, nationally.* When adding -*ly* to a word that ends in -*l,* keep both *l*'s: *actual* + -*ly* = actually; *real* + -*ly* = really.

3 Forming plurals according to spelling rules

Most English nouns are made plural by adding -*s: book, books; page, pages.* There are, however, many exceptions. Fortunately, most of these follow the general rules described here.

General rules for plurals

Nouns ending in *ch, s, sh,* or *x* usually are made plural by adding -*es.*

church, churches	glass, glasses	wish, wishes	box, boxes

Nouns ending in *y* are made plural by adding -*s* if the letter before the *y* is a vowel. Otherwise, the plural is formed by changing the *y* to *i* and adding -*es.*

day, days	dairy, dairies
alloy, alloys	melody, melodies

Nouns ending in *o* are often made plural by adding -*s.*

video, videos	trio, trios	duo, duos
burro, burros	Latino, Latinos	inferno, infernos

However, several nouns ending in *o* preceded by a consonant form their plurals by adding -*es.*

embargo, embargoes	hero, heroes
veto, vetoes	potato, potatoes
tomato, tomatoes	

Other nouns ending in *o* may take either -*s* or -*es* in forming the plural.

cargo, cargos, cargoes
volcano, volcanos, volcanoes

tornado, tornados, tornadoes
zero, zeros, zeroes

Many writers make it a habit to refer to a dictionary for the accepted plural form of words ending in *o.*

Nouns ending in *f* sometimes change the *f* to *v* and add *-es* to make the plural.

calf, calves leaf, leaves self, selves
half, halves loaf, loaves thief, thieves

Other nouns ending in *f* simply add *-s.*

belief, beliefs chief, chiefs proof, proofs
brief, briefs oaf, oafs reef, reefs

Still others form the plural either way: *hoof, hooves, hoofs.*

Nouns ending in *fe* may change the *f* to *v* before adding *-s: wife, wives; life, lives; knife, knives.* But not all nouns ending in *fe* follow this pattern: *safe, safes; fife, fifes.*

Irregular and unusual plural forms

A few nouns are made plural without adding an *-s* or *-es.*

child, children goose, geese mouse, mice
foot, feet man, men woman, women

A handful of words have the same form for singular and plural.

deer, deer series, series
moose, moose sheep, sheep

Many loan words are made plural according to the rules of their original language. Words borrowed from Latin keep the endings used in Latin when forming plurals: *alumnus, alumni; alumna, alumnae; alga, algae; datum, data; medium, media.* Words from the Greek also keep their original endings: *analysis, analyses; criterion, criteria; phenomenon, phenomena.*

However, some loan words have Anglicized plurals that are more widely accepted than their original Latin or Greek plurals: *stadiums* rather than *stadia.* Some foreign plurals are regarded as singular in English because the singular form is so rarely used: *The agenda is brief.*

Plurals of proper nouns

In general, proper nouns form plurals by adding -s or -es. Adding -s when forming the plural does not create an extra syllable in pronunciation: *the Simpsons, the Kims, several Lisas.* When the plural is pronounced with one more syllable than the singular, add -es. This usually occurs with proper nouns that end in *ch, s, sh, x,* or *z: the Bushes, the Joneses, the Koches, the Ruizes.* Do not use an apostrophe to indicate the plural of a proper name.

Plurals of compound nouns

A **compound noun** consists of two or more words regularly used together. If the compound is written as one word, make the last part plural: *newspapers, henhouses, notebooks.* An exception to this rule is the word *passersby.*

If a compound noun is written as separate words or if it is hyphenated, make plural the word that expresses the central idea. This is usually the noun in the compound: *attorneys general, presidents-elect, professors emeritus.* When both parts of the compound are nouns, make plural the word that is modified by another word or by a prepositional phrase: *bath towels, sisters-in-law, soldiers of fortune.*

Plurals of letters, numbers, and words

To form the plural of a letter, number, or symbol, use an apostrophe and -s.

There are two *m*'s in *programmer.*
No sentence should end with two *?*'s.

For the plural of numbers referring to decades or centuries expressed in numerals, an apostrophe and *s* may be used, but the letter *s* alone is preferred. Be consistent.

the 1700s   the 1700's
the nineties

Plurals of abbreviations

If an abbreviation includes periods, form its plural with an apostrophe and *s.*

Several of my classmates have become M.D.'s.

Abbreviations without periods simply add *s.*

She keeps her money in two IRAs.

SPELLING TIPS

- Always consult a dictionary when you are in doubt about how to spell a word.

- When checking the spelling of an unfamiliar word, note its *etymology*, or origin, and the history of its usage. This information will help you understand why a word is spelled in a particular way and thus fix the correct spelling in your mind.

- In your notebook or journal keep a personal spelling list of difficult words you encounter. Check to see whether a word that you find troublesome shares a root, prefix, or suffix with a word you already know; the connection helps you learn the meaning, as well as the spelling, of the new word.

- Use the spell checker on your word processor to proofread your papers. It locates transposed or dropped letters as well as some misspellings.

- Proofread your work carefully, even when you use a spell checker. If your spelling is right but the word is wrong, even the computer can't help. For example, if you confuse *to, too,* and *two,* or *its* and *it's,* the spell checker won't catch the error because it can't recognize the context in which a word is used.

EDITING 2: PRACTICE

Edit the following passage, using basic spelling rules to eliminate misspelled words.

Of all the holidaies, one of my least favorite is Thanksgiving. I know that it is traditionnal to beleive in Thanksgiving as a time for shareing a hearty meal with family and freinds, but to me all that outragous food—the huge turkies with two different gravies, the spicey dressing, the rich potatos, along with the butterred vegetables, the breads and rolls, and the multiple peices of pumpkin pie—just excedes the boundarys of civilized dinning. Then after the guestes have all stuffed themselfs, one group—usualy the women, of course—spends the rest of the afternoon cleanning up while the others—mostly the man, naturally—head for the den, ploping down in front of the television for a truely stimulateing afternoon of armchair quarterbackking. I conceed that I am in the minority, but I just can't concieve what anyone possibly enjoies about Thanksgiving.

EDITING 3: APPLICATION

Keep a word list for one week. Look up in a dictionary any unfamiliar words that you encounter in your reading or writing, noting the origin and spelling of each word. Record these words on your word list. At the end of the week, review your list. Have a friend give you a spelling test, and cross off the words you get right. Start a new list with any you miss.

46   Capitalization

Capital letters are conventionally used to indicate the beginning of a sentence and to distinguish names, titles, and certain other words. (For information on the capitalization of abbreviations, see 49c–49g.)

46 a   Capitalizing the first word of a sentence

Use a capital letter at the beginning of a sentence.

The gymnast could not have been more pleased.

In a series of fragmentary questions, it is equally acceptable to begin each fragment with a capital or lowercase letter.

What was the occasion? a holiday? someone's birthday?

Whichever style of capitalization you choose for such questions, be consistent throughout your paper.

Sentences following colons

When two independent clauses are joined by a colon, capitalizing the first word of the second clause is optional, but be consistent throughout a paper.

The senators' courage failed them: the [*or* The] reform bill was dead for another decade.

Always capitalize a numbered list of sentences (but not phrases) following a colon.

His philosophy can be reduced to three basic rules: (1) Think for yourself. (2) Take care of your body. (3) Never hurt anyone.

Sentences between parentheses or dashes

Capitalize the first word of a complete sentence within parentheses if it is not inside another sentence.

Congress attacked sex discrimination in sports with a 1972 law called Title IX. (Changes added in 1974 are called the Bayh amendments.)

Do not capitalize the first word of a complete sentence set off by parentheses or dashes when it falls within another sentence.

Title IX (the name refers to a section of U.S. civil rights law) has changed collegiate sports a great deal over thirty years. On many campuses Title IX has increased the number of competitive sports offered to women—even opponents of the law agree this is true—but its effect on men's sports is more difficult to assess.

46 b Capitalizing quotations and lines of poetry

1 Quotations

Capitalize the first word of a quoted sentence wherever it falls in your own sentence.

"We'd like to talk to you about the budget for women's sports," Jeannine told the athletic director. "The first question is from Ryan."

Ryan asked, "How many sports are offered?"

Do not capitalize the first word of the continuation of a quotation interrupted by attributory words.

"Indeed," Mr. Kott responded, "we field men's and women's teams in track, swimming, tennis, and golf."

If the first word of a quotation does not begin a sentence of yours or a sentence in the original, do not capitalize it.

Recognizing details familiar from his childhood, E. B. White feels "the same damp moss covering the worms in the fishing can."

When quoting from published prose sources, you may have to change the capitalization of the original to fit into your sentence. If you use a capital letter where the original has a lowercase letter, or vice versa, use brackets to show the change. (See 44d.)

2 Capitalizing quotations from poetry

When quoting poetry, always follow the capitalization of the original.

> The poem opens with Frost's usual directness and rhythmic formality: "Whose woods these are, I think I know. / His house is in the village, though." Compare this to Lucille Clifton's offhanded "boys / i don't promise you nothing. . . ."

(See Chapters 43 and 44 for more on punctuating quotations.)

46 c Capitalizing proper nouns and their derivatives

Proper nouns name particular persons, places, or things: *Toni Cade Bambara, Gulf of Mexico, Mercedes Benz.* In general, proper nouns are capitalized. (Articles, coordinating conjunctions, and prepositions in proper nouns are not capitalized.) **Common nouns,** on the other hand, name general classes of persons, places, or things: *writer, gulf, automobile.* Common nouns are not capitalized unless they are part of a proper noun.

In general, the following should be capitalized.

Names of individual people and animals

Catherine the Great	Eleanor Roosevelt
Snoopy	Vincent van Gogh

Note that capitalization of *van, de, la,* and so on varies, so consult a reliable print source for the conventional spelling of a particular name.

FAMILY MEMBERS

Words describing family relationships are capitalized only when they are used as names, not when they are preceded by a possessive pronoun.

The family gave a party for Dad and Uncle Fritz.

My dad and my uncle are twins.

Religions, religious terms, deities, and sacred works

Allah	the Bible
Christianity, Christians	God
Judaism, Jews	the Koran
Protestant	Roman Catholic

Nationalities, ethnic groups, and languages

African Americans	Chicano	Chinese
French	Hindustani	Seminole

Titles

Formal and courtesy titles and their abbreviations are capitalized when they are used before a name and not set off by commas.

Coach Bill Walsh	Dame Agatha Christie
Dr. Wu	Prof. Mitchell Cox
Judge Marilyn Harris	Senator Dianne Feinstein

They are lowercased when used alone or separated from the name by commas.

Dianne Feinstein, senator from California

my physics professor, Mitchell Cox

Titles indicating high station or office may be capitalized when they are not followed by a name: *the President of the United States, the Queen, the Pope.* Derivatives of such titles, however, are not capitalized: *presidential, papal.*

Months, days of the week, and holidays

August 12, 1914	the Fourth of July
Presidents' Day	Tuesday, the twentieth of April

Seasons are not capitalized: *summer, fall.*

Geographic names

the Colorado River	the Grand Canyon
Little Rock, Arkansas	Madison Avenue
the Midwest	Puerto Rico
the Western Hemisphere	the Windy City

Note that *the* is generally not capitalized in these names. Common nouns like *river, avenue,* and *street* are lowercase when they

are preceded by two or more proper nouns: *Bleecker and MacDougal streets.*

Although direction words are capitalized when they name a region (*the South*), they are not when they indicate compass directions: *We headed south on U.S. 61.*

Institutions, organizations, businesses, and trade names

Aquafresh toothpaste	Congress
Big Mac	Habitat for Humanity
the League of Women Voters	Microsoft Corporation
the United Nations	Wesleyan University

Be sure to capitalize only the proper name of an institution, not a generic term referring to it: *Kenyon is ranked among the best small colleges in the country.*

Words such as *company, incorporated,* and *limited* and their abbreviations are capitalized when they are used as part of a business's formal name: *Jones Brothers Limited.* They are not capitalized when they are not part of the formal name: *The company is on the verge of bankruptcy.*

Historical documents, legislation, events, periods, and movements

the Constitution	Public Law 100-13
the Norman Conquest	the Renaissance
the Rationalist movement	the Stamp Act
an Impressionist painter	World War II

Ships, aircraft, spacecraft, and trains

the *Challenger*	the *Orient Express*
the *Spirit of St. Louis*	the *U.S.S. Constitution*

(See 48b for guidelines on italicizing names of vehicles.)

Derivatives of proper nouns

Beatlemania	Marxist
Newtonian	Texan

Prefixes before derivatives of proper nouns are not capitalized: *neo-Marxist, anti-American.* (See 47b for information on hyphenating prefixes before proper adjectives.)

Words derived from proper nouns that have taken on independent meanings often are no longer capitalized: *french fries, herculean, quixotic, ohm, vulcanization.*

46 d Capitalizing titles

For the title of a book, play, essay, story, poem, movie, television series, piece of music, or work of art, capitalize the first word, the last word, and all other words except articles (*the, a, an*), coordinating conjunctions (*and, or, for, but, nor, so, yet*), prepositions (*in, on, with,* and so on), and the *to* in infinitives. Some publishers capitalize prepositions of five or more letters (*within, among,* and so on). Check the title if possible.

Beauty and the Beast	"The East Is Red"
Home Improvement	*Nude Descending a Staircase*
"What I Did for Love"	*The Taming of the Shrew*

Follow the same rule for subtitles, including capitalizing the first word: *Women Playwrights: The Best Plays of 2002.*

If a title contains words joined by a hyphen, both words usually are capitalized, with the exception of articles, conjunctions, and prepositions (*The One-Minute Grammarian; The Social History of the Jack-in-the-Box*).

(See 43c and 48a on the use of quotation marks and italics for titles.)

I AND *O*

Always capitalize the personal pronoun *I*, no matter where it falls in a sentence.

Whatever I play, I play to win.

Also capitalize the interjection *O*, used in prayers and to express wonder and surprise.

Descend on us, O Spirit of Peace.

Note that the interjection *oh* is not capitalized unless it begins a sentence: *We didn't succeed, but oh, how we tried.*

> ✔ **WHAT NEEDS CAPITALIZATION?**
>
> As you edit, make sure you've capitalized the following words:
>
> - The first word of every sentence
> - The first word of a quoted sentence within a sentence
> - Proper nouns and their derivatives
> - Important words in titles of books and other works

EDITING 1: PRACTICE

Edit the following passage, capitalizing correctly.

The Library of congress, established in Washington in 1800, has been called the National Library of the United states. Primarily responsible for its creation was vice president Thomas Jefferson (He was himself an avid book collector), who also supported it strongly during the course of his Presidency. When a fire destroyed much of the Collection in 1814, Jefferson donated his own personal library as a replacement. Ruined by another fire in 1851—Some 35,000 volumes were lost—the library languished until congress passed the copyright act of 1870, which required that all material copyrighted in the Country be deposited there. Today the imposing building on Independence avenue—beloved by many washingtonians—contains some 75 million items, including maps, prints, photographs, and an extensive collection of asian art and artifacts. Of course, it also houses such diverse prose works as a rare edition of *The Federalist papers* and a copy of Gary Larsen's *It Came From The Far Side.*

EDITING 2: APPLICATION

Examine a paper you are working on for mistakes in capitalization. Is there one kind of mistake in using capitalization that you consistently make? If so, think about how best to identify words that should and should not be capitalized when you edit your work. Edit any sentences in which you have made capitalization mistakes.

47 Hyphenation

The hyphen helps readers understand how words are to be read. A hyphen can link parts of a word that might otherwise be seen as separate, can separate parts of a word that might be misleading or hard to read if written together, and can be used conventionally in numbers, fractions, and units of measure.

47 a Hyphenating words at the ends of lines

If a word is too long to fit at the end of a line, you can divide it, using a hyphen to signal that the word continues on the next line. It is better not to divide words, but if you must, be sure to do so at an acceptable point. When in doubt, consult a dictionary. The divisions in the entry word indicate where it may be hyphenated. Here are a few guidelines:

- **Follow pronunciation.** Divide between pronounced syllables: *ro-dent, jew-el.* Generally, divide between two consonants—*car-pen-ter, or-bit*—unless the two consonants produce a single sound: *broth-er, tro-phy.* Divide between double letters: *mas-sive, car-ry.* (See prefixes and suffixes below for an exception involving *-ing* endings.)

- **Do not leave just one letter on a line.** Such words as *amount* (*a-mount*), *ideal* (*i-deal*), and *opaque* (*o-paque*) should not be hyphenated; *abandon* can only be divided as *aban-don, idolize* only as *idol-ize.*

- **Divide compounds between words.** If a compound is hyphenated, divide at the hyphen: *self-/esteem, son-/in-law,* or *son-in-/law.* Divide a one-word compound between its parts: *mother-land,* not *mo-therland*

- **Divide at prefixes or suffixes.** Try to leave both parts of the word recognizable: not *an-tibody* but *anti-body,* not *hy-phenate* but *hyphen-ate.* Before *-ing* endings, generally hyphenate after double

letters that end a root word: *roll-ing,* not *rol-ling.* But if a consonant is doubled in adding the *-ing* ending, keep the added consonant with the suffix; *hit-ting, cut-ting.* (See 45b for rules on doubling consonants.)

Most computer word processing programs can automatically hyphenate a document. If you choose not to hyphenate any words, most programs allow you to turn off hyphenation. If you take advantage of your computer's ability to hyphenate, be sure to double-check its choices, which may be less than perfect.

EDITING 1: PRACTICE

Indicate all possible hyphenation points, if any, for the following words. If there is more than one point, indicate the preferable hyphenation. Then check against a dictionary.

1. coordinated	5. crossbones	9. commitment
2. acquitted	6. minibus	10. antidote
3. preparedness	7. ignite	11. damming
4. width	8. overcast	12. damning

47 b Hyphenating after some prefixes

Although most prefixes are attached to root words without hyphens, there are a few exceptions. When in doubt, consult your dictionary. The following guidelines cover most of the common uses of hyphens following prefixes.

Use a hyphen to attach a prefix to a capitalized word or to a date. (The prefix itself is usually not capitalized.)

anti-Washington sentiment   post-1994 guidelines

Use a hyphen to attach a prefix to a term of more than one word. (See 47c.)

pro-school-choice candidates   pre-space-age technology

Use a hyphen after *all-, ex-* (when used to mean "former"), *self-,* and *quasi-.*

all-inclusive   ex-convict   self-hypnosis   quasi-judicial

A hyphen may be used when a prefix ends with the same letter that begins the base word: *anti-intellectual, co-ownership.* However,

the hyphen has been dropped from many such words (*cooperate, preexisting, unnatural*). Check a dictionary.

A hyphen is occasionally used to distinguish between two different words spelled with the same letters, especially when there is a strong chance of a misreading.

> We asked them to *refund* [give back] our money.

> Congress will *re-fund* [fund again] the program for another year.

When two prefixes separated in a sentence by a conjunction apply to the same base word, add a hyphen after both prefixes, with a space after the first prefix.

> We compared the *pre-* and *post-election* analyses.

> An exception is *him-* or *herself;* the second word is closed up.

47 C Hyphenating compound words

Two or more words used as a single unit form a **compound word.** A compound rewritten as one word is called a *closed compound: workhorse, schoolteacher.* Other compounds are written as two words, or *open compounds: hope chest, lunch break, curtain rod.* Others are hyphenated: *great-grandson, mother-in-law,* and *stick-in-the-mud.*

In deciding whether to hyphenate **compound nouns,** check a dictionary. If the compound is not listed in the dictionary, write it as separate words. Note that most compound nouns consisting of three or more words are hyphenated: *will-o'-the-wisp, jack-in-the-box.*

Compound adjectives consist of two or more words that function together as a single adjective before a noun: *a well-written essay, a late-night party, a touch-and-go-situation.* They are usually hyphenated to make it clear which words go together to form the adjective. It is often necessary to do this to prevent a misreading. For example, compare the meanings of the following sentences:

> Mr. Donovan is an old car collector.

> *He is an* old *person who* collects cars.

> Mr. Donovan is an old-car collector.

> *He is a person who* collects old cars.

Note, however, that where a well-established compound noun functions as an adjective, misreading is unlikely and no hyphen is needed.

high school student   post office box

Also, a hyphen is never used between an adverb ending in *-ly* and the adjective it modifies.

highly motivated employees   a strongly worded statement

When multiple-word modifiers come *after* a noun, they are generally not hyphenated.

The out-of-work actor auditioned every day.

The actor was out of work for over a year.

When two compound adjectives before a noun have the same base word and are linked by a conjunction, the base word can be dropped from the first and a space added after the hyphen.

full- and part-time employees

Coined compounds are compounds made up by writers to express an idea in a particularly concise or vivid way. Such coinages are generally hyphenated.

We worked to the whirr-whoosh-click of the packing machine.

47 d Hyphenating numbers, fractions, and units of measure

Hyphenate two-word numbers from twenty-one to ninety-nine. Do not hyphenate before or after the words *hundred, thousand,* or *million.*

fifty-seven   twenty-two hundred
two hundred fifty-seven   six hundred twenty thousand

Remember that long numbers are often easier to read when expressed in figures. (See 49a.)

Use a hyphen between the numerator and denominator of a spelled-out fraction unless one of them is already hyphenated.

one-half   two-thirds   twenty-one fiftieths

When a number includes a unit of measure (feet, inches, miles, pounds), hyphenate modifiers but not nouns.

An ordinary dump truck has a *nine-cubic-yard* bed.

Only a gardener would delight in *nine cubic yards* of manure.

Use a hyphen in ages when the expression functions as a noun or as an adjective preceding a noun.

I threatened to trade in my *ten-year-old* twins for one *twenty-year-old.*

Do not hyphenate when the word indicating time—in this case *years*—is plural: *The boy is ten years old.*

A hyphen can be used to suggest a range between numbers: *1987–90, 120–140 times a year.* However, readers generally find it clearer if the range is described in words: *from 1987 to 1990; between 120 and 140 times a year.* Do not combine the two methods: *They attended the college from 1987 to 1990* (not *from 1987–1990*).

 GUIDELINES FOR HYPHENATION

As you edit, make sure you have used hyphens appropriately for the following:

- For dividing words at the ends of lines, if necessary
- After certain prefixes
- In certain compound words
- In some fractions, numbers, and units of measure

EDITING 2: PRACTICE

Edit the following passage, hyphenating all words where necessary and deleting unnecessary hyphens. You may have to consult a dictionary.

Widely-available desktop publishing systems have led to an explosion in the publication of *zines,* the low tech equivalent of magazines. Generally published out of the editor owner's home, the average zine has a small print run (from 250–350 copies) and very low production costs (around $500). Zines, which are similar to under-ground publications of the 1960s

and 1970s, reflect the offbeat personalities of their owners. Most make very-little money but enjoy a devoted reader-ship, approximately two thirds of which is under thirty-years-old in most cases. One of the best known zines is *Ersatz,* published by Sam Pratt, twenty seven, out of his loft in Manhattan's Hells' Kitchen. Reflecting the ir-reverent sensibilities of the postReagan era, *Ersatz* has included such pieces as a quasiserious article on the deeper significance of the Trix rabbit. As zines become more-and-more popular, bigger publishers have begun to look for ways to coopt their ideas.

EDITING 3: APPLICATION

Examine a paper you are working on for hyphenation mistakes. Is there one kind of mistake in using hyphens that you consistently make? If so, think about how best to remember hyphenation rules when you edit your work. Edit any sentences in which you have misused or omitted hyphens.

48 Italics

Most publications use a **roman** typeface—like this one—for the main body of the text. **Italic** typeface—*which looks like this*—is used to distinguish certain words, usually to indicate that they must be interpreted somewhat differently.

The equivalent of italics in typed and handwritten work is underlining. Many word processing programs now allow writers to shift to italic type, but make sure this is acceptable to your instructor; he or she may still prefer underlining to italics in student work.

48 a Italicizing titles

Italicize the titles of books, long poems considered to be independent works, plays, operas and other long musical works, movies, CDs or long-playing recordings, newspapers, magazines and journals, television or radio series, and works of art. Use quotation marks rather than italics for titles that are subdivisions of a larger work. (See 43c for more on using quotation marks for titles and for marking titles within titles.)

The titles of sacred works, parts of sacred works, and ancient manuscripts are not italicized.

the Bible   the Koran   Genesis

The titles of public documents also are not in italics.

the Constitution   the Declaration of Independence

Most academic stylebooks recommend neither capitalizing nor italicizing the article (*a, an,* or *the*) in the name of a newspaper or magazine, even if the newspaper or magazine includes it in its own name, as does [*The*] *New York Times.* However, when writing to or for a publication, follow its particular style.

ITALICS AND QUOTATION MARKS FOR TITLES

ITALICS	QUOTATION MARKS
Holy the Firm (book)	"Newborn and Salted" (chapter)
Here Lies (story collection)	"Big Blonde" (short story)
North of Boston (poetry collection)	"Mending Wall" (poem)
Song of Roland (long poem, independent work)	
Waiting for Godot (play)	
Porgy and Bess (opera)	
Carmina Burana (long musical work)*	
Pulp Fiction (movie)	
Voodoo Lounge (CD recording)	"Mean Disposition" (song)
Los Angeles Times (newspaper)	"Icy Words on Global Warming" (article)
New Republic (magazine)	
The Simpsons (television series)	"Homer Meets Godzilla" (episode)
All Things Considered (radio series)	
The Boating Party (painting)	
Reclining Nude (sculpture)	

*Note that a musical work identified by form and key is neither italicized nor put in quotation marks: Beethoven's Symphony No. 5 in D Minor.

 Italicizing the names of individual trains, ships, airplanes, and spacecraft

Italicize the official names of individual trains, ships, airplanes, and spacecraft but not the names of classifications of such vehicles.

a Polaris rocket	the *Shasta Daylight* (train)
Spirit of St. Louis (airplane)	a Trident submarine
the U.S.S. *Arizona* (ship)	*Voyager* (spacecraft)

48 c Italicizing for emphasis and clarity

Italics can be used to indicate that a certain word or words should receive special emphasis in a sentence.

Despite popular perception, the rate of violent crime is actually *lower* today than it was twenty years ago.

Whether something *is* true is less important than whether people *believe* it to be true.

Such emphasis can also help clarify a point.

Then Ms. Dillon asked *me* to sing.

Of all people, me!

Then Ms. Dillon asked me to *sing*.

Of all things, sing!

Be careful not to overuse italics for such purposes. Emphasis can often be achieved through other means. (See Chapter 26.)

48 d Italicizing words, numerals, and letters used as words

Use italics when you refer to a word or numeral itself. Also italicize letters referred to as part of the alphabet or as mathematical symbols.

How would you define the terms *liberal* and *conservative?*

Because I read the *1* as a *7,* my calculations were incorrect.

When I type quickly, I often substitute *w* for *s.*

Let *x* stand for test scores and *y* for hours of study.

48 e Italicizing words from other languages

Words and phrases from languages other than English are usually italicized unless they have become a familiar part of English usage.

Many old castles in Spain have been turned into *paradores* where visitors can spend the night.

The *Mille Miglia* was an auto race of a thousand miles.

The menu offered spaghetti, lasagne, and *pasticcio di faglioni.*

In deciding whether to italicize words from other languages, check a recent English dictionary. Words that do not appear should be italicized. Words that do appear should be italicized only if they are clearly not part of the English language and are seldom used by English speakers.

Always italicize a word or phrase from another language that you are defining for the first time.

The Hawaiian word for that smooth, ropelike lava is *pahoehoe*.

The Latin names used to classify plants and animals by genus and species are also italicized.

The biologists named their discovery *Symbian pandora*.

 COMMON USES OF ITALICS

As you edit, check for your use of italics with the following:

- Titles of long published works, musical works, and works of art
- Names of trains, ships, and other specific vehicles
- Specific words you wish to give special emphasis
- Words, numerals, and letters used as words
- Words from languages other than English

EDITING 1: PRACTICE _____

Edit the following passage, making sure words are italicized according to convention.

Before planting a garden, it is a good idea to consult a reputable source for tips on successful gardening. Many newspapers, such as the New York Times, have a weekly column devoted to gardening. There are also many useful books, such as "A Guide to Growing Gorgeous Greenery," with its especially helpful introductory chapter, *Plan Before You Plant.*

First a gardener should learn about the different types of plants. Annuals is the term given to plants that complete their lifetime in one year; the term perennials is used for plants that grow back every year. Many annuals are popular with gardeners, especially the Begonia semperflorens and the Petunia hybrida.

Another issue for gardeners to consider is pesticides. Environmentally conscious gardeners are not opposed to pesticides *per se*, but they use only organic pesticides, which derive from *natural* rather than *synthetic* substances.

Gardening books are useful, *sans doute*, and they may prevent the worst *faux pas* in the garden, but in the end there is no one way to make a garden—*chacun à son goût*!

EDITING 2: APPLICATION

Examine a paper you are working on for mistakes in italicizing. Is there one kind of mistake in using italics that you consistently make? If so, think about how best to remember which words to italicize when you edit your work. Edit any sentences in which you have misused or omitted italics.

49 Numbers and Abbreviations

Analysis and persuasion often depend on numbers. When doing research, you need to present the numbers that describe your findings. As you write, you include statistics that support your position. When you edit, you must ensure that numbers are presented effectively and clearly. The more numbers used in a piece of writing, the more likely readers are to become confused or intimidated.

49 a Choosing between figures and words according to context

Conventions for choosing between figures and words for numbers vary according to discipline. For more information, consult the style guide for your discipline (Chapters 54–60).

In most nontechnical academic writing (including writing in literature and the humanities), spell the numbers one to one hundred as well as all fractions. (See 47d about using hyphens in numbers.)

thirty universities   fifty-three graduates
three-fourths of the class

Also spell out round numbers over one hundred if they can be expressed in two words. Otherwise, use figures.

five hundred students   517 students
more than fifty thousand trees   52,317 trees

In some publications, figures are used for numbers over ten and for numbers used with measurements of time (*7 hours, 3 weeks*) and size, including weight (*20 pounds, 6 grams*), length (*5 feet*), area (*2 square meters*), and volume (*1 teaspoon, 2 liters*).

It is sometimes clearer to express very large round numbers using a combination of words and figures: *The Census Bureau says that the U.S. population exceeds 250 million.*

In most technical writing (including writing in the social and natural sciences), most numbers, especially measurements and statistics, are written in figures.

The pressure increased by 3 kilograms per square centimeter.

Fewer than 5 percent of the eggs failed to hatch.

In both nontechnical and technical writing, spell out any number that begins a sentence. If doing so is awkward, rewrite the sentence.

Five hundred forty-seven
~~547~~ students attended the concert.
^

Attending the concert were
547 students ~~attended the concert.~~
^   ^

Consistency is important. Express any numbers that readers must compare with each other in the same way. If convention requires using figures for one number, do the same for the other numbers.

                               87
In Midville last year, ~~eighty-seven~~ cats and 114 dogs were destroyed by the city pound.
                               ^

FIGURES OR SPELLED-OUT NUMBERS?

When trying to choose between spelling out numbers or using figures, ask yourself the following questions:

- Is it a round number that can be expressed in one or two words? For most writing situations, spell these out.
- Does the number begin a sentence? Spell it out or edit the sentence so that it appears elsewhere.
- Am I addressing a technical audience? Use the conventions for technical writing and those explained in the discipline's documentation guidelines. (See Chapters 56 and 57.)

SINGULAR AND PLURAL FORMS OF NUMBERS

When the word for a number is used as a plural noun without another number before it, use the plural form of the word. You may also need to use the word *of* after it.

The news report said there were only a few protesters at the nuclear power plant, but we saw *hundreds*.

Dozens of geese headed south today.

When the word for a number is preceded by another number, use the singular form of the word, and do not use *of* with it.

There were approximately *two hundred* protesters.

At least *three dozen* geese flew over the lake today.

In a hyphenated adjective that includes a number, use the singular for the unit of measure.

That movie lasted *three hours*.

It was a *three-hour* movie.

 49 b Using figures when required by convention

The following cases, by convention, require the use of figures, even in nontechnical writing.

In dates

11 April 1999   July 16, 1896   the year 2001

In addresses

2551 Polk Street, Apt. 3

San Francisco, CA 94109

With abbreviations and symbols

3500 rpm	37°C
65 mph	$62.23
74%	53¢

In discussions that use numbers infrequently, you may use words to express percentages and amounts of money if you can do so in two or three words: *seventy-four percent* and *fifty cents,* but not *sixty-two dollars and twenty-three cents.* If you spell out numbers, also spell out *percent, dollars,* and *cents.*

For time

12:15 A.M.   2330 hours

Note that numbers used with *o'clock, past, to, till,* and *until* are generally written out as words.

at seven o'clock   twenty past one

For decimal fractions

2.7 seconds   35.4 miles

For cross-references and citations

Chapter 56   line 25
volume 3, pages 13–17   act 3, scene 2

(See Chapters 54–60 for specific documentation formats.)

ESL **PUNCTUATING NUMBERS**

Numbering systems throughout the world differ in their punctuation. Some numbering systems use a period to mark divisions of thousands, so that *ten thousand* is written *10.000.* In the United States, commas are used to mark divisions of thousands.

In 1989, the population of Ecuador was 10,262,271.

In the United States, the period is used as a decimal point to separate whole numbers from decimal fractions.

Seven and a half can also be written 7.5.

EDITING I: PRACTICE

Edit the following passage, making sure all numbers are handled appropriately for nontechnical writing.

For the last 10 years, I have been running at least five miles a day, six days a week, fifty-two weeks a year. That adds up to eighteen hundred twenty miles yearly. I figure that by the year two thousand, I will have run well over 20,000 miles. My running schedule almost never varies. I hit the streets just after I awaken, at 6 o'clock, and run for 3/4 of an hour. Then I make a ten-minute stop at a nearby diner for a quick orange juice before circling back toward home. 1,750 footfalls later I arrive home to shower and get ready for the day.

EDITING 2: PRACTICE

Examine a paper you are working on for numbers that you have handled incorrectly. Is there one kind of mistake in using numbers that you consistently make? If so, think about how best to remember how to handle numbers when you edit your work. Edit any sentences in which you have handled numbers incorrectly.

49 **c** **Limiting abbreviations in nontechnical texts**

Abbreviations—shortened forms of words—are frequently used in tables, footnotes, endnotes, and bibliographies to help readers proceed through the material quickly and easily. (Documentation and its acceptable abbreviations are discussed in Chapters 54–60.) They are also used often in scientific and technical writing. With a few exceptions, however, you should avoid abbreviations in the body of a general, nontechnical essay, paper, or report. This chapter discusses abbreviations that are acceptable in nontechnical text.

When using an abbreviation, be sure it is appropriate for the particular writing situation, is easy for readers to understand, and is correctly punctuated and capitalized.

49 **d** **Abbreviating titles and degrees**

Personal or courtesy titles such as *Mr., Mrs., Dr.,* and *St.* may be abbreviated when they precede a full name. For such titles, capitalize the first letter and end with a period.

Mr. Samuel Taylor Darling	Dr. Leslie Hunter
St. Francis of Assisi	Prof. Karen Greenberg
Gen. Tommy Franks	Rep. Tom DeLay
the Rev. Martin Luther King, Jr.	Sen. John McCain

Never abbreviate *president* or *mayor.* (Note that *Miss* is not an abbreviation, so it is written without a period. The courtesy title *Ms.* ends with a period even though it is not an abbreviation.)

Except for *Mr., Mrs.,* and *Dr.,* spell out titles used before a surname alone: *Professor Greenberg, Senator Boxer.*

Titles that do not precede a name are not abbreviated or capitalized.

> professor
> **Raisha Goldblum has been named assistant ~~prof.~~ of chemistry.**
> ^

Titles or degrees such as *Esq, MD, LLD, JD,* and *PhD* that follow a name are always abbreviated, as are generational titles such as *Jr.* and *Sr.* They are set off by commas in a sentence. MLA guidelines omit periods in degree titles.

> A new book by Dana Clark, MD, criticizes animal testing.

Do not use both *Dr.* and a degree.

> **~~Dr.~~ Barry Qualls, PhD, will speak at commencement.**

The following abbreviations and symbols are used only preceding or following numbers.

Time

Use A.M. and P.M. (or *a.m.* and *p.m.*) for specific times of day.

> 12:15 P.M. (*or* p.m.)   9:00 A.M. (*or* a.m.)

Avoid using these abbreviations without a specific hour or with *o'clock.* (See 49b.)

> night.
> **We studied late into the ~~P.M.~~**
> ^

> in the evening.
> **The ceremony will begin at seven o'clock ~~P.M.~~**
> ^

Dates

Use B.C. (*before Christ*) and A.D. (*anno Domini,* Latin for "in the year of the Lord") when necessary to distinguish dates. To avoid a religious reference, some writers substitute the abbreviations B.C.E. (*before Common Era*) and C.E (*Common Era*). Note that A.D. precedes the date, except when *century* is used.

425 B.C. (or 425 B.C.E.)

A.D. 376 (or 376 C.E.)

the first century A.D.

Amounts or numbers

Acceptable abbreviations with amounts or numbers in nontechnical writing include *F* for *degrees Fahrenheit* and *C* for *degrees Celsius* in temperatures; *mph* (or *m.p.h.*) for *miles per hour;* and *No.* or *no.* for *number.*

The speed limit has been raised from 55 mph to 75 mph.

The British prime minister's official address is No. 10 Downing Street.

In scientific and technical writing, units of measure are abbreviated when they follow amounts, usually without periods.

To 750 ml of this solution was added 200 mg of sodium cyanate.

In other situations, abbreviations are often acceptable if they are clearly defined at the first mention.

The engine develops maximum torque at 2900 revolutions per minute (rpm). Peak power is achieved at 6500 rpm.

Symbols can also be used as abbreviations with amounts. Symbols acceptable in nontechnical writing include those for degrees (°), percentage (%), and dollars ($), when they are used with figures denoting specific quantities. Spell out the words for symbols when they are used without figures.

By definition, 100°C equals 212°F, the boiling point of water.

The bill came to $35.99.

The percentage of positive responses was surprising.

It is acceptable to abbreviate geographic names (except cities) in addresses on mail. For state names, use abbreviations recommended by the U.S. Postal Service (see the box in this section.)

Lila Martin
100 W. Glengarry Dr.
Birmingham, MI 48009

When presenting a full address in text, spell out everything but the state name. When presenting less than a full address, spell out everything.

 STATE ABBREVIATIONS

Use these U.S. Postal Service abbreviations (capitalized, with no periods) for the names of the fifty states and the District of Columbia only on mail, in full addresses in text, or in documentation.

STATE	ABBRE-VIATION	STATE	ABBRE-VIATION
Alabama	AL	Montana	MT
Alaska	AK	Nebraska	NE
Arizona	AZ	Nevada	NV
Arkansas	AR	New Hampshire	NH
California	CA	New Jersey	NJ
Colorado	CO	New Mexico	NM
Connecticut	CT	New York	NY
Delaware	DE	North Carolina	NC
District of Columbia	DC	North Dakota	ND
Florida	FL	Ohio	OH
Georgia	GA	Oklahoma	OK
Hawaii	HI	Oregon	OR
Idaho	ID	Pennsylvania	PA
Illinois	IL	Rhode Island	RI
Indiana	IN	South Carolina	SC
Iowa	IA	South Dakota	SD
Kansas	KS	Tennessee	TN
Kentucky	KY	Texas	TX
Louisiana	LA	Utah	UT
Maine	ME	Vermont	VT
Maryland	MD	Virginia	VA
Massachusetts	MA	Washington	WA
Michigan	MI	West Virginia	WV
Minnesota	MN	Wisconsin	WI
Mississippi	MS	Wyoming	WY
Missouri	MO		

His address was 1109 West Green Street, Harrisburg, PA 17102.

She was born in Harrisburg, Pennsylvania.

It is acceptable to abbreviate *District of Columbia* in text: *Washington, D.C.* Also, *United States* may be abbreviated to *U.S.* when used as an adjective, but it is generally spelled out as a noun.

The U.S. government is divided into three branches.

Voter turnout in the United States is disturbingly low.

49 g Abbreviating common Latin terms

The following abbreviations for common Latin terms are not generally used in text but may be used in documentation or notes. (See Chapters 54–60.)

ABBREVIATION	LATIN	MEANING
c. or ca.	*circa*	about
cf.	*confer*	compare
e.g.	*exempli gratia*	for example
et al.	*et alii*	and others
etc.	*et cetera*	and so forth
ibid.	*ibidem*	in the same place
i.e.	*id est*	that is
N.B.	*nota bene*	note well
vs. or v.	*versus*	against (used in legal case names)

49 h Using initials and acronyms

Initials or *initial abbreviations* consist of the first letter of each word in a phrase or name, such as *IMF* for International Monetary Fund, *U.K.* for the United Kingdom, or *CD* for compact disc. An **acronym** is a word consisting of initials and pronounced as a word: *NATO* for North Atlantic Treaty Organization, *UNICEF* for United Nations International Children's Emergency Fund. Both initials and acronyms consist entirely of capital letters.

Most initial abbreviations and all acronyms are written without periods. Abbreviated names of some countries do use periods: *U.S., U.K.* Initials that stand for people's names also use periods, followed by a space: *B. B. King, George W. Bush.* (Note, however, that

conventional references to American presidents by their three initials use neither periods nor spaces: *JFK*.) If you are not sure how to punctuate an abbreviation, consult a dictionary.

Unfamiliar initials or acronyms can bewilder readers. Before using one, decide whether it will be recognizable and whether it is essential to your writing. It is often helpful to provide the full name at the first mention in your text followed by the abbreviation or acronym in parentheses.

> World commerce is governed in large part by a set of treaties called the General Agreement on Tariffs and Trade (GATT).

In later references you can then use just the abbreviation or acronym.

> GATT keeps countries from imposing unilateral import duties.

EDITING 3: PRACTICE

Look for examples of abbreviations in your textbooks as well as in popular writing in magazines, newspapers, and fiction. Does the use of abbreviations in both types of writing follow the rules outlined in this chapter? Why do you think words have been abbreviated as they have in each kind of writing?

EDITING 4: PRACTICE

Edit the following passage, using abbreviations correctly.

> Although the United States Constitution is supposed to guarantee equal rights to all people regardless of color, in the first half of this century most African Americans in the southern U.S. lived in deplorable conditions. E.g., African Americans had to use separate washrooms, and they could not attend schools with whites. Not until the 1940s did the United States Supreme Court finally begin to outlaw practices that deprived African Americans of their rights. One small step toward equality was made when representatives from the National Association for the Advancement of Colored People (N.A.A.C.P.) persuaded the Court that maintaining separate schools for African Americans and whites was not equal. In 1954, under Chief Justice Earl Warren of Calif., the Court ordered the desegregation of schools in the U.S. Despite the new legislation, however, the southern states still resisted integration, and only Senator Lyndon Johnson from TX and two sen. from Tenn. (Estes Kefauver and Albert Gore, Senior) were in favor of desegregating the schools. Racial conflict raged throughout

ESL **USING ARTICLES WITH DEGREE ABBREVIATIONS, INITIALS, AND ACRONYMS**

Before **degree abbreviations** in the singular, you need to use an article: *a, an,* or *the.* The choice of *a* or *an* depends on how the first letter in the abbreviation is pronounced.

- Use *an* if the first letter of the abbreviation is a vowel or is a consonant that is pronounced with a vowel sound at the beginning.

He just finished *an* AA degree.

An MS is a Master of Science degree. [*The letter* M *is pronounced "em."*]

- Use *a* if the first letter of the abbreviation is a consonant that is pronounced with a consonant sound.

She has *a* PhD in physics.

For **initials** and **acronyms,** check a reference book to see whether an article is needed before them.

- Many of these words do not require an article when they are used as nouns.

I just read a new article about *NATO.* [not *the NATO*]

- Some initial abbreviations require the article *the* just as the spelled-out version would.

The FBI was called in to investigate the fire.

If you spelled it out, you would write The Federal Bureau of Investigation.

- If you use an abbreviation as an adjective, you may need to add the article *a* or *an* before it, depending on the meaning of the noun that follows. As with degrees, pronunciation of the abbreviation determines whether you should use *a* or *an.*

Both of my parents work in television, my mother at *an* NBC affiliate and my father at *a* CBS station. [N *is pronounced "en";* C *is pronounced "see."*]

The photograph on the front page showed *a* NATO session.

The acronym NATO *is pronounced as a word, not as individual letters.*

the southern states over the issue of integration; one area of conflict was Little Rock, Ark., where resistance was so great that the National Guard had to be used to enforce integration. Even this drastic step did not solve the problem, however, and the struggle for equal education and other civil rights for African Americans went on for many years.

EDITING 5: PRACTICE

Examine a paper you are working on for misused or omitted abbreviations. Is there one kind of mistake in using abbreviations that you consistently make? If so, think about how, in editing your work, you might best remember to abbreviate words correctly. Edit any sentences in which you have made errors in abbreviating.

PART SEVEN

Presenting Your Work

www.prenhall.com/fulwiler

Presenting Your Work

www.prenhall.com/fulwiler

On *The Blair Handbook, Fourth Edition,* Web site you can find

- Tips to create your own Web pages
- Suggestions to design documents
- Ways to give effective presentations

50 Designing Documents

The process of arranging and presenting your writing for others to read is **design.** Whether you present your writing as a college paper, a newsletter, or a Web page, you are creating a *document* of one kind or another. Your objectives in designing are to present your work in a neat, attractive form that is easy for readers to navigate and understand.

50 a Objectives of design

Good design is *transparent:* it calls attention to your work, not to itself. When a magazine cover catches your eye, you probably don't think, "What a well-designed magazine." But if your reaction is "That looks interesting—I want to read it," the design is doing its job.

Here are some objectives of good design and sample ways to achieve them:

- **Attract attention.** Think about a newspaper front page or magazine cover that attracts your attention. What catches your eye? A strong headline or an intriguing title? A compelling illustration? Even in a college paper, typography, illustrations, and graphics can help spark interest.

- **Create flow.** Once you have readers' attention, help them move easily through your document. Remove obstacles from the main path you want readers to follow. For example, put background information or statistics in tables or boxes, where they don't disrupt your main narrative or argument.

- **Show hierarchy.** Make items of similar importance resemble each other, and vary the appearance of items that are more or less important. In this book, the chapters, main sections, and subsections each have titles in distinctive sizes and styles of type. The typography and spacing reinforce the pattern of organization so

that readers can move easily from area to area and decide what to explore in depth. In a college paper, setting off major sections with subheadings, white space, or initial capitals can help keep readers oriented.

- **Show relationships.** Group related ideas together, and separate them from other elements by white space or distinguish them with a variation of layout style. (This list is one example of such grouping.)

- **Reinforce contrast.** If your paper advances with one side of an argument but fairness compels you to summarize the opposing view, consider presenting it in a box or "sidebar." Graphics can highlight changes over time or illustrate proportions.

- **Create emphasis.** A pull-out quotation calls attention to an important fact or a piece of supporting evidence.

- **Offer choices** to readers. If your writing is completely linear, readers feel obliged to start at the beginning and slog through to the end. By selecting elements that can be removed from the main path, you improve flow and allow readers to choose whether, for example, they want to read the background information or stay with your main thread. It is much easier to offer alternative paths through your writing on the World Wide Web than it is in print. **Links** to related material, charts, or sidebars can provide such choices.

- **Hold attention.** By giving readers information in varied forms and allowing them to follow their own interest, you are more likely to hold their attention. This is especially true when you publish information on the Web, since it will probably be read on a computer screen. Research suggests that computer readers have shorter attention spans than print readers and are less likely to read through a long document from beginning to end. For this reason, good design becomes especially important on the Web.

50 b Tools for designing

Picking a design for your writing involves selecting a **layout,** the basic arrangement of type and graphics on the page. The next step is **typography,** picking typefaces and choosing styles for paragraphs and headings. The third step is creating **graphics,** which include charts and graphs. **Illustrations** include drawings, clip art, and photographs. Finally, consider what, if any, use of **color** is appropriate to your purpose and audience.

Layout

Most college instructors expect papers to be submitted on 8½″ × 11″ paper. Pick paper heavy enough to prevent type on following pages from showing through. If you are using a word processor, use an ink-jet or laser printer to produce the most legible results.

Set page **margins** of one inch at the top, bottom, and sides of body text. Most word processors will show you a "page layout" view in which you can see the proportion of type to white space.

Double spacing lines of text is often required in college assignments. Check with your instructor.

Typography

Once upon a time, most instructors preferred typewritten papers, and a few would accept handwritten ones. For most students

---

✔ **RULES FOR INDENTING AND SPACING**

- Indent the first word of each paragraph five spaces.
- Space once after each word; space once after end punctuation if you write on a computer; otherwise check with your instructor.
- Space once after a comma, semicolon, or colon.
- Do not space between words and quotation marks, parentheses, or brackets. (See Chapter 43, 44a, 44d.)
- Do not space between quotation marks and end punctuation or between double and single quotation marks. (See 43a.)
- Do not space after a hyphen except in a suspended construction: *The rest of the staff are half- and quarter-time employees.* (See 47b–47d.)
- Do not space on either side of a dash, which may be typed as two hyphens: *Only two players remained—Jordan and Mario.* (See 44b.)
- Space before and after a slash only when it separates lines of poetry. (See 44e.)
- To display quotations of more than four typed lines, use block format. (See 43a2.)
- Underlining spaces between underlined words is optional, but be consistent.

COLUMNS

Setting type in multiple columns offers greater design flexibility. By tradition rooted in the use of the typewriter, college papers are usually produced in a single column of type, but with the permission of your instructor, you may use other formats. Newsletters and brochures are often set newspaper style with two, three, or more columns per page. Setting type in multiple columns provides shorter lines of text, which can be easier to read, and offers greater design flexibility. You can use your word processing program to specify the number of columns and the width of the gutter between them.

today, the word processing computer program has replaced the typewriter. Such programs let you present your work in a much more sophisticated and attractive form than typing.

For the body of your paper, select a **type font** and determine a **point size** that is easy to read, usually 12 points. A font consists of a typeface in various sizes along with variations such as **bold** and *italic*. A **serif font** has little bars at the ends of the lines of each letter. A **sans serif font** consists of type without serifs. For large blocks of text, serif type is easier to read. Sans serif type is useful in informal settings and for captions and labels.

Typefaces come with *proportional spacing*, in which the space allotted to each letter varies with the letter's shape, or *fixed spacing*, like a typewriter's in which each letter takes up the same amount of horizontal space. Unless your instructor specifies a typeface that looks like a typewriter's, such as Courier, pick a proportionally spaced font such as Times New Roman, Marin, Bookman, Palatino, or New Century Schoolbook.

As a rule of thumb, the wider each line of type, the larger the point size needed for easy reading. Avoid unusual typefaces, and don't introduce unnecessary typefaces within a document.

```
12-point
Courier
(serif,
fixed
spacing)
```

12-point
Century
Schoolbook
(serif,
proportional)

12-point
News Gothic
(sans serif,
proportional)

Title pages and headings

After you have selected the body type, pick a typeface for your title and for subheadings within text.

Designing Documents	Chapter title, 16-point News Gothic bold
Tools for designing	First-level heading, 12-point News Gothic bold
Typography	Second-level heading, 12-point News Gothic
Title pages and headings	Third-level heading, 12-point Times New Roman bold

Some instructors ask you to put your name, the date, and the title on the first page of a paper rather than on a separate title page. Start at the upper left-hand corner, using your regular typeface. Without indenting, add your name, your instructor's name, the course title, and the paper's due date, each on a separate, double-spaced line. On the next double-spaced line, center the title of the paper. Use a typeface slightly larger than your body type, but don't overdo it. Don't underline your title, and don't put it in quotation marks. Double-space again, and begin the body of text. (For an example of this style, see 18b.)

If your instructor asks for a separate title page, follow his or her guidelines or those of your discipline. (See 18a and 18c for examples in MLA and APA formats.)

In the upper right-hand corner of your manuscript, put your last name or an abbreviated title followed by the page number, separated by a single space. Do not use slashes, parentheses, periods, the abbreviation *p.,* or the word *page.* (See Chapter 18 for models.) Your word processor can automatically insert your last name or title and a page number in a "header."

Pull-out quotations

One way to renew readers' interest in a long passage of text is to use a pull-out quotation. You can set off your own words, emphasize an important statistic, or select a compelling quotation. Pull-out quotations are easily created on a word processor. Within a passage of text, you can draw a box approximately the size you need, then copy the words you want and paste them into the box.

JUSTIFIED OR RAGGED?

Your word processor can set type **ragged right,** with an uneven right margin, like this, or **justified,** with even margins on both sides, like the body text of this book. Justified type is attractive and is easier to read than ragged-right type, especially if you use a proportional font. Make sure, however, that the computer does not leave large spaces between words, especially on short lines of type. Also check for correct hyphenation. If your word processor makes many hyphenation errors, turn off hyphenation and hyphenate manually.

(If you use a quotation, be sure to cite the source.) Using slightly larger type provides greater contrast. Then "flow" the text around the box. Your word processor may allow you to specify the weight, color, and shading of the lines

> You can set off your own words . . . or select a compelling quotation.

that outline the box and to determine how type is wrapped around the box.

Another way to introduce a new section is to use a large initial capital letter or "drop cap" several sizes larger than the body type, with the text flowing around it. An initial capital can be set within the margin with text flowing around it, like the one in this paragraph, or outside the margin.

Lists and tables

A **list** of related items—ingredients, choices, or steps to be taken in a specific order—can be displayed using a few simple typesetting techniques. Indent the list to set it off from the body type. Select a symbol to introduce each list element, and make sure all the elements are written in parallel grammatical form. Once you select the typographical element, most word processors can format the list automatically with bullets or numbers.

DESIGNING YOUR DOCUMENT

1. Set page layout.
2. Set line spacing.
3. Select type fonts.
4. Plan tables and graphics.

DESIGN CHECKLIST

- Instructor's preferences
- Title page elements
- Page numbering
- Graphics, illustrations

A paragraph full of numbers will make most readers' eyes glaze over. Indeed, numbers in text can be very hard to understand.

A **table** can display data in a way that makes numbers easier to understand.

To set up a table, you can use tab stops or your word processor's "table" function. The array of numbers in the following table is four columns wide and seven rows deep. Place the table as close as possible to the portion of text that it illustrates.

MEDIAN INCOME BY AGE OF HOUSEHOLDER, 1993–2000

Age	1993	1999	2000
15–24	$22,740	26,017	27,689
25–34	36,793	43,591	44,473
35–44	48,063	52,582	53,240
45–54	54,350	58,829	58,218
55–64	39,373	46,095	44,992
65+	20,879	23,578	23,048

Source: Bureau of the Census.

3 Graphics

The term **graphics** refers to ways of presenting information in nonverbal form, including charts, graphs, and illustrations.

A **line graph** (sometimes called a *fever graph*) can make data easy to see.

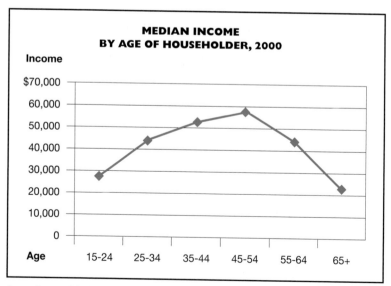

Source: Bureau of the Census, 2000

A **bar graph** can compare multiple sets of data.

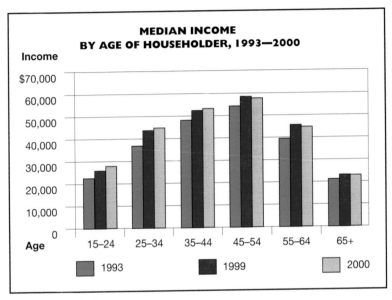

Source: Bureau of the Census.

A **pie chart,** which translates proportions into sections of a circle, compares parts to a whole.

Many computer programs can create graphs like these. You can enter the underlying data in a spreadsheet program, use software tools to create a graph, and copy the graph into a word-processed document. You can choose the type of chart, give it a title, and decide how you want it to appear.

If you don't have graphing software, you can make simple graphs and charts by hand and include them in your paper. Be sure to make them neat and easy to read, and always cite the source of your data.

Like all design elements, **color** should be used for a reason, not for its own sake. Color can convey information, as it does a photograph. It also can reinforce design objectives: the colors in the bar graph and pie chart reproduced in this section help distinguish elements and help tie them together with their descriptions. If your software or printer cannot produce color, many graphics programs can differentiate areas with shading or patterns of lines.

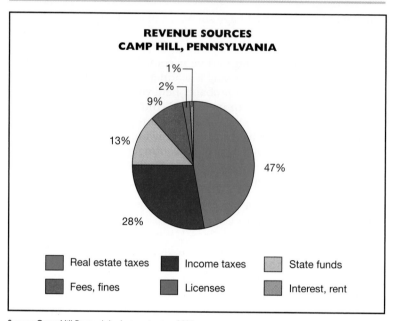

Source: Camp Hill Borough budget projection, 2001.

4 Illustrations

Illustrations include drawings, photographs, and clip art. For example, including a sketch that shows how you set up the equipment for an experiment might allow you to shorten a tedious description. In describing personal experience, a drawing or a snapshot can quickly establish a mood or a point of view. If you are writing about a visual experience—perhaps seeing a piece of art or a work of architecture—a picture really can be worth a thousand words.

Another source of illustration is **clip art,** a term that refers to simple stock illustrations. You may already have some clip art that came packaged in a software suite; you can download more over the Internet or purchase specialized collections. But be careful—some widely circulated clip art is so banal as to be virtually worthless.

Once again, the familiar guideline applies. Use an illustration not just to decorate your work but for a specific purpose—to make to something more understandable or easier to visualize, or to convey information or emotion. An illustration that relates specifically to your writing ("We climbed this path up Pikes Peak") is more

effective than a generic image such as a piece of clip art or a "stock" photograph ("We climbed a mountain that looked something like this one").

To reproduce an image on your computer, you might need to copy it in electronic form using a scanner or a digital camera. Your school's computer lab can probably help you. Once your graphic is in electronic form, you can use image-editing software to adjust it, and your word processing program can place it on the page. Mounting a photographic print or a drawing on a page of your paper is another acceptable way of presenting an illustration.

EDITING: EXPLORATION ━━━━━━━━━━━━━━━━━━━━━━━━━━━━

Look for examples of different kinds of design in newspapers and magazines. If your school library has a collection of student papers, look at some of them as

---

 DESIGN RESOURCES ONLINE

Combining text, headlines, and images on your computer to create papers or publications is sometimes called **desktop publishing.**

- Resources for designing paper and Web documents can be found at http://desktoppublishing.com/open.html. The site contains technical tips, theoretical discussions, free type fonts and clip art, and electronic bulletin boards you can use to discuss design questions.

- Another desktop publishing site is http://desktoppub.about.com/. Follow the series of links that begins with "Getting started."

- Learn about the history and the uses of various type styles at Typographic. http://www.rsub.com/typographic/

- The online version of Patrick J. Lynch and Sarah Horton's *Web Style Guide: Basic Design Principles for Creating Web Sites* gives an overview, much of which applies to publishing on paper as well. http://www.med.yale.edu/caim/manual/index.html

- Terry Sullivan's site All Things Web explains how design for Web pages differs from that of print documents. http://www.pantos.org/atw/basics.html

- The site of newspaper designer Ron Reason contains links to current front newspaper front pages, including the print and digital editions of several college newspapers. http://www.ronreason.com/livepages.html

- The Yahoo! directory has links to collections of graphic elements and tips at http://dir.yahoo.com/Arts/Design_Arts/Graphic_Design/Web_Page_Design_and_Layout/Graphics/

well. What design techniques appeal to you, and which ones are unappealing? Which ones look dated or appear to be trying too hard? Pick a half-dozen examples, and for each one write down two or three things you think the designer or author is trying to achieve through design.

50 C Proofreading

When you **proofread,** you check for errors. The key to proofreading is to see what is *actually* on the page rather than what you *intended* to put there. Somehow you must look with fresh eyes at words you have already read several times. Plan to proofread twice: once on the final, edited draft from which you prepare your final manuscript, and once on the final manuscript itself.

Proofread to correct punctuation and typographical errors, but of course fix any others you find as well. Listing errors in your journal may help you avoid them in the future. Here are some useful techniques to help you proofread:

- **Proofread on hard copy.** If you have been composing on a computer, proofread on a printout. You will be surprised how many errors or awkward passages leap out at you from the printed page. Make changes on the computer text as you go, or note all the changes on the printout before going back to enter them on the screen.

- **Read your paper aloud.** One test of good writing is whether it sounds clear and natural when read aloud. Reading aloud is also an effective way to find dropped words, misspellings, and punctuation errors.

- **Ask someone else to read your paper.** You can get a pair of fresh eyes by borrowing someone else's. Ask a friend to proofread your final draft for errors, omissions, or passages that seem unclear. Have your friend read your work aloud, and listen for awkward wordings, usage problems, and unclear punctuation.

- **Read your text backward.** In proofreading for spelling, read the manuscript one word at a time. In practice, this is hard to do, since most people read at the level of phrases and sentences. To avoid being distracted by meaning, try reading backward, starting at the last word and proceeding to the first. Some writers use a ruler to help them focus on one line at a time; other writers use a pencil to point out each word.

- **Use your computer's spell checker.** A computer's spell-checking function will never make the mistake of seeing what it expects to see instead of what is there. However, be aware that it can tell you only when you have misspelled a word, not when you have used the wrong word (such as *their* for *there*) or left one out. Most spell

STANDARD PROOFREADING MARKS

To mark errors in punctuation, mechanics, or spelling, use the proofreading marks listed here. (See also the editing symbols listed on the page facing the inside back cover.) Then incorporate the changes as you prepare your final manuscript. If you find errors in the final manuscript itself, you may also use these marks to make corrections; however, if you have to make more than two corrections on a page, retype or reprint the page.

Mark	Meaning
⌒	cl͡ose up space
#	add#space between words
	these words insert at this point ∧
— or ⌐ℯ	delete this ~~unneeded~~ material
⌐ or ℊ	delete and clo͜ose up
⌃ or ⌃ℯ	make a cha͡nge
∿	tra͡nps͡ose letters⌒words⌐or⌐
≡	c͟apitalize
/	⫽owercase
___	_italicize_
¶	¶ start a new paragraph

Add any symbols that are not available on computer or type-writer—such as accent marks—to your final manuscript neatly by hand, using dark blue or black ink.

checkers point out repeated words, but you must reread the sentence to determine whether the repetition is an error. (See Chapter 45 for more on spelling and using a spell checker.)

* **Make corrections.** Use standard proofreading marks to fix errors. (See the box above.) To correct a misspelled word, draw a line through it and write out the whole word.

This word is ~~misspeled.~~ *misspelled* ∧

If you make more than two corrections on a page, retype or reprint the page.

ESL **STRATEGIES FOR PROOFREADING**

In addition to the suggestions given in this section for effective proofreading, you may need to read your paper very carefully to check for common grammatical errors and incorrect word forms.

- Plan to read your paper several times to look for grammatical errors.
- Make a list of any frequent errors you are aware of. For example, you may consistently leave the final -s off plural nouns. Or you may use a verb tense that is not appropriate for the context. If you are not sure of your frequent errors, ask your instructor or tutor to help you create a list of them.
- Read your paper through once for each of these error types. In other words, concentrate on only one error type at a time. At first this process will be slow, but gradually your proofreading skills will improve; you will be able to proofread faster and to check more items at one time.
- You could also make a list of words that you frequently misspell. When you proofread for spelling, refer to your list and pay special attention to such words.

EDITING 1: PRACTICE _____

Proofread the following passage, correcting all errors in spelling, grammar, punctuation, and mechanics. Use standard proofreading marks.

Marian Anderson, who died in 1993 was the first black opera singer to preform at the Metropoliton Opera 1955 and became an inspiracion to generations of black performers throughout the U.S. Yet she was not able to make a name for herself in her own county until late in her life because of raical discrimmination. Althrough her grate talent was recognised early in her life (she won a voice contest in New York in 1925,) she could not get any rolls in opera, and her carrer was going nowhere. In the 1930s, Anderson decided to go to Europe to perform, and she quicky became an international singing star. When she returned to the U.S. and was invited to sing in Washington, DC, the D.A.R. (Daughters of the American Revolution) denied her acess to Constitution Hall, it's national headquarters. Eleanor Roosvelt (along with several other women) resined from the D.A.R. over this disgracefull incident, and she aranged for Anderson to perform outside at the Lincoln Memorial. 75,000 people came to hear Anderson sing, and her peformence in front of Lincolns statute became a powerful cymbal of the civil right's movement.

50 **d** Choosing a printing method and paper

1 Printing, typing, or handwriting

Computer printing generally gives excellent results. Corrections are easy, since you can reprint a single page if necessary. If your printer's output is faint and hard to read—as is that of many dot-matrix printers—put in a fresh ribbon, or take a copy of your manuscript on diskette to someone who has better equipment, perhaps even to a commercial copy shop.

Typing yields good results too, but accuracy is harder to achieve than with a computer. You can save time and effort by making some corrections before removing each page from the typewriter. Lift-off film works better than correction fluid, which in turn works better than erasure.

No matter how neat, a *handwritten paper* will seem less formal than a printed paper; submit a printed manuscript whenever you can. If you must submit a handwritten paper, make sure it will be acceptable to your instructor. Take special care to write simply, uniformly, and legibly.

2 Paper

For computer printing or typing, use $8\frac{1}{2}$" × 11" white bond paper of medium weight and good quality. Do not use very light paper, onionskin, or so-called erasable paper, all of which are hard to handle and make writing corrections or comments difficult. Unless your instructor specifies otherwise, double-space your manuscript no matter whether you print from a computer, type, or write by hand.

If your printer uses continuous paper, remove the perforated edges, separate the pages, and put them in the proper order.

If you write longhand, use blue or black ink on white, ruled paper, using only one side. Do not use legal-sized paper or paper torn from a spiral binder.

EDITING 2: APPLICATION ——————————————————————————

As you prepare the final manuscript of your next paper, look at it from a design perspective. Are the page layout and typeface appropriate? Does the design reinforce your paper's organization? Is your presentation orderly and neat? Make sure that you have followed all of the conventions of format and style discussed in this chapter. Pay attention to the indentation and spacing, as well as the positioning of the various elements on the page (heading, titles, page numbers). Make sure that you have corrected all typographical errors and that your paper is neat and legible.

Portfolios and Publishing

Revised and edited final drafts are written to be read. At the minimum, your audience is your instructor; at the maximum, it's the whole world—an audience for student writing now made possible by everyone's access to the Internet. In writing classes, the most common audience, in addition to the instructor, is the class itself. This chapter explores two common avenues of presenting your work in final published form via writing portfolio and class books.

51 a Writing portfolios

In simplest terms, a **writing portfolio** is a collection of your writing contained within a single folder. This writing may have been done over a number of weeks, months, or even years. A writing portfolio may contain writing that you wish to keep for yourself; in this case you decide what's in it and what it looks like. Or a portfolio may contain work you intend to share with an audience to demonstrate your writing and reasoning abilities.

One kind of writing portfolio, accumulated during a college course, presents a record of your work over a semester and will be used to assign a grade. Another type of portfolio presents a condensed, edited story of your semester's progress in a more narrative form. In addition, portfolios are often requested by prospective employers in journalism and other fields of professional writing; these samples of your best work over several years may determine whether or not you are offered a job as a writer or editor.

51 b Preparing a course portfolio

The most common type of portfolio assigned in a writing course contains the cumulative work collected over the semester plus a

cover letter in which you explain the nature and value of these papers. Sometimes you will be asked to assign yourself a grade based on your own assessment.

The following suggestions may help you in preparing a course portfolio:

Make your portfolio speak for you. If your course portfolio is clean, complete, and carefully organized, that's how you will be judged. If it's unique, colorful, creative, and imaginative, that, too, is how you'll be judged. So, too, will you be judged if your folder is messy, incomplete, and haphazardly put together. Before giving your portfolio to somebody else for evaluation, consider whether it reflects how you want to be presented.

Attend to the mechanics of the portfolio. Make sure the folder containing your writing is the kind specified and that it is clean and attractive. In the absence of such specification, use a pocket folder, which is an inexpensive means of keeping the contents organized and secure. Put your name and address on the outside cover. Organize the material inside as requested. And turn it in on time.

Include exactly what is asked for. If an instructor wants three finished papers and a dozen sample journal entries, that's the minimum your course portfolio should contain. If an employer wants to see five samples of different kinds of writing, be sure to include five samples. Sometimes you can include more than asked for, but do not include fewer.

Add supplemental material judiciously. Course portfolios are among the most flexible means of presenting yourself. If you believe that supplemental writing will present you in a better light, include that too, but only after the required material. If you include extra material, attach a note to explain why it is there. Supplemental writing might include journals, letters, sketches, or diagrams that suggest other useful dimensions of your thinking.

Include perfect final drafts. At least make them as close to perfect as you can. Show that your own standard for finished work is high. Final drafts should be printed double spaced on one side only of high-quality paper, be carefully proofread, and follow the language conventions appropriate to the task—unless another format is requested.

Demonstrate growth. This is a tall order, of course, but course portfolios, unlike most other assessment instruments, can demonstrate positive change. The signal value of portfolios in writing classes is that they allow you to demonstrate how a finished paper came into being. Consequently, instructors commonly ask for early drafts to be attached to final drafts of each paper, the most recent on top, so they can see how you followed revision suggestions, how

much effort you invested, how many drafts you wrote, and how often you took risks. To build such a record of your work, date every draft of each paper and keep it in a safe place.

Demonstrate work in progress. Course portfolios allow writers to present partially finished work that suggests future directions and intentions. Both instructors and potential employers may find such preliminary drafts or outlines as valuable as some of your finished work. When you include such tentative drafts, be sure to attach a note explaining why you still believe it has merit and in which direction you want to take it.

Attach a table of contents. For portfolios containing more than three papers, attach a separate table of contents. For those containing only a few papers, embed your table of contents in the cover letter.

Include a cover letter. For many instructors, the cover letter will be the most important part of your course portfolio since it represents your own most recent assessment of the work you completed over the semester. A cover letter serves two primary purposes: (1) as an introduction describing and explaining the portfolio's contents and organization, including an accounting of any missing or supplemental pieces; and (2) as a self-assessment of the work, from earliest to latest draft of each paper, and from earliest to latest work over the course of the semester. The following excerpt is from Kelly's letter describing the evolution of one paper:

In writing the personal experience paper, I tried three different approaches, two different topics, and finally a combination of different approaches to my final topic. My first draft [about learning the value of money] was all summary and didn't show anything actually happening. My second draft wasn't focused because I was still trying to cover too much ground. At this point, I got frustrated and tried a new topic [the hospital] but that didn't work either. Finally, for my last draft, I returned to my original topic, and this time it worked. I described one scene in great detail and included dialogue, and I liked it better and so did you. I am pleased with the way this paper came out when I limited my focus and zeroed in close.

The following excerpt describes Chris's assessment of her work over the whole semester:

As I look back through all the papers I've written this semester, I see how far my writing has come. At first I thought it was stupid to write so many different drafts of the same paper, as if I would beat the topic to death. But now I realize that all these different papers on the same topic went in

different directions. This happened to some degree in the first paper, but I especially remember in my research project, when I interviewed the director of the Ronald McDonald House, I really got excited about the work they did there, and I really got involved in the other drafts of that paper.

I have learned to shorten my papers by editing and cutting out needless words. I use more descriptive adjectives now when I'm describing a setting and try to find action verbs instead of "to be" verbs in all of my papers. I am writing more consciously now—I think that's the most important thing I learned this semester.

EDITING 1: APPLICATION

Using the guidelines in 51b and in the box below, select the papers and other writings to be included in a course portfolio. Make notes about the reasons for your selections as a reference for preparing a cover letter.

GUIDELINES FOR CREATING COURSE PORTFOLIOS

- **Date, collect, and save in a folder** all papers written for the course.
- **Arrange papers in chronological or qualitative order,** depending on the assignment, last drafts on top, earlier drafts in descending order behind.
- **In an appendix, attach supplemental writing** such as journal excerpts, letters, class exercises, quizzes, or other relevant writing.
- **Review your writing and compose a cover letter** explaining the worth or relevance of the writing in the portfolio. Consider the strengths and weaknesses of each individual paper as well as of the combined collection. Provide a summary statement of your current standing as a writer as your portfolio represents you.
- **Attend to the final presentation.** Include all writing in a clean, attractive folder; organize contents logically; attach a table of contents; write explanatory memos to explain unusual materials, and make sure the portfolio meets the minimum specifications of the assignment.

5 1 C Preparing a story portfolio

A story portfolio is a shorter, more fully edited and finely crafted production than a cumulative course portfolio. Instead of including a cover letter and all papers and drafts written during the term as evidence for your self-assessment, a story portfolio presents the evolution of your work and thought over the course of the semester in narrative form. In a story portfolio, you include excerpts of your papers insofar as they illustrate points in your development as a writer. In addition, you include excerpts of supplemental written records accumulated at different times during the semester, including such items as the following:

- Early and dead-end drafts of papers
- Journal entries
- Lecture and discussion notes
- In-class writing and freewriting
- Comments on papers from your instructor
- Letters to or from your instructor
- Comments from classmates about your papers

In other words, to write a story portfolio, you conduct something like an archeological dig through the written remains of your work in a class. By assembling this evidence in chronological order and choosing the most telling snippets from these various documents, you write the story that explains, amplifies, or interprets the documents included or quoted. The best story portfolios commonly reveal a theme or set of issues that run from week to week or paper to paper throughout the semester. As you can see, a story portfolio is actually a small research paper, presenting a claim about your evolution as a writer with the evidence coming from your own written sources.

We encourage students to write their story portfolios using an informal voice as they might in a journal or letter. However, some students choose a more formal voice. Some prefer to write in the third person, analyzing the semester's work as if it were someone else's. We also encourage them to experiment with the form and structure of their story portfolios, so that some present their work as a series of dated journal entries or snapshots while others write a more fluid essay with written excerpts embedded as they illustrate this or that point. The following pages from Karen's

portfolio exemplify the format and content of one type of story portfolio:

> When I entered English 1, I was not a confident writer and only felt comfortable writing factual reports for school assignments. Those were pretty straightforward, and personal opinion was not involved. But over the course of the semester I've learned that I enjoy including my own voice in my writing. The first day of class I wrote this in my journal:
>
>> 8/31 Writing has always been hard for me. I don't have a lot of experience writing papers except for straightforward things like science reports. I never did very well in English classes, usually getting B's and C's on my papers.
>
> But I began to feel a little more comfortable when we read and discussed the first chapter of the book—a lot of other students besides me felt the same way, pretty scared to be taking English in college.
>
> Our first assignment was to write a paper about a personal experience that was important to us. At first, I couldn't think where to start, but when we brainstormed topics in class, I got some good ideas. Three of the topics listed on the board were ones I could write about:
>
> - high school graduation
> - excelling at a particular sport (basketball)
> - one day in the life of a waitress
>
> I decided to write about our basketball season last year, especially the game that we lost. Here is a paragraph from my first draft:
>
>> We lost badly to Walpole in what turned out to be our final game. I sat on the bench most of the time.
>
> As I see now, that draft was all telling and summary—I didn't show anything happening that was interesting or alive. But in a later draft I used dialogue and wrote from the announcer's point of view and the result was fun to write and my group said fun to read:
>
>> Well folks, it looks like Belmont has given up, the coach is preparing to send in his subs. It has been a rough game for Belmont. They stayed in it during the first quarter, but Walpole has run away with it since then. Down by twenty with only six minutes left, Belmont's first sub is now approaching the table.

You were excited about this draft too, and your comment helped me know where to go next. You wrote:

> Great draft, Karen! You really sound like a play-by-play announcer—you've either been one or listened closely to lots of basketball games. What would happen if in your next draft you alternated between your own voice and the announcer's voice? Want to try it?

This next excerpt comes from a story portfolio that included twelve pages of discussion and writing samples and concluded with this paragraph:

> I liked writing this story portfolio at the end of the term because I can really see how my writing and my attitude have changed. I came into class not liking to write, but now I can say that I really do. The structure was free and we had plenty of time to experiment with different approaches to each assignment. I still have a long way to go, especially on my argument writing, since neither you nor I liked my final draft, but now I think I know how to get there: rewrite, rewrite, rewrite.

SUGGESTIONS FOR PREPARING A STORY FORTPOLIO

- **Assemble your collected writing in chronological order,** from beginning to end of each paper, from beginning to end of the semester.
- **Reread all your informal work** (in journals, letters, instructor comments) and highlight passages that reflect the story of your growth as a writer.
- **Reread all your formal work** (final papers, drafts) and highlight passages that illustrate your growth as a writer. Note especially if a particular passage had evolved over several drafts in the same paper—these would show you learning to revise.
- **Arrange all highlighted passages in order** and write a story that shows (a) how one passage connects to another and (b) why each passage is significant.
- Before writing your conclusion, reread your portfolio and **identify common themes or ideas or concerns** that have occurred over the semester; include these in your portfolio summary.

EDITING 2: APPLICATION ─────────────────────

Using the guidelines in 51c and in the box above, select the items to be included in a story portfolio. You may wish to use your computer's copy function to assemble a manuscript of selected extracts from papers, journal entries, freewriting, and other writing stored in your hard drive files or on disk. Make notes on this new manuscript of where you want to insert writing that is available only on hard copy, such as handwritten notes from instructors and classmates. Also make notes of the reasons for your selections for use in writing the narrative of a story portfolio.

EDITING 3: APPLICATION ─────────────────────

Depending on your instructor's assignment, prepare a course portfolio, using your work for editing assignment 1, or a story portfolio, using your work for editing assignment 2. Refer to 51a to complete your preparations.

51 **d** Publishing class books

Publishing a class book is a natural end to any class in which interesting writing has taken place. A **class book** is an edited, bound collection of student writing, usually featuring some work from each student in the class. When the book is published before the last class of the semester, a class discussion can be organized to examine the themes, style, and structure of the finished book. Responsibility for compiling and editing such a book is commonly assigned to class volunteers, who are given significant authority for design and production of the book. Volunteers who edit class books may find the following guidelines helpful:

- **Establish manuscript guidelines.** Discuss with the class what each submitted paper should look like: single- or double-spaced typing, typeface, font size, margins, justification, and title and author names.

- **Set page limits.** Since printing charges are usually made on a per-page basis, discussion of page length is related to final publication cost.

- **Ask for camera-ready copy.** To simplify and speed the publishing process, have each student prepare his or her own manuscript to submit to the editors.

- **Set deadlines.** Arrange for manuscript deadlines (when papers are due from contributors to editors) as well as final publication deadlines (when published books are available to students).

- **Organize the essays.** Arrange collected essays according to some logic—theme, content, quality, or author's last name.

- **Establish a graphics policy.** Discuss with the class how much space to leave in each essay for clip art, downloaded Web pictures, or taped-in photos.

- **Write an introduction.** Write an introduction to explain to readers the nature of the reading experience to follow. Introductions vary in length from a paragraph to several pages.

- **Prepare a table of contents.** Include author's name, essay title, and first page number for each essay.

- **Ask the instructor to write an afterword.** Instructors may write about the assignment objectives, impressions of the essays, or reactions to the class or add any other observation that seems relevant to the book.

- **Collect student writer biographies.** Conclude with short (50–100 word) serious, semiserious, or comical biographies of the student writers.

- **Design a cover.** Design the cover or commission a classmate to do so. (Color cardboard covers cost extra but are usually worth it.)

- **Arrange for publication.** Explore with local print shops the production costs and a timetable to produce copies for all students in the class.

- **Divide editorial responsibilities.** Class books are best done by editorial teams consisting of two or more students who arrange among themselves the various duties described above.

 SUGGESTIONS FOR DISCUSSING CLASS BOOKS

The following questions can help to generate critical discussions of class books:

- Which are your favorite titles and why?
- What, besides your own, is your favorite essay and why?
- What ideas or techniques did you learn from classmates' essays?
- In your own essay, what are your favorite passages?
- In your own essay, what would you like to change?
- In which essays are graphics used most effectively and why?

52 Writing for the World Wide Web

The World Wide Web is changing the way academic writers interact with their audiences. Before the Internet was widely available, student writers had to rely on college libraries, literary magazines, and academic journals to share their work. Publishing on the Internet, and the Web in particular, enables scholars and students alike to reach wider audiences, to learn from and to share ideas with people all over the world.

There are many reasons you might choose to publish your writing on the Web. You might want to put your writing where others in your class or your school can find it easily, without making dozens of copies. You might want to find other people with similar interests and, through your writing and theirs, become acquainted and build a community. You might want to find an audience that will give you feedback, encouragement, support, and criticism. You might use Web publishing simply out of pride in your work or to promote your writing and editing skills as part of a search for a job.

This chapter first presents some basic ideas about organizing your writing for the World Wide Web. First, we believe organizational clarity and an understanding of your audience are keys to good Web writing, as they are to all writing. With these concepts in mind, you can thoroughly map out your project's organization before you write a single line of text or computer code.

The next part of the chapter introduces the technical aspects of Web publishing, offers resources for coding and design, and provides examples.

52 a Organizing for the Web

Writing for the Web differs from writing for print. How? In print, we are accustomed to writing from the beginning to the middle to the end. That's true of narratives, of course, but it's also true of something as un-narrative as this book. Its pages are bound in a

certain order, and even though readers are expected and encouraged to skip around, that first-to-last order remains its basic organizational scheme.

When you write for the Web, you are creating **Web pages** consisting of text, graphics, images, and background that are presented simultaneously on a computer screen. A group of related pages is called a **Web site.** The program that displays such pages is called a **Web browser,** such as Netscape's *Navigator* or Microsoft's *Internet Explorer.* The coding system that creates Web pages is called *HyperText Markup Language,* or **HTML.**

1 Manageable chunks

Imagine how unwieldy a textbook or a novel would be if it were simply reproduced on the Web without organizational changes. Envision a 300-page text file with no way to get from place to place except by scrolling up or down on your computer screen and no landmarks except the page numbers and chapter titles to let you know where you were. Sounds pretty awful, doesn't it?

Holding the attention of a Web audience demands that you break up your writing into smaller, more easily comprehensible *chunks.* Research on reading habits has shown that people don't usually read as intensely or as long on a computer screen as they do on a printed page. Readers also seem to prefer examining a single screen of information rather than scrolling through text. Reading electronic text just seems to be a little harder, so people's attention spans are effectively shorter.

2 Nonlinear writing

By breaking information into chunks, you can give readers a choice of routes through your material. They can read background information first or skip to your conclusions. They can examine your sources to judge the quality of your research. They can go first to illustrations to get a visual sense of your material. But they can do these things only if you anticipate these moves and create paths for them.

Picking paths through Web material is called *navigation.* The navigation tricks we have developed for books, such as holding our place with one finger while we turn back a few pages to check something we missed, don't work well on the computer screen. But Web pages can offer better navigation tools.

ALTERNATIVE ENDINGS

In fiction, one kind of nonlinear writing creates points in a story at which readers must choose what happens and thus how the story proceeds. Depending on what choices the reader makes, the story leads to different endings. In nonfiction writing, nonlinear writing means giving a choice of which information to read first, which to read later, and which to skip.

3 Linking

Links, or *hypertext,* are the key navigational tool of the Web. Using the HTML coding system, you can make any word or image serve as a path that takes the reader to another place on the page, to another page on the same site, or to another page entirely. These paths are called **hyperlinks** or just **links.** (Actually, links don't literally take the reader anywhere. A click of the computer mouse on a link causes new files to be loaded into the browser, but the metaphor of "jumping" through "hyperspace" is pervasive.)

Using links, any Web page can be "next to" any other page or any number of other pages. For example, on a Web page we might set up a word as a link to take you to its own definition. A word that is a link usually shows up in colored text or underlined. Thus you needn't scroll through the text to find out what a term means; a click on a hyperlink can bring up the word's definition: "a word or image used to invoke a command to load a new file, usually one related by subject." After you read the definition, a click on the browser's "Back" button leads back to the main text. Readers who know what the word means can skip the definition. Those who don't know the term can click on the word, see the definition, and resume reading. This is how hypertext allows readers to choose the paths they take through your writing.

4 Anticipating readers' needs

The trick of Web writing, then, is to *anticipate* what paths your readers might want and to provide them. To do so, use the concepts of audience you're already familiar with. (See 6b.) With a target audience in mind, write for that audience. Then anticipate the needs of readers outside the target group. For those who know less about the topic, provide additional background. For those who are

skeptical, address key objections directly. For those with greatest interest, provide further information.

Suppose you're writing about the Henry Clay and the Whig Party primarily for your history professor and classmates. The Whig Party may be familiar to some of them, but other visitors to your site might need more background. Link keywords in your text to the relevant information.

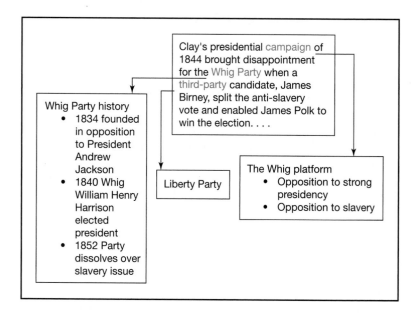

Clay's presidential campaign of 1844 brought disappointment for the Whig Party when a third-party candidate, James Birney, split the anti-slavery vote and enabled James Polk to win the election. . . .

Whig Party history
- 1834 founded in opposition to President Andrew Jackson
- 1840 Whig William Henry Harrison elected president
- 1852 Party dissolves over slavery issue

Liberty Party

The Whig platform
- Opposition to strong presidency
- Opposition to slavery

5 Clustering information

A map or **cluster diagram** is a good place to begin your Web site planning. (See 5f.) Make sure you have a spot for every major element.

On the main page, you can concentrate on Clay's stand on slavery and his efforts to preserve the Union in the Compromise of 1850. The biographical data, the story of the Whig Party, Clay's relationship with fellow senator Daniel Webster, and the collapse of the party all make attractive side journeys for your reader. By placing them on separate pages, you can streamline your main section.

Then think about what paths through the material readers are most likely to take. If the path branches into two choices, make

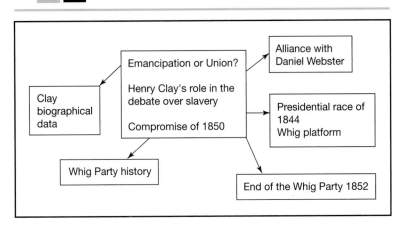

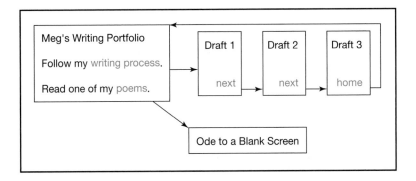

that choice clear with two links. If you have a preferred sequence in mind, you can set that up with a series of links.

6 Navigation tools

You don't want readers to get lost in your pages. Thus a Web site usually includes a central page referred to as a *home page,* the starting point for the site. A **navigation bar** is a consistent set of links to all pages in a site. The anchors for navigation links can be words, graphic images such as buttons, or pictures. Here's what a simple navigation bar for the Henry Clay site might look like:

Home:		
Emancipation or Union	The Whig Party	1844 presidential race
Clay biography	Daniel Webster	End of the Whig Party

Consider putting a navigation bar at the top and bottom of every page. If it's at the top, readers see it right away and can move on after reading one screen. If it's at the bottom, readers don't have to scroll back to the top after reading the page. Make navigation tools visually consistent, and locate them in the same position or positions on every page. (For an introduction to coding links, see 52b5.)

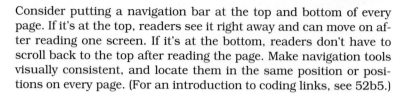

A Web page consists of a text file employing HTML commands, along with any photos, graphics, and audio or video elements. Some word processing programs can automatically create an HTML page for you.

1 Parts of a Web address

The unique filename of a page is called its *Web address* or uniform resource locator (URL). The URL tells the browser where on the Internet to find the page you want. A typical URL looks like this:

http://hotwired.lycos.com/webmonkey/teachingtool/index.html

Here's what the parts mean:

http://	"Hypertext transfer protocol" signifies a Web address.
hotwired.lycos.com	Second, first, and top-level domain names identify the computer with the desired file.
/webmonkey/teachingtool/	Directory and subdirectory on the target computer.
index.html	The name of the page itself. The suffix *.html* identifies a Web page written in HTML. The URL of the main or home page of a site usually ends with *index.html* or *index.htm.*

2 File organization

Make a separate text file for each page of your Web site. Store all the page files in one folder on your computer's hard drive. You

can put all your graphics and photos in the same folder or in a sub-folder. (See in 52b4.)

When you publish your page, you'll transfer the contents of this folder to a Web server, a computer that will send copies of the pages to any Web surfer who requests them. Your school's computer department or your Internet service provider can help you with the transfer. Ask whether space for your site is available on your school's host computers.

Basic HTML commands

There's no great mystery about HTML. Every command, or *tag*, consists of words or letters contained in angle brackets < > to distinguish it from surrounding text. Almost all tags come in pairs, one at the beginning and the other at the end of the text they control.

For example, the command <HTML> marks the beginning of an HTML page. The command </HTML> marks the document's end. Note the slash / signifying an ending tag. Everything on an HTML page happens between those two commands.

The next command is <HEAD>, which contains elements that don't appear on the page itself. One such element is <TITLE>, which sets the words that appear in the colored bar at the top of the page. The text and all other visible elements on the page follow the command <BODY>.

Here is the HTML code for a simple Web page:

```
<HTML>

<HEAD>

<TITLE>HTML Demo Page</TITLE>

</HEAD>

<BODY>

<H1>This is a level 1 heading, the largest.</H1>

<H6>The smallest is level 6.</H6>

<P>A new paragraph starts here. The paragraph command sets a
double line break. Paragraph commands don't come in pairs.

</BODY>

</HTML>
```

The text on the page will look like this:

This is a level 1 heading, the largest.

The smallest is level 6.

A new paragraph starts here. The paragraph command sets a double line break. Paragraph commands don't come in pairs.

You can see the HTML code used to create any Web page. In *Internet Explorer,* load the page into your browser and select "Source" from the "View" menu. A plain text file will appear, and you can examine each command.

4 Images

Suppose you want to include a photograph on your page. The photo is in digital form in a file named *snap.jpg* in your site's main folder. Use the image source tag:

```
<IMG SRC="snap.jpg">
```

If you have put your photos in a subdirectory named *pix* in the main folder, the tag should read <IMG SRC>="pix/snap.jpg">. This is a *relative address* for the photo. Whatever the browser's current directory is, it will look in a subdirectory called *pix* for a digital photo (*.jpg*) called *snap.*

You can also "call" a photo or graphic that does not reside on your site. To do this, you specify an *absolute address,* the complete URL at which the photo can be found: for example, <IMG SRC>=<http://www.microserve.com/users/alan/snap.jpg>. If you include links to material that belongs to someone else, be sure you have permission.

5 Links

A link, the basic element of Web navigation, consists of an anchor and a target. The **anchor** is the text or image the reader clicks on. The **target** is the destination Web address. Suppose you want readers to be able to click on the words "Click here!" to see a page whose address is <http://www.list.com/index.html>. Here's how you code the link:

```
<a href="http://www.list.com/index.html">Click here!</a>
```

The text "Click here!" is the anchor. In this code, *href* stands for *hypertext reference,* meaning the target address. Note the quotation marks around the URL and the absence of spaces from *href* to the closing angle bracket. On the Web page, this line shows up as Click

here! Clicking on it takes you to the page <http://www.list.com/index.html>.

6 Online and print tutorials

Complete instruction in writing HTML is beyond the scope of this book, but good instructions are available online and in print.

- Webmonkey

  http://hotwired.lycos.com/webmonkey/teachingtool/index.html

  A thorough online tutorial from *Hot Wired* magazine.

- A Beginner's Guide to HTML

  http://archive.ncsa.uiuc.edu/General/Internet/WWW/HTMLPrimer.html

  A primer from the National Center for Supercomputing Applications at the University of Illinois at Urbana-Champaign, birthplace of the first graphical Web browser.

In print, consult *HTML 4 for the World Wide Web* by Elizabeth Castro (Berkeley: Peachpit, 2000).

7 A sample Web page

To illustrate what a simple Web page looks like on the browser and as a text file, we asked Anna Fulwiler, daughter of author Toby Fulwiler, for permission to show two of her Web pages and the coding for one page. Of course, she graciously agreed. Compare the HTML code on page 736 with Anna's first page to see how various elements are produced.

Anna Fulwiler

"And these children that you spit upon as they try to change their worlds are immune to your consultations, they're quite aware of what they're going through" -David Bowie

My interests are:
• camping
• snowboarding
• kickboxing
• ER
• flowers
• eating

<u>Click Here</u> to read my debate on Women in the Work Force.

<u>Click here</u> to read my interpretation of "We Real Cool."

<u>Click here</u> to read my self-profile.

<u>Click Here</u> for more stuff.

Women in the Work Force

Are We Catching Up?

No, if...

• Society still tells girls they have a choice as to whether or not they will work for pay. Yet, women are nine times as likely as men to be single parents.

• Women continue to be clustered into traditionally female occupations.

• If present trends continue and girls are not encouraged to study math and science and computer programming, they will be trained only for the data and information-retrieval capabilities of the computer. There are still secretarial/clerical skills, and women will remain at the low end of the service-oriented pay scale.

Yes if...

• Nine out of ten women will work at some time during their lives.

• Employment growth in women-owned firms exceeds the national average by a substantial margin. 1991-1994 employment grew by 11.5% among commercially active women-owned firms in the United States compared to 5.4% among all firms.

• Eight out of ten women between the ages of 20 and 44 are working.

• The last twenty years witnessed the women's invasion in the working market. In 1985 the women made up 36.9% of the labor force. According to statistics, women represent 41.4% of today's economically active population. Most women are employed by the service sector (65.7%), followed by the industrial (19%) and agricultural (15.3%) sectors.

Click here to find more statistics of women in the labor force.

Click here to return to my home page.

Pages published on the World Wide Web by Anna Fulwiler

`<HTML>`	**`<HTML>` tag:** indicates this is an HTML file.
`<HEAD>`	**header tag:** title and comments placed in header.
`<TITLE>Anna's Home Page</TITLE>`	**title tag:** title displayed at top of the Web page; `</TITLE>` closes tag.
`<!creation date: 11/30/97>`	**comment tag:** does not display when file is viewed by a Web browser. Usually used by Web editors to make notes to themselves.
`</HEAD>`	
`<BODY>`	**body tag:** the majority of Web page follows.
`<H1>Anna Fulwiler</Hl><P>`	**heading tag `<Hl>`:** enlarges text and sets it apart from other text. H1 is the largest text size, down to H6, the smallest.
	paragraph tag `<P>`: equivalent of two returns or double line breaks.

`<B>"And these children that you spit upon as they try to change <BR> their worlds are immune to your consultations, they're quite<BR> aware of what they're going through" -David Bowie</B><P>`

bold tag `<B>`: makes text bold; same for italics `<I>`, underlined `<U>` and center `<CENTER>`.

break tag `<BR>`: makes one line break; equivalent of one return.

graphic tag: displays graphic from file.

list tag `<LI>`: bullets each item.

`<IMG ALIGN=RIGHT SRC="fish515.gif">`

align tag `<align=right>`: aligns picture (or text)

```
<B>My interests are:</B>
<LI><B>camping</B>
<LI><B>snowboarding</B>
<LI><B>kickboxing</B>
<LI><B>ER</B>
<LI><B>flowers</B>
<LI><B>eating</B><P>
<H4><A HREF="http://www.uvm.edu/~afulwile/women.htm"
>Click here</A>to read my debate on Women in the Work
Force. </H4><P>
<H4><A HREF="http://www.uvm.edu/~afulwile/realcool.html"
>Click here</A> to read my interpretation of "We   Real
Cool."</H4><P>
<H4><A HREF="http://www.uvm.edu/~afulwile/self.html"
>Click here</A> to read my self-profile.</H4><P>
<H4><A HREF="http://www.uvm.edu/~afulwile/annie.htm"
<Click here<A/A>for more stuff </H4><P>
```

links `<A HREF>`: links to other Web sites.

```
</BODY>
</HTML>
```

The HyperText Markup Language (HTML) code used to prepare Anna's home page

53 Making Oral Presentations

Public speaking is another way of "publishing" ideas that originate in written form. In speaking, as in writing, it's important to present ideas with confidence, clarity, accuracy, and grace: in the professions, in business, and in government, good writers and speakers get listened to, promoted, and rewarded; poor ones do not. While the art of public speaking can be addressed more comprehensively in speech class, we believe all writers should pay some attention to the oral publication of their ideas.

If asked to present a report to your classmates and teacher, approach it as you would the writing of a paper—in stages. Allow time to analyze the assignment's purpose and scope as well as your audience; time to research, organize, and add visual aids; and time to rehearse for timing, delivery, and understanding.

53 a Interpreting the assignment

The following suggestions have proved useful to successful public speakers:

Identify your purpose. Know the objective of your oral report task: What is your report supposed to accomplish? Is the purpose to present information, raise questions, argue a position, or lead the class in an activity? If you are not sure, reread the assignment and check with your instructor (after class or via e-mail). Regardless of your instructor's reason for making this assignment, to do a good job you'll need to believe in, understand, and know your subject—just as in any writing assignment. Choose a subject and a point of departure that you care about and believe in so you have the curiosity to do effective research and the passion to speak with conviction. If you don't care about gun control legislation, don't choose that for your topic.

Know your audience. Exactly what you say and how you say it depends upon to whom you are speaking. In most class settings,

your audience is composed of your instructor and your classmates; the best oral report will reach both effectively. Use your time in front of the class to teach them something they don't already know. Consequently, don't spend much time covering material already covered in class or in the textbook. At the other extreme, don't cover material that's totally unrelated to the course. Instead, build deliberately on issues, ideas, or information that stems from familiar class material, and present new information in that context. For example, if the class has been discussing multicultural issues, report on a small but specific and, to them, unfamiliar example.

Collaborate. If collaboration is called for or allowed—a common practice in classroom oral reporting—follow these procedures: (1) Arrive at a consensus understanding of what your task entails, and don't proceed until all of you know what is expected. (2) Divide tasks according to ability; do your own part promptly, and hold others accountable for doing theirs. (3) Meet often enough outside class so that your material is ready when the oral report is due. (4) Plan in advance who will report what and for how long.

53 b Preparing a speaking text

Texts that are spoken need to be simple, clear, and direct. The best way to prepare such a text is to follow essentially the same process as that for writing a paper: invent, draft, research, revise, and edit the material for your oral report until you know and trust it. The following ideas follow such a process:

Invent. Allow time for thinking, planning, inventing, discovering—don't try to prepare your whole oral report the night before it is due. Use your journal, notebook, or computer to brainstorm and discover the best ideas to speak about and the best strategies for preparing these ideas.

Draft. Use your computer to draft and develop ideas. Even if you don't intend to read your report out loud, it makes good sense to write it out in full to see how it looks and where it's going. Once a talk is drafted, it's easy to make an outline from it from which to speak.

Research. To teach audience members something they don't already know, research your topic so that you have fresh and detailed information to convey. Cite textual sources, quote local experts, report survey results, explain on-site visits. The more you've prepared, the more your audience will believe you.

Outline. The most effective oral reports are spoken rather than read, with the speaker making eye contact with the audience as much as possible. Consequently, the "final draft" of an oral report is not a polished, proofread paper but a "speaking outline" or notes to be glanced at as needed.

Create listening signposts. The old advice for making speeches goes like this: "Tell what you're gonna tell 'em. Tell 'em. Then tell 'em what you've told 'em." It makes sense to be repetitious in this way with oral presentations because it's hard for audiences to remember and keep track of what they hear. **Listening signposts—** words that signal what's coming—will help you do this. For example, tell your audience you are going to make three points about gun control legislation, then enumerate each as you get to it: "The first point in favor of [or against] gun control is . . . ; the second point is . . . ," and so on.

Prepare note cards. In a short report a one-page speaking outline may be the only thing you need. If your report is longer, is more complex, or includes quotations and statistics, organize note cards (3″ × 5″ or 4″ × 6″ index cards) to follow as you move from point to point in your talk.

Start strong. In speaking, as in writing, your opening sets the tone and expectations for what is to follow. In oral delivery it's especially important to get everyone listening at the same time, so speakers commonly use questions, stories, or jokes to catch quick attention. If you tell a story or joke, make sure it pertains to your subject.

Finish strong. Once they know their topic, their point, their audience, and the time available, many speakers map out their conclusion first, then work backward to make sure the text leads them there. With only five, ten, or fifteen minutes, be sure that when time is up, you've made the point you intended.

Write simply for oral delivery. Write an outline and notes with an emphasis on simplicity of language and repetition of main ideas, because listening audiences cannot pause as readers can to double-check what you mean. Simple jargon-free language is easiest to understand at a single hearing; repeating key words and phrases helps reinforce the listening memory.

Edit your reading text. If your material is complex and your time short, you may choose to read your report out loud. Reading is often less engaging than speaking, but it does guarantee that you say exactly what you wrote and meant precisely and economically. Be sure to double- or triple-space your reading copy, leave wide margins to pencil in extra notes, and start new paragraphs on new pages. For timing purposes, plan two and a half minutes for each page of double-spaced text ($8\frac{1}{2}$″ × 11″).

WRITING 1: EXPLORATION

What do the professionals say in a speech? Evaluate the content of a speech delivered by a professional public speaker, such as a guest lecture at your college, a television or radio news anchor's report of a single story, or a speech broadcast on CNN, C-Span, or Court TV. Take notes on what the speaker did to identify the theme or thesis of the speech and to capture the audience's attention at the beginning. Jot down listening signposts. Consider whether the speech ended with a strong conclusion.

EDITING 2: PRACTICE

Select a short paper, no longer than five pages, that you have written recently. Edit it for oral presentation in a speech of three minutes. Be prepared to explain in a small group discussion the reasons for your changes.

53 c Speaking in public

Once your talk is prepared, you need to present it, usually at the front of the classroom, which means leaving your comfortable seat and moving front and center for attention. A recent poll identified public speaking as the greatest fear of most Americans. Even famous actors and speakers feel anxiety before performing before live audiences, and they learn to use their nervous energy to keep a sharp edge while performing. Nervousness is unavoidable; accept it and try to harness this energy to help your performance. The following suggestions may help to alleviate this fear.

Rehearse. Run through your oral presentation in the privacy of your room to check your understanding and to set your pace to make sure you can deliver the talk in the time allotted. Rehearsing your talk out loud several times beforehand will help you understand your own material better as well as give you confidence when you walk to the front of the room. And in rehearsing, don't be afraid to revise, edit, rearrange ideas that looked good on paper but now strike you as wrong for an oral delivery. Rehearsing in front of a mirror and recording your rehearsals can help you to see your presentation from the perspective of a listener.

Make the room your own. Set up the room to suit the purpose of your presentation. If that means rearranging desks, tables, screens, or lecterns, then don't hesitate to do so. If there is a lectern front and center but you don't plan to use it, move it to one side. If you use the lectern, stand still and rest your hands on it—that will help you control any shaking. If you prefer your audience

in a semicircle or in groups instead of straight rows, ask them to sit that way. Taking control of your space makes you comfortable and gives you ownership of your time in front of the class.

Maintain eye contact with friendly audience members. While it's important to look around at the whole audience and make everyone feel as if you are addressing him or her, return periodically to the faces most receptive to your words—to smiles or nods or friends—for these will boost your confidence and keep you going smoothly.

Speak point by point. The reason for sticking to your outline or note cards is to present information in an economical and orderly fashion. If your report is supposed to last ten minutes, jot the starting time on your notes and stick to ten minutes. If you speak

---

ESL **DEVELOPING ORAL PRESENTATION SKILLS**

Giving presentations in a language that is not your native one can be a special challenge. Here are some suggestions for improving your skills:

- Remember that in English **your voice should rise on important words and syllables,** perhaps in a pattern that is different from the one in your language. Give a lower tone to less important words such as pronouns (she, them, it, and so on), auxiliary verbs (be, have, can, and so on), prepositions (of, in, with, and so on), and articles (a, an, the).

- Find time to **practice your presentation aloud.** Ask a native speaker of English to listen and write down any words that you say unclearly. Tape-record your presentation as well as the listener's corrections and suggestions. Then practice again, making the corrections.

- **Review the use of transitions** (See 23c2.) Then check your written text or notes to see that you have connected parts of your talk clearly. When you speak, pause slightly after a transition.

- **Speak loudly enough** so that every person in the audience can hear you easily. At first, you may find it difficult to do this, but you could practice with a friend listening from ten to fifteen feet away. Always ask your listeners in the beginning if they can hear you. If they can't, increase your volume to a level that is adequate for them. Also, **speak a bit more slowly than in conversation.** Your audience will appreciate your efforts.

too fast, the audience can't follow you; if you speak too slowly, people get restless—so strive for balance.

Leave time for questions. When giving oral reports, it is customary to allow your audience time to ask questions. Plan for this time, show your willingness to discuss further what you know, and always answer succinctly and honestly; if you don't know an answer, say so.

53 d Selecting creative options

Depending on your task and time, you may want to enhance your presentation with some of the following materials or activities:

Use handouts. Many talks are augmented by handouts (outlines, poems, stories, ads, articles, illustrations) illustrating points made in the talk or as a text to attend to at some time during the presentation. Prepare handouts carefully; make sure they are legible; document them properly if they are borrowed from another source, and make enough for everyone in your audience.

Use prepared visual aids. Many talks are made more powerful when accompanied by illustrations or examples of what is being talked about. What aids you use will depend on your purpose and topic, audience knowledge and size, and the physical setting available. Any of these visual aids may help: videos, films, maps, charts, sketches, photographs, posters, computer graphics, or transparencies shown on overhead projectors. With computer programs such as *PowerPoint,* it is possible to prepare professional-quality visual aids. Carefully prepare the aids in advance; order machines if necessary, and mark in your speaking text where you plan to use them.

Use process visual aids. It often helps to illustrate something on the spot in front of your audience. This device may be especially effective during a question-and-answer session. Media that help you write or sketch things out include blackboards, flip charts, and overhead projectors. Arrange for these aids in advance.

Use an overhead projector. The single most versatile visual aid is the overhead projector, which facilitates the use of prepared material as well as on-the-spot composing. You might even consider putting your speaking outline on one or more transparencies (available along with water-soluble marking pens in bookstores), projecting to your classmates your topic, key words, organization, and specific facts. Using an overhead projector has several distinct advantages for oral presentation: (1) it makes your notes easy to read; (2) it provides a visual record to aid your audience in

understanding, note taking, and retention; and (3) it divides audience attention between you and the lighted screen, thereby relieving you of some of the pressure of public scrutiny.

Use audio aids. Some talks are best advanced when accompanied by music or oral recordings. Audience attention picks up noticeably when you introduce sounds or voices other than your own into your presentation. A sound or visual recording may be the featured text in your presentation, or it may provide useful accompaniment. Order any necessary recording equipment, and rehearse in advance.

Be a visual and audio aid. For some topics, a live demonstration may be appropriate. Be sure to have all the props, supplies, and equipment you need for your demonstration, whether it involves how to play the trombone or how to dress for in-line skating. Even if you do not demonstrate a process, you can use *body language* to your advantage. Smiling at your audience, in addition to making eye contact, will help to establish a friendly connection. Natural gestures can help you maintain your audience's interest and can reinforce what you are saying. For example, if you say you are

---

TIPS FOR PUBLIC SPEAKING

- **Plan.** Know your purpose, analyze your audience, and allow time to create and discover the best ideas and approach to your talk.

- **Write.** Whether you intend to read from text or notes, write your way through the planning, drafting, revision, and editing stages so that you understand fully what you are saying and how much time it will take.

- **Research.** Add specific facts, observations, testimony, data, and ideas derived from library and field research to interest your audience and teach them something they don't already know.

- **Simplify.** Your audience will hear you only one time, so edit, arrange, and condense to make your points and conclusion as clear, direct, and simple as possible.

- **Rehearse.** To understand and pace your talk, practice it out loud in private before you deliver it in public.

- **Persuade.** To make your audience understand and believe you, speak not only from knowledge but from personal conviction.

- **Illustrate.** To increase audience interest and understanding, supplement your talk with visual or audio aids or both.

going to make three points, you can count them on your fingers. Body language also includes the sound of your voice; volume, speed of delivery, emphasis, tone, and pitch all add meaning to the words you say.

Ask your audience to write. If you want to engage your audience quickly and relax yourself at the same time, ask people to write briefly before you speak. For example, on the subject of "alcohol on campus," ask people to jot down their own experience with or knowledge of the subject on scratch paper, telling them their notes will remain private. After a few minutes, ask them to talk about— not read—their ideas with a neighbor for several more minutes. Writing for even five minutes pulls people into your topic by causing them to think personally about it. Talking aloud to seatmates pulls them in deeper still, and the oral buzz in the room makes everyone—especially you—more comfortable. To resume control, ask for several volunteer opinions and use these as a bridge to your own presentation.

The best preparation for oral presentations is encouraging and regularly joining class discussions and asking questions out loud. The more you work in small groups, discuss with neighbors, and participate in all class discussion, the easier and more natural oral reporting will be.

PART EIGHT

Writing Across the Curriculum

www.prenhall.com/fulwiler

Writing Across the Curriculum

www.prenhall.com/fulwiler

On *The Blair Handbook, Fourth Edition,* Web site you can find

- Discipline-specific Web links for research
- The official MLA, APA, CSE, and COS Web sites
- Sample documented papers

54 Understanding the College Curriculum

Good writing satisfies the expectations of an audience in form, style, and content. But different audiences come to a piece of writing with different expectations, so writing that is judged "good" by one audience may be judged "less good" by another. Although all college instructors value good writing, each area of study has its own set of criteria by which writing is judged. For instance, the loose form, informal style, and speculative content of a reflective essay that please an English instructor might not please an anthropology instructor, who expects form, style, and assertions to follow the more formal structures established in that discipline. This chapter provides a broad outline of these different criteria and points to some important similarities for writing across the curriculum.

54 a Understanding differences among the disciplines

As a rule, knowledge in the humanities focuses on texts and on individual ideas, speculations, insights, and imaginative connections. Interpretation in the humanities is thus relatively subjective. Accordingly, good writing in the humanities is characterized by personal involvement, lively language, and speculative or open-ended conclusions.

In contrast, knowledge in the social and physical sciences is likely to focus on data and on ideas that can be verified through observing, measuring, and testing. Interpretation in these disciplines needs to be objective. Accordingly, good writing in the social and physical sciences emphasizes inferences based on the careful study of data and downplays the personal opinion and speculation of the writer.

But boundaries between the disciplines are not absolute. For example, at some colleges history is considered one of the humanities, while at others it is classified as a social science. Geography is

a social science when it looks at regions and how people live, but it is a physical science when it investigates the properties of rocks and glaciers. Colleges of business, engineering, health, education, and natural resources all draw on numerous disciplines as their sources of knowledge.

The field of English alone includes not only the study of literature but also literary theory and history, not only composition but also creative and technical writing. In addition, English departments often include linguistics, journalism, folklore, women's studies, Afro-American studies, and sometimes speech, film, and communications. In other words, within even one discipline, you might be asked to write several distinct types of papers: personal experience essays for a composition course, interpretations for a literature course, abstracts for a linguistics course, short stories for a creative writing course. Consequently, any observations about the different kinds of knowledge and the differing conventions for writing about them are only generalizations. The more carefully you study any one discipline, the more complex it becomes, and the harder it is to make a generalization that doesn't have numerous exceptions.

Formal differences exist among the styles of writing for different disciplines, especially in the conventions for documenting sources. Each discipline has its own authority or authorities, which provide rules about such issues as spelling of technical terms and preferred punctuation and editing mechanics, as well as documentation style. In addition, if you write for publication in a magazine, professional journal, or book, the publisher will have a *house style,* which may vary in some details from the conventions listed in the authoritative guidelines for the discipline in which you are writing. The following table lists the sources of style manuals for various disciplines:

DISCIPLINE	STYLE
Languages and literature	Modern Language Association (MLA) (See Chapter 55.)
Humanities	*Chicago Manual of Style* (CMS) (See Chapter 56.)
Social sciences	American Psychological Association (APA) (See Chapter 57.)
Sciences	
Life sciences	Council of Science Editors (CSE)
Chemistry	American Chemical Society
Physics	American Institute of Physics (AIP) (See Chapter 58.)

Business	Varies (See Chapter 59.)
Journalism	Associated Press (AP)
Medicine	American Medical Association (AMA)

54 b Understanding similarities among the disciplines

Regardless of discipline, certain principles of good writing hold true across all areas of academic study.

Knowledge

Each field of study attempts to develop knowledge about a particular aspect of the physical, social, or cultural world. For example, history courses focus on human beings living in particular time periods; sociology courses focus on human beings in groups; psychology courses focus on the operation and development of the individual human mind. In writing for a particular course, keep in mind the larger purpose of the field of study, especially when selecting, introducing, and concluding your investigation.

Method

Each field has accepted methods of investigation. Perhaps the best known is the scientific method, used in most of the physical and social sciences. One who uses the scientific method first asks a question, then poses a possible answer (a hypothesis), then carries out experiments to test this answer, and finally, if it cannot be disproved, concludes that the hypothesis is correct. However, while research in the social sciences follows this scientific pattern, some disciplines, such as anthropology, rely instead on the more personal approach of ethnographic study. Literary research may be formal, historical, deconstructive, and so on. It is important to recognize that every discipline has its accepted—and its controversial—methods of study. Any conclusions you discuss in your writing should reflect that awareness.

Evidence

In every field, any claim you make about the subject of your study needs to be supported by evidence. If, in order to identify an unknown rock, you scrape it with a known rock in the geology laboratory, the scratch marks of the harder rock on the softer will be

part of your evidence to support your claims about the unknown rock. If you analyze Holden Caulfield on the basis of his opening monologue in *The Catcher in the Rye*, his words will be evidence to support your interpretation. If you conduct a survey of students to examine college study habits, your findings will be evidence to support your conclusions. In other words, although the *nature* of evidence varies greatly from one discipline to another, the *need* for evidence is constant. In some cases, when you need to support an assertion, you will consult certain sources for evidence and will need to have clear documentation for these sources. (Chapters 55–60 provide detailed guidelines for documenting sources in various disciplines.)

4 Accuracy

Each field values precision and correctness, and each has its own specialized vocabulary for talking about knowledge. Writers are expected to use terms precisely and to spell them correctly. In addition, each discipline has developed formats in which to report information. You should know the difference in form between a literary analysis in English, a research report in sociology, and a laboratory report in chemistry. Each discipline also values conventional correctness in language. Your writing must always reflect standard use of grammar, punctuation, and mechanics.

55 Writing in Languages and Literature

This chapter describes the aims, style, and forms required for most kinds of writing in English, comparative literature, and foreign languages where the primary focus is on the study of texts. Many specialized areas, such as film and cultural studies, also follow the conventions described here. Papers in language and literature use the documentation system of the Modern Language Association (MLA).

55 a The aims of writing in languages and literature

Language and literature courses are concerned with reading and writing about texts such as poems, novels, plays, and essays written by published authors as well as by students. (The term *text* is defined here broadly to include films, visual arts, advertisements—anything that can be read and interpreted.) What sets literary studies apart from most other disciplines, including others in the humanities, is the attention devoted to all elements of written language. In these courses, writing is not only the means of study but often the object of study as well: works are examined for their *form* and *style* as well as their *content*. Texts are read, listened to, discussed, and written about so students can discover what these texts are, how they work, what they mean, and what makes them exceptional or flawed. Moreover, literary studies often draw on ideas from other disciplines. For instance, reading a single novel such as Charles Dickens's *David Copperfield* or Toni Morrison's *Beloved* can teach readers a little about sociology, psychology, history, geography, architecture, political science, and economics as well as the esthetics of novel writing.

When you write in language and literature, you can examine texts from a variety of perspectives. You can focus on a text's ideas, authors, formal qualities, or themes. For such essays, you usually

refer mainly to **primary sources,** the text itself and perhaps other works to which you may compare it. You can also consider the culture that produced the text, the text's relationship to other texts, its place in history, and its politics. You may refer to **secondary sources,** writing by others about the text or about the context in which the primary text was written. Modern literary study may engage in any of five basic activities with texts:

- You can **appreciate** texts. You can write about the text's most moving or interesting features, the beauty or strangeness of the setting, the character with whom you most identify, the plot as it winds from beginning to end, or the turns and rhythms of the language.

- You can **analyze** texts, asking questions such as *How is it put together?* or *How does it work?* Analysis involves looking at a text's component parts (chapters, for example) and the system that makes it work as a whole (such as the plot), defining what they are, describing what they are like, and explaining how they function.

- You can **interpret** texts, asking questions such as *What does it mean? How do I know what it means?* and *Why was it made?* Interpretations often vary widely from reader to reader and may provoke quite a bit of disagreement.

- You can **evaluate** texts, asking questions such as *How good is it? What makes it worth reading?* and *How does it compare with other texts?* These are questions of judgment, based on criteria that might differ considerably from person to person. For example, you might judge a poem good because its pattern of rhythm and imagery is pleasing (esthetic criteria). Another reader may praise the same poem because it subverts common assumptions about power relationships (political criteria), and a third may do so because it evokes fond childhood memories (personal criteria). However, a fourth reader might look for underlying assumptions or values (philosophical criteria), and a fifth might contrast it to another poet's work (comparative criteria).

- You can **study the culture** that produced the text, asking such questions as *What are the values of the people depicted in the text?* and *How do the scenes, settings, and characters reveal the author's values?* To find answers to these and other questions, it is common to compare the text with other texts produced at the same or different times.

All of these activities come together when you are asked to write critical or analytical essays about the literature you read.

55 b The style of writing in languages and literature

Writing in languages and literature demands clarity, variety, and vitality to create a strong connection between the writer and reader. Direct, unpretentious language and an engaging tone are valued over obscure terminology and an artificially formal style. Observing the standard conventions of grammar, punctuation, and mechanics is also expected.

All that said, greater freedom and variety of style are allowed in language and literature study than perhaps in any other discipline. Because literary studies center so closely on the multitude of ways readers approach texts, writing can range from the highly personal to the highly theoretical, from deeply impressionistic to sharply rational, from journalistic to experimental to political. Indeed, a single essay may knit together all these styles.

As a student, you may do much of your writing in language and literature in a relatively conventional style—asserting a thesis and supporting it with textual evidence and reasoned insight. But do not be surprised if you find yourself responding in different styles and voices for different kinds of assignments.

55 c Common forms of writing in languages and literature

As we said, there are five common aims of writing about texts: appreciation, analysis, interpretation, evaluation, and cultural study. Addressing any one of these aims, the essays you are assigned in language and literature courses are likely to fall into two categories: those in which you focus on your own responses to one or more texts without consulting any outside sources, and those in which you research and synthesize additional material before coming to your own conclusions about a particular text or texts. (See Chapter 10 for more on writing about texts.)

Essays that focus on a writer's responses

When you focus on your own responses to a text, you may be expected to be subjective and to incorporate your own experiences, cultural background, and gender in your analysis. Or you may be asked to be objective, basing your response exclusively on the way a text is put together, its form, and its imagery. (See 10d.) Either way, be sure to quote from the work directly whenever doing so can help clarify a point you are making.

GLOSSARY OF LITERARY TERMS

- **alliteration** The repetition of initial consonant sounds ("*On the bald street breaks the blank day.*")
- **antagonist** A character or force opposing the main character (the *protagonist*) in a story.
- **climax** A moment of emotional or intellectual intensity or a point in the plot where one opposing force overcomes another and the conflict is resolved.
- **epiphany** A flash of intuitive understanding by narrator or character in a story.
- **figurative language** Language that suggests special meanings or effects such as metaphors or similes; not literal language. ("*She stands like a tree, solid and rooted.*")
- **imagery** Language that appeals to one of the five senses, especially language that reproduces something the reader can see or imagine. ("*His heart was an open book, pages aflutter and crackling in the wind.*")
- **narrator** Someone who tells a story; a *character narrator* tells the story from a personal perspective (Huckleberry Finn) while an *omniscient narrator* tells a story about other people.
- **persona** A *mask*, not the author's real self, worn by the author to present a story or poem.
- **plot** The sequence of events in a story or play.
- **point of view** The vantage point from which a story or event is perceived and told.
- **protagonist** The main character or hero of a plot.
- **rhyme** The repetition of sounds, usually at the ends of lines in poems, but also occurring at other intervals in a line (*moon, June, noon*).
- **rhythm** The rise and fall of stress sounds within sentences, paragraphs, lines, and stanzas.
- **symbol** An object that represents itself and something else at the same time. A *black rose* is both the color of the rose and the suggestion of something evil or death-like.
- **theme** The meaning or thesis of a text.

Aim to go beyond summarizing the text or what may have already been covered in class discussions. Your particular insights into what a text means, how it works, and how well it works should constitute the body of any such paper. Your conclusions may be

tentative and exploratory rather than assertive and conclusive, but they should always represent a careful, detailed reading.

2 Essays that incorporate secondary sources

Assignments that ask you to go beyond a primary text to consider *secondary source* material require you to read, evaluate, and synthesize what other critics have said about a work or to compare the work with other works or with historical events. In doing so, be careful not to let these additional sources overwhelm your own insights and viewpoint. You will be expected to develop your own thesis based on your close reading of the work and to introduce secondary sources as a way of supporting, expanding, or contrasting your views with those of other critics.

You may also be required (or choose) to consult other kinds of sources: biographies, letters, journals, and interviews about the writer; studies and documents that provide historical or social context; popular responses to the text; or recordings and dramatizations of the text. Such sources should serve to help you develop and support a thesis or point of view that is ultimately your own.

55 d Documenting sources: MLA style

The Modern Language Association (MLA) system is the preferred form for **documenting** research sources when you write about literature or language.

- All sources are briefly documented in the text by an identifying name and page number (generally in parentheses).

- A Works Cited section at the end of the paper lists full publication data for each source cited.

- Additional explanatory information provided by the writer of the paper (but not from external sources) goes either in footnotes at the foot of the page or in a Notes section after the close of the paper.

The MLA system is explained in more detail in the *MLA Handbook for Writers of Research Papers*, 5th ed. (New York: MLA, 1999).

The MLA system provides a simple, concise, and thorough way for writers to acknowledge the sources they use in research-based papers. In the MLA system, authors use footnotes and/or endnotes to provide additional, explanatory information, but not to cite information provided by external sources. Whenever possible,

DIRECTORY FOR MLA DOCUMENTATION GUIDELINES; INDEX TO SAMPLE FORMATS THAT FOLLOW

(Continued)

(Continued)

MLA MLA MLA

49. Online encyclopedia
50. Online work of art
51. Online interview
52. Online film or film clip
53. Online cartoon
54. Online television or radio program

DOCUMENTING OTHER SOURCES

55. Cartoon
56. Film or videocassette
57. Personal interview
58. Published or broadcast interview
59. Print advertisement
60. Unpublished lecture, public address, or speech
61. Personal or unpublished letter
62. Published letter
63. Map
64. Performance
65. Audio recording
66. Television or radio broadcast
67. Work of art

the MLA system includes explanatory information in the text itself and limits the use of footnotes or endnotes. Pay careful attention to the practical mechanics of documentation so that readers can readily identify, understand, and locate your sources.

Conventions for in-text citations

In-text citations identify ideas and information borrowed from other writers. They also refer readers to the Works Cited list at the end of the paper, where they can find complete publication information about each original source. The languages and literature are not primarily concerned with *when* something was written; instead, these fields of study focus on writers and the internal qualities of texts. Therefore, in-text citations following the MLA style feature author names, text titles, and page numbers. MLA style is economical, providing only as much in-text information as readers need in order to locate more complete information in the Works Cited list. Following are some examples of how in-text citation works; see the following pages for the format of entries in the Works Cited list. A sample paper using MLA documentation appears in 18b.

1. Single work by one or more authors

When you quote, paraphrase, or summarize a source, include in the text of your paper the last name of the source's author, if known, and, in parentheses, the page or pages on which the original information appeared. Do not include the word *page* or the abbreviation *p.* or *pp.* You may mention the author's name in the sentence or put it in parentheses preceding the page number(s).

Carol Lea Clark explains the basic necessities for the creation of a page

on the World Wide Web (77).

Provided one has certain "basic ingredients," the Web offers potential

worldwide publication to individuals (Clark 77).

Note that a parenthetical reference at the end of a sentence comes before the period. No punctuation is used between the author's last name and the page number(s).

If you cite a work with two or three authors, your in-text parenthetical citation must include all authors' names: (*Rombauer and Becker 715*), (*Child, Bertholle, and Beck 215*). For works with more than three authors, you may list all the authors or, to avoid awkwardness, use the first author's name and add *et al.* without a comma: (*Britton et al. 395*). *Et al.* is an abbreviation for the Latin *et alii,* translated "and others."

2. Two or more works by the same author

If your paper has references to two or more works by the same author, you should clearly identify the specific work in your citation. Either mention the title of the work in the text or include a shortened version of the title (usually the first one or two important words) in the parenthetical citation.

According to Lewis Thomas in <u>Lives of a Cell</u>, many bacteria become

dangerous only if they manufacture exotoxins (76).

According to Lewis Thomas, many bacteria become dangerous only if

they manufacture exotoxins (<u>Lives</u> 76).

Many bacteria become dangerous only if they manufacture exotoxins

(Thomas, <u>Lives</u> 76).

If both the author's name and a shortened version of the title are in a parenthetical citation, a comma separates them, but there is no comma before the page number.

3. Unknown author

When the author of a work you are citing is unknown, use either the complete title in the text or a shortened version of it in the parenthetical citation, along with the page number.

According to <u>Statistical Abstracts</u>, the literacy rate for Mexico stood at

75 percent in 1990, up 4 percent from census figures ten years earlier (374).

The literacy rate for Mexico stood at 75 percent in 1990, up 4 percent

from census figures ten years earlier (<u>Statistical</u> 374).

4. Corporate or organizational author

When no author is listed for a work published by a corporation, organization, or association, indicate the group's full name in any parenthetical reference: (*Florida League of Women Voters* 3). If the name is long, cite it in the sentence and put only the page number in parentheses.

5. Authors with the same last name

When you cite works by two or more authors with the same last name, include the first initial of each author's name in the parenthetical citation: (*C. Miller 63; S. Miller 101–04*).

6. Works in more than one volume

When your sources are in more than one volume of a multivolume work, indicate the pertinent volume number for each citation. Place the volume number before the page number and follow it with a colon and one space: (*Hill 2: 70*). If your source is in only one volume of a multivolume work, you need not specify the volume number in the in-text citation, but you should specify it in the Works Cited list.

7. One-page works

When you refer to a work that is only one page long, you need not include the page number in your citation. Author or title identification is sufficient for readers to find the exact page number on the Works Cited list.

8. Quotation from an indirect source

When a quotation or any information in your source is originally from another source, use the abbreviation *qtd. in.*

Lester Brown of Worldwatch believes that international agricultural

production has reached its limit and that "we're going to be in trouble on the

food front before this decade is out" (qtd. in Mann 51).

9. Literary works

In citing literary prose works available in various editions, provide additional information (such as chapter number or scene number) for readers who may be consulting a different edition. Use a semicolon to separate the page number from this additional information: (*331; bk. 10, ch. 5*). In citing poems, provide only line numbers for reference; include the word *line* or *lines* in the first such reference. Providing this information will help your audience find the passages *in any source where those works are reprinted,* which page references alone cannot provide.

In "The Mother," Gwendolyn Brooks remembers "[. . .] the children you

got that you did not get" (line 1); children that "never giggled or planned or

cried" (30).

Cite verse plays using act, scene, and line numbers, separated by periods: (*Hamlet 4.4.31–39*).

10. More than one work in a citation

To cite more than one work in a parenthetical reference, separate them with semicolons: (*Aronson,* Golden Shore *177; Didion 49–50*).

11. Long quotation set off from text

Set off quotations of four or more lines by indentation. Indent the quotation one inch or ten spaces from the left margin of the text (not from the paper's edge), double-space, and omit quotation marks. The parenthetical citation follows end punctuation (unlike shorter, integrated quotes) and is not followed by a period.

Fellow author W. Somerset Maugham, admiring Austen, but not blindly,

had this to say about her dialogue:

> No one has ever looked upon Jane Austen as a great stylist. Her
> spelling was peculiar and her grammar often shaky, but she had a
> good ear. Her dialogue is probably as natural as dialogue can ever
> be. To set down on paper speech as it is spoken would be very
> tedious, and some arrangement of it is necessary. (434)

2 Conventions for endnotes and footnotes

In MLA citation style, notes are used primarily to offer comments, explanations, or additional information (especially source-related information) that cannot be smoothly or easily accommodated in the text of the paper. You might use notes also to cite several sources within a single context if a series of *in-text* references might detract from the readability of the text. In general, however, you should omit additional information, outside the "mainstream" of your text, unless it is necessary for clarification or justification.

If you conclude that a note is necessary, insert a raised (superscript) numeral at the reference point in the text; introduce the note itself with a corresponding raised numeral, and indent it. Many word processing programs provide footnote functions, which greatly simplify the entire procedure.

TEXT WITH SUPERSCRIPT

The standard ingredients for guacamole include avocados, lemon juice,

onion, tomatoes, coriander, salt, and pepper.[1] Hurtado's poem, however,

gives this traditional dish a whole new twist (lines 10–17).

NOTE

[1]For variations see Beard 314, Egerton 197, Eckhardt 92, and Kafka

26. Beard's version, which includes olives and green peppers, is the

most unusual.

The references listed in the notes should appear in the Works Cited list along with the other sources referred to in your text.

Notes may come at the bottom of the page on which the text reference appears—as footnotes—or be included as endnotes, double spaced, on a separate page at the end of your paper. Endnote pages should be placed between the text of the paper and the Works Cited, with the title "Note" or "Notes." (For more on the format for footnotes, see 55c–55f.)

55 e Conventions for list of works cited

All sources mentioned in an academic essay (and other types of formal or professional writing) should be identified on a concluding list of works cited. These entries follow specific rules for formatting and punctuation so that the reader can readily find information.

Format. After the final page of the paper, title a separate page "Works Cited," an inch from the top of the page, centered, but not underlined and not in quotation marks. Exception: If you are required to list all the works you have read in researching the topic—not just those to which you have actually referred in your text or notes—you should title this list "Works Consulted" rather than "Works Cited." Number the page, following in sequence from the last page of your paper.

Double-space between the Works Cited title and your first entry. Begin each entry at the left margin, indenting the second and all subsequent lines of each entry five spaces. Double-space both between and within entries (in other words, double-space all lines of the Works Cited list). If the list runs to more than one page, continue numbering pages in sequence but do not repeat the title.

Order of entries. Alphabetize the entries according to authors' last names. If two or more authors have the same last name, alphabetize by first name or initial. For entries by an unknown author, alphabetize according to the first word of the title, excluding an initial *A, An,* or *The.*

MLA MLA MLA

Format for entries. There are many variations on the following general formats, given the additional information needed to identify various kinds of sources. These formats are the four most common and are shown for general illustrative purposes:

GENERAL FORMAT FOR BOOKS

one space   one space   one space   one space

Author(s). Book Title. Place of publication: Publisher, year

indent
5 spaces ———— of publication.

GENERAL FORMAT FOR JOURNAL ARTICLES

one space   one space   one space   one space

Author(s). "Article Title." Journal Title volume number (year of

indent
5 spaces ———— publication): inclusive page numbers.

one space

GENERAL FORMAT FOR MAGAZINE AND NEWSPAPER ARTICLES

one space   one space   one space   one space

Author(s). "Article Title." Publication Title date of publication:

indent
5 spaces ———— inclusive page numbers.

GENERAL FORMAT FOR ONLINE SOURCES

one space   one space

Author(s). "Title of Site." Print source (same as printed

one space   one space

indent
5 spaces ———— citation). Description of site. Date of electronic

one space   one space

publication. Page, paragraph, or section number.

one space   no period

Sponsoring body. Date of access <electronic address>.

Authors. Authors are listed last name first, followed by a comma and the rest of the name as it appears on the publication. A period follows the full name. If a work has more than one author, list the subsequent names first name first, and separate the names with a comma. When the Works Cited list has more than one work by the same author, substitute three hyphens for the author's name after the first entry.

Titles. List the titles and subtitles fully, capitalizing them as in the original. Underline the titles of entire books and periodicals: put quotation marks around the titles of essays, poems, and other works that are part of a larger (entire) work. Put a period after a book or article title; no punctuation should follow a journal, magazine, or newspaper title.

Places of publication. For books, always give the city of publication. If several cities are listed on the title or copyright pages, give only the first. If the name of the city alone could be unfamiliar or confusing to your readers, add an abbreviation for the state or country. (See the section on abbreviations in 49f.) Use a comma to separate the city from the state or country and a colon to separate the place of publication from the publisher.

Publishers. Abbreviate publishers' names as discussed in the section on abbreviations below. If the title page indicates that a book is published under an imprint—for example, Arbor House is an imprint of William Morrow—list both imprint and publisher, separated by a hyphen (*Arbor-Morrow*). For books, use a comma to separate the publisher from the publication date.

Dates and page numbers. For books and periodicals, give only the year of publication. Place a period after the year of publication for a book; place the year of publication for periodicals within parentheses, followed by a colon and a space. For dates of newspapers, use no commas between the elements and put the day before the month (*14 June 1995*). For magazines and newspapers, place a colon and a space after the date of publication. Separate inclusive page numbers with a hyphen (*42-54*). Up to 99, use all the digits for the second page numbers, and above 99 list the last two digits only (*130-38*) unless the full sequence is needed for clarity (*198-210*). If the page numbers are not consecutive (as in a newspaper), place a plus sign after the final consecutive page (*39+, 52-55+*). The plus sign represents *all* subsequent pages in the work cited, regardless of how many there are or how they are arranged.

Abbreviations. To follow MLA conventions, abbreviate state and country names—using established postal abbreviations—in the place of publication. Also abbreviate publishers' names by

dropping the words *Press, Company,* and so forth (e.g., use *Blair* for *Blair Press*); by using only the first in a series of names (*Farrar* for *Farrar, Straus, & Giroux*); and by using only the last name of a person (*Abrams* for *Harry N. Abrams*). *University Press* is abbreviated UP (*Southern Illinois UP; U of Chicago P*). In periodical dates, abbreviate all months except May, June, and July—to the first three letters followed by a period (*Jan., Apr.*). If no publisher, place of publication, date of publication, or page numbers are provided for a book, use the abbreviations *n.p.* (for both publisher and place, to be clarified by its relation to the separating colon), *n.d.,* or *n.pag.*

Following are examples of the Works Cited format for specific types of sources. For a sample Works Cited list, see 54h.

Documenting books

1. Book by one author

Benjamin, Jessica. The Bonds of Love: Psychoanalysis, Feminism, and the

Problem of Domination. New York: Prometheus, 1988.

2. Book by two or three authors

Zweigenhaft, Richard L., and G. William Domhoff. Blacks in the White

Establishment. New Haven: Yale UP, 1991.

Author names after the first are identified first name first, and the final author's name is preceded by *and.*

3. Book by more than three authors

Belenky, Mary Field, et al. Women's Ways of Knowing: The Development of

Self, Voice, and Mind. New York: Basic, 1986.

If a work has more than three authors, you may use the Latin abbreviation *et al.* or list all the authors' names in full as they appear on the title page.

4. More than one book by the same author

Nelson, Mariah Burton. Are We Winning Yet?: How Women Are Changing

Sports and Sports Are Changing Women. New York: Basic, 1991.

---. The Stronger Women Get, The More Men Love Football: Sexism and the

American Culture of Sports. New York: Harcourt, 1993.

Selfe, Cynthia L., and Billie J. Wahlstrom. "An Emerging Rhetoric of

Collaboration: Computer Collaboration and the Composing Process."

Collegiate Microcomputer 4 (1986): 289-96.

If your Works Cited list contains more than one source by the same author or authors, in the second and all additional entries by that author replace the author's name with three hyphens (no spaces) followed by a period. The hyphens represent the *exact* name of the author in the preceding entry. If a source's author is not identical to that in the preceding entry, list author names in full. Two or more works with the same author are alphabetized according to title; a work by a single author precedes works by that author and one or more collaborators.

5. Book by a corporation, association, or organization

Society of Automotive Engineers. Effects of Aging on Driver Performance.

Warrendale, PA: Society of Automotive Engineers, 1988.

Alphabetize by the name of the organization.

6. Revised edition of a book

Peek, Stephen. The Game Inventor's Handbook. 2nd ed. Cincinnati:

Betterway, 1993.

For second or any subsequent editions of a book, place the appropriate numerical designation (*2nd ed., 3rd ed.,* etc.) after the name of the editor, translator, or compiler, if there is one. If not, place it after the title.

7. Edited book

Schaefer, Charles E., and Steven E. Reid, eds. Game Play: Therapeutic Use of

Childhood Games. New York: Wiley, 1986.

For books with a listed editor or editors but no author, place the name of the editor(s) in the author position, followed by *ed.* or *eds.*

8. Book with an editor and an author

Hemingway, Ernest. Conversations with Ernest Hemingway. Ed. Matthew J.

Bruccoli. Jackson: UP of Mississippi, 1986.

Books with both an editor and an author should be listed with the editor following the title, first name first, preceded by the abbreviation *Ed.* This convention holds true whether one or more editors are listed.

9. Book in more than one volume

Waldrep, Tom, ed. Writers on Writing. 2 vols. New York: Random, 1985–88.

The total number of volumes is listed after the title. When separate volumes were published in different years, provide inclusive dates.

10. One volume of a multivolume book

Waldrep, Tom, ed. Writers on Writing. Vol. 2. New York: Random, 1988.

When each volume of a multivolume set has an individual title, list the volume's full publication information first, followed by series information (number of volumes, dates).

Churchill, Winston S. Triumph and Tragedy. Boston: Houghton, 1953. Vol. 6 of

The Second World War. 6 vols. 1948-53.

11. Translated book

Hammarskjold, Dag. Markings. Trans. Leif Sjoberg and W. H. Auden. New

York: Knopf, 1964.

12. Book in a series

McLeod, Susan, ed. Strengthening Programs for Writing Across the

Curriculum. New Directions for Teaching and Learning Ser. 36. San

Francisco: Jossey-Bass, 1988.

Immediately after the title, add the series information: the series name, neither underlined nor in quotation marks, and the series number, both followed by periods. Book titles within an underlined title are not underlined.

13. Reprinted book

Evans, Elizabeth E. G. The Abuse of Maternity. 1875. New York:

Arno, 1974.

Add the original publication date after the title; then cite the current edition information.

14. Introduction, preface, foreword, or afterword

Gavorse, Joseph. Introduction. The Lives of the Twelve Caesars. By

Suetonius. New York: Book League of America, 1937. vii-xvi.

Jacobus, Lee A. Preface. Literature: An Introduction to Critical Reading. By

Jacobus. Upper Saddle River, NJ: Prentice, 1996. xxvii-xxxiii.

Nabokov, Vladimir. Foreword. A Hero of Our Time. By Mihail Lermontov.

Garden City, NY: Doubleday-Anchor, 1958. v-xix.

List the author of the introduction, preface, foreword, or afterword first, followed by the title of the book. Next insert the word *By*, followed by the full name of the author of the whole work if different from the author of the piece or the last name only if the same as the author of the shorter piece.

15. Work in an anthology or chapter in an edited collection

Charen, Mona. "Much More Nasty Than They Should Be." Popular Writing in

America: The Interaction of Style and Audience. 5th ed. Ed. Donald

McQuade and Robert Atwan. New York: Oxford UP, 1993. 207-08.

Gay, John. The Beggar's Opera. British Dramatists from Dryden to Sheridan.

Ed. George H. Nettleton and Arthur E. Case. Carbondale: Southern

Illinois UP, 1975. 530-65.

Enclose the title of the work in quotation marks unless it was originally published as a book, in which case it should be underlined.

The title of the anthology follows the book title and is underlined. At the end of the entry, provide inclusive page numbers for the selection. For previously published nonscholarly works, you may, as a courtesy to your reader, include the year of original publication after the title of the anthologized work. Follow this date with a period.

16. Two or more works from the same anthology or collection

Kingston, Maxine Hong. "No Name Woman." Kirszner and Mandell 46-56.

Kirszner, Laurie G., and Stephen R. Mandell, eds. The Blair Reader. 2nd ed.

Ed. Laurie G. Kirszner and Stephen R. Mandell. Upper Saddle River, NJ:

Prentice, 1996.

Tannen, Deborah. "Marked Women." Kirszner and Mandell 362-67.

When citing two or more selections from one anthology, list the anthology separately under the editor's name. Selection entries will then need to include only a shortened cross-reference to the anthology entry, as illustrated above.

17. Periodical article reprinted in a collection

Atwell, Nancie. "Everyone Sits at a Big Desk: Discovering Topics for Writing."

English Journal 74 (1985): 35-39. Rpt. in Rhetoric and Composition: A

Sourcebook for Teachers and Writers. 3rd ed. Ed. Richard Graves.

Portsmouth, NH: Boynton/Cook, 1990. 76-83.

Include the full citation for the original periodical publication, followed by *Rpt. in* ("Reprinted in") and the book publication information. Provide inclusive page numbers for both sources.

18. Article in a reference book

"Behn, Aphra." The Concise Columbia Encyclopedia. 1983 ed.

"Langella, Frank." International Television and Video Almanac. 40th ed. New

York: Quigley, 1995.

For signed articles in reference books, begin with the author's name. For commonly known reference works (*Concise Columbia*), you need not include full publication information or editors' names. Page and volume numbers are also unnecessary when the entries in the reference book are arranged alphabetically.

19. Anonymous book

The End of a Presidency. New York: Bantam, 1974.

Alphabetically arrange anonymous books (and most other sources lacking an author name) in the Works Cited list by title, excluding *A, An,* or *The.*

20. Government document

United States. Cong. House. Committee on Energy and Commerce. Ensuring

Access to Programming for the Backyard Satellite Dish Owner.

Washington: GPO, 1986.

If the author is identified, begin with that name. If not, begin with the government (country or state), followed by the agency or organization. Most U.S. government documents are printed and published by the Government Printing Office in Washington, DC. You may abbreviate this office *GPO.*

21. Dissertation
UNPUBLISHED

McGuire, Lisa C. "Adults' Recall and Retention of Medical Information." Diss.

Bowling Green State University, 1993.

Enclose the title of an unpublished dissertation in quotation marks, followed by the abbreviation *Diss.* and the name of the university and the year.

PUBLISHED

Boothby, Daniel W. The Determinants of Earnings and Occupation for Young

Women. Diss. U. of California, Berkeley, 1978. New York: Garland, 1984.

For a published dissertation, underline the title, list the university and year as for an unpublished dissertation, and then add publication information as for a book, including the order number if the publisher is University Microfilms International (UMI). The descriptive abbreviation *Diss.* still follows the title.

22. A pamphlet

McKay, Hughina, and Mary Brown Patton. <u>Food Consumption of College</u>

<u>Men</u>. Wooster: Ohio Agricultural Experiment Station, 1943.

Cite a pamphlet just as you cite a book. Remember the abbreviations *n.p., n.d.,* and *n.pag.,* where publication information is missing. Also see item 23.

23. A book with missing publication information

Palka, Eugene, and Dawn M. Lake. <u>A Bibliography of Military Geography</u>.

[New York?]: Kirby, [198-?].

The MLA practice is to provide missing publication information if possible. If the information you provide does not come from the source itself—that is, if you succeed in finding missing information through another source—you should enclose this information in brackets in the Works Cited entry [*198-?*]. If a date of publication can only be approximated, place a *c.* before it, the abbreviation for the Latin *circa,* or "around." You may also use the abbreviations *n.p.*—depending on placement in your entry, this abbreviation stands for either "no place" or "no publisher"—*n.d.* ("no date"), or *n.pag.* ("no pages").

2 Documenting periodicals

24. Article, story, or poem in a monthly or bimonthly magazine

Hawn, Matthew. "Stay on the Web: Make Your Internet Site Pay Off."

<u>Macworld</u> Apr. 1996: 94-98.

Abbreviate all months except May, June, and July. Hyphenate months for bimonthlies, and do not list volume or issue numbers.

25. Article, story, or poem in a weekly magazine

Updike, John. "His Mother Inside Him." <u>New Yorker</u> 20 Apr. 1992: 34-36.

The publication date is inverted.

26. Article in a daily newspaper

Finn, Peter. "Death of a U-Va. Student Raises Scrutiny of Off-Campus

Drinking." <u>Washington Post</u> 27 Sept. 1995: D1.

If an article in a newspaper is unsigned, begin with its title. Give the name of the newspaper as it appears on the masthead, excluding *A, An,* or *The.* If the city is not in the newspaper's name, it should follow the name in brackets: *Blade* [*Toledo, OH*]. Include with the page number the letter that designates any separately numbered sections; if sections are numbered consecutively, list the section number (*sec. 2*) before the colon, preceded by a comma.

27. Article in a journal paginated by volume

Nelson, Jennie. "This Was an Easy Assignment: Examining How Students

Interpret Academic Writing Tasks." Research in the Teaching of English

34 (1990): 362-96.

If page numbers are continuous from one issue to the next throughout the year, include only the volume number and year, not the issue or month.

28. Article in a journal paginated by issue

Tiffin, Helen. "Post-Colonialism, Post-Modernism, and the Rehabilitation of

Post-Colonial History." Journal of Commonwealth Literature 23.1 (1988):

169-81.

If each issue begins with page 1, include the volume number followed by a period and the issue number. Do not include the month of publication.

29. Anonymous article

"Fraternities Sue Hamilton College over Housing Rule." Chronicle of Higher

Education 41.46 (1995): A39.

As with an anonymous book, if no author is listed for an article, begin your entry with the title and alphabetize by the first word, excluding *A, An,* and *The.*

30. Microform or microfiche article

Mayer, Caroline E. "Child-Resistant Caps to Be Made 'Adult-friendly.'"

Washington Post 16 June 1995: A3. CD-ROM. Newsbank. (1995) CON

16: B17.

If the listing is derived from a computer-based reference source such as *Newsbank*, you may treat it exactly as you would any other periodical. To help your audience locate the source as quickly as possible, however, you should include the descriptor *CD-ROM*, the name of the service (*Newsbank*), and the available section/ grid information.

31. Editorial

"Sarajevo Reborn." Editorial. <u>New York Times</u> 21 Feb. 1996, natl. ed.: A18.

If the editorial is signed, list the author's name first.

32. Letter to the editor and reply

Kempthorne, Charles. Letter. <u>Kansas City Star</u> 26 July 1992: A16.

Massing, Michael. Reply to letter of Peter Dale Scott. <u>New York Review of</u>

<u>Books</u> 4 Mar. 1993: 57.

33. Review

Rev. of <u>Bone</u>, by Faye Myenne Ng. <u>New Yorker</u> 8 Feb. 1992: 113.

Rosen, Steven. "Dissing 'HIStory.' " Rev. of <u>HIStory: Past, Present, and</u>

<u>Future—Book I</u>, by Michael Jackson. <u>Denver Post</u> 3 July 1995: F8.

Works Cited entries for reviews should begin with the reviewer's name, if known, followed by the title of the review, if there is one. *Rev. of* precedes the title of the work reviewed, followed by a comma, then the word *by* and the name of the work's author. If the work of an editor, translator, etc. is being reviewed instead of an author's, an abbreviation such as *ed.* or *trans.* replaces the word *by*. If a review is unsigned and untitled, list it as *Rev. of* [title] and alphabetize it by the name of the work reviewed. If the review is unsigned but titled, begin with the title. If the review is of a performance, add pertinent descriptive information such as director, composer, or major performers.

3 Documenting electronic sources

Electronic sources include both databases, available in portable forms such as CD-ROM, diskette, or magnetic tape, and online sources accessed with a computer connected to the Internet.

Databases

The Works Cited entries for electronic **databases** (newsletters, journals, and conferences) should be listed like entries for articles in printed periodicals: cite the author's name; the article or document title in quotation marks; the newsletter, journal, or conference title; the number of volume or issue; the year or date of publication (in parentheses); and the number of pages if available.

Portable databases are much like books and periodicals. Their entries in Works Cited lists are similar to those for printed material, except you must also include the following items:

- The medium of publication (*CD-ROM, diskette, magnetic tape*)

- The name of the vendor, if known (this may be different from the name of the organization that compiled the information, which must also be included)

- The date of electronic publication, in addition to the date the material originally may have been published (as for a reprinted book or article)

34. CD-ROM database, periodically updated

James, Caryn. "An Army as Strong as Its Weakest Link." New York Times

16 Sept. 1994: C8. New York Times Ondisc. CD-ROM. UMI-ProQuest.

Oct. 1994.

If a database comes from a printed source such as a book, periodical, or collection of bibliographies or abstracts, cite this information first, followed by the title of the database (underlined), the medium of publication, the vendor name (if applicable), and the date of electronic publication. If no printed source is available, include the title of the material accessed (in quotation marks), the date of the material (if given), the underlined title of the database, the medium of publication, the vendor name, and the date of electronic publication.

35. CD-ROM nonperiodical

"Rhetoric" The Oxford English Dictionary. 2nd ed. CD-ROM. Oxford: Oxford

UP, 1992.

List a nonperiodical CD-ROM as you would a book, adding the medium of publication and information about the source, if applicable. If citing only part of a work, underline the title of the selected portion or place it within quotation marks, as appropriate.

36. Diskette or magnetic tape

Doyle, Roddy. The Woman Who Walked into Doors. Magnetic tape. New York:

Penguin Audiobooks, 1996.

List on the Works Cited page as you would a book, adding the medium of publication (e.g., *Diskette, Magnetic tape*).

Online sources

Documenting information from the Internet follows the same basic guidelines as documenting other texts—you list who said what, where, and when. However, in citations of online sources, whether from the World Wide Web or electronic mail (e-mail), two dates are important—the date the text was created or published and the date you found the information (the access date). When both publication and access dates are available, provide them both. However, many WWW sources are often updated or changed, leaving no trace of the original version, so always provide the access date to show when this information was available. Thus, most electronic source entries will end with an access date immediately followed by the electronic address: *23 Dec. 1999* <http://www.cas.usf.edu/english/walker/mla.html>. The angle brackets (< >) identify the source as the Internet.

The following guidelines are derived from the MLA Web site at <http://www.mla.org>. To identify a World Wide Web source, include all the relevant items in the following order, each followed by a period except the date of access:

1. **Author** (or editor, compiler, or translator). Give the person's full name, if known, last name first; if the name is unknown, include any alias given.

2. **Title.** Enclose the title of a poem, short story, or article in quotation marks. Include the title of a posting to a discussion list or

forum in quotation marks, followed by *Online posting.* Underline book titles.

3. **Editor, compiler, or translator.** Include the full name, if not cited earlier, followed by the appropriate abbreviation (*Ed., Comp.,* or *Trans.*). Also see items 7 and 8 on pages 785-786.

4. **Print source information.** Include the same information you would give for a printed citation.

5. **Title of scholarly project, database, personal or professional site** (underlined). If there is no title, include a description such as *Home page.* Include the name of an editor if available.

6. **Identifying number.** For a journal, include the volume and issue numbers.

7. **Date of electronic publication.**

8. **Discussion list information.** Include the full name or title of the list or forum.

9. **Page, paragraph, or section numbers.**

10. **Sponsorship or affiliation.** Include the name of any organization or institution sponsoring this site.

11. **Date of access.** Include the date you visited this site.

12. **Address.** Enclose in angle brackets.

37. Personal or professional site

Fulwiler, Anna. Home page. 1 Feb. 1998 <http://www.uvm.edu/~afulwile>.

Yellow Wall-Paper Site. U of Texas. 1995. 4 Mar. 1998 <http://www.cwrl

.utexas.edu/~daniel/amlit/wallpaper/wallpaper.html>.

38. Government or institutional site

Zebra Mussels in Vermont. Home page. State of Vermont Agency of Natural

Resources. 3 May 1998 <http://www.anr.state.vt.us/dec/waterq/

smcap.htm>.

39. Article in a journal

Erkkila, Betsy. "The Emily Dickinson Wars." The Emily Dickinson Journal 5.2

(1996) 14 pars. 2 Feb. 1998 <http://www.colorado.edu/EDIS/Journal>.

40. Book

Twain, Mark. The Adventures of Tom Sawyer Internet Wiretap Online

Library. Carnegie Mellon U. 4 Mar. 1998 <http://www.cs.cmu.edu/Web/

People/rgs/sawyr-table.html.>.

41. Poem

Poe, Edgar Allan. "The Raven." American Review, 1845. The Poetry Archives.

4 Mar. 1998 <http://tqd.advanced.org/3247/cgibin/dispgi?poet=poe

.Edgar&poem=10.html&frame=none>.

42. Article in a reference database

"Jupiter." Britannica Online. Vers. 97.1.1 Mar. 1997. Encyclopaedia

Britannica. 29 Mar. 1998 <http://www.eb.com:180>.

43. Posting to a discussion list

"New Virginia Woolf Discussion List." Online posting. 22 Feb. 1996. The

Virginia Woolf Society, Ohio State U. 4 Mar. 1998 <gopher://dept.english

.upenn.edu:70//OrO-1858-?Lists/20th/vwoolf>.

44. E-mail, listserv, or newsgroup (Usenet) message

Fulwiler, Toby. "A Question About Electronic Sources." E-mail to Alan

Hayakawa. 23 Jan. 2002.

Superman. <superman@200.uvm.edu>. "Writing Committee Meeting."

Distribution list. University of Vermont. 24 Jan. 1998.

Include the author's name or Internet alias (if known, alias first, period) followed by the subject line (in quotation marks) and the date of the posting. Identify the type of communication (*Personal e-mail, Distribution list, Office communication*) before the access date. The source's e-mail address is optional, following the name in angle brackets; secure permission before including an e-mail address.

45. File transfer protocol (FTP), telnet, or gopher site

King, Jr., Martin Luther. "I Have a Dream Speech." 28 Aug. 1963. 30 Jan. 1996

    <telnet://ukanaix.cc.ukans.edu>.

Substitute the abbreviation *ftp, telnet,* or *gopher* for *http* before the
site address.

46. Synchronous communications (MUD, MOO, IRC)

StoneHenger. The Glass Dragon MOO. 6 Feb. 1999. Personal interview. 6 Feb.

    1999 <telnet://surf.tstc.edu>.

Synchronous communications take place in real time; when they
are over, an archive copy may remain, or they may simply be
erased. After the posting date, include the type of discussion (e.g.,
Personal interview, Group discussion) followed by a period.

47. Online newspaper

Sandomir, Richard. "Yankees Talk Trades in Broadcast Booth." New York

    Times on the Web 4 Dec. 2001. 5 Dec. 2001 <http://www.nytimes.com/

    pages/business/media/index.html>.

48. Online magazine

Epperson, Sharon. "A New Way to Shop for a College." Time.com 4 Dec.

    2001. 5 Dec. 2001 <http://www.time.com/time/education/article/

    0,8599,183955,00.html>.

49. Online encyclopedia

Standford Encyclopedia of Philosophy. Ed. Edward N. Zalta. 1995. Standford

    U. 5. Dec. 2001 <http://plato.stanford.edu/contents.html>.

50. Online work of art

Van Gogh, Vincent. The Olive Trees. 1889. Museum of Modern Art, New York.

    5 Dec. 2001 <http://www.moma.org/docs/collection/paintsculpt/

    recent/ c463.htm>.

51. Online interview

Plaxco, Jim. Interview. Planetary Studies Foundation. Oct. 1992. 5 Dec. 2001

<http://www.planets.org/>.

52. Online film or film clip

Columbus, Chris, dir. Harry Potter and the Sorcerer's Stone. Trailer. Warner

Brothers, 2001. 5 Dec. 2001 <http://hollywood.com>.

53. Online cartoon

Bell, Darrin. "Rudy Park." Cartoon. New York Times on the Web 5 Dec. 2001.

5 Dec. 2001 <http://www2.uclick.com/client/nyt/rk/>.

54. Electronic television or radio program

Chayes, Sarah. "Concorde." All Things Considered. Natl. Public Radio. 26

July 2000. 7 Dec. 2001 <http://www.npr.com/programs/atc/archives>.

4 Documenting other sources

55. Cartoon

Davis, Jim. "Garfield." Cartoon. Courier [Findlay, OH] 17 Feb. 1996: E4.

Roberts, Victoria. Cartoon. New Yorker 13 July 1992: 34.

56. Film or videocassette

Casablanca. Dir. Michael Curtiz. Perf. Humphrey Bogart and Ingrid Bergman.

Warner Bros., 1942.

Fast Food: What's in It for You. Prod. The Center for Science in the Public

Interest and Churchill Films. Videocassette. Los Angeles: Churchill, 1988.

Begin with the title, followed by the director, the studio, and the year released. Optionally, you may include the names of lead actors, producer, and the like between the title and the distribution information. If your essay is concerned with a particular person's work on a film, begin with that person's name, arranging all other information accordingly.

Lewis, Joseph H., dir. Gun Crazy. Screenplay by Dalton Trumbo. King

Bros., 1950.

57. Personal interview

Holden, James. Personal interview. 12 Jan. 1993.

Morser, John. Professor of Political Science, U of Wisconsin. Telephone

interview. 15 Dec. 1993.

Begin with the interviewee's name and specify the kind of interview and the date. Identify the interviewee's position if relevant to the purpose of the interview.

58. Published or broadcast interview

Sowell, Thomas. "Affirmative Action Programs." Interview. All Things

Considered. NPR. WGTE, Toledo. 5 June 1990.

Steinglass, David. Interview. Counterpoint 7 May 1970: 3-4.

For published or broadcast interviews, begin with the interviewee's name. Include appropriate publication information for a periodical or book and appropriate broadcast information for a radio or television program.

59. Print advertisement

Cadillac DeVille. Advertisement. New York Times 21 Feb. 1996, natl. ed.: A20.

Begin with the name of the product, followed by the description *Advertisement* and normal publication information for the source.

60. Unpublished lecture, public address, or speech

Graves, Donald. "When Bad Things Happen to Good Ideas." National Council

of Teachers of English Convention. St. Louis, 21 Nov. 1989.

Begin with the speaker, followed by the title (if any), the meeting (and sponsoring organization, if needed), the location, and the date. If it is untitled, use a descriptive label (such as *Speech*) with no quotation marks.

61. Personal or unpublished letter

Friedman, Paul. Letter to the author. 18 Mar. 1992.

Personal letters and e-mail messages are handled nearly identically in Works Cited entries. Begin with the name of the writer, identify the type of communication (e.g., *Letter*), and specify the audience. Include the date written if known, and the date received if not. To cite an unpublished letter from an archive or private collection, include information that locates the holding (for example, *Quinn-Adams Papers. Lexington Historical Society. Lexington, KY*).

62. Published letter

King, Jr., Martin Luther. "Letter from Birmingham Jail." 28 Aug. 1963. Civil

Disobedience in Focus. Ed. Hugo Adam Bedau. New York: Routledge,

1991. 68-84.

Cite published letters as you would a selection from an anthology. Specify the audience in the letter title (if known). Include the date of the letter immediately after its title. Place the page number(s) after the publisher information. If you cite more than one letter from a collection, cite the entire work in the Works Cited list, and indicate individual dates and page numbers in your text.

63. Map

Ohio River: Foster, KY, to New Martinsville, WV. Map. Huntington: U.S. Corps

of Engineers, 1986.

Cite a map as you would a book by an unknown author. Underline the title, and identify the item as a map or chart.

64. Performance

Rumors. By Neil Simon. Dir. Gene Saks. Broadhurst Theater, New York. 17

Nov. 1988.

Bissex, Rachel. Folk Songs. Flynn Theater. Burlington, VT. 14 May 2000.

Identify the pertinent details, such as title, place, and date of performance. If you focus on a particular person in your essay, such as the director or conductor, lead with that person's name. For a recital or individual concert, lead with the performer's name.

65. Audio recording

Marley, Bob, and the Wailers. "Buffalo Soldier." Legend. Audiocassette.

Island Records, 422 846 210-4, 1984.

Depending on the focus of your essay, begin with the artist, composer, or conductor. Enclose song titles in quotation marks, followed by the recording title, underlined. Do not underline musical compositions identified only by form, number, and key. If you are not citing a compact disc, specify the recording format. End with the company label, the catalog number if known, and the date of issue.

66. Television or radio broadcast

"Emissary." Star Trek: Deep Space Nine. Teleplay by Michael Pillar. Story by

Rick Berman and Michael Pillar. Dir. David Carson. Fox. WFLX, West

Palm Beach, FL. 9 Jan. 1993.

If the broadcast is not an episode of a series or the episode is untitled, begin with the program title. Include the network, the station and city, and the date of broadcast. The inclusion of other information—such as narrator, writer, director, or performers—depends on the purpose of your citation.

67. Work of art

Holbein, Hans. Portrait of Erasmus. Musée du Louvre, Paris. The Louvre

Museum. By Germain Bazin. New York: Abrams, n.d., 148.

Begin with the artist's name. Follow with the title, and conclude with the location. If your source is a book, also give pertinent publication information.

---

55 **f** Research essay: MLA style

The following research essay was written by a first-year college student, Andrew Turner, in response to an assignment to write about a major American author using both primary and secondary sources in formal MLA style. The inclusion of a title page and an outline are optional under MLA guidelines.

The Two Freedoms of Henry David Thoreau

Thesis statement: The writings of Henry David Thoreau inspire modern readers by arguing for freedom from government intervention and freedom from social conformity.

I. "Civil Disobedience" advocates political freedom while Walden argues for social freedom.

II. "Civil Disobedience" ("CD") advocates freedom from government interference in daily life.

    A. The premise of "CD" is "That government is best which governs least."

    B. Thoreau is arrested for not paying poll tax and is put in jail.

        1. Thoreau protests war with Mexico and the institution of slavery.

        2. The doctrine of passive resistance is articulated in "CD."

    C. The case is made in "Slavery in Massachusetts" and "A Plea for John Brown."

    D. The influence of "CD" is felt throughout world.

        1. "CD" inspires Gandhi and King.

        2. "CD" is the basis for the British Labour Party platform.

        3. "CD" supports underground resistance to Nazi Germany.

III. Walden (W) argues against social conformity and for simple living.

    A. Thoreau confronts the "essential facts of life."

        1. W provides an example of economical living.

        2. W provides an example of living alone.

    B. Thoreau lives deliberately at Walden Pond.

        1. Thoreau tends a bean patch.

        2. Thoreau chases loons.

    C. Living at Walden Pond is not an option today.

IV. Thoreau's ideals inspire modern readers.

Outline of a student essay in MLA format (optional)

TITLE IS CENTERED, LEFT TO RIGHT, ONE-THIRD DOWN PAGE.

The Two Freedoms of Henry David Thoreau

by

NAME

Andrew Turner

INSTRUCTOR

Professor Stephany

COURSE

English 2

DATE

3 October 200x

1"

Title page of a student essay in MLA format (optional). Note that margins shown are adjusted to fit space limitations of this book. Follow actual dimensions shown and your instructor's directions.

MLA MLA MLA

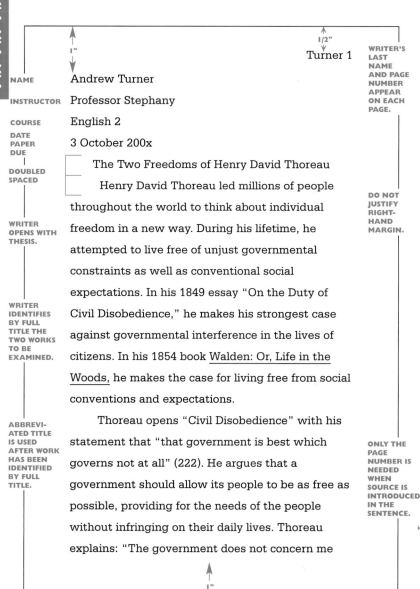

Turner 1

NAME — Andrew Turner

INSTRUCTOR — Professor Stephany

COURSE — English 2

DATE PAPER DUE — 3 October 200x

DOUBLED SPACED

The Two Freedoms of Henry David Thoreau

WRITER OPENS WITH THESIS.

Henry David Thoreau led millions of people throughout the world to think about individual freedom in a new way. During his lifetime, he attempted to live free of unjust governmental constraints as well as conventional social expectations.

WRITER IDENTIFIES BY FULL TITLE THE TWO WORKS TO BE EXAMINED.

In his 1849 essay "On the Duty of Civil Disobedience," he makes his strongest case against governmental interference in the lives of citizens. In his 1854 book Walden: Or, Life in the Woods, he makes the case for living free from social conventions and expectations.

ABBREVIATED TITLE IS USED AFTER WORK HAS BEEN IDENTIFIED BY FULL TITLE.

Thoreau opens "Civil Disobedience" with his statement that "that government is best which governs not at all" (222). He argues that a government should allow its people to be as free as possible, providing for the needs of the people without infringing on their daily lives. Thoreau explains: "The government does not concern me

WRITER'S LAST NAME AND PAGE NUMBER APPEAR ON EACH PAGE.

DO NOT JUSTIFY RIGHT-HAND MARGIN.

ONLY THE PAGE NUMBER IS NEEDED WHEN SOURCE IS INTRODUCED IN THE SENTENCE.

1/2"

1"

1"

Turner 2

much, and I shall bestow the fewest possible thoughts on it. It is not for many moments that I live under a government" ("Civil" 238).

SHORT TITLE IS ADDED TO PAGE NUMBER BECAUSE TWO WORKS BY THE AUTHOR APPEAR ON THE WORKS CITED PAGE.

In other words, in his daily life he attends to his business of eating, sleeping, and earning a living and not dealing in any noticeable way with an entity called "a government."

Because Thoreau did not want his freedom overshadowed by governmental regulations, he tried to ignore them. However, the American government in 1845 would not let him. He was arrested and put in the Concord jail for failing to pay his poll tax—a tax he believed unjust because it supported the government's war with Mexico as well as the immoral institution of slavery. Instead of protesting his arrest, he celebrated it and explained its meaning by writing "Civil Disobedience," one of the most famous English-language essays ever written. In it, he argues persuasively that "under a government which imprisons any unjustly, the true place for a just man is also a prison" (230). Thus the doctrine of passive resistance was formed, a doctrine that advocated protest against the government by nonviolent means:

PAGE NUMBER ONLY (SENTENCE IDENTIFIES THE WORK)

Turner 3

> How does it become a man to behave
> toward this American government today?
> I answer that he cannot without disgrace
> be associated with it. I cannot for an
> instant recognize that political
> organization as my government which is
> the slave's government also. (224)

INDENTED 10 SPACES BECAUSE QUOTATION IS MORE THAN 4 LINES

SIGNAL PHRASE INTRODUCES AUTHOR

According to Charles R. Anderson, Thoreau's other writings, such as "Slavery in Massachusetts" and "A Plea for Captain John Brown," show his disdain of the "[N]ortherners for their cowardice on conniving with such an institution" (28). He wanted all free American citizens, North and South, to revolt and liberate the slaves.

In addition to inspiring his countrymen, Thoreau's view of the sanctity of individual freedom affected the lives of later generations who shared his beliefs (King). "Civil Disobedience" had the greatest impact because of its "worldwide influence on Mahatma Gandhi, the British Labour Party in its early years, the underground in Nazi-occupied Europe, and Negro leaders in the modern

PARTIAL QUOTATION IS WORKED INTO SENTENCE IN GRAMMATIC-ALLY SMOOTH WAY.

MLA MLA MLA

Turner 4

[S]outh" (Anderson 30). In other words, for nearly 150 years. Thoreau's formulation of passive resistance has been a part of the human struggle for freedom ("Gandhi").

Thoreau also wanted to be free from the everyday pressure to conform to society's expectations. He believed in doing and possessing only the essential things in life. To demonstrate his case, in 1845 he moved to the outskirts of Concord, Massachusetts, and lived by himself for two years on the shore of Walden Pond (Spiller et al. 396-97). Thoreau wrote Walden to explain the value of living simply, apart from the unnecessary complexity of society: "Simplicity, simplicity, simplicity! I say, let your affairs be as two or three, and not a hundred or a thousand" (66). At Walden, he lived as much as possible by this statement, building his own house and furniture, growing his own food, bartering for simple necessities, attending to his own business rather than seeking employment from others (Walden 16-17).

IDENTIFICATION OF WORK WITH MORE THAN THREE AUTHORS.

ABBREVIATED SHORT TITLE AFTER FIRST REFERENCE

SHORT TITLE IS INCLUDED BECAUSE MORE THAN ONE TITLE APPEARS ON WORKS CITED PAGE.

Turner 5

Living at Walden Pond gave Thoreau the chance to formulate many of his ideas about living the simple, economical life. At Walden, he lived simply in order to "front only the essential facts of life" (66) and to center his thoughts on living instead of on unnecessary details of mere livelihood. He developed survival skills that freed him from the constraints of city dwellers whose lives depended on a web of material things and services provided by others. He preferred to "take rank hold on life and spend [his] day more as animals do" (117).

While living at Walden Pond, Thoreau was free to occupy his time in any way that pleased him, which for him meant writing, tending his bean patch, and chasing loons. He was not troubled by a boss hounding him with deadlines or a wife and children who needed support. In other words, "he wasn't expected to be anywhere at any time for anybody except himself" (Franklin). His neighbors accused him of being selfish and did not understand that he sought most of all "to live deliberately" (Walden 66), as he felt all people should learn to do.

PAGE NUMBERS SUFFICE WHEN CONTEXT MAKES SOURCE CLEAR.

BRACKETS INDICATE CHANGE IN WORDING SO PRONOUN CONFORMS TO SENTENCE GRAMMAR.

Turner 6

Then as now, most people had more responsibilities than Thoreau had, and they could not just pack up their belongings and go live in the woods—if they could find free woods to live in. Today, people are intrigued to read about Thoreau's experiences and are inspired by his thoughts, but few people can actually live or do as he suggests in Walden. In fact, most people, if faced with the prospect of spending two years removed from society—from modern plumbing, automobiles, television, telephone, and e-mail—would think of it as punishment or banishment rather than freedom (Poger).

WRITER'S CONCLUSION REPEATS THESIS.

Practical or not, Thoreau's writings have inspired countless people to reassess how they live and what they live for. Though unable to live exactly as he advocated, readers everywhere remain inspired by his vision of independence, equality, and, above all, freedom.

MLA MLA MLA

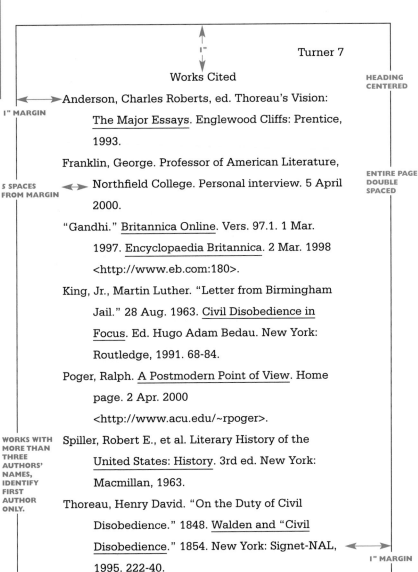

Turner 7

Works Cited

HEADING
CENTERED

I" MARGIN

Anderson, Charles Roberts, ed. Thoreau's Vision:

The Major Essays. Englewood Cliffs: Prentice,

1993.

Franklin, George. Professor of American Literature,

5 SPACES
FROM MARGIN

Northfield College. Personal interview. 5 April

2000.

ENTIRE PAGE
DOUBLE
SPACED

"Gandhi." Britannica Online. Vers. 97.1. 1 Mar.

1997. Encyclopaedia Britannica. 2 Mar. 1998

<http://www.eb.com:180>.

King, Jr., Martin Luther. "Letter from Birmingham

Jail." 28 Aug. 1963. Civil Disobedience in

Focus. Ed. Hugo Adam Bedau. New York:

Routledge, 1991. 68-84.

Poger, Ralph. A Postmodern Point of View. Home

page. 2 Apr. 2000

<http://www.acu.edu/~rpoger>.

WORKS WITH
MORE THAN
THREE
AUTHORS'
NAMES,
IDENTIFY
FIRST
AUTHOR
ONLY.

Spiller, Robert E., et al. Literary History of the

United States: History. 3rd ed. New York:

Macmillan, 1963.

Thoreau, Henry David. "On the Duty of Civil

Disobedience." 1848. Walden and "Civil

Disobedience." 1854. New York: Signet-NAL,

I" MARGIN

1995. 222-40.

MLA MLA MLA

Turner 8

AUTHOR'S NAME IS NOT REPEATED. NAME IS REPLACED BY 3 HYPHENS FOLLOWED BY A PERIOD.

---.Walden: Or, Life in the Woods. New York:

Harcourt, 1987.

56 Writing in the Humanities

This chapter describes the aims, style, forms, and documentation conventions associated with the humanities disciplines other than languages and literature: history, philosophy, religion, the fine arts.

56 a The aims of writing in the humanities

The purpose of studies in the humanities is to understand the human experience as it is expressed and interpreted in a variety of media. History examines the many documents that a civilization produces that provide clues to how its people thought and lived. Philosophy and religion examine the nature of humanity by scrutinizing texts produced by past thinkers and prophets. Studies in art and communications examine texts that are often nonverbal, including paintings, sculptures, and films.

In all humanities disciplines, writing is a primary means of interpreting meaning. Students of history and philosophy, for example, spend a lot of time reading texts, reading about texts, listening to lectures based on texts, and writing texts that demonstrate an understanding of historical or philosophical knowledge.

Studies in languages and literature have much in common with the other humanities. In all these disciplines, texts are analyzed, interpreted, and evaluated. (See 55a.) However, texts in history, philosophy, and the other humanities are often a stepping-stone toward defining a broader context, a larger issue, or a fuller understanding of some aspect of human life or thought. They are seen as documents to be argued with.

Issues in the humanities involve matters of interpretation and debate rather than proofs and truths. Interpretive papers need to be carefully reasoned and well supported so that the work will be believed.

56 b The style of writing in the humanities

In the humanities, thoughtfulness, variety, and vitality of expression are especially important. Though writing in the humanities is often explicitly argumentative, your tone should be fair and objective, presenting issues or positions reasonably, completely, and with a minimum of bias and subjectivity. Neutral and analytical writing encourages readers to take your ideas seriously. When you treat a text objectively, even one with which you disagree, you lay the foundation for strong and believable criticism. Treating texts, ideas, or people fairly invites readers to listen more carefully when you do interpret or evaluate your subject in a critical fashion.

Although you should try to write fairly and rationally in the humanities, understand that the stylistic rules in the humanities are more variable than in most social science and science writing. In many of the humanities, individuality and uniqueness of expression are highly prized.

56 c Common forms of writing in the humanities

Two common forms of writing in the humanities are the critical analysis (or review) and the research paper.

1 Writing about texts

As with language and literature studies, writing about texts in the other humanities requires analysis, interpretation, and evaluation. However, essays in the humanities generally focus on nonliterary works, commenting on the persuasiveness or relevance of the ideas expressed in these texts.

Critical analyses require a thorough and objective summary of the ideas expressed in a text; such a summary often involves less direct quotation and more evaluation of the work. The writer questions connections among ideas, underlying assumptions, and contradictions within the text and notes persuasive or enlightening arguments. The thesis of the essay may be tentative or qualified, but it should be a clear assertion of a well-reasoned viewpoint.

Reviews most often focus on contemporary interpretations of events, ideas, or works. For example, you might review a dramatized version of a historic event or a biographical analysis of an artist's work. You will need to express an overall judgment based on your analysis of both strengths and weaknesses of your subject.

2 Research papers

Most research papers in the humanities require a *synthesis* of **primary sources** (such as original documents, historical accounts, and statements of ideas) and **secondary sources** (what other writers have said about those primary sources). The aim may be analytical (for example, tracing the effect of a particular invention on a society's economic or cultural life) or may offer an argument (for example, positing a radically different interpretation of a philosopher's beliefs). Whatever your aim, remember that the best research papers demonstrate originality of thought, suggest new insights, and point to further areas of study.

56 d Documentation and format conventions: Chicago (CMS) style

The most widely used documentation system in history, philosophy, religion, and the fine arts is found in *The Chicago Manual of Style* (14th ed., University of Chicago Press, 1993). This manual actually includes two documentation systems, one using notes and bibliographies, the other using in-text citations with reference lists similar to those of the MLA and APA styles, but with subtle differences. Since Chicago style—as this set of guidelines is commonly called—is the only major system that still uses the note/bibliography format, that is the one described briefly here. The full note appears in close proximity to the reference—at the bottom of the page or the end of the chapter—so it is the easiest system for readers who want to know quickly the full source of a citation. Sample pages in Chicago style are provided at the end of this chapter. If you are required to write a major project using Chicago style, we recommend consulting the latest edition of *The Chicago Manual of Style* or checking their Web site at <www.press.uchicago.edu>.

1 Conventions for marking in-text citations

Each time you quote, paraphrase, or summarize source material in your text, you need to mark it by inserting a raised (superscript) Arabic number immediately after the sentence or clause containing the information. The superscript number must follow all punctuation except dashes. Each new reference to source material requires a new number, and numbers are arranged consecutively throughout the text.

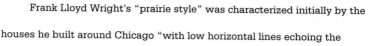
Frank Lloyd Wright's "prairie style" was characterized initially by the houses he built around Chicago "with low horizontal lines echoing the landscape."[1] Vincent Scully sees the suburban building lots for which Wright was designing as one of the architect's most important influences.[2]

Each superscript number corresponds to a note at the end of the paper, or sometimes at the foot of the page on which the number appears.

    1. Concise Columbia Encyclopedia, s.v. "Wright, Frank Lloyd."

    2. Vincent Scully, Architecture: The Natural and the Manmade (New York: St. Martin's, 1991), 340.

The first note does not require a page reference because it cites an alphabetized reference book. (See item 8 in 56d3.)

2 Conventions for positioning notes and bibliography

Endnotes are typed as a single list at the end of a text. Endnotes are easy to format since they can be typed separately on a sheet of paper without calculating the space needed on each page. Footnotes can be difficult to place because the space taken up by the notes sometimes moves a footnote marker-number to the next page, requiring you to refigure the placement of your text. Some word processing programs have a built-in footnote-formatting function, but endnotes are more convenient—they allow you to use the full page for text rather than taking up space with footnotes. Also, endnotes can be added to or deleted from your paper without affecting the body of the text.

The *endnote page* follows the last page of text and is numbered in sequence with the rest of the paper. Title the first page of the endnote section "Notes"—centered, without quotation marks, and one inch from the top of the page. Double-space throughout—between this title and the first entry, within the notes or entries themselves, and between entries. Order your entries consecutively according to the note numbers in your paper. Indent the first line of each entry five spaces from the left margin, and place each subsequent entry line flush with the margin.

Footnotes are convenient because instead of turning to the back of a text to check a numbered source, readers can find the information simply by glancing at the bottom of the page they are reading. Footnotes must always be placed at the bottom of the same page on which the marker-number appears, four lines below the last line of text and single spaced.

Some instructors and/or programs require a separate, alphabetically arranged list of sources, or **bibliography,** in addition to endnotes or footnotes. If you are asked to include in your bibliography *only* sources consulted in researching for your paper, you may title your bibliography list "Works Consulted."

3 Conventions for endnote and footnote format

Different style manuals offer a number of minor variations for the format of endnotes and footnotes. The following guidelines are based on *The Chicago Manual of Style,* which follows the endnote and footnote format similar to that found in the *MLA Handbook for Writers of Research Papers:*

Numbers and spacing. Each entry is preceded by an Arabic number with a period that is indented five spaces and followed by a space. Any subsequent lines for an entry begin at the left margin. Double-space endnotes throughout. Single-space individual footnotes and double-space between footnotes.

Authors. List all authors' names first name first, spelling them as they appear in their book. You may spell out the first name or use initials.

Punctuation. Separate authors' names and all titles with commas, and enclose all book publication information and periodical dates in parentheses. For papers submitted in college courses, it is customary to underline titles of books and periodicals. In published works, you will see these titles in italics. Titles of articles in a periodical or anthology are set within quotation marks. (See 43c.) Use colons to separate the place of publication from the publisher and commas to separate the publisher from the date. Colons should also be used to separate journal dates from page numbers. End all entries with a period.

Page numbers. Each entry for a book or periodical should end with the page number(s) on which the cited information can be found. (Note that according to the *Chicago Manual* style, *p.* or *pp.* is used only with the actual page numbers for material from journals that do not use volume numbers.)

The following are examples of the most common endnote citations required in undergraduate humanities papers.

DIRECTORY FOR CMS DOCUMENTATION GUIDELINES; INDEX TO SAMPLE FORMATS THAT FOLLOW

CMS CMS CMS

DOCUMENTING BOOKS: FIRST REFERENCE

1. Book by one author

1. Jessica Benjamin, The Bonds of Love: Psychoanalysis, Feminism, and the Problem of Domination (New York: Prometheus Books, 1988), 76.

2. Book by two or more authors

2. Richard L. Zweigenhaft and G. William Domhoff, Blacks in the White Establishment (New Haven: Yale University Press, 1991), 113.

For three or more authors, follow each name with a comma.

3. Revised edition of a book

3. S. I. Hayakawa, Language in Thought and Action, 4th ed. (New York: Harcourt Brace Jovanovich, 1978), 77.

4. Edited book and one volume of a multivolume book

4. Tom Waldrep, ed., Writers on Writing, vol. 2 (New York: Random House, 1988), 123.

5. Translated book

5. Albert Camus, The Stranger, trans. Stuart Gilbert (New York: Random House, 1946), 12.

6. Reprinted book

6. Elizabeth E. G. Evans, The Abuse of Maternity (1875; reprint, New York: Arno Press, 1974), 74-78.

7. Work in an anthology or chapter in an edited collection

7. Mona Charen, "Much More Nasty Than They Should Be," in Popular Writing in America: The Interaction of Style and Audience, 5th ed., ed. Donald McQuade and Robert Atwan (New York: Oxford University Press, 1993), 207-8.

8. Article in a reference book

8. <u>The Film Encyclopedia</u>, 2nd ed. "Beaty, Ned" (HarperCollins

Publishers, 1994).

No page number is needed for an alphabetically arranged book. Begin the entry with the author's name, if available.

9. Anonymous book

9. <u>The World Almanac and Book of Facts</u> (New York: World Almanac-

Funk & Wagnalls, 1995).

DOCUMENTING PERIODICALS: FIRST REFERENCE

10. Article, story, or poem in a popular or general-circulation magazine

10. Matthew Hawn, "Stay on the Web: Make Your Internet Site Pay

Off," <u>Macworld</u>, April 1996, 94-98.

11. John Updike, "His Mother Inside Him," <u>New Yorker</u>, 20 April 1992, 34.

11. Article in a daily newspaper

12. Peter Finn, "Death of a U-Va. Student Raises Scrutiny of Off-Campus

Drinking," <u>Washington Post</u>, 27 September 1995, sec. D, p. 1.

12. Article in a journal paginated by volume

13. Jennie Nelson, "This Was an Easy Assignment: Examining How

Students Interpret Academic Writing Tasks," <u>Research in the Teaching of</u>

<u>English</u> 34 (1990): 362-96.

13. Article in a journal paginated by issue

14. Helen Tiffin, "Post-Colonialism, Post-Modernism, and the

Rehabilitation of Post Colonial History," <u>Journal of Commonwealth Literature</u>

23, no. 1 (1988): 169-81.

14. Review

15. Review of <u>Bone</u>, by Faye Myenne Ng, <u>New Yorker</u>, 8 February

1992, 113.

16. Steven Rosen, "Dissing 'HIStory,'" review of <u>HIStory: Past, Present,</u>

<u>and Future--Book I</u>, by Michael Jackson, <u>Denver Post</u>, 3 July 1995, sec. F, p. 8.

DOCUMENTING ELECTRONIC SOURCES: FIRST REFERENCE

Because the nature of electronic sources can vary so widely
and because technology is so rapidly changing the ways in which
research can be done, *The Chicago Manual of Style* recommends
following the most recent published guidelines of the International
Standards Organization (ISO). In general, the ISO recommends
spelling and punctuating in a manner consistent with the language
in which the information is found. The latest ISO information is
available from:

ISO TC46/SC 9
Secretariat: Office of Library Standards
National Library of Canada
Ottawa, K1A ON4
Canada

The authors have constructed the following examples of electronic
sources commonly used in student research papers by extrapolat-
ing from examples in the fourteenth edition of *The Chicago Manual
of Style.*

15. Material on CD-ROM database, periodically updated

17. Oregon Trail II, Ver. 1.0 Mac. (Minneapolis: Educational Computing

Corp., 1995), ERIC, CD-ROM, SilverPlatter, March 1996.

Software titles are not italicized (underlined) in CMS style.

16. Material on diskette

18. Diane Greco, <u>Cyborg: Engineering the Body Electric</u> [diskette];

(Watertown: Eastgate, 1996).

17. World Wide Web (WWW) site

19. Victorian Women Writers Project. Ed. Perry Willett. April 1997. Indiana

U. [cited 5 March 1998]; available at http://www.indiana.edu/~letrs/vwwp.

List the author's full name in normal order (if available), site title, date of publication (if available), date of access, and electronic address.

18. E-mail, listserv, or newsgroup (Usenet) message

20. Robert Jones. "Writing Guidelines." University of Vermont, 1998

[cited 29 March 1998]; available from jones213@rocket.pu.edu.

If you quote a personal message sent by somebody else, be sure to get permission before including his or her address on the reference page.

19. Synchronous communications (MUD, MOO, IRC)

21. Andrew Harnack. "Words." [Group discussion.] 1996 [visited 12

June 1996]; available from telnet. moo.du.org/port=8888.

Before the posting date, include the type of discussion (e.g., personal interview, group discussion), date visited, and electronic address.

DOCUMENTING OTHER SOURCES: FIRST REFERENCE

20. Personal interview

22. John Morser, interview by author, Chicago, 15 December 1993.

21. Personal or unpublished letter

23. Paul Friedman, letter to author, 18 March 1992.

22. Work of art

24. Hans Holbein, Portrait of Erasmus, Musée du Louvre, Paris, in The

Louvre Museum, by Germain Bazin (New York: Abrams, n.d.), p. 148.

DOCUMENTING SUBSEQUENT REFERENCES TO THE SAME WORK

23. Subsequent references to a work

The second and any subsequent times you refer to a source, the Chicago style calls for you to include the author's last name, a

comma, a shortened version of the title, another comma, and the page number(s).

> 25. Benjamin, <u>Bonds</u>, 76.
>
> 26. Evans, <u>The Abuse</u>, 74-78.

The traditional Latin abbreviations *ibid.* ("in the same place") and *op. cit.* ("in the work cited") are seldom used in contemporary scholarly writing.

56 e Sample page with endnotes

The illustration that follows shows how citations are documented by endnotes.

         Owsley 2

recorded "in exultant tones the universal neglect that had overtaken pagan learning."[2] It would be some time, however, before Christian education would replace classical training, and by the fourth century, a lack of interest in learning and culture among the elite of Roman society was apparent. Attempting to check the demise of education, the later emperors established municipal schools, and universities of rhetoric and law were also established in major cities throughout the Empire.[3]

The beginning of a page from the middle of a paper in CMS format. The superscript numbers 2 and 3 indicate that citations are documentated in endnotes.

56 f Sample page with footnotes

Footnotes appear on the same page with the citations, as the illustration on this page shows.

Owsley 12

Notes

1. Rosamond McKitterick, The Carolingians and the Written Word (Cambridge: Cambridge University Press, 1983), 61.

2. J. Bass Mullinger, The Schools of Charles the Great (New York: Stechert, 1911), 10.

3. James W. Thompson, The Literacy of the Laity in the Middle Ages (New York: Franklin, 1963), 17.

4. O. M. Dalton, introduction, The Letters of Sidonius (Oxford: Clarendon, 1915), cxiv.

5. Pierre Riche, Education and Culture in the Barbarian West (Columbia: University of South Carolina Press, 1976), 4.

6. Riche, Education and Culture, 6.

Endnote page with references in numerical order in CMS format

Kelly 5

The Teatro Olimpico was completed in 1584, the statues, inscriptions, and bas-reliefs for the <u>frons-scena</u> being the last details completed. Meanwhile, careful plans were made for an inaugural, which was to be a production of <u>Oedipus</u> in a new translation.[10] Final decisions were made by the Academy in February of 1585 for the seating of city officials, their wives, and others, with the ruling that "no masked men or women would be allowed in the theatre for the performance."[11]

The organization of the audience space was "unique among Renaissance theaters, suggesting . . . its function as the theater of a 'club of equals' rather than of a princely court."[12] The Academy is celebrated and related to Roman grandeur by the decorating over the monumental central opening, where its motto, "Hoc Opus," appears.[13] It is difficult to make out the entrances.

10. J. Thomas Oosting, <u>Andrea Palladio's Teatro Olimpico</u> (Ann Arbor, MI: UMI Research Press, 1981), 118-19.

11. Oosting, <u>Palladio's Teatro</u>, 120.

12. Marvin Carlson, <u>Places of Performance: The Semiotics of Theater Architecture</u> (Ithaca, NY: Cornell University Press, 1989), 135.

13. Simon Tidworth, <u>Theaters: An Architectural and Cultural History</u> (London: Praeger, 1973), 52.

A sample page from a paper using footnotes in CMS format

57 **Writing in the Social Sciences**

This chapter describes the aims, style, forms, and documentation conventions associated with disciplines in the social sciences: psychology, sociology, anthropology, political science, and economics. The system of documentation described here is based on guidelines published by the American Psychological Association (APA).

57 a The aims of writing in the social sciences

The social sciences examine the fundamental structures and processes that make up the social world. Sociology examines social groups; political science examines the methods of governance and social organizations; anthropology examines social cultures; economics examines the allocation and distribution of resources among social groups; and psychology examines the mind as both a biological and social construction. The social sciences use methodical and systematic inquiry to examine and analyze human behavior, commonly asking questions such as the following:

- What is society? Can it be isolated and observed? How can it be described?

- How do social and psychological systems function? What forces hold them together or lead to their breakdown?

- Why do social organizations and individuals behave the way they do? Can governing laws be identified, explained, and understood?

Most writing in the social sciences explains findings based on factual research: either *empirical research*—that is, research based on firsthand observation and experimentation—or the wide reading that results in a *literature review*. Social scientists must also interpret their factual findings. As with any other field of academic

study, individual interpretations and opinions must be carefully reasoned and based on clear evidence that is objectively presented.

As a student in the social sciences, you will be writing for instructors and graduate students who are themselves social scientists and who are knowledgeable about the concepts and information you present. They will expect current, accurate information that is presented concisely and interpreted reasonably.

57 b The style of writing in the social sciences

Writing in the social sciences must be clearly organized. Connections among ideas should be explicitly stated. Language is expected to be precise—informal diction is discouraged. However, social science writing need not be dull or dry. Readers of the social sciences look for clarity, smoothness, and economy of expression. Writers should therefore avoid unnecessary jargon, wordiness, and redundancy.

STYLISTIC GUIDELINES FOR WRITING IN THE SOCIAL SCIENCES

As you write and revise, keep the following guidelines in mind:

- Write from a **third-person point of view.** (First-person experience is considered inappropriate for conveying empirical data because, in calling attention to the writer, it distracts from the information.)
- Use the **past tense** to describe methods and results ("Individuals responded by . . ."); use the **past** or **past perfect tense** for literature reviews ("The study resulted in . . . ," "Jones has suggested . . ."); use the **present tense** to report established knowledge or to discuss conclusions ("The evidence indicates . . ."). Use tenses consistently.
- Use the **technical language** of the discipline correctly, but avoid excessive jargon. Use plain, direct language. Choose synonyms with care.
- Include **graphs, charts,** and **illustrations** when they convey information more readily than words. Label them clearly.
- Incorporate **numbers, statistics,** and **equations** clearly and accurately. Include explanations.

57 **c** **Common forms of writing in the social sciences**

Two common forms of social science writing are reports of original research and reviews of published research.

Research reports

Empirical studies, those based on surveys and experiments, are common in the social sciences. In political science, a study might be based on an opinion poll about an election; in psychology, on the effects of a particular stimulus on behavior. The conventional form for research reports varies somewhat from discipline to discipline. However, many social science reports use the following basic structure:

Title page. The title of your report summarizes the topic of the paper. Center the title on the page, and underneath it type your name, your instructor's name, the course title, and the date.

Abstract. Your abstract summarizes the study and its results in approximately 100 words. A good abstract will explain what you did and what you found in simple, direct language so readers can then decide whether to read the report for details. It is best to write it after you complete the text itself. The abstract page follows the title page.

Introduction. Begin the report by defining the problem the study examines and outline how you set out to solve that problem. Discuss the background of the problem and include a brief literature review of any previously reported studies of the problem or issue. End by discussing your own purpose and rationale for the study and stating your hypothesis. The introduction has no heading.

Method. Explain how you studied the problem your report addresses. This section is often divided into three subsections: subjects or participants (describing the type, number, and selection of people in the study); apparatus (including any materials or statistical programs and their function); and procedure (summarizing the steps involved in conducting the study).

Results. In this section (headed "Results"), report the findings and conclusions of your study, including any findings that do not support your hypothesis. Use tables to present your results when doing so is clearer or more concise than a description in words. In this section, remain descriptive, not interpretive or evaluative.

Discussion. In this final section (headed "Discussion"), interpret what the results mean. Begin with a statement of whether or not your study supported your hypothesis. Consider what your work

contributes to an understanding of the problem you set out to study. You may speculate on any theoretical implications or implications for further experiments. (This is the only section of a formal report in which the *first person* may be appropriate, as you may want to identify an opinion or theory as your own.)

References. List all the references cited in the report at the end on a separate page (headed "References"; see 57d3.)

2 Literature reviews

In addition to being included as part of research reports, literature reviews (sometimes called surveys) are often written as independent documents. Preparing a literature review will expose you to knowledge generated by social science methodology and will also acquaint you with the conventions of experimentation and documentation.

Reviews are generally written in the style of an essay, with one paragraph devoted to each article surveyed. While the precise form, length, and name of these papers may vary slightly in different disciplines, they will generally contain the following parts:

Title. Create a title that concisely describes the subject area that is surveyed in the paper.

Introduction. Begin the report with a brief introduction to the subject and a chronological listing of the articles to be reviewed.

Summary. Summarize the main conclusion of each article reviewed. Include brief quotations that succinctly state the researchers' findings, and make some suggestion of how you interpret their implications.

Conclusion. Conclude the report with a cumulative summary of the survey. Assess the most important articles in the review and suggest possible implications for further research.

References. List all the articles cited in the report on a separate page titled "References." (See 57d3.)

57 d Documentation and format conventions: APA guidelines

Most disciplines in the social sciences—psychology, sociology, anthropology, political science, and economics—use the name-and-date system of documentation put forth by the American Psychological Association (APA). The discipline of education also uses

DIRECTORY FOR APA DOCUMENTATION GUIDELINES; INDEX TO SAMPLE FORMATS THAT FOLLOW

(Continued)

APA APA APA

this system. This citation style highlights dates of publication because the currency of published material is of primary importance in these disciplines. Also, listing *all* the authors is more strongly emphasized in the APA than in the MLA system; collaborative authoring is common in the social sciences, and it has been conventional to recognize the efforts of all collaborators. For more about the foundations and purposes of the APA system, see the *Publication Manual of the American Psychological Association*, 5th edition (Washington DC: APA 2001). For APA help on the Internet, consult http://www.apa.org/journals which includes answers to frequently asked questions about APA style. For guidelines focusing on electronic citations, see http://www.library.wisc.edu/libraries/ Memorial/citing.htm.

Conventions for in-text citations

1. Single work by one or more authors

Whenever you paraphrase or summarize material in your text, you should give both the author's last name and the date of the source. For direct quotations, you should also provide specific page numbers. You may also provide page references, as a convenience to your readers, whenever you suspect they might want to consult a source you have cited. Page references in the APA system are always preceded, in text or in the reference list, by the abbreviation

p., in the case of a single page, or *pp.,* in the case of multiple pages.

According to the APA system, authors' names, publication dates, and page numbers (when listed) should be placed in parentheses following citable material. If any of these elements are identified in the text referred to in the parenthetical citation, they are not repeated in the citation.

> Exotoxins make some bacteria dangerous to humans (Thomas, 1974).

> According to Thomas (1974), "Some bacteria are only harmful to us if they make exotoxins" (p. 76).

> We need fear some bacteria only "if they make exotoxins" (Thomas, 1974, p. 76).

For a work by *two authors,* cite both names each time the source is cited.

> Smith and Hawkins (1990) agree that all bacteria producing exotoxins are harmful to humans.

> All known exotoxin-producing bacteria are harmful to humans (Smith & Hawkins, 1990).

The authors' names are joined by *and* within your text, but APA convention requires an ampersand (&) to join authors' names in parentheses.

For a work by *three to five authors,* identify all the authors by last name the first time you cite a source. In subsequent references, identify only the first author followed by *et al.* ("and others").

> The most recent study supports the belief that alcohol abuse is on the rise (Dinkins, Dominic, Smith, Rogers, & White, 1989). . . . When homeless people were excluded from the study, the results were the same (Dinkins et al., 1989).

If you are citing a source by *six or more authors*, identify only the first author in all the references, followed by *et al.*

2. Two or more works by the same author published in the same year

To distinguish between two or more works published in the same year by the same author or team of authors, place a lowercase letter (*a, b, c,* etc.) immediately after the date. This letter should correspond to that in the reference list, where the entries will be alphabetized by title. If two appear in one citation, repeat the year.

(Smith, 1992a, 1992b)

3. Unknown author

To cite the work of an unknown author, use the first two or three words of the entry as appears in the reference list (usually by the title). If the words *are* from the title, enclose them in quotation marks or underline them, whichever is appropriate.

Statistical Abstracts (1991) reports the literacy rate for Mexico at 75% for 1990, up 4% from census figures 10 years earlier.

Many researchers now believe that treatment should not begin until other factors have been dealt with ("New Evidence Suggests," 1987).

4. Corporate or organizational author

If a citation refers to a work by a corporation, association, organization, or foundation, spell out the name of the authoring agency. If the name can be abbreviated and remain identifiable, you may spell out the name the first time only and put the abbreviation immediately after it, in brackets. For subsequent references to that source, you may use only the abbreviation.

(American Psychological Association [APA], 1993) . . . (APA, 1994)

5. Authors with the same last name

To avoid confusion in citing two or more authors with the same last name, include each author's initials in every citation.

(J. M. Clark, 1994)   (C. L. Clark, 1995)

6. Quotation from an indirect source

Use the words *as cited in* to indicate when a quotation or any information in your source is originally from another source.

Lester Brown of Worldwatch believes international agriculture

production has reached its limit and that "we're going to be in trouble on the

food front before this decade is out" (as cited in Mann, 1993, p 51).

7. More than one work in a citation

As a general guideline, list two or more sources within a single parenthetical reference in the same order in which they appear in your reference list. List more than one work by the same author in chronological order with the author's name mentioned once and the dates separated by commas.

(Thomas, 1974, 1979).

Works by different authors in the same parentheses are listed in alphabetical order by the author's last name, separated by semicolons:

(Miller, 1990; Webster & Rose, 1988)

8. Long quotation set off from text

Introduce long quotations (40 or more words) with a signal phrase that names the author and ends in a colon. Indent this entire block quotation five spaces. If you quote more than one paragraph, indent the first sentence of each subsequent paragraph five spaces. At the end of the quotation, after the final punctuation mark, indicate in parentheses the location of the quotation in the source—page numbers for a print document, a section and part number for an online source.

According to Langlacker:

> Language is everywhere. It permeates our thoughts, mediates our
> relations with others, and even creeps into our dreams. The
> overwhelming bulk of human knowledge is stored and transmitted in
> language. Language is so ubiquitous that we take it for granted, but
> without it, society as we now know it would be impossible. Despite its
> prevalence in human affairs, language is poorly understood (1968, p. 3).

2 Conventions for footnotes

Footnotes are used to provide additional information that cannot be worked into the main text, information highly likely to be of
interest to some readers but also likely to slow down the pace of
your text or obscure your point for other readers. Therefore, even
the footnotes you do choose to provide should be as brief as possible; when the information you wish to add is extensive, it is better
to present it in an appendix. Footnotes are indicated by an asterisk
to avoid confusion with endnote notations. Endnotes should
be numbered consecutively with superscript numbers, should follow the reference list on a page headed "Endnotes," should be
double spaced, and should have their first line indented five to
seven spaces.

3 Conventions for the reference list

All works mentioned in a paper should be identified on a reference list according to the following general rules of the APA documentation system.

Format. After the final page of the paper, title a separate page "References," with no underline or quotation marks. Center the title an
inch from the top of the page. Number the page in sequence with
the last page of the paper.

Double-space between the title and the first entry. Set the first
line flush with the left margin; the second and all subsequent lines
of an entry should be indented five spaces from the left margin.
This format is called a hanging indent.

Also double-space both between and within entries. If your reference list exceeds one page, continue listing your references in

sequence on an additional page or pages, but do not repeat the title "References."

Order of entries. Alphabetize the list of references according to authors' last names, using the first author's last name for works with multiple authors. For entries by an unknown author, alphabetize by the first word of the title, excepting nonsignificant words (e.g., *A, An, The*).

Format for entries. The three most common of several variations on general formats are the following.

GENERAL FORMAT FOR BOOKS

Author(s). (Year of publication). *Book title.* City of publication: Publisher.

GENERAL FORMAT FOR JOURNAL ARTICLES

Author(s). (Year of publication). Article title. *Journal Title, volume number,*

inclusive page numbers.

GENERAL FORMAT FOR MAGAZINE AND NEWSPAPER ARTICLES

Author(s). (Year, month of publication). Article title. *Publication Title,*

inclusive page numbers.

GENERAL FORMAT FOR ELECTRONIC SOURCES

Author(s). (date). Title. [On-line]. Any information for corresponding print

source.

Authors. List the author's last name first, followed by a comma and the author's initials (not first and middle names). When a work has more than one author, list all authors in this way, separating the names with a comma. When listing multiple authors for a single work, place an ampersand (&) before the last author's name. A period follows the author name(s).

Titles. List the complete titles and subtitles of books and articles, but capitalize only the first word of the title and any subtitle, as well as all proper nouns. Italicize book titles and journal or publication titles, but do not underline article titles or place quotation marks around them. Place a period after the title.

Publishers. List publishers' names in shortened form, omitting words such as *Company.* Spell out the names of university presses and organizations in full. For books, use a colon to separate the city of publication from the publisher.

Dates. For magazines and newspapers, use commas to separate the year from the month and day, and enclose the publication dates in parentheses: (*1954, May 25*). If no date is given in the document, write (*n.d.*) in parentheses.

Page numbers. Inclusive page numbers should be separated by a hyphen with no spaces: *361-375*. Full sequences should be given for pages and dates (not *361-75*.) If pages do not follow consecutively (as in newspapers), include subsequent page numbers after a comma: *pp. 1, 16*. Note that *pp.* precedes the page numbers for newspaper articles but not for journal articles.

Abbreviations. State and country names are abbreviated, but months are not. Use U.S. postal abbreviations for state abbreviations.

Following are examples of the reference list format for a variety of source types.

DOCUMENTING BOOKS

I. Book by one author

Benjamin, J. (1988). *The bonds of love: Psychoanalysis, feminism, and the*

　problem of domination. New York: Prometheus Books.

2. Book by two or more authors

Zweigenhaft, R. L., & Domhoff, G. W. (1991). *Blacks in the white*

　establishment. New Haven, CT: Yale University Press.

Include all authors' names in the reference list, regardless of the number of authors associated with a particular work.

3. More than one book by the same author

List two or more works by the same author (or the same author team listed in the same order) chronologically by year in your reference list, with the earliest first. Arrange any such works published in the same year alphabetically by title, placing lowercase letters after the dates. In either case, give full identification of author(s) for each reference listing.

Bandura, A. (1969). *Principles of behavior modification.* New York: Holt,

　Rinehart, and Winston.

Bandura, A. (1977a). Self-efficacy: Toward a unifying theory of behavioral

change. *Psychological Review, 84,* 191-215.

Bandura, A. (1977b). *Social learning theory.* Englewood Cliffs, NJ: Prentice

Hall.

If the same author is named first but has different co-authors, subalphabetize by the last name of the second author. Works by the first author alone are listed before works with co-authors.

4. Book by a corporation, association, or organization

American Psychological Association. (1994). *Publication manual of the American

Psychological Association* (4th ed.). Washington, DC: Author.

Alphabetize corporate authors by the corporate name, excluding the articles *A, An,* and *The.* When the corporate author is also the publisher, designate the publisher as *Author.*

5. Revised edition of a book

Peek, S. (1993). *The game inventor's handbook* (Rev. ed.). Cincinnati, OH:

Betterway.

6. Edited book

Schaefer, Charles E., & Reid, S. E. (Eds.). (1986). *Game play: Therapeutic use

of childhood games.* New York: Wiley.

Place (*Ed.*) or (*Eds.,*) capitalized, and in parentheses, after the singular or plural name of the editor(s) of an edited book.

7. Book in more than one volume

Waldrep, T. (Ed.). (1985-1988). *Writers on writing* (Vols. 1-2). New York:

Random House.

For a work with volumes published in different years, indicate the range of dates of publication. In citing only one volume of a multi-volume work, indicate only the volume cited.

Waldrep, T. (Ed.). (1988). *Writers on writing* (Vol. 2). New York: Random

House.

8. Translated or reprinted book

Freud, S. (1950). *The interpretation of dreams* (A. A. Brill, Trans.). New York:

Modern Library-Random House. (Original work published 1900)

The date of the translation or reprint is in parentheses after the author's name. Indicate the original publication date parenthetically at the end of the citation, with no period. In the text, parenthetically cite the information with both dates: (*Freud 1900/1950*).

9. Chapter or article in an edited book

Telander, R. (1996). Senseless crimes. In C. I. Schuster & W. V. Van Pelt (Eds.),

Speculations: Readings in culture, identity, and values (2nd ed., pp. 264-

272). Upper Saddle River, NJ: Prentice Hall.

The chapter or article title is not underlined or in quotation marks. Editors' names are listed in normal reading order (surname last). Inclusive page numbers, in parentheses, follow the title of the larger work.

10. Anonymous book

Stereotypes, distortions and omissions in U.S. history textbooks. (1977). New

York: Council on Interracial Books for Children.

11. Government document

U.S. House of Representatives, Committee on Energy and Commerce. (1986).

Ensuring access to programming for the backyard satellite dish

owner (Serial No. 99-127). Washington, DC: U.S. Government Printing

Office.

For government documents, provide the higher department or governing agency only when the office or agency that created the document is not readily recognizable. If a document number is available, list it after the document title in parentheses. Write out the name of the printing agency in full, as the publisher, rather than using the abbreviation *GPO*.

DOCUMENTING PERIODICALS

In citing periodical articles, use the same format for listing author names as for books.

12. Article in a journal paginated by volume

Hartley, J. (1991). Psychology, writing, and computers: A review of research.

Visible Language, 25, 339-375.

If page numbers are continuous throughout volumes in a year, use only the volume number, underlined, following the title of the periodical.

13. Article in a journal paginated by issue

Lowther, M. A. (1977). Career change in mid-life: Its impact on education.

Innovator, 8(7), 1, 9-11.

Include the issue number in parentheses if each issue of a journal is paginated separately.

14. Magazine article

Garreau, J. (1995, December). Edgier cities. *Wired,* 158-163, 232-234.

For nonprofessional periodicals, include the year and month (not abbreviated) after the author's name.

15. Newspaper article

Finn, P. (1995, September 27). Death of a U-Va. student raises scrutiny of off-

campus drinking. *The Washington Post,* pp. D1, D4.

If an author is listed for the article, begin with the author's name, then list the date (spell out the month); follow with the title of the newspaper. If there is a section, combine it with the page or pages, including continued page numbers as well.

DOCUMENTING FIXED ELECTRONIC SOURCES

APA conventions for documenting fixed electronic sources such as CD-ROMs, diskettes, and magnetic tapes list author, date, and title followed by the type of electronic source—for example, *[CD-ROM]*—in brackets and the complete information for the corresponding print source if available.

16. CD-ROM

Krauthammer, C. (1991). Why is America in a blue funk? [CD-ROM]. *Time, 138,*

83. Abstract from UMIACH file: Periodical Abstracts Item: 1126.00

17. Computer software

HyperCard (Version 2.2) [Computer software]. (1993). Cupertino, CA: Apple

Computer.

Provide the version number, if available, in parentheses following the software name. Add the descriptive term [*Computer software*] in brackets, followed with a period. Do not underline the names of computer programs.

DOCUMENTING ONLINE SOURCES

An APA Internet citation should provide essentially the same information as any textual source: author (when identified), date of site creation, title (or description of document), date of retrieval, and a working address (URL).

Try to reference specific documents or links, whenever possible, rather than general home or menu pages since such pages commonly contain many links, only one of which you are citing.

To transcribe a URL correctly, keep your word processing file open and copy the URL directly from the Internet site to your paper. (Make sure your word processor's automatic hyphenation feature is turned off since an automatically inserted hyphen will change the URL; if you need to break a URL, do so after a slash or before a period.) APA does not recommend using angle brackets to indicate an Internet address.

APA provides two general formats for listing online sources, which closely follow the conventions for their printed equivalents. (Keep in mind that all APA citations follow the general structure of *who, when,* said *what,* and *where.*)

ONLINE PERIODICAL

Author, A. A., Author, B. B., & Author, C. C. (2000). Title of article. *Title of*

Periodical, vol., pages. Retrieved month, day, year, from source (URL).

ONLINE DOCUMENT

Author, A. A. (2000). *Title of work.* Retrieved month, day, year, from source

(URL).

If electronic sources don't provide page numbers, use paragraph numbers: (*para 4*). If the source is divided into chapters, use chapter and paragraph numbers: (*chap 2. 12*). If the source is divided into sections, use section and paragraph numbers to identify the source location: *(section 6, 8)*.

For more details than the following examples can provide, consult the APA's Web page at http://www.apa.org/journals/webref.html.

18. Online periodical article

Kapadia, S. (1995, November). A tribute to Mahatma Gandhi: His views on

women and social exchange. *Journal of South Asia Women's*

Studies, 1(1). Retrieved December 2, 1995, from

http://www.shore.net/~india/jsaws

Indicate the number of paragraphs in brackets after the title, and add the term [*On-line serial*] in brackets between the journal name and the volume number.

If you have viewed the article only in its electronic form, you should add *Electronic version* in brackets after the article title as in the following example:

Smithsonian Institution's Ocean Planet: A special report. (1995). [Electronic

version]. *Outdoor Life 3,* 13-22. Retrieved November 1, 1999, from

http://www.epinions.com/mags-Outdoor Life

19. World Wide Web site

To document a specific file, list the author, the date of publication, the titles of the document and the complete work (if any). Add relevant information such as volume or page numbers of a print source. Conclude with a retrieval statement.

Williams, Scott. (1996, June 14). Back to school with the quilt. *AIDS Memorial*

Quilt Website. Retrieved June 14, 1996, from http://www.aidsquilt.org/

newsletter/stories/backto.html

Start with the title if no author is identified.

GVU's 8th WWW user survey. (n.d.). Retrieved August 8, 2000, from http://

www.cc.gatech.edu/gvu/usersurveys/survey1997-10/

20. E-mail messages

Under current APA guidelines, electronic conversations are not listed on the References page. Cite e-mail messages in the text as you would personal letters or interviews.

R. W. Williams, personal communication, January 4, 1999.

Following is an in-text parenthetical reference to a personal e-mail message:

James Holden (personal communication, November 2, 2002) told me that the

practice of dowsing has a scientific basis.

21. File transfer protocol (FTP), telnet, or gopher site

After the retrieval date, supply the FTP, telnet, or gopher search path.

Altar, T. W. (1993). *Vitamin B12 and vegans.* Retrieved May 28, 1996, from

ftp://ftp.cs.yale.edu

Clinton, W. (1994, July 17). Remarks by the President at the tribute dinner for

Senator Byrd. Washington, DC: Office of the White House Press

Secretary. Retrieved February 12, 1996, from

gopher://info.tamu.edu.70/00/.data/ politics/1994/byrd.0717

King, Jr., M. L. (1963 August 28). I have a dream [speech] Retrieved January

2, 1996, from telnet://ukanaix.cc.ukans.edu

22. Synchronous communications (MOO, MUD, IRC)

To document a *real-time communication,* such as those posted in MOOs, MUDs, and IRCs, describe the type of communication (e.g., *Group discussion, Personal interview*) if it is not indicated elsewhere in the entry.

Harnack, A. (1996, April 4). Words [Group discussion]. Retrieved April 5,

1996, from telnet://moo.du.org/port=8888

23. Web discussion forum

Holden, J. B. (2001, January 2). The failure of higher education [Formal

discussion initiation]. Message posted to http://ifets.mtu.edu/

archives

24. Listserv (electronic mailing list)

Weston, Heather (2002, June 12). Re: Registration schedule now available.

Message posted to the Chamberlain Kronsage dormitory electronic

mailing list, archived at http://listserv.registrar.uwsp

.edu/archives/62.html

Note that APA prefers the term *electronic mailing list* to *listserv.*

25. Newsgroup

Hotgirl (2002, January 12). Dowsing effort fails. Message posted to

news://alt.science.esp3/html

DOCUMENTING OTHER SOURCES

26. Film, recording, and other nonprint media

Curtiz, M. (Director). (1942). *Casablanca* [Film]. Hollywood, CA: Warner Bros.

Alphabetize a film listing by the name of the person or persons with primary responsibility for the product. Identify the medium in brackets following the title, and indicate both location and name of the distributor (as publisher). Other identifying information should appear in parentheses.

27. Electronic newspaper article

Kolata, G. (2002, February 12). Why some people won't be fit despite

exercise. *New York Times*. Retrieved February 12, 2002, from

http://www.nytimes.com

28. Document available on university program or department Web site

McClintock, R. & Taipale, K.A. (1994). *Educating America for the 21st century:*

A strategic plan for educational leadership 1993–2001. Retrieved

February 12, 2002, from Columbia University, Institute for

Learning Technologies Web site: http://www.ilt.columbia.edu/ilt/

docs/ILTplan.html

57 e Informational research paper: APA style

The research essay "Green Is Only Skin Deep: False Environmental Marketing," by Elizabeth Bone, was written in response to an assignment to identify and explain one problem in contemporary American culture. Elizabeth's essay is documented according to the conventions of the American Psychological Association (APA). This sample includes title page, abstract, and outline page; check with your instructor to find out whether these are required for course papers. The References page shows so-called hanging indent style, with each first line full measure and subsequent lines in an entry indented 5 to 7 spaces. In APA style, student papers may use a first-line indent instead. Check to see which style your instructor prefers.

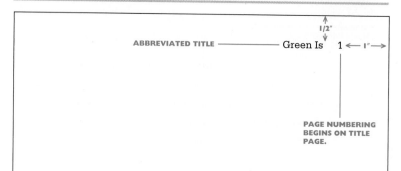

1/2"

PAGE NUMBERING
BEGINS ON TITLE
PAGE.

Green Is Only Skin Deep: TITLE

TITLE PAGE IS
CENTERED TOP TO
BOTTOM, LEFT TO
RIGHT, AND IS DOUBLE
SPACED.

False Environmental Marketing

Elizabeth Bone   AUTHOR

Professor John Clark   INSTRUCTOR

English 1   COURSE

December 6, 200X   DATE

APA APA APA

Title page for a student essay in APA format

ABSTRACT SHOULD BE PRINTED
ON A SEPARATE PAGE
FOLLOWING THE TITLE PAGE.

1"

1/2"

Green Is   2 ⟵ 1" ⟶

Abstract   HEADING CENTERED

DOUBLE
SPACE

NO
PARAGRAPH
INDENT

THE
ABSTRACT
SUMMARIZES
THE MAIN
POINT OF
THE PAPER.

Most Americans consider themselves environmentalists

and favor supporting environmentally friendly or "green"

companies. However, companies use a number of false

advertising practices to mislead the public about their

green practices and products by (1) exaggerating claims,

(2) masking false practices behind technical terminology,

(3) mis-sponsoring green events, (4) not admitting

responsibility for real problems, (5) advertising green by

association, and (6) solving one problem while creating

others. Consumers must be skeptical of all advertisements

and take the time to find out the truth behind advertising.

APA APA APA

Abstract for a student essay in APA format

OUTLINE SHOULD FOLLOW THE TITLE
PAGE AND ABSTRACT AND CONFORM
TO TRADITIONAL OUTLINE FORMAT.

1/2"

1"

Green Is   3 ⟵ 1" ⟶

Outline HEADING CENTERED

I.   Environmental consciousness is strong in

Americans.

DOUBLE
SPACE

A.   Gallup poll finds 75% are environmentalists.

B.   False advertising betrays consumers.

II.   Definitions are exaggerated by the media and

government.

A.   Biodegradable plastic is false advertising.

B.   Federal Trade Commission regulates

definitions.

ROMAN
NUMERALS
INDICATE
MAJOR
DIVISIONS.

III. Terminology is highly technical.

A.   CFCs threaten our ozone layer.

B.   Chrysler advertising misleads us about

chemicals.

IV.   Some companies are green by sponsorship yet not

green.

OUTLINE
USES
SENTENCE
FORMAT.

A.   Ford supports the Smithsonian Institution's

Ocean Planet.

B.   Ford is guilty of pollution in Michigan.

V.   It's not my problem.

A.   CFCs are not caused by natural gas.

B.   Natural gas causes other pollution.

VI.   Many companies are green only by association.

LETTERS
INDICATE
SUBDIVISIONS
AND
SUBORDINATE
POINTS.

A.   Advertising has nothing to do with product.

B.   Chevrolet logo implies relationship.

APA APA APA

Outline for a student essay in APA format

Green Is   4 ←— 1″ —→

VII. Some companies are insincere in their environmentalism.

   A. Chevron employees do good in Mississippi.

   B. Chevron pollutes Santa Monica Bay.

VIII. Environmental image does not match reality.

   A. Earth First! educates consumers.

   B. Federal Trade Commission regulates.

   C. Consumers beware!

(Continued)

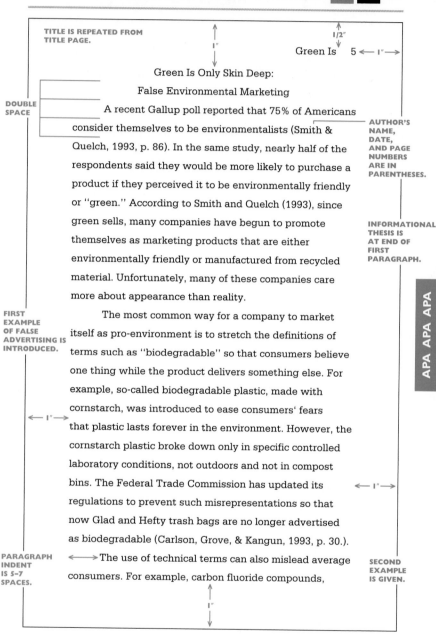

TITLE IS REPEATED FROM
TITLE PAGE.

1"

1/2"

Green Is   5 ← 1" →

Green Is Only Skin Deep:

False Environmental Marketing

DOUBLE
SPACE

A recent Gallup poll reported that 75% of Americans

consider themselves to be environmentalists (Smith &

Quelch, 1993, p. 86). In the same study, nearly half of the

respondents said they would be more likely to purchase a

product if they perceived it to be environmentally friendly

or ''green.'' According to Smith and Quelch (1993), since

green sells, many companies have begun to promote

themselves as marketing products that are either

environmentally friendly or manufactured from recycled

material. Unfortunately, many of these companies care

more about appearance than reality.

AUTHOR'S
NAME,
DATE,
AND PAGE
NUMBERS
ARE IN
PARENTHESES.

INFORMATIONAL
THESIS IS
AT END OF
FIRST
PARAGRAPH.

FIRST
EXAMPLE
OF FALSE
ADVERTISING IS
INTRODUCED.

The most common way for a company to market

itself as pro-environment is to stretch the definitions of

terms such as ''biodegradable'' so that consumers believe

one thing while the product delivers something else. For

example, so-called biodegradable plastic, made with

cornstarch, was introduced to ease consumers' fears

← 1" →

that plastic lasts forever in the environment. However, the

cornstarch plastic broke down only in specific controlled

laboratory conditions, not outdoors and not in compost

bins. The Federal Trade Commission has updated its

← 1" →

regulations to prevent such misrepresentations so that

now Glad and Hefty trash bags are no longer advertised

as biodegradable (Carlson, Grove, & Kangun, 1993, p. 30.).

PARAGRAPH
INDENT
IS 5–7
SPACES.

→ The use of technical terms can also mislead average

consumers. For example, carbon fluoride compounds,

SECOND
EXAMPLE
IS GIVEN.

1"

APA APA APA

First text page of a student essay in APA format

Green Is   6

called CFCs, are known to be hazardous to the protective
layer of ozone that surrounds the earth, so their
widespread use in air conditioners is considered an
environmental hazard (Decker & Stammer, 1989). Chrysler
Corporation advertises that it uses CFC-free refrigerant in
its automobile air conditioners to appeal to
environmentally concerned consumers ("Ozone Layer,"
1994). However, Weisskopf (1992) points out that the
chemical compounds that replace CFCs in their air
conditioners pose other environmental hazards that are
not mentioned.

Another deceptive greening tactic is the sponsoring
of highly publicized environmental events such as animal
shows, concerts, cleanup programs, and educational
exhibits. For example, Ocean Planet was a well-publicized
exhibit put together by the Smithsonian Institution to
educate people about ocean conservation. Ford Motor
Company helped sponsor the event, which it then used in
its car advertisements: "At Ford, we feel strongly that
understanding, preserving, and properly managing
natural resources like our oceans should be an essential
commitment of individuals and corporate citizens alike"
(Smithsonian Institution's Ocean Planet, 1995, para 8).

While sponsoring the exhibit may be a worthwhile
public service, such sponsorship has nothing to do with
how the manufacture and operation of Ford automobiles
affect the environment. In fact, Ford was ranked as among
the worst polluters in the state of Michigan in 1995

(Continued)

Green Is   7

(Parker, 1995).

Some companies court the public by mentioning environmental problems and pointing out that they do not contribute to those problems. For example, the natural gas industry describes natural gas as an alternative to the use of ozone-depleting CFCs ("Don't You Wish," 1994). However, according to Fogel (1985), the production of natural gas creates a host of other environmental problems from land reclamation to carbon dioxide pollution, a major cause of global warming. By mentioning problems they don't cause while ignoring ones they do, companies present a favorable environmental image that is at best a half-truth, at worst an outright lie.

SHORTENED TITLE IS USED WHEN NO AUTHOR IS CREDITED ON REFERENCES PAGE.

Other companies use a more subtle approach to misleading green advertising. Rather than make statements about environmental compatibility, these companies depict the product in unspoiled natural settings or use green quotations that have nothing to do with the product itself. For example, one Chevrolet advertisement shows a lake shrouded in mist and quotes an environmentalist: "From this day onward, I will restore the earth where I am and listen to what it is telling me" ("From This Day," 1994, p. 19). Below the quotation is the Chevy logo with the words "Genuine Chevrolet." Despite this touching appeal to its love of nature, Chevrolet has a history of dumping toxic waste into the Great Lakes (Allen, 1991). Has this company seriously been listening to what the earth has been telling it?

QUOTATION OF FEWER THAN 40 WORDS IS INTEGRATED INTO THE TEXT.

APA APA APA

(Continued)

The most common manner in which companies attempt to prove they have a strong environmental commitment is to give a single example of a policy or action that is considered environmentally sound. Chevron has had an environmental advertising campaign since the mid-1970s. Most recently the company's ads feature Chevron employees doing environmental good deeds (Smith & Quelch, 1993, p. 94). For example, a recent ad features ''a saltwater wetland in Mississippi at the edge of a pine forest . . . the kind of place nature might have made'' and goes on to explain that this wetland was built by Chevron employees (''Shorebirds Who Found,'' 1998, para 1). However, LaGanga (1993, p. A1) points out that during the time this advertisement was running in magazines such as *Audubon,* Chevron was dumping millions of gallons of nasty chemicals (carcinogens and heavy metals) into California's Santa Monica Bay, posing a health risk to swimmers. The building of the wetland in one part of the country does not absolve the company of polluting water somewhere else.

ELLIPSIS POINTS INDICATE MISSING WORDS IN QUOTATION.

It should be clear that the environmental image a company projects does not necessarily match the realities of the company's practice. The products produced by companies such as Chrysler, Ford, General Motors, and Chevron are among the major causes of air and water pollution: automobiles and gasoline. No amount of advertising can conceal the ultimately negative effect these products have on the environment (Kennedy &

APA APA APA

(Continued)

Green Is   9

Grumbly, 1988). According to Shirley Lefevre, president of
the New York Truth in Advertising League:

DOUBLE
SPACE

It probably doesn't help to single out one
automobile manufacturer or oil company as
significantly worse than the others. Despite small
efforts here and there, all of these giant corporations,
as well as other large manufacturers of metal and
plastic material goods, put profit before environment
and cause more harm than good to the environment.
(Personal communication, May 1995)

Consumers who are genuinely interested in buying
environmentally safe products and supporting
environmentally responsible companies need to look
beyond the images projected by commercial advertising in
magazines, on billboards, and on television. Organizations
such as Earth First! attempt to educate consumers to the
realities by writing about false advertising and exposing
the hypocrisy of such ads (''Do People Allow,'' 1994), while
the Ecology Channel is committed to sharing ''impartial,
unbiased, multiperspective environmental information''
with consumers on the Internet (Ecology, n.d.).
Meanwhile the Federal Trade Commission is in the
process of continually upgrading truth-in-advertising
regulations (Carlson, et al., 1993). Americans who are truly
environmentally conscious must remain skeptical of
simplistic and misleading advertisements while
continuing to educate themselves about the genuine
needs of the environment.

**INDENT
5–7 SPACES.**

**COLON IS
USED TO
INTRODUCE
A LONG
QUOTATION.**

**INTERVIEW
CONDUCTED
BY AUTHOR
IS NOT LISTED
ON THE
REFERENCES
PAGE.**

APA APA APA

**WHEN NO DATE
IS FOUND
ON A SOURCE,
WRITE *N.D.***

**SECOND
CITATION
OF MORE
THAN
THREE
AUTHORS IS
SHORTENED
TO FIRST
AUTHOR'S
NAME AND
*ET AL.***

**THESIS IS
REPEATED
IN MORE
DETAIL AT
END.**

(Continued)

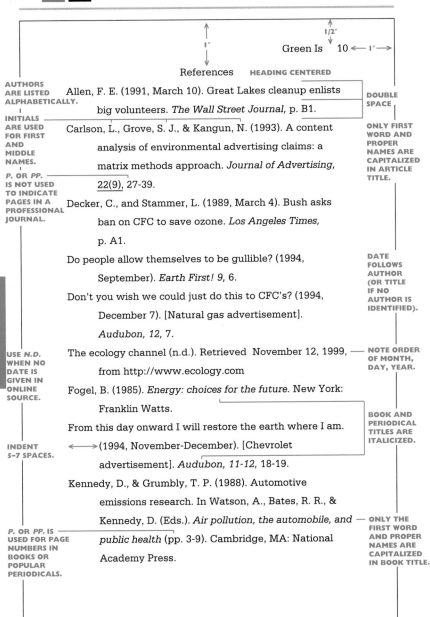

AUTHORS ARE LISTED ALPHABETICALLY.

INITIALS ARE USED FOR FIRST AND MIDDLE NAMES.

P. OR PP. IS NOT USED TO INDICATE PAGES IN A PROFESSIONAL JOURNAL.

USE N.D. WHEN NO DATE IS GIVEN IN ONLINE SOURCE.

INDENT 5–7 SPACES.

P. OR PP. IS USED FOR PAGE NUMBERS IN BOOKS OR POPULAR PERIODICALS.

1″

½″

Green Is   10 ← 1″ →

References   **HEADING CENTERED**

Allen, F. E. (1991, March 10). Great Lakes cleanup enlists
big volunteers. *The Wall Street Journal*, p. B1.

DOUBLE SPACE

Carlson, L., Grove, S. J., & Kangun, N. (1993). A content
analysis of environmental advertising claims: a
matrix methods approach. *Journal of Advertising*,
22(9), 27-39.

ONLY FIRST WORD AND PROPER NAMES ARE CAPITALIZED IN ARTICLE TITLE.

Decker, C., and Stammer, L. (1989, March 4). Bush asks
ban on CFC to save ozone. *Los Angeles Times*,
p. A1.

Do people allow themselves to be gullible? (1994,
September). *Earth First! 9*, 6.

DATE FOLLOWS AUTHOR (OR TITLE IF NO AUTHOR IS IDENTIFIED).

Don't you wish we could just do this to CFC's? (1994,
December 7). [Natural gas advertisement].
Audubon, 12, 7.

The ecology channel (n.d.). Retrieved November 12, 1999,
from http://www.ecology.com

NOTE ORDER OF MONTH, DAY, YEAR.

Fogel, B. (1985). *Energy: choices for the future*. New York:
Franklin Watts.

BOOK AND PERIODICAL TITLES ARE ITALICIZED.

From this day onward I will restore the earth where I am.
⟵→ (1994, November-December). [Chevrolet
advertisement]. *Audubon, 11-12*, 18-19.

Kennedy, D., & Grumbly, T. P. (1988). Automotive
emissions research. In Watson, A., Bates, R. R., &
Kennedy, D. (Eds.). *Air pollution, the automobile, and
public health* (pp. 3-9). Cambridge, MA: National
Academy Press.

ONLY THE FIRST WORD AND PROPER NAMES ARE CAPITALIZED IN BOOK TITLE.

APA APA APA

References list from a student essay in APA format   *(Continued)*

LaGanga, M. (1993), February 4). Chevron to stop dumping waste near shoreline. *Los Angeles Times,* pp. A1, A10.

The ozone layer has protected us for 1.5 billion years: It's time we returned the favor. (1994, November-December). [Chrysler advertisement]. *Audubon, 11-12,* 40-41.

Parker, L. (1995, March 28). GM, Ford among top polluters in state. *Detroit News,* p. A2.

The shorebirds who found a new wetland. (1998). Retrieved November 12, 1999, from http://www.audubon.com/water

Smith, N. C., & Quelch, J. A. (1993). *Ethics in marketing.* Boston, MA: Richard D. Irwin.

Smithsonian Institution's Ocean Planet: A special report. (1995). [electronic version]. *Outdoor Live, 3,* 13-22. Retrieved November 1, 1999, from http://www.epinions.com/mags-Outdoor_Life

Weisskopf, M. (1992, February 23). Study finds CFC alternatives more damaging than believed. The Washington Post, p. A3.

TITLES OF PERIODICALS ARE CAPITALIZED NORMALLY.

TITLE IS USED WHEN NO AUTHOR IS IDENTIFIED IN THE SOURCE.

INCLUDE THIS NOTE WHEN ONLY THE ONLINE SOURCE OF A PUBLISHED SOURCE HAS BEEN CONSULTED.

APA APA APA

58 Writing in the Physical Sciences

This chapter describes the general aims and style of scientific writing and provides an overview of common forms and specialized documentation systems shared by the scientific community. If you write extensively in the sciences, consult one of the more detailed style manuals listed in 58d2.

58 a The aims of writing in the sciences

Scientific study examines the fundamental structures and processes of the natural world. In analyzing particular phenomena and organisms, scientists ask questions such as the following:

- What is it? Can it be isolated and observed? How can it be described?

- How does it function? What forces are in operation? How can these forces be explained?

- Why does it function the way it does? Can governing principles be identified, explained, and understood? Can predictions be made?

- What can be learned about other phenomena or organisms based on the evidence of particular studies?

Scientists approach and attempt to answer such questions using the *scientific method* of observation, prediction, experimentation, and analysis.

Observation. A chemist notices, for example, that when liquid A is mixed with liquid B, the solution of the two (C) has a higher temperature than A or B alone.

Prediction. On the basis of this observation, the chemist predicts that whenever these amounts of A and B are mixed together, C will

always have a higher temperature. This prediction is called a *hypothesis*—a preliminary generalization or explanation based on the observed phenomena.

Experimentation. To test the hypothesis, the chemist devises an experiment (in this example, the mixing of the two liquids under controlled conditions), watches the results, and carefully notes what happens.

Analysis and conclusions. The results of the experiment may lead the scientist to conclude, "Yes, when specific amounts of A and B are mixed, reaction C occurs." This finding can be shared with other scientists and could provide the basis for further hypotheses. If the results are different from the hypothesis, new questions must be asked and new hypotheses formulated to explain why the results differed from the initial observations.

Writing plays a central role throughout the investigative and experimental process. To develop a hypothesis, scientists record observations, questions, and possible explanations. In conducting an experiment, scientists take full and accurate notes to keep a running account of methods, procedures, and results. To understand the significance of the results, scientists report or publish the results so other scientists can read about them and respond.

Scientific writing does not report the writer's opinions, values, or feelings; it aims for objectivity and accuracy when reporting observations and findings. When you write in the sciences, try to separate your observations from your expectations or biases. Record only what you see and hear and what the instruments tell you, not what you hope to discover. Keep in mind that your primary purpose is to present information accurately—not to persuade, argue, or entertain.

SCI SCI SCI

58 b The style of writing in the sciences

Most science writing seeks to convey information specifically, directly, economically, and accurately. But this common goal does not mean that the style of all science writing is uniform. For example, the form and style of a laboratory report is quite different from the laboratory notebook on which it is based. An article in *Scientific American* (written for a general readership) is quite different from one in *The Journal of Chemical Education* (written for college chemistry instructors).

STYLISTIC GUIDELINES FOR WRITING IN THE SCIENCES

In writing in the sciences, keep the goals of clarity and directness in mind.

- Choose **simple words** rather than complex words when the meaning is the same, and use disciplinary terminology carefully and accurately.
- Prefer **simple sentences** to complex.
- Maintain a **third-person point of view,** to avoid the pronoun *I.* Use the **passive voice** when necessary to describe procedures: *The liquids were brought to a temperature of 35°C.*
- Use the **present tense** to refer to established knowledge or to discuss conclusions. Use the **past tense** to describe methods and results.
- Insert **subheadings** to help readers predict what is coming.
- Include **tables** and **figures** when they can help explain your methods or results. Label each of these clearly, and mention them at appropriate points in the text.

58 c Common forms of writing in the sciences

Scientific reports have set forms that allow readers to locate information in predictable places. Two common forms of writing in college science courses are laboratory notebooks and laboratory reports.

1 Laboratory notebooks

Laboratory notebooks are journals that scientists keep to monitor day-to-day laboratory work and experimentation. They are used to record data—dates, times, temperatures, quantities, measurements—as well as to aid memory and provide records. These notebooks are also used to speculate about the meaning of the data. The privately kept notes serve as the basis for the information made public in formal laboratory reports.

- Laboratory notebook pages are usually numbered and bound rather than loose-leaf. This unalterable order guarantees an accurate record of exactly what happened in the laboratory, when it happened, and in what order.

- Double-entry notebooks, with a vertical line down the center of each page, are especially useful. Record data on the left; on the right make notes and speculations about the data.

- Laboratory notebooks must be complete and detailed. It is crucial to record all information about an experiment or observation.

Laboratory reports

Laboratory reports are formal reports that describe exactly what happened in any given experiment. The reader of a laboratory report should be able to replicate (or duplicate) the experiment by following the information in the report. While *labs* (as they are commonly called) vary slightly in format conventions from discipline to discipline, they all follow the same basic structure.

Introduction. The first section of the report defines the reasons for conducting the particular study, summarizes the findings of previous studies (a literature review), and states the researcher's hypothesis.

Methods and materials. Sometimes called "Procedure," this section details how the experiment was conducted and identifies all the equipment used. The experimental design is explained, and the methods of observation and measurement are described.

Results. Next, the researcher reports the specific factual findings of the study, describing the data and patterns that emerged but refraining from any judgment or interpretation.

Discussion. The final section of a laboratory report examines whether or not the results support the hypothesis. It can be somewhat speculative, focusing on the possible implications and limitations of the experiment and its results. It may also point out the relationship of the current study to other researchers' results, suggest further hypotheses that could be tested, and draw theoretical conclusions.

References cited. If you have mentioned published sources in your report, you need to include a list of *references cited*. (See 58d2.)

SCI SCI SCI

| 58 | d | **Documentation and format conventions: number systems** |

The life sciences (biology, botany, zoology), the applied sciences (chemistry, computer science, mathematics, and physics), and the medical sciences (medicine, nursing, general health) all use a number system of documentation.

1 Conventions for number citation

In the number system of citation, writers alert readers to the use of other sources by citing a number, either in parentheses or with a *superscript,* a character raised a small space above the baseline of the surrounding text: [2] (as you can see, superscript numbers are also typically reduced in size for a neater appearance). This citation number corresponds to a numbered list of sources at the end of the paper. Math and life science disciplines generally prefer parenthetical numbers; chemistry, physics, the medical fields, and computer science disciplines generally prefer superscript numbers.

If, in using the number system, you use an author's name in a sentence, place the number immediately after the name, if possible.

Linhoffer (3) reported similar results.

Linhoffer [3] reported similar results.

If no author's name is used in the sentence, place the number immediately after the use of the source material. Science writers using parenthetical numbers have the option of including the author's last name before the number: (*Smith 3*).

According to the conventions of scientific writing, the numbers cited in the text can be organized either sequentially or alphabetically. In *sequential arrangement,* the first source cited in the text is numbered *1,* the second cited source is numbered *2,* and so on. Any subsequent reference to an already cited source is given the same number. Sequential reference is preferred by writers in chemistry, computer science, physics, the life sciences, and medicine.

In *alphabetic arrangement,* writers assign numbers according to the alphabetical order of the authors' last names as they appear on the reference page(s). For example, a reference to an author named Smith, even if the first source cited in the text, should be accompanied by the number *12* if Smith is the twelfth name on the alphabetical list of references. Alphabetical arrangement is preferred in mathematical writing.

When using the sequential system, number the bibliography sequentially as you write, and continue to use the same number each time you cite that authority. When using the alphabetical system, arrange your bibliography alphabetically and number accordingly.

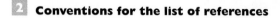

2 Conventions for the list of references

The Literature Cited or References section provides publication information for all sources cited in the text.

Each scientific discipline has its own format for documenting sources; select the style appropriate to your discipline or consult your instructor. The following brief examples are illustrative only; they suggest that minor differences occur from discipline to discipline within scientific fields. Should you need to write a substantial paper in any of these disciplines, consult the appropriate reference source listed below.

Life sciences

Biology, botany, zoology, anatomy, and physiology follow the documentation system recommended in the *CBE Style Manual*, 6th ed. (New York: Cambridge University Press, 1994), published by the Council of Science Editors. In-text number citations are given sequentially in parentheses. Title the list of references "Literature Cited," "References Cited," or "References," and use the following general styles.

BOOK ENTRIES

1. Quammen, D. Natural acts: a sidelong view of science and nature. New York: Schocken Books; 1985. 221p.

Book with more than one author

2. Martini FH, Timmons MJ, McKinley MP. Human anatomy, third edition. Upper Saddle River, NJ: Prentice Hall; 1999. 886 p.

Book with an editor

3. Roberts GG, editor. The Prentice Hall anthology of science fiction and fantasy. Upper Saddle River, NJ: Prentice Hall; 2001. 1184 p.

Do not underline titles, and capitalize only the first word. Place a semicolon after the name of the publisher, and place a colon after the date if page range numbers are given. Leave no space(s) on either side of the colon that follows the date.

PERIODICAL ENTRIES

4. Brown, SG; Wagsten, MV. Socialization processes in a female lowland gorilla. Zoo Biol 1986;5(12):269-80.

SCI SCI SCI

Newspaper article

5. Garfinkel P. Medical students get taste of real-life doctoring. New York Times 2001 Oct 23;Sect F:7(col 2).

Magazine article

6. Kinsley M. In Defense of Denial. Time 2001 Dec 17:72-3.

Do not place in quotation marks or underline article or journal titles. Use no space(s) between year, volume and page numbers, and place an issue number, if required, immediately after the volume number, in parentheses.

ELECTRONIC SOURCES

An online journal article

7. Alfred J. Fast fly maps at SNP. Nature reviews genetics [serial online] 2001 Dec. Available from: http://www.nature.com/cgitaf/DynaPage.taf?file=/nrg/journal/v2/n12/full/nrg1201-912b_fs.html. Accessed 2001 Dec 7.

An online book

8. Olson S. Shaping the future: biology and human values [book online]. Washington DC: National Academy Press; 1989. Available from: http://www.nap.edu/books/0309039479/html. Accessed 2001 Dec 7.

Chemistry

Documentation style in chemistry is based on the American Chemical Society's *The ACS Style Guide: A Manual for Authors and Editors*, 2nd edition (Washington, DC: American Chemical Society, 1998). In-text citations should be superscript numbers and arranged either sequentially or by author name and date. For entries on the reference list, which should be titled "Literature Cited," use the following general styles.

BOOK ENTRIES

1. Siggia, S.; Hanna, J. G. Quantitative Organic Analysis via Functional Groups, 4th ed.; R. E. Krieger: Malabar, FL, 1988; pp. 55-60.

PERIODICAL ENTRIES

2. Scott, J. M. W. J. Chem. Ed. 1992(69)600-602.

For papers in the chemistry style, do not include article titles. If an issue number is required, place it immediately after the volume

number (*69* in this example), in parentheses. Leave no spaces between date, volume, and page numbers for periodicals, and use all digits for page sequences.

Physics

Physics writing follows the style of the *AIP Style Manual*, 4th ed. (New York: American Institute of Physics, 1990). Following this citation style, number in-text citations in sequence and in superscript. In the reference page, which is titled "References," use the following styles.

BOOK ENTRIES

[1] Pagels, H. R. Perfect Symmetry: The Search for the Beginning of Time
(Bantam, New York, 1986), pp. 78-86.

PERIODICAL ENTRIES

[2] Crawford, F. S. Am. J. Phys. (60)751-752(1992).

In the physics system of citation, article titles are not included in the entries. If issue numbers are required, place them immediately after the volume number, in parentheses, and follow them with a comma. Place the date last, with single spaces between volume, page number(s), and date.

59 Writing in Business

This chapter describes the aims, style, and common forms of writing in the business and professional world. Like writing in the social and physical sciences, business writing puts a premium on information; like writing in the humanities, it is highly influenced by the relation between writer and reader.

59 a The aims of writing in business

The guiding objectives of successful companies are efficiency, accuracy, and responsibility: procedures are designed for minimal waste of time and energy, care is taken to avoid errors, and transactions are conducted fairly.

Communication in business mirrors these precepts. Business writing is primarily practical and instrumental, because its goal is to get things done. For efficiency, it should be simple, direct, and brief; for accuracy, it should convey correct information and conform to standard conventions; and for responsibility, it should be honest and courteous.

Business writers must be aware of their audience. They must ask: To whom is the communication being written? What information do they already have? What else do they need to know? What does this communication need to include in order to have its intended effect? What, if any, secondary audience is likely to read this communication? Business writers must also be concerned about presentation. To make a good impression, any piece of writing must be neat, clean, and correct.

59 b The style of writing in business

Because clear communication is highly valued, writing for business purposes should be simple, direct, economical, and

STYLISTIC GUIDELINES FOR BUSINESS WRITING

For most business writing, the following guidelines should be considered:

- **Start fast.** State the main point immediately, and avoid digression or repetition. In business your reader's time—as well as your own— is valuable.
- **Write in a simple, direct style.** Keep your sentences as straightforward and readable as possible.
- **Choose the active voice** (*start fast*) rather than the passive voice (*fast starting is a principle to be followed*).
- **Use technical terminology or jargon sparingly.** Write out complete names of companies, products, and titles. Explain any terms that could be misunderstood.
- **Avoid emotional or biased language** (sexist, racist) as well as stereotypes and clichés. Try to maintain a level of courtesy even when lodging a complaint.
- **Use numbers, bullets, or descriptive headings** to help readers locate information quickly.
- **Use graphs, charts, and other illustrations** when they convey information more clearly than verbal language.

conventional. In general, the preferred tone is objective and fairly formal (although when addressing someone you know well, a more personal, informal tone may be appropriate).

59 **c** **Common forms of writing in business**

Common forms of writing in business include letters, résumés, memos, and reports.

Business letters

Business letters commonly are written to request, inform, or complain, in many cases to an audience unknown to the letter writer. State the purpose clearly and provide all information needed to make responding easy for the reader.

Business letters are typed on $8\frac{1}{2}'' \times 11''$ paper, one side only. Most business letters use *block format,* in which every element of

the letter is typed flush with the left margin and paragraphs are not indented. All business letters contain the following elements:

Heading. The sender's address (but not name) and the date are typed single spaced approximately one inch from the top of the first page of the letter. Spell out all street and town names and months in full; abbreviate state names using the standard postal abbreviations. Zip codes should be included.

If you are using *letterhead* stationery, type the date two line spaces below the letterhead address.

Inside address. Type the recipient's address two or more line spaces below the heading (depending on how much space is needed to center the letter on the page). Include the person's full name (and a courtesy title, if appropriate), followed by his or her position (if needed). When writing to an unknown person, always try to find out the name, perhaps by calling the company switchboard. If doing this is impossible, use an appropriate title (*Personnel Director* or *Claims Manager,* for example) in place of a name. If you don't know the appropriate courtesy title—for example, if you don't know whether the addressee is a man or a woman—you may omit a courtesy title.

The name of the division within the company; the company name; the full street address, including suite, room, or floor number; and city, state, and zip code are typed on separate lines.

Greeting. Type the opening salutation two line spaces below the inside address (*Dear Dr. Jones, Dear James Wong*) followed by a colon. If you and the recipient are on a first-name basis, it is appropriate to use only the first name. If you do not know the recipient's name, use some variation of *Dear Claims Manager:* or *Attention: Director of Marketing* (the latter without a second colon) or *To Whom It May Concern:*. Avoid the old-fashioned *Dear Sir:* or *Dear Sir or Madam:*.

Body. Begin the body of the letter two line spaces below the greeting. Single-space within paragraphs; double-space between paragraphs. If your reason for writing is clear and simple, state it directly in the first paragraph. If it is absolutely necessary to detail a situation, to provide background, or to supply context, do so in the first paragraph or two, and the move on to describe your purpose in writing.

If your letter is more than one page long, type the addressee's last name, the date, and the page number flush with the right margin of each subsequent page.

Closing. Type the complimentary closing two spaces after the last line of the body of the letter. The most common closings are *Sincerely, Cordially, Yours truly, Respectfully yours* (formal), and *Best*

Doyle Advertising Services
1011 Oakhollow Road
Norman, OK. 73071   LETTERHEAD
405-555-1966 telephone
405-555-1982 fax

October 11, 2003   DATE

Ms. Tamara Blackburn

Marketing Director

Tamlyn Foods   INSIDE
                     ADDRESS
6850 Amberly Way

Cordova, TN 38018

Dear Ms. Blackburn: GREETING

BODY, UNINDENTED

Tony Adamo, your account representative, asked that I give you an update about the direct mail campaign for Tamlyn's Muffin Chips.

During the week of September 2, our direct mail contractor sent mailings to approximately 7500 homes in the Oklahoma City/Little Rock test markets. As you know, these mailings contained a sample-size package of the chips, along with a postage-paid questionnaire that recipients could return to receive a cents-off coupon for other Tamlyn products.

As of October 9, 2267 questionnaires had been returned, a very high response rate. We are currently compiling the questionnaire results and should have a formal report ready for you by October 15. The cents-off coupons will be mailed out October 22.

If you have any other questions, please give me a call at extension 557.

Sincerely,   CLOSING

Casey Dorris   SIGNATURE

Casey Dorris

Direct Mail Coordinator

Business letter: block format on letterhead

405 Martin Street
Lexington, Kentucky 40508 HEADING
February 12, 2002

Ms. Barbara McGarry, Director
Kentucky Council on the Arts INSIDE ADDRESS
953 Versailles Road
Box 335
Frankfort, Kentucky 40602

Dear Ms. McGarry: GREETING

BODY, UNINDENTED

John Huff, one of my professors at the University of Kentucky, recommended that I write to you regarding openings in the Council's internship program this summer. I would like to apply for one of these positions and have enclosed my résumé for your consideration.

As you will note, my academic background combines a primary concentration in business administration with a minor in art history. My interest in the arts goes back to childhood when I first heard a performance by the Lexington Symphony, and I have continued to pursue that interest ever since. My goal after graduation is a career in arts administration, focusing on fund-raising and outreach for a major public institution.

I hope you'll agree that my experience, particularly my work with the local Community Concerts association, is strong preparation for an internship with the Council. I would appreciate the opportunity to discuss my qualifications with you in greater detail.

I will call your office within the next few weeks to see about setting up an appointment to meet with you. In the meantime, you can reach me at the above address or by phone at (606) 555-4033.

Thank you for your attention.

Sincerely, CLOSING
Chris Aleandro SIGNATURE
Chris Aleandro
enc. ADDITIONAL INFORMATION

Cover letter

regards (informal). Capitalize only the first word of the closing; follow it with a comma.

Signature. Type your full name, including any title, four line spaces below the closing. Sign the letter with your full name (or just the first name if you have addressed the recipient by first name) in blue or black ink in the space above your typed name.

Additional information. You may provide additional brief information below your signature, flush with the left margin. Such information may include recipients of copies of the letter (*cc: Jennifer Rodriguez*); the word *Enclosures* (or the abbreviation *enc.*) to indicate you are also enclosing additional material mentioned in the letter; and, if the letter was typed by someone other than the writer, both the writer's and the typist's initials (*TF/jlw*).

2 Résumés

A *résumé* is a brief summary of an applicant's qualifications for employment. It outlines education, work experience, and other activities and interests so a prospective employer can decide quickly whether or not an applicant is a good prospect for a particular job. Try to tailor your résumé for the position you are seeking by emphasizing experience that is most relevant to the position. Preparing a résumé on a computer lets you revise it easily and quickly.

Generally, a résumé is sent out with a *cover letter* that introduces the applicant, indicates the position applied for, and offers additional information that cannot be accommodated on the résumé itself. Print out your résumé and cover letter on good-quality $8\frac{1}{2}'' \times 11''$ stationery. Even if you fax these documents to prospective employers, you should have attractive copies to take with you on interviews. Examples of a résumé and cover letter appear in 59c1.

Résumés should be brief and to the point, preferably no more than a page long (if relevant experience is extensive, more than one page is acceptable). Résumé formats vary in minor ways, but most include the following information:

Personal information. Résumés begin with the applicant's name, address, and phone number, usually centered at the top.

Objective. Many résumés include a line summarizing the applicant's objective, either naming the specific job sought or describing a larger career goal.

Education. Most first-time job applicants list their educational background first, since their employment history is likely to be fairly limited. Name the last two or three schools attended (including dates of attendance and degrees), starting with the most recent. Indicate major areas of study, and highlight any relevant courses. Also consider including grade point average, awards, and anything else that shows you in a good light. When employment history is more detailed, educational background is often placed at the end of the résumé.

Work experience. Starting with the most recent, list all relevant jobs, including company name, dates of employment, and a brief job description. If you are applying for your first full-time job, listing summer jobs, work-study programs, and similar employment, even in a different industry, will show prospective employers that you have some work experience. Unpaid volunteer work may also be relevant. Use your judgment about listing jobs where you had difficulties with your employer.

Special skills or interests. It is often useful to mention special skills, interests, or activities that provide additional clues about your abilities and personality.

References. The line *References available on request* indicates that you have obtained permission from two or three people—teachers, supervisors, employers—for prospective employers to contact them for a recommendation. To avoid embarrassment, select people who are likely to speak well of you, and secure their permission well in advance of your job search. Listing references on your résumé is acceptable but is not recommended. Most employers include a place to list references on their application form, and some have specific requirements such as listing only people who know you through previous work experience or not using relatives as references.

3 Memos

Memo is short for *memorandum,* which is defined as a short note or a reminder to someone to do something. Memos are used in business and college offices to suggest that actions be taken or to alert one or more people about a change in policy or an upcoming meeting. Part of the value of the memo is that the memo writer retains a record (a memory) that something was communicated to certain people on such and such a date.

Memo format is simple and direct. Names of both receiver and sender, along with the date and subject, are included at the top of

Chris Aleandro

405 Martin Street

Lexington, Kentucky 40508

(606) 555-4033

Objective: Internship in arts administration.

Education

University of Kentucky: 1998 to present.

Currently a sophomore majoring in business administration with a minor in art history. Degree expected May 2003.

Henry Clay High School (Lexington, KY.): 1995 to 1998.

College preparatory curriculum, with emphasis in art and music.

Related Work Experience

Community Concerts, Inc.: 1998 to present.

Part-time promotion assistant, reporting to local director. Responsibilities include assisting with scheduling, publicity, subscription/ticketing procedures, and fund-raising. Position involves general office duties as well as heavy contact with subscribers and artists.

Habitat for Humanity: September to November 1998.

Co-chaired campus fund-raising drive that included a benefit concert, raising $55,000.

Art in the Schools Program: 1998-1999.

Volunteer, through the Education Division of the Lexington Center for the Arts. Trained to conduct hands-on art appreciation presentations in grade school classrooms, visiting one school a month.

Other Work Experience

Record City: 1995 to 1998 (part-time and summers).

Salesclerk and assistant manager in a music store.

Special skills: WordPerfect 5.1; desktop design of brochures, programs, and other materials.

References: available on request.

Résumé

the page so that the receiver knows instantly what this message is about:

Date flush right

To: Name of person or persons to whom it will be sent

From: Name of memo sender

Re: Regarding what subject

Following is a typical memo:

January 25, 2003

To: Nancy, Bill, and Sue

From: Albert

Re: Curriculum Committee meeting

Our last meeting will be Tuesday (1/27) at 3:30 p.m. in Old Mill, room

117. The agenda is to plan discussion items for the spring semester.

59 d Documentation and format conventions

The format and style of documentation for business reports usually follow the guidelines of the American Psychological Association (APA). (See 57d.)

60   Columbia Online Style

*T*he *Columbia Guide to Online Style* (COS) by Janice R. Walker and Todd Taylor (Columbia UP, 1998) provides comprehensive coverage of how to cite electronic sources accurately. COS uses many of the same elements present in predominantly print documentation styles such as MLA and APA to cite works, including the author's name, title of the work, and date of publication, when these elements are known. In fact, COS provides sufficient information to document print sources, and alternative humanities and science guidelines make COS easy to use for writers accustomed to a variety of older documentation styles. COS accounts for the differences between print and electronic publications by including newer and necessary elements such as the electronic address and date of access.

When a research paper is assigned, find out which documentation style your instructor prefers. You can save yourself time and effort by using that style from the outset of your research.

60   a   Citing sources in the body of a paper in COS style

Many electronic sources do not include reference elements such as the author's last name and the page number of the cited work, so COS compensates for these differences. For instance, if an author's name is unknown, the material is referred to by its title. Also, most electronic sources are not numbered, so page references may be irrelevant. If page numbers, sections, or other navigational aids *are* available, however, include them in the citation as well, separated by commas. If the publication date of an electronic source is unavailable, use the date of access in day-month-year order. If available, COS in-text citations will use solely the author's name for humanities style and the author's name and the date of publication for scientific style.

HUMANITIES STYLE

According to the survey, over 80 percent of first-year students waited until

the night before an exam to begin studying (Jani).

SCIENTIFIC STYLE

The research proved conclusively that individuals deprived of sleep were

as dangerous as those driving under the influence of drugs or alcohol

(Rezik, 2000).

When the author's name is included in the sentence, the in-text citation is unnecessary. If there is more than one work by the author, use the work's title.

Distinctions between print and electronic citations

Most elements in a bibliographic reference remain the same for the various styles of documentation—the name of the author, the title, and the place of publication. However, the order of these elements depends on the needs of the field for which the style has been designed.

Citations for electronic sources use different elements from print sources to make it easier to track the source. The following chart lists the elements most commonly used in both print and

---

✔ DIFFERENCES BETWEEN CITATIONS FOR PRINT AND ELECTRONIC SOURCES

Print Source	**Electronic Source**
Place of publication and name of publisher	Protocol and address
(Upper Saddle River, NJ: Prentice Hall)	http://www.prenhall.com
Date of publication	Dates of publication and access (do not include access date if identical to publication date)
Author's name	Author's name or alias
Complete title of source	Title of Web site or file
Page numbers	Page or paragraph numbers if available

electronic citations. If you are not sure what needs to be included in the citation, provide as much information as possible. It is better to give too much information than too little.

60 b Guidelines for compiling a COS Works Cited list

Title. The title *Works Cited* appears centered at the top of your bibliography page. It should not be enclosed in quotation marks, boldfaced, italicized, or underlined.

Format and content. If your paper is presented in print, the Works Cited list should begin on a separate page numbered sequentially with the rest of the paper. For a hypertext publication, a separate file is often used for the Works Cited list, with a link provided in the table of contents.

Follow the MLA guidelines in Chapter 55 for content and format as well as arrangement of entries in the Works Cited list.

Authors' names. If an author's name is given, use it. Keep in mind that finding the author of a source may not be simple. Often, online writers use an alias or go by their login or user name. You may list a source by these alternative names if they are the only ones you can find.

In humanities style, the author's full first and middle names (if available) and last name are listed, and in scientific style, the author's full last name and first and middle initials are used. When there is more than one author, the second and subsequent authors are listed by first name (humanities style) or first initial (scientific style) followed by the full last name. If an author's name cannot be identified, cite the source by its title.

Capitalization and special treatment of titles. With the title of complete works (books, periodicals), use italics rather than underlining. (Since hypertext links are underlined online, an underlined title might confuse your audience.) Also italicize the titles of online sites and the names of information services.

In humanities style, titles of articles should be enclosed in quotation marks and all major words should be capitalized. In scientific style, titles of articles should not be distinguished in any way (i.e., no boldface, italics, or underlining), and only the first word of the title and proper nouns need to be capitalized. If a title is not available, use the file name.

Place of publication, publisher, and electronic address. The city of publication and publisher often do not apply to Web sites and other electronic sources. In those cases, the electronic address or uniform resource locator (URL) is used to find documents.

The URL must be provided so that readers trying to access a Web site will be able to find it themselves. For long addresses that exceed a line, follow MLA style: break only after slashes and do not hyphenate.

For electronic sources such as software and certain electronic publications, a publisher and city are usually listed and should be cited.

Version or file number. When applicable, provide the specific version or file number of a program you cite.

Document date or date of last revision. Cite a page's publication date or date of last revision, when available, only if it is different from the access date. This date is often found at the bottom of a source.

Date of access. Because online sources often change, locating material may be difficult. Always provide the date of access for a source so that your audience has a better idea of the version to which you refer. The date falls at the end of a citation in parentheses and follows a day-month-year format (for example, *22 Feb. 2001*).

Navigation points. On the World Wide Web, a given site is usually considered to be one page, regardless of its length. When available, cite any helpful navigational aids, such as page references, paragraph numbers, or parts. These aids should appear at the end of your citation, separated by commas. Keep in mind that often these aids are not available.

60 C Preparing a COS bibliography

Citations in a COS-style bibliography should adhere to the following models.

HUMANITIES STYLE

Author's Last Name, First and Middle Names. "Title of Docu-

INDENT 5 ———— ment" *Title of Complete Work* [if applicable]. Version or
SPACES

file number [if applicable]. Document date or date of last

revision [if different from access date]. Protocol and

URL, access path or directories (date of access).

SCIENTIFIC STYLE

Author's Last Name, First and Middle Initial(s). (Date of

INDENT 5 ———— document [if different from date accessed]). Title of
SPACES

document. *Title of complete work* [if applicable]. Version or file number [if applicable]. (Edition or revision [if applicable]). Protocol and URL, access path, or directories (date of access).

For more specific examples, refer to the models that follow.

■ COS humanities format

1. A site on the World Wide Web

Blackmon, Samantha. *Cows in the Classroom? MOOs and MUDs and MUSHes*

. . . *Oh My!* 24 Aug. 2000. http://www.sla.purdue.edu/people/engl/

blackmon/moo/index.html (11 Mar. 2001).

2. A revised or modified Web site

Grant, William E., and Ken Dvorak. *The American 1890s:* A *Chronology.* Mod.

Spring 2000. http://www.bgsu.edu/departments/acs/1890s/america

.html (22 Nov. 2000).

If the site is revised, use the abbreviation *Rev.* instead of *Mod.*

3. A maintained or compiled Web site

E-Zine-List. Maint. John Labovitz. 8 Mar. 2000. http://www.meer.net/~johnl/

e-zine-list (15 Sep. 2000).

If the site is compiled, use the abbreviation *Comp.* instead of *Maint.*

4. An article from a periodical

Kaplan, Carl S. "Suit Considers Computer Files." *The New York Times.* 28 Sep.

2000. http://www.nytimes.com/2000/09/28/technology/29CYBERLAW

.html (13 Oct. 2000).

5. An article in an online journal

Winickoff, Jonathan P., et al. "Verve and Jolt: Deadly New Internet Drugs."

Pediatrics 106:4 (Oct. 2000). http://www.pediatrics.org/cgi/content/

abstract/106/4/829 (10 May 2000).

6. A work by a group or organization

SIL International. "Ethnomusicology: 'Studying Music from the Outside In

and from the Inside Out.'" 7 May 1999. http://www.sil.org/anthro/

ethnomusicology.htm (20 Feb. 2000).

7. Corporate home pages and information

Pearson PLC. "Pearson Home page." 1999. http://www.pearson.com (12 Apr.

2001).

8. Government information and sites

Central Intelligence Agency. "Speeches and Testimony." 6 Oct. 2000.

http://www.cia.gov/cia/public_affairs/speeches/speeches.html (18 Dec.

2000).

9. A book

A BOOK PREVIOUSLY PUBLISHED IN PRINT

Brontë, Charlotte. *Jane Eyre.* London: Service & Paton, 1887. 1999. *University*

of Maryland ReadingRoom. http://www.inform.umd.edu/EdRes/Reading

Room/Fiction/Cbronte/JaneEyre/ (15 Sep. 2000).

AN ONLINE BOOK

Shires, Bob. *CPR (Cardiopulmonary Resuscitation) Guide.* 17 Jan. 2000.

http://www.memoware.com/Category=Medicine_ResultSet=1.htm

(17 Apr. 2000).

10. A graphic, video, or audio file on the page

owl.gif. 2000. "Original Free Clipart." *Clipart.com.* http://www.free-clip-

art.net/index4.shtml (27 Oct. 2000).

11. Personal electronic mail (e-mail)

Torres, Elizabeth. "Re: Puerto Rican Baseball History." Personal e-mail (11

Sep. 2000).

12. A posting to a discussion list

Sheldon, Amy. "Re: Request for Help on Sexism Inscription." 2 Jan. 2000.

FLING List for Feminists in Linguistics. http://listserv.linguistlist.org (14

Nov. 2000).

13. A posting to a newsgroup or forum

Markowitz, Al. "The Changing Face of Work: A Look at the Way We Work."

28 Sep. 2000. http://yourturn.npr.org/cgi-bin/WebX?50@121

.HjNGardZdaj^0@.ee7a9aa (8 Jan. 2001).

14. An archived posting

Radev, Dragomir R. "Natural Language Processing FAQ." 16 Sep. 1999.

Institute of Information and Computing Sciences. http://www.cs.ruu.nl/

wais/html/na-dir/natural-lang-processing-faq.html (27 Jan. 2000).

15. Online reference sources (encyclopedias, dictionaries, thesauruses, and style manuals)

Nordenberg, Tamar. "Make No Mistake! Medical Errors Can Be Deadly

Serious." *Brittanica.com.* Sep./Oct. 2000. Ebsco Publishing.

http://britannica.com/bcom/original/article/0,5744,12430,00.html (16

Nov. 2000).

16. Computer information services and online databases

Raintree Nutrition, Inc. "Pata de Vaca." Jun. 2000. *Raintree Tropical Plant*

Database. http://www.rain-tree.com/patadevaca.htm (9 Sep. 2000).

17. Gopher site

"Elections." May 1996. gopher://israel-info.gov.il/00/facts/state/st4 (27 Dec.

2000).

18. FTP site

Project Gutenberg. *Ibiblio.org.* 26 Mar. 2000. ftp://metalab.unc.edu/pub/docs/

books/gutenberg/ (12 Aug. 2000).

The abbreviation *FTP* stands for *file transfer protocol.*

19. A telnet site

Schweller, Kenneth G. "How to Design a Bot." *Collegetown MOO.* 28 May

1999. telnet://galaxy.bvu.edu.7777 (16 Nov. 2000).

20. A synchronous communication

Dominguez, Jose. "Interchange." *Daedalus Online.* http://daedalus.

pearsoned.com (11 Mar. 2001).

21. Software

Wresch, William. *Writer's Helper.* Vers. 4.0. Upper Saddle River, NJ: Prentice

Hall, 1998.

2 COS scientific format

1. Web site

Blackmon, S. (2000, August 24). Cows in the classroom? MOOs and MUDs

and MUSHes . . . oh my! http://www.sla.purdue.edu/people/engl/

blackmon/moo/index.html (11 Mar. 2001).

2. A revised or modified Web site

Grant, W. E., and K. Dvorak. (2000). The American 1890s: A chronology. (Mod.

Spring 2000). http://www.bgsu.edu/departments/acs/1890s

america.html (22 Nov. 2000).

If the site is revised, use the abbreviation *Rev.* instead of *Mod.*

3. A maintained or compiled Web site

E-zine-list. (2000, March 8). (John Labovitz, Maint.). http://www.meer.net/

~johnl/e-zine-list (15 Sep. 2000).

If the site is compiled, use the abbreviation *Comp.* instead of *Maint.*

4. An article from a periodical

Kaplan, C. S. (2000, September 28). Suit considers computer files. *The New*

York Times. http://www.nytimes.com/2000.09/28/technology/

29CYBERLAW.html (13 Oct. 2000).

5. An article in an online journal

Winickoff, J. P., et al. (2000, October). Verve and jolt: Deadly new Internet

drugs. *Pediatrics, 106*(4). http://www.pediatrics.org/cgi/content/

abstract/106/4/829 (10 May 2000).

6. A work by a group or organization

SIL International. (1999, May 7). Ethnomusicology: "Studying music from the

outside in and from the inside out." http://www.sil.org/anthro/

ethnomusicology.htm (20 Feb 2000).

7. Corporate home pages and information

Pearson PLC. (1999). Pearson home page. http://www.pearson.com (12 Apr.

2001).

8. Government information and sites

Central Intelligence Agency. (2000, October 6). Speeches and testimony.

http:5//www.cia.gov/cia/public_affairs/speeches/speeches.html (18

Dec. 2000).

9. A book

A BOOK PREVIOUSLY PUBLISHED IN PRINT

Brontë, C. (1887). *Jane Eyre.* London: Service & Paton (1999). *University of*

Maryland ReadingRoom. http://www.inform.umd.edu/EdRes/

ReadingRoom/Fiction/Cbronte/JaneEyre/ (15 Sep. 2000).

AN ONLINE BOOK

Shires, B. (2000, January 17). CPR (cardiopulmonary resuscitation) guide.

http://www.memoware.com/Category=Medicine_ResultSet=1.htm (17

Apr. 2000).

10. A graphic, video, or audio file on the page
owl.gif [graphic file]. (2000). Original free clipart. *Clipart.com.*

http://www.free-clip-art.net/index4.shtml (27 Oct. 2000).

11. Personal electronic mail (e-mail)
Torres, E. Re: Puerto Rican baseball history. [Personal e-mail]. (11 Sep. 2000).

12. A posting to a discussion list
Sheldon, A. (2000, January 2). Re: Request for help on sexism inscription.

FLING List for Feminists in Linguistlist. http://listserv.linguistic.org (14

Nov. 2000).

13. A posting to a newsgroup or forum
Markowitz, A. (2000, September 28). The changing face of work: A look at the

way we work. http://yourturn.npr.org/cgi-bin/WebX?50@121

.HjNGardZdaj^0@.ee7a9aa (8 Jan. 2001).

14. An archived posting
Radev, D. R. (1999, September 16). Natural language processing FAQ.

Institute of Information and Computing Sciences. http://www.cs.ruu.nl/

wais/html/na-dir/natural-lang-processing-faq.html (27 Jan. 2000).

15. Online reference sources (encyclopedias, dictionaries, thesauruses, and style manuals)
Nordenberg, T. (2000, October). Make no mistake! Medical errors can be

deadly serious. In *Britannica.com.* Ebsco Publishing. http://britannica

.com/bcom/original/article/0,5744,12430,00.html (16 Nov. 2000).

16. Computer information services and online databases

Raintree Nutrition, Inc. (2000, June). Pata de Vaca. *Raintree Tropical Plant*

Database. http://www.rain-tree.com/patadevaca.htm (9 Sep. 2000).

17. Gopher site

Elections. (1996, May). gopher: //israel-info.gov.il/00/facts/state/st4 (27 Dec.

2000).

18. FTP site

Project Gutenberg. (2000, March 26). *Ibiblio.org.* ftp://metalab.unc.edu/pub/

docs/books/gutenberg/ (12 Aug. 2000).

19. A telnet site

Schweller, K. G. (1999, May 28). How to design a bot. *Collegetown MOO.*

telnet://galaxy.bvu.edu:7777 (16 Nov. 2000).

20. A synchronous communication

Dominguez, J. Interchange. *Daedalus Online.* http://daedalus.pearsoned.com

(11 Mar. 2001).

21. Software

Wresch, W. (1998). *Writer's Helper.* (Vers. 4.0). Upper Saddle River, NJ:

Prentice Hall.

61 Writing Essay Examinations

Essay examinations are common writing assignments in the humanities, but they are important in the social and physical sciences as well. Such exams require students to sit and compose responses to instructors' questions about information, issues, and ideas covered in the course. Instructors assign essay exams instead of "objective" tests (multiple choice, matching, true/false) because they want students to go beyond identifying facts and to demonstrate mastery of concepts covered in the course and the ability to draw their own conclusions about what they have studied.

The best preparation for taking an essay exam is to acquire a thorough knowledge of the subject matter. If you have attended all the classes, done all the assignments, and read all the texts, you should be in a good position to write such essays. If you have also kept journals, annotated your text, discussed course material with other students, and posed possible essay exam questions, you should be in even better shape for such writing. Equally important is your strategic thinking about the course and its syllabus. If the course was divided into different topics or themes, think of a general question on each one; if it has been arranged chronologically, create questions focusing on comparisons or cause-and-effect relations within a particular period or across periods. Consider, too, the amount of class time spent on each topic, and pay proportionately greater attention to emphasized areas.

While there is no substitute for careful preparation, using certain writing strategies will enhance your presentation of information in virtually any exam. This chapter outlines suggestions for writing under examination pressure.

61 a Understanding the question

1 Read the whole examination

Before answering a single question, quickly read over the whole exam to assess its scope and focus. Answering three of four questions in fifty minutes requires a different approach from answering, say, five of eight questions in seventy-five minutes. If you are given a choice among several questions, select questions that together will demonstrate your knowledge of the whole course rather than answering two that might result in repetitious writing. Finally, decide which questions you are best prepared to answer, and respond to those first. Budget your time, however, so you can deal fully with the others later.

Starting with the questions you know you can answer relaxes you, warms you up intellectually, and often triggers knowledge about the others in the process.

2 Attend to direction words

Once you decide which questions you will answer, take a moment to analyze each one before you begin to write. Then focus closely on one particular question; read it several times. Underline the direction word that identifies the task you are to carry out, and understand what it is telling you to do.

Define or *identify* asks for the distinguishing traits of a term, subject, or event but does not require an interpretation or judgment. Use appropriate terminology learned in the course. For example, the question *Define John Locke's concept of tabula rasa* is best answered by using some of Locke's terminology along with your own.

Describe may ask for a physical description (*Describe a typical performance in ancient Greek theater*), or it may be used more loosely to request an explanation of a process, phenomenon, or event (*Describe the culture and practices of the mound builders*). Such questions generally do not ask for interpretation or judgment but require abundant details and examples.

Summarize asks for an overview or a synthesis of the main points. Keep in mind that *Summarize the impact of the Battle of Gettysburg on the future conduct of the war* asks only that you hit the highlights; avoid getting bogged down in too much detail.

Compare and contrast suggests that you point out both similarities and differences, generally between two subjects but sometimes among three or more. Note that questions using other direction

words may also ask for comparison or contrast: *Describe the differences between the works of Monet and Manet.*

Analyze asks that you write about a subject in terms of its component parts. The subject may be concrete (*Analyze the typical seating plan of a symphony orchestra*) or abstract (*Analyze the ethical ramifications of Kant's categorical imperative*). In general, your response should examine one part at a time.

Interpret asks for a discussion or analysis of a subject based on internal evidence and your own particular viewpoint: for example, *Interpret Flannery O'Connor's short story "Revelation" in terms of your understanding of her central religious and moral themes.*

Explain asks what causes something or how something operates. Such questions may ask for an interpretation and an evaluation. *Explain the function of color in the work of Picasso,* for example, clearly asks for interpretation of the artist's use of color; although it does not explicitly ask for a judgment, some judgment might be appropriate.

Evaluate or *critique* asks for a judgment based on clearly articulated analysis and reasoning. *Evaluate Plato's concept of the ideal state* and *Critique the methodology of this experiment,* for example, ask for your opinions on these topics. Be analytical and lead up to a final statement, but don't feel that your conclusion must be completely one-sided. In many cases, you will also want to cite more experienced judgments to back up your own.

Discuss or *comment on* is a general request, which allows you considerable latitude. Your answers to questions such as *Discuss the effects of monetarist economic theories on current Third World development* often let you demonstrate what you know especially well. Use terms and ideas as they have been discussed during the semester, and add your own insights with care and thoughtfulness.

61 b Writing a good answer

Instructors give essay exams to find out not only how much students know about course content but how thoroughly they understand and can discuss it. If they were interested in testing only for specific facts and information, they could give true/false or multiple choice tests. Therefore, the best essay answers will be accurate but also highly focused, carefully composed, and easy to follow. The following are two examples of answers to an essay question from a music history examination. Which do you think is the better answer?

Explain the origin and concept of neoclassicism, and identify a significant composer and works associated with the development of this music.

ESSAY 1   Neoclassicism in music is a return to the ideas of the classical period of earlier centuries. It is dry and emphasizes awkward and screeching sounds and does not appeal to the listener's emotions. It does not tell a story but presents only a form. It is hard to listen to or understand compared to more romantic music such as Beethoven composed. Neoclassical music developed in the early part of the twentieth century. Stravinsky is the most famous composer who developed this difficult music.

ESSAY 2   Neoclassical music developed as a reaction against the romantic music of the nineteenth century. Stravinsky, the most famous neoclassical composer, took his style and themes from the eighteenth-century classical music of Bach, Handel, and Vivaldi rather than Beethoven or Brahms. Stravinsky emphasizes technique and form instead of story or image, with his atonal compositions appealing more to the intellect than the emotions. Rite of Spring (1913) and Symphony of Psalms (1940) are good examples.

Both answers are approximately the same length, and both are approximately correct. However, the second answer is stronger for the following reasons: it is more carefully organized (from general to specific); it includes more information (names, works, dates); it uses more careful disciplinary terms (*form, technique, image*); and it answers all parts of the question (the first answer omits the titles of works). It also does not digress into the writer's personal value judgments (that neoclassical is hard to listen to), which the question did not ask for.

The following strategies will help you write more carefully composed answers.

▮ Planning and outlining

Take one or two minutes per question to make a potential outline of your answer. For example, if asked to compare and contrast three impressionist painters, decide in advance which three you will write about and in which order. While ideas will come as you start writing, having a plan of organization at the beginning allows you to write more effectively. If you create a quick outline in the margins of your paper or even just hold it in your head, your writing will include more focused information, presented in a more

logical order (as in essay 2 above) rather than scattered randomly throughout (as in essay 1 above).

2 Leading with a thesis

The surest way to receive full credit on an essay question is to answer the question briefly and directly in your first sentence. In other words, state your answer in a **thesis** statement which the rest of your essay explains, supports, and defends. In the example on page 869, essay 2 opens with a thesis statement: *Neoclassical music developed as a reaction against the romantic music of the nineteenth century.* The rest of the essay explains and supports this statement.

3 Writing with specific detail, examples, and illustrations

Remember that most good writing contains specific information that lets readers see for themselves the evidence for your position. Use as many supportive specifics as you can; memorize names, works, dates, and ideas as you prepare for the exam so you can recall them accurately if they are needed. Individual statistics alone are not worth much, but when used as evidence along with strong reasoning, these specifics make the difference between mediocre and good answers.

4 Providing context

In answering a question posed by an instructor who is an expert in the field, it is tempting to assume your instructor does not want a full explanation and thus to answer too briefly. However, you are being asked to demonstrate how much *you* understand; you should view each question as an opportunity to show how much you know about the subject. Briefly explain any concepts or terms that are central to your answer. Take the time to fit any details into the larger scheme of the subject. In essay 2 on page 869, for instance, it is clear that the second writer understood the relation of each musical movement to the century that produced it.

5 Using the technical terminology of the discipline

Be careful not to drop in names or terms gratuitously, unless these names and terms have been an integral part of the course. Make sure you define any other terms, use them appropriately, and

spell them correctly. Essay exams also test your facility with the language and concepts peculiar to a particular discipline. In the music example on page 869, it pays to know the correct terms for historical periods (*classical, romantic, neoclassical*) as well as technical terms used in discussing music (*image, tone*).

 STRATEGIES FOR WRITING ESSAY EXAMINATIONS

1. Skim the whole examination and block your time. Read quickly through the whole exam so that you know what you're being asked to do, and allot blocks of time for tackling each section.

2. Choose your essay questions carefully. The essay questions you answer should allow you to write on what you know best. Choose a mix of answers to show your range of knowledge.

3. Focus on direction words. For each question you have chosen, it is important to recognize what your instructor is really asking, for this understanding enables you to answer the question successfully.

4. Plan and outline each essay. Prepare a rough outline of your answer by identifying the key points you need to make and organizing them well.

5. Write thesis-first essays. Doing this illustrates your confidence in knowing the answer and setting out to prove it. (For more information on thesis-first-organized essays, see 9f1.)

6. Include specifics—details, examples, illustrations. Backing up statements with evidence shows your mastery of the subject matter. Include short, accurate, powerful quotations where relevant, citing each by author, title, and date, as necessary. To help you remember, focus on key words and jot them in the margins near your answer.

7. Use the terms and methods used by the discipline. Enter in the conversation of a particular discipline by using its accepted terms and methods.

8. Provide context but stay focused. Explain all your points as if your audience did not have the understanding your instructor does, but keep all your information focused on simply answering that one question. If you know more than time allows you to tell, end your answer with an outline of key points that you would discuss if you had more time.

9. Proofread your answers in the last five minutes before handing in the finished exam. Even this short step back from composing will allow you to spot errors and omissions.

6 Staying focused

Answer what the question asks. Attend to all parts of an answer, cover those parts, and once you have done that, do not digress or add extraneous information. While it may seem interesting to hear your other ideas on the subject at hand, some instructors may consider this digressing as reflecting unfocused attention.

PART NINE

A Grammar Reference

www.prenhall.com/fulwiler

A Grammar Reference

www.prenhall.com/fulwiler

On *The Blair Handbook, Fourth Edition,* Web site you can find

- Information on nouns, pronouns, and verbs
- Sentence elements
- Sentence structure

62 Parts of Speech

There are two basic approaches to English grammar. One looks at individual words and asks, "What kind of word is this?" This way looks at words as **parts of speech:** nouns, pronouns, verbs, adjectives, prepositions, conjunctions, and interjections. The other approach asks, "What function does each word or group of words serve in the sentence?" This question leads to an analysis of **sentence elements.** (See Chapter 63.)

To know what part of speech a word is, you must look not only at the word itself but also at its meaning, position, and use in a sentence. The word *ride,* for example, can be either a verb or a noun.

NOUN   They went for a *ride.*

VERB   They *ride* their horses.

62 a Nouns

Nouns are words that name persons, animals, places, things, or ideas: *woman, Lassie, Grand Canyon, tree,* and *virtue* are all nouns.

Common nouns, or **generic nouns,** can apply to any member of a class or group: *scientist, horse, state, ship, religion.* They are generally not capitalized. **Proper nouns** name particular people, animals, places, or things: *Marie Curie, Black Beauty, Kentucky, USS Constitution, Catholicism.* They are almost always capitalized. (See 46c.)

Concrete nouns refer to things that can be seen, heard, touched, smelled, or tasted: *butterfly, telephone, ice, fudge.* **Abstract nouns** refer to ideas or concepts that cannot be directly sensed: *nature, communication, temperature, temptation.* (For the uses of concrete and abstract nouns, see 27a.)

Count nouns refer to items that can readily be counted: *one book, two books; one idea, several ideas.* **Noncount nouns** (or *mass*

nouns) refer to entities that cannot be counted individually: _sand, water, fame._ These are seldom made plural.

Collective nouns, such as _crowd, couple,_ and _flock,_ refer to groups of similar things. (See 34n for a discussion of when to treat collective nouns as singular and when to treat them as plural.)

Singular and plural nouns

Nouns that refer to a single unit are **singular:** _boy, town, box._ Those that refer to two or more are **plural:** _boys, towns, boxes._

Most nouns add _-s_ or _-es_ to the singular to create the plural. A few nouns change spelling in other ways to form the plural: _goose, geese; child, children; man, men; medium, media._ And a few stay the same regardless of number: _sheep, sheep._ (For more on forming plurals, see 42b and 45b3.)

Possessive forms of nouns

Nouns change form to show possession, ownership, or connections, usually by adding an apostrophe and an _-s: the king's son, the town's mayor._ This form is called the **possessive case.** (For guidelines on forming possessives of plural nouns and nouns that end in _-s_, see 42b and 45b3.)

62 b Pronouns

A **pronoun** is a word that substitutes for a noun or another pronoun. The word for which the pronoun substitutes is called its **antecedent.**

                antecedent   pronoun

Sean helped Aspasia paint her room.

                pronoun   antecedent

Because of its construction, the boat was unsinkable.

Usually an antecedent appears before the pronoun, but it may also follow the pronoun. (For a description of pronoun reference to clear antecedents, see 36a.) A pronoun must agree with (or correspond to) its antecedent in terms of person, number, and gender. (See 36f–36j.)

Kinds of pronouns

Personal pronouns

Personal pronouns, such as *me, you, their,* and *it,* refer to specific people, animals, places, things, or ideas.

I asked *you* to buy *it.*

Personal pronouns change their form to show **person.** First-person pronouns refer to the speaker or writer directly: *I, we.* Second-person pronouns refer to those being addressed: *you.* Third-person pronouns refer to someone other than the speaker or writer or those being addressed: *he, she, it, they.*

Personal pronouns also change form to show **number.** They are either singular (*I, he, she, it*) or plural (*we, they*). The pronoun *you* is the same whether it is plural or singular.

Singular personal pronouns change form to show **gender.** They are masculine (*he*), feminine (*she*), or neuter (*it*).

Personal pronouns also change form to show **case.** They are subjective (*he*), objective (*him*), or possessive (*his*). (See 36k–36r and 61b2.)

Indefinite pronouns

Indefinite pronouns, such as *anyone, everybody, something, many, few,* and *none,* do not require antecedents because they do not refer to any specific person, animal, place, thing, or idea. Often they are used to denote a quantity.

Many are called, but *few* are chosen.

Indefinite pronouns change form to indicate the possessive case by adding an apostrophe and an -*s: anyone's idea, everyone's preference.* They do not change form to show person, number, or gender. Most are either always singular (*someone*) or always plural (*many*). A few can be either singular or plural, depending on context. (See 36j.)

Demonstrative pronouns

Demonstrative pronouns, such as *this, that, these,* and *those,* point out a specific person, place, or thing.

This is the largest box we have.

This and *that* are singular; *these* and *those* are plural.

These words are demonstrative pronouns only when they are not immediately followed by a noun, in which case they are adjectives: *I enjoyed reading* this *book.*

Relative pronouns

A **relative pronoun,** such as *who, which,* or *that,* introduces a dependent clause and "relates" that clause to an antecedent elsewhere in the sentence.

He chose the tool *that* worked best.

Some relative pronouns are also indefinite: *whoever, what, whatever, whichever.* Some relative pronouns change form to show case. (See 61b2.)

Interrogative pronouns

Interrogative pronouns, such as *who, what,* and *whose,* are used to ask questions. They change form only to show case.

Who is there?

Reflexive and intensive pronouns

Pronouns ending in *-self* or *-selves,* such as *myself, yourself,* and *themselves,* are **reflexive pronouns** when they refer back to, or "reflect," the subject of the sentence.

Dave cut *himself* while shaving.

The same pronouns are called **intensive pronouns** when they are used to emphasize, or "intensify," an antecedent.

I talked to the president *herself.*

Reflexive and intensive pronouns change form to show *person, number,* and *gender,* just as personal pronouns do.

Reciprocal pronouns

The **reciprocal pronouns** *each other* and *one another* are used to describe an action or state that is shared between two or more people, animals, places, things, or ideas.

The investigators helped *one another* with the research.

Reciprocal pronouns have possessive forms: *each other's, one another's.* Otherwise, they do not change form.

PRONOUNS

PERSONAL

I, me, my, mine	it, its
you, your, yours	we, us, our, ours
he, him, his	they, them, their, theirs
she, her, hers	

INDEFINITE

all	each	many	none	some
any	either	more	no one	somebody
anybody	everybody	most	nothing	someone
anyone	everyone	much	one	something
anything	everything	neither	several	what
both	few	nobody		

DEMONSTRATIVE

this	that	these	those

RELATIVE

that	whatever	whichever	whoever	whomever
what	which	who	whom	whose

INTERROGATIVE

what	which	who	whom	whose
whatever	whichever	whoever	whomever	

REFLEXIVE AND INTENSIVE

myself	yourself	himself	herself	itself
ourselves	yourselves	themselves	oneself	

RECIPROCAL

each other	one another

2 Pronoun case

Case indicates the role a word plays in a sentence, whether it is a subject, an object, or a possessive. To show the possessive case, nouns change form, usually by adding an apostrophe and -s to the end of the word. In the subjective and objective cases, nouns have the same form. Personal pronouns, indefinite pronouns, and the

relative or interrogative pronouns *who* and *whoever* change form to show all three cases.

subjective   possessive

The book she found was not hers.

objective

The class was easy for her.

Indefinite pronouns ending in *-one* and *-body* form the possessive case by adding *'s* just as nouns do: *somebody's, anyone's, someone's.* The other indefinite pronouns form possessives by using *of.*

He has the admiration *of many* but the confidence *of none.*

(For a list of personal pronouns by case, see the box in 36k.)

The **subjective case** indicates that a pronoun is the subject of a clause or is a subject complement.

We should leave now.

It was *she who* wanted to leave.

The **objective case** indicates that a pronoun is the object of a verb, a preposition, or a verbal.

Whom did they *choose?*

The judging seemed unfair *to us.*

Seeing her made the holiday complete.

The **possessive case** indicates possession, ownership, or connection. Possessive personal pronouns have two forms: adjective forms (*my, your*) modify a noun or gerund; noun forms (*mine, yours*) stand alone as a subject or complement.

That is *my* hat.

The hat is *mine.*

(For more on choosing pronoun case, see 36k–36r.)

A **verb** describes an action or state of being.

The logger *chops* the tree.

The air *is* fragrant with the scent of pine.

The verb of a sentence changes form to show person, number, tense, voice, and mood. The *person* indicates who performed the action. The *number* indicates how many people performed the action. The **tense** indicates when the action was performed. The **voice** indicates whether the grammatical subject of the sentence acts or is acted upon. The **mood** indicates the speaker's reaction to or opinion of the action.

PERSON	I *write.* She *writes.*
NUMBER	He *sings.* They *sing.*
TENSE	She *argues.* She *argued.*
VOICE	She *wrote* the book. The book was *written.*
MOOD	I *am* a millionaire. If I *were* a millionaire . . .

A verb with a specific person and number is called a **finite verb.** A verb form without these properties is called a **verbal.** (See 62c5.) For complete information on verb person, number, tense, and mood, see Chapter 34. For information on verb voice, see 27c and 62c4.

In addition to one-word verbs, English has many **phrasal verbs** or *multiple-word verbs.* These consist of a verb plus a **particle,** a word that may serve as a preposition in other contexts but which is so important to the meaning of the phrasal verb that it is considered a part of it. Both the verb and the particle are necessary to convey the meaning of the phrasal verb, and that meaning usually cannot be determined by examining the parts individually. In the sentence *That performance came off very well,* for example, *came off* is a phrasal verb; its meaning (*succeeded*) is not easy to determine by considering the separate meanings of the words *come* and *off.*

▋ Auxiliary verbs

In some sentences, the verb may be more than one word. Such verbs are called **verb phrases.** They consist of a **main verb,** which expresses the action or state of the subject of the sentence, and one

or more **auxiliary verbs** (or *helping verbs*), which precede the main verb to indicate certain forms of the verb.

We washed the dishes, but we could have helped more with the housekeeping chores.

Forms of the verbs *be, do,* and *have* are the most common auxiliary verbs. These auxiliaries are used to form certain tenses, add emphasis, ask questions, make negative statements, and form the passive voice. These verbs can also stand alone as main verbs. When used as auxiliaries, these verbs change to show person, number, and tense.

Certain auxiliary verbs, called **modal auxiliaries** or *modals,* add to the verb the meanings of desire, intent, permission, possibility, or obligation. Modals are not usually used alone as main verbs. English has both *one-word modals* and *phrasal modals* (or *multiple-word modals*).

ONE-WORD MODALS

can	may	must	should	would
could	might	shall	will	

PHRASAL MODALS

be able to	be supposed to	have got to
be allowed to	had better	ought to
be going to	have to	used to

The one-word modals do not change form to show person, number, or tense: *I can sing, and you can dance.* Most of the phrasal modals do change form to show person, number, and tense: *I am able to sing, and you are able to dance.* The phrasal modals *had better, ought to,* and *used to* do not change form.

2 Transitive and intransitive verbs

Some verbs require a **direct object,** a word or words that indicate who or what received the action of the verb. (See 63c.)

direct object

She threw the ball.

A verb that has a direct object is a **transitive verb.** A verb that does not have a direct object is an **intransitive verb.** Many verbs may be transitive or intransitive, depending on the context.

TRANSITIVE   Joey *grew* tomatoes last summer.

INTRANSITIVE   The tomatoes *grew* rapidly.

3 Linking verbs

Linking verbs include *be, become, seem,* and verbs describing sensations—*appear, look, feel, taste, smell, sound,* and so on. They link the subject of a sentence to an element, called a **subject complement,** that renames or identifies the subject. Subject complements can be nouns or adjectives. (See 63d.)

4 Voice

Most transitive verbs may be used in either the active or the passive voice. In a sentence using the **active voice,** the subject of the sentence is the person or thing performing the action or state expressed by the verb. In a sentence using the **passive voice,** the subject of the sentence is the person or thing acted upon.

ACTIVE   The keeper *blocked* the shot.

PASSIVE   The shot *was blocked* by the keeper.

The passive voice uses the past participle of the verb with a form of the verb *be* as an auxiliary verb. (See 62c1.) The object of the sentence in the active voice becomes the subject of the passive-voice sentence. The subject of the active-voice sentence, if it appears at all in the passive-voice sentence, is usually an *agent* following the preposition *by: Whales can be harmed by pollution.* Some passive-voice sentences do not have agents: *Many are found on beaches.*

5 Verbals

A *verbal* is a special verb form. It does not change form to show person or number. There are three types of verbals:

- **Infinitives:** the base form of the verb, usually preceded by the word *to* (*I like* to read)

- **Gerunds:** the *-ing* form of the verb, functioning as a noun (*I like* reading)

- **Participles:** either the past participle (usually ending in -ed or -d) or the present participle (ending in -ing) (*freshly* baked *bread, the* rising *moon*)

The infinitive changes form to show tense.

PRESENT
INFINITIVE
To sing at Carnegie Hall is her ambition.

PAST INFINITIVE
To have sung so well last night is something you should be proud of.

After prepositions and certain verbs, the *to* of an infinitive does not appear: *He did everything except wash the floor. She let them visit their cousins.*

A verbal can function as a noun or modifier, but it cannot function as the main verb of a sentence or clause.

NOUN
Jogging is a great form of exercise.

ADJECTIVE
We had *boiled* eggs for breakfast.

Verbals can form **verbal phrases** by taking objects, complements, and modifiers. (For more on verbal phrases, see 63e.)

62 d Adjectives and adverbs

Adjectives and **adverbs** modify—that is, they further describe, identify, or limit the meaning of other words. They have many similar properties, so sometimes adjectives and adverbs are grouped together as **modifiers.** The difference lies in what they modify. Adjectives modify nouns, pronouns, or phrases and clauses used as nouns.

The tourist spotted *scarlet* tanagers. [Modifies noun *tanagers*]

They were *beautiful.* [Modifies pronoun *they*]

To see them would be *delightful.* [Modifies phrase *to see them*]

Adverbs modify verbs, adjectives, verbals, or other adverbs; they can also modify clauses or entire sentences.

His judgment was made *hastily.* [Modifies verb *was made.*]

The feathers are *quite* beautiful. [Modifies adjective *beautiful.*]

Writing *well* takes practice. [Modifies verbal *writing.*]

She sings *very* nicely. [Modifies adverb *nicely*.]

Surprisingly, the band played for hours. [Modifies entire sentence.]

(See 35a for more on distinguishing adjectives and adverbs.)

Adjectives and adverbs come in three **degrees:** positive, comparative, and superlative. A modifier that makes no comparison is known as the **positive** form. A **comparative** adjective or adverb makes a comparison between two things. A **superlative** adjective or adverb distinguishes among three or more things.

POSITIVE   He lives in an *old* house.

COMPARATIVE   It is *older* than mine.

SUPERLATIVE   It is the *oldest* house in the county.

(See 35e for more on forming comparatives and superlatives.)

Kinds of adjectives

Adjectives that describe qualities or attributes are called **descriptive adjectives:** *gray* sky, *beautiful* garden. Adjectives that do not describe qualities but instead identify or specify the words they modify are called **limiting adjectives:** *this* sky, *my* garden.

Limiting adjectives include the **articles** *a, an,* and *the.* The word *the* is called the **definite article** because it identifies, or "defines," precisely which person or thing is being referred to. The words *a* and *an* are called **indefinite articles.** The choice between *a* and *an* depends on the initial sound of the following word: *a* precedes a consonant sound or a long *u* sound (*a monster, a university*) and *an* precedes any other vowel sound (*an apron*). (See the ESL box in 35a for more about using articles.)

Several types of *pronouns* can serve as limiting adjectives:

PERSONAL   She is going to buy *her* dog today.

RELATIVE   She hasn't decided *which* dog she will take.

DEMONSTRATIVE   She likes *that* dog very much.

INDEFINITE   But *every* dog looks good to her.

Numbers can also be limiting adjectives: *two dogs.*

Adjectives derived from proper nouns are called **proper adjectives:** *Alaskan, Shakespearean, British.* Like proper nouns, proper adjectives are capitalized. (See 46c.)

Sometimes a noun is used as an adjective without any change of form. Such a noun is called a *noun modifier*.

He works as a *masonry* contractor and employs six *concrete* finishers.

The police dispersed the rioters with a *water* cannon.

2 Kinds of adverbs

In addition to the usual kind of descriptive adverb (*quickly, often*), there are several special groups of words that are classified as adverbs. The **negators** *no* and *not* are considered adverbs. **Conjunctive adverbs,** such as *however* and *therefore,* modify an entire clause and express its relationship to another clause. (For a list of common conjunctive adverbs, see Chapter 25.) **Relative adverbs,** such as *where, why,* and *when,* introduce adjective or adverb clauses. (See 62f.)

NEGATOR   We were *not* ready.

CONJUNCTIVE
ADVERB   *However,* the train was leaving.

RELATIVE ADVERB We were visiting the house *where* I grew up.

62 e Prepositions

Words such as *to, with, by,* and *of* are **prepositions.** In addition to one-word prepositions such as these, English has several **phrasal prepositions** or *multiple-word prepositions,* which are made up of two or more words: *because of, except for, instead of.*

A preposition shows the relationship between a noun or pronoun—the **object** of the preposition—and other words in the sentence. The preposition, its object, and any associated modifiers are together called a **prepositional phrase.** In the sentence *I sat on the bed,* for example, *on* is a preposition, *bed* is the object of the preposition, and *on the bed* is a prepositional phrase. (For more on prepositional phrases, see 63e.)

A word is a preposition only if it introduces a phrase containing an object. Words that are commonly used as prepositions may also function as adverbs and as particles (parts of phrasal verbs).

PREPOSITION   I looked *up* the street.

ADVERB   The woman looked *up.*

PARTICLE   He looked *up* the word in the dictionary.

(For more on adverbs, see 62d. For more on phrasal verbs, see 62c.)

COMMON PREPOSITIONS

aboard	beneath	including	past
about	beside	in front of	regarding
above	besides	inside	since
according to	between	inside of	through
across	beyond	in spite of	throughout
after	but	into	till
against	by	like	to
ahead of	concerning	near	together with
along with	despite	next to	toward
among	down	notwithstanding	under
apart from	due to	of	underneath
around	during	off	unlike
as	except	on	until
as for	except for	onto	up
at	for	on top of	upon
away from	from	other than	up to
because of	in	out	via
before	in addition to	out of	with
behind	in back of	outside	within
below	in case of	over	without

62 f Conjunctions

The word **conjunction** comes from Latin words meaning "join" and "with." Conjunctions join two or more words, phrases, or clauses with one another. The **coordinating conjunctions**—*and, but, or, nor, for, so,* and *yet*—imply that the elements linked are equal or similar in importance.

Bill *and* I went shopping.

The bus will take you to the market *or* to the theater.

Correlative conjunctions appear in pairs: *either . . . or, neither . . . nor, both . . . and, not only . . . but also, whether . . . or.* Correlative conjunctions join pairs of similar words, phrases, or clauses.

Neither Jack *nor* his brother was in school this morning.

She *not only* sings *but also* dances.

Subordinating conjunctions, such as *after, before, when, where, while, because, if, although,* and *unless,* introduce ideas in dependent clauses. (See 25b for a list of subordinating conjunctions. See 62f for more on dependent and independent clauses.)

While you finish sewing, I will start dinner.

I left *because* I was angry.

Conjunctive adverbs, such as *however, therefore,* and *furthermore,* link independent clauses. The clauses they link must be separated by a semicolon or a period. (See 33b2 and 40a.)

I am finished; *therefore,* I am going home.

62 **g** Interjections

Interjections are words inserted, or "interjected," into a sentence. They may show surprise, dismay, or strong emotion. They most often appear in speech or dialogue, and their presence often calls for an exclamation point.

Ouch! That pipe is hot!

Gosh, you're muddy all over!

Yes, it does.

63 The Elements of a Sentence

The principal elements of a sentence are the subject and the predicate. In general, the **subject** names who or what performs the action of the sentence or tells whom or what the sentence is about. The subject consists of a noun, a pronoun, or another word or group of words that can serve as a noun, along with all of its modifiers. The **predicate** contains the verb of the sentence, along with its objects, its modifiers, and any words that refer to it. Both subject and predicate can be one word or many.

subject predicate

Rain fell.

subject   predicate

A woman in a yellow raincoat ran to catch the bus.

As in these examples, the subject usually comes at the beginning of a sentence and the predicate at the end. Sometimes, as in questions, the subject may follow part of the predicate.

predicate

subject

Do you know a good roofing contractor?

63 a Subjects

The **simple subject** of a sentence is the person or thing that acts, is described, or is acted upon. Usually this is a noun or pronoun, but it can also be a verbal, a phrase, or a clause that is used as a noun.

NOUN   Long *shadows* crept along the lawn.

PRONOUN   *He* looked exactly like a cowboy.

VERBAL	*Singing* is enjoyable.
PHRASE	*To work hard* is our lot in life.
CLAUSE	*That LeeAnn could dance* amazed us all.

The **complete subject** consists of the simple subject and all words that modify or directly relate to it. Elements of a complete subject can be adjectives, adverbs, phrases, or clauses.

Winning the last game of a dreadful season that included injuries, losing streaks, and a strike was small consolation to the team.

Here, the simple subject is *Winning. The last game* is the object of *Winning;* the prepositional phrase *of a dreadful season* modifies *game;* and the clause *that included injuries, losing streaks, and a strike* modifies *season;* thus, all are part of the subject.

A **compound subject** includes two or more subjects linked by a coordinating conjunction such as *and* or *or.*

Books, records, and *videotapes* filled the room.

An **implied subject** is one that is not stated directly but may be understood.

Come to the meeting to learn about the preschool program.

In this example, the subject is understood to be *you.* Commands have the implied subject *you.*

63 b Predicates

The **simple predicate** consists of the main verb of the sentence and any auxiliaries.

The candidate who wins the debate *will win* the election.

The **complete predicate** consists of the simple predicate and all words that modify or directly relate to it. Objects and complements are part of the predicate. Modifiers, including phrases, clauses, and single words, are part of the predicate if they modify the verb, object, or complement.

The farmer *gave the pigs enough food to last the weekend.*

The verb *gave* is the simple predicate. *Food* is the direct object of the verb and *pigs* is the indirect object of the verb. (See 63c.) The

words *the* and *enough* modify *pigs* and *food,* respectively. The phrase *to last the weekend* also modifies *food.*

A predicate in which two or more verbs have the same subject is a **compound predicate.** The following sentence has four verbs with the same subject:

> At the beach we *ate* our picnic, *swam* in the surf, *read* to each other, and *walked* on the sand.

Ate, swam, read, *and* walked *all have the subject* we.

63 c Objects of verbs

A **direct object** receives the action of a transitive verb.

> The company paid its *workers* earlier than usual.

Without the direct object *workers* and its modifiers, this sentence would be incomplete. If you read *The company paid,* you would not think it was a complete sentence. You would ask, *Whom or what did the company pay?* Asking a *Whom?* or *What?* question about the verb of a sentence is a good way to find its direct object. (For more on transitive verbs, see 62c2.)

An **indirect object** is a person or thing to whom (or for whom) the action of the verb is directed. It must be a noun or a pronoun that precedes the direct object. It cannot be accompanied by a preposition (or it becomes the object of the preposition, not an indirect object of the verb).

indirect object   direct object

The quarterback threw Lionel Fischer the ball.

To find an indirect object, identify the verb and the direct object and ask *To or for whom?* or *To or for what?* The answer is the indirect object. *He threw the ball to whom?* He threw it to *Lionel Fischer.*

63 d Complements

A **complement** renames or describes a subject or an object. A complement can be a noun, a pronoun, or an adjective.

A **subject complement** renames or describes the subject of a sentence. It follows a **linking verb,** a verb such as *be, become, seem,* or *appear.* (See 62c3.) A linking verb can be thought of as an

equal sign, linking two equivalent terms. Whatever is on the left of the equal sign, before the linking verb, is the subject; whatever is on the right is the subject complement.

subject   subject complement

My mother's uncle is the factory foreman.

subject   subject complement

The factory foreman is my mother's uncle.

An **object complement** appears following a direct object, modifying it or renaming it.

Tonight we will paint the town *red.*

In this example, the complement *red* describes the direct object *town.*

A noun or pronoun used as a complement is sometimes called a **predicate noun.** An adjective used as a complement is sometimes called a **predicate adjective.**

63 e Phrases

A group of related words lacking a subject, a predicate, or both is a **phrase.**

Verb phrase

A **verb phrase** consists of the main verb of a clause and its auxiliaries. It functions as the verb of a sentence.

verb phrase

The college has been having a difficult year.

Noun phrase

A **noun phrase** consists of a noun, a pronoun, or an infinitive or gerund serving as a noun, and all its modifiers.

noun phrase

The venerable and well-known institution is bankrupt.

Noun phrases may function as subjects, objects, or complements.

SUBJECT	*The college's president* is distraught.
OBJECT	He addressed *the board of trustees.*
COMPLEMENT	They became *a terrified mob.*

Prepositional phrase

A **prepositional phrase** consists of a preposition, its object, and any related modifiers.

prepositional phrase

The new book was hailed with great fanfare.

A prepositional phrase may function as an adjective or an adverb.

ADJECTIVE	He knows the difficulty *of the task.*
ADVERB	She arrived *at work* a little early.

Modifier phrase

A **modifier phrase** is any phrase that functions in a sentence as an adjective or an adverb. Prepositional phrases, infinitive phrases, participial phrases, and absolute phrases can be modifier phrases. Appositive phrases are considered modifier phrases.

Verbal phrase

A **verbal phrase** is one that contains a verbal plus any objects, complements, or modifiers. There are three kinds of verbals: infinitives, gerunds, and participles. (See 62c5.)

An **infinitive phrase** is one built around an **infinitive,** the base form of the verb usually preceded by *to.* Infinitive phrases can function as nouns, adjectives, or adverbs. When they function as nouns, they are usually subjects, complements, or direct objects.

NOUN	*To raise a family* is a lofty goal.
ADJECTIVE	He has the duty *to protect his children.*
ADVERB	My father worked *to provide for his family.*

A **gerund phrase** is one built around a gerund, the *-ing* form of a verb functioning as a noun. Gerund phrases always function as nouns; they are usually subjects, subject complements, direct objects, or the objects of prepositions.

SUBJECT	*Studying these essays* takes a lot of time.
SUBJECT COMPLEMENT	The key to success *is reading all the assignments.*
DIRECT OBJECT	My roommate likes *reading novels.*
OBJECT OF PREPOSITION	She can forgive me *for preferring short stories.*

A **participial phrase** is one built around a participle, either the past participle (usually ending in *-ed* or *-d*) or the present participle (ending in *-ing*). A participial phrase always functions as an adjective.

ADJECTIVE	*Striking a blow for freedom,* the Minutemen fired the "shot *heard round the world.*"

Appositive phrase

An **appositive** appears directly after a noun or pronoun and renames or further identifies it. (See 36m, 39c3.)

appositive phrase

Ralph Nader, a longtime consumer advocate, supports the new auto emissions proposal.

Absolute phrase

An **absolute phrase** modifies an entire sentence or clause. It consists of a noun or pronoun and a participle, together with any accompanying modifiers, objects, or complements.

absolute phrase

The work done, the boss called for a celebration.

63 f Clauses

Any group of related words with a subject and a predicate is a **clause.** A clause that can stand alone as a complete sentence is called an **independent clause** or a **main clause.**

The moon rose.

The best candidate will win the election.

A clause that cannot stand by itself as a complete sentence is called a **dependent clause** or a **subordinate clause.** It is dependent because it is introduced by a subordinating word, usually

either a subordinating conjunction (such as *because, when, unless*) or a relative pronoun (such as *who, which,* or *that*). (For lists of subordinating conjunctions and relative pronouns, see 25b.)

> The little girl laughed *when the moon rose.*

> I know *that the best candidate will win the election.*

Dependent clauses must be joined to independent clauses. They can be classified by the role they play in the sentence: they may be used as nouns, adjectives, or adverbs.

Noun clause

A **noun clause** is used as a noun would be—as a subject, an object, or a subject complement. A noun clause is usually introduced by a relative pronoun (such as *who, what,* or *which*) or by the subordinating conjunctions *how, when, where, whether,* or *why*.

SUBJECT   *What I want* is a good job.

DIRECT OBJECT   In class we learned *how we should write our résumés.*

SUBJECT
COMPLEMENT   English history is *what I know best.*

Adjective clause

An **adjective clause** modifies a noun or pronoun elsewhere in the sentence. Most adjective clauses begin with relative pronouns such as *who, whose,* or *that.* They can also begin with the relative adverbs *when, where,* or *why.* Adjective clauses are sometimes called **relative clauses.** Usually, an adjective clause directly follows the word it modifies.

The book that you reserved is now available.

The graduating seniors, who had just completed their exams, were full of high spirits.

Adjective clauses, along with adverb clauses, are also known as **modifier clauses.**

Adverb clause

An **adverb clause** modifies a verb, an adjective, an adverb, or an entire clause. Adverb clauses tell when, where, why, or how, or

they specify a condition. They are introduced by subordinating conjunctions (such as *although, than,* or *since*).

The fish ride the tide as far as it will carry them.

Now they can be caught more easily than at any other time.

Elliptical clauses

Clauses with words deliberately omitted are called *elliptical clauses.* The word left out of an elliptical clause may be the relative pronoun or subordinating conjunction introducing it, or it may be part of the predicate.

The man [that] I saw had one black shoe.

Marcia is as tall as I [am].

64 Sentence Classification and Sentence Patterns

Understanding how sentences are put together is particularly useful when you are editing for effectiveness and grammar. Sentences can be classified in two ways: by function and by grammatical structure. They can also be described in terms of their patterns.

64 a Classifying sentences by function

Declarative sentences make statements.

The road is long.

The Yankees have won the Eastern Division.

The normal word order for a declarative sentence is subject followed by predicate, although this order is occasionally inverted: *At the top of the hill stood a tree.* (See 64c.)

Interrogative sentences ask questions.

Who goes there?

Is there life on Mars?

Can pigs really fly?

An interrogative sentence can be introduced by an interrogative pronoun, as in the first example. (See 62b.) Or the subject can follow part of the verb, as in the second and third examples.

Imperative sentences make commands or requests.

Drive slowly.

Signal before changing lanes.

In commands, the subject is *you;* it is usually not stated but is implied: [*You*] *drive slowly.* The verb form used is always the base form.

Exclamatory sentences exclaim (and usually end with an exclamation point).

Oh, how I hate to get up in the morning!

(See 26c for more on the uses of these different types of sentences.)

64 b Classifying sentences by grammatical structure

Sentences are classified by grammatical structure according to whether they contain one or more dependent or independent clauses. (See 63f.)

A **simple sentence** consists of a single independent clause and no dependent clauses. Some simple sentences are brief. Others, if they contain modifier phrases or compound subjects, verbs, or objects, can be quite long.

Marmosets eat bananas.

Benny and Griselda, marmosets at our local zoo, eat at least fifteen bananas a day, in addition to lettuce, nuts, and sometimes each other's tails.

A **compound sentence** has two or more independent clauses and no dependent clauses.

     independent   independent

They grew tired of waiting, so they finally hailed a taxi.

A **complex sentence** contains one independent clause and at least one dependent clause.

     independent   dependent

The students assemble outside when the bell rings.

A **compound-complex sentence** contains at least two independent clauses and at least one dependent clause.

             independent

The first motorcyclists to finish never ordered anything to eat; they

   independent   dependent

just sat quietly until their hands stopped shaking.

64 c Understanding sentence patterns

Most independent clauses are built on one of five basic patterns. (See Chapter 63 for more on the sentence elements mentioned here.)

The simplest pattern has only two elements, a subject and a verb (S–V).

    s   v

Rain fell.

Even when expanded by modifying phrases, the basic pattern of an independent clause may still be only subject–verb.

       s   v

Heavy tropical rain fell Tuesday and Wednesday in the Philippines, causing mud slides and killing hundreds of people.

The next simplest pattern includes a subject, a verb, and a direct object (S–V–DO).

   s   v   do

Gloria read the book.

   s   v   do

Robins eat worms.

A third pattern is subject, verb, indirect object, and direct object (S–V–IO–DO).

    s   v   io   do

The committee sent the mayor its report.

    s   v   io   do

The waiter brought her an appetizer.

A fourth pattern is subject, verb, and subject complement (S–V–SC).

    s   v   sc

The commissioner seems worried.

s v sc

She is a Republican.

The fifth basic pattern is subject, verb, direct object, and object complement (S–V–DO–OC).

s v do oc

His friends call him an achiever.

s v do oc

That makes him proud.

GLOSSARY OF USAGE

This glossary provides information about words that are frequently confused, words that are often used incorrectly, and words that are not considered appropriate for formal academic writing. If you are unsure about how to use a word or are having trouble choosing between words, check here first.

Like any other aspect of editing, good usage is usually more than a matter of clear-cut distinctions and unvarying rules. Some usages described here would be considered incorrect by any knowledgeable speaker or writer in any context. For example, *discreet* means "prudent" and *discrete* means "separate"; no one who knows that these are two different words would argue that they are interchangeable. On the other hand, some usages are considered acceptable by some authorities but not by others. For example, some writers prefer to use *farther* only when referring to physical distances and *further* only when referring to the more abstract distances of time, quantity, or degree. However, respected writers have been using them interchangeably for hundreds of years. To decide what is appropriate for your writing, carefully consider the expectations of your audience. Instructors will appreciate your using words as carefully and precisely as possible.

Some of the usages described in this glossary are acceptable or common outside formal academic writing. For example, **nonstandard** usages (such as *anyways* instead of the standard *anyway*) reflect the speech patterns of a particular community but do not follow the conventions of the dominant American dialect. **Colloquial** usages (such as *flunk* meaning "to fail" or *awfully* meaning "very") are often heard in speech but are usually considered inappropriate for academic writing. **Informal** usages (such as using *can* and *may* interchangeably) may be acceptable in some papers but not in formal research essays or argument papers. Except where otherwise noted, the usages recommended in this glossary are those of **standard** written English, that is, the usages that most closely follow the rules and conventions of the

language. Standard written English is appropriate for formal academic papers.

a, an   Use *a* before words that begin with a consonant sound (*a boy, a hero, a shining star*), even if the first letter of the word is a vowel (*a useful lesson*). Use *an* before words that begin with a vowel sound (*an antelope, an umbrella*).

accept, except   *Accept* is a verb meaning "to receive" or "to approve" (*I accept your offer*). *Except* is a verb meaning "to leave out" or "to exclude" (*He excepted all vegetables from his list of favorite foods*) or a preposition meaning "excluding" (*He liked to eat everything except vegetables*).

adapt, adopt   *Adapt* means "to adjust" or "to accommodate"; it is usually followed by *to* (*It is sometimes hard to adapt to college life*). *Adopt* means "to take into a relationship" (*My parents are adopting another child*) or "to take and use as one's own" (*I have adopted my roommate's habits*).

adverse, averse   *Adverse* is an adjective meaning "unfavorable" or "unpleasant," generally used to describe a thing or situation (*Adverse weather forced us to cancel the game*). *Averse*, also an adjective, means "opposed to" or "feeling a distaste for" and usually describes feelings about a thing or situation; it is usually followed by *to* (*We are averse to playing on a muddy field*).

advice, advise   *Advice* is a noun meaning "recommendation" or "information given"; *advise* is a verb meaning "to give advice to" (*I advise you to take my advice and study hard*).

affect, effect   *Affect* as a verb means "to influence" or "to produce an effect" (*That movie affected me deeply*). *Affect* as a noun means "feeling" or "emotion," especially in psychology. *Effect* is commonly used as a noun meaning "result," "consequence," or "outcome" (*That movie had a profound effect on me*); it is also sometimes used as a verb meaning "to bring about" (*Dr. Johnson effected important changes as president*).

aggravate   *Aggravate* is a verb meaning "to make worse." *Aggravate* is sometimes used colloquially to mean "to irritate" or "to annoy," but in formal writing use *irritate* or *annoy* (*I was irritated by my neighbors' loud stereo; my irritation was aggravated when they refused to turn it down*).

ain't   *Ain't* is a nonstandard (colloquial) contraction for *am not, is not, are not, have not,* or *has not. Ain't* is not acceptable in formal writing except in reproducing dialogue.

all ready, already   *All ready* means "full prepared" (*The children were all ready for bed*). *Already* means "previously" (*The children were already in bed when the guests arrived*).

all right, alright   The two-word spelling is preferred; the one-word spelling is considered incorrect by many.

all together, altogether   *All together* means "all gathered in one place" (*The animals were all together in the ark*). *Altogether* means "thoroughly" or "completely" (*The ark was altogether too full of animals*).

allude, elude   *Allude* is a verb meaning "to refer to something indirectly"; it is followed by *to* (*Derek alluded to the rodent infestation by mentioning that he'd bought mousetraps*). *Elude* is a verb meaning "to escape" or "to avoid" (*The mouse eluded Derek at every turn*).

allusion, illusion *Allusion* means "an indirect reference" or "the act of alluding to, or hinting at, something" (*Derek's allusion to lunchtime was not lost on his companions*). *Illusion* is a noun meaning "misapprehension" or "misleading image" (*Mr. Hodges created an optical illusion with two lines*).

a lot *A lot* should be written as two words. Although *a lot* is used informally to mean "a large number," avoid using it in formal writing (*The prisoners had many* [not *a lot of*] *opportunities to escape*).

a.m., p.m. or A.M., P.M. Use these abbreviations only with numbers to indicate time (6:30 P.M.). Do not use them as substitutes for *morning, afternoon, evening,* or *night.* Do not use them with *o'clock.*

among, between *Among* should be used when three or more individuals are being discussed (*It was difficult to choose among all the exotic plants*). *Between* is generally used when only two individuals are being discussed (*There were significant differences between the two candidates*).

amount, number *Amount* should be used to refer to quantities that cannot be counted or cannot be expressed as a single number (*Fixing up the abandoned farmhouse took a great amount of work*). *Number* is used for quantities that can be counted (*A large number of volunteers helped*).

an See *a, an.*

and/or *And/or* is used in technical and legal writing to connect two terms when either one or both apply (*Purchasers must select type and/or size*). Avoid this awkward phrasing by using the construction "A or B or both" (*Students may select chemistry or physics or both*).

anxious, eager *Anxious* is an adjective meaning "worried" or "uneasy" (*Lynn is anxious about her mother's surgery*). Do not confuse it with *eager,* which means "enthusiastic," "impatient," or "marked by strong desire" (*I am eager* [not *anxious*] *to leave*).

anybody, anyone; any body, any one *Anybody* and *anyone* are singular indefinite pronouns that refer to an unspecified person (*Anybody may apply for the new scholarship. Anyone on the hill could have seen our campfire*). *Any body* and *any one* are noun phrases consisting of the adjective *any* and the noun *body* or the pronoun *one;* they refer to a specific body or a single member of a group (*Each child may select any one toy from the toy box*).

anyplace, anywhere In formal writing, do not use *anyplace;* use *anywhere* (*We could not find the game piece anywhere* [not *anyplace*]).

anyways, anywheres; nowheres Use the standard terms *anyway, anywhere* and *nowhere* in writing.

as *As* may be used to mean "because" (*We did not go ice skating as the lake was no longer frozen*), but only if no confusion will result. For example, *We canceled the meeting as only two people showed up* could mean that the meeting was canceled either at the moment when the two people showed up or because only two showed up.

as . . . as . . . In a comparison, use the word *as* twice to show that the items being compared are equal; the second *as* should not be dropped if the comparison is continued (*The American literature course is as popular as, if not more popular than, the English literature course*).

as, as if, like To indicate comparisons, *like* should be used only as a preposition followed by a noun or noun phrase to compare items that are

similar but not equivalent (*Ken, like his brother, prefers to sleep late*). In formal writing, *like* should not be used as a conjunction linking two clauses. Use *as* or *as if* instead (*Anne talks as if* [not *like*] *she has read every book by Ernest Hemingway*).

assure, ensure, insure   *Assure* is a verb meaning "to reassure" or "to convince" (*The lawyer assured her client that the case was solid*). *Ensure* and *insure* both mean "to make sure, certain, or safe," but *insure* generally refers to financial certainty (*John hoped his college degree would ensure him a job, preferably one that would insure him in case of injury or illness*).

as to   Do not use *as to* as a substitute for *about* (*We had questions about* [not *as to*] *the company's affirmative action policies*).

averse   See *adverse, averse.*

awful, awfully   *Awful* is an adjective meaning "inspiring awe." In formal writing, do not use it to mean "disagreeable" or "objectionable." Similarly, the adverb *awfully* means "in an awe-inspiring way"; in writing, do not use it in the colloquial sense of "very."

awhile, a while   The one-word form *awhile* is an adverb that can be used to modify a verb (*We rested awhile*). Only the two-word form *a while* can be the object of a preposition (*We rested for a while*).

bad, badly   *Bad* is an adjective, so it must modify a noun or follow a linking verb, such as *be, feel,* or *become* (*John felt bad about holding the picnic in bad weather*). *Badly* is an adverb, so it must modify a verb (*Pam played badly today*).

because of, due to   *Due to* is an adjective phrase that is generally used after forms of the verb *be* (*The smaller classes were due to a decline in enrollment*). In formal writing, *due to* should not be used as a prepositional phrase meaning "because of" (*Class size decreased because of* [not *due to*] *a decline in enrollment*).

being as, being that   *Being as* and *being that* are nonstandard expressions for *because* (*Anna withdrew from the tournament because* [not *being as*] *her shoulder was injured*).

beside, besides   *Beside* is a preposition meaning "by the side of" or "next to" (*The book is beside the bed*). *Besides* can be used as a preposition meaning "other than" or "in addition to" (*No one besides Linda can build a good campfire*). *Besides* can also be used as an adverb meaning "furthermore" or "in addition" (*The weather is bad for hiking; besides, I have a cold*).

better   The phrasal auxiliary verb *had better* denotes obligation (*You had better hurry*). Do not use *better* alone in this sense.

between   See *among, between.*

biannual, biennial   *Biannual* refers to something that happens twice a year (*The biannual adjustments for daylight saving time occur in April and October*). The term *biennial* refers to something that happens every two years (*The Whitney Museum opens its biennial exhibit of American art next month*).

breath, breathe   *Breath* is a noun (*I had to stop to catch my breath*). *Breathe* is a verb (*It became difficult to breathe at higher elevations*).

bring, take   The verb *bring* describes movement from a distant place to a nearer place; the verb *take* describes movement away from a place (*Dr. Gavin asked us to bring our rough sketches to class; she said we may take them home after class*).

busted   *Busted* is a nonstandard past tense for *burst* (*The state Senate chamber was flooded when a water line burst*). As a synonym for *arrested*, *busted* is also nonstandard.

but, however, yet   Each of these words should be used alone, not in combination (*We finished painting the house, but* [not *but however*] *there is still much work to do*).

can, may   In informal usage, *can* and *may* are often used interchangeably to indicate permission, but in formal writing, only *may* should be used this way (*May I borrow your dictionary?*). *May* is also used to indicate possibility (*It may snow tomorrow*). *Can* is used only to indicate ability (*I can see much better with my new glasses*).

capital, capitol   *Capital* is an adjective meaning "punishable by death" (*capital punishment*) or referring to uppercase letters (*A, B*). As a noun it means "accumulated wealth" (*We will calculate our capital at the end of the fiscal year*) or "a city serving as a seat of government" (*Albany is the capital of New York*). *Capitol* is a noun for the building in which lawmakers meet (*The civics class toured the capitol last week*).

censor, censure   *Censor* is a noun or verb referring to the removal of material that is considered objectionable; *censure* is a verb meaning "to blame or condemn sternly" (*Plans to censor song lyrics have been censured by groups that support free speech*).

center around, center on   *Center around* is colloquial for *center on* (*The discussion centered on the meaning of Darwin's theory to his scientific contemporaries*).

cite, site, sight   *Cite* is a verb meaning "to quote for the purposes of example, authority, or proof" (*Tracy cites several landmark cases in her treatise on capital punishment*). *Site* is usually used as a noun meaning "place" or "scene" (*Signs of prehistoric habitation were found at the site*). *Site* can also be used as a verb meaning "to place on a site." *Sight* is a verb meaning "to see" or a noun meaning "vision" (*Bligh's party finally sighted an island. The mariners thought it a beautiful sight*).

climactic, climatic   *Climactic* is an adjective derived from *climax*; it refers to a moment of greatest intensity (*In the climactic scene of the play, the murderer's identity is revealed*). *Climatic* is an adjective derived from the noun *climate*; it refers to weather conditions (*Some people fear that climatic changes are a sign of environmental dangers*).

compare to, compare with   *Compare to* means "to liken" or "to represent as similar" (*Jim compared our new puppy to an unruly child*). *Compare with* means "to examine to discover similarities or differences" (*We compared this month's ads with last month's*).

complement, compliment   *Complement* is a verb meaning "to fill out or complete"; it is also a noun meaning "something that completes or fits with" (*The bouquet of spring flowers complemented the table setting*). *Compliment* is a verb meaning "to express esteem or admiration" or a noun meaning "an expression of esteem or admiration" (*Russ complimented Nancy on her choice of flowers*).

compose, comprise   *Compose* means "to constitute or make up"; *comprise* means "to include or contain" (*Last year's club comprised fifteen members; only eight members compose this year's club*).

conscience, conscious   *Conscience* is a noun referring to a sense of right and wrong (*His conscience would not allow him to lie*). *Conscious* is an adjective meaning "marked by thought or will" or "acting with critical awareness" (*He made a conscious decision to be more honest*).

contact   *Contact* is often used informally as a verb meaning "to get in touch with." Avoid it in formal writing; use verbs such as *write* or *telephone.*

continual, continuous   *Continual* means "recurring" or "occurring repeatedly" (*Liz saw a doctor about her continual headaches*). *Continuous* means "uninterrupted in space, time, or sequence" (*Eventually we grew used to the continuous noise*).

council, counsel   *Council* is a noun meaning "a group meeting for advice, discussion, or government" (*The tribal council voted in favor of the new land rights law*). As a noun, *counsel* means "advice" or "a plan of action or behavior" (*The priest gave counsel to the young men considering the priesthood*). *Counsel* may also be used as a verb meaning "to advise or consult" (*The priest counseled the young man*).

could have, must have, should have, would have   Do not use the preposition *of* instead of the auxiliary verb *have* (*I could have danced* [not *I could of danced*] *all night*).

credible, incredible; credulous, incredulous   *Credible* and *incredible* describe whether something is believable or trustworthy (*His descriptions of life at sea seem credible enough, but his tales of his own heroism in battle are incredible*). *Credulous* means "willing to believe" and carries the connotation of "too willing to believe" (*Such a charismatic leader depends on credulous followers*). *Incredulous* means "unwilling to believe" (*The claim of controlled, low-temperature fusion was challenged by incredulous physicists around the world*).

criteria   *Criteria* is the plural of *criterion*, which means "a standard on which a judgment is based" (*Many criteria are used in selecting a president, but a candidate's hair color is not an appropriate criterion*).

data   *Data* is the plural of *datum*, which means "a fact" or "a result in research." Some writers now use *data* as both a singular and a plural noun; in formal usage it is still better to treat it as plural (*The data indicate that a low-fat diet may increase life expectancy*).

device, devise   *Device* is a noun meaning "mechanism" or "invention" (*McCormick's reaper was an ingenious device for harvesting grain*). The verb *devise* means "to invent or discover" (*Perhaps you can devise a way to make an omelet without breaking eggs*).

different from, different than   *Different from* is preferred to *different than* (*Hal's taste in music is different from his wife's*). But *different than* may be used to avoid awkward constructions (*Hal's taste in music is different than* [instead of *different from what*] *it was five years ago*).

differ from, differ with   *Differ from* means "to be unlike" (*This year's parade differed from last year's in many ways*). *Differ with* means "to disagree with" (*Stephanie differed with Tom over which parade was better*).

discreet, discrete   *Discreet* is an adjective meaning "prudent" or "modest" (*Most private donors were discreet about their contributions*). *Discrete* is an adjective meaning "separate" or "distinct" (*Professor Roberts divided the course into four discrete units*).

disinterested, uninterested   *Disinterested* is an adjective meaning "unbiased" or "impartial" (*It will be difficult to find twelve disinterested jurors for such a highly publicized case*). *Uninterested* is an adjective meaning "indifferent" or "unconcerned" (*Most people were uninterested in the case until the police discovered surprising new evidence*).

don't   *Don't* is a contraction for *do not*, not for *does not*. The contraction for *does not* is *doesn't* (*He doesn't* [not *don't*] *know where she's living now*).

drug   *Drug* is a nonstandard past tense of the verb *drag* (*The weary hikers dragged themselves back into camp*).

due to   See *because of, due to*.

each   *Each*—whether adjective or pronoun—is singular (*Each tool goes in its own place; each has to be put away properly*).

effect   See *affect, effect*.

e.g.   *E.g.* is the Latin abbreviation for *exempli gratia*, which means "for the sake of example." In formal writing, use *for example* or *for instance*.

elicit, illicit   *Elicit* is a verb meaning "to draw forth" or "to bring out" (*The investigators could not elicit any new information*). *Illicit* is an adjective meaning "unlawful" or "not permitted" (*The investigators were looking for evidence of illicit drug sales*).

elude   See *allude, elude*.

emigrate from, immigrate to   *Emigrate* means "to leave one's country to live or reside elsewhere" (*His grandparents emigrated from Russia*). *Immigrate* means "to come into a new country to take up residence" (*His grandparents immigrated to the United States*).

eminent, imminent   *Eminent* means "lofty" or "prominent" (*Her operation was performed by an eminent surgeon*). *Imminent* means "impending" or "about to take place" (*The hurricane's arrival is imminent*).

ensure   See *assure, ensure, insure*.

enthused, enthusiastic   In formal writing, *enthused*, a past-tense form of the verb *enthuse*, should not be used as an adjective; use *enthusiastic* (*Barb is enthusiastic* [not *enthused*] *about her music lessons*).

especially, specially   *Especially* is an adverb meaning "particularly" or "unusually" (*The weather was especially cold this winter*). *Specially* is an adverb meaning "for a special reason" or "in a unique way" (*The cake was specially prepared for Sandy's birthday*).

etc.   An abbreviation for the Latin expression *et cetera*, *etc.* means "and so forth." In formal writing, avoid ending a list with *etc.;* indicate that you are leaving items out of a list with *and so on* or *and so forth*. Use *etc.* alone, not with *and*, which is redundant.

eventually, ultimately   Although these words are often used interchangeably, *eventually* means "at an unspecified later time" while *ultimately* means "finally" or "in the end" (*He knew that he would have to stop running eventually, but he hoped that he would ultimately win a marathon*).

everybody, everyone, every one   *Everybody* and *everyone* are singular indefinite pronouns that refer to an unspecified person (*Everybody wins in this game*). *Every one* is a noun phrase consisting of the adjective *every* and the pronoun *one;* it refers to each single member of a group (*Every one of these toys must be picked up*).

except   See *accept, except.*

expect   *Expect* means "to anticipate or look forward to." Avoid using it colloquially to mean "to think or suppose." (*I suppose* [not *expect*] *I should go study now*).

explicit, implicit   *Explicit* means "perfectly clear, direct, and unambiguous" (*Darrell gave me explicit directions to his house*). *Implicit* means "implied" or "revealed or expressed indirectly" (*His eagerness to see me was implicit in his cheerful tone of voice*).

farther, further   Although these words are often used interchangeably, some writers prefer to use *farther* to refer to physical distances (*Boston is farther than I thought*) and *further* to refer to quantity, time, or degree (*We tried to progress further on our research project*).

fewer, less   *Fewer* is an adjective used to refer to people or items that can be counted (*Because fewer people came to the conference this year, we needed fewer programs*). *Less* is used to refer to amounts that cannot be counted (*We also required less space and less food*).

finalize   Many writers avoid using *finalize* to mean "to make final." Use an alternative phrasing (*We needed to complete* [not *finalize*] *our plans*).

firstly, secondly, thirdly   These expressions are awkward; use *first, second, third,* and so on instead.

former, latter   *Former* is used to refer to the first of two people, items, or ideas being discussed, *latter* to refer to the second (*Monet and Picasso were both important painters; the former is associated with the Impressionist school, the latter with Cubism*). *Former* and *latter* should not be used when referring to more than two items.

further   See *farther, further.*

get   The verb *get* has many colloquial uses that should be avoided in formal writing. For example, *get* can means "to provoke or annoy" (*He gets to me*), "to start" (*We should get going on this project*), or "to become" (*She got worried when he didn't call*). *Have got to* should not be used in place of *must* (*I must* [not *have got to*] *finish by five o'clock*) or in place of *have* (*Do you have* [not *Have you got*] *a dollar for the toll?*).

goes, says   The verb *goes* is sometimes used colloquially for *says,* but avoid this usage in formal writing (*When the coach says* [not *goes*] *"Now," everybody runs*).

good and   *Good and* should not be used for *very* in formal writing (*My shoes were very* [not *good and*] *wet after our walk*).

good, well   *Good* is an adjective; it should not be used in place of the adverb *well* in formal writing (*Mario is a good tennis player; he played well* [not *good*] *in the tournament*).

half a, half of, a half a   For distance, use *a half* (*They had walked a half mile in pitch darkness*). For other quantities, use *half of, a half,* or *half of a* (*Half of the audience was not amused. Half of an apple was plenty for Eve. A half ton of coal takes up a lot of room*). Avoid using *a half a.*

hanged, hung *Hanged* is the past-tense and past-participle form of the verb *hang* meaning "to suspend by the neck until dead" (*Two prisoners were hanged at this spot*). *Hung* is the past-tense and past-participle form of the verb *hang* meaning "to suspend" or "to dangle" (*All her clothes were hung neatly in the closet*).

hardly, scarcely *Hardly* and *scarcely* are adverbs meaning "barely," "only just." Do not use double negatives, such as *can't scarcely* and *not hardly*, in formal writing. (*I can scarcely* [not *can't scarcely*] *keep my eyes open*).

has got, have got See *get*.

have, of The auxiliary verb *have* (not *of*) should be used in verb phrases beginning with *could, would, should,* and *might* (*We could have* [not *of*] *gone to the concert*).

healthful, healthy *Healthful* means "tending to promote good health" (*I try to eat a healthful diet*). *Healthy* means "having good health" (*By doing so, I hope to stay healthy*).

he/she, s/he, his/her When you require both female and male personal pronouns in formal writing, use *he or she* (or *she or he*) and *his or her* (or *her or his*) instead of a slash. For more on avoiding sexist language.

height Use *height*, not *heighth* (*The temple was roughly six meters in height, ten in length, and twelve in width*).

herself, himself, itself, myself, ourselves, themselves, yourself, yourselves These reflexive or intensive pronouns should be used only to reflect the action of a sentence back toward the subject (*He locked himself out of the apartment*) or to emphasize the subject (*I myself have no regrets*). Do not use these pronouns in place of personal pronouns such as *I, me, you, her,* or *him* (*He left an extra key with Bev and me* [not *myself*]).

hisself *Hisself* is nonstandard; use *himself*.

hopefully *Hopefully* is an adverb meaning "in a hopeful manner" (*The child looked hopefully out the window for her mother*). In formal writing, do not use *hopefully* to mean "I or we hope that" or "It is hoped that" (*I hope that* [not *hopefully*] *Bob will remember his camera*).

however See *but, however, yet*.

hung See *hanged, hung*.

i.e. *I.e.* is an abbreviation for the Latin phrase *id est,* which means "that is." In formal writing, use *that is* instead of the abbreviation (*Hal is a Renaissance man; that is* [not *i.e.*], *he has many interests*).

if, whether Use *if* in a clause that refers to a conditional situation (*I will wear my new boots if it snows tomorrow*). Use *whether* (or *whether or not*) in a clause that expresses or implies an alternative (*I will decide whether to wear my boots when I see what the weather is like*).

illicit See *elicit, illicit*.

illusion See *allusion, illusion*.

immigrate See *emigrate from, immigrate to*.

imminent See *eminent, imminent*.

implicit See *explicit, implicit*.

imply, infer *Imply* is a verb meaning "to express indirectly" or "to suggest"; *infer* is a verb meaning "to conclude" or "to surmise" (*Helen implied that she had time to visit with us, but we inferred from all the work on her desk that she was really too busy*). Speakers *imply;* listeners *infer.*

incidents, incidence, instance *Incidents* are occurrences or events; *incidence* (usually singular) refers to the extent or frequency with which something occurs; an *instance* is an example (*The incidence of crime has decreased this year. For instance, our town had 30 percent fewer incidents involving armed robbery than we experienced last year*).

incredible, incredulous See *credible, incredible.*

infer See *imply, infer.*

ingenious, ingenuous *Ingenious* means "resourceful" or "clever" (*Elaine came up with an ingenious plan*). *Ingenuous* means "innocent" or "simple" (*It was a surprisingly deceptive plan for such an ingenuous person*).

in, into Use *in* to indicate position (*The sun is low in the sky*). Use *into* to suggest motion or change of position (*The rats moved cautiously into the maze*). The use of *into* to mean "involved in" or "interested in" is slang (*She is interested in* [not *into*] *astrology*).

in regards to *In regards to* is an incorrect combination of two phrases, *as regards* and *in regard to* (*In regard to* [or *As regards*] *the first question, refer to the guidelines you received*).

inside, inside of; outside, outside of The prepositions *inside* and *outside* should not be followed by *of* (*The suspect is inside* [not *inside of*] *that building*).

insure See *assure, ensure, insure.*

irregardless, regardless The nonstandard *irregardless* is often mistakenly used in place of *regardless* (*We will have the party regardless* [not *irregardless*] *of the weather*).

is when, is where Avoid these awkward expressions in formal writing to define terms (*Sexual harassment refers to* [not *is when someone makes*] *inappropriate sexual advances or suggestions*).

its, it's *Its* is the possessive form of the pronoun *it; it's* is a contraction for *it is* or *it has* (*It's hard to tear a baby animal away from its mother*).

itself See *herself, himself. . . .*

kind, sort, type *Kind, sort,* and *type* are singular nouns; each should be used with *this* (not *these*) and a singular verb (*This kind of mushroom is* [not *These kind of mushrooms are*] *very expensive*). The plural forms—*kinds, sorts,* and *types*—should be used with *these* and with a plural verb (*These three types of envelopes are the only ones we need*).

kind of, sort of In formal writing, avoid using the colloquial expressions *kind of* and *sort of* to mean "somewhat" or "rather" (*My paper is rather* [not *kind of*] *short; my research for it was somewhat* [not *sort of*] *rushed*).

later, latter *Later* means "after some time"; *latter* refers to the second of two people, items, or ideas (*Later in the evening, Jim announced that the latter of the two speakers was running late*). See also *former, latter.*

lay, lie The transitive verb *lay* means "to put or set down" and is followed by an object; the principal forms of *lay* are *lay, laid, laid* (*Lay the blanket on this spot and lie down; She laid the book next to the spot where he lay on*

the bed). The verb *lie* meaning "to recline" or "to rest in a horizontal position" has the principal forms *lie, lay, lain. Lie* should not be confused with *lay.*

lead, led As a verb, *lead* means "to go first" or "to direct"; as a noun, it means "front position" (*Hollis took the lead in organizing the files*). *Lead* is also a noun for the metallic element. Be careful not to confuse this form of *lead* with *led*, which is pronounced the same way. *Led* is the past-tense and past-participle form of the verb *lead* (*He led me to the cave*).

learn, teach Students *learn;* teachers *teach.* Do not use *learn* in place of *teach* (*In Sunday school the preacher taught* [not *learned*] *us right from wrong*).

leave, let *Leave* means "to depart"; it should not be used in place of *let*, which means "to allow" (*When you are ready to leave, let* [not *leave*] *me give you a ride*). The expressions *leave alone* and *let alone*, however, may be used interchangeably (*I asked Ben to leave* [or *let*] *me alone while I worked on my paper*).

led See *lead, led.*

less See *fewer, less.*

let See *leave, let.*

liable, likely *Liable* means "inclined" or "tending," generally toward the negative (*If you do not shovel the sidewalk, you are liable to fall on the ice*). *Liable* is also a legal term meaning "responsible for" or "obligated under the law" (*The landlord is liable for the damage caused by the leak*). *Likely* is an adjective meaning "probable" or "promising" (*The school board is likely to cancel classes if the strike continues*).

lie See *lay, lie.*

like See *as, as if, like.*

likely See *liable, likely.*

loose, lose *Loose* is an adjective meaning "not securely attached"; it should not be confused with the verb *lose*, which means "to misplace," "to fail to keep," or "to undergo defeat" (*Be careful not to lose that loose button on your jacket*).

lots, lots of *Lots* and *lots of* are colloquial expressions meaning "many" or "much"; avoid them in formal writing (*The senator has much* [not *lots of*] *support; she is expected to win many* [not *lots of*] *votes*).

man, mankind These terms were once used to refer to all human beings. Now such usage is considered sexist; use terms such as *people, humanity*, and *humankind* instead (*What has been the greatest invention in the history of humanity* [not *mankind*]*?*).

may See *can, may.*

may be, maybe *May be* is a verb phrase (*Charles may be interested in a new job*); *maybe* is an adverb meaning "possibly" or "perhaps" (*Maybe I will speak to him about it*).

media The term *media*, frequently used to refer to various forms of communication—newspapers, magazines, television, radio—is the plural form of the noun *medium*; it takes a plural verb (*Some people feel that the media were responsible for the candidate's loss*).

mine, mines   *Mine* is a pronoun meaning "belonging to me." Avoid *mines*, a nonstandard form (*Did you find yours? I found mine*).

moral, morale   *Moral* is the message or lesson of a story or experience (*The moral is to treat others as you wish to be treated*). *Morale* is the mental condition or mood of a person or group (*The improvement in the weather lifted the crew's morale*).

most   In formal writing, do not use *most* to mean "almost." (*Prizes were given to almost* [not *most*] *all the participants*).

myself   See *herself, himself. . . .*

nausea, nauseated, nauseating, nauseous   The noun *nausea* refers to the feeling of being sick to one's stomach. Something that makes you sick to your stomach is *nauseous* or *nauseating*. If you are sick to your stomach, you are *nauseated* (not *nauseous*).

nor, or   *Nor* should be used with *neither* (*Neither Paul nor Sara guessed the right answer*); *or* should be used with *either* (*Either Paul or Sara will have to drive me home*).

nowhere near   *Nowhere near* is an informal usage. Use *not nearly* instead (*This year's class is not nearly as unruly as last year's*).

number   See *amount, number.*

of   See *have, of.*

off of   Use *off* alone; *of* is not necessary (*The child fell off* [not *off of*] *the playground slide*).

OK, O.K., okay   All three spellings are acceptable, but this colloquial term should be avoided in writing (*John's performance was all right* [or *adequate* or *tolerable*; not *okay*], *but it wasn't his best*).

on account of   In formal writing, avoid *on account of* to mean "because of" (*The course was canceled because of* [not *on account of*] *lack of interest*). Also see *because of, due to.*

or   See *nor, or.*

outside, outside of   See *inside, inside of; outside, outside of.*

passed, past   *Passed* is the past-tense form of the verb *pass* (*She passed here several hours ago*). *Past* may be an adjective or a noun referring to a time before the present (*She has forgotten many details about her past life; the past is not important to her*).

people, persons   A *person* is an individual human being. Groups are usually *people* (*Only one person came, although we had hoped many people would attend*) except when emphasizing the individuality of the members of a group of people (*Three persons were injured in a single-vehicle accident on Rohrer Road*).

per   The Latin term *per* should be reserved for commercial or technical use (*miles per gallon, price per pound*). Avoid it elsewhere in formal writing (*Kyle is exercising three times each* [not *per*] *week*).

percent, percentage   The term *percent* refers to a specific fraction of one hundred; it is always used with a number (*We raised nearly 80 percent of our budget in one night*). Do not use the symbol % in formal writing except in tables, formulas, or technical writing. The term *percentage* is not used with a specific number (*We raised a large percentage of our budget in one night*).

perspective, prospective *Perspective* is a noun meaning "a view"; it should not be confused with the adjective *prospective*, meaning "potential" or "likely" (*Mr. Harris's perspective on the new school changed when he met his son's prospective teacher*).

phenomena *Phenomena* is the plural of the noun *phenomenon*, meaning "an observed fact, occurrence, or circumstance" (*Last month's blizzard was an unusual phenomenon; there have been several such phenomena this year*).

plenty *Plenty* means "full" or "abundant"; in formal writing, do not use it to mean "very" or "quite" (*The sun was quite* [not *plenty*] *hot*).

plus *Plus* is a preposition meaning "increased by" or "with the addition of" (*With wool socks plus your heavy boots, your feet should be warm enough*). Do not use *plus* to link two independent clauses; use *besides* or *moreover* instead (*Brad is not prepared for the advanced class; moreover* [not *plus*], *he can't fit it in his schedule*).

p.m., a.m. or P.M., A.M. See *a.m., p.m. or A.M., P.M.*

precede, proceed *Precede* is a verb meaning "to go or come before"; *proceed* is a verb meaning "to move forward or go on" or "to continue" (*The attendants preceded the bride into the church; when the music started, they proceeded down the aisle*).

pretty In formal writing, avoid *pretty* to mean "quite" or "somewhat" (*Dave is quite* [not *pretty*] *tired this morning*).

principal, principle *Principal* is an adjective meaning "first" or "most important"; it is also a noun meaning "head" or "director" or "an amount of money" (*My principal reason for visiting Gettysburg was my interest in the Civil War; my high school principal suggested the trip*). *Principle* is a noun meaning "a rule of action or conduct" or "a basic law" (*I also want to learn more about the principles underlying the U.S. Constitution*).

proceed See *precede, proceed.*

quotation, quote *Quotation* is a noun, and *quote* is a verb. Avoid using *quote* as a noun (*Sue quoted Jefferson in her speech, hoping the quotation* [not *quote*] *would have a powerful effect on her audience*).

raise, rise *Raise* is a transitive verb meaning "to lift" or "to increase"; it takes a direct object (*The store owner was forced to raise prices*). *Rise* is an intransitive verb meaning "to go up"; it does not take a direct object (*Prices rise during periods of inflation*).

rarely ever Do not use *rarely ever* to mean "hardly ever"; use *rarely* alone (*We rarely* [not *rarely ever*] *travel during the winter*).

real, really *Real* is an adjective meaning "true" or "actual" (*The diamonds in that necklace are real*). *Really* is an adverb, used informally to mean "very" or "quite"; do not use *real* as an adverb (*Tim was really* [not *real*] *interested in buying Lana's old car*). In formal writing, it is generally best to avoid *really* altogether.

reason is because *Reason is because* is redundant; use *reason is that* or *because* instead (*The reason I am late is that* [not *because*] *I got stuck in traffic. Yesterday I was late because* [not *The reason I was late yesterday was because*] *I overslept*).

reason why   *Reason why* is redundant; use *reason* alone (*The reason* [not *The reason why*] *we canceled the dance is that no one volunteered to chaperone*).

regardless   See *irregardless, regardless.*

relation, relationship   *Relation* is a connection or association between things; *relationship* is a connection or involvement between people (*The analyst explained the relation between investment and interest. The relationship between a mother and child is complex*).

respectably, respectfully, respectively   *Respectably* means "in a manner worthy of respect" (*Although we did not win, we performed respectably*). *Respectfully* means "in a manner characterized by respect" (*Even when you disagree, you should listen respectfully*). *Respectively* means "in the order given" (*The programs on the environment, woodcraft, and herpetology are at 10 A.M., noon, and 3 P.M., respectively*).

rise   See *raise, rise.*

says   See *goes, says.*

scarcely   See *hardly, scarcely.*

sensual, sensuous   *Sensual* means "arousing or exciting the senses or appetites"; it is often used in reference to sexual pleasure (*His scripts often featured titillating situations and sensual encounters*). *Sensuous* means "experienced through or affecting the senses," although it generally refers to esthetic enjoyment or pleasure (*Her sculpture was characterized by muted colors and sensuous curves*).

set, sit   *Set* is a transitive verb meaning "to put" or "to place"; it takes a direct object, and its principal forms are *set, set, set* (*Mary set her packages on the kitchen table*). *Sit* is an intransitive verb meaning "to be seated"; it does not take a direct object, and its principal forms are *sit, sat, sat* (*I sat in the only chair in the waiting room*).

shall, will   In the past, *shall* (instead of *will*) was used as a helping verb with the first-person subjects I and *we*. Now *will* is acceptable with all subjects (*We will invite several guests for dinner*). *Shall* is generally used in polite questions (*Shall we go inside now?*) or in legal writing (*Jurors shall refrain from all contact with the press*).

since   *Since* should be used to mean "continuing from a past time until the present" (*Carl has not gone skiing since he injured his knee*). Do not use *since* to mean "because" if there is any possibility that readers will be confused about your meaning. For example, in the sentence *Since she sold her bicycle, Lonnie has not been getting much exercise, since* could mean either "because" or "from the time that." Use *because* to avoid confusion.

sit   See *set, sit.*

site   See *cite, site, sight.*

so, so that   The use of *so* to mean "very" can be vague; use *so* with a *that* clause of explanation (*Gayle was so depressed that she could not get out of bed*). *So that* means "with the intention that" (*Gayle got out of bed early so that she would be in class on time*).

somebody, someone, something   These singular indefinite pronouns take singular verbs (*Somebody calls every night at midnight and hangs up; I hope something is done about this problem before someone in my family becomes frightened*).

someplace, somewhere Do not use *someplace* in formal writing; use *somewhere* instead (*The answer must lie somewhere* [not *someplace*] *in the text*).

some time, sometime, sometimes The phrase *some time* (an adjective and a noun) means "a length of time" (*We have not visited our grandparents in some time*). *Sometime* is an adverb meaning "at an indefinite time in the future" (*Let's get together sometime*); *sometimes* is an adverb meaning "on occasion" or "now and then" (*Sometimes we get together to talk about our assignments*).

sort See *kind, sort, type.*

sort of See *kind of, sort of.*

stationary, stationery *Stationary* is an adjective meaning "not moving" (*All stationary vehicles will be towed*). *Stationery* is a noun meaning "writing materials" (*Karen is always running out of stationery*).

supposed to, used to Both of these expressions consist of a past participle (*supposed, used*) followed by *to*. Do not use the base forms *suppose* or *use* (*Ben is supposed* [not *suppose*] *to take the garbage out; he is used* [not *use*] *to his mother's reminders by now. He used to do his chores without being reminded*).

sure, surely In formal writing, do not use the adjective *sure* to mean "certainly" or "undoubtedly"; use the adverb *surely* or *certainly* or *undoubtedly* instead (*It is certainly* [or *surely;* not *sure*] *cold today*).

sure and, try and *Sure and* and *try and* are colloquial expressions for *sure to* and *try to*, respectively; avoid them in formal writing (*Be sure to* [not *and*] *come to the party; try to* [not *and*] *be on time*).

take See *bring, take.*

than, then *Than* is a conjunction used in comparisons (*Dan is older than Eve*). *Then* is an adverb indicating time (*First pick up the files and then deliver them to the company office*).

that, which A clause introduced by *that* is always a restrictive clause; it should not be set off by commas (*The historical event that interested him most was the Civil War*). Many writers use *which* only to introduce nonrestrictive clauses, which are set off by commas (*His textbook, which was written by an expert on the war, provided useful information*); however, *which* may also be used to introduce restrictive clauses (*The book which offered the most important information was an old reference book in the library*).

thataway, thisaway Both these terms are colloquial. Use *that way* or *this way.*

that there, these here, them there, this here By themselves, the demonstrative adjectives or demonstrative pronouns *that, these, them,* and *this* indicate position (*this* means something close to the speaker, and *that* means something farther away), so the colloquial constructions *that there, this here,* and so forth are redundant.

their, there, they're *Their* is the possessive form of the pronoun *they* (*Did they leave their books here?*). *There* is an adverb meaning "in or at that place" (*No, they left their books there*); it may also be used as an expletive with a form of the verb *be* (*There is no time to look for their books*). *They're* is a contraction of *they are* (*They're looking all over for their books*).

theirselves, themselves *Theirselves* is nonstandard; use *themselves*.

then See *than, then.*

'til, till, until *Till* and *until* are both acceptable spellings; *'til*, however, is a contraction and should be avoided in formal writing (*We will work until we are finished; you should not plan to leave till then*).

to, too, two *To* is a preposition, often used to indicate movement or direction toward something (*Nancy is walking to the grocery store*). *Too* is an adverb meaning "also" (*Sam is walking too*). *Two* is a number (*The two of them are walking together*).

toward, towards *Toward* is preferred, but both forms are acceptable.

try and See *sure and, try and.*

type In colloquial speech, *type* is sometimes used alone to mean "type of," but avoid this usage in formal writing (*What type of* [not *type*] *medicine did the doctor prescribe?*). Also see kind, sort, type.

ultimately See *eventually, ultimately.*

uninterested See *disinterested, uninterested.*

unique *Unique* is an adjective meaning "being the only one" or "having no equal." Because it refers to an absolute, unvarying state, it should not be preceded by a word that indicates degree or amount (such as *most, less,* or *very*) (*Her pale blue eyes gave her a unique* [not *very unique*] *look*). The same is true of other adjectives that indicate an absolute state: *perfect, complete, round, straight,* and so on.

until See *'til, till, until.*

usage, use The noun *usage* means "an established and accepted practice or procedure" (*He consulted the glossary whenever he was unsure of the correct word choice or usage*). Do not substitute it for the noun *use* (*Park guidelines forbid the use* [not *usage*] *of gas grills*).

used to See *supposed to, used to.*

utilize The verb *utilize*, meaning "to put to use," is often considered inappropriately technical for formal writing; it is generally better to use *use* instead (*We were able to use* [not *utilize*] *the hotel kitchen to prepare our meals*).

wait for, wait on *Wait for* means "to await" or "to be ready for." *Wait on* means "to serve"; in formal writing they are not interchangeable (*You are too old to wait for* [not *on*] *your mother to wait on you*).

way, ways Do not use *ways* in place of *way* when referring to long distances (*Los Angeles is a long way* [not *ways*] *from San Francisco by car*).

well See *good, well.*

where *Where* is nonstandard when used in place of *that* (*I read that* [not *where*] *several of the company's plants will be closed in June*).

where . . . at, where . . . to *Where* should be used alone, not in combination with *at* or *to* (*Where did you leave your coat?* [not *Where did you leave your coat at?*] *Where are you going next?* [not *Where are you going to next?*]).

whether See *if, whether.*

which See *that, which.*

which, who, that Use the relative pronoun *which* to refer to places, things, or events; use *who* to refer to people or to animals with individual qualities or given names; use *that* to refer to places, things, or events or to groups of people (*The parade, which was rescheduled for Saturday, was a great success; the man who* [not *which*] *was grand marshal said it was the best parade that he could remember*). *That* is also occasionally used to refer to a single person (*Beth is like the sister that I never had*). See also *that, which.*

who See *which, who, that.*

who, whom; whoever, whomever Use *who* and *whoever* for subjects and subject complements; use *whom* and *whomever* for objects and object complements (*Who revealed the murderer's identity? You may invite whomever you wish*).

who's, whose *Who's* is a contraction of *who is* (*Who's coming for dinner tonight?*). *Whose* is the possessive form of *who* (*Whose hat is lying on the table?*).

will See *shall, will.*

-wise The suffix *-wise* indicates position or direction in words such as *clockwise* and *lengthwise*. In formal writing, do not add it to words to mean "with regard to" (*My personal life is rather confused, but with regard to my job* [not *jobwise*], *things are fine*).

yet See *but, however, yet.*

your, you're *Your* is the possessive form of the pronoun *you* (*Your table is ready*). *You're* is a contraction of *you are* (*You're leaving before the best part of the show*).

yourself, yourselves See *herself, himself. . . .*

GLOSSARY OF TERMS

abbreviation   A shortened form of a word. See Chapter 49.

absolute   A modifier indicating a quality that cannot be made larger or smaller (*entire, unique, superior*). An absolute does not have a comparative or superlative form. See 35e4.

absolute phrase   A phrase that consists of a noun or pronoun and a participle and that modifies an entire sentence, not just one part of it. See 63e.

abstract database   See *database*.

abstract noun   See *abstract word*.

abstract word   A word referring to something that cannot be perceived by one of the five senses: *liberty, education, exciting*. See 27a, 62a.

acronym   An abbreviation that forms a word out of the initials of the name or title that it shortens: *LILCO, MoMA, MADD*. See 38a, 49h.

active voice   See *voice*.

adjective   A modifier that describes nouns and pronouns. There are three types of adjectives: **descriptive** (*green, tall*), **proper** (*Italian, Buddhist*), and **limiting** (*few, all, a, the*). See also *article* and *modifier*. See 27d, Chapter 35, 62d.

adjective clause   A dependent clause introduced by a relative pronoun (*who, which, that*) and functioning as an adjective. See 63f.

adverb   A modifier that describes a verb, adjective, another adverb, or a whole sentence. See also *modifier*. See Chapter 35, 62d.

adverb clause   A dependent clause introduced by a subordinating conjunction and functioning as an adverb. See 63f.

agent   The person or thing that performs an action. In a sentence in which the verb is in the passive voice, the agent, if indicated, is usually the object of the preposition *by*. See also *voice*; see 27c.

agreement   Grammatical correspondence in number, person, and gender between subjects and their verbs and between pronouns and their antecedents. See 34h–34u, 36f–36j.

analogy   See *figurative language*.

analytical interpretation   See *interpretive essay*.

anecdote   A brief story that illustrates the theme or thesis of a piece of writing. See 24a3.

annotating Writing comments on a text to record one's responses during critical reading.

antecedent The noun, noun phrase or clause, or pronoun that a pronoun replaces. Pronouns agree with their antecedents in person, number, and gender. Also called *referent*. See also *agreement, gender, number,* and *person*. See Chapter 36, 62b.

antithesis A thesis presented in opposition to another thesis in a position paper. See *synthesis*.

antonyms Words whose meanings are the opposite of each other's. See 30b.

appositive A word or phrase following a noun or pronoun that describes or renames it: *Cliff, an old family friend, always helps out at harvest time.* See 36m, 39c2.

argument paper An essay whose purpose is to persuade readers regarding one side of an issue or regarding one answer to a question. See also *interpretive essay, position paper*. See Chapter 9.

argument research Research undertaken to collect information to support an argument. See also *informational research;* see Chapter 9, 11c.

argument thesis See *thesis*.

article *A, an* **(indefinite articles)**, or *the* **(definite article)** are considered adjectives and also called *determiners*. See 62d1.

attributory words Words that indicate the person who is quoted in a direct quotation: *I said, Jonathan wrote*. See 39g.

audience The readers to whom a piece of writing is directed. See 6b, 19c2.

automatic phrase A phrase that is used habitually but adds little to a sentence's meaning. See 28b.

auxiliary verb A form of the verb *be, do,* or *have* or the verb *can, could, may, might, must, shall, should, will,* or *would*. An auxiliary verb together with a main verb or a participle constitutes a *verb phrase*. Also called *helping verb*. See 34c1, 61c.

base form The first- and second-person, singular, and the plural present-tense form of a verb: *go, stop, sit, stand*. Also called *plain form* or *simple form*. See 34a.

biased language Writing in which meaning is expressed by connotation, sterotype, or prejudice rather than by direct statements of fact, inference, or evidence. See Chapter 31.

bibliographic database See *database*.

bibliography A complete, alphabetically arranged list of works on a topic, or sources consulted in conducting research. See 12b2, 55e, 56d2.

Boolean operators Words such as *AND, OR,* and *NOT* that limit the combination of words used in an Internet search to those most likely to locate the topic of interest. See 13b.

brainstorming An invention and discovery technique in which the writer makes a list of possible solutions to a problem or answers to a question. See 5a.

browser   A client program that can be installed on a computer to allow the user to gain access to information from servers. See also *server, World Wide Web.* See 13a.

bureaucratese   Jargon or pretentious language that is typical of governmental or institutional writing. See *doublespeak, euphemism.* See 28e.

case   The form of a pronoun that shows whether it functions as a subject **(subjective case)** or an object **(objective case)** or whether it indicates ownership **(possessive case)**. Nouns change form only to show ownership (possessive case). See 36k–36r, 42a, 62a, 62b2.

cause-and-effect analysis   A writing strategy in which the writer identifies the action or actions (cause) that bring about a certain condition (effect). See 7e1, 8d5.

chronological order   See *sequence of events.*

claim   A statement or assertion made in support of an argument. The argument's central claim is its *thesis.* A **counterclaim** is a claim made against the thesis. See 9a.

class book   An edited, bound collection of student writing, usually featuring some work from each student in a class. See 51d.

classification and division   A writing strategy in which the writer puts ideas, things, or people in a category or class with similar items (classification) and identifies distinguishing features (division). See 8d4.

clause   A group of words that includes both a subject and a predicate. See also *dependent clause, independent clause;* see 63f.

cliché   An expression used so often and for so long that it is no longer striking, vivid, or meaningful. See 30i.

climactic order   Presentation of specific details in order of increasing importance, ending with a dramatic statement, a climax. See 23b.

clustering   An invention and discovery technique in which ideas are grouped nonlinearly, with relationships among them indicated by lines and circles. See 5f.

coherence   The connection between ideas established by clear, focused, logical development and careful transitions. See 23c.

coined compound   A compound word (generally hyphenated) made up by a writer to express an idea in a particularly concise or vivid way. See 47c.

collaborating   Working as a group with other writers. See 11b, 17d, 53a.

collective noun   A singular noun that names a group of things or people: *fleet, team, family.* See 34n, 36i, 62a.

colloquialism   A term or expression used in spoken language but not accepted in formal writing. See 30g.

command   See *imperative sentence.*

comma splice   The joining of two independent clauses with only a comma. See Chapter 33.

common noun   A noun that names a general person, place, or thing. Also called *generic noun.* See also *proper noun.* See 46c, 62a.

communicative writing   Writing whose primary purpose is to communicate information and ideas. The most common communicative purposes

are to recount an experience, to report information, to explain an idea, and to argue a position. See 6a2.

comparative form   See *modifier.*

comparison and contrast   A writing strategy in which the writer describes similarities between two or more things or people (comparison) and then the differences between them (contrast). See 8d3.

complement   A word or phrase that renames a subject or object. **A subject complement** is an adjective or noun that follows a linking verb and renames the subject: *Tom is patient.* An **object complement** is an adjective or noun that follows an object and renames it: *They named him captain.* See also *linking verb.* See 34k, 36l3, 39j1, 63d.

complete predicate   See *predicate.*

complete subject   See *subject.*

complex sentence   A sentence that includes one independent clause and one or more dependent clauses. See 26c, 64b.

compound adjective   See *compound word.*

compound antecedent   An antecedent made up of two or more nouns or pronouns joined by a coordinating conjunction. See 36g–36h.

compound-complex sentence   A sentence containing two or more independent clauses and at least one dependent clause: *While you were gone, your mother called and the sink overflowed.* See 26c, 64b.

compound noun   See *compound word.*

compound object   An object of a verb or preposition composed of two or more nouns or pronouns joined by a coordinating conjunction. See 36l2.

compound predicate   Two or more predicates that share a subject and that are joined by a coordinating conjunction: *My uncle Ron shaved and dressed.* See also *predicate.* See 63b.

compound sentence   A sentence containing two or more independent clauses and no dependent clauses: *I went to John's house, but he wasn't home.* See 25a, 26c, 64b.

compound subject   Two or more subjects that share a predicate and that are joined by a coordinating conjunction: *Her dog and her cat got sick.* See also *subject.* See 34l–34m, 36l1, 63a.

compound word   A single unit formed by combining two or more words. A *closed compound* is written as one word; an *open compound* is written as two or more separate words; other compounds are hyphenated. A **compound noun** is composed of a noun plus a modifier or modifiers. See 45b3, 47c. A **compound adjective** consists of two or more words that function together as a single adjective before a noun. See 47c.

concise   In writing, use of the fewest words possible to achieve one's purpose. See Chapter 28.

conclusion   The final section of a paper, in which the writer summarizes what has gone before and makes general statements about the topic that are needed to complete the paper's purpose. See 24c–24d.

concrete noun   See *concrete word.*

concrete word   A word referring to something that can be perceived by the senses: *rain, rocks, sunlight.* See 27a, 62a.

conjunction A word or pair of words that joins two sentence elements and sets up a relationship between them. A **coordinating conjunction** joins elements of equal grammatical weight: *and, but, or, nor, so, for, yet*. A **correlative conjunction** is a pair of words that joins two grammatically equivalent elements: *both . . . and, either . . . or, neither . . . nor, not only . . . but also, whether . . . or*. A **subordinating conjunction** introduces a dependent clause and indicates its relationship to an independent clause. Subordinating conjunctions include *although, because, when,* and *while*. See also *conjunctive adverb*. See Chapter 25, 33a, 34l–34m, 36h–36i, 36l, 62f.

conjunctive adverb A conjunctive adverb, together with a semicolon, joins two independent clauses: *however, therefore, furthermore*. See 39d, 62f.

connotation A word's associations in addition to its literal meaning. See also *denotation*. See 30d.

context Background information or setting provided for readers to understand a whole work. See 6b, 9c1.

contraction A word or phrase shortened by the omission of one or more letters, which are replaced with an apostrophe. See 29c, 42c1.

contrast See *comparison and contrast*.

convention The accepted, standard, or customary way of doing something. *Academic conventions* call for an objective style and a clear thesis statement. See 20e. Conventions for writing are a language's set of customs for using words, grammar, and punctuation. See 22b.

coordinate adjectives Two or more adjectives with distinct meanings modifying a noun or pronoun separately: *The tired, discouraged, disgusted ballplayer slumped on the bench*. Coordinate adjectives are separated by commas. See also *cumulative adjectives*. See 39f2.

coordinating conjunction See *conjunction*.

coordination The grammatical connection of two or more ideas to give them equal emphasis and importance. See 25a, 25c.

correlative conjunction See *conjunction*.

counterclaim See *claim*.

count noun A noun that names something that can be counted by unit or instance: *fifty laps, thirty-nine flavors, two apples*. See also *noncount noun*. See 62a.

creative writing Writing whose primary purpose is the creation of a text that is enjoyable and rewarding in and of itself, apart from the information or ideas it conveys. Fiction, poetry, and drama are commonly identified as creative writing, but all writing can be creative. See 6a3.

critical essay See *interpretive essay*.

critical reading An analysis of an author's assumptions, ideas, arguments, and conclusions to understand them better, test them, and determine their meaning in an overall sense. See Chapter 2.

critical thinking The process of gathering, synthesizing, and evaluating information and its sources and reaching one's own conclusions.

cross-referencing Finding relationships among text passages.

cumulative adjectives Two or more adjectives that build on one another and together modify a noun: *The unsightly green chair had been in the family for five generations.* See also *coordinate adjectives.* See 39f2.

cumulative sentence A sentence in which the main idea is stated at the beginning. See also *periodic sentence.* See 26c.

dangling modifier A modifier, often a participle or participial phrase, that does not modify a clearly stated noun or pronoun: *Driving down the highway, the radar detector went off.* See 35g.

database A large, structured collection of related information in print or electronic form. A **bibliographic database** lists articles or books by subject, title, and author. An **abstract database** contains brief summaries of the articles listed in addition to the bibliographic information. A **full-text database** contains a complete or nearly complete text of the articles listed. See 12b3, 12c.

declarative sentence A sentence that presents facts or assertions. See 26c, 64a.

deductive reasoning Reasoning in which a general statement supports a conclusion about a specific case: *All cats purr. Rex is a cat. Rex must purr.* See also *inductive reasoning.*

definite article See *article.*

definition A writing strategy in which the writer describes something so that it can be distinguished from similar things. See 8d1.

degree See *modifier.*

demonstrative adjective See *demonstrative pronoun.*

demonstrative pronoun A pronoun that distinguishes its antecedent from similar things: *this, that, these, those.* When the word precedes a noun, it is a **demonstrative adjective:** *these apples.* See 62b1.

denotation A word's literal meaning. See also *connotation.* See 30d.

dependent clause A clause containing a subject and a verb but introduced by a subordinating conjunction or a relative pronoun. A dependent clause cannot constitute a complete sentence. Also called *subordinate clause.* See 25b, 26c, 28c, 32b, 33e, 63f.

description A writing strategy in which the writer creates an image of something, using words that appeal to the five senses. See 8d2.

descriptive modifier See *adjective.*

design Decide how to present written material visually, including selection of paper, type fonts, spacing, and placement of headings and titles among the considerations. See Chapter 50.

desktop publishing The art of using computers and computer-based programs to design documents visually. See Chapter 50.

determiner See *article.*

direct address A word or phrase that indicates a person or persons who are spoken to: *Don't forget, Amy, to lock the door.* See 39e.

direct discourse See *quotation.*

direct object See *object.*

direct question   A sentence that asks a question and ends with a question mark: *Which way is north?* See also *indirect question, tag sentence;* see 38b.

direct quotation   See *quotation.*

discovery writing   Writing whose primary purpose is to uncover ideas and information stored in the writer's memory. See also *invention;* see Chapter 5.

disruptive modifier   A modifier placed in such a way as to make the phrase or clause it modifies difficult to follow. See also *split infinitive;* see 35h.

division   See *classification and division.*

documentation   The practice and procedures for crediting and identifying source materials used in research writing. Standard documentation styles are MLA style for writing in language and literature, Chicago (CMS) style for writing in other humanities, and APA style for writing in the social sciences. See 16g, 55d, 56d, 57d, 58d, 59d.

double negative   The nonstandard use of two negative modifiers that, in effect, cancel each other out. See 35d.

doublespeak   An extreme form of euphemism that purposely describes things so they seem the opposite of what they actually are. See 28f.

drafting   The stage of the writing process in which the writer begins to produce a text. The complete text is called a **draft;** each subsequent revision of the piece of writing is considered a new draft. See also *editing, revising;* see 3c.

dynamic verb   See *verb.*

editing   The stage of the writing process in which the writer improves a draft by making sentences and words clearer, more powerful, and more precise. See also *revising;* see 3f, Chapter 22.

effect   See *cause-and-effect analysis.*

effectiveness   The quality of writing that makes it clear, interesting, and readable. See 3f, Chapters 23–31.

editorial *we*   Reference to the writer in the first-person plural, even when only one person is writing. Used to indicate that the writing represents the work or opinions of the writer and his or her colleagues. See 37a1.

elements of contrast   Words, phrases, or clauses that emphasize a point by describing what it is not or by citing an opposite condition. Usually set off by commas. See 39d.

ellipsis   The omission of one or more words from a quoted phrase or clause. An ellipsis must be indicated by ellipsis points (. . .). See also *elliptical construction;* see 44c.

elliptical construction   A phrase or clause from which one or more words are omitted and are assumed to be understood: *I ordered the shrimp; Angelo, the lobster.* See 25f, 26f.

e-mail   A system for transmitting messages electronically via the Internet. Participants have an e-mail address for sending and receiving messages.

endnotes   Notes at the end of a chapter or paper that list, in numerical sequence, sources cited by superscript numbers in the text. A documentation system that follows CMS style. See 56d2.

end punctuation   One of three marks of punctuation—a period, a question mark, or an exclamation point—used to indicate a full stop at the end of a sentence. See Chapter 38.

error   Departure from a rule. See 22b.

etymology   The source and development of a word. See 30b4.

euphemism   A polite term substituted for one considered unpleasant or impolite. See 28f.

evaluation   Comment that places a value or rating on a piece of work or judges it. See also *suggestion.*

evidence   Information presented in support of an argument. The most important types of evidence are facts, examples, inferences, informed opinions, and personal testimony. See 9a4, 9e.

evocative detail   A description of setting or character that relies on an appeal to the senses to make the subject vivid.

exclamatory sentence   A sentence that expresses strong feeling and that usually ends with an exclamation point. See 26c, 64a.

explanatory writing   A presentation of information and ideas that will help readers understand the subject. Explanatory essays are sometimes called *informative papers, expository papers,* or *reports.* See Chapter 8.

expletive construction   A sentence beginning with *it* or *there* (called an *expletive* when used in this manner), followed by a form of the verb *be* and the subject of the sentence: *There is a delay on Route 24 this morning.* See 27b1, 28c, 34j.

expository paper   See *explanatory writing.*

fact   A verifiable piece of information that most readers will accept without further argument.

fallacy   Incorrect logic or weak reasoning. See 9e.

faulty predication   A mixed construction in which the subject and verb do not make sense together. See 37b3.

field research   Research conducted outside of the library by **interviewing** people who have information about a topic or by **observing** people and activities related to the topic. See Chapter 14.

figurative language   Any use of language that makes surprising comparisons or describes things in unexpected ways. The main types of figurative language are analogy, hyperbole, irony, metaphor, paradox, personification, simile, and understatement. See 8d, 30h, 55c.

finite verb   A verb that changes form to indicate person, number, tense, and mood. See also *verbal;* see 62c.

first person   See *person, point of view.*

flashback   See *sequence of events.*

footnote   A note at the bottom of a page listing, in numerical sequence, sources cited by superscript number in the text on that page. A documentation system that follows CMS style. See 56d2.

formal   See *level of formality.*

fragment   A word group that is grammatically incomplete but is punctuated as a sentence. See Chapter 32.

freewriting An invention and discovery technique in which the writer writes quickly without stopping. See 2b, 5b.

full-text database See *database.*

fused sentence Two or more independent clauses joined without a conjunction or proper punctuations. Also called *run-on sentence.* See Chapter 33.

gender (1) The categorization of a noun or pronoun as masculine, feminine, or neuter. See also *agreement.* See 36f, 62b. (2) The categorization of a person as male or female. See 31c. Pronouns must agree with their antecedents in gender.

general Categorization of a word or statement that includes or refers to an entire group, type, or category. See also *specific;* see 22a, 27a.

generality A very broad generalization that is essentially meaningless or empty. See 28a.

generalization A conclusion based on a number of specific facts or instances. Sometimes called *inference.* When a generalization becomes so broad as to be empty or meaningless, it is called a *generality.* See 9e, 28a, Chapter 31.

gerund The *-ing* form of a verb functioning as a noun: *Painting is her life.* See also *participle, verbal.* See 34b, 36o, 62c.

gerund phrase A gerund, its modifiers, complements, and objects. See 63e.

governing pronoun Predominance of first, second, or third person used to convey a point of view in a piece of writing. See 29b.

grammar A system for describing how sentences are organized and structured. See 22a11, Chapters 32–37, 61–64.

helping verb See *auxiliary verb.*

homonym A word that sounds like another word but has a different spelling and meaning. See 30e.

hyperbole See *figurative language.*

idiom A customary phrase or usage that does not make literal sense or follow strict rules. See 30f.

imperative mood See *mood.*

imperative sentence A sentence that gives an order or instruction. Also called *command.* See 26c, 64a.

implied subject A subject that is not stated but that can be inferred from context. In imperative sentences (commands), the subject *you* is usually implied: *Shut the door.* See also *subject;* see 63a.

indefinite article See *article.*

indefinite pronoun A pronoun that refers to a nonspecific person or thing and therefore does not have a clear antecedent: *anybody, no one, everything, some, none.* See 34o, 36j, 62b1.

independent clause A clause with a subject and a predicate which can stand alone as a complete sentence. Also called *main clause.* See also *dependent clause;* see Chapters 32–33, 63f.

indicative mood   See *mood.*

indirect discourse   See *quotation.*

indirect object   See *object.*

indirect question   A sentence that reports a question, usually in a dependent clause, and ends with a period: *She asked whether I would go along.* See also *direct question, tag sentence;* see 38b.

indirect quotation   See *quotation.*

inductive reasoning   Reasoning in which specific facts support a probable general conclusion: *The alarm has rung at 8:30 on the past five mornings. The alarm will probably ring at 8:30 this morning.* See also *deductive reasoning.*

inference   See *generalization.*

infinitive   The base form of a verb preceded by *to.* An infinitive functions as a noun, adverb, or adjective. See also *verbal;* see 34b, 36o.

infinitive phrase   An infinitive, its modifiers, and its objects or complements. See 63e.

informal   See *level of formality.*

informational research   Research undertaken to collect information needed to answer a research question. See also *argument research;* see 11b.

informational thesis   See *thesis.*

informative paper   See *explanatory writing.*

initials   The first letter of each word in a phrase or name. See 49g.

intensive pronoun   A pronoun ending in *-self* or *-selves* used for emphasis: *I myself prefer steak.* See also *reflexive pronoun;* see 36r, 62b1.

interior monologue   A portrayal of unspoken thoughts, often expressed with sentence fragments and made-up words; described as talking to oneself.

interjection   A term inserted into a sentence or standing alone that expresses strong feeling or reaction: *wow, jeepers.* See 39e3, 62g.

Internet   The international network by which computers send and receive information, in the form of data, images, and sound. Called the Net for short. See also *online, World Wide Web;* see Chapter 13, 15b.

interpretive community   Any group that shares a set of beliefs or approaches to analyzing, discussing, and interpreting ideas. See 10c.

interpretive essay   An essay whose purpose is to analyze a text and present a persuasive explanation of its meaning. Sometimes called *analytical essay, critical essay, critical analysis, literary interpretation,* or *review.* A **personal interpretation** uses the writer's beliefs, experiences, and viewpoint to give meaning to the text. An **analytical interpretation** deemphasizes the writer's personal relationship to the text and focuses on the work being interpreted. See Chapter 10.

interrogative pronoun   A pronoun used to introduce a question: *who, whose.* See 36q1, 62b1.

interrogative sentence   A sentence that asks a question. See also *direct question, indirect question, tag sentence.* See 26c3, 64a.

interview See *field research.*

intransitive verb A verb that expresses action or being with no object or recipient. See also *transitive verb.* See 34b3, 62c2.

introductory element A dependent clause, phrase, or word that precedes and introduces an independent clause. Usually ends with a comma. See 39b.

invention Writing or other activities undertaken to help the writer develop solutions to questions and problems encountered in the writing process. See also *discovery writing.* See Chapter 5.

inverted word order The placement of words in a sentence in an unexpected sequence for emphasis. The most common inverted order is verb before subject. See 26c2.

invisible writing An invention and discovery technique in which the writer uses a word processor for freewriting but darkens the screen so that the words on it are invisible. See 5b.

irony See *figurative language.*

irregular verb A verb that does not follow the usual *-d* or *-ed* pattern in spelling its past tense and past participle. See also *regular verb.* See 34b2.

I-search essay A piece of writing that focuses on the process of the search instead of the result. See 11e4, 18b.

issue A topic that can be argued about, often stated in the form of a question. It raises a real question that has at least two distinct answers, one of which the writer is interested in advocating. See 9a1, 9b–9c.

italics An aspect of a typeface characterized by slanted letters. For uses, see Chapter 48; see also *roman.*

jargon Terms and expressions that arise within a specialty or field, often essential language for people in that field but not understood by others. See 30g.

journal A record of a person's thoughts and ideas on any aspect of life, work, or studies. See Chapter 4.

judgment See *evaluation.*

keyword An important word related to a research topic, used to search for references. See 12b.

level of formality A quality of language created by word choice and sentence structure and ranging from the very formal (or ceremonial) to the familiar. See 29c.

limiting modifier A modifier that distinguishes the word modified from other similar things. See also *adjective;* see 35f, 62d1.

linking verb A verb that connects a subject to a complement, which is a word that renames or describes the subject. See also *complement;* see 34k, 35b, 36l3, 62c3.

listening signposts Words in a speech that signal to the audience what is coming next. See 52b.

listserv An e-mail program that automatically sends copies of messages to every subscriber on a list. See also *newsgroup;* see 13a4.

literary interpretation See *interpretive essay.*

literary present The present tense used to describe the events of a literary work. See 34d.

logic Systematic thinking that bases conclusions on reasonable relationships between pieces of evidence.

looping An invention and discovery technique in which the writer creates a series of freewritings, each building on the most important idea uncovered in the previous one. Sometimes called *loop writing*. See also *freewriting;* see 5c.

main clause See *independent clause.*

main verb The verb in a verb phrase that expresses the action or state of the subject of the sentence. See also *verb phrase;* see 62c1.

mechanics The standardized features of written language, other than punctuation, that are used to clarify meaning. Elements of mechanics are spelling, capitalization, hyphenation, and italics. See 22a13, Chapters 45–49.

metaphor See *figurative language.*

misplaced modifier A modifier that is placed in a sentence in such a way that it is unclear what it describes or which word it modifies. See also *dangling modifier;* see 35f.

mixed construction A sentence that combines two or more types of sentence structure that do not fit together grammatically. See 37b.

mixed metaphor An implied comparison in which unrelated elements are introduced from a different implied comparison: *We're all in the same boat, so we mustn't fumble.* See also *figurative language;* see 30h.

modal auxiliary An auxiliary verb that does not change form for person or number. The one-word modals are *can, could, may, might, must, shall, should, will,* and *would.* See 34c1, 62c1.

modifier A word or group of words that describes another word, phrase, or clause. The most common modifiers are adjectives and adverbs. Modifiers have three forms: *positive,* which simply states a quality (*He worked hard*); **comparative,** which compares the degree of that quality between two persons or things (*He worked harder than his sister*); and **superlative,** which compares the degree of the quality among three or more persons or things (*He worked hardest of all the company's employees*). See Chapter 35, 62d.

modifier clause A dependent clause that functions as an adjective or adverb. See 63f.

modifier phrase A phrase that functions as an adjective or adverb. See 63e.

mood The characteristic of a verb used to indicate whether it is stating fact **(indicative),** giving an order or instruction **(imperative mood),** or expressing a wish or condition contrary to fact **(subjunctive).** See 34f–34g, 62c.

multiple-word verb See *phrasal verb.*

newsgroup A collection of postings on the Internet about a single topic. Also called a *usenet group.* See also *listserv;* see 13a4.

nominalization The construction of a noun from a verb root plus a suffix: *estrange* plus *-ment* equals the noun *estrangement.* See 27b3.

noncount noun   A noun that names something concrete that cannot be counted and given a number: *silver, tobacco, information*. Also called *mass noun*. See 34a, 62a.

nonfinite verb   See *verbal*.

nonrestrictive clause   See *restrictive and nonrestrictive clauses*.

nonsexist language   See *sexist language*.

nonstandard English   Usage that reflects the speech patterns of a particular community but does not follow the conventions of the dominant American dialect. Nonstandard English is inappropriate for academic writing.

noun   A word that names a person, animal, place, or idea. See also *common noun, count noun, noncount noun, proper noun*. See 62a.

noun clause   A dependent clause that functions as a noun (as a subject, object, or complement). See 34r, 63f.

noun cluster   A group of words consisting of a noun and several other nouns used as modifiers: *hardwood maple ballroom dance floor*. See 27d.

noun phrase   A noun and its modifiers functioning as a noun. See 34r, 63e.

number   The characteristic of a noun, pronoun, or verb that indicates whether it is *singular* (referring to one person or thing) or *plural* (referring to more than one). See also *agreement*. See 34h–34u, 36f–36j, 62b–62c.

object   A noun, pronoun, or noun phrase or clause that receives the action of or is influenced by a verb, a verbal, or a preposition. A **direct object** receives the action of a verb or verbal: *She read the newspaper.* An **indirect object** indicates to or for whom or what the action of the verb is directed: *She gave him the newspaper.* The **object of a preposition** follows a preposition: *The newspaper had a story about the peace plan.* The preposition, its object, and any associated modifiers together form a **prepositional phrase:** *The newspaper had a story about the peace plan.* See 62e, 63c.

object complement   See *complement*.

objective case   See *case*.

objective stance   See *stance*.

observation   See *field research*.

online   Connected to the Internet. See 12b3, Chapter 13.

opening   The beginning of an essay, which establishes the subject, the tone, and sometimes the theme or thesis of the essay. See 19d7, 24a–24b.

opinion   An idea that reflects an author's personal beliefs and conclusions.

organize   Arrange in a clearly perceptible order. See *sequence of events;* see also *climactic order, spatial order;* see 23b.

outline   Organized list showing the points made about a topic, the information supporting each point, and the organization of this material. Outlining is useful as an invention and discovery technique, a means of organizing materials before drafting, and a revision technique. See 5e, 16b1, 19d.

paradox   See *figurative language*.

paragraph   A group of sentences about a single topic. Good paragraphs are unified, coherent, and well organized. See Chapter 23.

parallelism   The use of similar grammatical elements or structures—words, phrases, clauses, sentences, or paragraphs—for emphasis. See 25e–25f.

paraphrase   A restatement of the ideas of a written or spoken source in the writer's own words. See also *quotation, summary;* see 12e3, 16d2.

parenthetical expression   A word or word group that comments on or adds information to a sentence but is not part of the sentence structure and does not alter the meaning of the sentence. Parenthetical elements appear between parentheses, commas, or dashes. See 39d, 44a–44b.

participial phrase   A present or past participle, including its modifiers, that functions as a modifier. See 63e.

participle   A verb form created by adding an ending to the base form to change tense; used with an auxiliary verb or as a verbal. A **present participle** is created by adding *-ing* to the base form. Used with auxiliary verbs, it forms the progressive tenses. Used without an auxiliary verb, a present participle is a modifier when functioning as an adjective or a gerund when functioning as a noun. See also *verbal.* See 34b, 34c, 36o, 61c. A **past participle** is created by adding *-d* or *-ed* to the base form in regular verbs. In irregular verbs the past participle is formed differently for each verb. Used with auxiliary verbs, it forms perfect tenses. Used without an auxiliary verb, it functions as a modifier. See also *verbal;* see 34a, 34e, 36o, 62c.

particle   See *phrasal verb.*

part of speech   Designation of a word as a noun, pronoun, verb, adjective, preposition, conjunction, or interjection. See Chapter 62.

passive voice   See *voice.*

past participle   See *participle.*

past tense   See *tense.*

perfect progressive tense   See *tense.*

perfect tense   See *tense.*

periodic sentence   A sentence in which the main idea is placed at the end. See also *cumulative sentence.* See 26c.

person   The characteristic of a noun, pronoun, or a verb that indicates whether the subject or actor is the one speaking (**first person:** *I, we*), spoken to (**second person:** *you*), or spoken about (**third person:** *he, she, it, they*). See also *agreement;* see 29b, 34a, 34h, Chapter 36, 62b–62c.

personal experience paper   A common college writing assignment whose purpose is to recount events experienced by the writer in an interesting and enlightening manner. See Chapter 7.

personal interpretation   See *interpretive essay.*

personal pronoun   A pronoun that refers to a particular person, group, or thing. See 62b1.

personification   See *figurative language.*

perspective The vantage point from which a paper is written. Perspective is established through point of view, tense, emphasis, and level of formality. See also *point of view, stance, tone;* see 7c, 8f.

persuasion See *argument paper.*

phrasal preposition A group of words that work together as a single preposition: *except for, according to.* See 62e.

phrasal verb A verb with more than one word. Phrasal verbs are formed by combining a one-word verb with one or more **particles** such as *to* or *off.* Together, the verb and the particle(s) create a meaning that is distinct from that of the original verb: *come to, come off.* Also called *two-word verb* or *multiple-word verb.* See 30f, 62c.

phrase Two or more words that do not include a subject and a verb but that work as a grammatical unit, serving as a noun, verb, adjective, or adverb. See also *absolute phrase, modifier phrase, noun phrase, object, verbal phrase, verb phrase;* see 63e.

plagiarism Any use of someone else's ideas or words without explicit and complete documentation or acknowledgment. See 12e3, 16g.

plain form See *base form.*

planning The stage of the writing process that consists of creating, discovering, locating, developing, organizing, and trying out ideas. See 3b.

plural See *number.*

point of view An indication of the writer's relation to and attitude toward his or her material. See also *person;* see 7c, 29b, 55b.

position paper A type of argument paper that sets forth a position on an issue of local or national concern. See Chapter 9.

positive form See *modifier.*

possessive case See *case.*

predicate The part of a sentence that specifies action or being. The **simple predicate** is the main verb of the sentence. The **complete predicate** is the simple predicate plus its modifiers, objects, and complements. See also *compound predicate;* see 63b.

predicate adjective An adjective functioning as a complement. See also *complement;* see 63d.

predicate noun A noun functioning as a complement. See also *complement;* see 63d.

prefix A word segment attached to the beginning of a word root to change its meaning. See 30c.

preposition A word that connects a noun or noun phrase (the **object** of the preposition) to another word, phrase, or clause and conveys a relation between the elements connected. See also *object;* see 62e.

prepositional phrase See *object.*

present participle See *participle.*

pretentious language Excessively formal, old-fashioned, or complicated words and expressions used not for their appropriateness but to impress the reader. See 28e.

primary source   Firsthand information and raw data on a topic. Many of the sources consulted in field research are primary sources. See also *secondary source*. See 11e, 55a, 56c2.

progressive tense   See *tense*.

pronoun   A word used in place of a noun or noun phrase. See also *agreement, antecedent, demonstrative pronoun, intensive pronoun, interrogative pronoun, personal pronoun, reciprocal pronoun, reflexive pronoun, relative pronoun*. See Chapter 36, 62b.

proofreading   The final stage in a writing project; it involves rereading the final draft to catch small errors such as typographical errors, misspellings, and incorrect capitalization. See 22a13, 50c.

proper adjective   See *adjective*.

proper noun   A name of a particular person, place, animal, organization, or thing. Proper nouns are capitalized. See also *common noun*. See 46c, 62a.

punctuation   A system of standardized marks used in written material to clarify meaning. The marks of punctuation used most often in English are the period, the exclamation point, the question mark, the comma, the semicolon, the colon, the apostrophe, quotation marks, the slash, the dash, ellipsis points, parentheses, and brackets. See 22a12, Chapters 38–44.

purpose   The reason for generating a piece of writing; the goal a writer wants to accomplish. Four general purposes for writing are to discover, to communicate, to persuade, and to create. See 6a, 6b.

qualifying phrase   An expression such as *I think* or *in my opinion* that distinguishes the statement to which it is related as being the writer's idea rather than the thoughts or beliefs of others. In presenting research, qualifying phrases may be useful as indicators of the writer's evaluation of ideas from sources, but otherwise these phrases tend to make writing unnecessarily wordy. See 24d3.

quotation   The reproduction of a writer's or speaker's exact words. In **direct quotation** (or **direct discourse**), a writer reproduces another person's words exactly and places them in quotation marks. In **indirect quotation** (or **indirect discourse**), a writer rephrases another person's words and integrates them grammatically and logically into his or her own sentence. See also *paraphrase, summary;* see 12e3, 16d1, Chapter 43.

reciprocal pronoun   A two-word pronoun that refers to one part of a plural antecedent: *each other, one another.* See 62b1.

recounting experience   See *personal experience paper.*

redundancy   Unnecessary repetition. See 28d.

referent   See *antecedent.*

reflective essay   A common college writing assignment in which the writer reflects on a significant subject, raises questions about it, and speculates on possible meanings. Sometimes called simply an *essay*. See Chapter 7.

reflexive pronoun   A pronoun ending in *-self* or *-selves* whose antecedent is the subject of the sentence it appears in: *I could kick myself.* See also *intensive pronoun;* see 36r, 62b1.

regionalism A form of language use that is common in one geographic area but is not used elsewhere. See 30g.

register See *level of formality.*

regular verb A verb that forms its past tense and past participles by adding *-d* or *-ed* to the base form. See also *irregular verb;* see 34b.

relative adverb An adverb that introduces an adjective clause. Common relative adverbs are *when, where,* and *how.* See 62d.

relative clause A dependent clause that functions as an adjective. See 62f.

relative pronoun A pronoun that introduces a dependent noun or adjective clause: *who, whose, which, what.* See 36b2, 62b1.

report See *explanatory writing.*

reporter's questions A set of questions that reporters use in gathering information and that can be used by any writer as an invention and discovery technique: *Who? What? Where? When? Why? How?* Also called *journalist's questions.* See 5d, 15b.

research essay A common college writing assignment in which students conduct research and write about their findings. Research essays are generally longer, require more extensive research, use a more formal style and format, and take more time than other papers. Sometimes called *research paper* or *research report.* See Chapter 11.

researching The stage of the writing process in which the writer gathers information and ideas about which to write. Research is a part of all writing assignments except those written completely from personal experience. See also *argument research, field research, information research, research essay.* See 3d, Chapters 11–18.

research question The question that research is designed to answer. See 11b3.

responding The act of offering comments on a writer's material, ideals, or drafts. See *collaborating, writing group;* see Chapter 21.

restrictive and nonrestrictive clauses *Restrictive clauses* are adjective clauses that limit the nouns they modify and that are essential to the meaning of a sentence: *I bought the books that were assigned.* Restrictive clauses are not set off with commas from the words they modify. *Nonrestrictive clauses* do not limit the nouns they modify and are not essential to the meaning of a sentence: *The assigned books, which were on a special shelf, cost sixty dollars.* Nonrestrictive clauses are set off with commas. See 36f, 39c.

review essay See *interpretive essay.*

revising The stage of the writing process in which the writer improves a draft by making changes to its direction, focus, argument, information, organization, or other important features. Revision generally occurs at the level of ideas. See also *editing;* see 3e, Chapters 19–21.

revision strategies Plans and methods for revising. See 19d, Chapter 20.

rhetoric The principles of effective use of language to communicate the writer's (or speaker's) purpose to an audience. See 3f.

rhetorical question A question that is not meant to be answered but sets up a response from the writer. See 24c1.

roman A typeface characterized by a vertical emphasis in the form of letters and other characters. In most printed material, the body of the text is set in roman type. See also *italic;* see Chapter 48.

root The part of a word that stays the same as the word changes form with the addition of prefixes and suffixes. *Route* is the root of *routing, routine, reroute.* Also called *base word.* See 31c, 50b.

rule A convention so widely accepted that not to follow it is considered wrong. See 22b.

run-on sentence See *fused sentence.*

sarcasm See *figurative language.*

search engine A computer program that searches for information about a topic based on a word or phrase. To narrow the search to useful information, users indicate by **Boolean operators,** such as *AND, OR,* and *NOT,* the combination of words that best limit search to the topic of interest. See 13b.

secondary source Reports and interpretations of and arguments about firsthand information and raw data. Many of the sources consulted in library research are secondary sources. See also *primary source;* see 11e, 55a, 56c2.

second person See *person, point of view.*

sentence A group of words containing a subject and a predicate and conveying a comprehensible, complete idea or thought.

sentence element Designation of a word or group of words according to its function in a sentence. See Chapter 63.

sequence of events The order in which events are related in an essay. The most straightforward sequence of events is **chronological order,** which presents events in the same order in which they happened. See 23b2. Another sequence of events is the **flashback,** in which earlier events are related after later ones. See 7e2.

sequence of tenses The relationship between the main verb and all the other verbs in a sentence. See also *governing tense* in **tense.** See 34e.

serial comma The comma that normally precedes the coordinating conjunction before the last item in a series. See 39f.

series A list of words, phrases, or clauses separated by commas or semicolons. See 25f, 39f1.

server A host computer that stores files of information and distributes them on request from client computers. See 13a1.

sexist language Any language in which assumptions about gender are embedded: *policeman, each must do his best.* Nonsexist alternatives are *police officer* and *his or her best.* See Chapter 31.

-s form The third-person singular, present-tense form of a verb, created by adding *-s* or *-es* to the base form. See also *base form;* see 34a.

shift Any change in verb tense, number, or person within a sentence or between sentences that results in confusion for the reader. See 37a.

simile See *figurative language.*

simple form See *base form.*

simple predicate See *predicate.*

simple sentence A sentence that contains one independent clause. See 26c, 64b.

simple subject See *subject.*

simple tense See *tense.*

singular See *number.*

slang Colorful, irreverent, informal expressions usually coined by small groups. Slang is not appropriate in formal writing. See 30g.

spatial order Organization of a physical description by moving from one detail to another. See 23b.

specific Categorization of a word or statement that refers to a single, particular thing. See also *general;* see 22a, 27a.

split infinitive A construction in which words intervene between the infinitive marker *to* and the verb. See 35h1.

squinting modifier An ambiguously placed modifier that does not clearly modify one sentence element but could modify more than one. See 35f.

stance The perspective adopted for a particular paper. An **objective stance** focuses on the topic under discussion rather than on the writer's own thoughts and feelings. A **subjective stance** incorporates the writer's thoughts and feelings into the account or analysis.

standard English Usage that follows the rules and conventions of written English. Standard English is appropriate for formal academic papers.

stative verb See *verb.*

stereotype Overgeneralization about a person or group based on gender, race, ethnicity, and so on. See 31a.

structure The way in which the content of a paper is put together, including the order and grouping of ideas. See 6b.

style (1) The distinctive way a writer expresses himself or herself, established primarily through the level of formality and the simplicity or complexity of words, sentences, and paragraphs. See also *level of formality;* see 6b2, 6c2. (2) In reference to the visual design of a document, the overall effect of such features as the type font, size of margins, and placement of headings, titles, page numbers, and notes. See Chapter 50.

subject (1) The noun or pronoun that performs the action of the verb, is acted upon by the verb, or is described by the verb. The **simple subject** is the noun or pronoun alone. The **complete subject** is the noun or pronoun plus its modifiers. See also *compound subject, implied subject;* see 63a. (2) The idea or thing about which a paper is written. See also *topic.*

subject complement See *complement.*

subjective case See *case.*

subjective stance See *stance.*

subjunctive mood See *mood.*

subordinate clause See *dependent clause.*

subordinating conjunction See *conjunction.*

subordination Connection of two or more ideas (usually clauses) to make one of them dominant and the other or others logically secondary or subordinate. See 25b–25c, 33e.

suffix A word segment attached to the end of a word root to change its meaning or form. See 30c, 45b.

suggestion A recommendation for revising a piece of work. See also *evaluation.*

summary A distillation of a source's ideas into a brief statement phrased in the writer's own words. See also *conclusion, paraphrase, quotation;* see 12e3, 16d3, 24c2.

superlative form See *modifier.*

survey A structured interview in which respondents, representative of a larger group, are all asked the same questions. Their answers are tabulated and interpreted in an effort to discover attitudes, beliefs, or habits of the larger population they represent. See 14c.

suspense A writing strategy that sustains readers' interest by raising a question or posing a problem and delaying the answer or solution.

symbol Something that stands for something else. In type, a character that represents a word or words. See 49e.

synonym Word with the same meaning as another word or with a similar meaning. See 30b.

synthesis An element of critical thinking in which a writer or reader applies the process of summary, analysis, and interpretation to prior beliefs to produce new ideas. See also *antithesis, thesis;* see 9a.

tag question See *tag sentence.*

tag sentence A brief sentence placed at the end of another sentence (after a comma) for the purpose of providing emphasis or eliciting a response. A tag sentence may be either a statement or a question: *Mark cannot join us, I'm afraid. You're tired, aren't you?* See 33b1, 38b, 39e1.

telling detail A fact or observation that advances the characterization of someone without the writer's having to render an obvious opinion. See 7a.

tense The form a verb takes to show when its action occurs. **Simple tenses** show events that occur in the past, present, or future: *I walked, I am walking, I will walk.* **Perfect tenses** indicate action completed in the past (*had sat*), present (*have sat*), and future (*will have sat*). **Progressive tenses** indicate action happening continuously, and not necessarily ending, in the past (*was sitting*), present (*am sitting*), and future (*will be sitting*). **Perfect progressive tenses** express actions happening over a period of time and then ending in the past (*had been sitting*), the present (*have been sitting*), or in the future (*will have been sitting*). **Perfect progressive tenses** describe action continuing up to a specific time of completion in the present, past, or future. The **governing tense** is the tense used in verbs describing most of the actions in a paper or story. See 7c, 34d–34e, 62c.

text Any symbolic work constructed by humans that is open to interpretation, specifically, written texts such as essays, novels, short stories, plays, and poems. See Chapter 10.

theme The central idea of a personal or reflective essay. It is not necessarily stated outright but is more often strongly implied. See 7f, 10d, 55b.

thesaurus A word reference that lists synonyms and may also list antonyms.

thesis   A statement, usually made early in a research or persuasive essay, that asserts the point the writer hopes to make in the essay. A **working thesis** is a statement of the point a writer thinks his or her finished essay will make; it is useful in the research and drafting phases of writing and often changes during the writing process. An **argument thesis** expresses an opinion about the issue the writer is exploring; the essay then serves to support that opinion. An **informational thesis** presents a factual statement that will be fleshed out with explanation and detail. See 6a, 8c, 9a, 10d, 11c.

third person   See *person, point of view.*

tone   The writer's attitude toward the subject and audience, conveyed through the piece of writing. Tone is established primarily through word choice, point of view, and level of formality. See also *level of formality, point of view;* see 6b2, Chapter 29.

topic   The specific issue, idea, fact, or situation about which a paper is written. See also *subject.* Also called **main idea.** See 2a, 23a, 24a.

topic sentence   The sentence that states the main idea of a paragraph. See 23a.

transitional expression   A word or phrase that connects separate ideas or statements and describes the relationship between them: *for example, as a result.* See 23c2, 39b, 39d.

transitive verb   A verb that expresses an action that has an object or recipient; many verbs can be both transitive and intransitive: *I walked the dog* (transitive); *I walked to the store* (intransitive). See also *intransitive verb;* see 34b3, 62c2.

two-word verb   See *phrasal verb.*

understatement   See *figurative language.*

unified   In reference to a paragraph, having all its sentences develop a single topic. See 23a.

URL (uniform resource locator)   The address of a Web site. A user can gain access to the site by typing the address in the appropriate space in the command line of a **browser** program or by selecting a *hypertext link* at another Web site. See also *World Wide Web;* see 13a2.

verb   A word that indicates action or existence, expressing what a subject does or is. See 62c. An *action verb* expresses motion or creates vivid images. See 27b. A **dynamic verb,** which usually appears in the *-ing* form, expresses actions, processes, or events that are in progress. See 34d. A **stative verb** expresses a subject's existence rather than action: *be, seem, become.* See 22a7, 27b.

verbal   A verb form that does not function as the main verb of a sentence. See also *gerund, infinitive, participle;* see 34b, 36o, 62c.

verbal phrase   A verbal plus its modifiers, objects, and complements. See also *gerund phrase, infinitive phrase, participial phrase.* See 63e.

verb phrase   A main verb plus any auxiliary verbs. See also *auxiliary verb;* see 34c1, 35h2, 62c1, 63e.

voice   (1) The sense of the writer conveyed to the reader through a piece of writing. See 6c, 7a1. (2) In grammar, an attribute of a verb showing whether the action of the verb is performed by the sentence's subject

(active voice) or is performed on the sentence's subject **(passive voice).** *Mary reads the book* (active); *The book is read by Mary* (passive). See 27c, 34a, 62c4.

vocabulary   The collection of words commonly used by an individual or group of people. See 30c.

wordy phrases   Phrases that use extra words that may make the meaning imprecise. Abstract nouns and the preposition *of* frequently appear in wordy phrases. See 28b.

working thesis   See *thesis.*

World Wide Web   The portion of the Internet made up of **Web pages** that can simultaneously present information as text, graphics, animation, photography, and sound. A **Web site** is a collection of Web pages from the same source. See Chapter 13, 51e.

writing group   A group of writers who work together to help one another improve their writing. Writers may respond to one another's work or they may collaborate on a piece of writing. See 21e.

writing portfolio   A collection of a writer's work contained within a single folder. See 51a.

writing process   The set of activities writers go through to produce a finished piece of writing. Writing processes vary from person to person and from situation to situation. However, the typical writing process can be described as having five discrete but overlapping stages: planning, drafting, researching, revising, and editing. See Chapter 3.

ACKNOWLEDGMENTS

ESL INDEX

A

Abbreviations, 699
Acronyms, 699
Active voice, 398
Adjectives
    labels from, 455
    order of, 401
Adverb phrases, 383
Adverbs
    of extent or degree, 383
    frequency, 536
    negative, 383
    of position, 383
Articles (*a, an, the*)
    with acronyms, 699
    with comparatives and
      superlatives, 529
    with degree abbreviation, 699
    with initial abbreviation, 699
    using with nouns, 522–23
Authority, becoming, 163
Auxiliary verbs, 383

B

Biased language, 324
Bilingual dictionaries, 434
British spellings, 661

C

Clauses
    conditional, 383
    strategies for reducing, 410
Collective nouns, 455
    plural verbs with, 518
Comparatives, 383, 529
Conditional clauses, 383
Count nouns, verb agreement
    with, 512

D

Definite articles (*the*), 455, 522,
    529
Degree abbreviation, 699
Dictionaries, bilingual, 434

E

Editing
    revising versus, 274
    writings of others, 329
Emphasis, subject-verb inversion
    and, 383

F

Freewriting, to develop fluency, 52
Frequency adverbs, 536

G

Gender bias, 324
Gender of possessive pronouns,
    549
Gerunds, 491–92

I

Indefinite articles (*a, an*), 522, 529
Infinitives, 491–92
Initial abbreviations, 699
Interviews, conducting in English,
    208
Intransitive verbs, 398

J

Journals, 46

L

Labels, derived from adjectives,
    455

M

Modals, phrasal, 495
Modifiers, 383
Multiple-word prepositions, 467

N

Native language skills, 27
Noncount nouns
    articles with, 522
    verb agreement with, 512
not, no, using, 527–28

INDEX

Note: **Boldface type** indicates page numbers for main text discussion of that topic.

NOTES

NOTES